Active Voice

Third Edition

Edited by

W.H. New and W.E. Messenger
University of British Columbia

Prentice-Hall Canada Inc. Scarborough, Ontario

Canadian Cataloguing in Publication Data
Main entry under title:

Active voice : an anthology of Canadian, American and
    Commonwealth prose

3rd ed.
ISBN 0-13-006461-0

1. College readers. 2. Exposition (Rhetoric).
I. New, W.H. (William Herbert), 1938- .
II. Messenger, William E., 1931- .

PE1122.A37 1991   808'.0427 C90-094805-1

Prentice Hall, Inc., Englewood Cliffs, New Jersey
Prentice-Hall International, Inc., London
Prentice-Hall of Australia, Pty., Ltd., Sydney
Prentice-Hall of India Pvt., Ltd., Sydney
Prentice-Hall of Japan, Inc., Tokyo
Prentice-Hall of Southeast Asia (Pte.) Ltd., Singapore
Editora Prentice-Hall do Brasil Ltda., Rio de Janeiro
Prentice-Hall Hispanoamericana, S.A., Mexico

ISBN 0-13-006461-0
Production Editor: Dick Hemingway
Editorial Coordinator: Linda Collins
Design: Bruce Farquhar
Production Coordinator: Anna Orodi
Desktop Publishing: Bonnie Way
Cover Image: The Stock Market Inc.

Printed and bound in Canada by Alger Press Limited

    2 3 4 5   AP   95 94 93 92

Michael J. Arlen: From *Living-Room War* by Michael J. Arlen. Copyright © 1966, 1967, 1968, 1969 by Michael J.
    Arlen. Reprinted by permission of Candida Donadio & Associates, Inc.
Margaret Atwood: © Radcliffe College 1980. Reprinted with permission of the Radcliffe Quarterly.
Margaret Atwood: From *The Handmaid's Tale* by Margaret Atwood. Used by permission of the Canadian
    Publishers, McClelland and Stewart, Toronto.
Nicholson Baker: "The Size of Thoughts," *The Atlantic Monthly* (March, 1983). Reprinted by permission of the
    author.
Isaiah Berlin: From Isaiah Berlin, *Concepts and Categories: Philosophical Essays*, London: Oxford University Press
    (1980). Oxford Paperback edition. Originally published by Hogarth Press. Reprinted by permission of the
    author.

Contents

Thematic Table of Contents
(excluding excerpts from novels)

HISTORY AND POLITICS

History:

Eiseley, Forster, Huxley, T. Macaulay, MacEwen, MacLennan, Mukherjee, Murdoch, Tuchman

Politics and Government, Nationalism, Colonialism:

Arlen, Atwood, Brink, Forster, Gordimer, Huxley, Kingsley, T. Macaulay, MacEwen, MacLennan, McClung, Murdoch, Orwell, Spence, Swift, Tuchman, Zinsser

Violence and Confrontation—War, Aggression, Competition, Power:

Arlen, Brink, Dryden, Eiseley, Gordimer, Huxley, Iyer, Lane, Ludwig, T. Macaulay, MacLennan, McClung, Morgan, Mukherjee, Sheehan, Spence, Stein, Tuchman, Zinsser

MIND AND THOUGHT

Ideas, Thinking, Logic:

Bierce, Baker, Brink, Carlyle, Davenport, Eiseley, Fulford, Gordimer, Huxley, Lopez (b), Morgan, Tuchman, Zinsser

Education, Learning:

Addison, Atwood, Brink, Cutschall, Gordimer, Newman, O'Connor, Thoreau

Philosophy and Religion:

Baker, Berlin, Brink, Carlyle, Cole, Cutschall, Davenport, Donne, Huxley, Kingston, St. Luke (Bible), Synge, L. Thomas (*NBW*)

Human Nature and the Human Condition:

Brink, Cutschall, Ecclesiastes (Bible), Eiseley, Fulford, Huxley, Kemble, Le Guin, Morgan, Newman, Rigby, Thurber

Self-Knowledge:

Cutschall, Dillard, Dryden, Eiseley, Fisher, Forster, Fulford, Gordimer, Haig-Brown, Haliburton, Laurence, Meigs, Mukherjee, Thoreau, White

Good and Evil:

Atwood, Brink, Cooper, Dillard, Eiseley, Huxley, Iyer, MacLennan, Meigs, Milton

Life and Death, Time and Change, Progress:

Arlen, Brink, Browne, Cutschall, Davenport, Dillard, Donne, Ecclesiastes (Bible), S. Gould, Kingston, Le Guin, MacLennan, McClung, Mitford, Morgan, Mukherjee, Ritter, Stein, L. Thomas (*NBW*), Thoreau, White

The Non-Rational—Feelings, Emotions, Instincts, Dreams, Illusions, the Absurd:

Cole, Cutschall, Davenport, Dillard, Forster, Fulford, Haig-Brown, Kael, Kingston, Lane, Le Guin, Ludwig, MacLennan, Meigs, Mukherjee, Sheehan, Thoreau, White, Zinsser

Myth:

Cutschall, Kingston, Meigs, Morgan, Synge, Tuchman

VALUES: JUDGMENT, BELIEF, TASTE, CHOICES, RESPONSIBILITY

Aesthetics:

Addison, Baker, Colombo, Cooper, Deacon, Frayn, G. Gould, Kael, Wilde, Woolf

Ethics:

Bierce, Breton, Brink, Cooper, Cutschall, Dillard, Dryden, Eiseley, Forster, Fulford, Gorman, Haig-Brown, Huxley, Iyer, Johnson, Kael, Kemble, Ludwig, MacLennan, McClung, Meigs, Milton, Newman, O'Connor, Ritter, Rooney, Sheehan, Stein, Swift, Szasz, L. Thomas (*NBW*), Tuchman

Freedom, Freedom and Necessity, Free Will, Duty:

Brink, Dillard, Eiseley, Kemble, McClung, Milton, Montagu, Mukherjee, Stevenson, Szasz, White

Definitions of Normality:

Iyer, Kingsley, Morgan, Szasz

SCIENCE

Health and Medicine:

Roueché, Szasz, L. Thomas (*NBW*)

Technology, Mathematics:

Cole, Gorman, S. Gould, Leacock, Le Guin, Ritter, Roueché, L. Thomas (*NBW*), Tuchman, Zinsser

Anthropology and Archaeology:

Cutschall, Eiseley, Morgan

Nature, Animals:

Cole, Deacon, Dillard, Gorman, S. Gould, Haig-Brown, Lopez (a), Morgan, L. Thomas (*NBW*), Thurber, Traill (a), Wilde

COMMUNICATION AND THE ARTS

The Media, Journalism, Advertising:

Arlen, Brink, Dryden, Fulford, Hornyansky, Mitford, Mukherjee, Spence, L. Thomas (*NP*), Zinsser

Language, Writing:

Baker, Brink, Carlyle, Cole, Colombo, Cooper, Davenport, Galbraith, Gordimer, Hornyansky, Leacock, Mitford, Mukherjee, Orwell, Piozzi, Stein, Synge, L. Thomas (*NBW, NP*), Thurber, Trillin

Literature:

Addison, Atwood, Bierce, Colombo, Cooper, Deacon, Forster, Frayn, Gordimer, Kingston, Lane, Meigs, Murdoch, O'Connor, Wilde, Woolf

Film, Painting, Music:

Baker, Colombo, Frayn, G. Gould, Huxley, Kael, Stein, Wilde

OCCUPATIONS AND PASTIMES, WORK AND LEISURE

Sport:

Dryden, Haig-Brown, Ludwig, Ritter, Sheehan

Everyday Life, Domesticity:

Bacon, Fisher, Montagu, Mukherjee, Rooney, Synge, D. Thomas, Traill, Updike

Business and Labour, Industry, Economics, Ownership; Rich and Poor:

Brink, Dryden, Eiseley, Forster, Galbraith, Huxley, Johnson, Kael, St. Luke (Bible), McClung, Mitford, Ritter, Spence, Stevenson, Swift, Szasz

Happiness:

Bierce, Fisher, St. Luke (Bible), Piozzi, Stevenson, D. Thomas

Table of Contents According to Methods of Development

Virtually all the essays and extracts use *Illustration and Example,* supplying *Details.* Most make use of several other methods as well. Indeed it is seldom possible to designate a single method as the main or overall one. Here are the authors who make most significant use of some particular methods. (We do not include all the selections from section VII.)

NARRATION

Arlen, Atwood, Cole, Cutschall, Davenport, Deacon, Dillard, Dryden, Eiseley, Fisher, Forster, Gordimer, Haig-Brown, Huxley, Kingston, Lane, Leacock, Ludwig, MacEwen, MacLennan, McClung, Mitford, Montagu, Mukherjee, Murdoch, Roueché, Sheehan, Synge, Szasz, D. Thomas, Trillin, White, Zinsser

DESCRIPTION

Davenport, Dillard, Eiseley, Fisher, Forster, Gordimer, Haig-Brown, Huxley, Lane, Leacock, Lopez (a), Ludwig, MacLennan, Mitford, Montagu, Mukherjee, Ruskin, Sheehan, Synge, D. Thomas, White

ANALYSIS

Addison, Brink, Cole, Colombo, Cooper, Cutschall, Davenport, Deacon, Eiseley, Forster, Galbraith, S. Gould, Hornyansky, Kemble, Lane, Le Guin, Ludwig, MacLennan, Mitford, Morgan, Mukherjee, Murdoch, O'Connor, Sheehan, Stein, Swift, L. Thomas (*NP*), Tuchman, Updike, Woolf

DEFINITION

Addison, Arlen, Atwood, Baker, Berlin, Bierce, Breton, Brink, Carlyle, Cole, Colombo, Cutschall, Davenport, Dillard, Donne, Dryden, Fulford, Galbraith, S. Gould, Hornyansky, Huxley, Iyer, Johnson, Kael, Ludwig, Meigs, Mitford, Morgan, Murdoch, O'Connor, Piozzi, Ritter, Rooney, Sheehan, Spence, Stein, Stevenson, Szasz, L. Thomas (*NBW, NP*), Trillin, Tuchman

CLASSIFICATION

Addison, Atwood, Bacon, Baker, Beerbohm, Berlin, Brink, Cole, Colombo, Cooper, Forster, Fulford, Galbraith, S. Gould, Hornyansky, Iyer, Kingsley, Leacock, Murdoch, Orwell, Rigby, Ritter, Spence, Szasz, L. Thomas (*NBW*), Tuchman, Woolf

COMPARISON AND CONTRAST

Atwood, Bacon, Berlin, Breton, Cole, Deacon, Dillard, Eiseley, Fisher, Gordimer, Gorman, S. Gould, Huxley, Iyer, Kael, Lane, Lopez (b), Ludwig, T. Macaulay, MacLennan, Meigs, Morgan, Mukherjee, Murdoch, Newman, Ritter, Rooney, Spence, Stevenson, Trillin, White, Zinsser

PROCESS

Beerbohm, Brink, Colombo, Cooper, Cutschall, Deacon, Frayn, Gordimer, G. Gould, Haig-Brown, Huxley, Kingsley, Leacock, MacLennan, Milton, Mitford, Morgan, Orwell, Roueché, Sheehan, Stein, Swift, Traill, Tuchman, White

CAUSE AND EFFECT

Addison, Arlen, Bacon, Berlin, Brink, Cooper, Cutschall, Dillard, Donne, Dryden, Eiseley, Forster, Fulford, Galbraith, Gordimer, Haig-Brown, Hornyansky, Huxley, Johnson, Kael, Kemble, Kingsley, Le Guin, T. MacCaulay, MacLennan, McClung, Mitford, Morgan, Mukherjee, Newman, O'Connor, Orwell, Rigby, Rooney, Roueche, Sheehan, Spence, Stevenson, Swift, Szasz, L. Thomas (*NBW*, *NP*), Traill (b), Tuchman, White, Woolf, Zinsser

SPECIAL FORMS

Some of the selections depend in whole or in part on certain special methods for generating their material and forms for presenting it.

Letters:
   Kemble, Montagu
Reviews:
   Cooper, Deacon, Frayn, Kael, Woolf
Editorial:
   Fulford
Interviews:
   Gordimer, Lane, Ludwig
Research Essays:
   Cooper, Cutschall

Lectures:
Atwood, Brink, Cutschall, Meigs, Stein, Tuchman
Instructions:
Traill
Lists:
Bierce, Rooney, Updike
Dialogue:
Haliburton, Wilde

A Note to the Reader

No book on its own can answer all your questions about writing or tell you once and for all how to write. People learn to write only by writing—by finding out what does reach readers and what does not. There are no rigid rules, no certain shortcuts, no guarantees of success, and for that matter, no inevitable pitfalls. But there are models. By reading attentively, and by responding—sympathetically, analytically, and inquiringly—to other writers' efforts to communicate, you can increase your understanding of the ways that writers and readers connect, and you can learn some of the practical strategies that successful writers use.

Active Voice gives you a cross-section of such models. It shows a variety of twentieth-century writers (Canadian, American, British, Australian, South African, Jamaican) dealing with a variety of subjects (science, history, language, medicine, politics, the arts, economics, psychology, race, sport, philosophy, nature, gender, the media, travel, food, mathematics, personal experience) in a variety of styles and forms (formal, informal, experimental; personal narrative, interview, letter, editorial, review, investigation, argument, explanation, entertainment). (See the alternative tables of contents.) But the thematic and the technical are only the most obvious among the many avenues of approach offered you here. For example, asking if Americans write differently from Canadians, or women from men, or writers of the 1920s from writers of the 1970s, might lead to an informed discussion on the biases of culture, sex, and fashion that sometimes colour a writer's attitude or affect the premises on which an argument rests. Exploring the nature of rhythm might lead to a greater understanding of the importance of sound to an essay's effect on a reader. Seeking the relation between technique and meaning might lead to a greater understanding of the nature of literacy and a greater appreciation of the need for verbal accuracy in all kinds of communication. Examining expository essays alongside poems and narratives, and even beside prose forms conventionally considered nonliterary, might help develop an appreciation for literary endeavour in general. Much depends on your willingness to invest effort and imagination in the process of reading. By asking questions, suggesting possibilities, affirming the open-endedness of literary inquiry, and giving some indication of the range of twentieth-century stylistic excellence, the readings in this book give you models to follow and places to begin learning about writing.

The essays and categories isolated here are not meant to impose limits on your powers of invention. Whatever the examples in this collection might imply, not all lectures have to be argumentative, nor all reviews sarcastic or humorous. It is important to emphasize that language is flexible, to assert again and again that the forms of composition overlap and that the categories by which we describe the varieties of prose form are not mutually exclusive. Many of the examples in this book have more than one aim: to explain *and* persuade, for example, or to describe *and* amuse. And many, with some difference of emphasis, could be classified differently: Haig-Brown's narrative could be considered explanatory, Orwell's argument explanatory, Lewis Thomas's explanation argumentative, Dylan Thomas's memoir humorous, and so on. Keep in mind that the organization of any anthology of essays is essentially an arbitrary structuring device, one which the good reader will both use and transcend.

The particular organization that we have adopted for *Active Voice* is meant to draw your attention to three features of the strategy of writing essays:

1. The large or overall purpose that motivates a writer to write (to tell a story, to explain a problem, to convince someone of something). This element of form governs the division of the book into its seven sections. Section I stresses the importance of observing closely, actively, and personally; all the essays show what the authors themselves see, hear, do, and remember. Section II stresses the art of indirect communication. The good interviewer, for example, can induce people to reveal the character that lies behind their public mask, or to demonstrate the set of values that governs their judgments and their behaviour; other essays can be personally revealing, or can adapt the revelatory techniques of the interview and the journal to more conventional essay forms. The writers of such essays address one subject on the surface, even apparently neutrally, but all the while they are drawing attention to their real subject (which lies at some tangent to the other) and implying a different (and often more judgmental) interpretation of the details they are assembling. Sections III and IV explore the tasks of persuasion, explanation, and instruction; they show how these apparently abstract enterprises can also be subjectively organized, sometimes deliberately and sometimes unconsciously—the art of persuasion being the most open to personal bias, and the art of explanation being the most neutral. The next two sections, V and VI, isolate particular formal problems—humorous writing and experimentation—for practical consideration, and encourage apprentice writers to experiment intelligently as they practise their way toward their own personal style. In section VI, too, appear examples of fable and other narrative, adaptations of form which call attention to the fine line separating some essays from fiction. And section VII constitutes a kind of appendix, assembling a gallery of samples of prose, mostly from previous centuries,

illustrating diverse styles and techniques, along with exercises for practising stylistic analysis.

2. The immediate purpose—the sense of audience—that governs the writer's choice of form (letter, recipe, reminiscence, editorial, review, feature article, research essay, *jeu d'esprit*). These forms range across the general categories; you will find other kinds of form—advertisement, poem, anecdote—also used as examples in various parts of the book, and you may find it instructive to compare the conventions of prose with other, often more exclusively visual or aural, conventions of communication.

3. The specific techniques by which writers develop and express their ideas. The principal methods of development, what we here call *internal strategies*, are

> analysis;
> definition;
> classification;
> comparison and contrast;
> process analysis; and
> cause and effect.

An essay may seem to have one or another of these as its overall purpose. Traill's "Masquinonge" (section VII), for example, is strictly a process; but its *purpose* is to inform, to give instructions. Both Brink's and Fulford's pieces (section III) engage in definition, but both have argument or persuasion as their overall purpose, and both use other strategies internally, as well. Gorman's "Man, Bytes, Dog" (section V) is an exemplary piece of comparison and contrast, but its governing intention is to entertain, to amuse. Nearly every piece of writing will use one or more of these internal strategies in order to develop its ideas, to realize its overall purpose. Forster's essay (section I), for example, depends largely on analysis and cause and effect, Mitford's (section IV) on explaining a process, Baker's (section IV) on classification. If you examine almost any essay in this book, or any essay you are engaged in writing, you will find these techniques at work in the service of an overall purpose.

Even narration and description, which we treat in section I as overall purposes, commonly function as internal strategies. A description of a person or a scene, or a brief illustrative anecdote, often works toward achieving a larger purpose. Any process analysis, for example, is necessarily narration; Roueché's expository essay (section IV) depends heavily on narration. And the most common internal strategy of all, the supplying of *illustrations and examples*, of *details*, to explain or support a thesis, is so broad as to be all-embracing; that is, the illustrations and examples themselves are often made up of bits of narration, description, cause-and-effect, classification, and so on—though of course they may also be simply lists of concrete particulars illustrating a generalization. As you read and study the essays in this book, look for examples of these strategies at work.

3

The introductions to each section establish this triple context. Rather than analyze the essays that follow or prescribe procedures for reading them, however, they suggest some of the terms of reference within which different kinds of analysis and discussion can take place. They do this in part by definition and discussion, and in part by technical example. Direction, like meaning, often lies in form. The introduction to section IV, for instance, concerns the need for explanations to be clear, which is a commonplace that will raise little argument and little cheering. How actually to write clearly is another question. The essays in this section provide examples of some successful techniques: using a precise vocabulary, making comparisons between unfamiliar and familiar things, telling illustrative anecdotes, and adopting an informal, person-to-person tone. The introduction at once generalizes about these methods and uses at least some of them in the process of talking about them. Hence it begins anecdotally in order to discuss the effect of anecdotal beginnings, and uses the vocabulary of its own anecdote as part of its process of exploring the language of explanation. Meaning and method unite. You will discover analogous techniques in the other introductions as well: an ironic quotation, quoted ironically, forms part of the commentary on humorous writing; sentence fragments appear in a section that asks if it is acceptable to break standard rules of composition; rhetorical questions and other deliberate devices—litotes, chiasmus, simile, antithesis—appear both as strategies for argument and as examples for analysis.

Some of these terms and techniques—such as litotes (the "negative positive": "not unusual") and chiasmus (an X-shaped structure: "He had a talent for making the easy difficult and the difficult easy")—will not be familiar to all readers. Some of the essays, too, might seem unusually difficult. To add to what the introductions can do to illuminate them, therefore, *Active Voice* provides at the end of each section some brief accounts of relevant terms and some suggestions for study, discussion, and composition. Like the introductions, these study sections neither assert easy answers nor suggest that all answers come easily; part of the function of this book is to encourage a little overreaching, for real learning seldom takes place without it. Wrestling with something difficult can be frustrating, of course. But if you consult not only the resources within yourself but also those provided by our questions and suggestions, you can return to your challenging subject with more of the tools you need in order to master it. Such a procedure can prove far more stimulating than simply making do with the knowledge and skills you already have.

Similarly, because your ability to express yourself depends partly on the words you can command, each study section begins with a list of words selected from the essays in that section—not technical, foreign, coined, or otherwise special words, but words that can be useful in your general vocabulary. You may know many of them already, but ask yourself whether they are part of your *recognition* vocabulary rather than your *working* vocabulary. That is, you may understand a word when you read it in a context; you may even be able to define it; but can you use it naturally and confidently in your own writing? To increase your ability as a reader and your power as a writer, stretch your vocabulary. Keep your own list. Include not only words from our lists but also any others you encounter that you aren't thoroughly at home with. Even if you think you know a word, look it up: it may have uses you weren't aware of; try *tonic*, for instance, or *confer*. And don't be surprised if you have to look up other than "big" words: for example, are *shun*, *akin*, *loath*, and *wry* in your working vocabulary? Look your words up in a good dictionary; write out their definitions if necessary. But don't stop there. In order to make words part of your active vocabulary you must practise using them. Make it a point to incorporate some words from your list in whatever you find yourself writing. Compose sentences using them; if a word has more than one meaning or usage, write a sentence for each. If a word has derivatives or forms that function as different parts of speech, practise with all of them. Don't stop with *bigot*; use *bigotry* and *bigoted* as well. When you learn *facile*, learn *facility*, *facilely*, and *facilitate*. Try *heresy*, *heretic*, and *heretical*; *evoke*, *evocation*, *evocative*, and *evocatively*; *prudent*, *prudence*, *prudently*, *prudential*, and *prudentially*; *derided*, *derision*, *derisive*, and *derisively*; *dogma*, *dogmatic*, and *dog-matism*; and so on. And use some words figuratively as well as in a narrowly limited literal sense, as when Baker (section IV) writes of a "hypotenuse of sunlight," or Dillard in her essay in section I writes of being "ensconced in the lap of lichen." Finally, when you look up a word look at its *etymology*; knowing a word's origin often makes it more interesting and memorable: consider for example the etymologies of *abject*, *candid*, *curfew*, *scrupulous*, and *subjugation*. Your dictionary should provide the sources and histories of words as well as their current definitions; if it doesn't, get a better dictionary, or consult an etymological dictionary such as Eric Partridge's *Origins*.

Throughout, *Active Voice* emphasizes the extent to which form embodies meaning. In particular, this idea is the central concern of the essays in section VI. Depending on one's approach, this section could provide a forceful beginning. So could section VII. The essays throughout the book offer variety and hence a variety of places to start. Most of all, they are enjoyable in their own right, whether as models for the apprentice writer or as inquiries and diversions for people who just like to read.

To conclude this introductory note, here are some terms that you should be familiar with at the outset:

Diction The choice and use of words. "Good diction" means the use of correct and specific words. The term "levels of diction" refers to formal, informal, colloquial, and slang usage.

Idiom A combination of words that constitutes the accepted way of saying something in a particular language, even though it may not be entirely grammatical or make literal sense. For example we say (informally) "There is loads of time," treating *loads* as if it were singular, like *plenty*. Certain verbs and other words take certain prepositions: *agree on*, *agree to*, and *agree with* have precise but different usages, as do *differ from* and *differ with*, *compare to* and *compare with*, *wait for* and *wait on*, and *part from* and *part with*;

5

one can have mastery *of* something but mastery *over* someone; one is *convinced of* something but *persuaded to* do something; one can be *capable of* doing something but *able to* do it; something can be *redolent of* something but not *redolent with* it. The word *idiom* also refers to expressions like *by and large, all but* (as in "all but finished," where the seemingly equivalent *except* will not work in place of *but*), *all in (worn-out)*, and *shut up!* which work in defiance of logical or literal sense. Others, like *give the high sign, be on edge, take the lion's share, go the whole hog, bottle up, switched on, wet blanket, get in high gear, here and now, hit-and-miss, lay of the land, go to the dogs, a dog's breakfast*, and *as the crow flies*, show that many idioms are metaphorical and that some can be classified as slang or cliché, or both. Clearly many idioms cannot be translated literally into another language, though some do have equivalents. For example a *brown study* would in French be a *sombre rêverie*; but the French also say *broyer du noir*, which wouldn't work translated into English even though it overlaps in meaning with "to be in a brown study." *Battre les buissons* means much the same as our "beat the bushes," but it also works as a counterpart of our "beat around (or about) the bush." Where we would say "Ay, there's the rub" or "You've hit the nail on the head," the French would probably say "C'est là que gît le lièvre" and Germans either "Da liegt der Hase im Pfeffer" or "Da liegt der Hund begraben." (For more on idioms, see Hornyansky's essay in section VI.)

Cliché A trite expression, one worn-out from overuse (a bolt from the blue, last but not least, pretty as a picture, nothing new under the sun, it's a small world).

Abstract, concrete Basically, an abstract word denotes something intangible, such as an idea, quality, or condition (honour, beauty, laziness, patriotism, sorrow), and a concrete word denotes something tangible, perceivable by one or more of the senses (chair, fir tree, hyena, flame, raindrop). Poetry works mainly with the concrete; philosophical discussion, in contrast, can be relatively abstract. Much amateur writing is weak because it lacks concreteness.

General, specific Relative terms, different from *abstract* and *concrete*, with which they partly overlap. A *general* term denotes a class (for example *art*) which has subclasses named by *less general*—or *more specific*—terms (*painting, literature, music*, etc.). The term *literature* can be further subdivided into the less general or more specific classes of *poetry, fiction, essays*, etc., until you get to a single, indivisible, concrete item such as the novel sitting on your desk or the book you are reading right now. Generalizations are necessary ("There seems to be a violent streak in human beings"), for we could scarcely communicate without them; but they are seldom of much use unless supported by specifics ("Two of the players started a fight over an imagined insult, but fortunately they cooled off before anyone got hurt").

Syntax The arrangement of words; the grammatical relations among words in phrases, clauses, and sentences. *Grammar* is simply the systematic study and description of the way a language works.

Active voice, passive voice Grammatical terms describing two ways some verbs (transitive ones) can work. A verb in the active voice acts upon an object: A woman *bought* the green sports car this morning. When a verb is in the passive voice, what would otherwise be the object of the verb becomes the subject of the sentence: The car *was bought* by a woman this morning. (The *by*-phrase is not always present: The car *was bought* this morning. The verb is nevertheless still in the passive voice.) Verbs in the passive voice are generally weaker than verbs in the active voice, though they are sometimes useful in controlling emphasis and in constructing sentences when the agent or actor is unknown or unimportant. (The title of this book does not refer only to this grammatical principle; there we also use the term figuratively, to suggest that good writers actively and consciously choose their style, their "voice," rather than passively letting the style do the choosing.)

Fragment A group of words lacking a subject or a verb, or both. A fragment that is acceptable, that is satisfactorily complete because of context (as would be a brief answer to a question), is sometimes referred to as a *minor sentence.*

Point of view The angle or perspective from which an author writes, which governs the way a reader receives information. Technically, for example, the author of a narrative may use first-person point of view ("I did so and so") or third-person point of view ("She, he, they did so and so").

Metaphor A figurative use of language in which things not usually thought of as alike or even related are identified with each other; that is, a word or phrase usually applied to one thing is applied to something quite different, as in "The ship *ploughed* through the rough sea." At the end of the first paragraph of "Living Like Weasels" (section I), Dillard refers to a weasel as "socketed" into a man's hand. A metaphor often not only helps clarify meaning but also provokes a sharp reappraisal of the subject. A metaphor usually forces a reader to perceive one thing as if looking at it through the filter of the other: the weasel with its teeth partakes of the qualities of the two-pronged plug gripping its socket; or "socketed" may suggest merely something firmly and tightly pushed in. Slang is a prolific source of metaphor: *ace in the hole, square, coffin nail, heel.* So is a poet's imagination: "tongues of consuming fire" not only suggests the shape and movement of flames ("licking," often) but also enforces the idea of consuming as an act of eating, devouring. And some metaphors are buried deep in the language: "daisy" is a collapsed form of "day's eye." A *simile* is a form of metaphorical language that states a similarity explicitly, usually with *like* or *as*: "His voice was *like thunder*." A metaphor would condense the likeness, for example

7

into a verb, adjective, noun, or adverb: "He (or his voice) *thundered*"; "In his *thundering* voice"; "The *thunder* of his voice"; "He spoke *thunderously*." An *extended metaphor* (or simile) is one in which an implicit (or explicit) comparison is continued, like an analogy, beyond a single statement: "His voice thundered. When he spoke, the clouds parted and the lightning of his wit flashed through. The resulting deluge of information and entertainment floated the audience's spirits." Extended metaphors can be dangerous in that they sometimes get out of control or distract by becoming too much of a good thing, drowning out the point being made.

Image A verbal representation, either literal or figurative, of something concrete, usually something visual. Metaphors often create figurative images. An image can also be aural, olfactory, gustatory, tactile, or kinesthetic.

Symbol An image that not only represents a concrete, empirical reality but also makes that reality stand for something else, usually something more abstract. A flag, for example, not only represents a country but also symbolizes, for many people, their country's political or ethical virtues. The word *rose* not only represents an actual flower but also, in many poems, symbolizes feminine beauty or the Virgin Mary. Don't confuse the verbs *symbolize* and *represent*.

Allusion An indirect or casual reference to something, usually something outside an immediate context. Writers often allude to figures and events from literature and other arts, from history, and from contemporary popular culture. When Forster in his essay "My Wood," for example (section I), alludes to particular passages in the Bible, he intends to call up in his readers' minds a wide array of associations that bear on what he is directly saying. When Dylan Thomas in his second paragraph (section I) rattles off a catalogue of well-known children's books, he expects it to help you conjure up memories of your own childhood Christmases and thus become more attuned to the mood and content of his essay. (But if you haven't read, or don't remember, *Struwwelpeter* and *Black Beauty* and the rest, you may have to do some homework in order to climb all the way aboard his memory-train.)

Tone An author's attitude toward his or her subject and audience. Tone is manifested by various stylistic qualities of a piece of writing. Tone can be formal, informal, relaxed, playful, serious, condescending, insulting, ironic, sarcastic, bitter, questioning, matter-of-fact, and so on. It is related to the general sense of point of view.

Rhythm The movement or cadence in an arrangement of words, sentences, or paragraphs; the movement one feels when reading (even if one is not reading aloud). Is there a regular, rhythmical, metrical beat from the patterns of stress on the syllables? The preceding sentence, for example, is dactylic. Besides the dactyl (/∪∪), the standard metrical feet are the iamb (∪/), the trochee (/∪), the anapest (∪∪/), and the spondee (//). Though regular metre is relatively rare in prose, other kinds of rhythm are not. For example is there a rising—or a falling—inflection to the words? Does a string of words move quickly, or does it, instead, move rather heavily, sluggishly, slowly? (Punctuation of course affects rhythm in a sentence.) Is there enough variety of sentence and paragraph length to prevent a monotonous rhythm?

Sound patterns The flow of prose can also be affected by such patterns of sound as *alliteration* (repetition of the same sound at the beginning of nearby words), *assonance* (similarity of vowel sounds within nearby words), *consonance* (similarity of consonant sounds within nearby words), and even *rhyme* (the same or similar sound at the ends of words, beginning with the last stressed vowel; night flight, dutiful and beautiful, the salvation of the nation). Such patterns often occur accidentally, of course, but they can be controlled.

If you want further explanation of these and other terms defined in this book, or if we have not provided definitions of terms you don't know, you should consult a good standard dictionary. Better yet, there are many dictionaries or glossaries of literary terms that will help you even more. Here are the names of a few of them, just to get you started:

M.H. Abrams, *A Glossary of Literary Terms*
Chris Baldick, *The Concise Oxford Dictionary of Literary Terms*
C. Hugh Holman and William Harmon, *A Handbook to Literature*

Once the terms are familiar to you, apply them to the essays and to your other reading, practise using the techniques yourself, and ask yourself how useful and effective they are for shaping your ideas in prose and for reaching your chosen reader.

Introduction: Audience and Purpose

To begin, here are six examples of how some people actually talk:

1. "Now, boys and girls . . . ."
2. "It has come to a point where the Prime Minister must begin to face matters and recognize that an election must be called forthwith."
3. "You have *no idea* how difficult it's been to arrange everything for this afternoon."
4. "Cold out by the bluff today, eh?"
5. "There's still a real relationship between him and I, irregardless of what he done."
6. "The organization metatalk of this is offered in terms of the recognition that composition situations will be met down the road, and persons without a game plan, on the basis of the correlation interface between their multivalent experimental factors and their societal age-group factors, will be quantified institution-wise."

Each utterance conveys a message—though the sixth example deeply buries it—and each conveys clearly the character of the speaker. Interestingly, however, the message that the speaker intends and the public face that he or she wishes to display often differ from the message an audience actually hears and the face it perceives. Consider again the six examples:

1. The first utterance demands a context before a listener can adequately interpret it. Who is the speaker, and who is he or she talking to? Is it a storyteller's conventional opening? Is it a sharp directive demanding instant attention—or action—from a group of children? Or is it a camp counsellor's experienced effort to cajole order out of chaos? Or could it even be a sign of condescension? How for example would a group of fifteen-year-olds respond to a camp counsellor who addressed them this way? How would you, as a reader of this book, react if we as editors

addressed *you* with these words? Clearly, given differences in milieu or in the age of the audience, this communication could break down.

2. The second utterance, clearly political, just as clearly comes from the mouth of someone not on the governing party's side. It will scarcely be effective. Compare it for a moment with the standard slogans of actual election campaigns: "Hold the Vote Now!" "Vote Them Out!" "Time for a Change!" The bluntly monosyllabic slogans appeal directly—hence personally—to the listener: "*You* vote them out." But any utterance that begins wordily (*It has come to a point where*), continues with vague words (*matters, forthwith*), and closes with a passive evasion (*must be called*—by whom???) dooms itself. No one will take it seriously. No one will hear the overt message; they will hear a waffling covert message instead, something like: "I know this is futile but the party requires me to make a mechanical gesture." The emphasis falls, finally, on the futility and the sense of obligation.

3. The third example, too, offers a personal glimpse of the speaker. Ostensibly it's about *you* ("You have no idea"), but really it's about *I*, the speaker. "It's been *difficult*, for me," the speaker is saying. "Admire *me* because *I've* done something difficult; *I've* put *myself* out." The message contains at least two further notions. The first —"I'm a martyr"—is a curiously perverse sort of self-aggrandizing. The second— "and it's *your fault*"—implies that the afternoon's event is less than successful. This last twist emerges because the message ("*no idea*," "*difficult*") is essentially negative. It occurs only when there's a problem. And whose problem is it? The speaker's, perhaps—certainly not *yours*—but the speaker has difficulty admitting to it. In any case, an afternoon event that's proceeding well will call forth an utterance more like "There was a lot to do, but *we* had a *good* time doing it." It is at once less defensive and less shrill.

4. The fourth example reveals no problem of personality. It's a colloquial fragment of conversation, informal in tone, designed not so much to impart or to ask for information—despite the fact that it's cast as a question—as to give a kind of ritual voice to a chance encounter. "How do you do?" offers a more formal parallel. Try to imagine yourself replying, "I do do well." The exchange is a social convention, varying according to the social circumstances. The speaker who says "Pleased to meet you" may not be. People who say "Charmed, I'm sure" convey the distinct impression that they aren't, and that they're stuffy to boot. What we know of the speaker who uses *bluff* and *eh*? has more to do with his nationality than his social status. He's likely Canadian. But there's another geographic variable here, for if he's a prairie speaker, *bluff* means a *grove of trees*, not a *cliff*. Without a context, the utterance is ambiguous.

11

5. In a conversational context, a sentence fragment—as in example number four—is perfectly acceptable. Provided it grows directly out of a previous utterance, its meaning will usually be clear. But the fifth example contains a grating combination of plain and fancy mistakes. Among some occupations and in some environments, grammatical errors do constitute a norm, of course; in such settings, correctly spoken English would sound curiously stiff. But in an environment where grammatical correctness is valued, an ungrammatical speaker sounds either boorish or ill-educated. Whether the simple mistakes in this example—mistakes of diction (*irregardless*) and of grammar (*what he done*)—derive from lack of education or from regional or cultural norms of usage would be hard to tell were it not for the presence of the more elaborate mistake (*between him and I*). The overcorrection here—which erases *me* even when syntax demands it—suggests some acquaintance with grammar and a conscious desire to appear "proper." But the ultimate effect is the same as that of tawdry paintings: of elegance wanted, and elegance still wanting.

6. The final example shows what happens when inflated notions of elegance and preciseness take over. The result is inelegance and impreciseness. Long words do not intrinsically sound better than short ones, nor do they somehow mean better. Yet these assumptions seem to lie behind every outburst of such bafflegab. Relying on the passive voice allows the speaker to evade responsibility for everything he says; relying on clichéd stock phrases (*game plan*), vague reference (*this*), noun clusters (*composition situation*), long words and invented words (*multivalent, metatalk*) allows him to create the illusion of complexity and great intelligence even when both are lacking. Listeners cannot just absorb a communication like this one; they have to decode it. And the message they decode is often crashingly pedestrian.

These examples draw attention to many of the points of connection between speakers and their audiences. Age, education, occupation, social standing, nationality, region, time, and taste can all bring speaker and listener together or irrevocably separate them. Speakers who condescend, either through the tone they adopt or by oversimplifying their subject, cause listeners to respond, at the very least, unsympathetically. Similarly, overestimating an audience's ability to handle the complexity of a subject or a certain level of vocabulary will estrange speakers from the people they are trying to reach. Waffling, evading the responsibility for thought, speaking too quickly, and speaking too slowly or quietly all interfere with the act of communicating. An audience distracted by a speaker's dress or gestures, by a strange or strained pitch of voice, by a failure to look at them (or at the television camera), or by a series of verbal tics (*er, um, y'know, like*) is not listening to the words. It is more likely counting the *ums*. Such speakers parody themselves, but may never realize it, nor recognize how much they are dissolving before their audience's eyes.

Other speakers, knowledgeable about body language, can cleverly manipulate their audience through their gestures rather than through their actual words. The earnest crease in the forehead, the expansively open gesture of the arms, the honest raising of the eyebrows or widening of the eyes: speakers can falsify their emotions as easily as they can leave them on display. The informed audience learns how to distinguish between the trustworthy and the deceptive, between the actual and the acted, between the event and the advertisement for the event. The social psychology of the relation between speaker and listener is far more complex than this simple declaration suggests, but the ability to recognize some of the links between them is increasingly necessary as North American culture comes to rely more and more on pictorial and oral communication.

The relation between writer and reader is not the same as that between speaker and listener. It is similar, but the act of writing things down has the effect of limiting an audience in further ways. Education, whether formal or informal, remains an issue, for writers almost always write to an audience that values the act of reading. Writing for a person who can't read is self-contradictory; writing for a person who won't read is probably futile. One might argue, therefore, that writing is essentially a middle-class act, and that the spoken rhetoric of the street, the wharf, the hustings, and the television set can reach a greater range of people than books, and reach them more directly. That may or may not be so; but what is undeniable is that writers, like speakers, face problems of reaching and holding their chosen audiences. And they are subject to many of the same variables of style. Tone, directness, accuracy, level, and movement all matter acutely if a writer intends to win a receptive audience. Merely writing things down, in the first words that come to mind and in whatever order they occur, will not suffice. An economics argument in current slang would not convince the people attending a businessmen's luncheon; producing a simile like "as barren as a plant sale reduced to its lowest common cactus" is not likely to amuse gardeners, especially cactus fanciers.

Writers write; but they write with both a purpose and a reader in mind. Knowing *why* they want to write and *what* they want to say, they make a series of decisions: to write a letter or an essay or a book, for children or adults, for a specialized group or the general public. Then, as they plan and write and revise, the fine rhetorical choices follow, and in making them, writers shape what they say until they are as sure as they can be that they have matched their intention with their audience. They have to consider the age, education, biases, ability, and expectations of their readers. They have to decide if they want to be funny or serious or neutral or sad. They have to decide whether they want to entertain or instruct or argue or describe or reveal. They have to decide if they want to announce their subject directly or to draw their readers into deducing conclusions. They have to know their subject and their grammar well enough to be accurate and clear. They have to decide whether to be personal, informal, and conversational, or distant and formal and objective. And they have to decide how to shape their rhetoric: whether to make it flow grandly or step in staccato phrases, to ring eloquently or murmur laconically, to dazzle with metaphor or convince by plain speaking. Only when they have made these decisions are they close to a strategy for writing effectively on a given occasion.

Whether consciously or unconsciously, writers question their choice of words (are they monosyllabic or polysyllabic? abstract or concrete? easy or difficult? objective or slanted? formal or informal? general or precise?), syntax and structure (are the sentences short or long? simple or complex? varied or unvaried? fragmentary or whole?), and the organization of their whole work (is it coherent? unified? clear? is the emphasis appropriate? do the paragraphs flow?). If they are true stylists they worry also about the sound and the cadence and the freshness of the arrangements they have devised. In short, they address themselves actively to their audience in their own voice and in a form they choose. The choices they make do not derive from some secret set of absolutes. There is no hidden writer's chart somewhere that reveals to a chosen few that polysyllables are "good" and informality "bad."

Nor do writers usually set out, as textbooks often imply, to tackle as vague a project as a "comparison-and-contrast essay." They seldom begin with a structural device; rather they have subjects to explore, and they know that substance and style are intrinsically related. They have audiences to satisfy, and they have particular tasks to do—letters to write, explanations to provide, stories to tell, arguments to deliver. In carrying out these tasks as articulately as possible, skilled writers can use an extraordinary variety of verbal techniques, even to the point of making deliberate errors to achieve particular effects. In the process they will demonstrate not only some of the many creative ways in which words work, but also the individuality that can invigorate all prose forms. Their work reveals the force of writing both for an audience and with a purpose in mind.

I

Writing to Relate and Describe

"Once upon a time..." and "Have you heard the one about..." are two of the most familiar ways in the language to begin a story. And they invite particular responses. The first, either part of a child's tale or else adopting the form of one, asks readers to suspend empirical judgments for the moment and to accept the possibilities of fantasy. The other nudges clearly toward the salacious bar-room jest or the simple corny joke. Like other preludes, they seize and settle the people in the taleteller's audience and establish the likely mood of the story to follow. These particular preludes, moreover, invite audiences to expect an ensuing narrative rather than an explanation or an argument. Only highly sophisticated writers manage to use such an opening for a different end.

Story, or narrative, rarely appears in as undiluted a form as it does in joking anecdotes. Even when constructed with a careful plot, as in novels and short stories, narratives contain more than the basic narrative elements of event, time, and sequence. Stories can, however, also appear in contexts other than purely narrative ones. The personal narrative, for example, contains a story, or stories, and conveys an individual personality. But it is not plotted. White, Thomas, Fisher, Haig-Brown, and Mukherjee, writing narrative memoirs and relating a variety of internal anecdotes, use an identifiable chronology and create individual characters. Plot, however, relies on causal relationships among episodes. One event makes another one happen, and part of the reader's task with a plotted narrative is to unravel how and why. In these essays, the writers focus primarily on something other than cause and effect. The events they write about may join to achieve a consistent single effect, therefore, but they do not connect into a plot. Fisher writes about food and family, Haig-Brown about the art of fishing and the temptations of pride, Mukherjee about familiarity, place, and the politics of privilege and custom. Characteristically, moreover, the narrative essayist employs descriptive as well as narrative techniques, and it is sometimes a moot point whether the essay that results should properly be called narrative or descriptive. In the long run, naming a proper category matters less than appreciating the essay itself, with its blend of techniques and the skilful balance which each author individually contrives.

Description begins in concrete observations; it delights in adjective and verb, and depends upon exact detail: smooth and elongated pebbles, squawking chimpanzees, lurching home late, the flash of jade-green thumb-nails, the muted thunder of my uncle's breathing. John Updike's verbal snapshot of Central Park is really an orchestration of just such details as these, cumulatively arranging an effect. But description, like narration, usually appears as an "impure" form. Narrative emphasizes temporal sequence but incidentally observes settings and records dramatic conversational exchanges; description emphasizes visual placement—direction, size, texture, and general appearance—but often for other than simply pictorial purposes. Hence in personal memoirs—and even in much fiction—descriptive passages frequently occur. They can heighten a reader's sense of both the place and the event a writer is recreating, intensify the mood that the writer is striving to convey, and often illustrate or epitomize, concretely and clearly, the writer's ideas. This excerpt from an 1883 feminist novel, Olive Schreiner's *The Story of an African Farm*, employs descriptive details for just such purposes:

> It was eight o'clock when they neared the farm-house: a red-brick building, with kraals to the right and a small orchard to the left. Already there were signs of unusual life and bustle: one cart, a waggon, and a couple of saddles against the wall betokened the arrival of a few early guests, whose numbers would soon be largely increased. To a Dutch country wedding guests start up in numbers astonishing to one who has merely ridden through the plains of sparsely-inhabited karroo.
>
> As the morning advances, riders on many shades of steeds appear from all directions, and add their saddles to the long rows against the walls, shake hands, drink coffee, and stand about outside in groups to watch the arriving carts and ox-waggons, as they are unburdened of their heavy freight of massive Tantes and comely daughters, followed by swarms of children of all sizes, dressed in all manner of print and moleskin, who are taken care of by Hottentot, Kaffir, and half-caste

nurses, whose many-shaded complexions, ranging from light yellow up to ebony black, add variety to the animated scene. Everywhere is excitement and bustle, which gradually increases as the time for the return of the wedding party approaches. Preparations for the feast are actively advancing in the kitchen; coffee is liberally handed round, and amid a profound sensation, and the firing of guns, the horse-waggon draws up, and the wedding party alight. Bride and bridegroom, with their attendants, march solemnly to the marriage chamber, where bed and box are decked out in white, with ends of ribbon and artificial flowers, and where on a row of chairs the party solemnly seat themselves. After a time bridesmaid and best man rise, and conduct in with ceremony each individual guest, to wish success and to kiss bride and bridegroom. Then the feast is set on the table, and it is almost sunset before the dishes are cleared away, and the pleasure of the day begins. Everything is removed from the great front room, and the mud floor, well rubbed with bullock's blood, glistens like polished mahogany. The female portion of the assembly flock into the side-rooms to attire themselves for the evening; and re-issue clad in white muslin, and gay with bright ribbons and brass jewellery. The dancing begins as the tallow candles are stuck up about the walls, the music coming from a couple of fiddlers in a corner of the room. Bride and bridegroom open the ball, and the floor is soon covered with whirling couples, and everyone's spirits rise. The bridal pair mingle freely in the throng, and here and there a musical man sings vigorously as he drags his partner through the Blue Water or John Speriwig; boys shout and applaud, and the enjoyment and confusion are intense, till eleven o'clock comes. By this time the children who swarm in the siderooms are not to be kept quiet longer, even by hunches of bread and cake; there is a general howl and wail, that rises yet higher than the scraping of fiddles, and mothers rush from their partners to knock small heads together, and cuff little nursemaids, and force the wailers down into unoccupied corners of beds, under tables, and behind boxes. In half an hour every variety of childish snore is heard on all sides, and it has become perilous to raise or set down a foot in any of the side-rooms lest a small head or hand should be crushed. Now, too, the busy feet have broken the solid coating of the floor, and a cloud of fine dust rises, that makes a yellow halo round the candles, and sets asthmatic people coughing, and grows denser, till to recognize any one on the opposite side of the room becomes impossible, and a partner's face is seen through a yellow mist.

To create the effect she wants, Schreiner chooses precise terms, often in Afrikaans (*kraal, karroo, Tantes*), specific numbers and colours (*one cart, brass jewellery*), exact and evocative details (*half-caste nurses, artificial flowers, bullock's blood*, and *John Speriwig*), and a whole array of verbs, both active and passive. The variety of adjectives lends colour and texture to the scene, but it is the verbs that give the passage its life. Schreiner marshalls the active verbs to contrive an illusion of speed and commotion: riders *appear, add, shake*, and *drink;* the wedding company *flock, reissue, mingle, sing, drag, shout*, and *applaud;*

mothers *rush, knock, cuff,* and *force.* Such verbs help her to perceive and define movement exactly and therefore to describe scenes effectively. She uses static verbs (*is, seem, appear*) sparingly. But somewhat surprisingly, she does use a number of verbs in the passive voice (coffee *is handed round,* the dishes *are cleared away,* everything *is removed* from the table), which ordinarily would have a dampening effect on the action; here, under creative control, they manage to generalize from the specific event, to imply that the events and relationships described never change in this society: the women, who are doing the work, disappear into the passive structures. It is not difficult, then, to see the relation between form and meaning, to see how the author makes the activity itself inherently misleading, and how she makes the paragraphs form part of her novel's general attack upon the static roles and relationships which society opens to women.

Essayists, like novelists, can use prose rhythm and precise detail evocatively. Thomas's attempt to capture the Welsh vernacular, Mukherjee's anecdotal representations of Indian speech, and MacLennan's choral invocation of the Québécois *ouais* all illustrate the effectiveness of rhythmic control. Forster's, White's, Eiseley's, and Dillard's mastery of simple verbs, their talent for metaphor, and their eye for significant detail all contribute to their transformations of experience into art. Good writers know, of course, that not all metaphors are valid. Many are inappropriate, clichéd, irrelevant, and unnecessary; and no good writer would be drawn into writing a mixed metaphor—as in the sentence "He's buttered his bread, and now he must lie in it"—without being aware of the ludicrous image it is likely to create. If the writer's intention is to amuse, or if the established situation is a little bizarre, the mixed metaphor's incongruity might reinforce the effect; but otherwise it will jolt a reader abruptly out of an essay. Good writers know, too, that not all details are significant. Much of the art of good writing is knowing when to leave things out. The wrong details, or too many or too few, will cause the reader to respond unfavourably or not at all. But leaving out the right things at the right time—as Eiseley does in his rhythmic account of the way the mind remembers and discovers—can at once intensify the effect of the remaining details and add to the suspense of the narrative memoir and the surprise of its conclusion.

Perhaps most important, because narrative tries above all else to interest and entertain, good writers know that not every personal experience intrinsically fascinates every reader; it is the *telling* of a story that is fascinating. When writers subtly transform experience, the process may appear effortless, but the transformations appear subtle and easy only because the writers have been so skillful at selecting and arranging details that the reader is willing to watch along with them, the listener willing to hear.

Central Park

John Updike

(March 1956)

On the afternoon of the first day of spring, when the gutters were still heaped high with Monday's snow but the sky itself was swept clean, we put on our galoshes and walked up the sunny side of Fifth Avenue to Central Park. There we saw:

Great black rocks emerging from the melting drifts, their craggy skins glistening like the backs of resurrected brontosaurs.

A pigeon on the half-frozen pond strutting to the edge of the ice and looking a duck in the face.

A policeman getting his shoe wet testing the ice.

Three elderly relatives trying to coax a little boy to accompany his father on a sled ride down a short but steep slope. After much balking, the boy did, and, sure enough, the sled tipped over and the father got his collar full of snow. Everybody laughed except the boy, who sniffled.

Four boys in black leather jackets throwing snowballs at each other. (The snow was ideally soggy, and packed hard with one squeeze.)

Seven men without hats.

Twelve snowmen, none of them intact.

Two men listening to the radio in a car parked outside the Zoo; Mel Allen was broadcasting the Yanks-Cardinals game from St. Petersburg.

A tahr (*Hemitragus jemlaicus*) pleasantly squinting in the sunlight.

An aoudad absently pawing the mud and chewing.

A yak with its back turned.

Empty cages labelled "Coati," "Orang-outang," "Ocelot."

A father saying to his little boy, who was annoyed almost to tears by the inactivity of the seals, "Father [Father Seal, we assumed] is very tired; he worked hard all day."

Most of the cafeteria's out-of-doors tables occupied.

A pretty girl in black pants falling on them at the Wollman Memorial Rink.

"BILL & DORIS" carved on a tree. "REX & RITA" written in the snow.

Two old men playing, and six supervising, a checkers game.

The Michael Friedsam Foundation Merry-Go-Round, nearly empty of children but overflowing with calliope music.

A man on a bench near the carrousel reading, through sunglasses, a book on economics.

Crews of shinglers repairing the roof of the Tavern-on-the-Green.

A woman dropping a camera she was trying to load, the film unrolling in the slush and exposing itself.

A little colored boy in aviator goggles rubbing his ears and saying, "He really hurt me." "No, he didn't," his nursemaid told him.

The green head of Giuseppe Mazzini staring across the white softball field, unblinking, though the sun was in its eyes.

Water murmuring down walks and rocks and steps. A grown man trying to block one rivulet with snow.

Things like brown sticks nosing through a plot of cleared soil.

A tire track in a piece of mud far removed from where any automobiles could be.

Footprints around a KEEP OFF sign.

Two pigeons feeding each other.

Two showgirls, whose faces had not yet thawed the frost of their makeup, treading indignantly through the slush.

A plump old man saying "Chick, chick" and feeding peanuts to squirrels.

Many solitary men throwing snowballs at tree trunks.

Many birds calling to each other about how little the Ramble has changed.

One red mitten lying lost under a poplar tree.

An airplane, very bright and distant, slowly moving through the branches of a sycamore.

Memories of Christmas

Dylan Thomas

One Christmas was so much like another, in those years, around the seatown corner now, and out of all sound except the distant speaking of the voices I sometimes hear a moment before sleep, that I can never remember whether it snowed for six days and six nights when I was twelve or whether it snowed for twelve days and twelve nights when I was six; or whether the ice broke and the skating grocer vanished like a snowman through a white trap-door on that same Christmas Day that the mince-pies finished Uncle Arnold and we tobogganed down the seaward hill, all the afternoon, on the best tea-tray, and Mrs Griffiths complained, and we threw a snowball at her niece, and my hands burned so, with the heat and the cold, when I held them in front of the fire, that I cried for twenty minutes and then had some jelly.

All the Christmases roll down the hill towards the Welsh-speaking sea, like a snowball growing whiter and bigger and rounder, like a cold and headlong moon bundling down the sky that was our street; and they stop at the rim of the ice-edged, fish-freezing waves, and I plunge my hands in the snow and bring out whatever I can find; holly or robins or pudding, squabbles and carols and oranges and tin whistles, and the fire in the front room, and bang go the crackers, and holy, holy, holy, ring the bells, and the glass bells shaking on the tree, and Mother Goose, and Struwelpeter—oh! the baby-burning flames and the clacking scissorman!—Billy Bunter and Black Beauty, Little Women and boys who have three helpings, Alice and Mrs Potter's badgers, penknives, teddybears—named after a Mr Theodore Bear, their inventor, or father, who died recently in the United States—mouth-organs, tin-soldiers, and blancmange, and Auntie Bessie playing 'Pop Goes the Weasel' and 'Nuts in May' and 'Oranges and Lemons' on the untuned piano in the parlour all through the thimble-hiding musical-chairing blind-man's-buffing party at the end of the never-to-be-forgotten day at the end of the unremembered year.

In goes my hand into that wool-white bell-tongued ball of holidays resting at the margin of the carol-singing sea, and out come Mrs Prothero and the firemen.

It was on the afternoon of the day of Christmas Eve, and I was in Mrs Prothero's garden, waiting for cats, with her son Jim. It was snowing. It was always snowing at Christmas; December, in my memory, is white as Lapland, though there were no reindeers. But there were cats. Patient, cold, and callous, our hands wrapped in socks, we waited to snowball the cats. Sleek and long as jaguars and terrible-whiskered, spitting and snarling they would slink and sidle over the white back-garden walls, and the lynx-eyed hunters, Jim and I, fur-capped and moccasined trappers from Hudson's Bay off Eversley Road, would hurl our deadly snowballs at the green of their eyes. The wise cats never appeared. We were so still, Eskimo-footed arctic marksmen in the muffling silence of the eternal snows—eternal, ever since Wednesday—that we never heard Mrs Prothero's first cry from her igloo at the bottom of the garden. Or, if we heard it at all, it was, to us, like the far-off challenge of our enemy and prey, the neighbour's Polar Cat. But soon the voice grew louder. 'Fire!' cried Mrs Prothero, and she beat the dinner-gong. And we ran down the garden, with the snowballs in our arms, towards the house, and smoke, indeed, was pouring out of the dining-room, and the gong was bombilating, and Mrs Prothero was announcing ruin like a town-crier in Pompeii. This was better than all the cats in Wales standing on the wall in a row. We bounded into the house, laden with snowballs, and stopped at the open door of the smoke-filled room. Something was burning all right; perhaps it was Mr Prothero, who always slept there after midday dinner with a newspaper over his face; but he was standing in the middle of the room, saying 'A fine Christmas!' and smacking at the smoke with a slipper.

'Call the fire-brigade,' cried Mrs Prothero as she beat the gong.

'They won't be there,' said Mr Prothero, 'it's Christmas.'

There was no fire to be seen, only clouds of smoke and Mr Prothero standing in the middle of them, waving his slipper as though he were conducting.

'Do something,' he said.

And we threw all our snowballs into the smoke—I think we missed Mr Prothero—and ran out of the house to the telephone-box.

'Let's call the police as well,' Jim said.

'And the ambulance.'

'And Ernie Jenkins, he likes fires.'

But we only called the fire-brigade, and soon the fire-engine came and three tall men in helmets brought a hose into the house and Mr Prothero got out just in time before they turned it on. Nobody could have had a noisier Christmas Eve. And when the firemen turned off the hose and were standing in the wet and smoky room, Jim's aunt, Miss Prothero, came downstairs and peered in at them. Jim and I waited, very quietly, to hear what she would say to them. She said the right thing, always. She looked at the three tall firemen in their shining helmets, standing among the smoke and cinders and dissolving snowballs, and she said: 'Would you like something to read?'

Now out of that bright white snowball of Christmas gone comes the stocking, the stocking of stockings, that hung at the foot of the bed with the arm of a golliwog dangling over the top and small bells ringing in the toes. There was a company, gallant and scarlet but never nice to taste though I always tried when very young, of belted and busbied and musketed lead soldiers so soon to lose their heads and legs in the wars on the kitchen table after the tea-things, the mince-pies, and the cakes that I helped to make by stoning the raisins and eating them, had been cleared away; and a bag of moist and many-coloured jelly-babies and a folded flag and a false nose and a tram-conductor's cap and a machine that punched tickets and rang a bell; never a catapult; once, by a mistake that no one could explain, a little hatchet; and a rubber buffalo, or it may have been a horse, with a yellow head and haphazard legs; and a celluloid duck that made, when you pressed it, a most unducklike noise, a mewing moo that an ambitious cat might make who wishes to be a cow; and a painting-book in which I could make the grass, the trees, the sea, and the animals any colour I pleased; and still the dazzling sky-blue sheep are grazing in the red field under a flight of rainbow-beaked and pea-green birds.

Christmas morning was always over before you could say Jack Frost. And look! suddenly the pudding was burning! Bang the gong and call the fire-brigade and the book-loving firemen! Someone found the silver three-penny-bit with a currant on it; and the someone was always Uncle Arnold. The motto in my cracker read:

> Let's all have fun this Christmas Day,
> Let's play and sing and shout hooray!

and the grown-ups turned their eyes towards the ceiling, and Auntie Bessie, who had already been frightened, twice, by a clockwork mouse, whimpered at the sideboard and had some elderberry wine. And someone put a glass bowl full of nuts on the littered table, and my uncle said, as he said once every year: 'I've got a shoe-nut here. Fetch me a shoe-horn to open it, boy.'

And dinner was ended.

And I remember that on the afternoon of Christmas Day, when the others sat around the fire and told each other that this was nothing, no, nothing, to the great snowbound and turkey-proud yule-log-crackling holly-berry-bedizined and kissing-under-the-mistletoe Christmas when *they* were children, I would go out, school-capped and gloved and mufflered, with my bright new boots squeaking, into the white world on to the seaward hill, to call on Jim and Dan and Jack and to walk with them through the silent snowscape of our town.

We went padding through the streets, leaving huge deep footprints in the snow, on the hidden pavements.

'I bet people'll think there's been hippoes.'

'What would you do if you saw a hippo coming down Terrace Road?'

'I'd go like this, bang! I'd throw him over the railings and roll him down the hill and then I'd tickle him under the ear and he'd wag his tail...'

'What would you do if you saw *two* hippoes...?'

Iron-flanked and bellowing he-hippoes clanked and blundered and battered through the scudding snow towards us as we passed by Mr Daniel's house.

'Let's post Mr Daniel a snowball through his letterbox.'

'Let's write things in the snow.'

'Let's write "Mr Daniel looks like a spaniel" all over his lawn.'

'Look,' Jack said, 'I'm eating snow-pie.'

'What's it taste like?'

'Like snow-pie,' Jack said.

Or we walked on the white shore.

'Can the fishes see it's snowing?'

'They think it's the sky falling down.'

The silent one-clouded heavens drifted on to the sea.

'All the old dogs have gone.'

Dogs of a hundred mingled makes yapped in the summer at the sea-rim and yelped at the trespassing mountains of the waves.

'I bet St Bernards would like it now.'

And we were snowblind travellers lost on the north hills, and the great dewlapped dogs, with brandy-flasks round their necks, ambled and shambled up to us, baying 'Excelsior.'

We returned home through the desolate poor sea-facing streets where only a few children fumbled with bare red fingers in the thick wheel-rutted snow and cat-called after us, their voices fading away, as we trudged uphill, into the cries of the dock-birds and the hooters of ships out in the white and whirling bay.

Bring out the tall tales now that we told by the fire as we roasted chestnuts and the gaslight bubbled low. Ghosts with their heads under their arms trailed their chains and said 'whooo' like owls in the long nights when I dared not look over my shoulder; wild beasts lurked in the cubby-hole under the stairs where the gas-meter ticked. 'Once upon a time,' Jim said, 'there were three boys, just like us, who got lost in the dark in the snow, near Bethesda Chapel, and this is what happened to them....' It was the most dreadful happening I had ever heard.

And I remember that we went singing carols once, a night or two before Christmas Eve, when there wasn't the shaving of a moon to light the secret, white-flying streets. At the end of a long road was a drive that led to a large house, and we stumbled up the darkness of the drive that night, each one of us afraid, each one holding a stone in his hand in case, and all of us too brave to say a word. The wind made through the drive-trees noises as of old and unpleasant and maybe web-footed men wheezing in caves. We reached the black bulk of the house.

'What shall we give them?' Dan whispered.

'"Hark the Herald"? "Christmas comes but Once a Year"?'

'No,' Jack said: 'We'll sing "Good King Wenceslas." I'll count three.'

One, two, three, and we began to sing, our voices high and seemingly distant in the snow-felted darkness round the house that was occupied by nobody we knew. We stood close together, near the dark door.

> Good King Wenceslas looked out
> On the Feast of Stephen.

And then a small, dry voice, like the voice of someone who has not spoken for a long time, suddenly joined our singing: a small, dry voice from the other side of the door: a small, dry voice through the keyhole. And when we stopped running we were outside *our* house; the front room was lovely and bright; the gramophone was playing; we saw the red and white balloons hanging from the gas-bracket; uncles and aunts sat by the fire; I thought I smelt our supper being fried in the kitchen. Everything was good again, and Christmas shone through all the familiar town.

'Perhaps it was a ghost,' Jim said.

'Perhaps it was trolls,' Dan said, who was always reading.

'Let's go in and see if there's any jelly left,' Jack said. And we did that.

A Thing Shared

M.F.K. Fisher

(1918)

Now you can drive from Los Angeles to my Great-Aunt Maggie's ranch on the other side of the mountains in a couple of hours or so, but the first time I went there it took most of a day.

Now the roads are worthy of even the All-Year-Round Club's boasts, but twenty-five years ago, in the September before people thought peace had come again, you could hardly call them roads at all. Down near the city they were oiled, all right, but as you went farther into the hills toward the wild desert around Palmdale, they turned into rough dirt. Finally they were two wheel-marks skittering every which way through the Joshua trees.

It was very exciting: the first time my little round brown sister Anne and I had ever been away from home. Father drove us up from home with Mother in the Ford, so that she could help some cousins can fruit.

We carried beer for the parents (it exploded in the heat), and water for the car and Anne and me. We had four blowouts, but that was lucky, Father said as he patched the tires philosophically in the hot sun; he'd expected twice as many on such a long hard trip.

The ranch was wonderful, with wartime crews of old men and loud-voiced boys picking the peaches and early pears all day, and singing and rowing at night in the bunkhouses. We couldn't go near them or near the pen in the middle of a green alfalfa field where a new prize bull, black as thunder, pawed at the pale sand.

We spent most of our time in a stream under the cottonwoods, or with Old Mary the cook, watching her make butter in a great churn between her mountainous knees. She slapped it into pats, and put them down in the stream where it ran hurriedly through the darkness of the butter-house.

She put stone jars of cream there, too, and wire baskets of eggs and lettuces, and when she drew them up, like netted fish, she would shake the cold water onto us and laugh almost as much as we did.

Then Father had to go back to work. It was decided that Mother would stay at the ranch and help put up more fruit, and Anne and I would go home with him. That was as exciting as leaving it had been, to be alone with Father for the first time.

He says now that he was scared daft at the thought of it, even though our grandmother was at home as always to watch over us. He says he actually

26

shook as he drove away from the ranch, with us like two suddenly strange small monsters on the hot seat beside him.

Probably he made small talk. I don't remember. And he didn't drink any beer, sensing that it would be improper before two unchaperoned young ladies.

We were out of the desert and into deep winding canyons before the sun went down. The road was a little smoother, following streambeds under the live-oaks that grow in all the gentle creases of the dry tawny hills of that part of California. We came to a shack where there was water for sale, and a table under the dark wide trees.

Father told me to take Anne down the dry streambed a little way. That made me feel delightfully grown-up. When we came back we held our hands under the water faucet and dried them on our panties, which Mother would never let us do.

Then we sat on a rough bench at the table, the three of us in the deep green twilight, and had one of the nicest suppers I have ever eaten.

The strange thing about it is that all three of us have told other people that same thing, without ever talking of it among ourselves until lately. Father says that all his nervousness went away, and he saw us for the first time as two little brown humans who were fun. Anne and I both felt a subtle excitement at being alone for the first time with the only man in the world we loved.

(We loved Mother too, completely, but we were finding out, as Father was too, that it is good for parents and for children to be alone now and then with one another...the man alone or the woman, to sound new notes in the mysterious music of parenthood and childhood.)

That night I not only saw my Father for the first time as a person. I saw the golden hills and the live-oaks as clearly as I have ever seen them since; and I saw the dimples in my little sister's fat hands in a way that still moves me because of that first time; and I saw food as something beautiful to be shared with people instead of as a thrice-daily necessity.

I forget what we ate, except for the end of the meal. It was a big round peach pie, still warm from Old Mary's oven and the ride over the desert. It was deep, with lots of juice, and bursting with ripe peaches picked that noon. Royal Albertas, Father said they were. The crust was the most perfect I have ever tasted, except perhaps once upstairs at Simpson's in London, on a hot plum tart.

And there was a quart Mason jar, the old-fashioned bluish kind like Mexican glass, full of cream. It was still cold, probably because we all knew the stream it had lain in, Old Mary's stream.

Father cut the pie in three pieces and put them on white soup plates in front of us, and then spooned out the thick cream. We ate with spoons too, blissful after the forks we were learning to use with Mother.

And we ate the whole pie, and all the cream...we can't remember if we gave any to the shadowy old man who sold water...and then drove on sleepily toward Los Angeles, and none of us said anything about it for many years, but it was one of the best meals we ever ate.

Perhaps that is because it was the first conscious one, for me at least; but the fact that we remember it with such queer clarity must mean that it had other reasons for being important. I suppose that happens at least once to every human. I hope so.

Now the hills are cut through with super-highways, and I can't say whether we sat that night in Mint Canyon or Bouquet, and the three of us are in some ways even more than twenty-five years older than we were then. And still the warm round peach pie and the cool yellow cream we ate together that August night live in our hearts' palates, succulent, secret, delicious.

Behind the Salmon

Roderick Haig-Brown

When the salmon turn into the estuary of a small stream one has a right to expect that some big cutthroat trout will be near them. Often they are, but often, too, they can be quite hard to find. Then, particularly if it is late in the season, one is likely to get an uneasy feeling that they have all moved up into the creek and that fishing the estuary may be a waste of time.

I know much better than to go up into the lower reaches of Cedar Creek and try to fish them, even though there are several pools that hold both cutthroats and steelheads really well. These pools are long and slow, for the most part too deep to wade and with steep slippery clay banks that support tangled crab-apple thickets on one side and over-hanging alders on the other side. Any kind of a backcast is out of the question and even a roll or spey cast is grossly inhibited by the precarious stance and crowding brush; it must also find a way into the water between the overhanging limbs. Inevitably one accepts all this and makes a cast or two. Just as inevitably, all goes well at first, one falls into easy admiration of the accurate and tidy way in which the fly settles close under the hazards of the far bank, its cunning search of likely places, the precariously smooth roll that sets it out again to search again. Then, and it can happen in various ways, from a slip on the clay bottom that fills waders to a hang-up in a high branch that catches the peak of the roll, all the ease and smoothness goes out of things and one recalls the forsaken resolve to stay away from such places.

As recently as last fall I found things too slow in Cedar Creek estuary and decided to take a quick look up the creek in the hope of finding a good fish or two to round out the day. It was well on in October and I knew that a strong run of humpback salmon had moved in, so it was reasonable to suppose the estuary cutthroats had all moved up behind them.

The head of the long pool is not too bad a place to get at. After a wild struggle with the crab apples I found myself in the water at the head of the pool, fairly securely placed and with a nice space between the alder limbs inviting my fly to a strongish run on the far side. The creek was flowing well with good fall water, dark but clear, and past experience suggested I should find the first fish twenty or thirty yards further downstream, probably near my own bank where the current spread. I had put up a Harger's Orange, one of several I had tied with claret-colored hair in the wing instead of orange a few years before and a fly I like particularly well for fall cutthroats as well as steelhead. It rolled out nicely, settled into the water and was immediately chased and taken by a fine cutthroat of about three pounds.

At this stage I wasn't really fishing—just getting my fly out. I did set the hook, but then I stood like a particularly dull-witted sheep while the fish ran off downstream. There was an impressive tangle of brush against my bank about forty yards downstream; before I came to and started to move, the line was well tangled in it and the fish was jumping below.

I had sense enough to forget him and work my way carefully downstream—after all, he could only break the leader and if he chose instead to lie quietly I might even be able to disentangle the line and tighten up on him again. The tangle was worse than I had expected, but I struggled with it in admirable calm, freed the worst of it with no more harm than my right arm wet to the armpit and saw my empty fly trailing in the current below. It was a mild disappointment, because it is always satisfying to free a mess of this sort and find that the fish has waited through one's patient efforts, but I knew very well I had earned nothing better—that recovering the fly was a good deal more than I deserved.

For a moment I considered working on down the pool from the brush pile, but that seemed wrong since I had made only one cast at the head of the pool, so I worked my way back up again to where I had started. I placed myself carefully, repeated my first cast exactly, watched my fly settle again neatly between the alder branches and began to think of the next cast and the next after that, when I might reasonably expect to find another fish. Then I saw the fish shouldering across behind the fly, an exact double of the one I had just lost. He took, I tightened; two minutes later my line was tangled in the same brush pile and I was floundering down, by no means calmly, to free it again. And again the fish was lost but the fly was there. In the end I did hook and kill a good fish far below the brush pile, almost at the tail of the pool, but I solemnly renewed all my resolutions about avoiding the crab apples and clay banks and other humiliations of Cedar Creek's most productive pools.

The next day I went about forty miles down along the coast of Vancouver Island to look at several small creeks and their estuaries, among them Sedge Creek. The sensible way to Sedge Creek estuary is to wade down the gravel bed of the creek itself from the highway bridge. It is clear and comfortable going, and one can make an occasional cast to where the creek deepens on a bend or under a root.

Just below the highway bridge the creek bed has been deepened by a bulldozer for several hundred yards to give the flood water an open, easy channel. To break the flow still more and prevent washing of the gravel there are heavy cross logs set into the high gravel banks at intervals of fifty or sixty yards. Behind these, long shallow pools of gently flowing water with a few deeper spots make good lying places for dog and coho salmon—and sometimes cutthroats.

On this particular day there was a school of some twenty or thirty dog salmon in the upper pool, big fish, moving a little, calm and lazy. There was every possible chance that a few cutthroats were lying somewhere amongst them, so I kept as well back from the water as I could and began to drop my Harger's Orange as nearly as I could behind individual members of the scattered, shifting school. Every so often a fish would move up under the swing of the fly and I would feel the fly or the leader scrape against him, but I slacked carefully at such times and for a while all went well. Then the inevitable happened. A fish moved up under the fly almost as it landed. For a moment of time Harger's Orange was swinging freely across the current, a moment later it had stopped, securely set in the dorsal fin of a fifteen-pound dog salmon.

At first neither I nor the fish was greatly concerned. I thought I should get my fly back without too much difficulty, he didn't think the slight restraint of the line was particularly significant. He began to swim slowly upstream. I left the line slack, hoping the fly would come free. Near the head of the pool he turned and began to swim, still quite slowly, downstream. I decided to tighten, again in the hope that the fly would come free. My fish resented this and swam a little harder, taking line nicely and stirring up the other fish in the pool. By the time he turned, just above the cross log at the tail, most of them were following him. By the time he had swum his majestic way back to the head of the pool they were tightly schooled around him, sympathetic or curious or both or neither.

The next trip down the pool was a lot faster and at the tail he broke with some violence, the school all about him still. He liked it down there and I had some difficulty in persuading him to come back up. In the end he came, the whole school still with him. And so it went on, up and down the pool, the school so closely together that it seemed I had hooked twenty fish at once on my single poor little fly. And my one fish felt like twenty. I had to accept that he was not tiring in the slightest and that my little eight foot rod was not going to bring him to beach or to hand within the foreseeable future. I tried my best, because I was really quite fond of that fly. I could direct him a little, turn him at the tail of the pool, even force him to break water, but that was about all. In the end I pointed the rod at him and broke.

Although I had kept fairly well back from the edge of the water throughout the performance, it seemed certain that the pool must be completely disturbed, so I climbed the high gravel bank on the left and started down it. I kept back in the shade of the timber, though, and watched curiously, because I wanted to see how the salmon settled down and how the fish behaved with my fly still in his dorsal fin. I found him easily, with the claret of hackle and wing in the fly showing up nicely, and he seemed just as calm as the others still schooled around him. They were already beginning to spread out through the pool and their movements were slow and lazy. As I turned my eyes from them to search the lower part of the pool I found the quiet, still shapes of two good cutthroats under the overhanging limbs of a small fir, some sixty feet up from the cross log.

These were the fish I had hoped to find among the salmon. They were flat on the bottom now, unmoving and apparently uninterested in anything about them. But it was not the sort of chance one passes up without a try of some

31

sort. I drew farther back into the brush and circled carefully around to the tail of the pool.

My first guess was a good big floating fly. The larger fish of the two was lying a little farther out and a little downstream, so I put it over him, accurately and carefully, with a right-hand curve cast that kept the leader upstream of the drifting fly. Neither fish made the slightest move and though I repeated the cast a dozen times I could not detect even the quiver of a fin to give me encouragement.

My next thought was a nymph, but I discarded this in favor of an orange fly with a weighted body. I aimed for the same right-hand curve cast, but forgot to allow for the reduced air resistance and greater weight of the new fly. It overshot badly and whipped round into a left-hand curve that dropped it in midstream, at least eight feet over from where the fish was lying. He moved like a flash the second it touched the water and took perfectly. I tightened, held him for a second or two, then the fly came away. To my surprise he returned at once to his old position, though the second fish had disappeared.

It seemed a safe assumption that I had mistimed the strike in the surprise of seeing him come so far for the fly. To expect him to take again was totally unreasonable, but I threw the fly up anyway. It landed about six inches to his left and a foot upstream of him, and again he was on it the second it touched the water. This time I was certain of my strike. He was a strong, very fast fish of rather over two pounds, but I controlled him after two or three good runs and moved to a favorable spot to beach him, just above the cross log. As I brought him in there, the fly came away. This time I looked at the fly and found that the point and barb were broken off, no doubt by touching the rocks of the high gravel banks on a backcast.

The lesson is, I suppose, that if you are as careless a fisherman as I seem to be you should stay away from the upstream reaches of the small creeks. If you do not, they will certainly temper your pride, test your vocabulary and perhaps humiliate you in other unforeseen ways. But in the fall they hold some very good fish and the slightly larger ones like Cedar Creek and Sedge Creek may present some very pretty and interesting situations. Any resolve to stay away is only good for a few days. One can so easily make a counterresolve to be careful, respectful, farsighted and extremely skillful. Beside this the frustrations of entangling brush, slippery banks and limited casting room fade into insignificant memory. Pride is completely restored and all is ready for the next fall.

Living Like Weasels

Annie Dillard

A weasel is wild. Who knows what he thinks? He sleeps in his underground den, his tail draped over his nose. Sometimes he lives in his den for two days without leaving. Outside, he stalks rabbits, mice, muskrats, and birds, killing more bodies than he can eat warm, and often dragging the carcasses home. Obedient to instinct, he bites his prey at the neck, either splitting the jugular vein at the throat or crunching the brain at the base of the skull, and he does not let go. One naturalist refused to kill a weasel who was socketed into his hand deeply as a rattlesnake. The man could in no way pry the tiny weasel off, and he had to walk half a mile to water, the weasel dangling from his palm, and soak him off like a stubborn label.

And once, says Ernest Thompson Seton—once, a man shot an eagle out of the sky. He examined the eagle and found the dry skull of a weasel fixed by the jaws to his throat. The supposition is that the eagle had pounced on the weasel and the weasel swiveled and bit as instinct taught him, tooth to neck, and nearly won. I would like to have seen that eagle from the air a few weeks or months before he was shot: was the whole weasel still attached to his feathered throat, a fur pendant? Or did the eagle eat what he could reach, gutting the living weasel with his talons before his breast, bending his beak, cleaning the beautiful airborne bones?

I have been reading about weasels because I saw one last week. I startled a weasel who startled me, and we exchanged a long glance.

Twenty minutes from my house, through the woods by the quarry and across the highway, is Hollins Pond, a remarkable piece of shallowness, where I like to go at sunset and sit on a tree trunk. Hollins Pond is also called Murray's Pond; it covers two acres of bottomland near Tinker Creek with six inches of water and six thousand lily pads. In winter, brown-and-white steers stand in the middle of it, merely dampening their hooves; from the distant shore they look like miracle itself, complete with miracle's nonchalance. Now, in summer, the steers are gone. The water lilies have blossomed and spread to a green horizontal plane that is terra firma to plodding blackbirds, and tremulous ceiling to black leeches, crayfish, and carp.

This is, mind you, suburbia. It is a five-minute walk in three directions to rows of houses, though none is visible here. There's a 55 mph highway at one end of the pond, and a nesting pair of wood ducks at the other. Under every bush is a muskrat hole or a beer can. The far end is an alternating series of fields and woods, fields and woods, threaded everywhere with motorcycle tracks—in whose bare clay wild turtles lay eggs.

So. I had crossed the highway, stepped over two low barbed-wire fences, and traced the motorcycle path in all gratitude through the wild rose and poison ivy of the pond's shoreline up into high grassy fields. Then I cut down through the woods to the mossy fallen tree where I sit. This tree is excellent. It makes a dry, upholstered bench at the upper, marshy end of the pond, a plush jetty raised from the thorny shore between a shallow blue body of water and a deep blue body of sky.

The sun had just set. I was relaxed on the tree trunk, ensconced in the lap of lichen, watching the lily pads at my feet tremble and part dreamily over the thrusting path of a carp. A yellow bird appeared to my right and flew behind me. It caught my eye; I swiveled around—and the next instant, inexplicably, I was looking down at a weasel, who was looking up at me.

Weasel! I'd never seen one wild before. He was ten inches long, thin as a curve, a muscled ribbon, brown as fruitwood, soft-furred, alert. His face was fierce, small and pointed as a lizard's; he would have made a good arrowhead. There was just a dot of chin, maybe two brown hairs' worth, and then the pure white fur began that spread down his underside. He had two black eyes I didn't see, any more than you see a window.

The weasel was stunned into stillness as he was emerging from beneath an enormous shaggy wild rose bush four feet away. I was stunned into stillness twisted backward on the tree trunk. Our eyes locked, and someone threw away the key.

Our look was as if two lovers, or deadly enemies, met unexpectedly on an overgrown path when each had been thinking of something else: a clearing blow to the gut. It was also a bright blow to the brain, or a sudden beating of brains, with all the charge and intimate grate of rubbed balloons. It emptied our lungs. It felled the forest, moved the fields, and drained the pond; the world dismantled and tumbled into that black hole of eyes. If you and I looked at each other that way, our skulls would split and drop to our shoulders. But we don't. We keep our skulls. So.

He disappeared. This was only last week, and already I don't remember what shattered the enchantment. I think I blinked, I think I retrieved my brain from the weasel's brain, and tried to memorize what I was seeing, and the weasel felt the yank of separation, the careening splash-down into real life and the urgent current of instinct. He vanished under the wild rose. I waited motionless, my mind suddenly full of data and my spirit with pleadings, but he didn't return.

Please do not tell me about "approach-avoidance conflicts." I tell you I've been in that weasel's brain for sixty seconds, and he was in mine. Brains are private places, muttering through unique and secret tapes—but the weasel and I both plugged into another tape simultaneously, for a sweet and shocking time. Can I help it if it was a blank?

What goes on in his brain the rest of the time? What does a weasel think about? He won't say. His journal is tracks in clay, a spray of feathers, mouse blood and bone: uncollected, unconnected, loose-leaf, and blown.

I would like to learn, or remember, how to live. I come to Hollins Pond not so much to learn how to live as, frankly, to forget about it. That is, I don't think I can learn from a wild animal how to live in particular—shall I suck warm blood, hold my tail high, walk with my footprints precisely over the prints of my hands?—but I might learn something of mindlessness, something of the purity of living in the physical senses and the dignity of living without bias or motive. The weasel lives in necessity and we live in choice, hating necessity and dying at the last ignobly in its talons. I would like to live as I should, as the weasel lives as he should. And I suspect that for me the way is like the weasel's: open to time and death painlessly, noticing everything, remembering nothing, choosing the given with a fierce and pointed will.

I missed my chance. I should have gone for the throat. I should have lunged for that streak of white under the weasel's chin and held on, held on through mud and into the wild rose, held on for a dearer life. We could live under the wild rose wild as weasels, mute and uncomprehending. I could very calmly go wild. I could live two days in the den, curled, leaning on mouse fur, sniffing bird bones, blinking, licking, breathing musk, my hair tangled in the roots of grasses. Down is a good place to go, where the mind is single. Down is out, out of your ever-loving mind and back to your careless senses. I remember muteness as a prolonged and giddy fast, where every moment is a feast of utterance received. Time and events are merely poured, unremarked, and ingested directly, like blood pulsed into my gut through a jugular vein. Could two live that way? Could two live under the wild rose, and explore by the pond, so that the smooth mind of each is as everywhere present to the other, and as received and as unchallenged, as falling snow?

We could, you know. We can live any way we want. People take vows of poverty, chastity, and obedience—even of silence—by choice. The thing is to stalk your calling in a certain skilled and supple way, to locate the most tender and live spot and plug into that pulse. This is yielding, not fighting. A weasel doesn't "attack" anything; a weasel lives as he's meant to, yielding at every moment to the perfect freedom of single necessity.

I think it would be well, and proper, and obedient, and pure, to grasp your one necessity and not let it go, to dangle from it limp wherever it takes you. Then even death, where you're going no matter how you live, cannot you part. Seize it and let it seize you up aloft even, till your eyes burn out and drop; let your musky flesh fall off in shreds, and let your very bones unhinge and scatter, loosened over fields, over fields and woods, lightly, thoughtless, from any height at all, from as high as eagles.

Intimations

Bharati Mukherjee

My life, I now realize, falls into three disproportionate parts. Till the age of eight I lived in the typical joint family, indistinguishable from my twenty cousins, indistinguishable, in fact, from an eternity of Bengali Brahmin girls. From eight till twenty-one we lived as a single family, enjoying for a time wealth and confidence. And since twenty-one I have lived in the West. Each phase required a repudiation of all previous avatars; an almost total rebirth.

Prior to this year-long stay in India, I had seen myself as others saw me in Montreal, a brown woman in a white society, different, perhaps even special, but definitely not a part of the majority. I receive, occasionally, crazy letters from women students at McGill accusing me of being "mysterious," "cold," "hard to get to know," and the letter writers find this mysteriousness offensive. I am bothered by these letters, especially by the aggressive desire of students to "know" me. I explain it as a form of racism. The unfamiliar is frightening; therefore I have been converted into a "mystery." I can be invested with powers and intentions I do not possess.

In a life of many cultural moves, I had clung to my uniqueness as the source of confidence and stability. But in India I am not unique, not even extraordinary. During the year, I began to see how typical my life had actually been, and given the limited options of a woman from my class and from my city, how predictably I had acted in each crisis. And I see how, even in the West, I have acted predictably. My writing is a satellite of my marriage and profession; I have chosen, or fallen into, the role of bourgeois writer, limited to a month of writing in a year, or one year of writing for every seven of teaching. The American alternative, *Mama Doesn't Live Here Anymore*, remains unthinkable.

Only the first eight years were spent in Ballygunge, in a flat crowded with relatives, and friends of relatives who needed a place for sleeping and eating while they went to college in the city, and hangers-on, whose connection with my family I did not have the curiosity to determine. I was not happy in that joint family. Perhaps some of my mother's frustration seeped down to me. People say that I look very much like her. Certainly I am, like her, a collector of resentments and insults, and am stubbornly unforgiving. I suspect that in those early years, it was more important to me to retain my position as my father's favorite daughter (he had written a poem about me, titled "Treasure of the Heart") than it was to imitate, in proper fashion, the personality of my mother. But I am sure that from her I learned only to feel relief when we could close the door of our bedroom and shut out the forty-odd relatives.

It was a small room after the corners and sides had been filled with the bulky furniture of my mother's dowry. Two beds—one was the bridal four-poster, the other was a simple *chowki*—were pushed together for the five of us, two adults and three daughters. I recall that because of shortage of space, my father used to store an untidy pile of scientific books and journals on the bridal bed itself and that we children had to be careful not to kick the books in our sleep. In a household where no one kept his opinions to himself, this room was our shrine of privacy.

Sometimes there were invasions by cousins or younger uncles. Once my mother, sisters, and I returned from our customary afternoon visit to Southern Avenue to find that my eldest sister's British-made painting book and paintbox, which she had won as a school prize, had been vandalized. Another time, the lock of the wooden cabinet in which my mother kept her jewelry and small cash savings had been forced open, and some money was missing. I was taught to think of these episodes as an assault on our desire to maintain slight separateness within the context of the joint family, rather than expressions of mischief by relatives.

Within the small perimeters of that room, it became clear to me that if I wished to remain sane I should not permit myself to squander my affections on too many people or possessions. With over-population of that sort, possessions and relationships could at best be fragile. I learned also to be always on my guard, and because I was small, shy, and the second youngest in the family, to stay in the background, out of danger's reach. During communal meals, when all the children sat on the floor of the corridor surrounding an inner courtyard, I did not demand the prized items—eyes and brain of carp—because I knew that if I set myself no goals, there could be no defeat. I had, I felt, an intimate knowledge and horror of madness. There was a mad aunt in the family, and during a long stay that she, her husband and four children inflicted on us (because there was some natural disaster, probably a flood, in the part of East Bengal where they lived), I had seen her chase her husband with an ugly piece of firewood. I cannot recall if I had actually seen her hit her husband on the head with the firewood before I was hustled off by my mother into the privacy of our bedroom, or if the aunt had only been standing, weapon poised, about to hit him. I did not think of the uncle, whom I disliked, as the victim. But I thought of madness as grotesque, and as shameful, for I had been told by my parents that if too many people came to know about the craziness in the family, it would be hard to marry us daughters off. I resolved immediately to fight in myself the slightest signs of insanity.

I was released from all that terrifying communal bonding by a single decisive act of my father's, shortly after my eighth birthday. Because of certain circumstances in the pharmaceutical company that he and his partner, a Jewish immigrant from the Middle East, had set up, circumstances that he did not explain to his daughters though he probably did to his wife, he brought home colorful brochures one day of an all-first-class boat on the Anchor Line, and within weeks we left the joint family, and Calcutta, in order to make a new start in London.

We were happy in Britain and Switzerland where my father worked on his research projects, and where we went to school and were remarkable for our good manners as well as our intelligence, and where my mother took night courses in flan baking and basket weaving. But my parents did not make for themselves a new life. The partner followed my father to London, for a while installed us in a company flat at the corner of Curzon and Half Moon streets, vacationed with us in Montreux, and was, I suspect, persuasive about his plan for the pharmaceutical company in Calcutta. And so, after almost three years abroad, we returned to Calcutta, not quite where we had left off, and certainly not to Ballygunge and the joint family.

That period abroad is the only time I have felt perfectly bilingual. It was a time of forgetting Bengali and acquiring English until I reached an absolute equilibrium. But that gradual erosion of the vernacular also contained an erosion of ideas I had taken for granted. It was the first time I was forced to see myself not reflected in people around me, to see myself as the curiosity that I must have seemed to the majority—a skinny brown child, in stiff school uniform and scarred knees, who could not do cartwheels. The sense that I had had of myself in Ballygunge, of being somehow superior to my cousins, was less destructive than this new sense of being a minority on account of my color. I felt I was a shadow person because I was not white. We were an extraordinarily close-knit family, but since I had been brought up to please, I felt I could not burden my parents with these anxieties. It would have made them unhappy, and I could not bear to do that. I could count only on myself for devising strategies of survival in London, our adopted city. I became less passive than I had been among relatives and friends in Ballygunge: I began to regard facility in English as my chief weapon for bending my own personality and for making friends among the British.

In sacrificing a language, we sacrifice our roots. On returning to Calcutta, we found that our image of ourselves had changed radically. It was not at all a question of money. *Jethoo*, my father's oldest brother, owned rice mills and lumber mills in Assam, but he would not be comfortable outside of Ballygunge. But to us, the thought of re-entry into that closed, conspiratorial joint-family world was unbearable. So we sublet a flat in fashionable Chowringhee, the break from the joint family being facilitated by a quarrel between my mother and another relative. We changed schools too, from the Anglicized Bengali school on the edge of Ballygunge to the most renowned girls' school on Middleton Row, a school where, it was rumored, Indian children had for a long time been denied admission. And in our new school, the foreign nuns treasured us for our faintly British accents which had survived the long homeward journey.

From our return to Calcutta after the false start in Europe until the middle of 1959, we lived in the compound of the pharmaceutical factory which my father and his partner had set up in Cossipore, on the outskirts of the city. My parents now refer to that phase of our lives as "the good days." I thought of the compound walls as the boundaries of a small constitutional monarchy in which my sisters and I were princesses. We presided at factory functions, such as sports events, religious celebrations, variety shows for workers, and looked on that as our necessary duty.

The pharmaceutical company had bought out the garden house and estate of a refined Bengali gentleman after whom a street had been named in happier times, but whose fortunes had now declined completely. His botanical gardens—full of imported rarities—were cut down and cleared, the snakes scared away, the pools filled, the immense Victorian house converted into a production plant for capsules, syrups, and pills. I saw the conversion as a triumph of the new order over the old, and felt no remorse. Nothing would return me to the drabness and tedium of Ballygunge.

For me, being part of the new order meant walking under arches of bougainvillaea with my sisters and a golden spaniel we had acquired immediately after moving in, while neighbors gawked at us from their rooftops. We were inviolable and inaccessible within our walled compound. To our neighbors, we were objects of envy, and probably freaks. There were screening devices to protect us: gates, guards, internal telephones. We were at home to only those we wished to see; others could be sent away from the front gate. Having been deprived of privacy in early childhood, I carried my privacy to an extreme; I did not even learn the names of the streets around the factory.

Every day we shuttled between this fortressed factory compound and the school compound in an old gray Rover, once owned by a British executive who had decided independent India was no longer the best place for him. Our privacy was guaranteed on these trips by a bodyguard who looked like Oliver Hardy. The ride from Cossipore to Middleton Row and back is very long, and the cityscape unusually unpleasant. I learned very quickly, therefore, to look out of the window and see nothing. During those rides, my sisters and I talked endlessly about the kinds of men we wanted to marry, and memorized passages from Shakespeare or from the Gospels for the morning's quizzes. My older sister, who is four years older than I and currently is a childless, working wife in Detroit, was the most romantic among us. She said that she did not care about money, but that the groom would have to have excellent table manners and be perfect at ballroom dancing. My younger sister and I knew what she meant by that: She wanted a "Westernized" groom who had studied abroad, and who could command for her a "Westernized" life-style in a pretty flat on Park Street or Chowringhee. Like us, she did not want to lapse into the self-contained vernacular world of Ballygunge.

During this period we were once visited by some female relatives of Mr. D. Gupta, former owner of the garden house that we had converted into a factory. My father arranged for the visiting women to be taken on a guided tour of the plant and then to have tea with us. It was intended by my father to be, and therefore was, an amiable occasion. We sat on the Georgian and Jacobean imported furniture that my parents had extravagantly selected from auction houses on Park and Free School streets, and we listened to the niece of the former owner describe how pretty the chute of colored syrups and capsules had been. It was amiable because the old and new orders had treated each other courteously. Confrontations would come later, and my sisters and I would one day not long after that tea, on our return from school, have to walk through a crowd of striking employees who had blocked our car and who carried placards we were too well-brought-up to read. This tea among the women of the former and current owners was an acknowledgment of another sort: the vulnerability of individual heroes or families in the face of larger designs. Having a street named after oneself was no permanent guarantee of dignity or survival.

That is why, on this 1973 trip back to India, when a newer order has replaced us within the walls of that same compound, I chose not to visit the factory, nor to walk once more under the flowering arches where my sisters and I dreamed about our "Westernized" grooms and "Westernized" lifestyles. On this latest trip, I was told that the neighborhood around the factory had become dangerous, and that during the recent Naxalite agitations, workers had been beaten up and that a chemist I recalled well had been knifed in the head a block and a half from the factory gates.

For me the walled factory compound, the guards at the gate office, the bodyguard inside our Rover, the neighbors staring at us from the rooftops, are now emblems. We were typical of a class in the city. There was surely nothing ignoble in our desire to better our condition. In a city that threatens to overwhelm the individual who is passive, there was nothing immoral in self-protection. But we had refused to merge with the city; we had cleared the snakes and shrubberies; we had preoccupied ourselves with single layers of existence—getting ahead, marrying well—and we had ignored the visionary whole. And now, years later, those of us who left and settled in far-off cities like Detroit and Montreal, as well as those of my school friends who stayed and who now live in flats on Park Street or own houses on Rawdon Street, are paying for having scared the snakes and gutted the shrubberies.

My parents moved out of Calcutta long ago. But the impulse to erect compound walls, to isolate and exclude, appears all around me in Calcutta in 1973. My friends live in mansions that the British had built in less volatile times to separate themselves from the bazaars and settlements of the natives. These mansions, even now, are fronted by spacious lawns, gravel driveways, enormous gates with wooden watch posts, and one or more uniformed guards. The guards are not always alert on the job. One rainy July morning as we swung into the driveway of the home of a managing director of a former British firm, we caught the guard urinating against the compound wall.

The cry these days is more for protection than for privacy, and this cry is more shrill than I have ever heard. The women who live in these mansions and whom I meet very regularly for lunch and charity work, study groups and cocktails on the lawn, tell me about the "troubled times" when everything was "topsy-turvy" because the Naxalite gangs took over. With manicured nails jabbing the air, they describe to me how the Naxals scared the guards, sometimes invaded the compounds, threw gravel against the bathroom windows, tore up the lawns by playing soccer. One elegant young woman wearing a delicate pink nylon sari and Japanese pearls (it is hard for me to adjust to this new image, for I had last seen her as a pigtailed schoolgirl with socks that kept sliding into her shoes) wants me to know that "the troubled times" are not over yet, that what I am seeing is simply a lull before the coming class confrontation. I do not disbelieve her; it is a common conviction all over Calcutta. A woman I had met a week before is now hiding out with her family in the house of another friend in order to avoid what she calls "mischievous acts"—acid bombs? sieges? kidnapings?—by striking employees in her husband's firm.

Here in Calcutta, my friends go out into the city in groups, beautiful women in well-waxed cars, and they pack pills for lepers for Mother Teresa. They supervise sewing workshops for destitute women, even clean streets in front of photographers and journalists in order to save and beautify Calcutta. "CALCUTTA IS FOREVER" announces a billboard on Ballygunge Circular Road, paid for by the Beautification Committee. "KEEP YOUR CITY CLEAN AND DESCENT" mocks a less-professional effort near Free School Street. They have made their commitment to this decayed and turbulent city. In exchange, they want protection for themselves and their children.

To protect oneself is to be sensible, I am told. It is a city-wide obsession. Even the Scholar's Guest House where Clark and I stay and which is run by the Ramakrishna Mission, a religious Hindu order, is set apart from the street by high walls. Outside the walls are the accouterments of Ballygunge life: hawkers, beggars, loiterers, squatters, sleepers, cows and pariahs, cars, taxis, buses, mini-buses, cycles, rickshaws, bullock carts, and heedless pedestrians. Inside there is greenery, flowers, a studied calm. The *durwan* at the gate sits on a stool and separates the two worlds. He has a register and pencil to keep track of all visitors. But still the brutal world invades the mission, and brass gas rings disappear from the secondary kitchen, and dissatisfied employees demonstrate on the edge of the judiciously kept lawn.

We do not seem to have heeded the message of the anonymous sculptor from Deoghar. We have confined ourselves to single obsessions. We have protected our territory, and posted uniformed servants to keep out the confusions of the city. We have forgotten that the guard himself is in an ambiguous position and that his loyalties may be fragile. In a city like this, an elderly relative tells me as he chews an endless mouthful of betel nuts, *You just can't be too careful. If you relax for a second, someone will snatch your gold necklace or your purse.* He advises me against certain doctors—there have been stories about nearly any doctor that I mention. *That man is too black, That man is unmarried, Never go to a doctor alone.* But to be so wise, I would like to answer, is also to distort.

Out there beyond our walled vision is a reality that disgusts and confounds the intellect, and a populace that is too illiterate, too hungry, too brutish, to be gently manipulated. Or, just as confounding, a populace too gentle to be brutishly commanded. The odds against survival for an individual are enormous, and rewards, at best, are uncertain.

Merge, commands the Deoghar sculptor, *there are no insides and outsides, no serpents, no gods.*

But at this time, we who consider ourselves more intelligent, more politically conscious, more sophisticated, more charming than the ancient stoneworker, know that to merge, to throw in our lot with Calcutta, is also to invite self-destruction. If we take down the compound walls and remove the ceremonial guard who relieves himself in the street and picks his nose while opening the gates to visitors, what will happen to our children?

It is at this point that I separate myself from the chorus of my old school friends in Calcutta. My sons will return to Montreal at the end of the year, study very little, ski a little more, watch Saturday cartoons on TV, and inherit the promises of the New World.

For the children of my friends who have chosen to remain in Calcutta, the range of future possibilities is infinitely more frightening. Though we never discuss it, we all know that this city will yield its rewards only to the strongest, the smartest, or the most powerful.

Bombay: May-June 1973

For me, 1973 was a year of luxurious nostalgia. This nostalgia could be triggered by the smallest objects, such as a Venetian liqueur glass bought at Staynor's auction house during the "good days" and transported with love during the reluctant move from Calcutta to Baroda and Bombay. Nostalgia could overtake me anywhere and transform the immediate surroundings until my parents' carelessly furnished Chembur living room became once more the room stocked with Jacobean sofas that I had lolled on as a teenager.

But for many Indians, 1973 was a year in which nostalgia gave way to bewilderment and anger. The papers and periodicals were full of stories of misunderstandings. I read that an eighteen-year-old pregnant woman who had been cooking supper on the platform of a clean, new railway station was kicked to death by an outraged railway official. And that a starving mother threw her four daughters and herself into a well but succeeded in killing only two.

Then there were the standard stories of rage and frustration, of men killing each other in movie house queues, of knifings among street sleepers because a child had cried too loud and too long or one man had made a pass at another man's wife. The time for good humor seemed about to disappear. There were endless complaints about endless shortages, and short fierce strikes all over India, but no one had yet taken radical, irrevocable measures.

In Chembur, where we spent the first month and a half seeing my family and preparing for the trip farther east to Calcutta, I learned that fear is not an affliction; it merely is a way of ordering a confused world. The wives I met in Bombay relied on fear to give meaning to lives that might otherwise have seemed, even to them, banal. Like my mother, these women lived in compounds of factories in which their husbands worked, in executives' quarters which were considered luxurious. The compounds had the usual paraphernalia of security: walls, sometimes topped with barbed wire and always with wicked shards of glass, check posts, emergency "hot lines" to the general manager, uniformed and ununiformed guards. These executives' wives thrilled to the lazy salute of the watchmen as they drove in and out of the main gate on their way to the bazaar: The salute was reassurance of status. These women were valuable while the millions outside the gates were not. The compound literally isolated them from the world of unassorted passions. The factory walls gave them their corporate identity, loyalty, and self-respect, created a calming communal village in a chaotic industrial zone. The women were grateful for the rigid security and for the group privacy, relieved to be cut off from the other Chembur in which degenerate or starving people burgled, murdered, cheated, used dirty words. They had intimations of danger each time they went to the bazaar in groups of two and three in private cars, or (because of gasoline prices) mostly in the factory's bus. More often than not the buses that bumped them along the narrow highways and city roads had windows covered with wire mesh to deflect any projectiles hurled by unhappy laborers.

Inside the compound, they lived in neatly kept houses, set in hierarchical rows, and separated from the noisy, smelly work site by trees or hill slopes or at least a bamboo grove. Their children watched television in the company's recreation room, and sometimes if there was a really good movie being run, the women joined the children for an hour or two, fighting mosquitoes that preyed on all the viewers. There was also a Ping-Pong table, and though none of the women played themselves, they took secretive, unacknowledged pride in the Ping-Pong skills of their husbands and sons. They did not worry that there were no telephones, except in the houses of perhaps the general manager and the managing director. Their husbands handled all their serious relationships with the outside world; all they needed was the factory intercom so that they could call each other to set up visits and call their husbands home for lunch.

The women I met in that preparatory period before Calcutta were friendly, anxious to let me know that they did not hold my eccentric marriage against me, though, when pressed, they admitted they did not want their daughters or younger sisters to marry outside their state and caste. Their friendliness took the form of solicitous advice to Clark and myself. They found us naive, helpless, untutored in strategies of self-defense. So they became our eager tutors.

"Don't let Bart and Bernie go off to the park with the servant. You never know what gets into servants' heads. They should post a guard there."

"Did you read about that murder? After six and a half years, a servant goes crazy and murders the lady when her husband is at work. I tell you, you simply can't trust anyone."

"Chembur is one of the worst areas, one of the very worst," agrees another.

"Chembur is nothing compared to Calcutta. I don't know why you want to go to Calcutta. It's so nice here."

"Never ride a taxi in Calcutta. Tell your old friends to send cars if they want to see you."

"Make sure Clark gets in first...."

"Have you told them about that European who lost his passport? Don't ever leave your hotel room for a visitor downstairs—make him come up."

"During the troubles people would just walk up to you on the street in broad daylight and snatch your gold necklace. They would cut off your fingers to get your rings."

"Things are better now, I must say. Hats off to Siddhartha Shankar Ray. He's been good and tough."

"Maybe a little bit better for the local people, but Bharati and Clark won't be able to manage. They are too trusting. I see Clark and I say to myself he is so open, always laughing, what will he do in Calcutta? He'll take his big Nikon camera to New Market and the *goondas* will beat him up. You tell him to be careful."

They told more stories. A niece whose earrings had been torn from her ears, shredding the flesh. An old widow whose gold chain was clipped from her neck in plain view of fifty people on a tram. For her complaints, she'd been lectured to by fellow passengers for having provoked the attack by wearing gold.

"Bharati, you better not wear *two* gold chains like that in Calcutta. It looks very nice—you have a very nice throat and collarbone area for necklaces—but in Calcutta that's an open invitation to burglars."

"There are so many gold smugglers around and they'll do anything."

"I'll tell you a story that happened to relatives of a friend of mine."

"Is this the one about prostitute rings?"

"No, this one is much worse."

She began the story; Clark was nearby, reading. It was all in Bengali, with a cluster of executives' wives hanging on every word.

"These people were quite young and the husband had a good job. One day they went to New Market to shop. They had an infant daughter who also went to the market with them. She was fast asleep, so the parents—and this is fate—left the baby locked in the car while they went in for a second to buy something, I've forgotten what—"

"They have *very* nice petticoats in New Market," my mother said. "It was probably petticoats."

"Anyway, they went to the store, and when they came back, there was no sign of the baby."

"It is fate," suggested another neighbor.

"Car was locked you said?"

"Completely locked. So there is absolute pandemonium. They informed the police, interrogated those Muslim chaps who hang around New Market acting as porters and touts, but no trace."

"They are absolute *goondas*—Mex, you hear that?"

44

"So, anyway these people had some important connections, and a real serious search was made, but still nothing turned up."

"That is good. These days in our country unless you have connections nobody will care."

"Nobody cares, that is right. It is terrible."

"Never let Bart and Bernie out of your sight for a minute."

"Every day, they had to drive here and there and everywhere to look at babies, but it was always the wrong baby. It gives you an idea how many stolen babies there are. Meanwhile the poor mother was so upset that she was almost mad, unable to eat or sleep. Then they got a call from the police to come out to the airport where a suspicious-looking mother and child had been detained. The husband and wife rushed out there, and sure enough, the mother recognized her daughter, and threw herself on the kidnaper—"

"Oh, thank God!" the women exclaimed.

"No, no—here comes the worst part. It was their baby all right, but she was dead."

"No! *Baapré-ba!*" They touched their foreheads.

"*Yes.* The smugglers—they were Muslims trying to get back to Abu Dhabi to get more gold—had taken out the baby's intestines and stuffed the cavity with gold bars, then sewn the stomach flaps back. Go ahead, translate it for Clark." He raised his head at the mention of his name. *"That's right, Clark, Calcutta no good. Calcutta full of goondas and very bad behavior."*

My mother likes to lock doors. Also windows, safes, cupboards, closets, trunks, valises. Her closest friend in Chembur has installed a padlock and chain around the door of her refrigerator. Foodstuffs such as sugar, gram flour, cloves, cardamom, and cigarettes that cannot be fitted with locks are poured into plastic canisters and placed in neat rows inside lockable cupboards. Keys to locked cupboards are stored in other locked cupboards. My mother carries only one key on her person; it is frail and black and hangs limply from a knot in her sari, just below her left shoulder. Heavier rings of keys, the ones that issue insolent challenges to potential burglars—for example, the ring of keys to get to the purse that contains the key to another cupboard and to another purse which holds the key to a steel cabinet with a safe fitted with a double lock where my mother has stowed my scratched German leather purse full of passports, health certificates, and the children's photographs—these remain out of sight.

Clark considers this paranoia. He tells me that since the gate office of the factory compound screens all those who try to enter, this elaborate security system is designed to discourage only the live-in servant and part-time maids who come to wash the dishes, do the laundry, and to clean floors and toilets. I know, of course, that Clark is wrong. He does not understand the apocalyptic vision of my mother. He is annoyed that he cannot get to his tape recorder without having the women unlock several cupboards, or that when he is ready and waiting in the car for the long drive downtown it takes my mother and me several extra minutes of coordinated effort to give him his traveler's checks and identification cards. I explain to him that if the servant wanted to burgle or murder, he could easily do so during the siesta hour. My mother, though heavy, is not at all strong. She is totally at the mercy of any sinister intruder. Locking is her way of integrating belief in karma and belief in individual resourcefulness. She is alert to the conditions of modern India; she assumes that disaster, which in her childhood had seemed to lie in some unrealizable future, is now about to occur in her lifetime. Perhaps she remembers those wooden cupboards back in the joint family, when the forcing of a door was an attack upon all her defenses. She will not set herself impossible goals about reversing her fate or the country's; she will simply use her common sense to minimize the personal effects of disaster.

We suffer an unacknowledged crisis over Bernie's electric train, which we bought in Geneva en route to India and which we cannot permit him to play with guiltlessly in Chembur because of the factory's policy of "voluntary" power restraint. Bernie, who is obsessed by trains and planes, lies on the cool floor of his room and pushes his locomotive with his finger. My mother would like us to store the train set in a locked wall cabinet whenever Bernie is not playing with it. Clark refuses to do that.

"But that *chokra*-boy will wreck it in no time," my mother objects (to me, never to Clark). "He's a very curious and careless boy."

"It's a toy, for God's sake," Clark explodes with undue passion.

He is correct; he wins the round. We leave the electric train set out, and in a matter of weeks, the monsoon deposits rust flowers on the tracks, stealthily adventurous fingers leave dents on the underpinnings of carriages (it is Rajan who encourages Bernie to pry the tops off the passenger cars; it would not surprise me if Rajan had expected miniature people inside, reading their German newspapers), and the locomotive seems clogged with fluff and hair balls. And so my mother and Bernie conspire to save the train from further damage. They wrap the broken set in an old cotton sari and place it on the top shelf of a cupboard; it is transformed from a toy that functions to a souvenir of a nearly perfect visit by the family of a favorite daughter. I try once more to explain the episode of the train to Clark. I paint him a middle-aged woman with an overwhelming sense of doom. A middle-aged woman who no longer reads, sews, goes to parties, sees films or television, visits friends, and whose children now lead independent lives in far-off cities or continents. Locking out hazard, locking in happiness. To deprive her of that would be brutal.

My mother has raised precaution to a high art. She has not only experimented with locks of various sizes and brands—on trips abroad to visit me or my sister, she has spent meticulous half-days at the key and padlock counters—but she has also extended the range of items to be locked out. In Chembur she locks out sunlight, insects, bats, toads, pariah dogs, servants' chums, and cobras. She is full of cautionary tales about the cobra that had slithered into the neighbor's bathroom because a window had been left unlatched. All her windows are still covered over with the heavy black paper that had been given out to all residents of the compound to block out house lights during the Indo-Pakistan war. During the war, she had supervised the cutting and pasting, making sure the servant did not let a single sliver of light slip through. You could develop film in some of those rooms, even in tropical daytime. Now when she shuts her windows during the day—and she does that by nine o'clock to keep out industrial soot and smells, heat, undesirable creatures—the house is peaceful, dark, and cavernous. With doors and windows battened down, and with her hands on the panel of fan and light switches, she can control her universe. Manipulation of breezes and light, she construes as a triumph of will over chaos. Each time she bars a window, causing the papered-over panes to cut off the sun, she sees it as a stalling of a future disaster.

The wartime paper, as it turns out, is destined to go. Clark does not like the paper; he cannot work behind closed windows. He likes to work, and he is more self-reliant than anyone else in the compound. Also, he has allies in the servant and the chauffeur, whose full names he, rather than my parents, has been the first to find out. After three weeks of writing longhand in bed under a ceiling fan that scattered his writing materials without cooling him, he has the chauffeur drive him out to the bazaar, where, without engaging in acrimonious and exhaustive comparison shopping, he buys a metal desk and a metal chair, and installs them himself in front of windows in our bedroom. Then, with Rajan's help, he rips aside the company curtains, unlocks the windows, peels off the black paper, takes a long gulp of the outside air, and writes uninterruptedly for five hours.

My mother looks in now and then and says in the direction of the servant, "Don't interrupt, *Sahib* at work here."

But to me she says, "Are you sure he'll be all right? All that black stuff from the factory chimney will make his eyes sore. Ask him, does he need anything? Shall I bring him some mangoes or sweet lime? Or how about tea? He needs to eat more."

Over the next few days, the servant continues with the paper-removing work that Clark began. The curtains in all the bedrooms start to bleach in window-sized rectangles. Those of us who suffer from nervous sick headaches in the sun suffer them more than usual. Clark, whose desk looks out over the rise and the chimney, develops itchy eyes and has to return to his original writing position on the bed under the fan. The children suffer continuous hay fever. Dust from the open window covers his desk, typewriter, arms, hands, and papers; he can't erase without smearing the page. The servant mops a great deal more than he has before. A window has been opened and a foreign element permitted indoors. Clark does not yet understand an Indian's relationship to "nature"; he still suffers from the American myth of nature's benevolence.

When it is time for Clark and me to fly from Santa Cruz Airport to Calcutta, I am not afraid to leave Bart and Bernie with my mother. She will, of course, be even more overprotective when she is their sole guardian. My father will be at his office until the boys' supper hour; so she will see herself as their principal custodian, and love will make her more fearful than usual.

I hear her shout as I pack my bags, "Bertie, don't play in the puddle. Hookworms will get you." And five minutes later, "Bernie, come back here darling, big, big cobras outdoors." These, I know, are her ways, and perhaps her only ways, of expressing affection to her stranger-grandsons. To love is also to minimize the beloved's exposure to danger. And, having been brought up in monsoon country, I know that hookworms and snakes slither in and out of maladied, middle-aged imaginations. Bernie has already shown me, five yards from our front door, six dead baby vipers (he called them "fat worms, Mommy"), washed down the hillsides by the heavy seasonal rains. So I do not shout out counterinstructions to the boys to go out into the rain and find their own adventure, to be resourceful and independent and not bother the grown-ups. I do not whisper to my mother to disguise or restrain the force of her love. This will probably be the last time that the boys, my hardy North American boys, will experience familial affection and not consider it burdensome.

But for many Indians, the excellent balance between fear and love is part of nostalgia. Extravagant, unrestrained love can no longer be expressed and extravagant fear has come to replace it. Only partially hidden under the stiff Indian-English of newspaper journalism, I see the spurts and flares of private terror in this year of threatened famine and deteriorating nerves.

Mr. Suprio Das, in *The Statesman* of August 1, 1973, writes that while out on the V.I.P. Road for his customary evening constitutional stroll, he had stumbled upon a decomposing corpse bearing obvious knife wounds, and that though he had done his civic duty by calling the police, he had not been able to arrange for immediate corpse removal. Three days later the corpse had disappeared, thanks to the efforts (he believed) of neighbor-hood pariah dogs and vultures. And now, the writer wants to know of the editor of that respected newspaper, what should he do if during another evening stroll, he happens on another corpse full of knife wounds?

In Habibur area, in the district of Malda, sixty-five-year-old landlord (*jotedar*) wins posthumous notice by becoming North Bengal's first fatal casualty during the crop-cutting and harvesting season. He is rumored to have been shot full of arrows by a tribal group who did not want him har-vesting in that area.

Hungry or simply immoral youths, in large gangs, attempt to hijack loaded trucks in the Siliguri area, by blockading the highway with boulders, then by throwing stones at the windshield of the stopped truck in order to injure the driver and his guard. This results in an organized protest by truck drivers who tie up traffic on Highway 31 and demand better protection. The protesters are finally persuaded to cease their demonstration in time for the motorcade of West Bengal's Chief Minister, Siddhartha Shankar Ray, who is making an official visit to Kalimpong.

In India, then, for some people at least, it is a year of eroding faith in inevitable destinies. The daily newspapers, still uncensored, publish scorching indictments of official pronouncements and heap abuse on ministerial fiats. The workers at Calico go out on strike. It is to last only a week, but it drags on and on, sharpening into a show of force. Six months later, after a death and several beatings, the workers will return, accepting the company offer. Force alone still carries the greatest respect.

Once More to the Lake

E.B. White

(August 1941)

One summer, along about 1904, my father rented a camp on a lake in Maine and took us all there for the month of August. We all got ringworm from some kittens and had to rub Pond's Extract on our arms and legs night and morning, and my father rolled over in a canoe with all his clothes on; but outside of that the vacation was a success and from then on none of us ever thought there was any place in the world like that lake in Maine. We returned summer after summer—always on August 1st for one month. I have since become a salt-water man, but sometimes in summer there are days when the restlessness of the tides and the fearful cold of the sea water and the incessant wind which blows across the afternoon and into the evening make me wish for the placidity of a lake in the woods. A few weeks ago this feeling got so strong I bought myself a couple of bass hooks and a spinner and returned to the lake where we used to go, for a week's fishing and to revisit old haunts.

I took along my son, who had never had any fresh water up his nose and who had seen lily pads only from train windows. On the journey over to the lake I began to wonder what it would be like. I wondered how time would have marred this unique, this holy spot—the coves and streams, the hills that the sun set behind, the camps and the paths behind the camps. I was sure that the tarred road would have found it out and I wondered in what other ways it would be desolated. It is strange how much you can remember about places like that once you allow your mind to return into the grooves which lead back. You remember one thing, and that suddenly reminds you of another thing. I guess I remembered clearest of all the early mornings, when the lake was cool and motionless, remembered how the bedroom smelled of the lumber it was made of and of the wet woods whose scent entered through the screen. The partitions in the camp were thin and did not extend clear to the top of the rooms, and as I was always the first up I would dress softly so as not to wake the others, and sneak out into the sweet outdoors and start out in the canoe, keeping close along the shore in the long shadows of the pines. I remembered being very careful never to rub my paddle against the gunwale for fear of disturbing the stillness of the cathedral.

The lake had never been what you would call a wild lake. There were cottages sprinkled around the shores, and it was in farming country although the shores of the lake were quite heavily wooded. Some of the cottages were owned by nearby farmers and you would live at the shore and eat your meals at the farmhouse. That's what our family did. But although it wasn't wild, it was a fairly large and undisturbed lake and there were places in it which, to a child at least, seemed infinitely remote and primeval.

I was right about the tar: it led to within half a mile of the shore. But when I got back there, with my boy, and we settled into a camp near a farmhouse and into the kind of summertime I had known, I could tell that it was going to be pretty much the same as it had been before—I knew it, lying in bed the first morning, smelling the bedroom, and hearing the boy sneak quietly out and go off along the shore in a boat. I began to sustain the illusion that he was I, and therefore, by simple transposition, that I was my father. This sensation persisted, kept cropping up all the time we were there. It was not an entirely new feeling, but in this setting it grew much stronger. I seemed to be living a dual existence. I would be in the middle of some simple act. I would be picking up a bait box or laying down a table fork, or I would be saying something, and suddenly it would be not I but my father who was saying the words or making the gesture. It gave me a creepy sensation.

We went fishing the first morning. I felt the same damp moss covering the worms in the bait can, and saw the dragonfly alight on the tip of my rod as it hovered a few inches from the surface of the water. It was the arrival of this fly that convinced me beyond any doubt that everything was as it always had been, that the years were a mirage and there had been no years. The small waves were the same, chucking the rowboat under the chin as we fished at anchor, and the boat was the same boat, the same color green and the ribs broken in the same places, and under the floorboards the same fresh-water leavings and débris—the dead helgramite, the wisps of moss, the rusty discarded fishhook, the dried blood from yesterday's catch. We stared silently at the tips of our rods, at the dragonflies that came and went. I lowered the tip of mine into the water, tentatively, pensively dislodging the fly, which darted two feet away, poised, darted two feet back, and came to rest again a little farther up the rod. There had been no years between the ducking of this dragonfly and the other one—the one that was part of memory. I looked at the boy, who was silently watching his fly, and it was my hands that held his rod, my eyes watching. I felt dizzy and didn't know which rod I was at the end of.

We caught two bass, hauling them in briskly as though they were mackerel, pulling them over the side of the boat in a businesslike manner without any landing net, and stunning them with a blow on the back of the head. When we got back for a swim before lunch, the lake was exactly where we had left it, the same number of inches from the dock, and there was only the merest suggestion of a breeze. This seemed an utterly enchanted sea, this lake you could leave to its own devices for a few hours and come back to, and find that it had not stirred, this constant and trustworthy body of water. In the shallows, the dark, water-soaked sticks and twigs, smooth and old, were undulating in clusters on the bottom against the clean ribbed sand, and the track of the mussel was plain. A school of minnows swam by, each minnow with its small individual shadow, doubling the attendance, so clear and sharp in the sunlight. Some of the other campers were in swimming, along the shore, one of them with a cake of soap, and the water felt thin and clear and unsubstantial. Over the years there had been this person with the cake of soap, this cultist, and here he was. There had been no years.

Up to the farmhouse to dinner through the teeming, dusty field, the road under our sneakers was only a two-track road. The middle track was missing, the one with the marks of the hooves and the splotches of dried, flaky manure. There had always been three tracks to choose from in choosing which track to walk in; now the choice was narrowed down to two. For a moment I missed terribly the middle alternative. But the way led past the tennis court, and something about the way it lay there in the sun reassured me; the tape had loosened along the backline, the alleys were green with plantains and other weeds, and the net (installed in June and removed in September) sagged in the dry noon, and the whole place steamed with midday heat and hunger and emptiness. There was a choice of pie for dessert, and one was blueberry and one was apple, and the waitresses were the same country girls, there having been no passage of time, only the illusion of it as in a dropped curtain—the waitresses were still fifteen; their hair had been washed, that was the only difference—they had been to the movies and seen the pretty girls with the clean hair.

Summertime, oh summertime, pattern of life indelible, the fadeproof lake, the woods unshatterable, the pasture with the sweetfern and the juniper forever and ever, summer without end; this was the background, and the life along the shore was the design, the cottages with their innocent and tranquil design, their tiny docks with the flagpole and the American flag floating against the white clouds in the blue sky, the little paths over the roots of the trees leading from camp to camp and the paths leading back to the outhouses and the can of lime for sprinkling, and at the souvenir counters at the store the miniature birch-bark canoes and the post cards that showed things looking a little better than they looked. This was the American family at play, escaping the city heat, wondering whether the newcomers in the camp at the head of the cove were "common" or "nice," wondering whether it was true that the people who drove up for Sunday dinner at the farmhouse were turned away because there wasn't enough chicken.

It seemed to me, as I kept remembering all this, that those times and those summers had been infinitely precious and worth saving. There had been jollity and peace and goodness. The arriving (at the beginning of August) had been so big a business in itself, at the railway station the farm wagon drawn up, the first smell of the pine-laden air, the first glimpse of the smiling farmer, and the great importance of the trunks and your father's enormous authority in such matters, and the feel of the wagon under you for the long ten-mile haul, and at the top of the last long hill catching the first view of the lake after eleven months of not seeing this cherished body of water. The shouts and cries of the other campers when they saw you, and the trunks to be unpacked, to give up their rich burden. (Arriving was less exciting nowadays, when you sneaked up in your car and parked it under a tree near the camp and took out the bags and in five minutes it was all over, no fuss, no loud wonderful fuss about trunks.)

Peace and goodness and jollity. The only thing that was wrong now, really, was the sound of the place, an unfamiliar nervous sound of the outboard motors. This was the note that jarred, the one thing that would sometimes break the illusion and set the years moving. In those other summertimes all motors were inboard; and when they were at a little distance, the noise they made was a sedative, an ingredient of summer sleep. They were one-cylinder and two-cylinder engines, and some were make-and-break and some were jump-spark, but they all made a sleepy sound across the lake. The one-lungers throbbed and fluttered, and the twin-cylinder ones purred and purred, and that was a quiet sound too. But now the campers all had outboards. In the daytime, in the hot mornings, these motors made a petulant, irritable sound; at night, in the still evening when the afterglow lit the water, they whined about one's ears like mosquitoes. My boy loved our rented outboard, and his great desire was to achieve single-handed mastery over it, and authority, and he soon learned the trick of choking it a little (but not too much), and the adjustment of the needle valve. Watching him I would remember the things you could do with the old one-cylinder engine with the heavy flywheel, how you could have it eating out of your hand if you got really close to it spiritually. Motor boats in those days didn't have clutches, and you would make a landing by shutting off the motor at the proper time and coasting in with a dead rudder. But there was a way of reversing them, if you learned the trick, by cutting the switch and putting it on again exactly on the final dying revolution of the flywheel, so that it would kick back against compression and begin reversing. Approaching a dock in a strong following breeze, it was difficult to slow up sufficiently by the ordinary coasting method, and if a boy felt he had complete mastery over his motor, he was tempted to keep it running beyond its time and then reverse it a few feet from the dock. It took a cool nerve, because if you threw the switch a twentieth of a second too soon you would catch the flywheel when it still had speed enough to go up past center, and the boat would leap ahead, charging bull-fashion at the dock.

We had a good week at the camp. The bass were biting well and the sun shone endlessly, day after day. We would be tired at night and lie down in the accumulated heat of the little bedrooms after the long hot day and the breeze would stir almost imperceptibly outside and the smell of the swamp drift in through the rusty screens. Sleep would come easily and in the morning the red squirrel would be on the roof, tapping out his gay routine. I kept remembering everything, lying in bed in the mornings—the small steamboat that had a long rounded stern like the lip of a Ubangi, and how quietly she ran on the moonlight sails, when the older boys played their mandolins and the girls sang and we ate doughnuts dipped in sugar, and how sweet the music was on the water in the shining night, and what it had felt like to think about girls then. After breakfast we would go up to the store and the things were in the same place—the minnows in a bottle, the plugs and spinners disarranged and pawed over by the youngsters from the boys' camp, the fig newtons and the Beeman's gum. Outside, the road was tarred and cars stood in front of the store. Inside, all was just as it had always been, except there was more Coca Cola and not so much Moxie and root beer and birch beer and sarsaparilla. We would walk out with a bottle of pop apiece and sometimes the pop would backfire up our noses and hurt. We explored the streams, quietly, where the turtles slid off the sunny logs and dug their way into the soft bottom; and we lay on the town wharf and fed worms to the tame bass. Everywhere we went I had trouble making out which was I, the one walking at my side, the one walking in my pants.

One afternoon while we were there at that lake a thunderstorm came up. It was like the revival of an old melodrama that I had seen long ago with childish awe. The second-act climax of the drama of the electrical disturbance over a lake in America had not changed in any important respect. This was the big scene, still the big scene. The whole thing was so familiar, the first feeling of oppression and heat and a general air around camp of not wanting to go very far away. In midafternoon (it was all the same) a curious darkening of the sky, and a lull in everything that had made life tick; and then the way the boats suddenly swung the other way at their moorings with the coming of a breeze out of the new quarter, and the premonitory rumble. Then the kettle drum, then the snare, then the bass drum and cymbals, then crackling light against the dark, and the gods grinning and licking their chops in the hills. Afterward the calm, the rain steadily rustling in the calm lake, the return of light and hope and spirits, and the campers running out in joy and relief to go swimming in the rain, their bright cries perpetuating the deathless joke about how they were getting simply drenched, and the children screaming with delight at the new sensation of bathing in the rain, and the joke about getting drenched linking the generations in a strong indestructible chain. And the comedian who waded in carrying an umbrella.

When the others went swimming my son said he was going in too. He pulled his dripping trunks from the line where they had hung all through the shower, and wrung them out. Languidly, and with no thought of going in, I watched him, his hard little body, skinny and bare, saw him wince slightly as he pulled up around his vitals the small, soggy, icy garment. As he buckled the swollen belt suddenly my groin felt the chill of death.

My Wood

E.M. Forster

A few years ago I wrote a book which dealt in part with the difficulties of the English in India. Feeling that they would have had no difficulties in India themselves, the Americans read the book freely. The more they read it the better it made them feel, and a cheque to the author was the result. I bought a wood with the cheque. It is not a large wood—it contains scarcely any trees, and it is intersected, blast it, by a public footpath. Still, it is the first property that I have owned, so it is right that other people should participate in my shame, and should ask themselves, in accents that will vary in horror, this very important question: What is the effect of property upon the character? Don't let's touch economics; the effect of private ownership upon the community as a whole is another question—a more important question, perhaps, but another one. Let's keep to psychology. If you own things, what's their effect on you? What's the effect on me of my wood?

In the first place, it makes me feel heavy. Property does have this effect. Property produces men of weight, and it was a man of weight who failed to get into the Kingdom of Heaven. He was not wicked, that unfortunate millionaire in the parable, he was only stout; he stuck out in front, not to mention behind, and as he wedged himself this way and that in the crystalline entrance and bruised his well-fed flanks, he saw beneath him a comparatively slim camel passing through the eye of a needle and being woven into the robe of God. The Gospels all through couple stoutness and slowness. They point out what is perfectly obvious, yet seldom realized: that if you have a lot of things you cannot move about a lot, that furniture requires dusting, dusters require servants, servants require insurance stamps, and the whole tangle of them makes you think twice before you accept an invitation to dinner or go for a bathe in the Jordan. Sometimes the Gospels proceed further and say with Tolstoy that property is sinful; they approach the difficult ground of asceticism here, where I cannot follow them. But as to the immediate effects of property on people, they just show straightforward logic. It produces men of weight. Men of weight cannot, by definition, move like the lightning from the East unto the West, and the ascent of a fourteen-stone bishop into a pulpit is thus the exact antithesis of the coming of the Son of Man. My wood makes me feel heavy.

In the second place, it makes me feel it ought to be larger.

The other day I heard a twig snap in it. I was annoyed at first, for I thought that someone was blackberrying, and depreciating the value of the undergrowth. On coming nearer, I saw it was not a man who had trodden on the twig and snapped it, but a bird, and I felt pleased. My bird. The bird was not equally pleased. Ignoring the relation between us, it took fright as soon as it saw the shape of my face, and flew straight over the boundary hedge into a field, the property of Mrs. Henessy, where it sat down with a loud squawk. It had become Mrs. Henessy's bird. Something seemed grossly amiss here, something that would not have occurred had the wood been larger. I could not afford to buy Mrs. Henessy out, I dared not murder her, and limitations of this sort beset me on every side. Ahab did not want that vineyard—he only needed it to round off his property, preparatory to plotting a new curve—and all the land around my wood has become necessary to me in order to round off the wood. A boundary protects. But—poor little thing—the boundary ought in its turn to be protected. Noises on the edge of it. Children throw stones. A little more, and then a little more, until we reach the sea. Happy Canute! Happier Alexander! And after all, why should even the world be the limit of possession? A rocket containing a Union Jack, will, it is hoped, be shortly fired at the moon. Mars. Sirius. Beyond which... But these immensities ended by saddening me. I could not suppose that my wood was the destined nucleus of universal dominion—it is so very small and contains no mineral wealth beyond the blackberries. Nor was I comforted when Mrs. Henessy's bird took alarm for the second time and flew clean away from us all, under the belief that it belonged to itself.

In the third place, property makes its owner feel that he ought to do something to it. Yet he isn't sure what. A restlessness comes over him, a vague sense that he has a personality to express—the same sense which, without any vagueness, leads the artist to an act of creation. Sometimes I think I will cut down such trees as remain in the wood, at other times I want to fill up the gaps between them with new trees. Both impulses are pretentious and empty. They are not honest movements towards money-making or beauty. They spring from a foolish desire to express myself and from an inability to enjoy what I have got. Creation, property, enjoyment form a sinister trinity in the human mind. Creation and enjoyment are both very very good, yet they are often unattainable without a material basis, and at such moments property pushes itself in as a substitute, saying, 'Accept me instead—I'm good enough for all three.' It is not enough. It is, as Shakespeare said of lust, 'The expense of spirit in a waste of shame': it is 'Before, a joy proposed; behind, a dream.' Yet we don't know how to shun it. It is forced on us by our economic system as the alternative to starvation. It is also forced on us by an internal defect in the soul, by the feeling that in property may lie the germs of self-development and of exquisite or heroic deeds. Our life on earth is, and ought to be, material and carnal. But we have not yet learned to manage our materialism and carnality properly; they are still entangled with the desire for ownership, where (in the words of Dante) 'Possession is one with loss.'

And this brings us to our fourth and final point: the blackberries.

Blackberries are not plentiful in this meagre grove, but they are easily seen from the public footpath which traverses it, and all too easily gathered.

Foxgloves, too—people will pull up the foxgloves, and ladies of an education-al tendency even grub for toadstools to show them on the Monday in class. Other ladies, less educated, roll down the bracken in the arms of their gentlemen friends. There is paper, there are tins. Pray, does my wood belong to me or doesn't it? And, if it does, should I not own it best by allowing no one else to walk there? There is a wood near Lyme Regis, also cursed by a public footpath, where the owner has not hesitated on this point. He has built high stone walls each side of the path, and has spanned it by bridges, so that the public circulate like termites while he gorges on the blackberries unseen. He really does own his wood, this able chap. Dives in Hell did pretty well, but the gulf dividing him from Lazarus could be traversed by vision, and nothing traverses it here. And perhaps I shall come to this in time. I shall wall in and fence out until I really taste the sweets of property. Enormously stout, end-lessly avaricious, pseudocreative, intensely selfish, I shall weave upon my forehead the quadruple crown of possession until those nasty Bolshies come and take it off again and thrust me aside into the outer darkness.

The Street-Car Conductor

Hugh MacLennan

The street-car rattling westward was almost empty, for it was the slack hour of the early afternoon. The conductor was half-sitting, half-standing in his cage at the back of the car. On his cuff were six tarnished service stripes. On his face was an expression of unfathomable calm.

A bell buzzed. A passenger rose, moved down the aisle to the rear of the car and stood by the conductor's cage. This citizen was short, square, elderly and decisive. He carried a worn brief-case in his left hand; the fingers of his right drummed firmly on the polished steel rail of the conductor's cage. His grey face was stern and his wide mouth had formed itself into the thin straight line of a man who has waited too long to buy a set of false teeth. He fixed the conductor with accusing eyes and spoke in a harsh, clear voice.

"*La situation internationale est terrible!*"

"*Ouais,*" the conductor said, not turning his head.

"*L'Angleterre est finie!*"

"*Ouais.*"

"*La France est manifestement finie!*"

"*Ouais.*"

"*La troisième guerre vient pour sûr!*"

"*Ouais.*"

"*Nous sommes donc tous finis!*"

"*Ouais.*"

The car stopped, the doors opened, the citizen stepped out, the doors closed, the car jerked forward, and as I looked at the conductor's quarter-profile from where I sat near the end of the long bench at the back of the car, I wondered why most of us take conductors for granted, seeing them but not seeing them, as though they were mechanical fixtures of their cars.

For thirty years, perhaps longer, this man had been half-sitting, half-standing in the sterns of street-cars in such a posture that he had always to watch the world recede from him as the car advanced. Summer and winter, fall and spring, millions of citizens had jostled him as his trams carried them to and from their work, to and from their sports and business *coups* and parties and love affairs. Girls with shining eyes had stared into the rapt faces of boys. Young married men with pay cheques in their pockets had stood cheerfully in the jam beside him thinking how happy they were going to make their wives that evening. Desperate men had plotted suicide and women in middle age had wondered how much longer they could stand it. The mothers of two generations had pushed children past him while they fumbled for tickets, and behind him old ladies had smiled when young men had risen to offer them seats. Billions of loves, hates, lusts, fears, hopes, boredoms and little private amusements had cavorted through the busy brains surrounding this man. And always *la situation internationale* had been *terrible.*

For thirty years, perhaps longer, this man had lived in the midst of it. In the headlines of newspapers tucked under arms or crunched before faces the epic of the twentieth century had been displayed in all editions and in both languages of the city. But because the papers were usually folded in the middle he had seen only half the headlines recording fires and floods, murders and rescues, rising and collapsing governments, and the land, sea and air battles of three wars. In the splintering anxieties of an apocalyptic epoch he had remained half-sitting, half-standing at his post in the stern of his car. On the morning in 1940 when France fell he was passing out his transfers. When the Third Reich dissolved in smoke and bomb-bursts he was calling out *Ghee—Guy—Côte des Neiges.* When the Chinese invaded Korea the world was still receding from him. Through all the tempests of his century he had ridden the street-cars of Montreal, half-sitting, half-standing, with an expression as mysterious, as remote, as profound as that of a Buddha in the jungle-infested ruins of Ankor Vat.

The car began to sway as it ran the straight passage of Sherbrooke Street past Westmount Park; it staggered a little as it took the curving slope towards Decarie; then it settled down for its run through Notre Dame de Grâce. Fifteen to twenty years ago this district had been loud and gay with the voices of children and adolescents, for it was the part of the city where young couples had moved to raise their families after the Old War. Now several thousands of those who had grown up in the nineteen-thirties had been killed in the Second War, and most of their brothers and sisters had married and moved away. The people on the sidewalks seemed to be in late middle age. For Notre Dame de Grâce *la situation internationale* had indeed been *terrible...*

We get into the habit of steeling ourselves for bad news, I thought, with the echo of the dour citizen's words still in my mind. The moment we stop worrying about something, we suspect we are losing our grip on reality. Troubles will arise—what would we do without them? but whatever evil we see in the near future can hardly rival the evils this conductor has been carrying about in the headlines of the papers his passengers have been reading over the past thirty years.

It was fashionable during the nineteen-thirties to talk of the death-wish that ruled the world. By feeding it with the incense of our fears we fattened it into a monster more frightening than Hitler's armies. Today we no longer consider it our master. Today we are tired of its company, and scorn ourselves for having invited it into our homes. But its strange and ghastly reign during the first forty years of the twentieth century will give historians of the future an opportunity to say some pretty nasty things about us.

When we first became aware, through Freud, of this thing in all of us which he called the death-wish—this thing which caused the dour citizen to assert with such relish *nous sommes tous finis*—it seemed romantic and exciting. In 1914 Rupert Brooke, most innocent of twentieth-century poets, sang of giving the world away and pouring out "the red, sweet wine of youth." The first of our wars gave many millions the opportunity of doing so. In the nineteen-twenties the face of the death-wish was painted with a false, bright gaiety, and young novelists like Ernest Hemingway began to glorify bullfights and hangovers, while older poets like T.S. Eliot chanted of the wasteland and hollow men with a loving eloquence which proclaimed that it was only in corruption and impotence that we could discover the seeds of beauty. The mask of the death-wish was weary and sophisticated in the first days of the depression when the blonde in Noel Coward's *Cavalcade* swung her pretty legs from the piano top and crooned "Twentieth Century Blues," asking what there was to strive for, love or keep alive for. By the late nineteen-thirties the death-wish had lost both its charm and its sophistication. Now it wore the mask of staring fear. It was distorted with fear on the day Chamberlain and Daladier flew back from Munich, when the populations of the two most civilized nations in the world cried out in rejoicing for the deal Hitler had made to destroy them.

The death-wish did more than make us act like cowards. It hypnotized us as though we were birds cowering before snakes. It sucked potency from our men and charm from our women. (Remember, those of you who can, the styles of the 1920's?) It made the old and rich ask only to be let alone. It persuaded the young and poor that every man in authority was their enemy. It made us pray for security instead of for courage. And when we discovered that we had courage nevertheless, we no longer talked about the death-wish, for by that time another generation had come along, and they took Freud for granted. But the old slogans glorifying security still had enough power to win elections. Worst of all, they persuaded Stalin, as they had persuaded Hitler, that we were ripe to be picked...

The tram began swaying again as it left Royal Avenue with the additional freight of three small boys who had been let out early at Lower Canada College. The conductor, half-sitting, half-standing, was concerned with his own cavernous thoughts as he watched the brick apartment buildings and small shops move away to his rear. From the folded front of my newspaper half of Winston Churchill's face stared upward. He looked older, but his expression was not much different from what it had been fifteen years ago when so many of us called him irresponsible merely because he was brave. The tendons in his neck were more prominent, but not much more than they had been in the days when he took the death-wish by the throat and choked it, and then turned and breathed some of his own courage into us as God breathed life into Adam.

"Were you working on this same route fifteen years ago?" I asked the conductor, wondering if he would know that my question was addressed to him.

"*Ouais.*"

Fifteen years ago Hemingway, our hero among the novelists of that time, had written that he was always embarrassed by words like "sacred," "glorious" and "sacrifice," for "the things that were glorious had no glory and the sacrifices were like the stockyards of Chicago if nothing was done with the meat except to bury it." Hemingway had written these words and we all knew that he himself was a brave man. We thought we knew everything in those days. We knew that Hitler and Mussolini had to be stopped and at the same time we knew that wars decide nothing. So we voted to stop Hitler and Mussolini and at the same time we voted to reduce the budget for armaments. *La situation internationale?* Today we shrug our shoulders and say, "But what do you expect?" Or merely, *"Ouais."*

The tram and its impassive guardian continued to sway onward and I got up as I saw my stop a few blocks ahead. The acres of apartments on the old Benny Farm slid past and sunlight glinted on snow in open spaces. Again we were in a district filled with children.

In Red River suits they played in the snow or were drawn on sleds by their mothers (younger mothers these days than when we were married, young enough to enjoy their families vigorously and to remain young when their children grow up, so that in their early forties they will be free to make full use of what the world has taught them). The tram was nearing my stop and I reached up to press the bell. I stood beside the conductor and spoke to him again.

"Things aren't so bad these days."

"Ouais," he said.

The car stopped, the doors opened and I stepped out into the street. The doors closed, the car jerked forward and I stood watching the conductor, half-sitting, half-standing, his image blurred behind the glass, riding off into the west.

The Creature from the Marsh

Loren Eiseley

I

The only thing strange about me is my profession. I happen to be one of those few persons who pursue the farther history of man on the planet earth, what Darwin once called "the great subject." But my business is not with the formal art of the history books. Take, for example, today.

Today I have been walking in the ruins of the city. The city still moves, it is true, the air drills ring against iron, and I am aware of laughter and of feet hurrying by at the noon hour. Nevertheless the city is in ruins. This is what the trained eye makes of it. It stands here in the morning sun while rust flakes the steel rails and the leaves of innumerable autumns blow mistily through the ribs of skyscrapers and over the fallen brick work lies a tangle of morning glories. I have seen this before in the dead cities of Mexico—the long centuries wavering past with the curious distortion of things seen through deep sea water. Even the black snake gliding down the steps of the cathedral seems a repetition, past and future being equally resolvable in the curious perspective of the archaeological eye.

But it was not for this that I hurried out to walk in the streets of the city. I wanted to find a symbol, something that would stand for us when the time came, something that might be proud after there was no stone upon another— some work of art, perhaps, or a gay conceit that the rains had not tarnished, something that would tell our story to whatever strange minds might come groping there.

I think I must have walked miles in those ruins. I studied a hundred shop windows. I weighed with a quarter century of digging experience the lasting qualities of metal, stone, and glass. I hesitated over the noble inscriptions upon public buildings, while the rain dissolved in the locked containers the files of treaties and the betrayal of all human trust. I passed by the signs of coruscating heat and the wilted metal of huge guns. I found the china head of a doll in the metal of a baby carriage that my mind took hold of and considered carefully, though later I realized I stood by a living nursemaid in the Park.

I looked at tools, and at flowers in the windows of tenements. (They will creep out and grow, I thought.) And I heard a dog howl in the waste streets for the comforting hand of man. I saw the vacant, ashy leaves of books blow by, but I did not pick them up. There were dead television screens and the curious detached loneliness of telephone receivers whose broken wires still thrummed in the winds over the Sierra.

It will never do, I thought; there was more to us than this—with all the evil, with all the cruelty. I remembered an inscribed gold ring in a pawnshop window. "From Tom to Mary," it had read, "for always." It is back there, I thought; that might be it—there was love in us, things we spoke to each other in the evening or on deathbeds, the eyes frank at last. It might be there. I turned and hurried back.

But the little shop was gone, and finally I came up short at a place where stones had tumbled in a peculiar way, half sheltering a fallen window. There were bones there, and at first this made no sense because bones in exposed places do not last well, and there are so many of them finally that the meaning escapes you.

There was a broken sign LED—Fi—Av—. And among the bits of glass, a little cluster of feathers, and under a shattered pane, the delicate bones of a woman's hand that, dying, had reached wistfully out, caught there, when the time came.

Why not? I mused. The human hand, the hand is the story. I touched one of the long, graceful bones. It had come the evolutionary way up from far eons and watery abysses only to perish here.

There was a little restless stirring beside me.

So it died after all that effort, I thought on. Five hundred million years expended in order that the shining thread of life could die reaching after a little creation of feathers in the window of a shop. And why not? Even my antique reptilian eye had a feel for something, a kind of beauty here.

The tugging at my sleeve continued. The slow, affectionate voice of my wife said to me, "Wait here. I want to go in."

"Of course," I said, and took and squeezed her slender hand as I returned from some far place. "It will look becoming," I said. "I will stand here and watch."

"The gloves to match it are of green lizard skin," she exulted.

"That will look just right," I ventured, and did not quite know what I meant. "I will stand here and watch."

A swinging light like a warning at a railroad crossing began flashing in the darkness below consciousness. A bell began jangling. Then it subsided. My wife was pointing, for the benefit of an attentive clerk, at a little cluster of feathers in the window. I came forward then and beckoned hastily. "But why—?" she said. "Another day," I said, wiping my forehead. It was just that—"Another time," I promised and urged her quickly away.

It is the nature, you see, of the profession—the terrible *déjà vu* of the archaeologist, the memory that scans before and after. For instance, take the case of the black skull, a retreat, some might say, in another direction.

II

The skull was black when they brought it to me. It was black from the irons and acids and mineral replacements of ice-age gravels. It was polished and worn and gleaming from the alterations of unnumbered years. It had made strange journeys after the death of its occupant; it had moved with glacial slowness in the beds of rivers; it had been tumbled by floods and, becoming an object of grisly beauty, had been picked up and passed from hand to hand by men the individual had never seen in life.

Finally it was brought to me.

It was my duty to tell them about the skull.

It was my professional duty to clothe these bones once more with the faint essence of a personality, to speak of a man or a woman, young or old, as the bones might tell the story. It was my task to read the racial features in a forgotten face, stare deep into the hollow sockets through which had once passed in endless procession the days and seasons and the shed tears of long ago.

The woman had been young. I could tell them that. I could tell them she had once fallen or been struck and that after a long time the bone had mended and she had recovered—how, it was difficult to say, for it had been a dangerous and compound fracture. Today such a wound would mean months of immobilization in a hospital. This woman had survived without medical attention through the endless marchings and journeyings of the hunters' world. Even the broken orbit of the left eye had dropped by a quarter of an inch—a serious disfigurement. Nevertheless she had endured and lived on toward some doom that had come fast upon her but was not written in the bones. It was, in all likelihood, a death by violence. Her skull had not been drawn from a grave. It had come from beneath the restless waters of a giant river that is known to keep its secrets well.

They asked me for the time of the events, and again, obediently, I went down that frail ladder which stretches below us into the night of time. I went slowly, by groping deductions and the hesitant intuitions of long experience that only scholars know. I passed through ages where water was wearing away the shapes of river pebbles into crystalline sand and the only sound in the autumn thickets was the gathering of south-flying birds. Somewhere in the neighborhood of the five thousandth millennium—I could place it no closer than that—the ladder failed me. The river was still there but larger—an enormous rolling waste of water and marshes out of which rose a vast October moon.

They interrupted me then, querulously, asking if archaeologists could do no better than this, and was it not true that there were new and clever methods by which physicists could call the year in the century and mark the passage of time by the tick of atoms in the substance of things. And I said, yes, within limits it was true, but that the methods were not always usable, and that the subtle contaminations possible among radioactive objects sometimes defeated our attempts.

At this point they shook their heads unwillingly, for, as I quickly saw, they had the passion of modern men for the precision of machines and disliked vagueness of any sort. But the skull lay there on the table between us, and over it one man lingered, fascinated in spite of himself. I knew what he was thinking: Where am I going? When shall I become like this?

I heard this in his mind for just an instant while I stared across at him from among my boxes of teeth and flint arrowheads that had grown chalky and dull with the passage of long centuries in the ground.

"Thank you," the visitor said finally, moving after his party to the door. He was, I saw, unsure for what it was he thanked me.

"You are quite welcome," I said, still returning slowly from that waste of forgotten water over which the birds of another century cried dolefully, so that I could hear them keening in my head. Like the man who asks a medium to bring back some whimpering memoryless ghost and make it speak out of a living mouth for the amusement of a group of curiosity seekers, he may have felt remorse. At any rate, he nodded uncertainly and fled.

I was the instrument. I had made this journey a hundred times for students who scrawled their initials on my skulls, a hundred times for reporters who wanted sensational accounts of monkey-men, a hundred times for people who came up at the end of lectures and asked, "How much money are the bones worth, doctor? Are they easy to find?"

In spite of this I have continued to make these journeys. It is old habit now. I go back into the past alone. I would do so if I fled my job and sought safety in some obscure room. My sense of time is so heightened that I can feel the frost at work in stones, the first creeping advance of grass in a deserted street. I have stood by the carved sarcophagi of dead knights in a European cathedral, men seven hundred years away from us with their steel and their ladies, and from that point striven to hurl the mind still backward into the wilderness where man coughs bestially and vanishes into the shape of beasts.

I cannot say I am a student of the dates in the history books. My life is mostly occupied with caves filled up and drifted over with the leaves of ten thousand thousand autumns. My speciality is the time when man was changing into man. But, like a river that twists, evades, hesitates through slow miles, and then leaps violently down over a succession of cataracts, man can be called a crisis animal. Crisis is the most powerful element in his definition. Of his entire history, this he understands the least. Only man has continued to turn his own definition around upon his tongue until, in the end, he has looked outside of nature to something invisible to any eye but his own. Long ago, this emotion was well expressed in the Old Testament. "Oh Lord," exclaimed the prophet Jeremiah, "I know that the way of man is not in himself." Therefore, I would add, as a modern evolutionist, "the way" only lies through man and has to be sought beyond him. It was this that led to a very remarkable experience.

III

"The greatest prize of all," once confessed the British plant explorer F. Kingdon Ward, "is the skull of primitive man." Ward forgot one thing: there are other clues to primitive men than those confined to skulls. The bones of fossil men are few because the earth tolerated them in scant numbers. We call them missing links on the road to ourselves. A little less tooth here, a little more brain there, and you can see them changing toward ourselves in that long historyless time when the great continental ice sheets ebbed and flowed across the northern continents. Like all the students of that age, I wanted to find a missing link in human history. That is what this record is about, for I stumbled on the track of one.

Some men would maintain that a vague thing called atmosphere accounts for such an episode as I am about to relate, that there are houses that demand a murder and wait patiently until the murderer and his victim arrive, that there are great cliffs that draw the potential suicide from afar or mountains of so austere a nature that they write their message on the face of a man who looks up at them. This all may be. I do not deny it. But when I encountered the footprint in the mud of that remote place I think the thing that terrified me most was the fact that I knew to whom it belonged and yet I did not want to know him. He was a stranger to me and remains so to this day. Because of a certain knowledge I had, however, he succeeded in impressing himself upon me in a most insidious manner. I have never been the same since the event took place and often at night I start up sweating and think uncannily that the creature is there with me in the dark. If the sense of his presence grows, I switch on the light, but I never look into the mirror. This is a matter of old habit with me.

First off, though, we must get straight what we mean by a missing link.

A missing link is a day in the life of a species that is changing its form and habits, just as, on a smaller scale, one's appearance and behavior at the age of five are a link in one's development to an adult man or woman. The individual person may have changed and grown but still the boy or girl of many years ago is linked to the present by a long series of steps. And if one is really alive and not already a living fossil, one will go on changing till the end of one's life and perhaps be the better for it. The term "missing link" was coined because some of the physical links in the history of man as a species are lost, and those people who, like myself, are curious about the past look for them.

My album is the earth, and the pictures in it are faded and badly torn and have to be pieced together by detective work. If one thinks of oneself at five years of age, one may get a thin wisp of disconnected memory pictures. By contrast, the past of a living species is without memory except as that past has written its physical record in vestigial organs like the appendix or a certain pattern on our molar teeth. To eke out what those physical stigmata tell us, we have to go grubbing about in caves and gravel for the bones of very ancient men. If one can conceive of the trouble an archaeologist might have in locating one's remains a half-million years from now, supposing they still existed, one will get an idea of the difficulties involved in finding traces of man before his bones were crowded together in cities and cemeteries.

I was wandering inland along a sunken shore when the thing happened— the thing I had dreamed of so long. In other words, I got a clue to man. The beaches on that coast I had come to visit are treacherous and sandy and the tides are always shifting things about among the mangrove roots. It is not a place to which I would willingly return and you will get no bearings from me. Anyway, what it was I found there could be discovered on any man's coast if he looked sharp for it. I had come to that place with other things in mind, and a notion of being alone. I was tired. I wanted to lie in the sun or clamber about like an animal in the swamps and the forest. To secure such rest from the turmoil of a modern city is the most difficult thing in the world to accomplish and I have only achieved it twice: once in one of the most absolute deserts in the world and again in this tropical marsh.

By day and night strange forms of life scuttled and gurgled underfoot or oozed wetly along outthrust branches; luminous tropical insects blundered by in the dark like the lamps of hesitant burglars. Overhead, on higher ground, another life shrieked distantly or was expectantly still in the treetops. Somehow, alone as I was, I got to listening as if all that world were listening, waiting for something to happen. The trees drooped a little lower listening, the tide lurked and hesitated on the beach, and even a tree snake dropped a loop and hung with his face behind a spider web, immobile in the still air.

A world like that is not really natural, or (the thought strikes one later) perhaps it really is, only more so. Parts of it are neither land nor sea and so everything is moving from one element to another, wearing uneasily the queer transitional bodies that life adopts in such places. Fish, some of them, come out and breathe air and sit about watching you. Plants take to eating insects, mammals go back to the water and grow elongate like fish, crabs climb trees. Nothing stays put where it began because everything is constantly climbing in, or climbing out, of its unstable environment.

Along drowned coasts of this variety you only see, in a sort of speeded-up way, what is true of the whole world and everything upon it: the Darwinian world of passage, of missing links, of beetles with soldered, flightless wings, of snakes with vestigial feet dragging slowly through the underbrush. Everything is marred and maimed and slightly out of focus—everything in the world. As for man, he is no different from the rest. His back aches, he ruptures easily, his women have difficulties in childbirth—all because he has struggled up upon his hind legs without having achieved a perfect adjustment to his new posture.

On this particular afternoon, I came upon a swamp full of huge waterlilies where I had once before ventured. The wind had begun to rise and rain was falling at intervals. As far as I could see, giant green leaves velvetly impervious to water were rolling and twisting in the wind. It was a species of lily in which part of the leaves projected on stalks for a short distance above the water, and as they rolled and tossed the whole swamp flashed and quivered from the innumerable water drops that were rolling around and around like quicksilver in the great cupped leaves. Everything seemed flickering and changing as if in some gigantic illusion, but so soft was the green light and so delicate the brushing of the leaves against each other that the whole effect was quite restful, as though one could be assured that nothing was actually tangible or real and no one in his senses would want it to be, as long as he could sway and nod and roll reflecting water drops about over the surface of his brain.

Just as I finally turned away to climb a little ridge I found the first footprint. It was in a patch of damp, exposed mud and was pointed away from

67

the water as though the creature had emerged directly out of the swamp and was heading up the shore toward the interior. I had thought I was alone, and in that place it was wise to know one's neighbors. Worst of all, as I stood studying the footprint, and then another, still heading up the little rise, it struck me that though undoubtedly human the prints were different in some indefinable way. I will tell you once more that this happened on the coast of another country in a place where form itself is an illusion and no shape of man or beast is totally impossible. I crouched anxiously in the mud while all about the great leaves continued to rotate on their stems and to flash their endlessly rolling jewels.

But there were these footprints. They did not disappear. As I fixed the lowermost footprint with every iota of scientific attention I could muster, it became increasingly apparent that I was dealing with some transitional form of man. The arch, as revealed in the soft mud, was low and flat and implied to the skilled eye an inadequate adjustment to the upright posture. This, in its turn, suggested certain things about the spine and the nature of the skull. It was only then, I think, that the full import of my discovery came to me.

Good Lord, I thought consciously for the first time, the thing is alive. I had spent so many years analyzing the bones of past ages or brooding over lizard tracks turned to stone in remote epochs that I had never contemplated this possibility before. The thing was alive and it was human. I looked uneasily about before settling down into the mud once more. One could make out that the prints were big but what drew my fascinated eye from the first was the nature of the second toe. It was longer than the big toe, and as I crawled excitedly back and forth between the two wet prints in the open mud, I saw that there was a remaining hint of prehensile flexibility about them.

Most decidedly, as a means of ground locomotion this foot was transitional and imperfect. Its loose, splayed aspect suggested inadequate protection against sprains. That second toe was unnecessarily long for life on the ground, although the little toe was already approximating the rudimentary condition so characteristic of modern man. Could it be that I was dealing with an unreported living fossil, an archaic ancestral survival? What else could be walking the mangrove jungle with a foot that betrayed clearly the marks of ancient intimacy with the arboreal attic, an intimacy so long continued that now, after hundreds of thousands of years of ground life, the creature had squiggled his unnecessarily long toes about in the mud as though an opportunity to clutch at something had delighted his secret soul.

I crouched by the footprint and thought. I remembered that comparisons with the living fauna, whenever available, are good scientific procedure and a great aid to precise taxonomy. I sat down and took off my shoes.

I had never had much occasion to look critically at my own feet before. In modern man they are generally encased in shoes—something that still suggests a slight imperfection in our adaptations. After all, we don't normally find it necessary to go about with our hands constantly enclosed in gloves. As I sat contemplating and comparing my feet with the footprints, a faintly disturbing memory floated hazily across my mind. It had involved a swimming party many years before at the home of one of the most distinguished comparative anatomists in the world. As we had sat on the bench alongside his pool, I had glanced up suddenly and caught him staring with what had seemed unnecessary fascination at my feet. I remembered now that he had blushed a deep pink under his white hair and had diverted my inquiring glance deftly to the scenery about us.

Why I should have remembered the incident at all was unclear to me. I thought of the possibility of getting plaster casts of a footprint and I also debated whether I should attempt to trail the creature farther up the slope toward which he appeared to have been headed. It was no moment for hesitation. Still, I did hesitate. The uneasy memory grew stronger, and a thought finally struck me. A little sheepishly and with a glance around to see that I was not observed, I lowered my own muddy foot into the footprint. It fitted.

I stood there contemplatively clutching, but this time consciously, the mud in my naked toes. I was the dark being on that island shore whose body carried the marks of its strange passage. I was my own dogging Man Friday, the beast from the past who had come with weapons through the marsh. The wind had died and the great green leaves with their rolling jewels were still. The mistake I had made was the mistake of all of us.

The story of man was not all there behind us in the caves of remote epochs. Even our physical bodies gave evidence that the change was not completed. As for our minds, they were still odd compounds of beast and saint. But it was not by turning back toward the marsh out of which we had come that the truly human kingdom was to be possessed and entered—that kingdom dreamed of in many religions and spoken of in many barbarous tongues. A philosopher once said in my presence, "The universe is a series of leaping sparks—everything else is interpretation." But what, I hesitated, was man's interpretation to be?

I drew a foot out of the little steaming swamp that sucked at it. The air hung heavily about me. I listened as the first beast might have listened who came from the water up the shore and did not return again to his old element. Everything about me listened in turn and seemed to be waiting for some decision on my part. I swayed a moment on my unstable footing.

Then, warily, I stepped higher up the shore and let the water and the silt fill in that footprint to make it, a hundred million years away, a fossil sign of an unknown creature slipping from the shadows of a marsh toward something else that awaited him. I had found the missing link. He walked on misshapen feet. The stones hurt him and his belly sagged. There were dreams like Christmas ornaments in his head, intermingled with an ancient malevolent viciousness. I knew because I was the missing link, but for the first time I sensed where I was going.

I have said I never look into the mirror. It is a matter of old habit now. If that other presence grows too oppressive I light the light and read.

TERMS and TOPICS

TERMS

1. **Vocabulary, Section I:** acrimonious, apocalyptic, asceticism, avaricious, balking, carnality, coruscating, destitute, dolefully, ensconced, giddy, grisly, grossly, hierarchical, ignoble, impassive, impervious, incessant, indelible, insidious, irrevocable, languidly, malevolent, meagre, meticulous, paranoia, paraphernalia, pensively, petulant, placidity, premonitory, pretentious, primeval, querulously, rudimentary, solicitous, squander, succulent, supple, tangible, taxonomy, teeming, tranquil, turmoil, vernacular, vestigial.

2. *Formal, informal, colloquial, slang* Think of these so-called "levels" of diction or style as occurring on a spectrum. One point on the spectrum is not intrinsically better (or worse) than another; rather each is right, or appropriate, for a given subject, audience, and purpose. Sharpen your sense of the distinctions between them as you read and write. Most writing today uses a relatively informal style. But for what kind of occasion would a relatively formal style be most appropriate? or a colloquial style? Can you think of an occasion for which you would want to mix formal diction and slang? Can you find any instances of such a mixture in the essays in this book?

3. *Synecdoche* A figurative use of language in which a part is made to stand for a whole, or sometimes a whole for a part. For example we speak of workers as "hands" or, slangily, of a car as "wheels"; the word "Ottawa" often means "the government" which is located there. Synecdoche is essentially a form of *metonymy*, in which one of a thing's attributes, or a cause or effect of it, or something associated with it, in fact or in fancy, is made to stand for it, as when we say "crown" when referring to the Queen or her government. When White says he has become a "salt-water man" he is not identifying himself with the sea metaphorically; rather he is declaring his literal association with it and for the moment letting that connection stand metonymically for his whole self. And when he refers to "the road under our sneakers," the word *sneakers*, though literally apt, also stands in place of "feet" or even "us," the whole bodies above the feet. When MacLennan writes that the new generation "took Freud for granted," the name *Freud* refers not so much to the man as to his works, his theories, his influence. Dillard gets a little metonymic twist by referring to Hollins Pond as "a remarkable piece of shallowness." Much descriptive writing is essentially metonymic, in that an author selects certain details from the great number available and uses them to stand for, suggest, or evoke the total reality of which they are a part, as when Mukherjee writes of "the walls" and "the accouterments of Ballygunge life" outside them: "hawkers, beggars, loiterers, squatters, sleepers, cows and pariahs, cars, taxis, buses, mini-buses, cycles, rickshaws, bullock carts, and heedless pedestrians. Inside," she adds, "there is greenery, flowers, a studied calm." Metonymy is often considered a form of metaphorical language, but it is better understood as fundamentally different, for whereas the effect of metaphor depends partly on the difference, the distance, between two things that are nonetheless being equated with each other (the ship and the plough, the weasel's teeth and the plug), metonymy depends on their contiguity, their sameness, their close association with each other: "shallowness" is an actual feature of the pond; "walls" are a prominent physical part of the scene.

4. *Personification* A form of metaphorical language in which human attributes are ascribed to something nonhuman—usually something inanimate or abstract. White assumes, about the camp as he remembers it, "that the tarred road would have found it out," as if the road could think and seek out its victim. He provides the rowboat with a "chin" under which it can be "chuck[ed]" by the waves, themselves thus personified. Forster refers to the boundary of his wood as a "poor little thing" that needs protection, as if it were a helpless child. Haig-Brown's fly conducts a "cunning search of likely places" to find a fish. In a more complicated metaphor, but one depending basically on personification, Eiseley writes of "mountains of so austere a nature that they write their message on the face of a man who looks up at them." Dylan Thomas refers to "the carol-singing sea." (Since Thomas was also a major poet, it isn't surprising to find his prose filled with metaphors of various kinds.) Animate creatures can, in effect, also be personified, as when Forster describes the bird as having "the belief that it belonged to itself." And the conclusion of Fisher's reminiscence includes a kind of personification when she speaks of "our hearts' palates"—even though the hearts are, strictly speaking, parts of human beings.

5. *Paradox* A statement that is seemingly illogical, self-contradictory, or otherwise absurd, but that is somehow actually or at least possibly true. Many proverbs, for example, express paradoxes: slow but sure wins the race; the shortest way round is the longest way home; he who cannot obey cannot command. Shakespeare's "Sweet are the uses of adversity" *(As You Like It)* is another. It is paradoxical, yet true, that the best person for a particular job might be the one who knows least about it, or that a difficult task often makes one do better work than if the task were easy.

6. *Rhetorical question* A question that does not expect an answer, because the answer is implicit in the question or in the context. Such a question is thus for rhetorical effect only.

7. *Subject, thesis* A *subject*, or a *topic* (a term often used to designate a narrowed-down subject area), is what is being written about; a *thesis* is a proposition about a subject which governs what a writer says about it. For example, a subject such as "modern travel" could have any number of theses: "Travel by ship is more romantic than travel by air," "Travel is safer today than it used to be," "Sometimes planning a trip is more fun than the actual travelling," and so on. But a thesis need not be so explicitly argumentative—for example, "Travel is broadening." Good writers almost always state their theses is some way, usually near either the beginning or the end of an essay—and often in both places. A thesis may, however, be partly or even entirely implicit. Look for the thesis in each of these essays. Make up several subjects of your own and then construct several possible theses for each.

8. *Subjective, objective* These adjectives, as they apply here, designate opposite qualities of a piece of writing or of a writer's attitude. *Objective* means independent of the mind, free of any influence by the attitudes, emotions, or special interests of the writer; *subjective* means just the opposite. An objective writer could be said to be writing from a detached point of view. Subjectivity or objectivity is almost always a matter of degree: one is relatively subjective or objective at any given time. Even a camera can lie.

9. *Parallelism* Parallel or repeated structure or phrasing, within a sentence or in successive sentences or paragraphs, to strengthen coherence and to create rhetorical effects, for example through emphasis. Parallelism obviously also affects rhythm.

TOPICS: On Individual Essays

JOHN UPDIKE   "Central Park"

1. Most of the details Updike lists are basically simple. Which ones would you call relatively complex? What makes them so?

2. Point out all the metaphors in this piece. Are there many? How do they work? What effects does each produce? Is the final item metaphorical? Who is Giuseppe Mazzini? Is treating his statue as if it were alive an instance of personification? Could the whole piece be considered an example of metonymy, depending for much of its effect on the process of association that goes on in a reader's mind? Could it be thought of along with those in section II, "Writing to Reveal"? What does it reveal about the place described? about the describer?

3. In 1956 the word "colored" was standard. When and why did it change? Is it still considered acceptable? What term would you use?

4. Updike's piece is proof that, to the observant eye, there are things all around us interesting enough to think about and write about. Try using his technique. Go for a walk. Make a descriptive list of the things you see. Or describe one of the following by assembling observed details: a shopping mall, a fast-food restaurant, a public beach, the view from a bridge, a post office, a downtown bus-stop during rush hour. Will you use every detail you record, or will you select from them? What principle of selection might you use? Will you let them stand in the order in which they came to you, or will you try to make some kind of pattern out of the sights you see? Use some metaphors, perhaps even personification.

DYLAN THOMAS   "Memories of Christmas"

1. Is *bombilating* a good word for the context? What is a *golliwog*? What is the point of the allusion to Pompeii? What are *trolls*? Is Thomas right about teddy-bears?

2. How does Thomas achieve the tone or outlook of a child without sounding childish? Consider for example his sentence structures.

3. Analyze the unusual metaphors at the beginning of the second paragraph. How do they work? Point out some metaphors elsewhere in the essay. Make up some metaphors imitating Thomas's.

4. What is the effect of the word *those* near the beginning of the first sentence (or paragraph)? What attitudes toward the writer and his subject does it virtually force a reader to adopt?

5. Does Thomas's essay have any "meaning" beyond evoking the past in a pleasant way? If so, how does he bring it out? Is the tone nostalgic? Does he avoid sentimentality?

6. To what extent does Thomas develop the other characters he mentions? Can you visualize them? Is it important?

7. Thomas was fond of compound adjectives. Examine some of them to see how much he achieved with how few words. Does he anywhere seem to you to overdo it? Does the style anywhere call too much attention to itself? Or do even the more striking turns of phrase contribute to the effect in justifiable ways?

8. Recall some recurring occasion of childhood—Christmas, birthdays, family reunions, camping holidays...—and describe those features that you have found particularly memorable.

9. Describe some setting that you remember from your childhood. Use as much metaphor and conscious rhythm as you feel the prose will bear; maybe even try a string of compound adjectives. Use as much narration as you wish, and put as many people into your scene as you need in order to create the effect you want. Does your piece have a thesis, even if only an implicit one?

M.F.K. FISHER "A Thing Shared"

1. Fisher is writing in 1943 about 1918. What is the point of her reference to "the September before people thought peace had come again"?

2. To what extent does this reminiscence constitute a comparison or contrast of *then* and *now*?

3. Write a brief memory-piece about a moment of discovery or happiness you shared with someone when you were five or six. Don't get caught up in sentimental nostalgia. Try to recapture some of your experiences and sensations and thoughts as a child, perhaps even focussing on a "first time" for one or more of them. What is the first meal you consciously remember eating? Why do you remember it?

4. Choose an event in your life that had unexpected significance for you, and try to recreate the experience and its impact on you at the time.

RODERICK HAIG-BROWN "Behind the Salmon"

1. For the uninitiated, are terms like "Harger's Orange," "backcast," spey cast," "set the hook," "shouldering," and "leader" unnecessarily confusing, or do they add authenticity? For a reader who doesn't fish, what is there to hold the attention? Is the essay more likely to appeal to someone who does fish?

2. What is the purpose of this essay? What is your interest focussed on? At what point or points does Haig-Brown state his thesis? What is the tone of the essay? Point out some of the stylistic features that create the tone.

3. Note how Haig-Brown moves from the pronoun *one* at the beginning, to *I*, and finally to *you* in the last paragraph, along with one final *one*. Does this indicate a careless inconsistency in his handling of point of view, or do you think it is intentional? Does he make it work?

4. The final sentence includes an allusive pun (see Terms, section V). Look back through the essay for earlier occurrences of the word *fall*, and remember that this essay is from the book *Fisherman's Fall*. Is a pun a cheap trick? How does this one function thematically?

5. Analyze Haig-Brown's descriptive technique. Note for example how paragraph 9 moves from general fact through increasingly specific details to the final focus on the possible fish. Do other paragraphs follow a similar pattern?

6. At the end of paragraph 10 and in the second sentence of paragraph 11, Haig-Brown uses a comma to join pairs of independent clauses. Technically these are comma splices, a serious writing error; but can his practice here be defended?

7. Write an essay about your engagement in some pursuit, some unusual hobby or sport or pastime that you believe is not an interest shared by many. Try to convey your enthusiasm to your audience.

ANNIE DILLARD *"Living Like Weasels"*

1. Who is Ernest Thompson Seton?

2. Analyze some of Dillard's metaphors, similes, and analogies. Does she ever seem to push too hard for an effective image? Comment on other details of her style. Does she pick up the metaphor of "socketed" (paragraph 1) elsewhere in the essay? What is the effect of the several questions scattered through the essay? Are they rhetorical questions? Why does she twice use the one word *So* as a sentence—once to begin a paragraph and once to end one?

3. Is Dillard's essay finally about "how to live," about living as we are meant to, by instinct rather than by choice? What is her thesis, either explicit or implicit? How effective is the ending? Is her advice "to grasp your one necessity" also implicit in Stephen Jay Gould's essay (section IV)? Is it comparable to what Brink (section III) quotes: "We must grasp what grips us?" Explain the paradox of the "perfect freedom of single necessity."

4. Notice how Dillard revivifies clichés. Comment for example on "held on for a dearer life" and "down is out." Are there any other clichés? Try playing in a similar way with several clichés; through context or variation, make them fresh and meaningful again.

5. Identify the various internal strategies or methods of development Dillard uses in this short essay: narration and description of course, and analogy. Does she use cause-and-effect? definition? contrast?

6. Write a short essay developing an analogy between human beings and some creature you know or know about.

7. Write a paragraph that starts with a description of something natural and moves from concrete to abstract by way of analogy or metaphor.

BHARATI MUKHERJEE *"Intimations"*

1. What are *avatars* (paragraph 1)? Explain the italicized allusion at the end of the third paragraph. What did Oliver Hardy look like (paragraph 15)? Explain the title, "Intimations."

2. How can "the aggressive desire of students to 'know' her" (paragraph 2) be explained "as a form of racism"?

3. In the chapter before the one reprinted here Mukherjee writes: "In Deoghar several time sequences coexist in what appears to be a single frieze." In this one she writes: "We do not seem to have heeded the message of the anonymous sculptor from Deoghar." What is the relation between this allusion and the way she handles time? Is time rendered in a simple narrative or historic line? through retrospect and prospect? Are there several "layers" of time? If so, is one more important than the others? Is time itself in any way a subject of her essay?

4. Nostalgia, along with associated feelings, is both explicit and implicit in this piece, but it is far from the simple nostalgia we commonly indulge in. Point out some instances where nostalgia is qualified and complicated in various ways.

5. To what degree is this piece "travel writing"? The focus is on Calcutta, but how does she illuminate it by contrasting it with other places?

6. Compare where you and your family live with modern Calcutta as Mukherjee describes it. How important is "protection" in your life? Can "privacy" itself be a kind of protection?

7. How does Mukherjee force us to see various things through eyes other than hers? What is the point of view? Does she succeed in juggling subjectivity and objectivity so as to make you see things through your own eyes? Note how she shifts from commenting on the ordinary to reflecting on the extraordinary, the unusual, the insane. How does she use anecdote to alter a reader's perception of what constitutes ordinariness? How does ordinariness relate to political, cultural, economic, or philosophical matters?

8. Write a brief narrative and descriptive essay about some event or condition that requires a similar adjustment of more than one point of view for full understanding.

E.B. WHITE *"Once More to the Lake"*

1. Consult one or more good dictionaries of quotations; then try to make a case for the title's including a literary allusion, possibly a multiple one.

2. The penultimate paragraph is almost pure description. What is its function in the essay? Why does White liken the scene to a "melodrama". What are the characteristic qualities or features of melodrama? Is White being melodramatic?

3. Try to decide how much of this essay is description and how much narration. Is it impossible to call some parts either one or the other? Is the overall purpose primarily narrative? descriptive? neither? Find or supply a thesis for it.

4. White's diction and syntax are basically simple; when he departs from that level he does so for a purpose. Find places where the level of diction or sentence structure shifts, and discuss the reason for the shifts.

5. What is the function of the last word of the second paragraph? What does White mean by "the grooves which lead back" (paragraph 2)?

6. Why does White repeatedly refer to time? In what different ways does he introduce the idea of time? How appropriate is the colloquial and cliché metaphor in "everything that had made life tick" (penultimate paragraph)?

7. Analyze the fourth sentence. Comment on its style and on its function in the opening and in the essay as a whole. What connection has it with the passage (paragraph 6) in which he says "the lake was exactly where we left it"? What saying or proverb is implicitly alluded to in these spots and elsewhere?

8. Describe a return (real or imagined) to a place you've not visited for several years, and explain the differences you perceive in the place or in yourself—or both.

9. Write a narrative of personal experience focussing on the effects of time on someone or something. Try to avoid merely stating or asserting your point; let your thesis remain implicit. But use as much description as necessary to make your meaning clear.

E.M. FORSTER   *"My Wood"*

1. Forster's first paragraph is a good example of the kind of introductory paragraph that begins broadly and gradually narrows down to a particular thesis—here partly by a process of elimination and partly by moving from general to increasingly specific. Practise writing this handy kind of opening paragraph, perhaps sometimes ending one, as Forster does here, with a thesis *question* rather than a thesis statement.

2. Is there any point to Forster's reference to his last novel, *A Passage to India*, or is it just a convenient anecdotal opening? Consider what he says about the novel's subject matter.

3. Does the short sentence "My bird," in paragraph 4, seem to you a deliberate echo of the essay's title? If so, what is the point of the similarity?

4. Using whatever reference books you need, analyze the complicated metaphor and allusion in the fourth sentence of the second paragraph. Find the other Biblical allusions and the literary and historical ones as well. Explain the function of each.

5. How would you characterize the tone of this essay? Is it consistent, or are there shifts? If there are shifts, do they jar, or is there a pattern and purpose to them?

6. In paragraph 2 Forster plays with words, punning on the word *weight*. Explain the pun. Is it fruitful? Does it fit the tone of the paragraph? Is there wordplay elsewhere in the essay? Forster has made the structure of his essay unusually obvious. How has he done this, and why do you think he did it? Does it work, or do you find it obtrusive?

7. Forster's essay could also be classified as writing to reveal. Write an essay that reveals how some attitude (hatred of or affection for something or someone?) or possession (a car? a dress? a computer? a collection of something? a swimming pool?) affects you. Model the structure of your essay as closely as possible on that of Forster's, and be just as obvious about it as he is.

HUGH MacLENNAN   *"The Street-Car Conductor"*

1. Do you think MacLennan means to blame Freud for the ills of the twentieth century? How valid was Freud's theory of the death instinct? Compare MacLennan's attitude with what Tuchman says (section III) about Freud and the influence of his ideas on the twentieth century, and with what is implicit in Szasz's essay (section III).

2. How much does the development of MacLennan's thesis depend on comparison and contrast of past and present? on cause and effect? Is it also in part a process analysis?

3. What is the effect of the parenthesis in the paragraph beginning "In Red River suits"? What are Red River suits?

4. Analyze the paragraph beginning "It was fashionable" for rhythm, sentence length and structure, coherence, parallelism, diction, metaphor, and any other stylistic feature you think worth mentioning. Discover all you can about the way the paragraph works. Does it use any internal strategy other than that of cause and effect? To what degree is it a substantive paragraph as well as a transitional one? What "nasty things" have historians said about the first forty years of this century?

5. What is the point of the final exchange, "Things aren't so bad these days" followed by the customary *"Ouais"*? Is this the beginning of the ending? How has MacLennan prepared for it, led up to it? Note for example the refrain of *la situation internationale* and *terrible*.

6. Analyze the essay's final sentence for everything you can find out about it and how it works.

7. Are you less likely in future to take for granted such an individual as this conductor? Has MacLennan made you "see" him? Or is he not the real subject of the essay? If not, what is?

8. Write an essay that focusses on some "little person" of your experience—perhaps a friend, a neighbour, or a relative—that is only nominally about that person, but instead uses him or her as a peg on which to hang other matter.

LOREN EISELEY   "The Creature from the Marsh"

1. How precisely can you define *eons*? What is a *déjà vu* experience? Have you ever had one? What is *keening*?

2. Do you know anyone you could describe as a "living fossil"?

3. Would you describe the way Eiseley begins his essay as strange, even bizarre? Why has he chosen to begin that way? He doesn't clearly announce his subject until part III (though it's suggested near the beginning). Can you justify so long a delayed beginning? What is the function of part I? of part II? Does the mystery-story technique seem appropriate to the essay's subject and purpose?

4. If you haven't already done so, re-read the essay. Do things that were puzzling the first time become clearer? Do you think Eiseley intended the essay to need two readings, or can a reader, with sufficient care, understand all the points the first time through? Is it imposing on readers to expect them to read something more than once? Does a third reading help still more?

5. In the paragraph beginning "On this particular afternoon" (part III), what is the proportion of monosyllabic words? Write a long descriptive paragraph using at least as large a proportion of monosyllables.

6. Note how, toward the end, Eiseley turns explicitly to *comparison* as a thematic technique—comparison of the footprint with his own foot. What other internal strategies does he use? Examine also his metaphors and his use of sound patterns and rhythm. Write sentences imitating the forms of some of his that you find particularly striking.

7. Write a short essay that doesn't fully reveal its subject until about halfway through and that doesn't state its thesis until the end. But don't be too obviously mysterious, and be sure that your readers, though somewhat in the dark, will be interested enough to read on.

TOPICS: General and Comparative

1. The writers in this section all make excellent use of concrete *details*. Updike's list, for example, necessarily consists of concrete details. How firmly is Fisher's memoir anchored in concrete? How does Haig-Brown's knowledge of the specifics of fly-fishing add visually or descriptively to his essay? What kinds of details does Mukherjee amass to support her evocations of feelings and attitudes? What is the force of the opening paragraph of White's essay, or almost any other paragraph, for example the third from the end? When you write descriptively and narratively, be especially alert to the need for details; it's difficult to overdo them.

2. *Rhythm* can derive from repetition (see MacLennan's essay), from the use of voice patterns (see Thomas's essay), and from paragraph length (see Forster's essay). What else determines rhythm? How for example do punctuation and sentence length affect rhythm? Point out some examples in Dillard's essay and elsewhere. How does a writer's choice of monosyllabic words affect rhythm? Find some examples of metrical patterns in Thomas's essay. Try scanning Mukherjee's final sentence. Look for effective uses of sound patterns—especially alliteration—in these essays (see "A Note to the Reader"). Do you find more in Thomas than elsewhere, as you might expect? How do such patterns affect rhythm? Analyze the rhythms and sound patterns in the short fourteenth paragraph of Haig-Brown's essay; could any of its rhythms be called metrical? How do rhythm and sentence length affect tone, for example in Thomas's and Forster's essays? How does rhythm affect meaning—for example through emphasis?

3. Consider the effectiveness of the *structure* of the essays in this section.

   (a) Has Updike arranged his details so as to make his piece more than a mere list of things observed?

   (b) See if you can discover any principle of form or structure in Thomas's essay. Why are things related in the order they are? Is it simply chronological? Or is it haphazard, a grab-bag, as Thomas implies?

   (c) Haig-Brown's essay is straightforwardly chronological. Would any other scheme have worked as well or better? Where is its climax?

   (d) Note how White relies on a shift in tone. Does the last paragraph look back to any earlier parts? How does it alter the tone and the effect of the essay?

   (e) The structure of Forster's essay is aggressively obvious. What is the rationale for the order of the four parts? Is there a progression of any kind? Point out how Forster controls emphasis through tone, proportion, and position. As he controls and alters the image of the wood, does he succeed in elevating it into a symbol?

   (f) Would you call MacLennan's essay "plotted"? Explain its organization and movement.

   (g) Note how Eiseley suspends the identification of his "discovery." What does this add to his inquiry? Suspense? Why is point of view important in this essay? And in White's?

4. Does history impose its own order on essays about historical subjects? Write an essay about some historical event, such as a battle, a journey of exploration and discovery, or an election. How does the chronology of the event affect the structure of your essay? Did you try using a flashback (analepsis) or flashforward (prolepsis)?

5. How does a knowledge of history benefit a reader of MacLennan and Mukherjee? Do you need it for Forster and Fisher? What historical allusions does MacLennan use? Compare the ways MacLennan and Mukherjee make thematic use of the ideas of *fear* and *security*.

6. Near the end of "My Wood" Forster refers to walls around a piece of property. Are Mukherjee's frequent references to walls at all similar? Analyze her short paragraph beginning "Out there beyond our walled vision." What does she mean by "walled vision"? Is it a simple metaphor? Is it akin to the gulf-traversing "vision" referred to by Forster? How important is seeing, or the way we see, in other essays? Dillard for example writes about observing nature. What does she see in it? Compare the way it functions in her essay with the way it works in others, for example those by Haig-Brown, White, and Eiseley.

7. Compare Fisher's treatment of memory and the past with that of others who write about their childhood—Dylan Thomas, White, Mukherjee, and Sheehan (section II). How importantly, for example, do parents figure in these essays? How do the writers use details and terms of another day to help evoke the past? What levels of diction and style do they use?

8. Consider the effects writers can achieve by using descriptive adjectives carefully. Do they ever overuse adjectives? Examine Eiseley's paragraph beginning "By day and night" (part III). On what words does the force, the vividness, of the description depend? What proportion of them are adjectives (excluding verbal adjectives)? The first half of Thomas's fourth paragraph has many adjectives, the last half few. Why the difference? What is the effect? Are there occasions when precise nouns and verbs are preferable to adjectives and adverbs? Examine your own style in light of this distinction. Try writing a description with few or no adjectives.

9. Take a representative passage from each of the essays and list and classify its verbs (as we do with the passage from Schreiner in the preface to this section). Try to justify what you find out about these verbs in terms of the purposes of the different essays.

10. Compare and discuss two or more of the essays in terms of some of the following features: sentence length, sentence structure, level of diction, frequency and length and kind of metaphor, proportion of concrete detail, handling of chronology. You can probably think of still other ways to make useful comparisons.

11. If you should see a traffic accident, would you make a good witness? Try to record exactly a sequence of events that you observed or a conversation you overheard this morning, or to describe exactly a person you saw several hours ago. What was your sister, brother, or roommate wearing yesterday?

12. Taking one of the writers in this section as your stylistic model, write a paragraph or two of personal narrative. Think about your subject first. What incident do you want to focus on? Why? What purpose or purposes do you want the incident to serve? Why do you want to share this particular incident with a reader? Which reader? How will you engage the reader? With detail? a certain tone? an anecdote? metaphoric language? transcribed conversation?

13. Try writing a few sentences to describe exactly some of the following:

> a red Frisbee, a screen door, the sound of moving water, warts, ice, a clear glass window, dirt, safety pins, escalator steps, sore feet, hair, a running-shoe, wheat, porridge, dogs' noses, a car tire, a glove compartment, fish scales, a soccer ball, a dime, night, oil, lemons, linen, a cup of tea, bees, dancing, moustaches, the income tax department, a line-up in a bank, a row of houses, lipstick, the 42nd floor, spaghetti sauce, gargling, blue, happiness, a butcher shop, a chess piece, an orange, anger, a blade of grass, bare feet, a hamburger, a tightrope walker.

What are the difficulties in each case? Finding the words to convey the appropriate sense impression? Making an abstract notion concrete? Avoiding clichés? What else? Where does the force of your description lie? In the verbs? adjectives? nouns? sentence rhythms? In some combination of these? Have you in each instance focussed on a *dominant impression* that you want to convey?

Now try writing advertising copy for some of these same items. How does your language differ?

II

Writing to Reveal

On bookstore shelves a few years ago, there appeared a work with an entire conversation for a title: *Where Did You Go? Out. What Did You Do? Nothing.* On the surface this brief exchange between parent and child does not appear to say much; the questions are pointedly clear, but the answers are evasive and unspecific. Indirectly, however, the conversation says a good deal more than the words alone declare. It *implies* rather than declares; it *reveals* more than it explains. Even the direct questions reveal the parent's concern; the answers suggest the child's desire for privacy. "I'm busy now—ask me later" is one way of psychologically interpreting these answers. Another is to hear the words that go unspoken—"Nothing *out of the ordinary* happened: don't be concerned"—and to realize that the covert message is essentially a reassuring one, even if the surface words appear to frustrate communication entirely.

Dialogues of all kinds depend on such indirect revelations, often as much as they depend on clear explanation and argument. For example, lawyers in cross-questioning witnesses sometimes strive to catch people in self-revelatory (and perhaps self-condemning) inconsistencies. Interviewers often seek to induce interviewees to reveal more of themselves than they might ordinarily put on public display. Gossips hint at dark secrets, and wait to see what seems embarrassing and might therefore be confirmed. Sophisticated listeners respond to body language as well as to verbal utterances, and the fact that television has made body language a manipulative art of communication in its own right has turned people into sophisticated watchers as well. It is the very sense of something hidden (and the accompanying promise of candidness, of the exposure of some behind-the-scenes truth) that constitutes the fascination of revelatory forms of address. But such forms are not simply accidents of conversation; they are open to shaping, and the results can be triumphs of psychological and political commentary.

Consider, for example, Robert Browning's 1842 poem "My Last Duchess." It is a *dramatic monologue,* a poem in which only one speaker is heard, one whose speech is an extraordinary act of unwitting self-revelation. It not only reveals the context of the conversation, but also (as with many a journal and diary) reveals far more of the speaker than he is himself aware of. In this particular poem the speaker is the Duke of Ferrara, and we know from context that he is speaking to an emissary from a prospective father-in-law:

FERRARA

That's my last Duchess painted on the wall,
Looking as if she were alive. I call
That piece a wonder, now: Frà Pandolf's hands
Worked busily a day, and there she stands.
Will't please you sit and look at her? I said
"Frà Pandolf" by design, for never read
Strangers like you that pictured countenance,
The depth and passion of its earnest glance,
But to myself they turned (since none puts by
The curtain I have drawn for you, but I)
And seemed as they would ask me, if they durst,
How such a glance came there; so, not the first
Are you to turn and ask thus. Sir, 'twas not
Her husband's presence only, called that spot
Of joy into the Duchess' cheek: perhaps
Frà Pandolf chanced to say, "Her mantle laps
Over my lady's wrist too much," or "Paint
Must never hope to reproduce the faint
Half-flush that dies along her throat": such stuff
Was courtesy, she thought, and cause enough
For calling up that spot of joy. She had
A heart—how shall I say?—too soon made glad,
Too easily impressed; she liked whate'er
She looked on, and her looks went everywhere.
Sir, 'twas all one! My favour at her breast,
The dropping of the daylight in the West,
The bough of cherries some officious fool
Broke in the orchard for her, the white mule
She rode with round the terrace—all and each
Would draw from her alike the approving speech,
Or blush, at least. She thanked men,—good!   but thanked
Somehow—I know not how—as if she ranked
My gift of a nine-hundred-years-old name

With anybody's gift. Who'd stoop to blame
This sort of trifling? Even had you skill
In speech—(which I have not)—to make your will
Quite clear to such an one, and say,"Just this
Or that in you disgusts me; here you miss,
Or there exceed the mark"—and if she let
Herself be lessoned so, nor plainly set
Her wits to yours, forsooth, and made excuse,
—E'en then would be some stooping; and I choose
Never to stoop. Oh sir, she smiled, no doubt,
Whene'er I passed her; but who passed without
Much the same smile? This grew; I gave commands;
Then all smiles stopped together. There she stands
As if alive. Will't please you rise? We'll meet
The company below, then. I repeat,
The Count your master's known munificence
Is ample warrant that no just pretence
Of mine for dowry will be disallowed;
Though his fair daughter's self, as I avowed
At starting, is my object. Nay, we'll go
Together down, sir! Notice Neptune, though,
Taming a sea-horse, thought a rarity,
Which Claus of Innsbruck cast in bronze for me!

Listening between the lines, readers can interpret what the Duke is saying and come quickly to understand him better than he might wish. We glimpse an egocentric and powerful man for whom people and art matter only as personal possessions. Power and his public position matter more. He needs to be admired. He thinks himself grand and needs to feel that others think so too. So he boasts, seeks praise, ensures that his power is known about, and yet pretends to be elegant, civilized, fastidious, perhaps even humane. But how does Browning make sure that his readers know better? And does the listener in the poem know the Duke as well as we do?

Occasional interviews and recorded everyday conversations are scarcely as compact and as finely organized as this poem is, but many essays nonetheless consciously adapt the techniques of revelation to similarly deliberate ends. Lane and Davenport, for example, seem to provide neutral accounts of the lives of Potter and Wittgenstein, yet they also offer their readers opportunities to draw other-than-neutral conclusions. McClung, not so neutrally, makes some direct and evaluative statements, but in reproducing parts of her conversations with the Premier, she not only lets him reveal the weaknesses of his attitudes and assumptions, but also indicates her own strength and determination. Lane addresses the very problem that an interviewee's masks can become for an interviewer; yet in recording interviews that have gone awry she still manages to reveal features of her subject's personality. And also her own?

Rooney, drawing up rules for others' lives, quite consciously puts much of his own personality on display. Sheehan, ostensibly writing about baseball, obliquely outlines a whole code of behaviour; baseball is only the surface subject, behind which lies a message of another order entirely. Doesn't it?

The other works in this section—the interview with Gordimer and the essays by Ludwig and Huxley—all in one way or another record the voices of people whom the authors have interviewed, listened to, observed, and overheard. In the interview, though the interviewer no doubt influences Gordimer's answers by the way she asks questions, she records the answers fairly faithfully. But each of the two essay writers, using a form something like that of a personal journal, notes down observed details and fragments of conversation; each then sets about to connect, weigh, and interpret them. But in so doing, each writer filters the revelations he perceives through his own social consciousness, making them part of a process of self-revelation as well. In none of the three essays is the covert message neutral; it is passionate, and it is political. The writers are *aware* of what they are doing. And it is a mark of their verbal craftsmanship that what sets out to be—or to appear to be—a personal and private record can turn so compellingly into an act of public persuasion.

Nadine Gordimer

An Interview by Jannika Hurwitt

INTERVIEWER: Do you have seasons in South Africa, or is it hot all year round?

GORDIMER: Oh no, we have seasons. Near the equator, there's very little difference in the seasons. But right down where we are, at the end of the continent, and also high up where I live in Johannesburg—6,000 feet up—you have very different seasons. We have a sharp, cold winter. No snow—it's rather like your late fall or early spring—sunny, fresh, cold at night. We have a very definite rainy season. But you don't see rain for about half the year. You forget that rain exists. So it's a wonderful feeling when you wake up one day, and you smell the rain in the air. Many of the old houses, like ours, have galvanized iron or tin roofs. It's very noisy when there's a heavy rain—it just gallops down on the roof. The house that I was brought up in had a tin roof, so it's one of my earliest memories, lying in bed and listening to the rain...and hail, which, of course, on a tin roof is deafening.

INTERVIEWER: When was your first trip out of South Africa?

GORDIMER: My first trip out was to what was then called Rhodesia—Zimbabwe. That might seem very much the same thing as South Africa to you, but it isn't. Zimbabwe is Central Africa, subtropical, shading into tropical. But my first real trip out was much later. I had already published two books—I was thirty years old. I went to Egypt, on my way to England, and America. Perhaps it was a good transition. In London I felt at home, but in an unreal way—I realized when I got there that my picture of London came entirely from books. Particularly Dickens and Virginia Woolf. The writers who, I'd thought, had impressed me with the features of English life, like Orwell, did not have this evocation when I was actually in the place; they were not writers with a strong sense of place. Woolf and Dickens obviously were. So that when I walked around in Chelsea I felt that this was definitively Mrs. Dalloway's country. I remember I stayed in a hotel near Victoria Station. And at night, these dark, sooty buildings, the dampness when one leant against a wall—absolutely decayed buildings...

INTERVIEWER: Were you as unprepared for this first trip off the African continent, and as awed by it, as Rebecca in your novel, *Guest of Honour?*

GORDIMER: No, my mother, who hadn't been back to England for about twenty years, prepared me. She provided me with woolly underwear and whatnot, which I threw away after I arrived. But Rebecca's trip to

Switzerland... I think descriptions of impressions from the air are something that writers nowadays have to be careful of. Like train journeys in mid-nineteenth century literature...they made such a change in people's lives. They produced a...leap in consciousness, especially so far as time was concerned. I can imagine what it must have been, the thought of taking a train that was to go rushing through the countryside. There were so many descriptions of trains in the literature of the day. But I think writers must be careful now not to overdo the use of travel as a metaphor for tremendous internal changes. "The journey" now is by air, and think of how many writers use this—in my own books it appears in *The Conservationist* and in *Guest of Honour*. And indeed, in *Burger's Daughter*, Rosa Burger takes her first trip out of South Africa; I had to resist the temptation to talk about the journey—I describe only the landing, because that particular piece of the landscape could be useful later on.

INTERVIEWER: Was this trip to England a sort of "back to the roots" expedition?

GORDIMER: No. But it brought an understanding of what I was, and helped me to shed the last vestiges of colonialism. I didn't know I was a colonial, but then I had to realize that I was. Even though my mother was only six when she came to South Africa from England, she still would talk about people "going home." But after my first trip out, I realized that "home" was certainly and exclusively—Africa. It could never be anywhere else.

INTERVIEWER: What brought your parents to South Africa?

GORDIMER: The same thing brought them both. They were part of the whole colonial expansion. My maternal grandfather came out in the 1890s with a couple of brothers. South Africa was regarded as a land of opportunity for Europeans. And indeed, he went prospecting for diamonds in Kimberley. I don't think he found very much—maybe some small stones. After that, his entire life was the stock exchange. He was what we call a "tickey-snatcher." A tickey was a tiny coin like a dime—alas, we don't have it anymore. It was equal to three English pence. "Tickey" is a lovely word, don't you think? Well, my grandfather was a tickey-snatcher on the stock exchange, which meant that he sat there all day, and that he bought and sold stocks—making a quick buck.

My father's story is really not such a happy one. He was born in Lithuania, and he went through the whole Jewish pogrom syndrome, you know. He had hardly any schooling. There wasn't any high school for Jewish kids in his village. His father was a shipping clerk and there were twelve children. I'm sure they must have been very poor. Their mother was a seamstress. As soon as my father was twelve or thirteen the idea was that he would just go—*somewhere*, either to America or wherever—it was the time of the great expansion, you know, the early 1900s. So his was the classic Ellis Island story—thirteen years old, not speaking a word of English, traveling in the hold of a ship, but all the way to Africa instead of America—it must have been extraordinary. He was a very unadventurous man; he didn't have a strong personality—he was timid. He still is a mystery to me. I wonder if he didn't burn himself out in this tremendous initial adventure, whether it wasn't really too much for him, and once having found a niche for himself somewhere, he just didn't have the guts to become much of a personality. There was something *arrested* about my father.

INTERVIEWER: What did he do once he got to Africa?

GORDIMER: Like many poor Jews—one either became a shoemaker, a tailor, or a watchmaker. He had learned watchmaking. All he had was a little bag with his watchmaking tools. He went to the Transvaal, to the goldfields. He took his little suitcase and went around the mines and asked the miners if anybody wanted a watch fixed. And he would take the watches away to a little room he had somewhere: he would just sit there and mend watches. Then he bought a bicycle and he'd go back round the mines. But by the time I came on the scene he had a little jeweler's shop and he was no longer a watchmaker—he employed one. Indeed, he imported his brother-in-law from Russia to do it. By now my father was the tycoon of the family. He brought *nine* sisters out of Lithuania—the poor man—saving up to bring one after the other. I found out later that he hated them all—we didn't ever have family gatherings. I don't know why he hated them so much.

INTERVIEWER: Where exactly was this jeweler's shop?

GORDIMER: In a little town called Springs, which was thirty miles from Johannesburg. I grew up in a small, gold-mining town of about 20,000 people.

INTERVIEWER: What were the schools like there?

GORDIMER: Well, I've had little formal education, really. I had a very curious childhood. There were two of us—I have an elder sister—and I was the baby, the spoiled one, the darling. I was awful—brash, a show-off, a dreadful child. But maybe that had something to do with having a lot of energy that didn't find any outlet. I wanted to be a dancer—this was my passion, from the age of about four to ten. I absolutely adored dancing. And I can still remember the pleasure, the release, of using the body in this way. There was no question but that I was to be a dancer, and I suppose maybe I would have been. But at the age of ten, I suddenly went into a dead faint one day, having been a very skinny but very healthy child. Nobody took much notice. But then it happened again. So I was taken to the family doctor, and it was discovered that I had an incredibly rapid heartbeat. Nobody had noticed this; it was, I suppose, part of my excitability and liveliness. It was discovered that I had an enlarged thyroid gland, which causes a fast heartbeat and makes one hyperactive. Well, I've since discovered that this isn't a serious malady at all. It happens to hundreds of people—usually at puberty. But my mother got very alarmed. This rapid pulse should have been ignored. But my mother was quite sure that it meant that I had a "bad heart." So she went immediately to the convent where I attended school and told the nuns, "This child mustn't have any physical training, she mustn't play tennis, she mustn't even swim." At ten, you know, you don't argue with your mother—she tells you you're sick, you believe her. When I would be about to climb stairs, she would say, "Now, take it slowly, *remember your heart*." And then of course the tragedy was that I was told I mustn't dance anymore. So the dancing stopped like that, which was a terrible deprivation for me.

It's really only in the last decade of my life that I've been able to face all this. When I realized what my mother had done to me, I went through, at the age of twenty, such resentment—this happens to many of us, but I *really* had reason. When I was thirty, I began to understand why she did it, and thus to pity her. By the time she died in '76 we were reconciled. But it was an extraordinary story.

In brief, my mother was unhappily married. It was a dreadful marriage. I suspect she was sometimes in love with other men; but my mother would never have dreamt of having an affair. Because her marriage was unhappy, she concentrated on her children. The chief person she was attracted to was our family doctor. There's no question. I'm sure it was *quite* unconscious, but the fact that she had this "delicate" daughter, about whom she could be constantly calling the doctor—in those days doctors made house calls, and there would be tea and cookies and long chats—made her keep my "illness" going in this way. Probably I was being wrongly treated anyway, so that what medication should have cleared up, it didn't, and symptoms persisted. Of course, I began to feel terribly important. By that time I was reading all sorts of books that led me to believe my affliction made me very interesting. I was growing up with this legend that I was very delicate, that I had something wrong with my heart.

When I was eleven—I don't know how my mother did this—she took me out of school completely. For a year I had no education at all. But I read tremendously. And I retreated into myself, I became very introspective. She changed my whole character. Then she arranged for me to go to a tutor for three hours a day. She took me there at ten in the morning and picked me up at one. It was such incredible loneliness—it's a terrible thing to do to a child. There I was, all on my own, doing my work; a glass of milk was brought to me by this woman—she was very nice, but I had no contact with other children. I spent my whole life, from eleven to sixteen, with older people, with people of my mother's generation. She carted me around to tea parties—I simply lived her life. When she and my father went out at night to dinner she took me along...I got to the stage where I could really hardly talk to other children. I was a little old woman.

INTERVIEWER: What about your sister's relationship to you during this time?

GORDIMER: My sister is four years older than I am. She went away to university; she wasn't really a companion to me. I stopped going to the tutor when I was fifteen or sixteen. So that was the extent of my formal education.

When I was twenty-one or twenty-two, already a published writer, I wanted to go to university to get a little more formal education. But since I hadn't matriculated, I could only do occasional courses at the University of the Witwatersrand—that's Afrikaans for "ridge of white waters." There was something called "general studies"—this was just after the war, and there were lots of veterans who had interrupted their education, and so it was very nice for me—there were people my own age mixed up with the others. A few years ago I gave a graduation address at that same university.

INTERVIEWER: Are you one of these writers to whom they're always trying to give honorary degrees?

GORDIMER: I don't accept them in South Africa. I've taken one—in Belgium in 1981, from the University of Leuven. It turned out to be quite extraordinary, because the man who got an honorary degree with me, Monsignor Oscar Romero, was assassinated two weeks later in El Salvador. In Belgium he had given the most marvelous address. He was such a striking man. He received a standing ovation for about eight minutes from the students. And two weeks later he was lying on the floor of a church, dead.

INTERVIEWER: How long did you go to university?

GORDIMER: One year. This was the first time in my life I'd mixed with blacks, and was more or less the beginning of my political consciousness. Perhaps the good thing about being carted around with my parents was that they would sit playing gin rummy or something while I wandered around the host's house seeing what I could find to read. I discovered everybody from Henry Miller to Upton Sinclair. It was Sinclair's *The Jungle* that really started me thinking about politics: I thought, good God, these people who are exploited in a meat-packing factory—they're just like blacks here. And the whole idea that people came to America, not knowing the language, having to struggle in sweat shops...I didn't relate this to my own father, because my father was bourgeois by then...but I related it to the blacks. Again, what a paradox that South Africa was the black's *own country,* but they were recruited just as if they had been migrant workers for the mines. So I saw the analogy. And that was the beginning of my thinking about my position vis-à-vis blacks. But though I didn't know anything—I was twelve or thirteen, and leading the odd kind of life I did, living in books—I began to think about these things before, perhaps, I was ready for them. When I got to university, it was through mixing with other people who were writing or painting that I got to know black people as equals. In a general and inclusive, nonracial way, I met people who lived in the world of ideas, in the world that interested me passionately.

In the town where I lived, there was no mental food of this kind at all. I'm often amazed to think how they live, those people, and what an oppressed life it must be, because human beings *must* live in the world of ideas. This dimension in the human psyche is very important. It was there, but they didn't know how to express it. Conversation consisted of trivialities. For women, household matters, problems with children. The men would talk about golf or business or horseracing or whatever their practical interests were. Nobody ever talked about, or even around, the big things—life and death. The whole existential aspect of life was never discussed. I, of course, approached it through books. Thought about it on my own. It was as secret as it would have been to discuss my parents' sex life. It was something so private, because I felt that there was nobody with whom I could talk about these things, just *nobody*. But then, of course, when I was moving around at university, my life changed. From Europe—it was just after the war—came Existentialism, and at home in South Africa there was great interest in movements of the Left, and black national movements. At that time, the Communist party and various other leftist movements were not banned. So there were all sorts of Marxist discussion groups. This was an area of thought and conviction I simply never had heard mentioned before. I'd only read about it. And there, of course, were people who were mixing with blacks. So it was through people who were writing, painting, or acting that I started mixing with blacks.

INTERVIEWER: What did you do after that year at university? Did you begin any political activity?

GORDIMER: No, you see I was writing then—a lot. I was concentrating tremendously on writing. I wasn't really interested in politics. My approach to living as a white supremacist, perforce, among blacks, was, I see now, the humanist approach, the individualistic approach. I felt that all I needed, in my own behavior, was to ignore and defy the color bar. In other words, my own attitude toward blacks seemed to be sufficient action. I didn't see that it was pretty meaningless until much later.

INTERVIEWER: Were you living on your own then?

GORDIMER: No, I wasn't. In that way I was extremely backward. But you have to look at the kind of dependency that had been induced in me at the crucial age of ten. When other kids were going off to the equivalent of what's known as "summer camp"—"Nadine can't go camping, she's got a *bad heart!* If people go on a hike, she can't go. She's got to stay with mama." A child like that becomes very corrupt, a kind of jester, an entertainer for grown-ups. Especially at the age of fifteen and sixteen. Adults find you charming. You flirt with other people's husbands instead of with boys your own age. It's a very corrupting thing. I was rather a good mimic. Perhaps it was the beginning of having an ear for dialogue? So I would take off people. Grown-ups would sit around at drink parties, getting a little tight, and there was Nadine prancing around, rather cruelly imitating people whom they knew. It didn't occur to them that the moment their backs were turned I was doing it to them as well.

At any rate, I was still living at home when I went to university, and I used to commute by train into Johannesburg. Then my sister got married and lived in Johannesburg, so that when I didn't want to go home I would go to her, which was very nice for me, to have a base there. But I still didn't have the guts, I don't know why, to move out of home, the mining town of Springs. And you see, I wasn't earning enough by my writing, heaven knows, to live on. I was doing something that no kid does nowadays—I was living off my father. On the other hand, my needs were so modest. It never occurred to me that one would want a car—now every kid has a jalopy—this was just not the kind of thing that I would have dreamt of. All I wanted was to buy books. I earned enough with my writing here and there to do this, and of course I also used the library tremendously, which, again, people don't seem to do so much anymore. When I talk to young writers, and I say, "Have you read this or that?"—"Well, no, but books are so expensive..."—I say, "Well for God's sake! The central library is a wonderful library. For heaven's sake, use it! You're never going to be able to write if you don't read!"

. . . .

INTERVIEWER: What role do you feel politics and the constant conflict it evokes in South Africa have played in your development as a writer?

GORDIMER: Well, it has turned out to have played a very important role. I would have been a writer anyway; I was writing before politics impinged itself upon my consciousness. In my writing, politics comes through in a didactic fashion very rarely. The kind of conversations and polemical arguments you get in *Burger's Daughter,* and in some of my other books—these really play a very minor part. For various reasons to do with the story, they had to be there. But the real influence of politics on my writing is the influence of politics on people. Their lives, and I believe their very personalities, are changed by the extreme political circumstances one lives under in South Africa. I am dealing with people; here are people who are shaped and changed by politics. In that way my material is profoundly influenced by politics.

INTERVIEWER: Do you see that as an advantage for a writer?

GORDIMER: Not really. Life is so apparently amorphous.But as soon as you burrow down this way or that...you know Goethe's maxim? "Thrust your hand deep into life, and whatever you bring up in it, that is you, that is your subject." I think that's what writers do.

INTERVIEWER: If you had grown up in a country that was not politically oppressed, might you have become a more abstract writer?

GORDIMER: Maybe. Take a writer whom I admire tremendously, the greatest American short-story writer ever, Eudora Welty. In a strange way, if she had lived where I've lived, she might have turned these incredible gifts of hers more outward—she might have written more, she might have tackled wider subjects. I hesitate to say this, because what she's done she's done wonderful-ly. But the fact is that she hasn't written very much; I don't think she ever developed fully her gifts as a novelist. She was not forced by circumstance to come to grips with something different. And I don't believe it's just a matter of temperament, because my early writing had qualities similar to hers. I got to hate that word about my work—"sensitive." I was constantly being com-pared to Katherine Mansfield. I am *not* by nature a political creature, and even now there is so much I don't like in politics, and in political people—though I admire tremendously people who are politically active—there's so much lying to oneself, self-deception, there has to be—you don't make a good political fighter unless you can pretend the warts aren't there.

INTERVIEWER: Do you have the same complaint about Virginia Woolf's novels as you do with Eudora Welty's?

GORDIMER: No, because Virginia Woolf extended herself the other way. I mean she really concentrated totally on that transparent envelope that she'd find for herself. There are two ways to knit experience, which is what writing is about. Writing is making sense of life. You work your whole life and perhaps you've made sense of one small area. Virginia Woolf did this incomparably. And the complexity of her human relationships, the economy with which she managed to portray them...staggering. But you can't write a novel like *Burger's Daughter* with the sensibility of a Virginia Woolf. You have to find some other way. You're always trying to find some other way. I'm interested in both ways of writing. I started off by being interested in that transparent envelope.

INTERVIEWER: Was Woolf a big influence when you began writing?

GORDIMER: Midway, I think—after I'd been writing for about five years. She can be a very dangerous influence on a young writer. It's easy to fall into the cadence. But the content isn't there. The same could be said for a completely different kind of writer like Dos Passos, or Hemingway. You've got to be very careful, or you do if you are a writer like me, starting out with an acute sensibility and a poor narrative gift. My narrative gift was weak in my early novels—they tend to fall into beautiful set pieces. It was only with *The Late Bourgeois World*, which was published in 1966, that I began to develop narrative muscle. From then on, my struggle has been not to lose the acute sensitivity—I mean the acuteness of catching nuance in behavior (not in description, because as you get more mature that falls into place) and to marry it successfully to a narrative gift. Because the kind of subjects that are around me, that draw me, that I see motivating me, require a strong narrative ability.

INTERVIEWER: Do you feel that your political situation—the political situation in South Africa—gave you a particular incentive as a writer?

GORDIMER: No. For instance, in *Burger's Daughter*, you could say on the face of it that it's a book about white Communists in South Africa. But to me, it's something else. It's a book about commitment. Commitment is not merely a political thing. It's part of the whole ontological problem in life. It's part of my feeling that what a writer does is to try to make sense of life. I think that's what writing is, I think that's what painting is. It's seeking that thread of order and logic in the disorder, and the incredible waste and marvelous profligate character of life. What all artists are trying to do is to make sense of life. So you see, I would have found my themes had I been an American or an English writer. They are there if one knows where to look...if one is pushed from within.

INTERVIEWER: How do you feel that fiction from relatively non-oppressed countries compares with that produced in countries where the political situation necessitates a certain amount of political consciousness?

GORDIMER: To me, it's all a matter of the quality of the writing. To me, that is everything. I can appreciate a tremendously subjective and apolitical piece of writing. If you're a writer, you can make the death of a canary stand for the whole mystery of death. That's the challenge. But, of course, in a sense you are "lucky" if you have great themes. One could say that about the Russians in the nineteenth century. Would they have been the wonderful writers they are if they hadn't had that challenge? They also had the restrictions that we chafe against in South Africa—censorship, and so on. And yet it seems on the face of it to have had only a good effect on writing. Then I think it depends. It can have a deleterious effect. In South Africa, among young blacks who are writing—it's difficult for them to admit it, but they know this—they have to submit to an absolute orthodoxy within black consciousness. The poem or the story or the novel must follow a certain line—it's a kind of party line even though what is in question is not a political party, but it *is*, in the true sense of the word, a party line. For example, nobleness of character in blacks must be shown. It's pretty much frowned upon if there's a white character who is human. It's easy enough to understand this and it's important as a form of consciousness-raising for young blacks to *feel* their own identity, to recite poems which simply exalt blackness and decry everything else, and often to exalt it in crude terms, in crude images, clichés. That's fine as a weapon of propaganda in the struggle, which is what such writing is, primarily. But the *real* writers are victims of this, because as soon as they stray from one or two clearly defined story lines,they're regarded as...

INTERVIEWER: Traitors. Are there many blacks writing and publishing in South Africa?

GORDIMER: There are a lot, and there's a fairly good relationship between black and white writers. Literature is one of the few areas left where black and white feel some identity of purpose; we all struggle under censorship, and most white writers feel a strong sense of responsibility to promote, defend, and help black writers where possible.

INTERVIEWER: *Burger's Daughter* was banned three weeks after it was published, wasn't it?

GORDIMER: Yes, and it remained banned for several months. Then it was unbanned. I was pleased, as you can imagine. Not only for myself, but because it established something of a precedent for other writers, since there are in that book blatant contraventions of certain Acts. In that book I published a document that was a real document, distributed by the students in the 1976 riots in Soweto, and banned by the government. It's in the book with all the misspellings and grammatical mistakes...everything exactly as it was; and indeed that's important because, as Rosa points out, these kids rioted because they felt their education wasn't good enough. And when you read the text of that pathetic little pamphlet you can see what the young blacks meant, because that's as well as they could write at the age of sixteen or seventeen, when they were ready to matriculate. So here is one example where, indeed, I flagrantly crossed the line to illegality. Now that the book has been unbanned, it's going to be a difficult thing for the censors to ban other books on evidence of such transgressions.

INTERVIEWER: Why was the book unbanned?

GORDIMER: If I hadn't been a writer who's known abroad and if this hadn't been a book that happened to receive serious attention at a high level abroad—it obviously made the censors feel rather foolish—the book would not have been released. So there we are.

INTERVIEWER: Is it common for a book to be unbanned?

GORDIMER: Well, not so quickly. Of my two previous books, one, *A World of Strangers*, was banned for twelve years, and the other, entitled *The Late Bourgeois World*, for ten; after that length of time most books are pretty well dead.

INTERVIEWER: How does a book get banned?

GORDIMER: First of all, if the book is imported, the authorities embargo it. In other words, it's just like any other cargo arriving at the docks. It is embargoed at Customs and the customs officer sends the book off to the Censorship Board. He's got a list of suspects. For instance, a South African writer like myself would be on it, you see, because they know the kind of subjects I've chosen, and, in any case, I've had three books banned previously. So would somebody like James Baldwin; several of his books were banned. Then there's another way that books get embargoed with the possible outcome of a ban. After normal distribution, somebody, some Mother Grundy, old busybody, reads a book that's already in the bookshops, objects to it, and sends it off to the Censorship Board with a complaint. On the recommendation of just one person, a committee will read the book to see if it's "objectionable." But while it's being read by the censors, it's under embargo, which means that although there are copies in the bookshops the bookseller can't sell them; he's got to put them away, take them off the shelves. Sometimes the book is then released. It happened to my novel, *A Guest of Honour*; it happened to *The Conservationist.* *The Conservationist*, I think, was held by the censors for ten weeks, which is iniquitous because the first ten weeks in a book's life are crucial from the point of view of sales. Then it was released by the director of the board. The members of the censor's committee—there are a number of those, usually with three people comprising a committee—read the book, each writes an independent report, and if these concur that the book should be banned or released, right, it's done. If they don't concur, then a fourth person has to be brought in. If they concur that the book is undesirable, then it is banned. The author isn't told. The decision is published in the government gazette, which is published once a week. And that's the end of the book.

INTERVIEWER: What happens then? Is it like what happened with *Ulysses?* Do people scrounge around frantically trying to get hold of it and hide it when policemen walk by?

GORDIMER: People do, people do. Books are usually banned only for sale and distribution but not for *possession,* so that if you've already bought the book you may keep it; but you may not lend it to me or the person across the road, and you may not sell it.

INTERVIEWER: You can't lend it?

GORDIMER: No. This, of course, is perfectly ridiculous. Everybody lends banned books all the time. But people are very nervous, for instance, about buying them abroad or having them sent. They're rather too timid about that. They don't like to have to smuggle them in.

INTERVIEWER: So there isn't much smuggling going on?

GORDIMER: Some people don't, some do. But with some of us, it's a point of honor always to do this.

INTERVIEWER: To smuggle?

GORDIMER: Yes, of course. It's a legitimate form of protest. But unfortunately, when a book is banned, very few copies get around.

. . . .

INTERVIEWER: I've noticed that sensual elements play a key role in your writing: smells, textures, sexuality, bodily functions. You don't write about the so-called "beautiful people," the leisured class of South Africa, and the beautiful environment in which they must live. In fact, I noticed that almost all of the white women in your *Selected Stories* are physically and mentally both highly unattractive and middle-class. Does this reflect the way in which you view white colonialists in your country?

GORDIMER: I don't make such judgments about people. After all, I'm a white colonial woman myself, of colonial descent. Perhaps I know us too well through myself. But if somebody is partly frivolous or superficial, has moments of cruelty or self-doubt, I don't write them off, because I think that absolutely everybody has what are known as human failings. My black characters are not angels either. All this role-playing that is done in a society like ours—it's done in many societies, but it's more noticeable in ours—sometimes the role is forced upon you. You fall into it. It's a kind of song-and-dance routine, and you find yourself, and my characters find themselves, acting out these preconceived, ready-made roles. But, of course, there are a large number of white women of a certain kind in the kind of society that I come from who...well, the best one can say of them is that one can excuse them because of their ignorance of what they have allowed themselves to become. I see the same kind of women here in the U.S. You go into one of the big stores here and you can see these extremely well-dressed, often rather dissatisfied-looking, even sad-looking middle-aged women, rich, sitting trying on a dozen pairs of shoes; and you can see they're sitting there for the morning. And it's a terribly agonizing decision, but maybe the heel should be a little higher or maybe...should I get two pairs? And a few blocks away it's appalling to see in what poverty and misery other people are living in this city, New York. Why is it that one doesn't criticize that American woman the same way one does her counterpart in South Africa? For me, the difference is that the rich American represents class difference and injustice, while in South Africa the injustice is based on both class *and* race prejudice.

INTERVIEWER: What about the "beautiful people" of South Africa?

GORDIMER: They're featured very prominently in an early book of mine called *A World of Strangers* but very rarely since then, until the character of Mehring in *The Conservationist*. They are not the most interesting people in South Africa, believe me...although they may regard themselves as such.

INTERVIEWER: Is it intentional that so often the physical details of characters are not brought home strongly in your work? One gets a very strong sense of the mind's workings in major characters, but often a very limited sense of what they actually look like.

GORDIMER: I think that physical descriptions of people should be minimal. There are exceptions—take Isaac Bashevis Singer. He very often starts off a story by giving you a full physical description. If you look very closely at the description, of course it's extremely good. He stamps character on a twist of the nose or a tuft of red beard. My own preference is for physical description to come piecemeal at times when it furthers other elements in the text. For instance, you might describe a character's eyes when another character is looking straight into them so it would be natural...a feature of that particular moment in the narrative. There might be another scene later, where the character whose eyes you've described is under tension, and is showing it by tapping her foot or picking at a hangnail—so if there was something particular about her hands, that would be the time to talk about them. I'm telling you this as if it were something to be planned. It isn't. It comes at the appropriate moment.

INTERVIEWER: In the introduction to your *Selected Stories,* you say that: "My femininity has never constituted any special kind of solitude, for me. In fact, my only genuine connection with the social life of the town (when I was growing up) was through my femaleness. As an adolescent, at least, I felt and followed sexual attraction in common with others; that was a form of communion I could share. Rapunzel's hair is the right metaphor for this femininity: by means of it I was able to let myself out and live in the body, with others, as well as—alone—in the mind." You go on to say you "question the existence of the specific solitude of woman-as-intellectual when that woman is a writer, because when it comes to their essential faculty as writers, all writers are androgynous beings."

What about the process of becoming a writer, of becoming an androgynous being? Isn't that a struggle for women?

GORDIMER: I hesitate to generalize from my own experience. I would consider it an arrogance to state my own experience as true for all women. I really haven't suffered at all from being a woman. It's inconceivable, for example, that I could ever have become interested in a man who regarded women as nonbeings. It's never happened. There would be a kind of war between us. I just take it for granted, and it has always happened, that the men in my life have been people who treated me as an equal. There was never any question of fighting for this. I'm somebody who has lived a life as a woman. In other words, I've been twice married, I've brought up children, I've done all the things that women do. I haven't avoided or escaped this, supposing that I should have wished to, and I don't wish to and never wished to. But, as I say, I don't generalize, because I see all around me women who are gifted and intelligent who *do* have these struggles and who indeed *infuriate* me easier. But I did manage to maintain it when my children were young, I suppose, by being rather ruthless. I think writers, artists, are very ruthless, and they have to be. It's unpleasant for other people, but I don't know how else we can manage. Because the world will never make a place for you. My own family came to understand and respect this. Really, when my children were quite small they knew that in my working hours they must leave me alone; if they came home from school and my door was closed, they left and they didn't turn on the radio full blast. I was criticized for this by other people. But my own children don't hold it against me. I still had time that I spent with them. What I have also sacrificed, and it hasn't been a sacrifice for me, is a social life; and as I've got older, I'm less and less interested in that. When I was young I did go through some years when I enjoyed party-going very much and stayed out all night. But in the end, the loss next day, the fact that I had a hangover and that I couldn't work, quickly outweighed the pleasure; and, as time has gone by, I've kept more and more to myself. Because a writer doesn't only need the time when he's actually writing—he or she has got to have time to think and time just to let things work out. Nothing is worse for this than society. Nothing is worse for this than the abrasive, if enjoyable, effect of other people.

INTERVIEWER: What conditions do you find to be most conducive to writing?

GORDIMER: Well, nowhere very special, no great, splendid desk and cork-lined room. There have been times in my life, my God, when I was a young divorced woman with a small child living in a small apartment with thin walls when other people's radios would drive me absolutely mad. And that's still the thing that bothers me tremendously—*that* kind of noise. I don't mind people's voices. But Muzak or the constant clack-clack of a radio or television coming through the door...well, I live in a suburban house where I have a small room where I work. I have a door with direct access to the garden—a great luxury for me—so that I can get in and out without anybody bothering me or knowing where I am. Before I begin to work I pull out the phone and it stays out until I'm ready to plug it in again. If people really want you, they'll find you some other time. And it's as simple as that, really.

. . . .

INTERVIEWER: Is there anything, new or otherwise, that you hope to do with your writing in the future?

GORDIMER: I would always hope to find the one right way to tackle whatever subject I'm dealing with. To me, that's the real problem, and the challenge of writing. There's no such feeling as a general achievement. You cannot say that because I have managed to say what I wanted to say in one book, that it is now inside me for the next, because the next one is going to have a different demand. And until I find out how to write it, I can't tackle it.

INTERVIEWER: In other words, you don't know the question until you have the answer?

GORDIMER: Yes. I would like to say something about how I feel in general about what a novel, or any story, ought to be. It's a quotation from Kafka. He said, "A book ought to be an ax to break up the frozen sea within us."

A Gentleman of the Old School

Nellie McClung

The big city gathered us in when the pleasant summer at the beach was over. Mark, our youngest child, was born in October of that year, and quickly became the idol of the family, with his blonde curls, blue eyes and quaint wisdom. The other children were all at school and Jack had started at Wesley College. Every day was full of interest. I enjoyed my association with the Canadian Women's Press Club, when we met once a week for tea in our own comfortable quarters. There great problems were discussed and the seed germ of the suffrage association was planted. It was not enough for us to meet and talk and eat chicken sandwiches and olives. We felt we should organize and create a public sentiment in favor of women's suffrage.

The visit of Mrs. Emmeline Pankhurst and of Miss Barbara Wiley, also one of the British Militant Suffragettes, created a profound impression. The immediate cause of our desire to organize was the plight of women workers in small factories. Some of our members had visited these and we were greatly stirred over the question of long hours, small wages and distressing working conditions.

Mrs. Claude Nash spoke one day on this subject at a Local Council meeting, and as a result of this meeting she and I were deputed to bring pressure to bear on the government for the appointment of a woman factory inspector. We decided to go to see Sir Rodmond Roblin, the Premier, and if possible, get him to come with us to see some of the factories. She knew him quite well and I had often listened to him in the Legislative Assembly from the visitors' gallery. He was a florid, rather good-looking man in his early sixties, somewhat pompous in manner but very popular with his party and firmly seated on the political throne by what was known as the "Machine." He believed in the patronage system and distributed governmental favors to the faithful in each riding. However, even in all the exposures which followed his defeat in 1914, there was no proof that he had ever enriched himself at the country's expense.

Mrs. Nash must have had some political standing, for I certainly had not, and we got an interview. We found Sir Rodmond in a very genial mood, and he expressed his delight at our coming. Mrs. Nash was a very handsome young woman, dressed that day in a grey lamb coat and crimson velvet hat. I wasn't looking so poorly myself for I, too, had youth on my side, and we could see that the old man was impressed favorably. I told him I had just come to live in the City from Manitou and I mentioned the name of W.H. Sharpe (afterwards Senator Sharpe) and I think that Sir Rodmond took it for granted that I, too, was a good Conservative, or, as he expressed it, was of the "household of faith." Sir Rodmond had once been a lay preacher in the Methodist Church, and scriptural references came natural to him. He balked a bit when we asked him if he would come with us to see some of the factories and tried to get us to be satisfied with one of his deputies, but Mrs. Nash and I held firm, and much to our surprise, he consented. He called his car and we set out. He looked very well in his beaver coat, and his car was the most pretentious I had ever ridden in. The cut glass vase filled with real carnations impressed my country eyes.

On the way to the first factory, the Premier, who sat between us, with his plump hands resting on a gold-headed cane, gave us his views on women working in factories. He believed in work, especially for young women. There was too much idleness now, with electricity and short cuts in labor. As a boy he had worked from sunrise, and before, until the shadows of evening fell, and enjoyed it. Happiest days of his life...running barefoot under the apple trees. Perhaps we were over-sentimental about factory conditions.... Women's hearts were often too kind...but he liked kind women—and hoped they would never change. And these young girls in the factories whom we thought were underpaid, no doubt they lived at home, and really worked because they wanted pin money. Anyway, working wouldn't hurt them, it would keep them off the streets...

Knowing what we did, we let the monologue go on. He advised us not to allow our kind hearts to run away with us. Most of the women in the factories, he understood, were from foreign countries, where life was strenuous (that word was in the first flush of its popularity then). They did not expect to be carried to the skies on a flowery bed of ease! It doesn't do women any harm to learn how money comes.... Extravagant women are the curse of this age.

We conducted the Premier down dark, slippery stairs to an airless basement where light in mid-day came from gaunt light bulbs, hanging from smoky ceilings. The floor was littered with refuse of apple peelings and discarded clothing. There was no ventilation and no heat. The room was full of untidy women operating sewing machines and equally unattractive men cutting out garments on long tables. We urged Sir Rodmond to speak to some of the workers, but he was willing to call it a day at the first glance. He was shocked at the filth of the place, and asked one of the women if anybody ever swept the floor? He had to shout to drown the sound of the machines. The woman shook her head and kept on working. Then we reminded him that all these people were on piece work.

We led the Premier through a side door into the foul passage where a queue had formed before a door marked "Toilet." We could see that Sir Rodmond was deeply shocked that we should know about such things but Mrs. Nash led the way, and I pushed him along from behind. We drew his attention to the fact that there was no separate accommodation for the women, and we did not need to mention that the plumbing had evidently gone wrong.

We knew that he was soon going to bolt away from us, so we didn't spare him anything.

"For God's sake, let me out of here," he cried at last. "I'm choking! I never knew such hell holes existed!"

"These people work from 8:30 to 6:00, Sir Rodmond. Six days a week," Mrs. Nash told him sweetly. "But no doubt they get used to it." I am afraid her sarcasm was lost on Sir Rodmond.

When we got him up on the street again, he remembered an important interview he had promised, but we coaxed him to come to one more factory where men's shirts were being made, and all the workers were young women, and by promising him that this would be the last one, he came with us. This workroom was in rather a better building and some daylight came in from the windows. We wanted him particularly to see these young girls who were being "kept off the streets." At one machine a girl worked with a bandaged hand, a badly hurt hand and a very dirty bandage. At another one a girl coughed almost continuously, I asked her how long she had had her cold and she said she had no cold, it was just a bit of bronchitis she had every winter, but she daren't stop work for there were plenty more to take her place, and someone had to earn some money in their family, as their father was out of work. She said she had been lucky to get the job. The manager came over to speak to us, anxious to show us the fine product they were turning out. Mrs. Nash asked him how often the factory inspector came around, but he didn't seem to know anything about factory inspectors. "In fact," he said, "we hardly need one. All the girls are glad of the work. I have no trouble with them."

"How about the girl who coughs so much?" I asked. "Couldn't she be given a few days off with pay to get built up a bit?"

The manager regarded me sternly.

"The company is not a charitable institution," he said, "and makes no provision for anything like that. If the girl is sick, she can always quit!" He threw out his hands expressively in a fine gesture of freedom.

Sir Rodmond was moving towards the door, and we followed. When we got back into the car we could see that the fine old gentleman of the old school was really shocked at what he had seen.

"Now, Sir Rodmond," we said, "do you still think that these women are pleasurably employed in this rich land of wide spaces and great opportunities?"

Sir Rodmond let down one of the windows of the car and said:

"I still can't see why two women like you should ferret out such utterly disgusting things."

"Your factory inspector knows about these places," we told him. "We mailed him a list of them and described them, but he has done nothing. He takes your attitude: Why should women interfere with what does not concern them? But we are not discouraged and have no intention of allowing these conditions to continue. We would like you to appoint a woman factory inspector, a real, trained social worker."

Sir Rodmond grew impatient at that. "I tell you it's no job for a woman. I have too much respect for women to give any of them a job like this.... But I don't mind admitting that I'm greatly disturbed over all this, greatly disturbed," he repeated. "I'll admit I didn't know that such places existed and I promise you that I will speak to Fletcher about it."

With this understanding we parted, thanking Sir Rodmond for giving us so much of his time.

Our investigations went on. We were only amateurs but we did find out a few things about how the "other half" lived. We made some other discoveries too. We found out that the Local Council of Women could not be our medium. There were too many women in it who were afraid to be associated with any controversial subject. Their husbands would not let them "go active." It might imperil their jobs. The long tentacles of the political octopus reached far. So one night at Jane Hample's house on Wolsley Avenue we organized the Political Equality League, with a membership of about fifteen. We believed that fifteen good women who were not afraid to challenge public opinion could lay the foundations better than a thousand. Some good work had been already done by the Icelandic women of the city, who had organized the first suffrage society many years before, and the W.C.T.U. women could always be counted on and the same was true of the Labor women.

We wanted to get first-hand information on the status of women in Manitoba, and, of course, the whole Dominion. Then it was our purpose to train public speakers and proceed to arouse public sentiment. We would be ready for the next election and hoped to make our influence felt. We had all the courage of youth and inexperience with a fine underpinning of simplicity that bordered on ignorance, but anything we lacked in knowledge we made up in enthusiasm.

On a sudden impulse one day I phoned to the Premier's office when the House was in session and asked for an interview with Sir Rodmond Roblin, and to my surprise I found myself speaking to the gentleman himself, who in his most gracious manner assured me he would be pleased to see me and I could come at once, which I did. There in his private office with its red plush hangings and heavy leather furniture, I told the head of the government what we were doing and what we hoped to do. He listened with amused tolerance, but I was grateful to him for listening.

"Sir Rodmond," I said, "the women of Manitoba are going to be given the vote, either by you or someone else, and as you are the present Premier, it can be your proud privilege to have this piece of progressive legislation to your credit. I know what you're thinking; you're not impressed with the importance of this matter but that's because you never thought of it and you really should begin to think about it. You can no longer afford to take this attitude of indifference, and that's why I came to see you."

He looked up at me then and said:

"What in the world do women want to vote for? Why do women want to mix in the hurly-burly of politics? My mother was the best woman in the world, and she certainly never wanted to vote! I respect women," he went on, "I honor and reverence women, I lift my hat when I meet a woman."

"That's all very nice to hear," I said, "but unfortunately that's not enough. The women of Manitoba believe that the time has come to make an effort to obtain political equality. The laws are very unfair to women. I would like to tell you about some of them, for I don't believe you know, and what I would really like to do this afternoon is to have a chance to talk to you and your cabinet. It wouldn't take me long; I think fifteen minutes would be enough, and if you and the cabinet could be convinced that it is the right thing to do, it would certainly be easier, more dignified and less disturbing than if we are compelled to make a fight for it. But that is what we are prepared to do, if that is the way you want it. I wish you would call them in, Sir Rodmond, there's plenty of room here in your office."

Sir Rodmond removed the dead cigar from his mouth and his eyes hardened.

"The cabinet wouldn't listen to you," he said.

"You'd be surprised," I answered. "I'm really not hard to listen to, and I don't believe the cabinet would mind at all. In fact," I said brazenly, "I think they'd like it. It would be a welcome change in the middle of a dull day."

He could scarcely find words to express his astonishment and disapproval.

"You surprise me," he said slowly. "Now who do you think you are?"

"At this moment," I said, "I'm one of the best advisers you ever had in all your life. I'm not asking you for a favor, I'm really offering you help."

"What if I tell you that I don't need your help?" he said severely. "And that I think you're rather a conceited young woman, who has perhaps had some success at Friday afternoon entertainments at country school houses, and so are laboring under the delusion that you have the gift of oratory. What would you say to that?"

"I wouldn't mind," I answered. "I wouldn't even resent it. But I wish to tell you again, Sir Rodmond, as clearly as I can make it, that we are going to create public sentiment in this province, which will work against you at the next election. Did you ever hear that quotation about there being a tide in the affairs of men, which taken at the flood leads on to fortune?"

We looked at each other across the wide space of his mahogany desk and the silence was eloquent. Then Sir Rodmond's mood changed. His self-confidence came back; for a moment a doubt had assailed him. But the absurdity of the situation gave him courage. After all, what had he to be afraid of? His party was firmly entrenched, having 29 of the 42 members. He grew jocular.

"It would never do to let you speak to the cabinet," he said in the tone that one uses to a naughty child. "Even if they listened to you, which I doubt, you would only upset them, and I don't want that to happen. They are good fellows—they do what they are told to do, now. Every government has to have a head, and I'm the head of this one; and I don't want dissension and arguments. I believe in leaving well enough alone. Take the Indians, for example, they were far happier eating muskrats and the bark of trees before the white man came with education and disturbing ideas. Now they've lost all their good old-fashioned ways. No, you can't come in here and make trouble with my boys, just when I have them trotting easy and eating out of my hand. Now you forget all this nonsense about women voting," he went on in his suavest tones. "You're a fine, smart young woman, I can see that. And take it from me, nice women don't want the vote."

His voice dripped fatness.

"By nice women," I said, "you probably mean selfish women who have no more thought for the underpaid, overworked women than a pussycat in a sunny window has for the starving kitten on the street. Now in that sense I am not a nice woman, for I do care. I care about those factory women, working in ill-smelling holes, and we intend to do something about it, and when I say 'we' I'm talking for a great many women, of whom you will hear more as the days go on."

I stood to go. Then he smiled good-humoredly at me and said:

"Now don't go away mad. You know you amuse me. Come any time, I'll always be glad to see you." My smile was just as good-natured as his when I said:

"I'll not be back, Sir Rodmond; not in your time. I hadn't much hope of doing any good by coming, but I thought it only fair to give you the chance. I'll not be back, but it's just possible that you will hear from me, not directly, but still you'll hear; and you may not like what you hear, either."

"Is this a threat?" he laughed.

"No," I said. "It's a prophecy."

The Ghost of Beatrix Potter

Margaret Lane

Most of the hallowed books of childhood lose something of their magic as we grow older. Beatrix Potter's never. She even, to the mature eye, reveals felicities and depths of irony which pass the childish reader by; the dewy freshness of her landscape recalls Constable; her animals, for all the anthropomorphism of their dress and behaviour, show an imaginative fidelity to nature, a microscopic truth that one finds in the hedgerow woodcuts of Thomas Bewick.

It would be unwise to say any of this if she were still alive. She died in 1943, her brief creative period (thirteen years in all) having come to a close some thirty years before, since when she had evolved into a rather crusty and intimidating person, interested mainly in acquiring land and breeding Herdwick sheep, and whom nothing annoyed more than to have her books appraised on a critical level.

Graham Greene was sharply rebuked when he wrote an essay (a more or less serious one, though Miss Potter took umbrage at what she interpreted as mockery) in which he discussed the period of the 'great comedies'— *Tom Kitten, The Pie and the Patty-Pan, Tiggy-Winkle*—and the subsequent 'dark period' of *The Roly-Poly Pudding* and *Mr. Tod*, the 'near-tragedies', using the tone of a sober scholar discussing Shakespeare. 'At some time between 1907 and 1909,' he wrote, 'Miss Potter must have passed through an emotional ordeal which changed the character of her genius. It would be impertinent to inquire into the nature of the ordeal. Her case is curiously similar to that of Henry James. Something happened which shook their faith in appearances.'

Miss Potter was affronted. Nothing, she told him in a 'somewhat acid letter', had disturbed her at the time of writing *Mr. Tod* save the after effects of 'flu, which had not altered her so-called genius in any way. She sharply deprecated any examination of her work by the 'Freudian school' of criticism. Yet the essay, despite its Gioconda smile, was a flattering one, and anybody but the author of *Peter Rabbit* would have been pleased. She had become, indeed, curiously ambivalent about the whole of her *oeuvre*. On the one hand, though she enjoyed the matter-of-fact acceptance of children, she was irritated to fury by any considered appraisal of her work; yet at the same time she could not have enough of the adulation which came to her in her latter years from America. Though she would see no others she would welcome reverent strangers from America, and the two or three poor-quality children's books of her late middle age all went to American publishers and were not in her lifetime allowed to be printed in this country. The reason for this, I believe, was that she was privately aware that they showed a sad falling-off, and while she was fairly confident of praise from the professional priestesses of 'kid lit.' in America she was unwilling to expose herself at home. Though she was impatient of serious attention from her compatriots, any hint of criticism exasperated her still more.

Miss Janet Adam Smith fell into this thorny trap in 1942 with an article in *The Listener*. 'Great rubbish, absolute bosh!' Beatrix Potter wrote to her publishers, who had thoughtfully sent her a copy, thinking she would be pleased to see herself placed, within her limits, in the 'same company as...Palmer, Calvert, Bewick and a host of earlier English artists'. To Miss Adam Smith she also wrote that she had read the article with 'stupefaction'. Her wrath was increased by a humourless misconception, since she plainly thought she was being accused of copying these artists. Much taken aback, Miss Adam Smith hastened to reassure her, explaining that 'your illustrations often give the reader the same kind of pleasure as the pictures of these earlier artists', and quoting a relevant passage from one of Constable's letters. Worse and worse. Miss Potter (or Mrs Heelis as she was in private life) now thought she was accused of copying Constable, and replied with a long expostulatory letter, ending with the tart postscript, 'When a person has been nearly thirty years married it is not ingratiating to get an envelope addressed to "Miss".' (An observation which would pass without comment in any of the several books about Tabitha Twitchet.)

I could, if asked, have warned anybody that it was unwise to meddle at all with Beatrix Potter, having nearly done so myself in 1939, when I was very sharply sent about my business. Like most people who have been wholly entranced by her little books in infancy, I had long believed that Beatrix Potter was dead. The occasional new production that one came across in bookshops (*A Fierce Bad Rabbit*, for example) was so egregiously bad compared with the early masterpieces as to strengthen the suspicion that they were written by somebody else. The bookshops denied this, and were not believed. It was no good asking questions about Beatrix Potter, because at that time nobody knew anything about her.

It was in the early days of the war that I first discovered that she was still alive, and living in the Lake District. My step-daughter was at school near Windermere, and brought home tempting scraps of some local legends that were current about her. She was very old. She was very rich. She was a recluse. She was a little mad. She drove round the lake on Sundays in an open carriage, wearing black lace and sitting very stiffly behind the coachman. (This, it turned out, was a memory of her mother, Mrs Rupert Potter, who had done exactly that.) Or alternatively, and this was the most popular legend of all, she did labourer's work in the fields, wearing sacks and rags.

It was very puzzling, but at least it seemed undeniable that she was still alive, and I fell, like Graham Greene and Miss Adam Smith soon after, into the innocent folly of wishing to write about her. Clearly, if she were as reclusive as people said, one must approach with care, and since it seemed desirable to go to the fountain-head as a precaution against inaccuracy or offence, I decided to write to her.

The sensible approach, indeed the only one, since I did not know where she lived, was through her publishers, and I wrote to Frederick Warne and Co. for her address. They replied with ill-concealed horror that on no account, in no possible circumstances, could her address be given. She lived in close retirement, she never saw anybody, they had her express instructions that nobody must ever be allowed to write her a letter.

This could have been final, but it was also rather a challenge to ingenuity, and since my intentions were of the most serious and respectful description I could not see why they should refuse to forward a letter. They did not refuse, though they clearly shrank from the impertinence, and in due course an extremely polite missive was forwarded to Sawrey. I told her of my lifelong pleasure in her books (addressing her, I am thankful to remember, as Mrs Heelis), expressed my admiration and my wish to write an essay on her work, and asked if I might one day call on her to check some facts and submit what I should write for her approval.

Back came, in a few days, the rudest letter I have ever received in my life. Certainly not, she said; nothing would induce her to see me. 'My books have always sold without advertisement, and I do not propose to go in for that sort of thing now.' Her reply could hardly have been more offensively worded if I had asked her to sponsor a deodorant advertisement.

Well, that was that, I thought. It would be impossible to write anything in the face of such hostility, a snub so out of proportion to the occasion. I tore up the letter in indignation, not knowing that I was only one of innumerable people who had had the breath knocked out of them by her acerbity.

And then, in 1943, she died; and Raymond Mortimer, at that time literary editor of *The New Statesman*, asked if I could write him an article on Beatrix Potter. I did my best but it was a poor best, for nobody seemed to know anything about her and the crumbs of fact I could gather were contemptible. I knew only that she had lived and farmed for years in the Lake District and was the wife of a country solicitor. I had to confine myself to an appreciation of her work, and even this contained some sad inaccuracies.

It soon became apparent, from the meagre obituary notices which followed, that I was not the only one who had failed to find out anything. The tone, everywhere, was one of surprise that she had been so recently alive, and it was suddenly borne in on me that what I wanted to do was to write her biography. Alas for such optimism! Here was a life so innocent, so uneventful that one would have supposed the only difficulty would be in finding something to say. Yet, when I approached her widower, the gentlest of men, who received me with a trembling blend of terror and courtesy, it appeared that he considered himself under oath to conceal the very few facts that he had in his possession. He knew remarkably little about her life before their marriage, which had taken place when she was approaching fifty, and what he did know he was unwilling to divulge. He impressed me as a man who for thirty years had lived under the rule of a fairly dominant feminine authority, and whenever, reluctantly, he imparted a scrap of information or a date, he would glance apprehensively over his shoulder, as though every moment expecting the door to open.

The house was indeed palpably haunted by her. She had not long been dead, and the imprint of her personality, clearly the more dynamic one in that marriage, was on every chair and table. Her clothes still hung behind the door, her geraniums trailed and bloomed along the windowsill, her muddles lay unsorted at one end of the table while he took his meals at the other, even a half-eaten bar of chocolate with her teeth-marks in it lay whitened and stale among the litter of letters on her writing-table.

Yet he had expressed himself willing, after much patient argument, that a biography should be written, and as a man of honour truly believed that he was doing his best. He had been, it is true, quite implacable at first, and had been at pains to explain, with the most considerate politeness, why such a project was impossible. She would not have wished it, he said; what was more, she would never have allowed it; and here he looked over his shoulder again and blew his nose in a large and dubious handkerchief. The argument which finally convinced him, in spite of his obvious misgiving that agreement was treachery, was that sooner or later, either in England or America, a biography would be written, and it was perhaps better to have it written while he was still alive and could presumably exercise some control over the biographer. He seemed relieved to think that by this means he might escape the attentions of some frantic American, but I had to promise that every word of every line should be subject to his inspection, and left the cottage after that first interview with my point gained, in the deepest possible dejection.

I knew exactly what he had in mind; the sort of biography he had at last brought himself, after the most scrupulous searching of conscience, to consider. It would be about a quarter of an inch thick, bound in navy blue boards with gilt lettering, and would be called *A Memoir of the late Mrs William Heelis*. We did not discuss the point, but I am sure he took it for granted that it would be for private circulation.

Then began a series of evenings which we spent together and which I look back on with misery. Every question, however innocuous, was met with the frightened response, 'Oh, you can't mention *that*!' Any detail of her parents, the date of her birth, even the fact of her marriage to himself fell under this extraordinary prohibition. Night after night I stretched my tact and ingenuity to breaking-point, feverishly changing from subject to subject, retreating at once when I saw his poor eyes watering in alarm, creeping back each night to my cold bedroom at the Sawrey inn to sleepless hours of knowing the whole thing to be impossible.

And then, after many evenings and by the merest accident, I changed my tune. Some tremulous negative, some futile protest over a harmless question, produced that sudden trembling which I have experienced only two or three times in my life and associate with the crisis known as losing one's temper. I found myself banging the table with clenched fist and crying 'Mr Heelis, you *must not obstruct me in this way!*' The moment it had happened, in the petrified silence, I was overcome with embarrassment. But the effect was magical. He jumped, looked over his shoulder again as towards a voice he knew, pulled himself together, blew his nose, apologized, and suddenly seemed to feel remarkably better. I had never meant to do it, but the inference was plain. Tact, compliance, the yielding deviousness that had cost me so much effort, were things he was unaccustomed to and could not deal with. With decision, with firm opinion, he felt at home, and responded in the most eager and obliging manner. Pleased at last to be able to express his pride in his wife's fame he brought out his boxes of letters, rummaged in the bottoms of wardrobes and at the backs of drawers for photographs, produced such addresses and names as from time to time crossed his uncertain memory. The thing was started; I breathed a sigh of relief; though not without foreboding that my difficulties were only begun.

They were indeed, for over his eager compliance, which even extended to giving me two of her water-colours, hung the cloud of that final inspection of the manuscript which I knew would mar all. Left to himself, with typescript before him, I knew how his trembling hand would score it through, how little, how very little would come back unscathed, how in despair I would fling that little into the wastepaper basket.

Outside the precincts of Castle Cottage there was no such reticence; there were many people living who had known her well, Potter cousins, the niece of her last governess, Miss Hammond, innumerable farm and cottage neighbours who thought of her only as the eccentric little figure that the Lake District remembers—the odd bundle of country clothing, clad in innumerable petticoats, full of good humour, of authority, of sudden acerbities which could flash out quite brutally and inflict hurts where she probably never intended them. 'I began to assert myself at seventy', she wrote to one of her cousins a few months before she died, but this was an understatement. She had been asserting herself for thirty years, and the Lake District had come to respect her as a person it was dangerous to oppose, but very safe to love.

Those who spoke of her with the most feeling were the shepherds and farmers with whom she was most akin in temperament, and to the poetry of whose lives she had always responded, almost with the nostalgia of an exile. On her deathbed she had scribbled a note of indecipherable farewell to her old Scottish shepherd, the 'lambing-time man' who had come to her every spring for nearly twenty years, and with whom she had kept up a long and affectionate correspondence. He had preserved all her letters, dated and wrapped up in little parcels in the recesses of his cottage, and he sent them to me as an act of piety, for love of her memory.

I took innumerable journeys, sometimes with Mr Heelis, more often (and more fruitfully) alone, over the fells and along the valleys, to cottages and farmhouses that she owned, talking to the people who had known her. She had been a workmanlike landlord, most practically interested in fences and gates, the felling and planting of timber, the repairing of walls. As a sheep-breeder she was knowledgeable and shrewd, and the farmers round about thought of her principally as a dangerous rival at sheep fairs and ram shows, an enigmatic and authoritative presence in the Keswick tavern where the Herdwick Sheep Breeders' Association held its meetings.

At the same time I embarked on a sea of correspondence, which ebbed and flowed for more than a year. Beatrix Potter, for all the crowded busyness of her later years, when she was managing a number of farms and doing important work for the National Trust in the Lake District, possessed that last-century sense of leisure which permitted her to write long and frequent letters to a great many people—sometimes even to people she had never met, but whose personalities, when they wrote to her, had taken her fancy. Now, these letters began to flow into my hands, not only from English senders, but from places as far afield as America and New Zealand; and the task of deciphering and sifting them for their shreds of biographical interest was for a time quite heavy.

To me, the series of letters which Warne's, her publishers for more than forty years, had kept without a gap since the day when they first accepted *Peter Rabbit*, was the most interesting of all, for they reflected her slow and painstaking development as an artist, her emotional growth from girl to woman, her emergence from unhappy and respectable nonentity into the kind of personality about whom biographies are written. The Warne family had played an important, and more than professional, part in her life, and without their help and confidence the book could never have been written.

But however much help I had from her publishers, relations and other friends, there was still to be faced the final confrontation with Mr Heelis, when, as I privately guessed, he would bring up reinforcements of prohibition and his mandate would fall on everything I had written.

I remember that on my last evening in Sawrey, returning from a walk with which I had tried in vain to recruit my spirits, I found a penny lying at the foot of a stile and decided to toss for it; whether I should give it up there and then or write the book as I saw it and be prepared to forget it for years in a locked drawer. The penny said heads, and I put it in my pocket as a charm. The drawer was the thing. I did not know how old Mr Heelis was, nor how I should explain my curious delay; but I resolved I would not expose myself, or him, to the long-drawn agony of his excisions.

As it turned out, the penny proved a true oracle, for the poor widower, left alone and at a loss without the mainstay on which his thoughts and decisions had so long depended, died a few months after, before the book was finished, and I never paid that final visit to Sawrey. I do not believe he turns in his grave, honest man, nor that the stout little ghost which haunts the place would still, after all this time, find it necessary to be angry.

Wittgenstein

Guy Davenport

Like the gentle Anton Bruckner, who counted leaves on trees to while away a Sunday afternoon, Ludwig Wittgenstein in odd moments calculated the height of trees by pacing off from the trunk the base of a right triangle, wheeling around and sighting along his walking stick (up the hypotenuse) to the tree's top, invoking then the majestic theorem of Pythagoras. Together with inventing a sewing machine (in his teens), designing a house in Vienna (still standing) that elicited the admiration of Frank Lloyd Wright, and following assiduously the films of the Misses Betty Hutton and Carmen Miranda, this is one of the few acts of the philosopher that was at all transparent. No mystery, however, surrounds either his life or his thought. If he was not the greatest philosopher of our age, he was the most significant. He founded (inadvertently) and disowned two major philosophies. He was "getting at something" when he died, just what we shall never know. At the end of his first book, the *Tractatus Logico-Philosophicus* (completed in a concentration camp during the First World War) he wrote: "My propositions serve as elucidations in the following way: anyone who understands me eventually recognizes them as nonsensical, when he has used them as steps to climb up beyond them." At the beginning of his other book, the *Philosophical Investigations,* he wrote: "It is not impossible that it should fall to the lot of this work, in its poverty and in the darkness of this time, to bring light into one brain or another—but, of course, it is not likely." Once, when a student posed a question during one of his classes at Cambridge, Wittgenstein said: "I might as well be lecturing to the stove." A box of slips of paper—*Zettel*—was found among Wittgenstein's effects. On each slip is written a thought. The order of the slips, if any, is of course unascertainable. To come to some understanding of them is not, as Sir Thomas Browne would cheer us on, beyond all conjecture, but we must go about it with the ghost of Wittgenstein whispering: "But, of course, it is not likely."

Wittgenstein before he came to philosophy was a mathematician, a musician, an architect, a sculptor, a mechanical engineer, a grade-school teacher, a soldier, and an aviator. He could have followed any of these careers doubtless with brilliant success; just before he came to Cambridge (they gave him a doctorate at the door) he was strongly inclined to "be an aeronaut." Every account of his strange life indicates that he *tried* to teach. He did not dine with the faculty, as the faculty in its grandeur always dines in academic gowns, black shoes, and neck tie. Wittgenstein was forever tieless and wore a suede jacket that opened and closed with that marvellous invention the zipper; and his shoes were brown. He held his lectures in his rooms, in the continental manner. As there was no furniture except an army cot, a folding chair, a safe (for the *Zettel*), and a card table, the students brought their own chairs. Philosophy classrooms in our century have frequently been as dramatic as stages: Santayana, Samuel Alexander, Bergson—men of passionate articulateness whose lectures fell on their students like wind and rain. But Wittgenstein, huddled in silence on his chair, stammered quietly from time to time. He was committed to absolute honesty. Nothing—nothing at all—was to be allowed to escape analysis. He had nothing up his sleeve; he had nothing to teach. The world was to him an absolute puzzle, a great lump of opaque pig iron. Can we think about the lump? What is thought? What is the meaning of *can*, of *can we*, of *can we think*? What is the meaning of *we*? What does it mean to ask what is the meaning of *we*? If we answer these questions on Monday, are the answers valid on Tuesday? If I answer them at all, do I think the answer, believe the answer, know the answer, or imagine the answer?

It was apparently not of the least interest to Wittgenstein that Plato had answered certain questions that philosophers need to ask, or that Kant or Mencius had answered them. He sometimes liked other philosophers' questions; he seems never to have paid any attention to their answers. Truth was stubborn; Wittgenstein was stubborn; and neither faced the other down. We have to look back to the stoic Musonius to find another man so nakedly himself, so pig-headedly single-minded. He actually taught for very little of his life. He was forever going off into the Norwegian forests, to Russia, to the west of Ireland where—and this is all we know of these solitudes—he taught the Connemara birds to come and sit in his hands. He mastered no convention other than speech, wearing clothes, and—grudgingly and with complaint— the symbols of mathematics. The daily chores of our civilization were wonders to him, and when he participated in them they became as strange as housekeeping among the Bantu. He liked washing dishes after a meal. He put the dishes and silverware in the bathtub, studied carefully the detergent, the temperature of the water, and spent hours at his task, and hours more in the rinsing and drying. If he was a guest for several days, all the meals had to be identical with the first, whether breakfast, lunch, or dinner. What he ate was of no matter, just so it was always the same. He listened carefully to human speech, and took it to pieces before one's eyes. Language, he decided, was a game men had learned to play, and he was always, like an anthropologist from Mars, trying to find out the rules. When he lay dying of cancer at his doctor's house, the doctor's kind wife remembered his birthday and baked him a cake. Moreover, she wrote on it with icing, "Many Happy Returns." When Wittgenstein asked her if she had examined the implications of that sentiment, she burst into tears and dropped the cake. "You see," Wittgenstein said to the doctor when he arrived on the scene, "I have neither the cake nor an answer to my question." Some days before, the doctor's wife, patient martyr in the history of philosophy, had shown Wittgenstein her new coat that she was to wear to a party that very evening. Silently he fetched the scissors, silently he snipped the buttons from the coat, silently he replaced the scissors. The sainted wife remarked that, yes indeed, come to think of it, the coat did look better without its buttons, but only when the seals are opened at Doom will the philosopher's skill with the scissors declare its meaning.

Except for the mathematician David Pinsent, to whom the *Tractatus* is dedicated and who was killed in the First World War, he was luckless in friends; he seems to have noticed women in order to know where to flee. The idea of a female philosopher made him close his eyes in despair. Insanity and suicide ran in his family. He pleaded with his students to take menial jobs (as he did from time to time, as a country schoolteacher and mechanic). Life was perhaps a strange disease which one suffered with heroism; thought was certainly a disease which philosophy, perhaps, could cure. Like Henry Adams he felt that a healthy intellect would be unaware of itself, and would get on with life's business, making beautiful machines, music, and poetry, without reflection. Whatever the truth of the world, it was simple in the sense that one can say, for instance, that death is not a part of life (one of the perceptions in the *Tractatus*) and that the world is independent of my will (another); and it was complex in the sense that all that happens is the result of many causes not all of which can ever be known.

It is only Wittgenstein's writing in the middle of his career that gives one fits—the part that gave birth (to his regret) to linguistic analysis, philosophy's darkest night. The early work—the *Tractatus*—is lucid and powerful. The newly discovered *Zettel* can only be compared to the fragments of Heraclitus. Indeed, Wittgenstein admired all his life the epigrams of the acid-tongued Lichtenberg, and felt that thought was basically perception. What the philosopher says about the world is not too different from the proverb, the old saw, the infinitely repeatable line of poetry. It is clear that the *Zettel* are a return to the manner of the *Tractatus,* back to the archaic period of philosophy, back before the talkative charm of Socrates. The philosopher, as Wyndham Lewis said of the artist, goes back to the fish. Physics in Wittgenstein's lifetime was going back to Heraclitus (a clue to cracking the atom was found in Lucretius by Niels Bohr); so was art; so was architecture. What could be more nakedly Pythagorean than the geodesic structures of Buckminster Fuller, what more household caveman than the paintings of Paul Klee? One definition of *modern* is a renaissance of the archaic (as *the* Renaissance was a reaching back to Hellenism, to Rome, to a ripened civilization rather than to the green springtime of that same civilization).

"The limits of any language are the limits of my world." "The most beautiful order of the world is still a random gathering of things insignificant in themselves." Which is Heraclitus, which Wittgenstein? "The philosopher," says one of the *Zettel*, "is not a citizen of any community of ideas. That is what makes him a philosopher." And: "What about the sentence—*Wie ist es mit dem Satz*—'One cannot step into the same river twice'?" That Heraclitean perception has always been admired for its hidden second meaning. *One* cannot step...; it is not only the flux of the river that makes the statement true. But is it true? No, Wittgenstein would smile (or glare), but it is wise and interesting. It can be examined. It is harmonious and poetic.

The more we read Wittgenstein the more we feel that he is *before* Heraclitus, that he deliberately began an infinite recession (in order, of course, to go forward when he found a footing). He bowed out of the tradition whereby all philosophers digest all other philosophers, refuting and enriching, forming allegiances and enmities, and emitting their version of what they have learned from a conquered vantage which must be defended night and day. Wittgenstein declined to inspect the history of philosophy. It is questionable if when he died he had ever come to any understanding of the number 2. Two *what*? Two things would have to be identical, which is absurd if identity has any meaning. One of the *Zettel* wonders what the phrase "friendly hand" could mean. Another, if the absence of feeling is a feeling. Another, if his stove has an imagination and what it means to assume that the stove does not have an imagination.

Wittgenstein did not argue; he merely thought himself into subtler and deeper problems. The record which three of his students have made of his lectures and conversations at Cambridge discloses a man tragically honest and wonderfully, astoundingly absurd. In every memoir of him we meet a man we are hungry to know more about, for even if his every sentence remains opaque to us, it is clear that the archaic transparency of his thought is like nothing that philosophy has seen for thousands of years. It is also clear that he was trying to be wise and to make others wise. He lived in the world, and for the world. He came to believe that a normal, honest human being could not be a professor. It is the academy that gave him his reputation of impenetrable abstruseness; never has a man deserved a reputation less. Disciples who came to him expecting to find a man of incredibly deep learning, found a man who saw mankind held together by suffering alone, and he invariably advised them to be as kind as possible to others. He read, like all inquisitive men, to multiply his experience. He read Tolstoy (always getting bogged down) and the Gospels and bales of detective stories. He shook his head over Freud. When he died he was reading *Black Beauty*. His last words were: "Tell them I've had a wonderful life."

The Calgary Stampede

Jack Ludwig

Start with its end, a July Saturday night, the Stampede cowboys packrolled, moving on, the rodeo pens and chutes empty, the chuckwagon races over. No race horses parade the track, people in the grandstand want broad-spectrum entertainment, "good fun," "real enjoyment." By 9 P.M. the Calgary Stampede has changed utterly. Now it's all tent show and provincial fair. Western sunset opens its sensational act, turning the uppermost third of the Ferris wheel into a burnished bridge, blinding the roller-coaster cowboys as, whooping up, they slingshot out of the shadowy lower depths. Gears mesh, lock, unlock, release, ratchet a coaster car slowly upward with the sound of a wooden stick rippling a picket fence, electronically augmented, a hundred times magnified, exploding then in a rush of screams and ooh's as subterfuge and centrifuge counterpoint the cry of "Come in, have your pitchur taken—hey, lady, take his pitchur so when he gets older he can see how much fun he had today."

But the barkers are bored, and the shills. That's the way it is at the fag end of any carnie stand. In these closing hours even the suckers may get an even break. A child losing at ringtoss is thrown a huge chartreuse hound dog with cerise tongue and pasted paper goo-goo eyes. A local hardball star has triumphed over the weighted milk bottles, and he and his woman friend walk off swathed in fuzzy Sicilian-tinted snakes and turtles luminous with purples, pinks, greens neither nature nor man ever expected or intended. Five bucks' worth of gaming has pecked out two bits' worth of kewpie dolls for the passing pigeons. Yet they come. Lines everywhere, ten, twelve deep for every blackjack seat at the Frontier Casino, as many or more waiting for a "color" of chips at the roulette tables. Those who never play from anything but "the farthest seat on the dealer's right" in blackjack will take any available place now; and those who never play any color but "blue" or "green" at roulette find all chips grey in the gathering dark. In only a matter of hours the Stampede will close, and who has the patience to wait till next year to lose a winter's stash of coins and bills?

Under canopies, in the few places one may sit and nurse a soft drink or beer without ransoming away an arm and a leg, the older folk stake claims to a seat, sip slowly, sagged and wilted. Arm in arm, leather-jacketed and blue-jeaned couples, parties, gangs, sweep through the crowd, in a great hurry to do it all before the chuckwagon horses change back to mice. Anyone dreaming of "one big break" must make his hit in the next few hours. So it's *hurry hurry, hurry scurry,* the rhythm on the midway, *click shuffle, scrape curse* in the casino, while in easy contrast, the young people space themselves out in front of the Sun Tree, make one joint service a dozen unhurried smokers while tired rock music ekes out its wobbly decibels. From time to time a pot-fogged dreamer floats off in the direction of food and finds lines—lines and lines here as elsewhere, sullen lines, giggly lines, crying lines (where the children wait for their last Stampede ride). The masses mass to pay out what was saved from bread to spend on circuses. In the Stampede's waning moments there are no good rides and bad rides, only short-line rides. If standards existed for what one eats, they're gone too. Soggy corn-on-the-cob turned sodden being served is sloshed over with watery butter, then devoured as if it were the manna. Cotton candy shows bald spots, iced drinks are warm, hot dogs clammy cool, ice cream runny, candy apples adhesive—the standard ingredients of "enjoyment." A massive burned onion cloud hangs over the spielway, memorializing every singed hamburger of Calgary's ten-day blow.

Calgary's a city on the tilt, sloping up from foothills to the Rockies, cowboy country, half cowboytown, and, eastward, flat as Saskatchewan, farmer country, half farmertown. Farmers and cowboys—even without the oil people—were never that easy to tell apart. Now, of course, the Western craze shrouds woman, man and child in blue denim. Farmboys regularly spruce up in boots, cowboy hats, string ties. To resemble their fathers, they part slicked-down hair just over the ear, then lay what's gained right across the forehead to look as up-to-date as dad's wig. Cowboys, farmers, oilmen still hang tight with Elvis sideburns. Women, to save the Stampede from going snooty, wear a metal clip on side curls, but, to prove the Stampede's a night out, forgo plastic rollers and curlers. The inevitable bikers loom up, black leather and studs, studded wristbands, silver zippers, black sunglasses, buckle boots, wartime/peacetime issue, worn by all male members of the enlarged nuclear family, the women in black leather, and democratically studded, everything but the receiving blankets a few have wrapped around infants.

These are the night people. In the morning and afternoon crowds summer was the dominant theme—short shorts, tank tops, cotton dresses, wash-and-wear dude shirts. What's ominous at night—the anachronistic freak show on the midway—in bright sunlight is only absurd. The flack for the Royal American Shows says that complaints "about bad taste from local patrons" persuaded the firm to cut out its "two-headed baby act," stout fellow! *And* its "chamber of horrors." Still, it offers midwayniks a Palace of Illusions featuring such nonbad taste items as Madam Twisto, whose thing is "revolving...alive," and another woman called "The Long Neck...alive," still another called "The Girl Without a Middle...alive," and several other "alives" who, it seems, survived electrocution, hanging, though presumably the biblical fates of stoning and beheading weren't considered worthy of midway display. Lined up to go into one of the Palace's "Main Entrances" is a man seemingly unaware he will soom be under contract—tiny of head, pigeon in the chest, and ballooned-out extravagantly in the middle. Madam Twisto will probably spin seeing him. He is not alone. That guy in glasses you always see coming out of peepshows and bumshows is with him—and several hundred others with forefinger upraised to catch the freaks on an Instamatic, "all alive"!

During its first days I came out to the Stampede when rain washed attendance away. The grandstand was new, all sorts of shifts and changes had been made since 1973's show. The result was little parking, a fair amount of inconvenience. Till more than 140,000 people turned up on closing day the Stampede seemed to be in deep trouble (as it was, attendance in 1974 was only 20,000 shy of the 1973 record—993,777). The new setup, good for horseracing, was, I found, far less suited to the rodeo events. Not till Paul Matte of the Stampede office sneaked me across the racetrack and I climbed into a TV tower just above the chutes was I able to see *the* Stampede. Behind those chutes sat the families, the friends of contestants, the rodeo aficionados as oblivious of the midway as the midway is of the rodeo.

These Calgarians and visitors know rodeo champions the way *Hockey Night in Canada* watchers have a legend on Bobby Orr, or Ken Dryden, or the guys in the "other league," Gordie Howe and Bobby Hull. Aficionados take it personally when the world champion bull rider, Bobby Steiner, doesn't compete in the 1974 Stampede. They want to know if it's because Bobby's hurt or because some other rodeo dares to compete on these dates with the Stampede. If it's the latter, they want to know if Steiner's absence doesn't downgrade the competing this year.

When they check down the program they look for the other "world" (*i.e.,* North American) champions, and, happily, find the champion of champions, Larry Mahan, of Dallas, Texas, on the premises. Mahan has been the All-Around champion five years in a row (six times in all), has won more money in a single year than any other competitor, and has won more money in total than any other competitor. Larry Mahan's presence more than makes up for Bobby Steiner's absence. The rodeo pushers call him, alas, "Mr. Supersaddle," and with a touch of Grand Old Opry refer to him as "the world's most winningest cowboy," but Larry Mahan doesn't need that breed of bull. At the 1974 Stampede he won the All-Around by winning the Bareback bronc championship and placing second in the bullriding (won by a Saskatoon rider, Brian Claypool, ranked fifth in the "world" behind Bobby Steiner).

There's a great deal of controversy about rodeos. The rodeo people have set up their own "humane" society to take the heat off the charges made by various local, national and international branches of the Society for the Prevention of Cruelty to Animals. Watching the bareback bronc and bull-riding events, I wondered if anybody thought to include man among those animals. There is no way for someone to sit a horse or a bull for eight seconds (or ten, when that's called for) without taking a lot of cruel and unusual punishment. Every rider—successful or instantly thrown—suffers disorientation on touching ground. A sine wave passes through a man's body, not smoothly but powerfully, whiplashing both ends against the humped-up, bucked and belted middle. That kind of violence sends shocks against the brain pan as severe, it seems to me, as a succession of uppercuts on the chin of a boxer. A rider goes against an animal who may be familiar to him, or strange. If strange, regardless of what other riders have told him about the animal's rhythm, he must key on that rhythm in about a second, and then, instantly programmed, adapt what he has learned to the variations in the animal's tricks. Think of the difficulty one has trying to figure an electric maze of complexity and trickiness: a bucking surging bronc or wildly spinning bull of the championship class is far more difficult to figure than a maze, and eight seconds, which, as punishment, may seem a century, is, as time allowed for problem-solving, incredibly short.

Larry Mahan's formula for bull-riding is pure Plato:

"I try," he says, "to picture a ride in my mind before I get on the bull. Then I try to do it by the picture."

Professional cowboys have among their rodeo icons not only the great cowboys but the great animals of circuit history, the most famous of which, a Canadian horse named Midnight, is mentioned whenever the serious challenges of the sport come up. Midnight is buried in the grounds of the Cowboy Hall of Fame in Oklahoma City, Oklahoma, his grave marked by a plaque,"1910-1936," and Angus Cameron, perhaps the most famous of horse book editors and a frequent visitor to the Hall of Fame, tells me the greatest attraction there is Midnight's grave. Cowboys talk about Midnight and such famous bulls as Tornado as "athletes": they characterize the animals as "honest," by which they mean nothing is held back, and boast of the bronc nobody could ride with almost the same enthusiasm they talk of those great animals someone eventually did stay on.

Transport, the horse Larry Mahan rode to win his bareback bronc riding championship, was such an "athlete." To ride him, Mahan lay back like a swimmer trying to float a whipping, powerful, spine-snapping wave. From fifty feet away I could hear the cracking and lashing sounds of Mahan's body as Transport strained and humped to shoot him off—this above the crowd shouts and the announcer's amplifiers. At the eight-second signal two pickup men charged toward Transport and swept Mahan off the still-bucking back, dropped him, stumbling, dazed, rocking on his feet, while they chased and steered the bronc out of the arena into a narrow runway.

Events in a rodeo follow upon one another with the speed and smoothness of a well-managed three-ring circus. At the Stampede I was as impressed by those who make a rodeo work as I was by the contestants. These were the professionals who keep the stock moving into the pens and chutes, who do the saddling, who measure the lengths of braided manila rope needed in bull-riding and saddle bronc-riding, who raise and lower the pen gates, who time an animal's release, who, on a Stampede afternoon when horseracing punctuates the rodeo events, use the putting up of the swinging gates as a rhythmic pause in the largely uninterrupted contests they must manage. The mounted pickup men in the bronc-riding and the rodeo clowns in the bull-riding were other pros absolutely essential to the continuity and safety of the bronc- and bull-riding events. By either accident or intent a bull could gore or trample a bucked-off rider, which means, of course, that the "clowns" in their

118

100-pound rubber barrels or running on cleated football shoes to divert the charging bulls are engaged in a serious and dangerous business. If, say, pickup men on horses tried to scoop up a fallen bull rider the horse would become a most vulnerable target. Therefore the clown operates on foot, always risking a stumble and a fall, and the almost certain injury that would follow. For this reason three clowns usually stand by for the bull-riding events. In the circus, clowns not only amuse but act as a diverting bridge between acts; in the rodeo the clown is an actor and participant. There could be no bronc- or bull-riding events without the pickup men and these clowns.

The rodeo, like a one-ring circus, aims at an illusion: that all contests dovetail, making the rodeo one continuous event, from the opening "Grand Parade" to the climactic bull-riding contest. The rodeo, like any other spectacle, structures its program, starts with "crowd-pleasers," leads into the main events—steer-wrestling, calf-roping, bareback and saddle bronc-riding, bull-riding—careful to intersperse "novice" and "boys" among the professional contests.

At the Stampede finale the Buffalo Ride, featuring young Canadian Indians, or pseudo-Indians mostly, served as "warm-up," "prelim," free-for-all show biz calculated to make an audience not only laugh but pay attention. In the insane confusion of buffalo charging, riders slipping and falling into the dirt, the crowd howled, egged on by the chortle and shout of the announcer. The Buffalo Ride and the Wild Cow Milking contest that followed, though connected to the rodeo, could as easily have been part of the midway hoke outside. The Buffalo Ride particularly, in which almost every contestant was tumbled, bumped, or fell staggering—running off, reeling, or limping—was something Nero's Roman compatriots might have enjoyed as a rather tame prelim for the bigger and better lion games that followed.

With the spectators still yowling and hooting like a studio audience at a TV participation show, the Buffalo Ride gave way to the Wild Cow Milking "fun," with the announcer's shouts even louder now, to encourage the aspiring hysterical. Only then, with the spectators ostensibly "delivered," did the rodeo proper begin, featuring "real" cowboys in a *real* contest directed to the *real* spectators in the rodeo seats behind *real* animals in their pens and chutes. Laughter stopped. Show biz disappeared. Everything, now, was between man and animal. Frequently a child's voice cut through, imploring a father or brother to be careful, or to "give 'im hell, Dad." During the boys' or novices' events women could be heard shouting, for the most part, *stay-on, stick-with-it, hang-in* encouragement. Nationalism touched the Stampede as it does most things Canadian: though the spectators wanted the big-time American rodeo contestants at the Stampede, they also wanted their Canadian heroes to knock them off.

In the first real rodeo event, bareback bronc-riding, the competition, curiously, fell into two groups—Canadian novices who hadn't scored *higher* than 138 in two previous short go-rounds (or heats), competitors who hadn't scored *lower* than 140. Yet even here, with little chance to beat the eventual winner, Mahan, Mel Hyland of Alberta cowboytown, Ponoka, the 1972 "world" saddle bronc champion, made a great try, actually outscoring Mahan on the short-go, 76-75. Every year, people in the stands told me, they look for signs that more Canadians are arriving as rodeo champions. If 1974 wasn't a good year for the bareback, it was an excellent year for the saddle bronc- and bull-riding events.

What Calgary saw were two young Saskatchewan competitors, eighteen-year-old Melvin Coleman, of Pierceland, and twenty-year-old Brian Claypool, of Saskatoon, win the saddle bronc- and bull-riding championships respectively. It was only Mel Coleman's first year as a non-novice competitor. A few old grizzled American cowboys grumbled that the judging seemed to favor Canadians but, for the most part, the results were conceived as fair. Brian Claypool, as I've already indicated, stood high among bull-riding competitors on the continent, so his victory wasn't all that surprising, though Coleman's, won in competition against such stars as Dennis Reiners and Marty Wood, was. Not only was Coleman young; this was his first try at a Stampede "North American" championship; in 1973 he was second in the *novice* competition.

"Hey," I hollered down from my tower platform at a cowboy who didn't look too happy when Coleman's high short-go score of 82 was announced, "what do you think of that?"

"He-e-ll," the man said in an accent I took for Texan, "they musta give him a little somethin' extra for wearin' that checker shirt."

A third Saskatchewan competitor, Richard Todd of Wood Mountain, had a superb short-go time of 4.2 in his last steer-wrestling try, actually beating the eventual champion, Tom Ferguson, the present "world" All-Around champ, by half a second, but in the aggregate and average lagged far behind Ferguson and another circuit star, Darryl Sewell.

Event followed event, each one settling a championship, each one meaning money. As usual, Larry Mahan's winnings put him in front of everybody else; but when one thinks of the punishment someone like Mahan has to absorb in order to win a total of, in Calgary, $7,468, it shivers the sports perspective. A successful rodeo rider will earn in a year what Johnny Miller or Jack Nicklaus walks off with winning a big stop on the golf tour—$50,000. Only a few top rodeo figures will earn in a year two-thirds of what Miller or Nicklaus get for coming out on top *twice*. No cowboy could hope to earn, in three or four years, the more than $300,000 Nicklaus and Miller have each won in their best tour years.

"We know it don't make sense," says Freckles Brown, a more or less retired rodeo cowboy, "get on another head o' stock, land on your shoulder, land on your head, pick yourself up, get on a rig, go another 900 miles, and get on another head o' stock…"

In the novice saddle bronc ride, a young Alberta rider, Tom Crowe, thrown from his mount before he knew he was on a "head o' stock," crashed to the ground, then crawled through the sunwarmed dirt to curl up like some hurt creature in the shade of the cement dugout under the grandstand stage. Stunned and huddled into himself, obviously hurting, Crowe spurned the stretcher bearers who raced out to help him. Cowboy *macho*. The code: *Walk off under your own legs, even if they is broke. Don't give no head o'stock the satisfaction o'knowin' he hurt you.* Shaky, doubled up, hobbling, Crowe made it out of the arena to much code applause, the spurned stretcher-bearers jogging beside him.

In the boys' steer-riding championship, though, the rodeo clown closest to the youngest, smallest contestant, Cam Bruce, snatched him off the steer's back at the horn, rather than risk the small boy being thrown that long fall from the animal roof. In the second half of the steer-riding, Daryl Schacher shot out of the chute, clinging two-handed (by the rules) as his steer bolted, smashing into the fence with Daryl still holding on tight, and everyone in the stands shouting. The clowns rushed in to pull Daryl free while other clowns chased the steer back through the runway. The result of it all? Daryl was given an official re-ride!

Sometimes the novices, disappointed, reacted like much younger boys. In the saddle bronc competition one competitor came in far ahead of everyone else but was penalized for a rule infraction on his final short-go, and assigned a zero. In a second the certain winner was turned into a loser. In disappointment and anger he began to cry, while his friends and fellow-competitors gathered to console him.

Only once—after the Buffalo Ride and the Wild Cow Milking show biz act—was anything in the arena arranged for Nero and his Romans, the Wild Horse Race. The rules called for several competing three men-with-a-wild-horse teams, each made up of:

1. a wild horse
2. an "ear man" who was supposed to bite the wild horse's ear in a Spockian touch intended to "distract and calm the animal"
3. the "shank man" who clings to the horse's shank while
4. the rider, or, one assumes, "ass man," tries to vault himself up into a saddle he himself has attached to the horse.

At the signal to begin, all aspiring riders try to saddle, mount, and then ride over a short designated "track," the first horse and rider to cross a white-washed line being the winner.

While the announcer chuckled and confounded, while the tucked-up-in-the-stands spectators screamed and laughed, terror dominated the arena below. I saw it in the ear man's face, the shank man's spine, the aspiring rider's eyes—because his face tried hard to show *macho*, arrogance, pugnaciousness. Knee-bent the ear man cringed. Terror showed in the team ducked beneath a rearing horse's flailing hooves in fear that the wild horse, and animal retribution, would come crashing down. And greater terror, of being trampled by frightened, swerving animals bolted free of aspiring saddlers. Ear men and shank men hanging on as horse body slammed up against horse body, dragging neverseated riders through the dust spitting dirt and clutching at empty saddles. A few horses charged about aimlessly, saddles slung below their bellies like mailman's pouches. Heels dug in the dirt, captive heroes skidded by like water skiers, or startled farmboys trying to hang onto a plow behind Secretariat. Loosed, horses struggled into an animal circle, a willed roundup full of nightmare Picasso images—teeth bared, streaming manes, frightened eyes, distended nostrils, taut vein-swollen necks, bodies shiny with sweat.

And what was it all for? The Emperor Nero, and many others in the stands, told the horses wouldn't kill anybody during their act, decided this was as good a time as any to go out for a hot dog and/or the men's room, and so missed the whole shebang. And those who run the midway "freak" show, interested in nothing *but* the Wild Horse Race, could now go back to their own exhibitionism, satisfied they had seen everything the rodeo had to offer.

Steer-wrestling and bull-riding slowly brought the rodeo back to the Stampede, and when those contests were over, so was the cowboy's Stampede—all but the chuckwagon races. But to see the chuckwagon races one had to leave the grandstand, wander the midway or casino areas for about three hours, spending, drinking, eating, and then, in order to watch the chuckwagons, pay another ticket's worth. The younger people around the Sun Tree wanted to see the chuckwagon races, they told me, but couldn't afford the price of another ticket. Some had already put out seven or eight dollars on little or nothing—without seeing any of the rodeo events they said they were most interested in seeing.

"It's all rip-off," an Edmonton girl told me. "This is supposed to be fun and we can't even make it into that grandstand. Why couldn't they have the rodeo and the chuckwagons all at once? Rip-off—just rip-off. Even this, that's free," she said, waving her hand at the Sun Tree, "this is supposed to be what young people want. It's insulting. It's the worst rip-off of all."

I left the Stampede grounds after the rodeo events, took a cab to a restaurant next to the Calgary Inn where a long line waited neatly to get in. Dates, twos, couples, all neat, all dressed up. I asked a couple what the line was all about.

"Cabaret," a young man said, beaming, "live entertainment."

He sounded as if he had just recently experienced the very opposite of live entertainment. Or, to put it another way, the Stampede midway.

When I got back to the Stampede the urgency of do-it-all-before-midnight-tolls had taken over. People were turning up for sweepstake draws, pots o'gold—that sort of thing. And the chuckwagon races.

From the very top of the grandstand I could see the racetrack, the stock pens, the stable area for racing horses, the river, everything now, in reddened sun tones, cast in the segment of the color spectrum that excludes anything blue. In the two symmetrical rodeo pens—one for horses, one for steers and calves—animal and earth and corral fence were all tinted brown, golden, orange. Everything was peaceful, serene—no hoke, no hype, no spiel, no violence, no show biz. The track, on which the chuckwagon race would begin, was in evening shade, but behind the pens the track lay in bright sunshine. Even as a recreation of something that might never have been, the chuckwagon race made it—the rig, the four horses, the hunched-forward driver, the tense outriders in helmets, cowboy hats or jockey caps getting ready to stow the stove and tent poles, mount, and race. Four wagons, everybody frozen except for the horses swishing tails at un-race-conscious flies.

All four teams broke at the start, inscribed their beautiful figure eights, then galloped onto the track, tails streaming, the drivers up and hollering, the outriders on their horses and out on the track in their race within the race. It took less than half an hour to run the four last heats of the chuckwagon finale and out of it emerged another young Canadian champion, Kelly Sutherland, 22, not only the grand winner but also the winner of the third spot, and a total of almost $11,500 out of a possible $67,000.

When the chuckwagon races ended, so, for many, did the Stampede. The midway was still open, the casino thrived, the rides went their appointed round, but the rodeo was gone. The year's peak flattened, the end of the circus that made the struggle for bread mean something special. At midnight the coach and horses were only pumpkin and mice—till summer '75.

A Penny Saved Is a Waste of Time

Andrew A. Rooney

What follows is some advice I forgot to give our kids before they left home:

—There is a Santa Claus but he doesn't always come.

—Being well dressed is like being six feet tall. You either are or you aren't and there isn't much you can do about it.

—Learn to drink coffee without sugar.

—Throw away the can of paint after you've finished painting something, no matter how much there is left in the can.

—Don't keep your watch five minutes fast.

—Go to bed. Whatever you're staying up late for isn't worth it.

—Don't expect too much from the company you work for even if it's a good company.

—You're almost always better off keeping your mouth shut, but don't let that stop you from popping off.

—There are few satisfactions in life better than holding a grudge. Pick them carefully but hold them.

—Don't fuss a whole lot with your hair.

—You're better off missing a bus or an airplane once in a while than you are getting there too early all the time.

—Don't save string. If you need string, buy it.

—Don't save pennies, either. They don't add up to anything.

—If you can't find comfortable shoes that are good-looking, buy comfortable shoes that aren't, but don't buy good-looking shoes that are uncomfortable.

—Don't call in sick except when you're sick.

—You aren't the only one who doesn't understand the situation in the Middle East.

—Nothing important is ever said in a conversation that lasts more than three minutes.

—Very few things you buy will be the answer to the problem you bought them to solve.

—There's seldom any good reason for blowing the horn on your car.

—If you work moderately hard you'll find a lot of people aren't working as hard as you are.

—It is unlikely that you'll have any success gluing a broken chair together.

—If you buy a book and feel like making marks in it with a pen or pencil, make them. It's your book and it doesn't ruin it for anyone else anyway.

—Be careful but don't be too careful.

—In a conversation, keep in mind that you're more interested in what you have to say than anyone else is.

—If nothing else works, take a hot shower.

—Don't keep saying, "I don't know where the time goes." It goes the same place it's always gone and no one has ever known where that is.

—If you own something useless which you like, don't throw it away just because someone keeps asking what you're keeping it for.

—The fewer, the merrier.

—Don't believe everything you read in the newspaper but keep in mind almost all of it is true.

—Keep the volume down on everything. It's like salt. You can get used to less of it.

—Money shouldn't be saved for a rainy day. It should be saved and spent for a beautiful day.

—Language is more important than numbers.

—Don't make a date for anything more than a month in advance.

—It's *i* before *e* except in the following words: "Neither leisure foreigner seized the weird height."

—Travel just for the sake of going somewhere is usually a disappointment.

—Use profanity sparingly and don't use any obscenities at all.

—If you can't afford the expensive one, don't buy it.

—Try to be aware of how you're being.

—You'll be better off in the long run making decisions quickly even if a lot of them are wrong. They probably won't be wrong any more often than if you took a lot of time making them.

—When you cross a street, look both ways...even on a one-way street.

How to Play Second Base

Laurence Sheehan

Second base is the most important position in baseball. Nobody realizes. A lot of coaches don't even bother to tell their second basemen the first thing about the job. They don't think second base is worth the effort.

The unfortunate name of second base is partly to blame. It just sounds like a hand-me-down. I think the ill-fated manager Joe McCarthy of the Boston Red Sox also once said something like second base is neither first nor third. That was the situation when I was playing for Centerville School, and I doubt if it's improved much since then, not at Centerville or in the majors.

Why is second base so important? Because when an easy grounder or a high pop-up is hit to that position, and you kick it away, or misjudge it and let it bounce on your head, the whole team gets demoralized. The shortstop comes over and says, Too bad the school bus didn't clip you this morning. The first baseman slaps his leg and laughs. The pitcher gives you the finger in front of everybody. Of course there may not be that many people at the game, so the public humiliation won't count for much. Centerville hardly ever drew a crowd because it was always in last place in its division, thanks in part to slight miscalculations by the second baseman.

I got my little sister Evie to come a lot when games were played at Legion Field in our neighborhood. But she didn't understand baseball. She would see me strike out on three consecutive pitches, or get run through by a steaming grounder. But she wouldn't find such happenings interesting enough to report to our parents. I'd have to tell them myself at supper.

You might say that for Evie my baseball failings went in one eye and out the other. She was a lousy fan. I sometimes wondered why I had her come to the games at all, which I did starting when I made the team in sixth grade and got my uniform. I don't think she even knew what number I wore (9—The Thumper's own!). Anyway, if it weren't for the bubble gum my black pal Herman kept giving her, she probably would have stopped coming long before she finally did. Herman played third. She would chew gum or eat an apple or orange from home, and watch out that no one stole our gloves when we were at bat, but basically Evie paid no attention to what was going on. She usually sat on the opposing team's bench, to my great embarrassment. It was closer to the water fountain.

Back to second base now. There are tips that can make anybody play this position better and I'd like to pass them along.

By the way, I didn't mean to imply I minded my teammates groaning and hooting at my errors. I mean I minded, but I understood. And basically we had a close-knit infield. It wasn't any dream infield, such as the Bosox built around the great Bobby Doerr and Johnny Pesky in the same years I was at Centerville, but we had a pretty good team feeling. Erwin, our regular pitcher, would put up with four or five errors in one inning before going to the finger. Lover Boy, the first baseman, would laugh at errors and kid a lot, but actually he didn't care where the ball went or even who won. His mind was always on his girlfriends who were waiting for him up in the nearly empty stands. Bert, our team captain at short, would come over after I'd let one go through my legs, and say, "All right, let's get back in this game now." And of course Herman, who never made an error himself over at third, would not get upset by anything I did. Or anybody did. He was the coolest cucumber on the squad.

Not even State Street's Butch Mendoza, the division's Home Run King and number-one razzer, could get through to Herman. We had no regular coaches on the bases. Older players on each team did the job. Mendoza liked to do it for State Street. He'd coach first base and rib Lover Boy about his shaggy hair and his white cleats, and Lover Boy would nod and smile, probably not even hearing Butch's taunts, too busy dreaming about those girls of his up in the stands and about his plans for them all after the game. When Butch coached third he liked to rib Herman about his color. "Hey, boy, where's your watermelon today?" he'd say, or "How come you're not picking cotton this week?" At that time blacks were few and far between in our town, no matter what grammar school you went to, and Butch probably thought of Herman as a foreigner. The important thing is, Herman paid no attention to Butch and never did make an error before his eyes.

I'll spare the outfielders on Centerville. Like most outfielders they were hotshots, and I suppose because they managed to get more hits and runs than anyone else, they had a right to parade around out there and editorialize on every move the infielders made.

Now, then, the hardest play to handle is the infield fly. I say anytime a ball goes higher than it goes farther, it is going to be a son of a gun to catch. In my playing days, half the time I wouldn't even know when one of those high pops was entering my territory. I'd need to hear Lover Boy call over, "Hey, little man, here comes trouble!"

Anyway, you've got to get set. A good thing is to get your feet in motion. And bend your neck back far enough so your eyes see more than the brim of the baseball cap. Everything about school uniforms is fine except the brims on the caps. They are made for adult heads, and if you stand 4 feet 3 and weigh 75 pounds, the hat will be like an awning on your forehead. The only thing you'll be able to see without any strain is your feet, which as I said should be in motion anyway—as you commence dancing into position to make a stab at the catch.

Of course, once you get your head tilted back far enough so you can see past the brim of your cap, you risk being temporarily blinded by the sun. Even on cloudy days it is possible for the sun to come out just at the crucial instant and make you lose sight of the damn ball, assuming you ever saw it in the first place.

Another bad thing about the high fly is that it gives you too much time to think. Like the drowning man, a ten-year-old tends to experience all the important moments in his life while waiting for a baseball to drop. Moments such as when you saw your name on the Centerville School baseball roster for the first time.

To tell the truth, the reason I got to play second base for Centerville for three years in a row is that my growth was stunted at the time, and provided I didn't swing at the ball when I was up to bat, opposing pitchers tended to walk me. My strike zone was about the size of a civics workbook. If I waited out the pitchers, I could count on getting on base almost every time.

Not that I wouldn't go for the hit once in a while. I would pretend to miss the signal telling me to wait for the walk that would invariably come from the third-base coach when I was up. The signal was always the same: doff cap, scratch left knee, blow nose in hanky, in that order. By the end of the season every team in the division knew all our coaching signals, but it was too confusing to try to change them.

Anyway, sometimes I would just ignore the signal and go for the hit. Each time I missed the ball, of course, the third-base coach would slam his cap on the ground or throw his hanky down, mad as can be. The opposing team's catcher would grin and hold the ball up in front of my eyes for my inspection before tossing it back to the mound. I would ignore all this and just dig in deeper with my cleats and take a couple of fierce practice swings. Digging in was itself a problem because the batter's box was furrowed over from other stances. Following the example of The Thumper and Vern Stephens and other Beantown sluggers, the boys in our division liked to get a really firm hold on the planet when at bat. They would dig and kick with their cleats like dogs tearing up the ground after peeing, and the result would be a set of gullies in the batter's box among which I was supposed to find a place to stand. I had the narrow stance that comes with a 4-foot, 3-inch frame, and sometimes I had one foot on a hillside and the other in a gully. No wonder my average was low.

That's really part of the story of how Herman and I got to be friends—we were built the same. We were the only two to make the team in sixth grade. Herman made it on his talent in spite of his size and I made it on my size in spite of my talent. In a way we came up together from the minors. Also we tended to sit right near each other in classrooms because our last names started with the same initial and in those days everything was done alphabetically, from choking on cod-liver-oil pills to taking cover in the lavatory during practice A-bomb attacks.

Now about the high fly. Your own thoughts are not the only distractions when you're looking for a ball somewhere up there in the blinding blue infinity of outer space. People are chattering all around you. Once I heard my sister call to me, "Hey, I'm going to play on the swings now, OK?" Another time, when we were playing State Street, Butch Mendoza hit a real rainmaker somewhere in my neighborhood. Running down the line to first, Butch had plenty of time on his hands, so he hollered, "Hey, kid, you're gonna miss it, you're gonna miss it!" Of course I was; nobody had to broadcast it.

State Street always won the division and usually went on to win the town title by beating the leader of the other division. They were tough boys at State Street. If they didn't beat you in the game, they'd beat you up afterwards. A lot of the State Street players had stayed back in grades a couple of times, which gave them the edge of experience over the boys at Centerville. I don't know how old Butch was. I did hear once that when he finally graduated from State Street he was eligible for the draft. That may have been an exaggeration, but no question, he was big. He would pole tremendous flies that our out-fielders wouldn't even bother running for. There was no proper fence at Legion Field such as they have at Fenway Park, and after a certain point, say 250 feet out, the field slanted sharply into an old cemetery and it was the devil finding the ball if it got that far.

Butch and one other boy in our division were the only ones who could reach the cemetery, so it really wasn't a problem. The other boy played for Mount Carmel but I don't remember his name. He missed a lot of the games, anyway, because he often had to work on his family's farm after school. Mount Carmel was in the town's last rural section and boasted a number of hayseeds on its squad, boys with eyebrows that grew together and hard bones.

The only other good team in our division was Spring Glen. It always amazed me how the rich families who lived in the Spring Glen section of town could produce so many ballplayers. As far as I could tell, Ted Williams, Dom DiMaggio, Walt Dropo, Birdie Tebbetts, Billy Goodman, and the rest all came from humble backgrounds. On that basis I used to think there was some connection between rough childhoods and good batting averages, which is why I sometimes wished my own house would burn down, to give me an edge.

My final advice on high pops is to play them on the first bounce. Just let the ball drop and say you thought the infield fly rule was in effect. Of course the infield fly rule is in effect only when two or more players are on base, and then the batter is automatically out. Actually, though, high infield flies are never hit to the second baseman when the rule happens to apply. That is one of the unfair parts a second baseman learns to live with.

I could go into what kind of glove to buy and how to keep it oiled and such, but you probably know all that. Anyway the glove doesn't make the ballplayer. When I was named to the team in sixth grade, I talked my folks into buying me a nice new glove with a big web and all, in honor of the miracle. But the only thing I ever caught in it was a cold—that's what Lover Boy always said. In comparison, Herman's glove looked like it had come off the world's last buffalo. It had no padding and hardly any webbing and one of the fingers was always coming unstitched. But Herman nabbed everything that came anywhere near third base.

I guess Evie knew Herman's glove was magical even though she hardly watched the action, because she would hold it in her lap for him between innings. Mine she just kept handy. Herman would pay her off in bubble gum for the service.

Now for grounders. I used to practice fielding grounders all winter by flinging a ball against the concrete wall in our basement. It drove my parents batty and scarred the patio furniture in storage and worst of all it taught me how to catch only one kind of grounder—the grounder that comes directly at you and bounces into your glove at knee level. In three years of play in our division, this particular type of ground ball was never once hit to my position.

The key thought at second is not to catch the grounder, anyway, but to stop it. That keeps the right fielder off your back and if you manage to find the ball after it's bounced off your knee or chest, you still might be able to get it to first in time for the out. A danger here is to get so excited about actually getting the ball in your bare hand that you send it sailing over the first baseman's head and over by the swings. So concentrate on the throw to first during infield warm-up at the start of every inning. This is when the first baseman throws a few grounders to the other infielders too loosen them up. Lover Boy was always careful to give me a grounder underhanded, so I would be more likely to catch it and not have to trot out into shallow centre to get the ball back again.

Maybe even more important than handling pops and stopping ground balls with your chin if necessary is the second baseman's role in boosting team spirit. A lot of boosting comes in the form of infield chatter in support of the pitcher. "Come on you kid, come on you babe," is a proven morale-booster. So are "No hitter no hitter up there" and "Chuck it in there, baby."

I was practically the psychological cornerstone of the Centerville infield because Erwin, our regular pitcher, was lefthanded. In the course of winding up, especially when there were men on base—as there usually were—Erwin would always pause briefly and be forced to look in my direction, as a southpaw, before collecting his energies for the assault on the strike zone. Sometimes he had a faintly disgusted look which seemed to say, "Well, I suppose you're getting ready to make another error." But I knew the importance of giving him confidence and I would stare right back and say, "Come on you kid come on you babe no hitter no hitter."

Erwin sucked on Life Savers during a game, which I don't approve of for a second baseman. If the second baseman gets knocked down by a runner, or happens to trip of his own accord, with a Life Saver in his mouth, it is quite possible he will get the candy jammed in his throat. I chewed gum and recommend the same. Chewing gum keeps your mouth from getting dry as a resin bag on those hot, dusty days when baseball was meant to be played, and it relaxes your jaw muscles, which are the first to freeze up under tension.

Covering the bag properly is another important duty. I never had much practice taking throws from the catcher, to put out base stealers, because in such cases the Centerville catchers either threw the ball way into the outfield or hit poor Erwin with it as he tried to get out of the way. I did handle throws from the outfield a lot. Naturally our outfielders had to show off their powerful throwing arms so, on an attempted double, say, I would face two means of extinction: (1) breaking my hand on the hard throw from the field, or (2) getting run over from behind by the base runner.

Actually I never got spiked or knocked down by runners, but there were many close calls. By far the most dangerous man on base in the division was Butch Mendonza, as you might have guessed by what I've mentioned about him already. Once Butch knocked Herman on his ass coming into third. Right away we had to bring in a young kid at Herman's position who was about as bad as I was out there. I remember Lover Boy saying, "My, my, we are now fielding a hole at second and a sieve at third!"

Herman was nowhere near the base and Butch should have been called out for running outside his normal course. He deliberately picked Herman off because of Herman's color and maybe even more because of Herman's indifference to Butch's many taunts. He should have been called out, but even the umpires were afraid of Butch Mendoza in those days. He was three times Herman's height and twice his weight, I'd guess. So Herman got carted off by Bert and Erwin and me, wind knocked out of him, and as it turned out, one arm busted.

In the meantime, I remember, Evie got up from the State Street bench, where she was sitting, naturally, and hit Butch with what was left of the apple she'd been chomping on. Got him in the face with her apple core after he'd crossed home plate. She turned and ran toward home and Butch was too surprised and out of breath anyway to do much about it. He just looked confused. I felt like catching up with Evie and buying her a Popsicle for trying to avenge Herman as she had done. I guess I knew, even as I helped cart off Herman, who was chewing his bubble gum like crazy at the time, to keep from crying probably—I guess I knew Butch had done something he would be ashamed of in later years, provided he ever stopped to think about it. And little Evie had done something she'd never stop to think about, because she was at that age when you can deal with villains cleanly.

In any case I couldn't have walked out on Centerville even though we were losing by about 12 to 3 at the time. We got Herman settled down and took the field again and finished the last two or three innings. I think State Street got a couple more runs off us, to rub it in. We never got on base again, but that didn't make any difference—we stuck it out. That's really about the last thing I wanted to pass along about the job of playing second base, whether you're winning or losing, or making five errors per game, or seeing one of your teammates get a bad break, or losing your only fan. Stick it out. That's what second base is all about.

Usually Destroyed

Aldous Huxley

Our guide through the labyrinthine streets of Jerusalem was a young Christian refugee from the other side of the wall, which now divides the ancient city from the new, the non-viable state of Jordan from the non-viable state of Israel. He was a sad, embittered young man—and well he might be. His prospects had been blighted, his family reduced from comparative wealth to the most abject penury, their house and land taken away from them, their bank account frozen and devaluated. In the circumstances, the surprising thing was not his bitterness, but the melancholy resignation with which it was tempered.

He was a good guide—almost too good, indeed; for he was quite remorseless in his determination to make us visit all those deplorable churches which were built, during the nineteenth century, on the ruins of earlier places of pilgrimage. There are tourists whose greatest pleasure is a trip through historical associations and their own fancy. I am not one of them. When I travel I like to move among instrinsically significant objects, not through an absence peopled only by literary references, Victorian monuments and the surmises of archaeologists. Jerusalem, of course, contains much more than ghosts and architectural monstrosities. Besides being one of the most profoundly depressing of the earth's cities, it is one of the strangest and, in its own way, one of the most beautiful. Unfortunately our guide was far too conscientious to spare us the horrors and the unembodied, or ill-embodied, historical associations. We had to see everything—not merely St Anne's and St James's and the Dome of the Rock, but the hypothetical site of Caiaphas's house and what the Anglicans had built in the 'seventies, what the Tsar and the German Emperor had countered with in the 'eighties, what had been considered beautiful in the early 'nineties by the Copts or the French Franciscans. But, luckily, even at the dreariest moments of our pilgrimage there were compensations. Our sad young man spoke English well and fluently, but spoke it as eighteenth-century virtuosi played music—with the addition of *fioriture* and even whole cadenzas of his own invention. His most significant contribution to colloquial English (and, at the same time, to the science and art of history) was the insertion into almost every sentence of the word 'usually.' What did he mean by it? The answer is, Nothing at all. What sounded like an adverb was in fact no more than one of those vocalized tics to which nervous persons are sometimes subject. I used to know a professor whose lectures and conversation were punctuated, every few seconds, by the phrase, "With a thing with a thing." "With a thing with a thing" is manifestly gibberish. But our young friend's no

132

less compulsive 'usually' had a fascinating way of making a kind of sense—much more sense, very often, than the speaker had intended. "This area," he would say as he showed us one of the Victorian monstrosities, "this area" (it was one of his favourite words) "is very rich in antiquity. St Helena built here a very vast church, but the area was usually destroyed by the Samaritans in the year 529 after Our Lord Jesus Christ. Then the Crusaders came to the area, and built a new church still more vast. Here were mosaics the most beautiful in the world. In the seventeenth century after Our Lord Jesus Christ the Turks usually removed the lead from the roof to make ammunition; consequently rain entered the area and the church was thrown down. The present area was erected by the Prussian Government in the year 1879 after Our Lord Jesus Christ and all these broken-down houses you see over there were usually destroyed during the war with the Jews in 1948."

Usually destroyed and then usually rebuilt, in order, of course, to be destroyed again and then rebuilt, *da capo ad infinitum*. That vocalized tic had compressed all history into a four-syllabled word. Listening to our young friend, as we wandered through the brown, dry squalor of the Holy City, I felt myself overwhelmed, not by the mere thought of man's enduring misery, but by an obscure, immediate sense of it, an organic realization. These pullulations among ruins and in the dark of what once were sepulchers; these hordes of sickly children; these galled asses and the human beasts of burden bent under enormous loads; these mortal enemies beyond the dividing wall; these priest-conducted groups of pilgrims befuddling themselves with the vain repetitions, against which the founder of their religion had gone out of his way to warn them—they were dateless, without an epoch. In this costume or that, under one master or another, praying to whichever God was temporarily in charge, they had been here from the beginning. Had been here with the Egyptians, been here with Joshua, been here when Solomon in all his glory ordered his slaves in all their misery to build the temple, which Nebuchadnezzar had usually demolished and Zedekiah, just as usually, had put together again. Had been here during the long pointless wars between the two kingdoms, and at the next destruction under Ptolemy, the next but one under Antiochus and the next rebuilding under Herod and the biggest, best destruction of all by Titus. Had been here when Hadrian abolished Jerusalem and built a brand-new Roman city, complete with baths and a theatre, with a temple of Jupiter, and a temple of Venus, to take its place. Had been here when the insurrection of Barcochebas was drowned in blood. Had been here while the Roman Empire declined and turned Christian, when Chosroes the Second destroyed the churches and when the Caliph Omar brought Islam and, most unusually, destroyed nothing. Had been here to meet the Crusaders and then to wave them goodbye, to welcome the Turks and then to watch them retreat before Allenby. Had been here under the Mandate and through the troubles of 'forty-eight, and was here now and would be here, no doubt, in the same brown squalor, alternately building and destroying, killing and being killed, indefinitely.

"I do not think," Lord Russell has recently written, "that the sum of human misery has ever in the past been so great as it has been in the last twenty-five years." One is inclined to agree. Or are we, on second thoughts, merely flattering ourselves? At most periods of history moralists have liked to boast that theirs was the most iniquitous generation since the time of Cain—the most iniquitous and therefore, since God is just, the most grievously afflicted. Today, for example, we think of the thirteenth century as one of the supremely creative periods of human history. But the men who were actually contemporary with the cathedrals and Scholastic Philosophy regarded their age as hopelessly degenerate, uniquely bad and condignly punished. Were they right, or are we? The answer, I suspect is: Both. Too much evil and too much suffering can make it impossible for men to be creative; but within very wide limits greatness is perfectly compatible with organized insanity, sanctioned crime and intense, chronic unhappiness for the majority. Every one of the great religions preaches a mixture of profound pessimism and the most extravagant optimism. "I show you sorrow," says the Buddha, pointing to man in his ordinary unregenerate condition. And in the same context Christian theologians speak of the Fall, of Original Sin, of the Vale of Tears, while Hindus refer to the workings of man's home-made destiny, his evil karma. But over against the sorrow, the tears, the self-generated, self-inflicted disasters, what superhuman prospects! If he so wishes, the Hindu affirms, a man can realize his identity with Brahman, the Ground of all being; if he so wishes, says the Christian, he can be filled with God; if he so wishes, says the Buddhist, he can live in a transfigured world where Nirvana and Samsara, the eternal and the temporal, are one. But, alas—and from optimism based on the experience of the few, the saints and sages return to the pessimism forced upon them by their observation of the many—the gate is narrow, the threshold high, few are chosen because few choose to be chosen. In practice man usually destroys himself—but has done so up till now a little less thoroughly than he has built himself up. In spite of everything, we are still here. The spirit of destruction has been willing enough, but for most of historical time its technological flesh has been weak. The Mongols had only horses as transport, only bows and spears and butchers' knives for weapons; if they had possessed our machinery, they could have depopulated the planet. As it was, they had to be content with small triumphs—the slaughter of only a few millions, the stamping out of civilization only in Western Asia.

In this universe of ours nobody has ever succeeded in getting anything for nothing. In certain fields, progress in the applied sciences and the arts of organization has certainly lessened human misery; but it has done so at the cost of increasing it in others. The worst enemy of life, freedom and the common decencies is total anarchy; their second worst enemy is total efficiency. Human interests are best served when society is tolerably well organized and industry moderately advanced. Chaos and ineptitude are anti-human; but so too is a superlatively efficient government, equipped with all the products of a highly developed technology.When such a government goes in for usually destroying, the whole race is in danger.

The Mongols were the aesthetes of militarism; they believed in gratuitous massacre, in destruction for destruction's sake. Our malice is less pure and spontaneous; but, to make up for this deficiency, we have ideals. The end proposed, on either side of the Iron Curtain, is nothing less than the Good of Humanity and its conversion to the Truth. Crusades can go on for centuries, and wars in the name of God or Humanity are generally diabolic in their ferocity. The unprecedented depth of human misery in our time is proportionate to the unprecedented height of the social ideals entertained by the Totalitarians on the one side, the Christians and the secularist democrats on the other.

And then there is the question of simple arithmetic. There are far more people on the earth today than there were in any earlier century. The miseries, which have been the usual consequence of the usual course of nature and the usual behaviour of human beings, are the lot today, not of the three hundred millions of men, women and children who were contemporary with Christ, but of more than two and a half billions. Obviously, then, the sum of our present misery cannot fail to be greater than the sum of misery in the past. Every individual is the centre of a world, which it takes very little to transform into a world of unadulterated suffering. The catastrophes and crimes of the twentieth century can transform almost ten times as many human universes into private hells as did the catastrophes and crimes of two thousand years ago. Moreover, thanks to improvements in technology, it is possible for fewer people to do more harm to greater numbers than ever before.

After the capture of Jerusalem by Nebuchadnezzar, how many Jews were carried off to Babylon? Jeremiah puts the figure at four thousand six hundred, the compiler of the Second Book of Kings at ten thousand. Compared with the forced migrations of our time, the Exile was the most trivial affair. How many millions were uprooted by Hitler and the Communists? How many more millions were driven out of Pakistan into India, out of India into Pakistan? How many hundreds of thousands had to flee, with our young guide, from their homes in Israel? By the waters of Babylon ten thousand at the most sat down and wept. In the single refugee camp at Bethlehem there are more exiles than that. And Bethlehem's is only one of dozens of such camps scattered far and wide over the Near East.

So it looks, all things considered, as though Lord Russell were right—that the sum of misery is indeed greater today than at any time in the past. And what of the future? Germ warfare and the H-bomb get all the headlines and, for that very reason, may never be resorted to. Those who talk a great deal about suicide rarely commit it. The greatest threat to happiness is biological. There were about twelve hundred million people on the planet when I was born, six years before the turn of the century. Today there are two thousand seven hundred millions; thirty years from now there will probably be four thousand millions. At present about sixteen hundred million people are underfed. In the nineteen-eighties the total may well have risen to twenty-five hundred millions, of whom a considerable number may actually be starving. In many parts of the world famine may come even sooner. In his Report on

135

the Census of 1951 the Registrar General of India has summed up the biological problem as it confronts the second most populous country of the world. There are now three hundred and seventy-five million people living within the borders of India, and their numbers increase by five millions annually. The current production of basic foods is seventy million tons a year, and the highest production that can be achieved in the foreseeable future is ninety-four million tons. Ninety-four million tons will support four hundred and fifty million people at the present sub-standard level, and the population of India will pass the four hundred and fifty million mark in 1969. After that, there will be a condition of what the Registrar General calls 'catastrophe'.

In the index at the end of the sixth volume of Dr Toynbee's *A Study of History*, Popilius Laena gets five mentions and Porphyry of Batamaea two; but the word you would expect to find between these names, *Population*, is conspicuous by its absence. In his second volume, Mr Toynbee has written at length on 'the stimulus of pressures'—but without ever mentioning the most important pressure of them all, the pressure of population on available resources. And here is a note in which the author describes his impressions of the Roman Campagna after twenty years of absence. "In 1911 the student who made the pilgrimage of the Via Appia Antica found himself walking through a wilderness almost from the moment when he passed beyond the City Walls....When he repeated the pilgrimage in 1931, he found that, in the interval, Man had been busily reasserting his mastery over the whole stretch of country that lies between Rome and the Castelli Romani....The tension of human energy on the Roman Campagna is now beginning to rise again for the first time since the end of the third century B.C." And there the matter is left, without any reference to the compelling reason for this 'rise of tension'. Between 1911 and 1931 the population of Italy had increased by the best part of eight millions. Some of these eight millions went to live in the Roman Campagna. And they did so, not because Man with a large M had in some mystical way increased the tension of human energy, but for the sufficiently obvious reason that there was nowhere else for them to go. In terms of a history that takes no cognizance of demographical facts, the past can never be fully understood, the present is quite incomprehensible and the future entirely beyond prediction.

Thinking, for a change, in demographic as well as in merely cultural, political and religious terms, what kind of reasonable guesses can we make about the sum of human misery in the years to come? First, it seems pretty certain that more people will be hungrier and that, in many parts of the world, malnutrition will modulate into periodical or chronic famine. (One would like to know something about the Famines of earlier ages, but the nearest one gets to them in Mr Toynbee's index is a blank space between Muhammad Falak-al-Din and Gaius Fannius.) Second, it seems pretty certain that, though they may help in the long run, remedial measures, aimed at reducing the birth-rate will be powerless to avert the miseries lying in wait for the next generation. Third, it seems petty certain that improvements in Agriculture (not referred to in Mr Toynbee's index, though Agrigentum gets two mentions and Agis IV,

King of Sparta, no less than forty-seven) will be unable to catch up with current and foreseeable increases in population. If the standard of living in industrially backward countries is to be improved, agricultural production will have to go up every single year by at least two and a half per cent, and preferably by three and a half per cent. Instead of which, according to the FAO, Far Eastern food production per head of population will be ten per cent less in 1956 (and this assumes that the current Five-Year Plans will be fully realized) than it was in 1938.

Fourth, it seems pretty certain that, as a larger and hungrier population 'mines the soil' in a desperate search for food, the destructive processes of erosion and deforestation will be speeded up. Fertility will therefore tend to go down as human numbers go up. (One looks up *Erosion* in Mr Toynbee's index but finds only Esarhaddon Esotericism and Esperanto; one hunts for *Forests*, but has to be content, alas, with Formosus of Porto.)

Fifth, it seems pretty certain that the increasing pressure of population upon resources will result in increasing political and social unrest, and that this unrest will culminate in wars, revolutions and counter-revolutions.

Sixth, it seems pretty certain that, whatever the avowed political principles and whatever the professed religion of the societies concerned, increasing pressure of population upon resources will tend to increase the power of the central government and to diminish the liberties of individual citizens. For, obviously, where more people are competing for less food, each individual will have to work harder and longer for his ration, and the central government will find it necessary to intervene more and more frequently in order to save the rickety economic machine from total breakdown, and at the same time to repress the popular discontent begotten by deepening poverty.

If Lord Russell lives to a hundred and twenty (and, for all our sakes, I hope most fervently that he will), he may find himself remembering these middle decades of the twentieth century as an almost Golden Age. In 1954, it is true, he decided that the sum of human misery had never been so great as it had been in the preceding quarter century. On the other hand, 'you ain't seen nuthin' yet.' Compared with the sum of four billion people's misery in the 'eighties, the sum of two billion miseries just before, during and after the Second World War many look like the Earthly Paradise.

But meanwhile here we were in Jerusalem, looking at the usually destroyed antiquities and rubbing shoulders with the usually poverty-stricken inhabitants, the usually superstitious pilgrims. Here was the Wailing Wall, with nobody to wail at it; for Israel is on the other side of a barrier, across which there is no communication except by occasional bursts of rifle fire, occasional exchanges of hand grenades. Here, propped up with steel scaffolding, was the church of the Holy Sepulchre—that empty tomb to which, for three centuries, the early Christians paid no attention whatsoever, but which came, after the time of Constantine, to be regarded, throughout Europe, as the most important thing in the entire universe. And here was Siloam, here St Anne's, here the Dome of the Rock and the site of the Temple, here, more ruinous than Pompeii, the Jewish quarter, levelled, usually, in 1948 and not

137

yet usually reconstructed. Here, finally, was St James's, of the Armenians, gay with innumerable rather bad but charming paintings, and a wealth of gaudily coloured tiles. The great church glowed like a dim religious merry-go-round. In all Jerusalem it was the only oasis of cheerfulness. And not alone of cheerfulness. As we came out into the courtyard, through which the visitor must approach the church's main entrance, we heard a strange and wonderful sound. High up, in one of the houses surrounding the court, somebody was playing the opening Fantasia of Bach's Partita in A minor—playing it, what was more, remarkably well. From out of the open window, up there on the third floor, the ordered torrent of bright pure notes went streaming out over the city's immemorial squalor. Art and religion, philosophy and science, morals and politics—these are the instruments by means of which men have tried to discover a coherence in the flux of events, to impose an order on the chaos of experience. The most intractable of our experiences is the experience of Time—the intuition of duration, combined with the thought of perpetual perishing. Music is a device for working directly upon the experience of Time. The composer takes a piece of raw, undifferentiated duration and extracts from it, as the sculptor extracts the statue from his marble, a complex pattern of tones and silences, of harmonic sequences and contrapuntal interweavings. For the number of minutes it takes to play or listen to his composition, duration is transformed into something intrinsically significant, something held together by the internal logics of style and temperament, of personal feelings interacting with an artistic tradition, of creative insights expressing themselves within and beyond some given technical convention. This Fantasia, for example—with what a tireless persistence it drills its way through time! How effectively—and yet with no fuss, no self-conscious heroics—it transfigures the mortal lapse through time into the symbol, into the very fact, of a more than human life! A tunnel of joy and understanding had been driven through chaos and was demonstrating, for all to hear, that perpetual perishing is also perpetual creation. Which was precisely what our young friend had been telling us, in his own inimitable way, all the time. Usually destroyed—but also, and just as often, usually rebuilt. Like the rain, like sunshine, like the grace of God and the devastations of Nature, his verbalized tic was perfectly impartial. We walked out of the courtyard and down the narrow street. Bach faded, a donkey brayed, there was a smell of undisposed sewage. "In the year of Our Lord 1916," our guide informed us, "the Turkish Government usually massacred approximately seven hundred and fifty thousand Armenians."

TERMS and TOPICS

TERMS

1. **Vocabulary, Section II:** abrasive, abstruseness, acerbity, acute, adroitly, adulation, aesthetes, affronted, ambivalent, amorphous, anachronistic, androgynous, anthropomorphism, arrested, assiduously, blighted, brash, brazenly, busybody, chortle, chronic, compliance, connived, contraventions, corrupt, counterpoint, definitively, deleterious, demoralized, deprecated, deprivation, didactic, dispassionate, dissension, diverting, dotage, egregiously, elicited, elucidations, embargo, enigmatic, epitome, existential, expostulatory, felicitous, flagrantly, forgo, frivolous, gratuitous, hallowed, humanist, icons, impinged, implacable, incentive, individualistic, ineptitude, iniquitous, innocuous, introspective, jalopy, maxim, mimic, ontological, orthodox, ostensibly, palpably, pathological, penury, piecemeal, piety, pogrom, polemical, profligate, psyche, puberty, pugnacious, recluse, reticence, sadism, superficial, sweat shops, syndrome, umbrage

2. What does the word *interview* mean? Does knowing its origins—its *etymology*—help you understand its full meaning?

3. *Irony*   Verbal irony consists in saying one thing and meaning another, usually with at least some humorous intent. If it is raining cats and dogs, and someone looks out the window and says, "It's a great day for a picnic!" everyone understands the intended meaning. Verbal irony that is lacking in wit or cleverness, that is particularly crude and obvious, or that is especially biting or brutal, is usually called **sarcasm**. There are other kinds of irony; for example *dramatic irony*, common in literature, is present when a character knows less about his or her circumstances than the audience does, or when expectations are aroused but not fulfilled. Irony always involves contrast.

4. *Mask*   Another kind of irony is **Socratic irony**, so called because in Plato's dialogues Socrates characteristically pretends to be naive or ignorant in order to trap an opponent during an argument. In other words, figuratively speaking he wears a *mask* of innocence, though beneath it he is very wise indeed. Writers often put on such a mask, present a particular kind of image of themselves, adopt a *persona* or character other than their true or everyday one, in order to achieve certain rhetorical effects. An extreme and obvious example: In Browning's poem it is of course not Browning himself speaking but the Duke of Ferrara, the persona that Browning has assumed for the occasion of the poem. Interestingly, even the character the Duke presents could be considered a mask covering this true self. Could such a mask be useful for an interviewer as well as an interviewee?

5. *Caricature*   Exaggeration, whether in a picture or in words, of certain prominent features of the subject. If the features exaggerated are outstanding defects, caricature can be used to ridicule a subject.

TOPICS: On Individual Essays

NADINE GORDIMER *An Interview by Jannika Hurwitt*

1. What are Gordimer's views of politics in South Africa? Compare Gordimer's views on South African society with those of André Brink (section III).

2. How does the interviewer elicit information on Gordimer's childhood and parents, and of what relevance is this information to Gordimer's attitudes to such issues as those of power, belonging, race, the sense of "inside" or "outside"?

3. Try reading one of Gordimer's novels—for example *Burger's Daughter* or *The Conservationist*. Then explain what Gordimer means by "you can't write a novel like *Burger's Daughter* with the sensitivity of a Virginia Woolf."

4. Explain what Gordimer means by the following statements: "Commitment is not merely a political thing. It's part of the whole ontological problem in life." Writing is "seeking that thread of order and logic in the disorder, and the incredible waste and marvelous profligate character of life." You may wish to consult Berlin's essay on "The Purpose of Philosophy" (section IV).

5. What does Gordimer reveal about her sense of class? of women's role in society?

6. Discuss her closing quotation from Kafka.

NELLIE McCLUNG *"A Gentleman of the Old School"*

1. What does *suffrage* mean? What is its etymology? What is McClung quoting when she refers to "a tide in the affairs of men, which taken at the flood leads on to fortune"?

2. Were you surprised that the feminist movement and concerns about "the status of women" were so strong so long ago? Investigate the history of women's rights in Canadian society— perhaps write a research report. How successful were McClung and the women's suffrage movement? When did women get the vote in Canada? in England? in the United States?

3. Is there today, eighty years or so after what McClung describes, still an "other half"? How does it live?

4. What is McClung's attitude toward the Premier? What effect does she have on him? McClung uses direct statement, but the dialogues and monologues are more dramatically revealing. What attitudes toward women do the Premier's words convey—for example his use of the verb "ferret out"? Show how McClung uses the record of conversation to reveal the character and attitudes and expectations of the speakers.

5. Point out some of the occurrences of irony in this chapter. How is the title ironic?

6. Write an account of someone you know or have had dealings with. Reveal character indirectly—for example through conversation and through seemingly objective, straightforward description that implies more than is said.

MARGARET LANE   "The Ghost of Beatrix Potter"

1. What are the predilections of the "Freudian School" of criticism? What is a "Gioconda smile"? Are Beatrix Potter's illustrations anything like Constable's paintings?

2. Read, or re-read, some of Beatrix Potter's better early works and try to reconcile their author's personality, insofar as you can infer it, with the character of Mrs. Heelis that peers out of Lane's memoir about not meeting her.

3. How would you characterize the tone of Lane's piece? On what grounds?

4. Are the details Lane mentions or quotes sufficient to support her statement that Mrs. Heelis's reply to her letter was "the rudest letter I have ever received"? Do the details Lane provides make it believable that Mr. Heelis could have undergone so sudden and complete a turnabout in his attitude toward her and her inquiries? If not, does it matter—that is, can we simply take her word for it?

5. Where does Lane reveal things about herself? Are any of these revelations implicit, indirect?

6. Try psychoanalyzing the author of some piece of children's literature you know well.

7. Compose a brief essay about not meeting someone.

8. Write a character sketch of someone you know only by hearsay, such as a grandparent who died before you were born. In order to gather data, you may need to interview some people who did know your subject.

GUY DAVENPORT   "Wittgenstein"

1. Do some research on Klee, Bohr, Fuller, and the rest in order to get a sense of the significance of Davenport's many allusions. Is he name-dropping? How do Betty Hutton and Carmen Miranda fit into the company of Pythagoras, Wright, Kant, Mencius, and the rest?

2. In the first paragraph Davenport calls Wittgenstein "the most significant" "philosopher of our time." But then he refers to "his strange life," his dish-washing routine, his odd behaviour as a guest, his saying that his propositions will be recognized as "nonsensical," and his being "stubborn," "pig-headedly single-minded," "absurd," and so on. How can one possibly reconcile these and other points? Look up Wittgenstein in some standard encyclopedia or other reference work. Does Davenport seem to reveal a different man than the one you find discussed there? Which seems the more real, the more human, the more interesting? As a result of reading Davenport's essay, are you "hungry to know more" about Wittgenstein? Would you like to have met Wittgenstein? Why, or why not? What does the essay *tell* of the man, and what does it imply and reveal?

3. Try to answer, in writing, some of the questions posed at the end of the second paragraph and elsewhere in the essay. Is the absence of feeling a feeling?

4. Evaluate the force of the ending. Where does the ending begin?

5. Write a short impressionistic profile or sketch of some notable person you've learned about from reading. Don't necessarily play down the learned or serious side, the reputation for great achievements, but select and arrange your details so as to bring out your subject's more human character. Be sure to acknowledge all your sources.

JACK LUDWIG   *"The Calgary Stampede"*

1. Analyze Ludwig's third paragraph in order to determine the techniques that make it effective. Note everything that contributes to the effect, for example the diction (including slang and neologisms), the puns and other wordplay, the metaphors, the rhythm, the descriptive details, the length and movement of the whole paragraph. Note too the allusions—to the Bible, ancient Rome, and fairy tale—two of which Ludwig echoes at the end of the essay. Would you call this paragraph strongly subjective? How and what does it *reveal*?

2. Does Ludwig's overall attitude toward the Stampede seem to you to be favourable, un-favourable, or simply neutral?

3. Write an essay in which you use a basic, overall contrast to support your point, as Ludwig uses the contrast with "the midway hoke outside" to point up the qualities of "*the* Stampede," "the rodeo proper." Make the contrast *reveal* qualities of the subject you're focussing on. Is Ludwig's essay really about the competition and heroism of the rodeo? What proportion of attention does he devote to the two aspects?

4. Conduct several interviews with people engaged in some activity or event (a sporting event, such as a race or a golf tournament; a church bazaar or some other fund-raising enterprise; a reunion or some other kind of party). From whatever notes or tapes you collect, write up the event and its atmosphere, trying to portray it as seen through the eyes of the participants, but avoiding long stretches of quotation.

ANDREW A. ROONEY   *"A Penny Saved Is a Waste of Time"*

1. Is the order of the items in this list random, or is it carefully controlled? Are the pieces of advice of similar importance or seriousness? If not, why do you think Rooney includes them all? Is he trying to be funny? Is he trying to provoke thought? argument? Are any items too vague, general, or abstract to seem meaningful? Are any just plain confusing? If so, why are they there?

2. What does this list reveal about the character of its author? Do you like the Andy Rooney who comes through, or do you dislike him? Why? Write a character sketch showing what you think he must be like, based on the kind of advice he *forgot* to give. What advice do you think he *did* give?

3. Choose one of these pieces of advice and use it as a thesis statement for a brief explanatory essay (perhaps partly argumentative). For example, what are the implications of the final item? Does it make a good note to end on? Or choose one piece of advice with which you instinctively disagree and compose a brief argument countering it. What proverb is Rooney twisting in the title? Is he right to disagree with it?

4. Devise a list of your own for someone you care for: advice you'd give if you had something to do all over again, or advice you weren't given and wish you had been. What does your list reveal about you?

LAURENCE SHEEHAN   *"How to Play Second Base"*

1. Sheehan purports to be writing an instructional essay about "How to Play Second Base," but he wanders from that topic a great deal. Why does he keep digressing—apparently? How

has he controlled the wandering? What *persona* and tone does he establish, and by what means? How important is humour in this essay? How would you characterize the humour? What level of diction or style is he operating on? Are there any allusions (besides perhaps that to Ted Williams as "The Thumper")?

2. What is the essay about? It consists mainly of a long series of anecdotes—but are they about baseball, or something else? What is the point of the many details that have nothing to do with baseball? What does the essay *reveal* about life, courage, shame, or the refusal to be humiliated? Does the moral stated in the final few sentences seem to you a satisfactory conclusion? Does it manage somehow to pull all the seemingly disparate elements together?

3. Write an autobiographical essay ostensibly about participating in some sport or other activity, but handle your material so that the true purpose is to reveal one or more things about yourself, your friends, your community, or even life itself.

ALDOUS HUXLEY   "Usually Destroyed"

1. Are you likely to use the words *pullulations* and *condignly*? What do they mean? Is such diction appropriate in the context of Huxley's essay? Is his tone overtly formal, or is he just learned? Do any other words he uses seem unlikely candidates for your vocabulary? Might you surprise yourself and use them?

2. Look up any of the historical references you don't already know about, if only to get a feeling for the wide-ranging quality of Huxley's mind. Identify the allusions in "By the waters of Babylon" and "you aint' seen nuthin' yet." Do they sit comfortably together in the same essay?

3. It has now been well over a generation since Huxley wrote this essay. Consult some current sources of information in order to assess the accuracy of his predictions and of the others he mentions.

4. Is Huxley's principal concern what we now call *ecology*? What does the word mean, and when did it become current?

5. Examine the structure of Huxley's essay. Obviously the title and the beginning and ending point up a principal theme, but much other matter comes in between. How is it ordered? What is the relevance of each part to the whole?

6. Write a short essay in which you make use of some recurrent or choric phrase in the way Huxley does, repeating it throughout, sometimes with different effects, but building cumulatively to the end. The phrase might be a friend's comment that you can apply more broadly, or a slogan from advertising or politics, or any other phrase that—with a little thought—will yield greater significance and resonances than at first appear.

TOPICS: General and Comparative

1. It has been said that the basic principle of good interviewing is to *listen*. Do you agree? Is the reader of an interview turned into a listener? What other successful interviewing techniques can you think of?

2. Consider the way some of the essays in this section begin.

(a) Is Lane's second sentence—a fragmentary or minor sentence—effective as such? Can you improve the opening by revising what some would call an awkward and egregious error? In her third sentence Lane refers to irony. How ironic is her essay?

(b) Do Davenport's style and his reference in the opening paragraph to the fact that the "order" of Wittgenstein's slips of paper is "unascertainable" suggest something about both his treatment of his subject and the subject himself—something about fragments as opposed to sustained coherence, randomness as opposed to order?

(c) Note how much the vivid and unusual verbs and adjectives contribute to the description in Ludwig's opening paragraph. Try your hand at writing a descriptive paragraph, first with no adjectives at all and with only quiet verbs, then with imaginative verbs and adjectives like those Ludwig uses.

(d) How effective is Sheehan's beginning? Is he being purposely misleading?

(e) Huxley uses the word *labyrinthine* in his first sentence. How does this establish an idea that the essay as a whole will embroider? How does it relate to his comments on the relation between music and time?

3. Compare the techniques used by McClung, Lane, and Davenport to reveal aspects of their biographical subjects. What about Frayn (section VI)? How do biographical and autobiographical forms differ? Compare for example the selections by Lane and Davenport with those by Fisher, Haig-Brown, Mukherjee, and White (section I), Sheehan (section II), Dryden and Atwood (section IV), and MacEwen (section VI). Is all autobiographical writing automatically revealing?

4. Is Huxley saying that we customarily go about looking at the history of mankind in the wrong way? Consider his criticism of Toynbee: how just is it? What do some of the other essays in this book have to say about history and the way we view it? Start with Tuchman's essay in section III. (Interestingly, in another essay, called "In Search of History," Tuchman disparages "the genus Toynbee" as "systematizers." Would she agree with Huxley's criticisms?) Look also at least at Mukherjee and MacLennan (section I), and Brink (section III).

5. Compare Huxley's attitude toward technology with that of Glenn Gould (section III) and Lewis Thomas (section IV).

6. Gordimer discusses the exploitation of blacks in South Africa and the sharp contrast between rich and poor in New York City; Szasz (section III) refers to "appalling inequities between our treatment of the rich and the poor"; and note that Roueché (section IV) remarks that the poor are more likely to produce premature babies. Do any other writers in the book deal with distinctions of class and wealth? You may want to write an essay about some other instance of an implicit but strong distinction between how things go for the rich and how things go for the poor—or do you believe that in our society it isn't true that there is, in effect, one law for the rich and another for the poor? And what about those in between—the ever-present middle class?

7. To what degree do you think some of the writers in this section are wearing masks, adopting *personae* for the occasion?

8. Record a conversation verbatim. Does it sound natural and convincing as you have it written down? How do writers create the illusion of ordinary speech?

III

Writing to Persuade

By way of a preface: 1. This is the longest section in the book, so it's probably the best, and besides, we put a lot of work into it. 2. The undeniable quality of this section is clearly a result of the fact that one of us was given a lucky rabbit's foot just before we started working on it. 3. Intelligent readers will immediately recognize the importance and value of this section. 4. Previous readers of this section—sincere and professional people, some of them ministers and doctors, with a European education—all endorsed it strongly. 5. So if you don't like this section, you must have anchovy paste in your head instead of a brain, and you're probably a subversive too.

Our thesis in this section is quite straightforward. It is easy to write argumentatively. It is also easy to write logically, but logic and successful persuasion do not always go hand in hand. Even saying this is easy. But how can we prove it? That's the function of argumentative prose: to set out a thesis or proposition and prove it, or at least to persuade a reader or listener of the value or validity of a point of view or of a body of information. More than for any other kind of writing, therefore, argument depends upon engaging an audience.

Of course, preaching to the party faithful is easy, because there's little need for persuasion, logical or otherwise; all that's necessary is to trot out the slogans and the buzzwords that will confirm listeners in their existing belief. People say logic is persuasive. But logic will have little effect if listeners are already converted, so to speak—nor will it be of much use on an audience so committed to a contrary point of view that not even an earthquake would shake their commitment or their faith. And though logic should give a speaker some advantage, it is also true that illogical and emotional appeals are often successful. Sometimes, on these occasions, strict logic dissipates in a cloud of passion. If people are persuaded under such circumstances, one might well ask the question: Why?

The simple fact is that people make up and change their minds for countless reasons, some of them open, some covert, some rationally argued, some subliminally suggested. Such things, moreover, as fear, shame, moral outrage, nationalism, and emotional upheaval are among the most potent weapons a would-be influencer can use. Consider the five sample sentences at the beginning of this section. Are any of them convincing? Are any contentious? Do any seem "reasonable"? All are in some way emotional. And none of them is logical. Separately, therefore, they might or might not (a little equivocation here) be effective openings to an essay. Together, they illustrate some of the common ways that illogicalities creep into persuasive prose. The wary reader will be on the watch for these fallacies, whatever their guise. The conscious persuader uses them all the time. They have names, which may be useful as a guide to recognizing them:

1. Sentence 1 is an example both of the ***non sequitur*** (meaning "does not follow": size is not necessarily an indication of quality) and of ***special pleading*** (why should it matter how much time we spent?). Watch for any flaw in a writer's reasoning; every time you see terms like *so, therefore, must be, obviously, clearly, of course,* and *because*—those tools-of-the-trade of the persuasive writer—check that the logical connections they imply in fact make sense in context. Is this sentence, for example, even accurate?

2. Sentence 2 begins by ***begging the question***, assuming as given, or proved, what in fact needs to be proved ("undeniable quality"). And it demonstrates a process called ***post hoc ergo propter hoc*** ("after this therefore because of this"), which assumes a cause-effect relationship based on mere sequence. Superstitions, such as wearing good-luck charms because they supposedly make good things happen, are examples of ***post hoc*** thinking. We could also have claimed that because section II is so good, section III is bound to be better. It is true that persuasive writing often organizes details in climactic order (strong first, weakest next, then on to strongest last); but things don't necessarily get better (or worse) because they're older, younger, nearer, bigger, or next.

3. Sentence 3 involves ***argumentum ad populum*** ("argument directed at the people"), or an appeal to the reader to identify with some approved quality of character (here, intelligence). Such arguments appeal to people's emotions, their prejudices and fears.

4. Sentence 4 also uses a kind of *argumentum ad populum*, the invitation to get on a ***bandwagon***. As with the word "intelligent" in sentence 3, the implied message is "don't be left out." (Why do advertisers so often rely on this message? Why do consumers respond?) Sentence 4 also employs a covert ***appeal to authority***. Appeals to authority frequently rely on precedent, and they depend upon people's faith in some model. (Perhaps covertly, they also imply people's lack of faith in themselves.) The "authority" can

be the Bible, Aristotle, scientists, tradition, pop stars, the mayor, your Grade One teacher, a European education, or a variety of other persons and things. But ask: is it relevant to the case at hand? Is it truly authoritative? And is the language of the appeal *slanted* in any way: is it culturally biased, sexually biased, emotionally loaded? Check to see if an argument adequately takes contrary possibilities or points of view into account. A barrage of *statistics* often appears as a "proof," too, when 95% of the time (are you sure?) the questions that lead to the statistics are loaded or misleading, the statistical sample is too small to be valid, or the results are interpreted one-sidedly. Don't be bamboozled into belief.

5. Sentence 5 illustrates a combination of a false *either-or* option with *argumentum ad hominem* ("argument against the man"), which tries to divert attention from the question being discussed to the character of some person. *Name-calling, mudslinging, innuendo*: these are the techniques of gutter journalism and sleazy political contests. Anything else? Be wary of insults, stated or implied. Also be wary when offered only two options: "If you're not for us, you're against us," "If you're not *one of us*, you're *one of them*," "If you don't agree, you must be..." (Fill in the blank: *a Communist, a fascist, a radical, anti-American, from Toronto*). Ask yourself if there isn't another alternative. Beware the *false dilemma*.

Such fallacies are not always as clear as they are here. Those masters of persuasive rhetoric—politicians, lawyers, advertisers, salespeople, editorial writers, cult leaders, fashion designers, publicists, and con men—are frequently artists with verbal illusion. They can also of course be artists with logic. But given the contexts of their arguments, the wary reader will ask: What purpose does their logic serve?

Writing logically, a person can present a range of examples and invite readers to come to general conclusions *inductively*. By an alternative procedure, a writer can present a generalization or a series of generalizations and ask readers to come *deductively* to conclusions about particular examples. A typical form of deductive reasoning is called the *syllogism,* or syllogistic argument. Using this pattern, a writer will draw conclusions from the apparent connections between two *premises*, or "axiomatic" presumptions. Baldly stated, the form looks like this:

1. All bananas grow on trees.
2. This is a banana.
3. Therefore it grew on a tree.

Obviously such a pattern is open to distortion. Look what happens if the first premise is faulty or if the second premise doesn't connect appropriately with the first:

1. All human beings have brown eyes.
2. My brother has blue eyes.

3. Therefore my brother isn't human.

1. All dogs have legs.
2. My canary has legs.
3. Therefore my canary is a dog.

The false reasoning here is easy to see and therefore easy to dismiss, or avoid. Fallacies that are less easy to recognize are often found in expressions of people's prejudices and fears; the conclusions derive from faulty—but concealed—syllogisms, as in the following:

1. Americans hate communists.
2. X is spreading socialist ideas.
3. Therefore X is anti-American.

or:

1. Businessmen approve of politically rightwing economic measures.
2. X is a businessman.
3. Therefore X is a fascist at heart.

or, multiplying the premises somewhat:

1. We are nice people.
2. We speak English.
3. Our neighbours speak another language.
4. Therefore they are (a) not nice people, (b) not worth knowing, (c) responsible for our problems—the garbage in the lane, violence in the streets, crowding in the stores, the loss of our jobs, etc.

This last example illustrates the process of faulty reasoning that leads to the making of *scapegoats*—a way of blaming others for a problem, and victimizing them for it, instead of looking for a reasonable solution. In such circumstances, the premises are sometimes not even expressed; instead they have been consciously or unconsciously suppressed, so that just the conclusions appear—making the conclusions look like axioms when in fact they are just the invalid results of faulty reasoning. It is easy to see why polemical writers would try to stir up emotionally based animosities. And why they would try, even while doing so, to appeal to people's sense of the logic of it all. People like to think that they think about what they believe and what they do. But sometimes they don't. And people who never stop to think about the process of persuasion are the most susceptible to being manipulated.

Yet it does not follow that people who are passionate about ideas are necessarily irrational, or that people who reason their way to conclusions are necessarily cold. The essays in this section—examples of reviewing, feminist polemics, political statement, feature journalism, formal lecture, editorial comment, and "scientific" organization of evidence—all take contentious stances, sometimes for emotional reasons, sometimes out of a deep-seated intellectual commitment, sometimes for debate. They vary in tone. Some are solemn; some are witty; some are passionate; some are acid. None is neutral. And none is grey. Their styles are as individual as the styles of personal narratives: argument does not imply an absence of personality. Indeed, the overt presence of an authorial perspective often greatly aids a writer or speaker in reaching and holding—and hence influencing—the members of an audience.

Glenn Gould, for example, introduces humour into his argument (does Kael's caustic wit interfere with her judgment of sentimentality? Morgan and Meigs analyze forms of sexual politics (how do they differ from each other in tone and perspective as well as in particular subject?). Fulford and Brink both write of racism (how do their different national and political backgrounds affect their methods of argument?). The essays on psychiatry and language probe assumptions about society and behaviour (are they arguing for greater thoughtfulness, greater attention to what is going on?). In each case, who is the writer's chosen audience? Are you? And are you persuaded? (You don't have to be; but if you disagree with what these writers say, how reasoned, how valid—and how emotional—are your objections?)

A final word is necessary. Lest the foregoing points imply that reason explains everything, that passion proves nothing, and that all discoveries and judgments ought to be based on rigorous processes of logical thought, let us remind you of the *Eureka*! principle. When Archimedes leaped from his bath with a mathematical solution to the problem of displaced water, he undoubtedly had at least a glimmer of logical proof at the back of his mind. But sometimes reason is a servant rather than a leader. Sometimes the glimmer is a magnificent, unbidden leap of imaginative insight. Reason, then, can only trudge along after.

Politics and the English Language

George Orwell

Most people who bother with the matter at all would admit that the English language is in a bad way, but it is generally assumed that we cannot by conscious action do anything about it. Our civilization is decadent and our language—so the argument runs—must inevitably share in the general collapse. It follows that any struggle against the abuse of language is a sentimental archaism, like preferring candles to electric light or hansom cabs to aeroplanes. Underneath this lies the half-conscious belief that language is a natural growth and not an instrument which we shape for our own purposes.

Now, it is clear that the decline of a language must ultimately have political and economic causes: it is not due simply to the bad influence of this or that individual writer. But an effect can become a cause, reinforcing the original cause and producing the same effect in an intensified form, and so on indefinitely. A man may take to drink because he feels himself to be a failure, and then fail all the more completely because he drinks. It is rather the same thing that is happening to the English language. It becomes ugly and inaccurate because our thoughts are foolish, but the slovenliness of our language makes it easier for us to have foolish thoughts. The point is that the process is reversible. Modern English, especially written English, is full of bad habits which spread by imitation and which can be avoided if one is willing to take the necessary trouble. If one gets rid of these habits one can think more clearly, and to think clearly is a necessary first step towards political regeneration: so that the fight against bad English is not frivolous and is not the exclusive concern of professional writers. I will come back to this presently, and I hope that by that time the meaning of what I have said here will have become clearer. Meanwhile, here are five specimens of the English language as it is now habitually written.

These five passages have not been picked out because they are especially bad—I could have quoted far worse if I had chosen—but because they illustrate various of the mental vices from which we now suffer. They are a little below the average, but are fairly representative samples. I number them so that I can refer back to them when necessary:

(1) I am not, indeed, sure whether it is not true to say that the Milton who once seemed not unlike a seventeenth-century Shelley had not become, out of an experience ever more bitter in each year, more alien [*sic*] to the under of that Jesuit sect which nothing could induce him to tolerate.

> Professor Harold Laski (Essay in *Freedom of Expression*)

(2) Above all, we cannot play ducks and drakes with a native battery of idioms which prescribes such egregious collocations of vocables as the Basic *put up with* for *tolerate* or *put at a loss* for *bewilder*.

> Professor Lancelot Hogben (*Interglossa*)

(3) On the one side we have the free personality: by definition it is not neurotic, for it has neither conflict nor dream. Its desires, such as they are, are transparent, for they are just what institutional approval keeps in the forefront of consciousness; another institutional pattern would alter their number and intensity; there is little in them that is natural, irreducible, or culturally dangerous. But *on the other side*, the social bond itself is nothing but the mutual reflection of these self-secure integrities. Recall the definition of love. Is not this the very picture of a small academic? Where is there a place in this hall of mirrors for either personality or fraternity?

> Essay on psychology in *Politics* (New York)

(4) All the 'best people' from the gentlemen's clubs, and all the frantic fascist captains, united in common hatred of Socialism and bestial horror of the rising tide of the mass revolutionary movement, have turned to acts of provocation, to foul incendiarism, to medieval legends of poisoned wells, to legalize their own destruction of proletarian organizations, and rouse the agitated petty-bourgeoisie to chauvinistic fervour on behalf of the fight against the revolutionary way out of the crisis.

> Communist pamphlet

(5) If a new spirit *is* to be infused into this old country, there is one thorny and contentious reform which must be tackled, and that is the humanization and galvanization of the B.B.C. Timidity here will bespeak canker and atrophy of the soul. The heart of Britain may be sound and of strong beat, for instance, but the British lion's roar at present is like that of Bottom in Shakespeare's *Midsummer Night's Dream*—as gentle as any sucking dove. A virile new Britain cannot continue indefinitely to be traduced in the eyes or rather ears, of the world by the effete languors of Langham Place, brazenly masquerading as 'standard English'. When the Voice of Britain is heard at nine o'clock, better far and infinitely less ludicrous to hear aitches honestly dropped than the present priggish, inflated, inhibited, school-ma'amish arch braying of blameless bashful mewing maidens!

> Letter in *Tribune*

Each of these passages has faults of its own, but, quite apart from avoidable ugliness, two qualities are common to all of them. The first is staleness of imagery: the other is lack of precision. The writer either has a meaning and cannot express it, or he inadvertently says something else, or he is almost indifferent as to whether his words mean anything or not. This mixture of vagueness and sheer incompetence is the most marked characteristic of modern English prose, and especially of any kind of political writing. As soon as certain topics are raised, the concrete melts into the abstract and no one seems able to think of turns of speech that are not hackneyed: prose consists less and less of *words* chosen for the sake of their meaning, and more and more of *phrases* tacked together like the sections of a prefabricated henhouse. I list below, with notes and examples, various of the tricks by means of which the work of prose-construction is habitually dodged:

DYING METAPHORS. A newly invented metaphor assists thought by evoking a visual image, while on the other hand a metaphor which is technically 'dead' (e.g. *iron resolution*) has in effect reverted to being an ordinary word and can generally be used without loss of vividness. But in between these two classes there is a huge dump of worn-out metaphors which have lost all evocative power and are merely used because they save people the trouble of inventing phrases for themselves. Examples are: *Ring the changes on, take up the cudgels for, toe the line, ride roughshod over, stand shoulder to shoulder with, play into the hands of, no axe to grind, grist to the mill, fishing in troubled waters, on the order of the day, Achilles' heel, swan song, hotbed.* Many of these are used without knowledge of their meaning (what is a 'rift', for instance?), and incompatible metaphors are frequently mixed, a sure sign that the writer is not interested in what he is saying. Some metaphors now current have been twisted out of their original meaning without those who use them even being aware of the fact. For example, *toe the line* is sometimes written *tow the line*. Another example is the *hammer and the anvil*, now always used with the implication that the anvil gets the worst of it. In real life it is always the anvil that breaks the hammer, never the other way about: a writer who stopped to think what he was saying would be aware of this, and would avoid perverting the original phrase.

OPERATORS OR VERBAL FALSE LIMBS. These save the trouble of picking out appropriate verbs and nouns, and at the same time pad each sentence with extra syllables which give it an appearance of symmetry. Characteristic phrases are: *render inoperative, militate against, make contact with, be subjected to, give rise to, give grounds for, have the effect of, play a leading part (role) in, make itself felt, take effect, exhibit a tendency to, serve the purpose of, etc., etc.* The keynote is the elimination of simple verbs. Instead of being a single word, such as *break, stop, spoil, mend, kill*, a verb becomes a *phrase*, made up of a noun or adjective tacked on to some general-purposes verb such as *prove, serve, form, play, render*. In addition, the passive voice is wherever possible used in preference to the active, and noun constructions are used instead of gerunds (*by examination of* instead of *by examining*). The range of verbs is further cut down by means of the *-ize* and *de-* formations, and the banal statements are given an appearance of profundity by means of the *not un-* formation. Simple conjunctions and prepositions are replaced by such phrases as *with respect to, having regard to, the fact that, by dint of, in view of, in the interests of, on the hypothesis that*; and the ends of sentences are saved from anticlimax by such resounding common-places as *greatly to be desired, cannot be left out of account, a development to be expected in the near future, deserving of serious consideration, brought to a satisfactory conclusion,* and so on and so forth.

PRETENTIOUS DICTION. Words like *phenomenon, element, individual* (as noun), *objective, categorical, effective, virtual, basic, primary, promote, constitute, exhibit, exploit, utilize, eliminate, liquidate,* are used to dress up simple statement and give an air of scientific impartiality to biased judgments. Adjectives like *epoch-making, epic, historic, unforgettable, triumphant, age-old, inevitable, inexorable, veritable,* are used to dignify the sordid processes of international politics, while writing that aims at glorifying war usually takes on an archaic colour, its characteristic words being: *realm, throne, chariot, mailed fist, trident, sword, shield, buckler, banner, jackboot, clarion.* Foreign words and expressions such as *cul de sac, ancien régime, deus ex machina, mutatis mutandis, status quo, gleichschaltung, weltanschauung,* are used to give an air of culture and elegance. Except for the useful abbreviations *i.e., e.g.,* and *etc.,* there is no real need for any of the hundreds of foreign phrases now current in English. Bad writers, and especially scientific, political and sociological writers, are nearly always haunted by the notion that Latin or Greek words are grander than Saxon ones, and unnecessary words like *expedite, ameliorate, predict, extraneous, deracinated, clandestine, subaqueous* and hundreds of others constantly gain ground from their Anglo-Saxon opposite numbers.[1] The jargon peculiar to Marxist writing (*hyena, hangman, cannibal, petty bourgeois, these gentry, lacquey, flunkey, mad dog, White Guard,* etc.) consists largely of words and phrases translated from Russian, German or French; but the normal way of coining a new word is to use a Latin or Greek root with the appropriate affix and, where necessary, the -ize formation. It is often easier to make up words of this kind (*deregionalize, impermissible, extramarital, non-fragmentatory* and so forth) than to think up the English words that will cover one's meaning. The result, in general, is an increase in slovenliness and vagueness.

MEANINGLESS WORDS. In certain kinds of writing, particularly in art criticism and literary criticism, it is normal to come across long passages which are almost completely lacking in meaning.[2] Words like *romantic, plastic, values, human, dead, sentimental, natural, vitality,* as used in art criticism, are strictly

---

[1] An interesting illustration of this is the way in which the English flower names which were in use till very recently are being ousted by Greek ones, snapdragon becoming antirrhinum, forget-me-not becoming myosotis, etc. It is hard to see any practical reason for this change of fashion: it is probably due to an instinctive turning-away from the more homely word and a vague feeling that the Greek word is scientific.

[2] Example: 'Comfort's catholicity of perception and image, strangely Whitmanesque in range, almost the exact opposite in aesthetic compulsion, continues to evoke that trembling atmospheric accumulative hinting at a cruel, an inexorably serene timelessness . . . . Wrey Gardiner scores by aiming at simple bull's-eyes with precision. Only they are not so simple, and through this contented sadness runs more than the surface bitter-sweet of resignation.' (*Poetry Quarterly*)

meaningless, in the sense that they not only do not point to any discoverable object, but are hardly ever expected to do so by the reader. When one critic writes, 'The outstanding feature of Mr X's work is its living quality', while another writes, 'The immediately striking thing about Mr X's work is its peculiar deadness', the reader accepts this as a simple difference of opinion. If words like *black* and *white* were involved, instead of the jargon words *dead* and *living*, he would see at once that language was being used in an improper way. Many political words are similarly abused. The word *Fascism* has now no meaning except in so far as it signifies 'something not desirable'. The words *democracy, socialism, freedom, patriotic, realistic, justice,* have each of them several different meanings which cannot be reconciled with one another. In the case of a word like *democracy,* not only is there no agreed definition but the attempt to make one is resisted from all sides. It is almost universally felt that when we call a country democratic we are praising it: consequently the defenders of every kind of régime claim that it is a democracy, and fear that they might have to stop using the word if it were tied down to any one meaning. Words of this kind are often used in a consciously dishonest way. That is, the person who uses them has his own private definition, but allows his hearer to think he means something quite different. Statements like *Marshal Pétain was a true patriot, The Soviet Press is the freest in the world, the Catholic Church is opposed to persecution,* are almost always made with intent to deceive. Other words used in variable meanings, in most cases more or less dishonestly, are: *class, totalitarian, science, progressive, reactionary, bourgeois, equality.*

Now that I have made this catalogue of swindles and perversions, let me give another example of the kind of writing that they lead to. This time it must of its nature be an imaginary one. I am going to translate a passage of good English into modern English of the worst sort. Here is a well-known verse from *Ecclesiastes*:

> I returned and saw under the sun, that the race is not to the swift, nor the battle to the strong, neither yet bread to the wise, nor yet riches to men of understanding, nor yet favour to men of skill; but time and chance happeneth to them all.

Here it is in modern English:

> Objective consideration of contemporary phenomena compels the conclusion that success or failure in competitive activities exhibits no tendency to be commensurate with innate capacity, but that a considerable element of the unpredictable must invariably be taken into account.

This is a parody, but not a very gross one. Exhibit (3), above, for instance, contains several patches of the same kind of English. It will be seen that I have not made a full translation. The beginning and ending of the sentence follow the original meaning fairly closely, but in the middle the concrete illustrations—race, battle, bread—dissolve into the vague phrase 'success or failure in competitive activities'. This had to be so, because no modern writer of the kind I am discussing—no one capable of using phrases like 'objective consideration of contemporary phenomena'—would ever tabulate his thoughts in that precise and detailed way. The whole tendency of modern prose is away from concreteness. Now analyse these two sentences a little more closely. The first contains forty-nine words but only sixty syllables, and all its words are those of everyday life. The second contains thirty-eight words of ninety syllables: eighteen of its words are from Latin roots, and one from Greek. The first sentence contains six vivid images, and only one phrase ('time and chance') that could be called vague. The second contains not a single fresh, arresting phrase, and in spite of its ninety syllables it gives only a shortened version of the meaning contained in the first. Yet without a doubt it is the second kind of sentence that is gaining ground in modern English. I do not want to exaggerate. This kind of writing is not yet universal, and outcrops of simplicity will occur here and there in the worst-written page. Still, if you or I were told to write a few lines on the uncertainty of human fortunes, we should probably come much nearer to my imaginary sentence than to the one from *Ecclesiastes*.

As I have tried to show, modern writing at its worst does not consist in picking out words for the sake of their meaning and inventing images in order to make the meaning clearer. It consists in gumming together long strips of words which have already been set in order by someone else, and making the results presentable by sheer humbug. The attraction of this way of writing is that it is easy. It is easier—even quicker, once you have the habit—to say *In my opinion it is a not unjustifiable assumption that* than to say *I think*. If you use ready-made phrases, you not only don't have to hunt about for words; you also don't have to bother with the rhythms of your sentences, since these phrases are generally so arranged as to be more or less euphonious. When you are composing in a hurry—when you are dictating to a stenographer, for instance, or making a public speech—it is natural to fall into a pretentious, Latinized style. Tags like *a consideration which we should do well to bear in mind* or *a conclusion to which all of us would readily assent* will save many a sentence from coming down with a bump. By using stale metaphors, similes and idioms, you save much mental effort, at the cost of leaving your meaning vague, not only for your reader but for yourself. This is the significance of mixed metaphors. The sole aim of a metaphor is to call up a visual image. When these images clash—as in The *Fascist octopus has sung its swan song, the jackboot is thrown into the melting pot*—it can be taken as certain that the writer is not seeing a mental image of the objects he is naming; in other words he is not really thinking. Look again at the examples I gave at the beginning of this essay. Professor Laski (1) uses five negatives in fifty-three words. One of these is superfluous, making nonsense of the whole passage, and in addition there is the slip *alien* for akin, making further nonsense, and several avoidable pieces of clumsiness which increase the general vagueness. Professor Hogben (2) plays ducks and drakes with a battery which is able to write prescriptions, and, while disapproving of the everyday phrase *put up with*, is unwilling to look *egregious* up in the dictionary and see what it means. (3), if one takes an uncharitable attitude towards it, is simply meaningless: probably one could work out its intended meaning by reading the whole of the article in which it occurs. In (4), the writer knows more or less what he wants to say, but an accumulation of stale phrases chokes him like tea leaves blocking a sink. In (5), words and meaning have almost parted company. People who write in this manner usually have a general emotional meaning—they dislike one thing and want to express solidarity with another—but they are not interested in the detail of what they are saying. A scrupulous writer, in every sentence that he writes, will ask himself at least four questions, thus: What am I trying to say? What words will express it? What image or idiom will make it clearer? Is this image fresh enough to have an effect? And he will probably ask himself two more: Could I put it more shortly? Have I said anything that is avoidably ugly? But you are not obliged to go to all this trouble. You can shirk it by simply throwing your mind open and letting the ready-made phrases come crowding in. They will construct your sentences for you—even think your thoughts for you, to a certain extent—and at need they will perform the important service of partially concealing your meaning even from yourself. It is at this point that the special connexion between politics and the debasement of language becomes clear.

In our time it is broadly true that political writing is bad writing. Where it is not true, it will generally be found that the writer is some kind of rebel, expressing his private opinions and not a 'party line'. Orthodoxy, of whatever colour, seems to demand a lifeless, imitative style. The political dialects to be found in pamphlets, leading articles, manifestos, White Papers and the speeches of under-secretaries do, of course, vary from party to party, but they are all alike in that one almost never finds in them a fresh, vivid, home-made turn of speech. When one watches some tired hack on the platform mechanically repeating the familiar phrases—*bestial atrocities, iron heel, bloodstained tyranny, free peoples of the world, stand shoulder to shoulder*—one often has a curious feeling that one is not watching a live human being but some kind of dummy: a feeling which suddenly becomes stronger at moments when the light catches the speaker's spectacles and turns them into blank discs which seem to have no eyes behind them. And this is not altogether fanciful. A speaker who uses that kind of phraseology has gone some distance towards turning himself into a machine. The appropriate noises are coming out of his larynx, but his brain is not involved as it would be if he were choosing his words for himself. If the speech he is making is one that he is accustomed to make over and over again, he may be almost unconscious of what he is saying, as one is when one utters the responses in church. And this reduced state of consciousness, if not indispensable, is at any rate favourable to political conformity.

In our time, political speech and writing are largely the defence of the indefensible. Things like the continuance of British rule in India, the Russian purges and deportations, the dropping of the atom bombs on Japan, can indeed be defended, but only by arguments which are too brutal for most people to face, and which do not square with the professed aims of political parties. Thus political language has to consist largely of euphemism, question-begging and sheer cloudy vagueness. Defenseless villages are bombarded from the air, the inhabitants driven out into the countryside, the cattle machine-gunned, the huts set on fire with incendiary bullets: this is called *pacification.* Millions of peasants are robbed of their farms and sent trudging along the roads with no more than they can carry: this is called *transfer of population* or *rectification of frontiers.* People are imprisoned for years without trial, or shot in the back of the neck or sent to die of scurvy in Arctic lumber camps: this is called *elimination of unreliable elements.* Such phraseology is needed if one wants to name things without calling up mental pictures of them. Consider for instance some comfortable English professor defending Russian totalitarianism. He cannot say outright, 'I believe in killing off your opponents when you can get good results by doing so'. Probably, therefore, he will say something like this:

'While freely conceding that the Soviet regime exhibits certain features which the humanitarian may be inclined to deplore, we must, I think, agree that a certain curtailment of the right to political opposition is an unavoidable concomitant of transitional periods, and that the rigours which the Russian people have been called upon to undergo have been amply justified in the sphere of concrete achievement.'

The inflated style is itself a kind of euphemism. A mass of Latin words falls upon the facts like soft snow, blurring the outlines and covering up all the details. The great enemy of clear language is insincerity. When there is a gap between one's real and one's declared aims, one turns as it were instinctively to long words and exhausted idioms, like a cuttlefish squirting out ink. In our age there is no such thing as 'keeping out of politics'. All issues are political issues, and politics itself is a mass of lies, evasions, folly, hatred and schizophrenia. When the general atmosphere is bad, language must suffer. I should expect to find—this is a guess which I have not sufficient knowledge to verify—that the German, Russian and Italian languages have all deteriorated in the last ten or fifteen years, as a result of dictatorship.

But if thought corrupts language, language can also corrupt thought. A bad usage can spread by tradition and imitation, even among people who should and do know better. The debased language that I have been discussing is in some ways very convenient. Phrases like *a not unjustifiable assumption, leaves much to be desired, would serve no good purpose, a consideration which we should do well to bear in mind*, are a continuous temptation, a packet of aspirins always at one's elbow. Look back through this essay, and for certain you will find that I have again and again committed the very faults I am protesting against. By this morning's post I have received a pamphlet dealing with conditions in Germany. The author tells me that he 'felt impelled' to write it.

I open it at random, and here is almost the first sentence that I see: '(The Allies) have an opportunity not only of achieving a radical transformation of Germany's social and political structure in such a way as to avoid a nationalistic reaction in Germany itself, but at the same time of laying the foundations of a co-operative and unified Europe.' You see, he 'feels impelled' to write— feels, presumably, that he has something new to say—and yet his words, like cavalry horses answering the bugle, group themselves automatically into the familiar dreary pattern. This invasion of one's mind by ready-made phrases (*lay the foundations, achieve a radical transformation*) can only be prevented if one is constantly on guard against them, and every such phrase anaesthetizes a portion of one's brain.

I said earlier that the decadence of our language is probably curable. Those who deny this would argue, if they produced an argument at all, that language merely reflects existing social conditions, and that we cannot influence its development by any direct tinkering with words and constructions. So far as the general tone or spirit of a language goes, this may be true, but it is not true in detail. Silly words and expressions have often disappeared, not through any evolutionary process but owing to the conscious action of a minority. Two recent examples were *explore every avenue* and *leave no stone unturned*, which were killed by the jeers of a few journalists. There is a long list of flyblown metaphors which could similarly be got rid of if enough people would interest themselves in the job; and it should also be possible to laugh the *not un*-formation out of existence,[3] to reduce the amount of Latin and Greek in the average sentence, to drive out foreign phrases and strayed scientific words, and, in general, to make pretentiousness unfashionable. But all these are minor points. The defence of the English language implies more than this, and perhaps it is best to start by saying what it does *not* imply.

To begin with it has nothing to do with archaism, with the salvaging of obsolete words and turns of speech, or with the setting up of a 'standard English' which must never be departed from. On the contrary, it is especially concerned with the scrapping of every word or idiom which has outworn its usefulness. It has nothing to do with correct grammar and syntax, which are of no importance so long as one makes one's meaning clear, or with the avoidance of Americanisms, or with having what is called a 'good prose style'. On the other hand it is not concerned with fake simplicity and the attempt to make written English colloquial. Nor does it even imply in every case preferring the Saxon word to the Latin one, though it does imply using the fewest and shortest words that will cover one's meaning. What is above all needed is to let the meaning choose the word, and not the other way about. In prose, the worst thing one can do with words is to surrender to them. When you think of a concrete object, you think wordlessly, and then, if you want to Probably it is better to put off using words as long as possible and get one's

---

[3] One can cure oneself of the *not un*-formation by memorizing this sentence: *A not unblack dog was chasing a not unsmall rabbit across a not ungreen field.*

meaning as clear as one can through pictures or sensations. Afterwards one can choose—not simply *accept*—the phrases that will best cover the meaning, describe the thing you have been visualizing you probably hunt about till you find the exact words that seem to fit it. When you think of something abstract you are more inclined to use words from the start, and unless you make a conscious effort to prevent it, the existing dialect will come rushing in and do the job for you, at the expense of blurring or even changing your meaning. and then switch round and decide what impression one's words are likely to make on another person. This last effort of the mind cuts out all stale or mixed images, all prefabricated phrases, needless repetitions, and humbug and vagueness generally. But one can often be in doubt about the effect of a word or a phrase, and one needs rules that one can rely on when instinct fails. I think the following rules will cover most cases:

(i) Never use a metaphor, simile or other figure of speech which you are used to seeing in print.

(ii) Never use a long word where a short one will do.

(iii) If it is possible to cut out a word, always cut it out.

(iv) Never use the passive where you can use the active.

(v) Never use a foreign phrase, a scientific word or a jargon word if you can think of an everyday English equivalent.

(vi) Break any of these rules sooner than say anything outright barbarous.

These rules sound elementary, and so they are, but they demand a deep change of attitude in anyone who has grown used to writing in the style now fashionable. One could keep all of them and still write bad English, but one could not write the kind of stuff that I quoted in those five specimens at the beginning of this article.

I have not here been considering the literary use of language, but merely language as an instrument for expressing and not for concealing or preventing thought. Stuart Chase and others have come near to claiming that all abstract words are meaningless, and have used this as a pretext for advocating a kind of political quietism. Since you don't know what Fascism is, how can you struggle against Fascism? One need not swallow such absurdities as this, but one ought to recognize that the present political chaos is connected with the decay of language, and that one can probably bring about some improvement by starting at the verbal end. If you simplify your English, you are freed from the worst follies of orthodoxy. You cannot speak any of the necessary dialects, and when you make a stupid remark its stupidity will be obvious, even to yourself. Political language—and with variations this is true of all political parties, from Conservatives to Anarchists—is designed to make lies sound truthful and murder respectable, and to give an appearance of solidity to pure wind. One cannot change this all in a moment, but one can at least change one's own habits, and from time to time one can even, if one jeers loudly enough, send some worn-out and useless phrase—some *jackboot, Achilles' heel, hotbed, melting pot, acid test, veritable inferno* or other lump of verbal refuse—into the dustbin where it belongs.

The Sound of...

The Sound of Music and
The Singing Nun

Pauline Kael

The Singing Nun will make you realize how good Fred Zinnemann's *The Nun's Story* was. Although the theme, the conflict and even the story line are similar, *The Singing Nun* reduces them to smiles, twinkles, banalities and falseness. It is almost a parody of *The Nun's Story* and, of course, without the courage of the conclusion of that earlier thoughtful, subtle film. Though *The Singing Nun* draws its ideas from *The Nun's Story*, its inspiration is obviously that movie phenomenon the trade press now refers to (very respectfully) as *The Sound of Money*. And perhaps to get at what goes on in a movie like *The Singing Nun*, we need to look at that phenomenon, which is so often called "wholesome" but which is probably going to be the single most repressive influence on artistic freedom in movies for the next few years.

The success of a movie like *The Sound of Music* makes it even more difficult for anyone to try to do anything worth doing, anything relevant to the modern world, anything inventive or expressive. The banks, the studios, the producers will want to give the public what it seems to crave. The more money these "wholesome" movies make, the less wholesome will the state of American movies be. "The opium of the audience," Luis Bunuel, the Spanish director, once said, "is conformity." And nothing is more degrading and ultimately destructive to artists than supplying the narcotic.

What is it that makes millions of people buy and like *The Sound of Music*—a tribute to "freshness" that is so mechanically engineered, so shrewdly calculated that the background music rises, the already soft focus blurs and melts, and, upon the instant, you can hear all those noses blowing in the theatre? Of course, it's well done for what it is: that is to say, those who made it are experts at manipulating responses. They're the Pavlovs of movie-making: they turn us into dogs that salivate on signal. When the cruel father sees the light and says, "You've brought music back into the house," who can resist the pull at the emotions? It's that same tug at the heartstrings we feel when Lassie comes home or when the blind heroine sees for the first time; it is a simple variant of that surge of warmth we feel when a child is reunited with his parents. It's basic, and there are probably few of us who don't respond. But it is the easiest and perhaps the most primitive kind of emotion that we are made to feel. The worst despots in history, the most cynical purveyors of mass culture respond

161

at *this* level and may feel pleased at how tenderhearted they *really* are because they do. This kind of response has as little to do with generosity of feeling as being stirred when you hear a band has to do with patriotism.

I think it is not going too far to say that when an expensive product of modern technology like *The Sound of Music* uses this sort of "universal" appeal, it is because nothing could be safer, nothing could be surer. Whom could it offend? Only those of us who, *despite the fact that we may respond*, loathe being manipulated in this way and are aware of how self-indulgent and cheap and ready-made are the responses we are made to feel. And we may become even more aware of the way we have been used and turned into emotional and aesthetic imbeciles when we hear ourselves humming those sickly, goody-goody songs. The audience for a movie of this kind becomes the lowest common denominator of feeling: a sponge. The heroine leaves the nuns at the fence as she enters the cathedral to be married. Squeezed again, and the moisture comes out of thousands—millions—of eyes and noses.

And the phenomenon at the center of the monetary phenomenon? Julie Andrews, with the clean, scrubbed look and the unyieldingly high spirits; the good sport who makes the best of everything; the girl who's so unquestionably good that she carries this one dimension like a shield. The perfect, perky schoolgirl, the adorable tomboy, the gawky colt. Sexless, inhumanly happy, the sparkling maid, a mind as clean and well brushed as her teeth. What is she? Merely the ideal heroine for the best of all possible worlds. And that's what *The Sound of Music* pretends we live in.

Audiences are transported into a world of operetta cheerfulness and calendar art. You begin to feel as if you've never got out of school. Up there on the screen, they're all in their places with bright, shining faces. Wasn't there perhaps one little Von Trapp who didn't want to sing his head off, or who screamed that he wouldn't act out little glockenspiel routines for Papa's party guests, or who got nervous and threw up if he had to get on a stage? No, nothing mars this celebration of togetherness. Not only does this family sing together, they play ball together. This is the world teachers used to pretend (and maybe still pretend?) was the real world. It's the world in which the governess conquers all. It's the big lie, the sugarcoated lie that people seem to want to eat. They even seem to think they should feed it to their kids, that it's healthy, wonderful "family entertainment."

And this is the sort of attitude that makes a critic feel that maybe it's all hopeless. Why not just send the director, Robert Wise, a wire: "You win, I give up," or, rather, "We both lose, we all lose."

Yet there was a spider on the valentine: the sinister, unpleasant, archly decadent performance Christopher Plummer gives as the baron, he of the thin, twisted smile—my candidate for the man least likely to be accepted as a hero. Even the monstrously ingenious technicians who made this movie couldn't put together a convincing mate for Super Goody Two-Shoes. The dauntless heroine surmounts this obstacle: in the romantic scenes, she makes love to herself. And why not? We never believed for a moment that love or marriage would affect her or change her. She was already perfection.

Debbie Reynolds, as the character based on Soeur Sourire in *The Singing Nun*, is less than perfection. Her eyes are not so clear and bright, indeed they're rather anxious and, yes, almost bleary; and her singing isn't pure and pretty, it's sort of tacky and ordinary. So is the whole production. Henry Koster doesn't succeed even in making it very convincingly "wholesome." The religion is a familiar kind of Hollywood Christianity. The nuns are even more smiley and giggly—like a mush-headed schoolteacher's dream of ideally happy schoolchildren; Ricardo Montalban is a simperingly simple priest; and though Agnes Moorehead plays a nun like a witch, she is more than balanced by Greer Garson as the Mother Prioress. With her false eyelashes and her richly condescending manner, Greer Garson can turn any line of dialogue into incomparable cant. It's a gift, of a kind.

The people in *The Singing Nun* behave like the animals in a Disney movie: they are so cute and so full of little tricks. There are chintzy little pedagogical songs that are supposed to be full of *joy*, and there is Debbie's excruciating humility. "I have a lot to learn," she tells us; but we didn't need to be told. She gives up her singing career—which was giving her too much attention and adoration—in order to find her simple faith again. And so, at the end, we see her working as a nurse in Africa, posed like a madonna holding a Negro baby, surrounded by attentive, adoring Africans....But then, of course, this movie is the kind of spiritual exercise in which the nuns say a little prayer for Ed Sullivan every day.

Why am I so angry about these movies? Because the shoddy falseness of *The Singing Nun* and the luxuriant falseness of *The Sound of Music* are part of the sentimental American tone that makes honest work almost impossible. It is not only that people who accept this kind of movie tend to resent work which says that this is not the best of all possible worlds, but that people who are gifted give up the effort to say anything. They attune themselves to *The Sound of Money*.

Total Effect and the Eighth Grade

Flannery O'Connor

In two recent instances in Georgia, parents have objected to their eighth- and ninth-grade children's reading assignments in modern fiction. This seems to happen with some regularity in cases throughout the country. The unwitting parent picks up his child's book, glances through it, comes upon passages of erotic detail or profanity, and takes off at once to complain to the school board. Sometimes, as in one of the Georgia cases, the teacher is dismissed and hackles rise in liberal circles everywhere.

The two cases in Georgia, which involved Steinbeck's *East of Eden* and John Hersey's *A Bell for Adano*, provoked considerable newspaper comment. One columnist, in commending the enterprise of the teachers, announced that students do not like to read the fusty works of the nineteenth century, that their attention can best be held by novels dealing with the realities of our own time, and that the Bible, too, is full of racy stories.

Mr. Hersey himself addressed a letter to the State School Superintendent in behalf of the teacher who had been dismissed. He pointed out that his book is not scandalous, that it attempts to convey an earnest message about the nature of democracy, and that it falls well within the limits of the principle of "total effect," that principle followed in legal cases by which a book is judged not for isolated parts but by the final effect of the whole book upon the general reader.

I do not want to comment on the merits of these particular cases. What concerns me is what novels ought to be assigned in the eighth and ninth grades as a matter of course, for if these cases indicate anything, they indicate the haphazard way in which fiction is approached in our high schools. Presumably there is a state reading list which contains "safe" books for teachers to assign; after that it is up to the teacher.

English teachers come in Good, Bad, and Indifferent, but too frequently in high schools anyone who can speak English is allowed to teach it. Since several novels can't easily be gathered into one textbook, the fiction that students are assigned depends upon their teacher's knowledge, ability, and taste: variable factors at best. More often than not, the teacher assigns what he thinks will hold the attention and interest of the students. Modern fiction will certainly hold it.

Ours is the first age in history which has asked the child what he would tolerate learning, but that is a part of the problem with which I am not equipped to deal. The devil of Educationism that possesses us is the kind that can be "cast out only by prayer and fasting." No one has yet come along strong enough to do it. In other ages the attention of children was held by Homer and Virgil, among others, but, by the reverse evolutionary process, that is no longer possible; our children are too stupid now to enter the past imaginatively. No one asks the student if algebra pleases him or if he finds it satisfactory that some French verbs are irregular, but if he prefers Hersey to Hawthorne, his taste must prevail.

I would like to put forward the proposition, repugnant to most English teachers, that fiction, if it is going to be taught in the high schools, should be taught as a subject and as a subject with a history. The total effect of a novel depends not only on its innate impact, but upon the experience, literary and otherwise, with which it is approached. No child needs to be assigned Hersey or Steinbeck until he is familiar with a certain amount of the best works of Cooper, Hawthorne, Melville, the early James, and Crane, and he does not need to be assigned these until he has been introduced to some of the better English novelists of the eighteenth and nineteenth centuries.

The fact that these works do not present him with the realities of his own time is all to the good. He is surrounded by the realities of his own time, and he has no perspective whatever from which to view them. Like the college student who wrote in her paper on Lincoln that he went to the movies and got shot, many students go to college unaware that the world was not made yesterday; their studies began with the present and dipped backward occasionally when it seemed necessary or unavoidable.

There is much to be enjoyed in the great British novels of the nineteenth century, much that a good teacher can open up in them for the young student. There is no reason why these novels should be either too simple or too difficult for the eighth grade. For the simple, they offer simple pleasures; for the more precocious, they can be made to yield subtler ones if the teacher is up to it. Let the student discover, after reading the nineteenth-century British novel, that the nineteenth-century American novel is quite different as to its literary characteristics, and he will thereby learn something not only about these individual works but about the sea-change which a new historical situation can effect in a literary form. Let him come to modern fiction with this experience behind him, and he will be better able to see and to deal with the more complicated demands of the best twentieth-century fiction.

Modern fiction often looks simpler than the fiction that preceded it, but in reality it is more complex. A natural evolution has taken place. The author has for the most part absented himself from direct participation in the work and has left the reader to make his own way amid experiences dramatically rendered and symbolically ordered. The modern novelist merges the reader in the experience; he tends to raise the passions he touches upon. If he is a good novelist, he raises them to effect by their order and clarity a new experience—the total effect—which is not in itself sensuous or simply of the moment. Unless the child has had some literary experience before, he is not going to be able to resolve the immediate passions the book arouses into any true, total picture.

It is here the moral problem will arise. It is one thing for a child to read about adultery in the Bible or in *Anna Karenina,* and quite another for him to read about it in most modern fiction. This is not only because in both the former instances adultery is considered a sin, and in the latter, at most, an inconvenience, but because modern writing involves the reader in the action with a new degree of intensity, and literary mores now permit him to be involved in any action a human being can perform.

In our fractured culture, we cannot agree on morals; we cannot even agree that moral matters should come before literary ones when there is a conflict between them. All this is another reason why the high schools would do well to return to their proper business of preparing foundations. Whether in the senior year students should be assigned modern novelists should depend both on their parents' consent and on what they have already read and understood.

The high-school English teacher will be fulfilling his responsibility if he furnishes the student a guided opportunity, through the best writing of the past, to come, in time, to an understanding of the best writing of the present. He will teach literature, not social studies or little lessons in democracy or the customs of many lands.

And if the student finds that this is not to his taste? Well, that is regrettable. Most regrettable. His taste should not be consulted; it is being formed.

Music and Technology

Glenn Gould

One Sunday morning in December 1950, I wandered into a living-room-sized radio studio, placed my services at the disposal of a single microphone belonging to the Canadian Broadcasting Corporation, and proceeded to broadcast "live" (tape was already a fact of life in the recording industry, but in those days radio broadcasting still observed the first-note-to-last-and-damn-the-consequences syndrome of the concert hall) two sonatas: one by Mozart, one by Hindemith. It was my first network broadcast, but it was not my first contact with the microphone; for several years I'd been indulging in experiments at home with primitive tape recorders—strapping the mikes to the sounding board of my piano, the better to emasculate Scarlatti sonatas, for example, and generally subjecting both instruments to whichever imaginative indignities came to mind.

But the CBC occasion, as I've hinted already, was a memorable one: not simply because it enabled me to communicate without the immediate presence of a gallery of witnesses (though the fact that in most forms of broadcasting a microphone six feet away stands as surrogate for an audience has always been, for me, prominent among the attractions of the medium) but rather because later the same day I was presented with a soft-cut "acetate," a disc which dimly reproduced the felicities of the broadcast in question and which, even today, a quarter-century after the fact, I still take down from the shelf on occasion in order to celebrate that moment in my life when I first caught a vague impression of the direction it would take, when I realized that the collected wisdom of my peers and elders to the effect that technology represented a compromising, dehumanizing intrusion into art was nonsense, when my love affair with the microphone began.

I suspect, indeed, that if I were to assign an absolute time to the moment of recognition, that time would relate to the occasion when, later in the day, rehearing the acetate for the third or fourth time, I discovered that if I gave it a bass cut at a hundred cycles or thereabouts and a treble boost at approximately five thousand, the murky, unwieldy, bass-oriented studio piano with which I had had to deal earlier in the day could be magically transformed on playback into an instrument seemingly capable of the same sonic perversions to which I had already introduced Maestro Scarlatti.

"A plausible approach qua Mozart," you say, "but entirely inappropriate for Hindemith!" Perhaps; perhaps not. I'm reluctant to argue the case on musical grounds, for my intentions, of course, were only secondarily musical;

they were primarily theatrical and illusory. I had prevailed upon the most primitive technology to sponsor a suggestion of that which was not; my own contribution as artist was no longer the be-all and end-all of the project at hand, no longer a fait accompli. Technology had positioned itself between the attempt and the realization; the "charity of the machine," to quote the theologian Jean Le Moyne, had interposed itself between "the frailty of nature and the vision of the idealized accomplishment." "Remarkable clarity—must have been an incredible piano," friends would say. "Believe me, you simply can't imagine," I would respond. I had learned the first lesson of technology; I had learned to be creatively dishonest.

Let me say straight off that I admit to no inherent contradiction in those terms. Technology, in my view, is not primarily a conveyor belt for the dissemination of information; it is not primarily an instantaneous relay system; it is not primarily a memory bank in whose vaults are deposited the achievements and shortcomings, the creative credits and documented deficits, of man. It is, of course, or can be, any of those things, if required, and perhaps you will remind me that "the camera does not lie," to which I can only respond, "Then the camera must be taught to forthwith." For technology should not, in my view, be treated as a noncommittal, noncommitted voyeur; its capacity for dissection, for analysis—above all, perhaps, for the idealization of an impression—must be exploited, and no area with which it is currently occupied better demonstrates the philosophical conflicts with which its practitioners and theorists have been too long preoccupied than the aims and techniques of recording.

I believe in "the intrusion" of technology because, essentially, that intrusion imposes upon art a notion of morality which transcends the idea of art itself. And before, as in the case of "morality," I use some other old-fashioned words, let me explain what I mean by that one. Morality, it seems to me, has never been on the side of the carnivore—at least not when alternative life-styles are available. And evolution, which is really the biological rejection of inadequate moral systems—and particularly the evolution of man in response to his technology—has been anticarnivorous to the extent that, step by step, it has enabled him to operate at increasing distances from, to be increasingly out of touch with, his animal response to confrontation.

A war, for instance, engaged in by computer-aimed missiles is a slightly better, slightly less objectionable war than one fought by clubs or spears. Not much better, and unquestionably more destructive, statistically, but better to the extent, at least, that, all things being equal, the adrenal response of the participants (we had better forget about the bystanders or the argument collapses) is less engaged by it. Well, Margaret Mead, if I read her rightly, disapproves of that distancing factor, of that sense of disengagement from biological limitation. But I do believe in it, and recordings, though they're rarely understood as such, are one of the very best metaphors we have for it.

A few months back, for instance, I was listening to the broadcast memoirs of the very distinguished and very venerable British conductor Sir Adrian Boult. At one point Sir Adrian was asked what he thought of recording, and he said, predictably enough, something to the effect that "Well, of course, it's fair game to make them, especially for those who can't get out to the concert hall, but they're never going to take the place of the concert, are they? I always say to my producer at the outset of the session, 'Look here, old man, it's my job to get the very best I can out of the band, and I shall strive to do that even if we need two or three takes. But I don't want any of this patching! That's all you young chaps seem to think of these days—patching. Should the horn fluff his part—well, bad luck, I say, and if time permits, we'll let him have another go at it. But I don't want you to repair the warts by patching, d'you see, because at all costs I must have the long line intact.'" (I hasten to add that I do not have Sir Adrian's transcript at hand, but the paraphrase is as accurate as memory can make it.)

In any case, Sir Adrian's attitude toward "patching"—which we call "editing" or "splicing" on this side of the water—and toward recording technology in general represents one of the more unbreachable sectors of the generation gap. He's wrong, of course—splicing doesn't damage lines. Good splices build good lines, and it shouldn't much matter if one uses a splice every two seconds or none for an hour so long as the result *appears* to be a coherent whole. After all, if one buys a new car, it doesn't really matter how many assembly-line hands are involved in its production. The more the better, really, insofar as they can help to ensure the security of its operation.

But what really bothers Sir Adrian, I suspect, is that since the splice divides the elements of a particular problem, it transcends the physical anxieties, the coordinative challenges, represented by that problem. It seems to preclude the possibility that man unaided is his own best advocate—the most unwarranted assumption of the post-Renaissance era—and for that reason to be, in some way, antihuman.

Of course, we very often tend to confuse a sense of humanity with the way in which human concerns are traditionally resolved. Traditionally, they're resolved by individual moments of enlightenment, of vision, and it's that almost mystical faith in the omnipotence of the enlightened moment, in the challenge honorably overcome, which makes people of Sir Adrian's generation distrust recording technology.

I mentioned already the generation gap, but there's also a geographical gap involved. The farther east you go, the more likely you are to find recordings which are in effect taped concerts. Of course, if you go far enough east, you get to Japan, and in that country, which has no inhibiting Westernized concert-hall tradition to reckon with, recordings are understood as indigenous experiences. But in general, as one heads east from the Rhine, the perspective becomes more distant, as in a concert hall, usually more reverberant, and less precise, for that reason, and the whole operation functions mainly as an exercise in memory.

Of course, there is nothing really wrong with making records for that purpose. Fifty years ago, most people thought that recording was essentially an archival operation, the better to remember Grandpapa's generation by.

And, as I've said, that's part of what it does, but not at all what the process is about.

I do quite a bit of fancy editorial footwork with the voices of characters that I interview for radio documentaries, and if I do it well, I defy anyone to find in my editorial "patching" something other than a tauter, more coherent character synthesis. It is of course true that the amount of work one does is often relative to the value of what's being said by the character in question, and that if virtually nothing is being said, the sense of portraiture could conceivably be enhanced by leaving the material uncut. If, for instance, one stumbled into an interview with a character who said, "Well, like, man, I sorta don't wanna go out on a limb to, like, answer da question, you know, because, like, well, it takes all kinds, you know, and, well, either you dig it or maybe not, am I right? But, like, man, if I were to give a real conclusive answer, I'd say that—well, could be, you know." If he said that, it might be tempting not to cut it, to keep it intact as a portrait. If, however, one happened to deduce that what he was really saying was "To be or—like, uh—not to be," and those words were bound within that quote, then I really think that "like, uh" should go.

Nobody Here but Us Dead Sheep

William Zinsser

Nerve gas in Okinawa. Nuclear explosions in Nevada. Chemical Mace in the eyes. Every day it's something else in American life which strikes me as outlandish, but which evidently began in logic. I can no longer tell where we cross over from the normal to the insane.

I remember back in May seeing a picture of a tank and some infantrymen on the front page of the morning paper. I didn't bother to read the caption because it was the same combat picture of Vietnam that I've seen every other morning. But, it wasn't Vietnam—it was a college in North Carolina. A few days later I saw a photograph of several hundred soldiers standing guard in gas masks. They were in gas masks because a helicopter was poised overhead to spray chemicals. It was the University of California at Berkeley. In 1969 the incongruous becomes routine almost overnight.

I never knew, for instance, that the American Army has been storing nerve gas at its bases in other countries. The only way the Army lets us know about its nerve gas is to leak a little by mistake, as it did last month in Okinawa, briefly hospitalizing 24 men. Just routine deployment of deterrent power, the Pentagon said, explaining its policy on chemical weapons—nobody should be surprised.

Well, *I* was surprised. More surprised, actually, than the Okinawans, who suspected something last summer when 200 Okinawa children suffered skin burns while swimming at a beach 12 miles south of our 137th Ordnance Company's camp. The unusual still strikes them as unusual.

Not us. In the spring of 1968, 6,400 sheep dropped dead one week in Utah—a mortality rate not common in sheep-raising—fairly near the Army's chemical warfare testing center. Queried about this coincidence, the Army said it couldn't imagine what could have possibly happened to those sheep. Luckily, a few people felt that the sudden death of 6,400 sheep taunted the laws of zoology, and they kept bringing the matter up, clinging to reason amid denials that persisted for 14 months, until finally the official lies were turned into official truths—as happened when the Pentagon admitted that it knew exactly what happened to those sheep. A valve malfunctioned. The wind changed. So sorry.

Should we laugh or cry? We teeter every day on the edge of absurdity and think it is solid ground. Recently the Army decided to get rid of 27,000 tons of obsolete chemical and bacteriological weapons stockpiled at a base in the Rockies—including 2,660 tons of rockets and 12,322 tons of bomb clusters, all filled with nerve gas—by hauling the whole load across the country in railroad cars and dumping it in the ocean off New Jersey. A routine operation, perfectly safe.

The Army didn't think anything could happen to those weapons as they moved secretly across the country by train, bouncing 1,500 miles through American cities and towns where the populace lay sleeping, snug in the belief that it was only the night mail. But actually the Army doesn't even have responsibility while its cargo is on a train. That belongs to the railroad—and anything *can* happen. Just a few weeks ago a cargo of Army "ammunition propellant" exploded on a freight train as it passed through Noel, Mo., killing one resident, injuring 100, and damaging all the businesses and most of the homes in town.

Maybe this is what finally nudged the Senate into realizing that the Army could use some supervision, and, with any luck, the measure approved last week—to restrict the storage, transportation and use of chemical weapons— will provide it. We'll need the luck because we obviously can't count on logic. Remember the grotesque shipment of nerve gas across the country? Apparently only one person heard about it and found it grotesque—Representative Richard D. McCarthy, Democrat of New York, who said there must be a safer way to get rid of the stuff. There was. The Pentagon gave it a second thought and decided that it could neutralize the gases without moving them anywhere at all.

Then there's the funny story about the atomic tests in Nevada. Somehow it never occurred to me that a hydrogen bomb explosion would be a spectacle that tourists would want to see, like Cypress Gardens or Colonial Williamsburg. But then I came upon an article in the travel and resort section of the New York *Times*—nestled among the Caribbean cruises and Riviera nights—which said that the Atomic Energy Commission has decided to let sightseers observe large-scale atomic tests at its new test site 200 miles north of Las Vegas.

I was surprised to see this announcement made in the travel section. I could only take it to mean that our nuclear arsenal has somehow crossed over from the realm of American defense to the realm of American leisure: a fun facility for Dad, Mom and the kids. Undecided about your vacation? Already done Disneyland? Why not go to Nevada for the blasts?

Unfortunately, "Observers will not experience the blinding flashes, awesome fireballs and deafening roars of the early aboveground tests," the *Times* article explained. "But even at a distance of 12 miles an underground megaton shot produces an artificial earthquake that makes the ground shudder and seemingly heave a couple of feet, a shock that can knock a man off his feet. A spectacular curtain of dust, miles wide, is sent up from the desert floor. There is always a possibility that the huge caverns blasted underground may cause a spectacular surface cave-in. The principal unexpected thing that can happen is a venting of radioactive gas through unpredictable fissures in the ground."

Well, I've got to admit that as a tourist attraction it goes far beyond your average gator farm or monkey jungle. There's the whole new element of surprise. I mean, we all know that Old Faithful is going to erupt every 65 minutes. So what else is new? And at Disneyland everything is so clean—you simply don't have the possibility of a surface cave-in or a curtain of dust.

I assume the AEC will build a luxury motel out at the site. It should have a name that will look folksy on billboards—Atomland, or Nuclear Village—and convey the idea of a resort where the whole family can come and have a good time between explosions. It would be a shame, after all, to arrive on a Monday and catch an ordinary megaton shot with just a medium earthquake. By waiting around for another test, the family might see a really decent cave-in and get some funny pictures for the photo album ("Me and Mom in front of atom bomb hole—that's Dad on the ground"). It might even open some unpredictable fissures that would vent enough radioactive gas to show up on Bobby's toy Geiger counter, the one he bought at the New Hiroshima Boutique & Coffee Shoppe where he got those wonderful blastburgers.

Got time for one more joke? Let's look at the droll story of Chemical Mace. Several congressional committees recently learned that Mace, used by more than 4,000 police departments, can cause permanent injury.

Now comes the funny part. Sixteen months ago—in April, 1968—the Army made a "biological assessment" of Chemical Mace Mark IV on rabbits, monkeys and dogs and found that it "could cause scarring of the corneal surface and scarring of the skin." Surgeon General William Stewart therefore advised all state, county and city health officers that Mace could cause "more than transient effects to the exposed individual unless treatment is prompt."

Now anyone might think that all those public health officers would try to get a substance banned which can scar the corneas of the public whose health they are officering. But evidently they all thought it was somebody else's business, and it was not until this spring—a year later—that the matter came up before the Senate Subcommittee on Executive Reorganization. (Where have *they* been all these years?)

Why, Surgeon General Stewart was asked by a reporter, did he not recommend discontinuing the use of Mace?

"I think there was a misunderstanding," he replied, "that we have some authority to ban Mace." Translation: "Don't look at me, I'm only the Surgeon General." Besides, he said, he wasn't asked to evaluate Mace. He was only asked "what were the health effects and what do you do with people who are Maced?" He pointed out that the Public Health Service has no control over Mace as a weapon used by police departments, partly because it does not fit the definition of a drug.

This was disputed by former Food and Drug Commissioner James Goddard, who told the Senate subcommittee that Mace does indeed fit the definition of a drug "as altering in some way the structure or function of the human body." He cited reports of "corneal scars, chemical burns and sharp rises in blood pressure—up to 100 points within seconds. I would have to say that it

173

is a dangerous substance and it does have potential for causing blindness, according to the reports I have read, and to cause death.

"To the best of my knowledge, Mr. Chairman," Goddard added, "no police officer has sprayed Mace at a citizen and then immediately flushed the victim's eyes with cool water and rinsed his clothing."

Meanwhile the head of the Federal Trade Commission, Paul Rand Dixon, said that his agency is trying to halt the "deceptive advertising of chemical sprays being sold to the general public," but that the job requires some cooperation. "The commission deplores the fact that all interested government agencies were not informed of the results of the Army's tests. Without the free and complete exchange of such information, the enforcement of our laws in the protection of the public interests is virtually an impossible task."

Again, I don't know whether to laugh or cry at an executive organization so hopelessly in need of reorganizing. I'm too old to cry, but it hurts too much to laugh—mainly around the cornea.

The Man-Made Myth

Elaine Morgan

According to the Book of Genesis, God first created man. Woman was not only an afterthought, but an amenity. For close on two thousand years this holy scripture was believed to justify her subordination and explain her inferiority: for even as a copy she was not a very good copy. There were differences. She was not one of His best efforts.

There is a line in an old folk song that runs: "I called my donkey a horse gone wonky." Throughout most of the literature dealing with the differences between the sexes there runs a subtle underlying assumption that woman is a man gone wonky; that woman is a distorted version of the original blueprint; that they are the norm, and we are the deviation.

It might have been expected that when Darwin came along and wrote an entirely different account of the *Descent of Man*, this assumption would have been eradicated, for Darwin didn't believe she was an afterthought: he believed her origin was at least contemporaneous with man's. It should have led to some kind of breakthrough in the relationship between the sexes. But it didn't.

Almost at once men set about the congenial and fascinating task of working out an entirely new set of reasons why woman was manifestly inferior and irreversibly subordinate, and they have been happily engaged on this ever since. Instead of theology they use biology, and ethology, and primatology, but they use them to reach the same conclusions.

They are now prepared to debate the most complex problems of economic reform not in terms of the will of God, but in terms of the sexual behavior patterns of the cichlid fish; so that if a woman claims equal pay or the right to promotion there is usually an authoritative male thinker around to deliver a brief homily on hormones, and point out that what she secretly intends by this, and what will inevitably result, is the "psychological castration" of the men in her life.

Now, that may look to us like a stock piece of emotional blackmail—like the woman who whimpers that if Sonny doesn't do as she wants him to do, then Mother's going to have one of her nasty turns. It is not really surprising that most women who are concerned to win themselves a new and better status in society tend to sheer away from the whole subject of biology and origins, and hope that we can ignore all that and concentrate on ensuring that in the future things will be different.

I believe this is a mistake. The legend of the jungle heritage and the evolution of man as a hunting carnivore has taken root in man's mind as firmly as Genesis ever did. He may even genuinely believe that equal pay will do something terrible to his gonads. He has built a beautiful theoretical construction, with himself on the top of it, buttressed with a formidable array of scientifically authenticated facts. We cannot dispute the facts. We should not attempt to ignore the facts. What I think we can do is to suggest that the currently accepted interpretation of the facts is not the only possible one.

I have considerable admiration for scientists in general, and evolutionists and ethologists in particular, and though I think they have sometimes gone astray, it has not been purely through prejudice. Partly it is due to sheer semantic accident—the fact that "man" is an ambiguous term. It means the species; it also means the male of the species. If you begin to write a book about man or conceive a theory about man you cannot avoid using this word. You cannot avoid using a pronoun as a substitute for the word, and you will use the pronoun "he" as a simple matter of linguistic convenience. But before you are halfway through the first chapter a mental image of this evolving creature begins to form in your mind. It will be a male image, and he will be the hero of the story: everything and everyone else in the story will relate to him.

All this may sound like a mere linguistic quibble or a piece of feminist petulance. If you stay with me, I hope to convince you it's neither. I believe the deeply rooted semantic confusion between "man" as a male and "man" as a species has been fed back into and vitiated a great deal of the speculation that goes on about the origins, development, and nature of the human race.

A very high proportion of the thinking on these topics is androcentric (male-centered) in the same way as pre-Copernican thinking was geocentric. It's just as hard for man to break the habit of thinking of himself as central to the species as it was to break the habit of thinking of himself as central to the universe. He sees himself quite unconsciously as the main line of evolution, with a female satellite revolving around him as the moon revolves around the earth. This not only causes him to overlook valuable clues to our ancestry, but sometimes leads him into making statements that are arrant and demonstrable nonsense.

The longer I went on reading his own books about himself, the more I longed to find a volume that would begin: "When the first ancestor of the human race descended from the trees, she had not yet developed the mighty brain that was to distinguish her so sharply from all other species...."

Of course, she was no more the first ancestor than he was—but she was no *less* the first ancestor, either. She was there all along, contributing half the genes to each succeeding generation. Most of the books forget about her for most of the time. They drag her onstage rather suddenly for the obligatory chapter on Sex and Reproduction, and then say: "All right, love, you can go now," while they get on with the real meaty stuff about the Mighty Hunter with his lovely new weapons and his lovely new straight legs racing across the Pleistocene plains. Any modifications in her morphology are taken to be imitations of the Hunter's evolution, or else designed solely for his delectation.

Evolutionary thinking has been making great strides lately. Archaeologists, ethologists, paleontologists, geologists, chemists, biologists, and physicists are closing in from all points of the compass on the central area of mystery that remains. For despite the frequent triumph dances of researchers coming up with another jawbone or another statistic, some part of the miracle is still unaccounted for. Most of their books include some such phrase as: "...the early stages of man's evolutionary progress remain a total mystery." "Man is an accident, the culmination of a series of highly improbable coincidences...." "Man is a product of circumstances special to the point of disbelief." They feel there is still something missing, and they don't know what.

The trouble with specialists is that they tend to think in grooves. From time to time something happens to shake them out of that groove. Robert Ardrey tells how such enlightenment came to Dr. Kenneth Oakley when the first Autralopithecus remains had been unearthed in Africa: "The answer flashed without warning in his own large-domed head: 'Of course we believed that the big brain came first! We assumed that the first man was an Englishman!'" Neither he, nor Ardrey in relating the incident, noticed that he was still making an equally unconscious, equally unwarrantable assumption. One of these days an evolutionist is going to strike a palm against his large-domed head and cry: "Of course! We assumed the first human being was a man!"

First, let's have a swift recap of the story as currently related, for despite all the new evidence recently brought to light, the generally accepted picture of human evolution has changed very little.

Smack in the center of it remains the Tarzanlike figure of the prehominid male who came down from the trees, saw a grassland teeming with game, picked up a weapon, and became a Mighty Hunter.

Almost everything about us is held to have derived from this. If we walk erect it was because the Mighty Hunter had to stand tall to scan the distance for his prey. If we lived in caves it was because hunters need a base to come home to. If we learned to speak it was because hunters need to plan the next safari and boast about the last. Desmond Morris, pondering on the shape of a woman's breasts, instantly deduces that they evolved because her mate became a Mighty Hunter, and defends this preposterous proposition with the greatest ingenuity. There's something about the Tarzan figure which has them all mesmerized.

I find the whole yarn pretty incredible. It is riddled with mysteries, and inconsistencies, and unanswered questions. Even more damning than the unanswered questions are the questions that are never even asked, because, as Professor Peter Medawar has pointed out, "scientists tend not to ask themselves questions until they can see the rudiments of an answer in their minds." I shall devote this chapter to pointing out some of these problems before outlining a new version of the Naked Ape story which will suggest at least possible answers to every one of them, and fifteen or twenty others besides.

The first mystery is, "What happened during the Pliocene?"

There is a wide acceptance now of the theory that the human story began in Africa. Twenty million years ago in Kenya, there existed a flourishing population of apes of generalized body structure and of a profusion of types from the size of a small gibbon up to that of a large gorilla. Dr. L.S.B. Leakey has dug up their bones by the hundred in the region of Lake Victoria, and they were clearly doing very well there at the time. It was a period known as the Miocene. The weather was mild, the rainfall was heavier than today, and the forests were flourishing. So far, so good.

Then came the Pliocene drought. Robert Ardrey writes of it: "No mind can apprehend in terms of any possible human experience the duration of the Pliocene. Ten desiccated years were enough, a quarter of a century ago, to produce in the American Southwest that maelstrom of misery, the dust bowl. To the inhabitant of the region the ten years must have seemed endless. But the African Pliocene lasted twelve million."

On the entire African continent no Pliocene fossil bed has ever been found. During this period many promising Miocene ape species were, not surprisingly, wiped out altogether. A few were trapped in dwindling pockets of forest and when the Pliocene ended they reappeared as brachiating apes—specialized for swinging by their arms.

Something astonishing also reappeared—the Australopithecines, first discovered by Professor Raymond Dart in 1925 and since unearthed in considerable numbers by Dr. Leakey and others.

Australopithecus emerged from his horrifying twelve-million year ordeal much refreshed and improved. The occipital condyles of his skull suggest a bodily posture approaching that of modern man, and the orbital region, according to Sir Wilfred le Gros Clark, has "a remarkably human appearance." He was clever, too. His remains have been found in the Olduvai Gorge in association with crude pebble tools that have been hailed as the earliest beginning of human culture. Robert Ardrey says: "We entered the Pliocene crucible a generalized creature bearing only the human potential. We emerged a being lacking only a proper brain and a chin. What happened to us along the way?" The sixty-four-thousand-dollar question: "What happened to them? Where did they go?"

Second question: "Why did they stand upright?" The popular versions skim very lightly over this patch of thin ice. Desmond Morris says simply: "With strong pressure on them to increase their prey-killing prowess, they became more upright—fast, better runners." Robert Ardrey says equally simply: "We learned to stand erect in the first place as a necessity of the hunting life."

But wait a minute. We were quadrupeds. These statements imply that a quadruped suddenly discovered that he could move faster on two legs than on four. Try to imagine any other quadruped discovering that—a cat? a dog? a horse?—and you'll see that it's totally nonsensical. Other things being equal, four legs are bound to run faster than two. The bipedal development was violently unnatural.

Stoats, gophers, rabbits, chimpanzees, will sit or stand bipedally to gaze into the distance, but when they want speed they have sense enough to use all the legs they've got. The only quadrupeds I can think of that can move faster on two legs than four are things like kangaroos—and a small lizard called the Texas boomer, and he doesn't keep it up for long. The secret in these cases is a long heavy counterbalancing tail which we certainly never had. You may say it was a natural development for a primate because primates sit erect in trees—but *was* it natural? Baboons and macaques have been largely ter-restrial for millions of years without any sign of becoming bipedal.

George A. Bartholomew and Joseph B. Birdsell point out: "...the extreme rarity of bipedalism among animals suggests that it is inefficient except under very special circumstances. Even modern man's unique vertical locomotion when compared to that of quadrupedal mammals, is relatively ineffective.... A significant nonlocomotor advantage must have resulted."

What was this advantage? The Tarzanists suggest that bipedalism enabled this ape to race after game while carrying weapons—in the first instance, presumably pebbles. But a chimp running off with a banana (or a pebble), if he can't put it in his mouth, will carry it in one hand and gallop along on the others, because even *three* legs are faster than two. So what was our ancestor supposed to be doing? Shambling along with a rock in each hand? Throwing boulders that took two hands to lift?

No. There must have been a pretty powerful reason why we were con-strained over a long period of time to walk about on our hind legs *even though it was slower*. We need to find that reason.

Third question: How did the ape come to be using these weapons, anyway? Again Desmond Morris clears this one lightly, at a bound: "With strong pressure on them to increase their prey-killing prowess...their hands became strong efficient weapon-holders." Compared to Morris, Robert Ardrey is obsessed with weapons, which he calls "mankind's most significant cultural endowment." Yet his explanation of how it all started is as cursory as anyone else's: "In the first evolutionary hour of the human emergence we became sufficiently skilled in the use of weapons to render redundant our natural primate daggers" (i.e., the large prehominid canine teeth).

But wait a minute—how? and why? Why did one, and only one, species of those Miocene apes start using weapons? A cornered baboon will fight a leopard; a hungry baboon will kill and eat a chicken. He could theoretically pick up a chunk of flint and forget about his "natural primate daggers," and become a Mighty Hunter. He doesn't do it, though. Why did we? Sarel Eimerl and Irven de Vore point out in their book *The Primates*:

"Actually, it takes quite a lot of explaining. For example, if an animal's normal mode of defense is to flee from a predator, it flees. If its normal method of defense is to fight with its teeth, it fights with its teeth. It does not suddenly adopt a totally new course of action, such as picking up a stick or a rock and throwing it. The idea would simply not occur to it, and even if it did, the animal would have no reason to suppose that it would work."

179

Now primates do acquire useful tool-deploying habits. A chimpanzee will use a stick to extract insects from their nests, and a crumpled leaf to sop up water. Wolfgang Köhler's apes used sticks to draw fruit toward the bars of their cage, and so on.

But this type of learning depends on three things. There must be leisure for trial-and-error experiment. The tools must be either in unlimited supply (a forest is full of sticks and leaves) or else in *exactly the right place*. (Even Köhler's brilliant Sultan could be stumped if the fruit was in front of him and a new potential tool was behind him—he needed them both in view at the same time.) Thirdly, for the habit to stick, the same effect must result from the same action every time.

Now look at that ape. The timing is wrong—when he's faced with a bristling rival or a charging cat or even an escaping prey, he won't fool around inventing fancy methods. A chimp sometimes brandishes a stick to convey menace to an adversary, but if his enemy keeps coming, he drops the stick and fights with hands and teeth. Even if we postulate a mutant ape cool enough to think, with the adrenalin surging through his veins, "There must be a better way than teeth," he still has to be lucky to notice that right in the middle of the primeval grassland there happens to be a stone of convenient size, precisely between him and his enemy. And when he throws it, he has to score a bull's-eye, first time and every time. Because if he failed to hit a leopard he wouldn't be there to tell his progeny that the trick only needed polishing up a bit; and if he failed to hit a springbok he'd think: "Ah well, that obviously doesn't work. Back to the old drawing board."

No. If it had taken all that much luck to turn man into a killer, we'd all be still living on nut cutlets.

A lot of Tarzanists privately realize that their explanations of bipedalism and weapon-wielding won't hold water. They have invented the doctrine of "feedback," which states that though these two theories are separately and individually nonsense, together they will just get by. It is alleged that the ape's bipedal gait, however unsteady, made him a better rock thrower (why?) and his rock throwing, however inaccurate, made him a better biped. (Why?) Eimerl and de Vore again put the awkward question: Since chimps can both walk erect and manipulate simple tools, "Why was it only the hominids who benefited from the feed-back?" You may well ask.

Next question: Why did the naked ape become naked?

Desmond Morris claims that, unlike more specialized carnivores such as lions and jackals, the ex-vegetarian ape was not physically equipped to "make lightning dashes after his prey." He would "experience considerable overheating during the hunt, and the loss of body hair would be of great value for the supreme moments of the chase."

This is a perfect example of androcentric thinking. There were two sexes around at the time, and I don't believe it's ever been all that easy to part a woman from a fur coat, just to save the old man from getting into a muck-sweat during his supreme moments. What was supposed to be happening to the female during this period of denudation?

Dr. Morris says: "This system would not work, of course, if the climate was too intensely hot, because of damage to the exposed skin." So he is obviously dating the loss of hair later than the Pliocene "inferno." But the next period was the turbulent Pleistocene, punctuated by mammoth African "pluvials," corresponding to the Ice Ages of the north. A pluvial was century after century of torrential rainfall; so we have to picture our maternal ancestor sitting naked in the middle of the plain while the heavens emptied, needing both hands to keep her muddy grip on a slippery, squirming, equally naked infant. This is ludicrous. It's no advantage to the species for the Mighty Hunter to return home safe and cool if he finds his son's been dropped on his head and his wife is dead of hypothermia.

This problem could have been solved by dimorphism—the loss of hair could have gone further in one sex than the other. So it did, of course. But unfortunately for the Tarzanists it was the stay-at-home female who became nakedest, and the overheated hunter who kept the hair on his chest.

Next question: Why has our sex life become so involved and confusing?

The given answer, I need hardly say, is that it all began when man became a hunter. He had to travel long distances after his prey and he began worrying about what the little woman might be up to. He was also anxious about other members of the hunting pack, because, Desmond Morris explains, "if the weaker males were going to be expected to cooperate on the hunt, they had to be given more sexual rights. The females would have to be more shared out."

Thus it became necessary, so the story goes, to establish a system of "pair bonding" to ensure that couples remained faithful for life. I quote: "The simplest and most direct method of doing this was to make the shared activities of the pair more complicated and more rewarding. In other words, to make sex sexier."

To this end, the Naked Apes sprouted ear lobes, fleshy nostrils, and averted lips, all allegedly designed to stimulate one another to a frenzy. Mrs. A.'s nipples became highly erogenous, she invented and patented the female orgasm, and she learned to be sexually responsive at all times, even during pregnancy, "because with a one-male—one-female system, it would be dangerous to frustrate the male for too long a period. It might endanger the pair bond." He might go off in a huff, or look for another woman. Or even refuse to cooperate on the hunt.

In addition, they decided to change over to face-to-face sex, instead of the male mounting from behind as previously, because this new method led to "personalized sex." The frontal approach means that "the incoming sexual signals and rewards are kept tightly linked with the identity signals from the partner." In simpler words, you know who you're doing it with.

This landed Mrs. Naked Ape in something of a quandary. Up till then, the fashionable thing to flaunt in sexual approaches had been "a pair of fleshy, hemispherical buttocks." Now all of a sudden they were getting her nowhere. She would come up to her mate making full-frontal identity signals like mad with her nice new earlobes and nostrils, but somehow he just didn't want to know. He missed the fleshy hemispheres, you see. The position was parlous, Dr. Morris urges. "If the female of our species was going to successfully shift the interest of the male round to the front, evolution would have to do something to make the frontal region more stimulating." Guess what? Right the first time: she invested in a pair of fleshy hemispheres in the thoracic region and we were once more saved by the skin of our teeth.

All this is good stirring stuff, but hard to take seriously. Wolf packs manage to cooperate without all this erotic paraphernalia. Our near relatives the gibbons remain faithful for life without "personalized" frontal sex, without elaborate erogenous zones, without perennial female availability. Why couldn't we?

Above all, since when has increased sexiness been a guarantee of increased fidelity? If the naked ape could see all this added sexual potential in his own mate, how could he fail to see the same thing happening to all the other females around him? What effect was that supposed to have on him, especially in later life when he noticed Mrs. A.'s four hemispheres becoming a little less fleshy than they used to be?

We haven't yet begun on the unasked questions. Before ending this chapter I will mention just two out of many.

First: If female orgasm was evolved in our species for the first time to provide the woman with a "behavioral reward" for increased sexual activity, why in the name of Darwin has the job been so badly bungled that there have been whole tribes and whole generations of women hardly aware of its existence? Even in the sex-conscious U.S.A., according to Dr. Kinsey, it rarely gets into proper working order before the age of about thirty. How could natural selection ever have operated on such a rickety, unreliable, late-developing endowment when in the harsh conditions of prehistory a woman would be lucky to survive more than twenty-nine years, anyway?

Second: Why in our species has sex become so closely linked with aggression? In most of the higher primates sexual activity is the one thing in life which is totally incompatible with hostility. A female primate can immediately deflect male wrath by presenting her backside and offering sex. Even a male monkey can calm and appease a furious aggressor by imitating the gesture. Nor is the mechanism confined to mammals. Lorenz tells of an irate lizard charging down upon a female painted with male markings to deceive him. When he got close enough to realize his mistake, the taboo was so immediate and so absolute that his aggression went out like a light, and being too late to stop himself he shot straight up into the air and turned a back somersault.

Female primates admittedly are not among the species that can count on this absolute chivalry at all times. A female monkey may be physically chastised for obstreperous behavior; or a male may (on rare occasions) direct hostility against her when another male is copulating with her; but between the male and female engaged in it, sex is always the friendliest of interactions. There is no more hostility associated with it than with a session of mutual grooming.

How then have sex and aggression, the two irreconcilables of the animal kingdom, become in our species alone so closely interlinked that the words for sexual activity are spat out as insults and expletives? In what evolutionary terms are we to explain the Marquis de Sade, and the subterranean echoes that his name evokes in so many human minds?

Not, I think, in terms of Tarzan. It is time to approach the whole thing again right from the beginning: this time from the distaff side, and along a totally different route.

Pandora was a Feminist

Mary Meigs

Secrets. The origin of secrets—a great puzzle that I'm trying to solve, for it seems to me that there is an urgent need to decide which, if any, are necessary and which spring from the ego's need to protect its truths and its lies, hence, the idea that every self is a sacred place and that all secrets have the same sacred character. Other people's secrets, as we know, beg to be told, make up the fabric of gossip and innuendo even if severe penalties are attached to telling them. As for our own, they are raided, so to speak, by others with their conjectures, their analyses that we so fiercely reject (like ours of them). One's secret self is guarded as closely as spies guard secrets in wartime, not because of a real penalty for telling (unlike the spies), but an imaginary one, because of the feeling that it belongs to oneself, like one's brain, one's heart, and the illusion that it is invisible to others. But, in fact, those others are nibbling away, like fishes around bait, so that it might be better to give them an authentic whole to nibble on. Better still, perhaps, to sit in one of those cages in which one is completely visible but protected from over-eager sharks, the cage of indifference to what other people think. I often wonder if the secret of oneself is worth keeping, if it shouldn't be released like the contents of Pandora's box. That story is a wonderful example of patriarchal ingenuity, which has invented yet another mythical explanation for the woes of *man*kind, i.e. the unbridled curiosity of womankind. Personally, I think of Pandora not as irresponsible and foolish but as a radical feminist, sister of Eve and Bluebeard's wives, of all women who *want to know*. We are all Pandoras, each with her box complete with instructions not to open it, the box of the secret self.

Pandora, according to Zimmerman's *Dictionary of Classical Mythology*, was made with clay by Hephaestus at the request of Zeus, who desired to punish Prometheus for stealing fire from heaven by giving him a wife. "All the gods and goddesses of Olympus vied in giving her gifts:" beauty, eloquence, the art of singing, beautiful clothes, a gold crown, etc., not to mention the famous box, a gift from Zeus himself. But Prometheus saw through Zeus, and Pandora ended by marrying his brother Epimetheus (which means Afterthought). "Don't open the box," said Zeus. Naturally, Pandora opened it. So do I open things: Christmas presents before Christmas, the last page of a book to see how it's going to end (I have to know whether it will have a happy ending, or whether so-and-so will still be alive at the end. I hate suspense, cannot read detective stories, cannot look at movies full of suspense without intolerable anxiety.) But to get back to Pandora. "When the box was opened, a host of

plagues escaped to harass hapless man; only Hope remained in the box."
Why? It seems to me it would have been much better to let Hope out, too.
"Women's curiosity is always punished," I remarked to Paul, a male friend.
"Pandora's, Eve's, Bluebeard's wives." "Of course," he says. "Evil is woman's
fault. That's part of history." He's making fun of me, of course. I say I think
people should be less possessive of their secrets, that Pandora was right to
open the box. And then he tells me a fascinating story about himself. He used
to dream, he says, to remember his dreams and write them down, until one
day a dream told him something about himself that he didn't want to know.
So he pushed it back into his subconscious. "And I never remembered another
dream!" Pandora couldn't possibly have been more curious about the contents
of her box than I am about this dream-truth that he doesn't want to think
about. I say to him that nothing in my dreams makes me want to censor them,
that there is nothing they tell me that I don't want to think about, that they
have helped me to think about the things I don't want to think about. And far
from wanting to turn them off, I want to stimulate them, I want them to tell
me the worst!

Curiosity, how it can be thought of as either a virtue or a vice, how it is a
virtue for men in men's eyes and a vice for women which must be punished,
and how the punishment becomes dogma until women, too, feel impatient
with Eve, Pandora and Bluebeard's wives for being so foolish, for wanting to
know. God or Zeus or Bluebeard loves to tempt them by inventing rules that
as high-spirited women, they are bound to break. Don't eat of the fruit of the
tree! Don't open that box! Don't look in the closet! Sometimes God, just for
good measure, tests a man. Don't ask me *why*, he says to Job. But much more
often, men's curiosity is rewarded and women's is punished. And yet when
it comes to opening the Pandora's box which is in each of us, men and women
are alike. Paul's self-censorship—the Pandora's box of his dreams—he seemed
to think it was wrong to know *too much* about himself and called on the Zeus
in himself to close the box forever. I wondered how often he had told this story,
whether each telling wasn't to reinforce the lock, whether the *thing* he wanted
to shut away didn't manage to reach out a paw under the lid like an angry
kitten in a basket. He told it smiling, with a kind of excitement, triumph, ha!
it almost got out! It seemed to me that *it* was amazingly discreet; it could be
talked about without betraying what it was even to Paul. Perhaps it had
become so tame that it was ready to be let out of the box; perhaps he told it as
a way of taming it?

I think about *it*, the beast, silenced but still there in the dreams that are not
allowed over the threshold of consciousness, and want to say, "Let it out. It
won't hurt you," want to say that secrets, once released, often sheath their
claws, stretch, rub against other people's ankles and finally curl up in a
comfortable chair and go to sleep. Interestingly, Pandora was not punished
(note that the plagues "escaped to harass hapless *man*"). Long after the affair
of the box, Zeus sent a deluge to destroy *man*kind and Pandora's daughter,
Pyrrha, and her husband, Deucalion (Prometheus' son), were the only survivors. They had the foresight to replace "the loss of mankind by throwing

stones behind their backs; those Deucalion threw became men; those Pyrrha threw became women." So the sexes, each reproduced by a kind of parthenogenesis (another case of patriarchal wish-fulfillment), were equal for a while, and Pandora was the grandmother of all the women in the world. True, the "host of plagues" was still at large, but Zeus himself had invented them and put them in the box, a cover-up, so to speak, and Pandora had the courage to show everybody what Zeus was up to. It was a tremendous victory over Zeus, just as Eve had won a victory over God by disobeying his senseless edict about eating the fruit of the tree. Confronted by boxes that are not supposed to be opened, we contemporary Pandoras say to ourselves, "Where did this rule come from? Was it Zeus who told me not open the box, and is he impersonating me so skillfully that I think his commands come from myself?"

Is History a Guide to the Future?

Barbara Tuchman

The commonest question asked of historians by laymen is whether history serves a purpose. Is it useful? Can we learn from the lessons of history?

When people want history to be utilitarian and teach us lessons, that means they also want to be sure that it meets scientific standards. This, in my opinion, it cannot do, for reasons which I will come to in a moment. To practice history as a science is sociology, an altogether different discipline which I personally find antipathetic—although I suppose the sociologists would consider that my deficiency rather than theirs. The sociologists plod along with their noses to the ground assembling masses of statistics in order to arrive at some obvious conclusion which a reasonably perceptive historian, not to mention a large part of the general public, knows anyway, simply from observation—that social mobility is increasing, for instance, or that women have different problems from men. One wishes they would just cut loose someday, lift up their heads, and look at the world around them.

If history were a science, we should be able to get a grip on her, learn her ways, establish her patterns, know what will happen tomorrow. Why is it that we cannot? The answer lies in what I call the Unknowable Variable—namely, man. Human beings are always and finally the subject of history. History is the record of human behavior, the most fascinating subject of all, but illogical and so crammed with an unlimited number of variables that it is not susceptible of the scientific method nor of systematizing.

I say this bravely, even in the midst of the electronic age when computers are already chewing at the skirts of history in the process called Quantification. Applied to history, quantification, I believe, has its limits. It depends on a method called "data manipulation," which means that the facts, or data, of the historical past—that is, of human behavior—are manipulated into named categories so that they can be programmed into computers. Out comes—hopefully—a pattern. I can only tell you that for history "data manipulation" is a built-in invalidator, because to the degree that you manipulate your data to suit some extraneous requirement, in this case the requirements of the machine, to that degree your results will be suspect—and run the risk of being invalid. Everything depends on the naming of the categories and the assigning of facts to them, and this depends on the quantifier's individual judgment at the very base of the process. The categories are not revealed doctrine nor are the results scientific truth.

The hope for quantification, presumably, is that by processing a vast quantity of material far beyond the capacity of the individual to encompass, it can bring to light and establish reliable patterns. That remains to be seen, but I am not optimistic. History has a way of escaping attempts to imprison it in patterns. Moreover, one of its basic data is the human soul. The conventional historian, at least the one concerned with truth, not propaganda, will try honestly to let his "data" speak for themselves, but data which are shut up in prearranged boxes are helpless. Their nuances have no voice. They must carry one fixed meaning or another and weight the result accordingly. For instance, in a quantification study of the origins of World War I which I have seen, the operators have divided all the diplomatic documents, messages, and utterances of the July crisis into categories labeled "hostility," "friendship," "frustration," "satisfaction," and so on, with each statement rated for intensity on a scale from one to nine, including fractions. But no pre-established categories could match all the private character traits and public pressures variously operating on the nervous monarchs and ministers who were involved. The massive effort that went into this study brought forth a mouse—the less than startling conclusion that the likelihood of war increased in proportion to the rise in hostility of the messages.

Quantification is really only a new approach to the old persistent effort to make history fit a pattern, but *reliable* patterns, or what are otherwise called the lessons of history, remain elusive.

For instance, suppose Woodrow Wilson had not been President of the United States in 1914 but instead Theodore Roosevelt, who had been his opponent in the election of 1912. Had that been the case, America might have entered the war much earlier, perhaps at the time of the *Lusitania* in 1915, with possible shortening of the war and incalculable effects on history. Well, it happens that among the Anarchists in my book *The Proud Tower* is an obscure Italian named Miguel Angiolillo, whom nobody remembers but who shot dead Premier Canovas of Spain in 1897. Canovas was a strong man who was just about to succeed in quelling the rebels in Cuba when he was assassinated. Had he lived, there might have been no extended Cuban insurrection for Americans to get excited about, no Spanish-American War, no San Juan Hill, no Rough Riders, no Vice-Presidency for Theodore Roosevelt to enable him to succeed when another accident, another Anarchist, another unpredictable human being, killed McKinley. If Theodore had never been President, there would have been no third party in 1912 to split the Republicans, and Woodrow Wilson would not have been elected. The speculations from that point on are limitless. To me it is comforting rather than otherwise to feel that history is determined by the illogical human record and not by large immutable scientific laws beyond our power to deflect.

I know very little (a euphemism for "nothing") about laboratory science, but I have the impression that conclusions are supposed to be logical; that is, from a given set of circumstances a predictable result should follow. The trouble is that in human behavior and history it is impossible to isolate or repeat a given set of circumstances. Complex human acts cannot be either reproduced or deliberately initiated—or counted upon like the phenomena of nature. The sun comes up every day. Tides are so obedient to schedule that a timetable for them can be printed like that for trains, though more reliable. In fact, tides and trains sharply illustrate my point: One depends on the moon and is certain; the other depends on man and is uncertain.

In the absence of dependable recurring circumstance, too much confidence cannot be placed on the lessons of history.

There *are* lessons, of course, and when people speak of learning from them, they have in mind, I think, two ways of applying past experience: One is to enable us to avoid past mistakes and to manage better in similar circumstances next time; the other is to enable us to anticipate a future course of events. (History could tell us something about Vietnam, I think, if we would only listen.) To manage better next time is within our means; to anticipate does not seem to be.

World War II, for example, with the experience of the previous war as an awful lesson, was certainly conducted, once we got into it, more intelligently than World War I. Getting into it was another matter. When it was important to anticipate the course of events, Americans somehow failed to apply the right lesson. Pearl Harbor is the classic example of failure to learn from history. From hindsight we now know that what we should have anticipated was a surprise attack by Japan in the midst of negotiations. Merely because this was dishonorable, did that make it unthinkable? Hardly. It was exactly the procedure Japan had adopted in 1904 when she opened the Russo-Japanese War by surprise attack on the Russian fleet at Port Arthur.

In addition we had every possible physical indication. We had broken the Japanese code, we had warnings on radar, we had a constant flow of accurate intelligence. What failed? Not information but *judgment*. We had all the evidence and refused to interpret it correctly, just as the Germans in 1944 refused to believe the evidence of a landing in Normandy. Men will not believe what does not fit in with their plans or suit their prearrangements. The flaw in all military intelligence, whether twenty or fifty or one hundred percent accurate, is that it is no better than the judgment of its interpreters, and this judgment is the product of a mass of individual, social, and political biases, prejudgments, and wishful thinkings; in short, it is human and therefore fallible. If man can break the Japanese code and yet not believe what it tells him, how can he be expected to learn from the lessons of history?

Would a computer do better? In the case of Pearl Harbor, probably yes. If one could have fed all the pieces of intelligence available in November 1941 into a computer, it could have hardly failed to reply promptly, "Air attack, Hawaii, Philippines" and probably even "December 7." But will this work every time? Can we trust the lessons of history to computers? I think not, because history will fool them. They may make the right deductions and draw the right conclusions, but a twist occurs, someone sneezes, history swerves and takes another path. Had Cleopatra's nose been shorter, said Pascal, the whole aspect of the world would have been changed. Can a computer account for Cleopatra?

Once long ago when the eternal verities seemed clear—that is, during the Spanish Civil War—I thought the lessons of history were unmistakable. It appeared obvious beyond dispute that if fascism under Franco won, Spain in the foreshadowed European war would become a base for Hitler and Mussolini, the Mediterranean would become an Italian lake, Britain would lose Gibraltar and be cut off from her empire east of Suez. The peril was plain, the logic of the thing implacable, every sensible person saw it, and I, just out of college, wrote a small book published in England to point it up, all drawn from the analogy of history. The book showed how, throughout the eighteenth and nineteenth centuries, Britain had consistently interposed herself against the gaining of undue influence over Spain by whatever power dominated the continent. The affair of the Spanish marriages, the campaigns of Wellington, the policies of Castlereagh, Canning, and Palmerston all were directed toward the same objective: The strongest continental power must be prevented from controlling Spain. My treatise was, I thought, very artful and very telling. It did not refer to the then current struggle, but let the past speak for itself and make the argument. It was an irrefutable one—until history refuted it. Franco, assisted by Hitler and Mussolini, *did* win, European war *did* follow, yet unaccountably Spain remained neutral—at least nominally. Gibraltar did not fall, the portals of the Mediterranean did *not* close. I, not to mention all the other "premature" anti-fascists, as we were called, while morally right about the general danger of fascism, had been wrong about a particular outcome. The lessons of history I had so carefully set forth simply did not operate. History misbehaved.

Pearl Harbor and Spain demonstrate two things: One, that man fails to profit from the lessons of history because his prejudgments prevent him from drawing the indicated conclusions; and, two, that history will often capriciously take a different direction from that in which her lessons point. Herein lies the flaw in systems of history.

When it comes to systems, history played her greatest betrayal on Karl Marx. Never was a prophet so sure of his premises, never were believers so absolutely convinced of a predicted outcome, never was there an interpretation of history that seemed so foolproof. Analyzing the effects of the Industrial Revolution, Marx exposed the terrible riddle of the nineteenth century: that the greater the material progress, the wider and deeper the resulting poverty, a process which could only end, he decided, in the violent collapse of the existing order brought on by revolution. From this he formulated the doctrine of *Verelendung* (progressive impoverishment) and *Zusammenbruch* (collapse) and decreed that since working-class self-consciousness increased in proportion to industrialization, revolution would come first in the most industrialized country.

Marx's analysis was so compelling that it seemed impossible history could follow any other course. His postulates were accepted by followers of his own and later generations as if they had been graven on the tablets of Sinai. Marxism as the revealed truth of history was probably the most convincing dogma ever enunciated. Its influence was tremendous, incalculable, continuing. The founder's facts were correct, his thinking logical and profound; he was right in everything but his conclusions. Developing events did not bear him out. The working class grew progressively better, not worse, off. Capitalism did not collapse. Revolution came in the least, not the most, industrialized country. Under collectivism the state did not wither but extended itself in power and function and in its grip on society. History, ignoring Marx, followed her own mysterious logic, and went her own way.

When it developed that Marx was wrong, men in search of determinism rushed off to submit history to a new authority—Freud. His hand is now upon us. The Unconscious is king. At least it was. There are new voices, I believe, claiming that the Unconscious is a fraud—iconoclasm has reached even Freud. Nevertheless, in his effect on the modern outlook, Freud, I believe, unquestionably was the greatest influence for change between the nineteenth and twentieth centuries. It may well be that our time may one day be named for him and the Freudian Era be said to have succeeded the Victorian Era. Our understanding of human motivation has taken on a whole new dimension since his ideas took hold. Yet it does not seem to me that unconscious sexual and psychological drives are as relevant in all circumstances as they are said to be by the Freudians, who have become as fixed in their system as were the orthodox Marxists. They can supply historians with insights but not with guidance to the future because men *en masse* cannot be relied upon to behave according to pattern. All salmon swim back to spawn in the headwaters of their birth; that is universal for salmon. But man lives in a more complicated world than a fish. Too many influences are at work on him to make it applicable that every man is driven by an unconscious desire to swim back to the womb.

It has always seemed to me unfortunate, for instance, that Freud chose the experiences of two royal families to exemplify his concept of the Oedipus and Elektra complexes. Royalty lives under special circumstances, particularly as regards the issue of power between the sovereign and his heir, which are not valid as universal experience. The legend of Oedipus killing his father may have derived from the observed phenomenon that every royal heir has always hated his father, not because he wants to sleep with his mother but because he wants to ascend the throne. If the parental sovereign happens to be his mother, he hates her just as much. She will dislike him equally from birth because she knows he is destined to take her place, as in the case of Queen Victoria and her eldest son, who became Edward VII. That is not Freudian, it is simply dynastic.

As for Elektra, it is hard to know what to make of that tale. The House of Atreus was a very odd family indeed. More was going on there than just Elektra being in love with her father. How about Orestes, who helped her to kill their mother, or killed her himself, according to another version? Was not that the wrong parent? How come he did not kill his father? How about Iphigenia, the sister, whom Agememnon killed as a sacrifice? What is the Freudian explanation for that? They do not say, which is not being historical.

A historian cannot pick and choose his facts; he must deal with all the evidence.

Or take Martin Luther. As you know, Professor Erik Erikson of Harvard has discovered that Luther was constipated from childhood and upon this interesting physiological item he has erected a system which explains everything about his man. This is definitely the most camp thing that has happened to history in years. It even made Broadway. Nevertheless I do not think Luther pinned the 95 Theses on the church door at Wittenberg solely or even mainly because of the activity, or inactivity rather, of his anal muscle. His personal motive for protest may have had an anal basis for all I know, but what is important historically is the form the protest took, and this had to do with old and deep social grievances concerned with the worldliness of the church, the sale of indulgences, corruption of the clergy, and so on. If it had not been Luther who protested, it would have been someone else; Protestantism would have come with or without him, and its causes had nothing whatever to do with his private physiological impediment. Professor Erikson, I am sure, was attempting to explain Luther, not Protestantism, but his book has started a fad for psycho-history among those without the adequate knowledge or training to use it.

Following Freud there flourished briefly a minor prophet, Oswald Spengler, who proclaimed the Decline of the West, based on an elaborate study of the lessons of history. Off and on since then people have been returning to his theme, especially since World War II and the end of colonialism. The rise of China and the rash of independence movements in Asia and Africa have inspired many nervous second looks at Spengler. Europe is finished, say the knowing ones; the future belongs to the colored races and all that.

People have been burying Europe for quite some time. I remember a political thinker for whom I had great respect telling me in the thirties that Europe's reign was over; the future belonged to America, Russia, and China. It was a new and awful thought to me then and I was immensely impressed. As I see it now, his grouping has not been justified. I do not think Russia and America can be dissociated from Europe; rather, we are extensions of Europe. I hesitate to be dogmatic about Russia, but I am certain about the United States. American culture stems from Europe, our fortunes are linked with hers, in the long run we are aligned. My impression is that Europe, and by extension the white race, is far from finished. Europe's vitality keeps reviving; as a source of ideas she is inexhaustible. Nuclear fission, the most recent, if unwanted, advance, came from the work of a whole series of Europeans: Max Planck, the Curies, Einstein, Rutherford, Fermi, Niels Bohr, Szilard. Previously the three great makers of the modern mind, Darwin, Marx, and Freud, were Europeans. I do not know of an original idea to have importantly affected the modern world which has come from Asia or Africa (except perhaps for Gandhi's concept of non-violent resistance or civil disobedience, and, after all, Thoreau had the same idea earlier).

It does not seem to me a passing phenomenon or an accident that the West, in ideas and temporal power, has been dominant for so long. Far from falling behind, it seems to be extending its lead, except in the fearful matter of mere numbers and I like to think the inventiveness of the West will somehow eventually cope with that. What is called the emergence of the peoples of Asia and Africa is taking place in Western terms and is measured by the degree to which they take on Western forms, political, industrial, and otherwise. That they are losing their own cultures is sad, I think, but I suppose it cannot be helped. The new realm is space, and that too is being explored by the West. So much for Spengler.

Theories of history go in vogues which, as is the nature of vogues, soon fade and give place to new ones. Yet this fails to discourage the systematizers. They believe as firmly in this year's as last year's, for, as Isaiah Berlin says, the "obstinate craving for unity and symmetry at the expense of experience" is always with us. When I grew up, the economic interpretation of history, as formulated with stunning impact by Charles Beard, was the new gospel—as incontrovertible as if it had been revealed to Beard in a burning bush. Even to question that financial interests motivated our Founding Fathers in the separation from Britain, or that equally mercenary considerations decided our entrance into the First World War, was to convict oneself of the utmost naïveté. Yet lately the fashionable—indeed, what appears to be the required—exercise among historians has been jumping on Beard with both feet. He and the considerable body of his followers who added to his system and built it up into a dogma capable of covering any historical situation have been knocked about, analyzed, dissected, and thoroughly disposed of. Presently the historical establishment has moved on to dispose of Frederick Jackson Turner and his theory of the Frontier. I do not know what the new explanation is, but I am sure there must be some thesis, for, as one academic historian recently ruled, the writing of history requires a "large organizing idea."

I visualize the "large organizing idea" as one of those iron chain mats pulled behind by a tractor to smooth over a plowed field. I see the professor climbing up on the tractor seat and away he goes, pulling behind his large organizing idea over the bumps and furrows of history until he has smoothed it out to a nice, neat, organized surface—in other words, into a system.

The human being—you, I, or Napoleon—is unreliable as a scientific factor. In combination of personality, circumstance, and historical moment, each man is a package of variables impossible to duplicate. His birth, his parents, his siblings, his food, his home, his school, his economic and social status, his first job, his first girl, and the variables inherent in all of these, make up that mysterious compendium, personality—which then combines with another set of variables: country, climate, time, and historical circumstance. Is it likely, then, that all these elements will meet again in their exact proportions to reproduce a Moses, or Hitler, or De Gaulle, or for that matter Lee Harvey Oswald, the man who killed Kennedy?

So long as man remains the Unknowable Variable—and I see no immediate prospect of his ever being pinned down in every facet of his infinite variety—I do not see how his actions can be usefully programmed and quantified. The eager electronic optimists will go on chopping up man's past behavior into the thousands of little definable segments which they call Input, and the machine will whirr and buzz and flash its lights and in no time at all give back Output. But will Output be dependable? I would lay ten to one that history will pay no more attention to Output than it did to Karl Marx. It will still need historians. Electronics will have its uses, but it will not, I am confident, transform historians into buttonpushers or history into a system.

The Intellectual and His World

André Brink

(1980)

To say that the last quarter of the twentieth century presents us with a tough and practical world, with tough and practical demands on both society and the individual, is to state the obvious. Yet the obvious may require as much scrutiny as the cryptic or the arcane, since its very obviousness may tend to its being taken too much for granted. The result may be intellectual laziness and moral slackness. And this world of ours, provisionally described as tough and practical, demands above all a particular form of intellectual and moral courage—especially when it is approached from the perspective of the academic.

It has become customary to sneer at the impotence of the individual in general and the intellectual in particular. In a world overrun by masses and requiring, for its practical needs, ever-increasing common denominators, the individual appears a paltry and insignificant creature indeed, more often a hindrance than a help. And in a world demanding urgent solutions for problems like hunger, racism, exploitation, ideological and territorial expansionism, aggression and repression, the activity of the intellectual may appear not only futile but redundant, a luxury society can ill afford.

This is the context within which Lorca told his famous anecdote about the rich man and his peasant neighbour taking a stroll through a particularly scenic landscape: the rich man stopped in ecstasy every few minutes to exclaim with genuine appreciation: 'How beautiful!' But all the poor man could do in response was to clutch his belly and repeat: 'I am hungry, I am hungry, I am hungry!' Again, this is the context within which one encounters the accusation: 'No book and no thought can stop a bullet from a gun!' Or: 'I was suffering, and you offered me a theory of relativity. I was oppressed, and you formed a Freedom and Justice Committee to debate the nature of oppression. I was put in jail and tortured by the Security Police, and you said liberty was a commendable thing.' It is the context within which a leading South African Sunday newspaper, reviewing the axing of staff and departments at a particular university, commented that this was only a logical and possibly even salutary step, in keeping with the practice in big business to eliminate non-profitable areas of production.

These arguments and accusations derive from a Cartesian rigorism which divides thought and action into two separate categories divided by an either/or. In each group one finds thoroughly well-meaning persons condemning what they regard as their opposite group: 'You are being merely intellectual...'/'You are being merely practical...' There seems to be an unfortunate tendency in the West to think in these linear terms, these neat opposites. If you oppose the Government you are a communist; if you don't oppose it you're a fascist. And when an effort towards reconciliation is made, the solution usually seems to lie in creating a sliding scale containing thought on one end and action on the other, with the logical inference that the validity of thought lies in the measure in which it evolves into action, or prompts or promotes action. It seems to me an impoverishment of our experience to think in these terms. In fact, I would suggest that it is a line of thought which develops from either a misunderstanding or an obfuscation of the concepts 'thought' and 'action'; hence, of the concept 'intellectual'. It is the same sort of misunderstanding which, for such a long time, clouded the concepts of 'form' and 'content' in the arts.

Approached in one particular way one might suggest that 'thought' and 'action' are really two sides of the same coin, and that what matters is neither heads nor tails but the solid metal in between. In this context thought would be seen as interiorized action; action as expressive thought, or thought made visible. And neither can exist without the other: it is only in our impoverished interpretation of empirical processes that we fatefully separate them. But perhaps even the coin image is too mechanical: perhaps one should think in terms of an iceberg, with nine-tenths of thought submerged in order to allow one-tenth of action to protrude.

Although this may be a truer image, we are left with the situation I outlined at the beginning of my talk, in terms of which certain *kinds* of action seem to be preferable to others: preferable, at least, within the frameworks of the 'practical' demands of organized society. We are left, in other words, with the hungry man who cannot be fed on beauty; the jailed prisoner who cannot be freed through noble dictums; the company that cuts staff in order to 'rationalize' and which demands the same of universities. But in this situation, too, it seems to me that an either/or approach defeats the purpose and is too easy a way out. No one disputes that a hungry man should be fed, an unjustly imprisoned man freed, or an ailing company be made profitable. But having fulfilled all these obligations, would society then be a more just and free place to live in? Would people automatically be more fulfilled or the much vaunted 'quality of life' be enhanced *sans plus*? Put in the simplest possible terms: can man really live by bread alone? To take it one step further, remaining within the framework of our set examples: if Lorca's hungry man is given his daily bread, can one deny his well-fed neighbour his delight in something beautiful? Can a climate for justice, in which the unjustly jailed are set free, be created without the dedicated activity of those who insist on the basic requirement of justice in society? And once our company has been made profitable, is there not another set of rules to measure the 'profitability' of an institution for higher education? Balanced books are a good and honourable thing, but these do not rule out other kinds of books which create a balanced mind. 'Bread for one yen' says the Japanese proverb, 'For the other yen, white hyacinths.'

* * *

And so we are really back where we started: 'the intellectual and his world'. It may seem that we are now entitled to ask: What is the function of the intellectual in his world? But in Hamlet's words: *Madam, I know not 'seems'.* For it is, indeed, as unseemly a question as was the suggested dichotomy between 'thought' and 'action'. To pose this question would, after all, be to revive the dichotomy I have tried to discredit: it would imply a difference between an 'intellectual' and, say, an 'ordinary man', whatever either of these terms may mean. When I was caught up in the student protests in Paris in 1968 there was one particular march in which a million people took part, just after Daniel Cohn Bendit had been expelled from France, and a million voices shouted: 'We are all German Jews'—probably the only occasion in history when the French showed any liking for the Germans. But obviously nobody was so ridiculous as to take this in its literal sense. A form of poetry was on the streets that day; and a million people affirmed their common humanity and their common opposition to a system of laws and a pattern of society which denied or threatened that humanity. In this sense, we are all either 'ordinary men' or 'intellectuals'—or both: even though, in Orwell's immortal term, some may be more equal than others.

All I am trying to clarify is that asking about the function of the intellectual may be posing the wrong question. Let us rather, more cautiously, enquire about the function of that part in each one of us which is involved with intellectual activity: an enquiry which obviously has particular relevance within the framework of a university. For however 'modern' or 'practical' or 'pragmatic' or 'society-oriented' we may have become, I should still like to see, glimmering through the gloom, something of the original 'universality' in the word 'university': and if, as an institution, it is also becoming, through need and necessity, a career-orientated machine, it cannot ever, without denying itself, shed its function of shaping, broadening, stimulating and directing intellectual enquiry as the submerged nine-tenths of its unwieldy iceberg.

In thus directing my brief exploration towards the 'intellectual' half or nine-tenths of 'universal man', I accept, with Sir Herbert Read, that 'I am not concerned with the practicability of a programme. I am only concerned to establish the truth.' This is an ambitious activity into which one can enter only as an individual: thought is as exclusive to the individual as birth or death; and, I should like to think, as definitive. It is only natural that this activity of the individual should more often than not find itself in conflict with the accepted patterns of society: it is within this context that teaching has, rightly I think, been termed 'a subversive activity'. For in that territory of the mind where man is utterly and adventurously alone—even though he may assume responsibility for all men in what he undertakes (just as Sir Edmund Hilary, in a sense, climbed Everest for all mankind) the individual, putting everything at stake, can be guided only by the full and overwhelming reality of *that situation*, and not by general rules or by tradition. It is a religious solitude which can lead to perdition or redemption: but precisely because the stakes are so high it is an adventure unequalled by any other. To speak once again with Read:

'Life depends on the agitation set up by a few eccentric individuals. For the sake of that life, that vitality, a community must take certain risks, must admit a modicum of heresy. It must live dangerously if it would live at all.'

Or elsewhere:

'I realize that form, pattern, and order are essential aspects of existence; but in themselves they are the attributes of death. To make life, to ensure progress, to create interest and vividness, it is necessary to break down form, to distort pattern, to change the nature of our civilization.'

This seems a lofty and confused ideal. But it is possible to be more specific. I have no intention to be exhaustive in suggesting a few possibilities of intellectual action: only to venture a couple of yards across the border of this 'undiscover'd country' which differs from Hamlet's in that its travellers do survive to tell the tale.

'We must grasp what grips us,' said the literary theoretician Emil Staiger: a concept which may be broadened to intellectual activity as a whole. It is surely not part of our human condition simply to endure what happens: even in circumstances where it would appear impossible actively to influence the course of events the simple but momentous act of clarification—of establishing *what* is happening, and *why*—may become the starting point of significant social action. It works in two stages: informing oneself; and transmitting that information to others. The entire momentum of social action against authoritarian silence or authoritarian lies begins with the establishment of these two series of facts: what is happening; and why. No authority should be allowed to create a set of circumstances within which it becomes possible for anyone to say: *I didn't know.* What seems a very simple, basic procedure may, in societies like our own, prove to be an act of courage. It was the starting point of the Fischers and Mandelas in a struggle for a modicum of sanity in an insane structure. (Had the challenge of their intellectual enquiry been met instead of thwarted, violence could have been avoided.) It was the principle to which Beyers Naudé and the Christian Institute dedicated themselves. The Black Consciousness Movement, the Students' Council of Soweto, *The World*, Steve Biko, Donald Woods, and a fair percentage of the thousands of books banned in this country have been silenced in their various ways for this same basic reason: that truth is unbearable in a society which is built upon the lie. And only through the action of dedicated individuals, through the unflinching moral and intellectual enquiry of an independent mind, can silence and the lie be countered. We have an elemental need to know what grips us.

This enquiry is not directed exclusively towards a world of so-called external or social fact. The courage of the mind, which implies in our time Tillich's 'courage to be', demands also an enquiry of its own processes: of language, and of thought itself. We all know, when dealing with an estate agent, that 'charming' really means 'bloody awful', 'functional' means 'falling to pieces', and 'interesting view' means an unrestricted view of your neighbour's fence. But we also have to probe the language of authoritarianism: we have followed the semantic metamorphosis of 'apartheid' into 'separate development' into 'parallel development' into 'equal opportunity' into 'constellation of states'; of BOSS into DONS (a curious upgrading which the Mafia would appreciate), etc. But these are only the more glaring, obtrusive examples; and in an authoritarian society semantics is a very subtle game. We need only look at words like 'state security', 'law and order' and others to become aware of it. Among other processes one should be wary of the process of *definition:* our own society reveals startling similarities with that of Stalinist Russia described thus by Roland Barthes:

> In the Stalinist world, in which *definition*, that is to say the separation of
> Good and Evil, becomes the sole content of language, there are no more
> words without values attached to them, so that finally the function of writing is to cut out one stage of a process: there is no more lapse of time between naming and judging, and the closed character of language is
> perfected.

The search for truth, which is the search of the individual's intellectual activity, implies also an attack on facile polarities. In our dangerous society almost everything is experienced in terms of either/or. The most glaring: black/white; segregation/integration, etc.... In such a closed situation, I suggest, intellectual activity can contribute to a defusing of the tension created by simplistic polarities by clarifying the complexity of the issues involved and by exploring other options.

In immediate, practical terms: several previously white-dominated societies on our borders have in recent years and even months demonstrated a variety of different options. On a limited scale it applies even to Namibia, where some white Afrikaners have scrapped laws and rules regarded by other white Afrikaners as guarantees of national identity. If Namibia can survive without pass laws, group areas or the relevant sections of the Immorality Act, why should we be the only country in the world to need them for our survival?

South Africa has entered an exciting period in which, for the first time in thirty years, a limited range of new possibilities is being debated and in which the word 'change' is no longer, in itself, anathema. Intellectual integrity would lie neither in summarily dismissing it nor in accepting it as sufficient in itself. Instead, the true adventure of the mind would ensure that the range of possibilities be expanded immeasurably both in width and in depth, and that not only matters of bread and of physical survival be explored but also, and above all, those matters of intellect and morality without which it would be presumptuous to claim for ourselves the name of *man*. Without quantity we may not be able to survive: without quality it would not be worth while to.

White Lies

Robert Fulford

Canada is not a racist society, cannot possibly be a racist society—except in the sense that all societies are racist. It's true that opinion polls tell us that a good many Canadians believe Canada should remain predominantly white, but those people hold their views so diffidently or so timidly that they have almost no affect on public policy. Ever since the liberalization of immigration laws under the Pearson government in 1967, Canada has become increasingly a multiracial community, not by historic accident (like the United States) but by the conscious choice of a generally popular government. Currently about half of new immigrants are non-whites. If Canadians were racist in any serious sense they would force their members of parliament to force the government to reject Vietnamese, Indians, Pakistanis, West Indians, and other non-whites or "visible minorities," as the cant phrase describes them.

In truth, Canadian immigration policy is for all its faults as liberal as any on earth, far more liberal than the policies of most European countries, where "guest workers" are imported from poor countries and then sent home when no longer needed. Canadian policy, while it has drawn criticism from a few fringe groups, has not been seriously opposed by even one major national institution or public figure. This summer, at the Conservative convention, where right-wing views of almost every kind were being tossed around, the idea of white supremacy didn't make an appearance.

But Canadians, in this regard as in others, are a long way from being perfect. Like all other people, they have feelings of racism, and sometimes they express them. Non-whites particularly feel discriminated against in employment and housing, and organizations have sprung up to express their feelings. This problem, like so many others, has become a subject for federal inquiry. In May, James Fleming, the minister responsible for multiculturalism and therefore the minister responsible for keeping minorities firmly at the side of the Liberal Party, announced plans for a seven-member all-party parliamentary committee on racism. The committee will travel across the country, hold public hearings, and listen to complaints from people who feel themselves victims of racism. After six months it will issue a report recommending ways to lessen intolerance.

Fleming, as he described his committee, noted that in various parts of Canada there have been outrageous incidents of racial discrimination, some of them violent. "The time is long past," he said, "when we can sit back and be comfortable with the thought that these incidents are aberrations....Parliamentarians, as the representatives of all Canadians, must acknowledge that we have wounds, and look for ways to heal those wounds."

What can the parliamentarians do? Until recently they might have acknowledged that visible minorities experience difficulty finding jobs and therefore recommended that Ottawa set an example of aggressive tolerance through an affirmative-action hiring programme. But, not long after Fleming's announcement, Ottawa declared that it was going in just that direction—although so far its programme encompasses only women, native people, and the handicapped. What, then, is left for this parliamentary committee? A kind of national teach-in, perhaps, an airing of grievances met by solemn promises to do better? At best this will be a media event, focussing the attention of television and newspapers on the views of racial minorities. For months people across the country will be talking, through the media, about racial issues. The committee will attempt to organize public opinion through mass communications. Not entirely a bad idea, but not so promising an idea as Fleming imagines.

Much of the research and writing on race centres on the mass media and their effects. The media are frequently blamed for creating or reinforcing stereotypes and frequently charged with the responsibility of reforming our attitudes. The media created this problem: let them solve it. That seems simple enough, but it may involve a mistaken view of both media and racism.

Marshall McLuhan made a remarkable career by demonstrating, among other things, that people do not take the media seriously enough. In the post-McLuhan era we may be committing the opposite error of taking them too seriously. An ignorant aloofness about the subject has been replaced, in many circles, by an ignorant dedication to the idea that the media are a kind of first cause, both the reason we are in trouble and the way we are going to get out of it. A recent issue of *Currents: Readings in Race Relations*, a magazine published in Toronto by the Urban Alliance on Race Relations, is devoted to the subject of the media and visible minorities. An editorial setting the tone for the issue attributes to the media powers that would be awe-inspiring if they in fact existed. "The media set norms, create stereotypes, build leaders, set priorities and educate the general public," the editorial says. "Mass media confer status on those individuals and groups they select for placement in the public eye, telling the viewer, or reader, who and what is important to know about, think about, and *have feelings about*. [Emphasis added.] Those who are made visible through the media become worthy of attention and concern; those whom the media ignore remain invisible."

This view, which is not atypical, seems to me outlandishly exaggerated. The persuasive powers of the media may be impressive, but they are not nearly so great as the editor of *Currents* and others like him imagine. We could argue, just as vehemently, that the media are remarkably impotent. For example, the national media concentrate much more of their attention on politics than on any other subject, implicitly urging us all to share this obsession. Yet a great many citizens remain entirely indifferent to politics;

there are elections in which fewer than half of those eligible bother even to vote. Far from directing public opinion, the media seek frantically to keep up with it—witness the endless public-opinion polling conducted by the most powerful newspapers and television networks. If the media could tell us what to "have feelings about," they might well do so; but they cannot. TV and the newspapers may sometimes reinforce our feelings, but they cannot direct them. If they could, most readers of *The Toronto Star* would by now be dedicated supporters of Canadian nationalism, most readers of *The Globe and Mail* would be passionately concerned about civil liberties, all readers of Allan Fotheringham and Richard Gwyn would vote against the Liberals, and all children weaned on *Sesame Street* would be free of racial bigotry.

Currents argues that the media in general, and the movie industry in particular, "constantly portray racial and ethnic minorities in the most base and distorted characterizations." That's partly true, but the media also portray majorities—women, to start with—in distorted ways. Distortion of reality, which is also called drama, is a necessary characteristic of television, film, theatre, and fiction—a writer or a director or a network executive is not a human-relations counsellor or a statistician. It matters not at all whether we consider dramatic literature at the highest or the lowest level: we would not look to Shakespeare for a fair, balanced view of everyday life in Elizabethan England, any more than we would look to *Dallas* for an account of what actually happens in Dallas. Fiction and drama deal routinely in stereotypes, and only fools rely on fiction and drama for their view of the world. When race-relations experts—whose attitudes are accurately reflected by *Currents*—place this much emphasis on the media, they imply that the public in its deepest and most atavistic feelings is entirely malleable, that it drifts from attitude to attitude at the suggestion of the media. The parliamentary committee will be forced to rely on this same malleability in its earnest efforts to "heal these wounds."

"It is difficult to combat past stereotypes," says *Currents*, "if the most influential and pervasive medium of them all [television] continues to feature movies which originated those stereotypes." The implication is that TV should sanitize itself by discarding all those films of the 1930s and 1940s in which racial minorities are occasionally shown in ways that offend the values of the 1980s. That would result in a serious loss—in knowledge of film, in knowledge of the past, and in ordinary enjoyment. To jettison those movies would be to place a pious attitude toward racial feelings above all other values. It would also be to admit that the media are a major cause of the problem.

Are they? It could as easily be argued that the media have promoted good race relations. If we examine only North America, which has been subjected to more mass media than any other part of the world, we can see the rise of the mass media occurring simultaneously with a rise in racial tolerance. Certainly the residents of this continent were much more subject to bigotry in, say, 1910 (before mass media) than today. If the media have had an effect it is in the direction of opening up and enlarging our view of the human race. We begin to think differently about people of other races when we see them as actors, musicians, comedians, commentators—or as the subjects of documentaries. Northrop Frye has said: "Television does have a profoundly civilizing aspect in that it compels people to look like people. I think of what an abstract notion I had of Eskimos when I was a student at school, or even college, and how that simply disappeared as soon as one began seeing them on television....You have to start whittling away your stereotypes." Of course television will not automatically produce tolerant or understanding citizens. If one is predisposed to bigotry one may remain a bigot; if one is otherwise predisposed, one may be broadened by the images of minorities on TV and outraged when those images are limited to stereotypes. In any case, whatever the effect of TV in propagating the most famous media stereotypes (the "bad Indian" and the "good Indian" in westerns, for instance), there are other stereotypes that persist without the help of media. A veteran politician has told me that in rural Ontario the most persistent bigotry he encounters is against Roman Catholics, about whom the media have traditionally had little to say.

My own experience suggests that there are factors in everyone's life more important than either the exhortations of government bodies (even when conveyed through we're-all-in-this-together anti-racist advertising) or the routine bombardment of media images. Parental example, personal experience, religious training, the attitudes of peers—each of these separately, certainly all of them together, amount to much more than the larger and vaguer messages of government and media, whether those messages are clumsy and inadvertent or carefully shaped by propagandists. It is in the world of private experience, not the media or government, that racism persists and that racism may eventually be defeated. One does not hear Newfie jokes or Polish jokes on television; one hears them in private. Racism is given its power in our lives not by something seen on television but by something heard at the coffee machine in the office. And racism is stripped of its power every time someone of one race meets someone of another and finds the meeting engaging, or enjoyable, or enriching. The poetry of private life, the decency possible in ordinary relationships—these are the best and perhaps the only answer to racism.

A friend of mine, dealing in frustration with an incompetent black on the telephone, realized recently that he himself was—in one sense, at least—a racist. He wanted to say to her: "You black bitch, get moving on this." He has an extremely expensive education which should, theoretically, have rooted out the racism in his soul—an MD, a residency in psychiatry, a long practice in a multiracial city. But he remains, as he knew in that moment, a racist. He did not *utter* those words, being far too civilized, but he thought them, and in the process understood the persistence of his racism. He disapproves of this part of himself, and rightly so, but in thinking about him (and millions like him) we should understand that there are different forms of racism. There is a distinction between instinct and behaviour, between feelings and policy, and the distinctions are crucial.

In the 1940s my parents told me that racism (we called it "intolerance" or "discrimination" in those days) was evil, and I accepted their teaching. Ever since, I have tried not to be a racist. Yet I still find myself more comfortable with and more reliant on people of my own race or closely related races. Logic suggests that in my dealings I probably favour those like me. In a sense I am, therefore, a racist—and would distrust anyone, of any colour, who claimed that he or she was not. We can consciously affect our behaviour and policy; we are, for the most part, unable to change our instincts and feelings, however shameful we may think them.

This distinction is lost in much of the public discussion of racism. For example, a report on racism in Toronto—one of eleven regional reports released by James Fleming when he announced his parliamentary committee—declared that there had been a recent and obvious improvement in race relations and then quickly denied that any encouragement could be taken from that improvement. "It is generally agreed by both the minority communities and the civic authorities," the report said, "that acts of racism in the streets, transportation system and public places have decreased. Some believe, however, that prejudiced persons have learned to conceal their prejudice, and that those Torontonians who have been traditionally 'polite racists' are even more polite now." The implication is that, since all racism is bad (right), one form of it is as bad as another (wrong). The report seems to say that polite racism is no better than pushing people under subway trains or beating them with baseball bats. In fact, polite racism is an enormous improvement on the other kind: it indicates that those who hold racist feelings have been instructed (by their peers, by society, by the media, or some other force) that these feelings are despicable and like all despicable feelings should be held in private if they must be held at all. If people can understand that it is required of them to—as the report scornfully puts it—"conceal their prejudice," then enormous progress has been made. That may be all, in this unjust and imperfect world, that we can hope for.

What Psychiatry Can and Cannot Do

Thomas S. Szasz

Psychiatry today is in the curious position of being viewed simultaneously with too much reverence and with undue contempt. Indeed, thoughtful Americans can be roughly divided between those who dismiss all forms of psychiatric practice as worthless or harmful, and those who regard it as a panacea for crime, unhappiness, political fanaticism, promiscuity, juvenile delinquency, and virtually every other moral, personal, and social ill of our time.

The adherents of this exaggerated faith are, I believe, the larger and certainly the more influential group in shaping contemporary social policy. It is they who beat the drums for large-scale mental health programs and who use the prestige of a massive psychiatric establishment as a shield of illusion, concealing some ugly realities we would rather not face. Thus when we read in the paper that the alcoholic, the rapist, or the vandal needs or will be given "psychiatric care," we are reassured that the problem is being solved or, in any event, effectively dealt with, and we dismiss it from our minds.

I contend that we have no right to this easy absolution from responsibility. In saying this I do not, as a practicing psychiatrist, intend to belittle the help that my profession can give to some troubled individuals. We have made significant progress since the pre-Freudian era, when psychiatry was a purely custodial enterprise.

However, our refusal to recognize the differences between medicine and psychiatry—that is, between deviations from biological norms, which we usually call "illness," and deviations from psychological or social norms, which we often call "mental illness"—has made it possible to popularize the simplistic clichés of current mental health propaganda. One of these, for instance, is the deceptive slogan "Mental illness is like any other illness." This is not true; psychiatric and medical problems are fundamentally dissimilar. In curing a disease like syphilis or pneumonia, the physician benefits both the patient and society. Can the psychiatrist who cures a "neurosis" make the same claim? Often he cannot, for in "mental illness" we find the individual in conflict with those about him—his family, his friends, his employer, perhaps his whole society. Do we expect psychiatry to help the individual—or society? If the interests of the two conflict, as they often do, the psychiatrist can help one only by harming the other.

II

Let us, for example, examine the case of a man I will call Victor Clauson. He is a junior executive with a promising future, a wife who loves him, and two healthy children. Nevertheless he is anxious and unhappy. He is bored with his job, which he believes saps his initiative and destroys his integrity; he is also dissatisfied with his wife, and convinced he never loved her. Feeling like a slave to his company, his wife, and his children, Clauson realizes that he has lost control over the conduct of his life.

Is this man "sick"? And, if so, what can be done about it? At least half a dozen alternatives are open to him: He could throw himself into his present work or change jobs or have an affair or get a divorce. Or he could develop a psychosomatic symptom such as headaches and consult a doctor. Or he could seek help from a psychotherapist. Which of these alternatives is the right one for him? The answer is not easy.

For, in fact, hard work, an affair, a divorce, a new job may all "help" him; and so may psychotherapy. But "treatment" cannot change his external, social situation; only he can do that. What psychoanalysis (and some other therapies) can offer him is a better knowledge of himself, which may enable him to make new and better choices in the conduct of his life.

Is Clauson "mentally sick"? If we so label him, what then is he to be cured of? Unhappiness? Indecision? The consequences of earlier, unwise decisions?

In my opinion, these are problems in living, not diseases. And by and large it is such problems that are brought to the psychiatrist's office. To ameliorate them he offers not treatment or cure but psychological counselling. To be of any avail, this process requires a consenting, co-operative client. There is, indeed, no way to "help" an individual who does not want to be a psychiatric patient. When treatment is imposed on a person, inevitably he sees it as serving not his own best interests, but the interests of those who brought him to the psychiatrist (and who often pay him).

Take the case of an elderly widow I will call Mrs. Rachel Abelson. Her husband was a successful businessman who died five years ago, bequeathing part of his estate of four million dollars to his children and grandchildren, part to charities, and one third to his wife. Mrs. Abelson has always been a frugal woman, whose life revolved around her husband. After he died, however, she changed. She began to give her money away—to her widowed sister, to charities, and finally to distant relatives abroad.

After a few years, Mrs. Abelson's children remonstrated, urging her to treat herself better, instead of wasting her money on people who had long managed by themselves. But Mrs. Abelson persisted in doing what she felt was "the right thing." Her children were wealthy; she enjoyed helping others.

Finally, the Abelson children consulted the family attorney. He was equally dismayed by the prospect that Mrs. Abelson might in this fashion dissipate all the funds she controlled. Like the children, he reasoned that if Mr. Abelson had wanted to help his third cousin's poverty-stricken daughters in Romania, he could have done so himself; but he never did. Convinced that they ought to carry out the essence of their father's intention and keep the money in the family, the Abelson children petitioned to have their mother declared mentally incompetent to manage her affairs. This was done. Thereafter Mrs. Abelson became inconsolable. Her bitter accusations and the painful scenes that resulted only convinced her children that she really was mentally abnormal. When she refused to enter a private sanitarium voluntarily, she was committed by court order. She died two years later, and her will—leaving most of her assets to distant relatives—was easily broken on psychiatric grounds.

Like thousands of other involuntary mental patients, Mrs. Abelson was given psychiatric care in the hope of changing behavior offensive to others. Indeed, what was Mrs. Abelson's illness? Spending her money unwisely? Disinheriting her sons? In effect, recourse to psychiatry provided Mrs. Abelson's children with a socially acceptable solution for their dilemma, not hers. To an appalling degree, state mental hospitals perform a like function for the less affluent members of our society.

Out of all too many comparable cases, I will cite that of a man we may call Tim Kelleher, who worked steadily as a truck driver for forty years, supporting a wife and nine children. In his early sixties Kelleher found jobs getting scarcer. Now in his late seventies, he has not worked for over a decade. Since his wife died a few years ago, he has lived with one or another of his children.

For two years his daughter Kathleen, mother of four, has been caring for him. Because the old man has grown progressively senile and burdensome, Kathleen's husband wants to shift the responsibility to the other children, but they all feel they've done their share.

Mr. Kelleher's future depends on what his family decides to do with him. One of them may still be willing to take care of him, but, if not, he will be committed to a state mental hospital. His case will be diagnosed as a "senile psychosis" or something similar. More than a third of the patients now in our mental hospitals are such "geriatric" cases. This is how psychiatry meets a purely socioeconomic need.

If Mr. Kelleher or one of his children were even moderately wealthy, they could hire a companion or nurse to care for him at home, or they could place him in a private nursing home. There would be no need to label him a "mental patient" and confine him to a building he will never again leave, and where he will doubtless die within a year.

But, for the poor, the mental hospital is often the only way. Such is the plight of Mrs. Anna Tarranti (this is not her real name). At thirty-two—but looking ten years older—she has just been delivered of her seventh child. Her husband is a construction worker, sporadically employed, and a heavy drinker. After each of the last three babies was born, Mrs. Tarranti was so "depressed" that she had to stay in the hospital an extra week or more. Now she complains of exhaustion, cannot eat or sleep, and does not want to see her baby. At the same time she feels guilty for not being a good mother, and says she ought to die.

The fact is that Mrs. Tarranti is overwhelmed. She has more children than she wants, a husband who earns only a marginal living, and religious beliefs that virtually prohibit birth control. What should she do? She knows that if she goes home, she'll soon be pregnant again, a prospect she cannot endure. She would like to stay in the hospital, but the obstetrical ward is too busy to keep her long without a bona fide obstetrical illness.

Again psychiatry comes to the rescue. Mrs. Tarranti's condition is diagnosed as a "post-partum depression" and she is committed to the state hospital. As in the case of Mr. Kelleher, society has found no more decent solution to a human problem than confinement in a mental hospital.

In effect, psychiatry has accepted the job of warehousing society's undesirables. Such, alas, has long been its role. More than a hundred and fifty years ago, the great French psychiatrist Philippe Pinel observed, "Public asylums for maniacs have been regarded as places of confinement for such of its members as have become dangerous to the peace of society."[1]

III

Nor have we any right to comfort ourselves with the belief that in our enlightened age confinement in a mental institution is really the same as any other kind of hospitalization. For even though we show more compassion and understanding toward the insane than some of our forebears, the fact is that the person diagnosed as mentally ill is stigmatized—particularly if he has been confined in a public mental hospital. These stigmata cannot be removed by mental health "education," for the root of the matter is our intolerance of certain kinds of behavior.

Most people who are considered mentally sick (especially those confined involuntarily) are so defined by their relatives, friends, employers, or perhaps the police—not by themselves. These people have upset the social order—by disregarding the conventions of polite society or by violating laws—so we label them "mentally ill" and punish them by commitment to a mental institution.

The patient knows that he is deprived of freedom because he has annoyed others, not because he is sick. And in the mental hospital he learns that until he alters his behavior he will be segregated from society. But even if he changes and is permitted to leave, his record of confinement goes with him. And the practical consequences are more those of a prison than a hospital record. The psychological and social damage thus incurred often far outweighs the benefits of any psychiatric therapy.

Consider, for example, the case of a young nurse I will call Emily Silverman, who works in a general hospital in a small city. Unmarried and lonely, she worries about the future. Will she find a husband? Will she have to go on supporting herself in a job that has become drudgery? She feels depressed, sleeps poorly, loses weight. Finally, she consults an internist at the hospital and is referred to a psychiatrist. He diagnoses her trouble as a case of "depression" and prescribes "anti-depressant" drugs. Emily takes the pills and visits

---

[1] Pinel, P.: A Treatise on Insanity (1801, 1809), transl. by D.D. Davis, facsimile of the London 1806 edition (New York: Hafner Publishing Co., 1962), pp. 3-4.z

the psychiatrist weekly, but she remains depressed and begins to think about suicide. This alarms the psychiatrist, who recommends hospitalization. Since there is no private mental hospital in the city, Emily seeks admission to the state hospital nearby. There, after a few months, she realizes that the "treatment" the hospital offers cannot help solve her problems. She then "recovers" and is discharged.

From now on, Emily is no longer just a nurse; she is a nurse with a "record" of confinement in a state mental hospital. When she tries to return to her job, she will probably find it filled and that there are no openings. Indeed, as an ex-mental patient, she may find it impossible to obtain any employment in nursing. This is a heavy price to pay for ignorance, yet no one warned her of the hazards involved before she decided to enter the hospital for her "depression."

Because the therapeutic potentialities of psychiatry are consistently exaggerated and its punitive functions minimized or even denied, a distorted relationship between psychiatry and the law has evolved in our time.

Years ago some people accused of serious crimes pleaded "insanity." Today they are often charged with it. Instead of receiving a brief jail sentence, a defendant may be branded "insane" and incarcerated for life in a psychiatric institution.[2]

This is what happened, for example, to a filling-station operator I will call Joe Skulski. When he was told to move his business to make way for a new shopping center, he stubbornly resisted eviction. Finally the police were summoned. Joe greeted them with a warning shot in the air. He was taken into custody and denied bail, because the police considered his protest peculiar and thought he must be crazy. The district attorney requested a pretrial psychiatric examination of the accused. Mr. Skulski was examined, pronounced mentally unfit to stand trial, and confined in the state hospital for the criminally insane. Through it all, he pleaded for the right to be tried for his offense. Now in the mental hospital, he will spend years of fruitless effort to prove that he is sane enough to stand trial. If he had been convicted, his prison sentence would have been shorter than the term he has already served in the hospital.

IV

This is not to say that our public mental hospitals serve no socially useful purpose. They do, in fact, perform two essential—and very different—functions. On the one hand, they help patients recover from personal difficulties by providing them with room, board, and a medically approved escape from everyday responsibilities. On the other hand, they help families, and society, care for those who annoy or burden them unduly. It is important that we sort out these very different services, for unfortunately their goals are not the same. To relieve people annoyed by the eccentricities, failings, or outright meanness

---

[2] Szasz, T.S.: *Psychiatric Justice* (New York: Macmillan, 1965).

of so-called mentally disturbed persons requires that something be done *to* mental patients, not *for* them. The aim here is to safeguard the sensibilities not of the patient, but of those he upsets. This is a moral and social, not a medical, problem. How, for example, do you weigh the right of Mr. Kelleher to spend his declining years in freedom and dignity rather than as a psychiatric prisoner, against the right of his children to lead a "life of their own" unburdened by a senile father? Or the right of Mrs. Tarranti to repudiate overwhelming responsibilities, against her husband's and children's need for the services of a full-time wife and mother? Or the right of Mrs. Abelson to give away her money to poor relatives, against her children's claim on their father's fortune?

Granting that there can often be no happy resolution to such conflicts, there is no reason to feel that we are as yet on the right road. For one thing, we still tolerate appalling inequities between our treatment of the rich and the poor. Though it may be no more than a dimly grasped ideal, both medicine and law strive to treat all people equally. In psychiatry, however, we not only fail to approximate this goal in our practice; we do not even value it as an ideal.

We regard the rich and influential psychiatric patient as a self-governing, responsible client—free to decide whether or not to be a patient. But we look upon the poor and the aged patient as a ward of the state—too ignorant or too "mentally sick" to know what is best for him. The paternalistic psychiatrist, as an agent of the family or the state, assumes "responsibility" for him, defines him as a "patient" against his will, and subjects him to "treatment" deemed best for him, with or without his consent.

Do we really need more of this kind of psychiatry?

TERMS and TOPICS

TERMS

1. **Vocabulary, Section III:** aberrations, absolution, adrenal, advocate, affluent, ameliorate, amenity, anaesthetizes, anathema, anxieties, arcane, arresting, atavistic, atrophy, banal, barbarous, bolstered, cajoled, capriciously, carnivore, chauvinistic, compendium, concomitant, contentious, cryptic, debasing, decadent, dichotomy, diffidently, disdain, dissection, dissemination, egregious, emasculate, evocative, fait accompli, flyblown, frugal, gross, hackneyed, humbug, immutable, incidence, incurred, indigenous, irrefutable, jeopardy, metamorphosis, modicum, noncommittal, obfuscation, obstreperous, omnipotence, paltry, panacea, pedagogical, perdition, perverting, preclude, precocious, preoccupied, priggish, ranting, repudiate, salutary, semantic, shirk, simplistic, slovenliness, sporadically, stigmatized, synthesis, traduced, unwarranted, utilitarian, vaunted, vehemently, venerable, virile, vogues, voyeur, welter, wonky

2. All kinds of writing use *rhetorical devices*, though argument probably makes the greatest use of them. Prominent among them is the *rhetorical question* (see Terms, section I), whereby a speaker or writer implicitly invites readers to strengthen an argument by themselves supplying a supposedly obvious answer. *Parallelism* (see Terms, section II) could be thought of as another. *Chiasmus* is used in "A Note to the Reader." A similar device is *antithesis*, a balanced structure whose two halves contrast, sometimes in parallel form and sometimes in the reverse order of chiasmus.

3. *Metaphor* and *simile* are defined in "A Note to the Reader," along with other terms. Are **symbols** and **allusions** also kinds of *figurative language* or *figurative thought*? Differentiate between *figurative language* and *rhetorical devices*. For example, is *paradox* (see Terms, section I) a figure of speech (or thought) or a rhetorical device, a figure of rhetoric? Is it, perhaps, a kind of *irony* (see Terms, section II)? Or can it be thought of as in a way all three?

4. *Analogy*   Reasoning from certain similarities between two things that they are alike in one or more other respects as well. For example, if one begins by assuming that a country is like a business in certain ways, one could then conclude, by analogy, that the qualities of a good business manager are the qualities needed in the leader of a country. Not all analogies are logically sound. Is this one?

5. *Denotation* and *connotation* are terms that it is important to understand and to keep in mind when deciding what words to use. *Denotation* is the literal, straightforward meaning of a word; *connotation* is what a word suggests or implies, sometimes by association of ideas or even of sound. For example, the words *fat, roly-poly, overweight, obese, chunky, heavy*, and *portly* all denote pretty much the same thing—but their connotations are quite different. Which do you think are negative? positive? neutral? What does *embonpoint* mean? What does it connote?

6. *Parody*   Imitation of a writer's style or of a specific work, either by exaggeration of style or by straightforward imitation of style with the subject altered—often (but not always) to ridicule the original.

7. *Axiom* A self-evident truth or established principle. How does an axiom differ from an *assumption* or a *presumption*? Distinguish between a *hypothesis* and a *theory*. Is there any place for *conjecture* in argumentative writing?

8. Distinguish between *journalism* and *journal.* What are the features of journalistic writing that make some people object to it? What are its advantages?

9. *Innuendo* A usually derogatory suggestion or hint; an insinuation. Is an innuendo a kind of *allusion* (see "A Note to the Reader"), or not?

TOPICS: On Individual Essays

GEORGE ORWELL *"Politics and the English Language"*

1. Near the end of his essay Orwell lists six "rules" of writing. Are they useful rules? Does Orwell obey his own rules in this essay?

2. Could Orwell be mistaken? What's wrong with jargon, foreign terms, plural structures, and Latinate diction? Are these all absolute evils in writing? Can you find something good to say for clichés? for euphemism?

3. Compare Orwell's views of style with those of Hornyansky (section VI).

4. Explain what Orwell means when he argues that language is political, or that the structures of language articulate some political assumptions, the more dangerous the more they are unexamined.

5. Using Orwell's rules, analyze the style of your local newspaper, or a recent issue of an established magazine such as *Saturday Night, Forbes,* or *The New Statesman.* Does your analysis reveal any "political" assumptions, especially any "undeclared" ones?

6. Can you write clearly without thinking clearly? If you don't think clearly, can you read clearly? Explain what you mean by "clear thinking."

7. Write an argument either agreeing or disagreeing with Orwell's assertion that "in our age.... all issues are political issues ...."

PAULINE KAEL *"The Sound of..."*

1. Identify these allusions: "the opium of the audience," "the best of all possible worlds." Is the allusion to Pavlov effective?

2. At the end of the review Kael says she is angry. Point out all you can find that makes her anger apparent throughout, long before she states it explicitly.

3. Is Kael guilty of using slanted or loaded diction in this review? Consider such forceful words as *cynical, purveyors, loathe, self-indulgent, imbeciles, shoddy, cant, sentimental.* Or does it depend on the reader—that is, is she preaching to the converted? (The review appeared originally in *The New Yorker.*) What should a review do? Whom is it written for? Why might Kael's review appeal to or alienate particular kinds of readers? Do you think it could persuade someone who initially disagreed?

4. Using the appropriate indexes and other aids in your library, look up others' reviews of these films. Do any differ substantially from Kael in their assessments? If so, what are their reasons? Are you convinced that these two movies are bad, and do you therefore not want to see them? Or, if you have already seen one or both, do you agree with Kael's assessment? If you don't, compose a counter-argument.

5. Write a two- or three-page review of one or two movies or television programs you have seen recently and that you feel are bad for other than obvious or technical reasons—that is, not because of poor acting, script, direction, or photography, but because of their implicit assumptions or projected values. Try to convince your readers, not that they won't be entertained, but that they shouldn't foster, condone, or submit themselves to such programs or movies.

FLANNERY O'CONNOR *"Total Effect and the Eighth Grade"*

1. Compose a sentence or two using *effect* as a verb.

2. From your own experience of reading fiction, both in and out of school, do you agree with O'Connor's assertions? Do you agree that a high-school student's taste, since it is in the process of being formed, should not be consulted? If so, at what point, if ever, should a student's taste be consulted?

3. In paragraph 6, is O'Connor correct, or fair, in using the word stupid? What she refers, near the end, to the high schools' "proper business of preparing foundations," is she begging the question—assuming as proved, or given, something that in fact needs to be proved? Who decides what is "proper," and on what grounds? What does "proper" mena? Try to defend her against the charge.

4. Pursue the ramifications of O'Connor's argument. Can you propose an acceptable counter-argument?

5. Write an essay in the form of a letter to a couple of cousins or other relatives two or three yers your junior in which you tell them of several books you think they should read, and why you think they should. Would it be more difficult to tell them what you think they should not read? Try it.

GLENN GOULD *"Music and Technology"*

1. Think about tone: How does Gould manage to be both wittily self-deprecatory and serious at the same time?

2. In what way does Gould dismiss the easy distinction once articulated by C.P. Snow—that science and art were "two cultures" that don't communicate with each other?

3. Write a research essay investigating the ways technology has changed the nature of art in the twentieth century—or in the eighteenth or nineteenth century—whether by altering equipment, the media used, the process of communicating, the character of perception, or whatever.

4. Listen to three recordings of Bach's *Goldberg Variations*, one by Gould. Write a review of the different versions, commenting on what you think are the strengths and limitations of each.

5. What is a documentary? Is *Lionheart Gal* (see Cooper's review in section VI) a documentary? In what ways do radio documentaries, television documentaries, and written documentaries differ?

6. Examine and discuss Gould's distinction between the human and the antihuman.

WILLIAM ZINSSER   *"Nobody Here but Us Dead Sheep"*

1. Note that Zinsser begins his article with three fragmentary or minor sentences. Effective? More such sentences occur farther on. Do the relatively short paragraphs work, or do they make the piece seem too choppy, too journalistic? (It first appeared in *Life* magazine, in a columnar format.)

2. Do the short sentences and paragraphs affect tone? Characterize Zinsser's tone, citing specific passages as examples. Does he seem to you to adopt any kind of mask or *persona*?

3. In a chapter on humour in his book *On Writing Well*, Zinsser says that the "heightening of some crazy truth—to a level where it will be seen as crazy—is at the heart of what the serious humorist is trying to do." Does that describe what he is doing in this essay? How can one be a "serious humorist"? Is Zinsser serious when he refers to "one more joke"? Is the joke funny? Examine the function of irony in this essay. Is irony necessarily funny?

4. What audience is Zinsser addressing? Do you think his article would be a persuasive argument for one audience and not for another? Explain. In just what way can it be considered an argument at all?

5. Write an argument describing something going on in your vicinity that you think is patently absurd but that is nonetheless officially sanctioned. Try to use some humour and irony the way Zinsser does. Or write a letter to a public figure or to a newspaper or magazine protesting some statement or act or article or advertisement that you feel strongly about. Use all the irony you can muster, and allow yourself at least one good burst of outright sarcasm. Consider sending the letter.

ELAINE MORGAN   *"The Man-Made Myth"*

1. Note how a recognizably argumentative tone and context is evident even in the kinds of terms Morgan uses—for example: *subtle underlying assumptions, distorted, eradicated, manifestly, conclusions, authoritative, homily, mistake, believe, theoretical, buttressed, authenticated, dispute the facts, ignore the facts, interpretation, ambiguous, prejudice, quibble, petulance, deduces, mesmerized, vitiated, speculation, theory, rudiments, cursory, nonsense, postulate, doctrine, alleged, quandary, questions, incompatible.* Find some others.

2. As the opening chapter of a book, this piece is obviously not complete in itself; the main arguments and evidence are still to come. But note how deftly Morgan piques the reader's curiosity. Point out some places where she does this.

3. Morgan seems to deal fairly with the opposition, quoting at length from the books by Ardrey and Morris that constitute her principal targets. If you know their books, or even if you know only what Morgan quotes, do you agree, after reading this introductory chapter, that their explanations are on the face of it "ludicrous," logically absurd?

4. In paragraph 8 Morgan says that one "cannot avoid" using the word *man* for the species and that the generic pronoun *he* is "a simple matter of linguistic convenience." Is she correct? Have things changed since 1972? How important is this point as part of her argument?

5. Write an argument attacking some popular or widely distributed book or article that you believe to be illogical, dangerous, or otherwise wrongheaded—for example something about dieting, a piece of self-praise by some government or industry, an editorial on some feature of public policy. Use sound, clear, and hard-hitting logic, but use wit rather than table-pounding anger. And remember that if you call something outrageous or ludicrous, you are obliged to demonstrate that it is so.

MARY MEIGS *"Pandora Was a Feminist"*

1. Look up and read the stories of Eve, Pandora, Bluebeard, and Prometheus. What does *Prometheus* mean? Why doesn't Meigs mention that, as she does for *Epimetheus*? How did God test Job?

2. Are Meigs's curiosity, impatience, and hatred of suspense common traits among other people? More common among women than among men? Do you agree that "Pandora was right to open the box"? Would you, in Pandora's place, have opened the box? Do you have a "box of the secret self"? Are you afraid to open it? Can it be dangerous to know "too much" about oneself? Or do you agree with Meigs that it's best to know everything? How convincing is her argument on this point?

3. Is it fair of Meigs to emphasize that "'plagues escaped to harass helpless *man*'"? What does the word *man* mean here? What does Meigs mean by referring to the reproduction of the sexes, in the myth of Deucalion and Pyrrha, "by a kind of parthenogenesis" as "another case of patriarchal wish-fulfillment"? Near the end Meigs says that Pandora had "the courage to show everybody what Zeus was up to," whereas earlier she follows the myth and calls it "curiosity." Is she stretching a point for the sake of her argument, or has she successfully made the transition from one term to the other?

4. Find another classical myth that you can use in an essay to illustrate some truth about modern people. Use it.

BARBARA TUCHMAN *"Is History a Guide to the Future?"*

1. Tuchman begins by using negative definition, saying what she thinks history is by saying what it is not: it is not sociology, it is not scientific, it is not quantification. Does her characterization of what sociologists do jibe with what you know about sociology? Is sociology a science? In the fourth and fifth paragraphs she points out some of the dangers and weaknesses of classification, or categorization, and of overdependence on machines such as computers. Now, twenty years later, would you be inclined to try to refute her argument by pointing to the increasing use and usefulness of computers? Do you believe that one *can* quantify behaviour and use the data to predict, reliably? If you do, compose an argument with some examples as evidence to support your position.

2. In paragraph 10 Tuchman acknowledges, with some qualification, that history can teach us lessons. What do you suppose she thought history could have taught Americans about Vietnam? Does hindsight help?

3. When Tuchman says (paragraph 9) that "*too* much confidence *cannot* be placed on the lessons of history," does she really mean that "too much confidence *can* be placed on the lessons of history" or that "*not* much confidence can be placed on the lessons of history"? (Our emphasis.) Could such a minor slip be attributable to the piece's being first delivered as a speech, and therefore being somewhat informal?

4. Can you think of any "modern" ideas that *have* come from Asia and Africa?

ANDRÉ BRINK " *The Intellectual and His World*"

1. What is the difference between *practical* and *practicable*? What does *cartesian* mean? Who is Sir Herbert Read? Paul Tillich? Identify the allusions in "can man really live by bread alone?" and "some may be more equal than others." If you know *Hamlet*, you will recognize the particular appropriateness of Brink's allusion in connection with the supposed dichotomy between thought and action. If you don't, read Hamlet's well-known "To be or not to be" soliloquy, for starters.

2. What is the role of thought in the life of a thinking person? Do you consider yourself an intellectual?

3. What kind of audience is Brink talking to? Does that help account both for his subject and for what he does with it?

4. Is it true that "truth is unbearable in a society which is built upon the lie"?

5. Sir Herbert Read was, among other things, a philosophical anarchist. Does it surprise you, then, that he should have been knighted? Why does Brink quote so much from Read, and how and why does he finally separate himself from Read?

6. Write an essay focussing on the weakness of an *either-or, black-white* approach as it is manifested in some issue in your community. Is something being pushed because it is "practical" or denounced because it is "impractical"?

ROBERT FULFORD "*White Lies*"

1. Define *racism*. What is "polite racism"? How can one know it's racism if it's completely concealed? How would you characterize the tone of the essay? Do you agree that most if not all of us are "in a sense" racists, that we each have our racial prejudices within us, however much we conceal them? Do you think it would be useful to you to talk or write about them? (Would Meigs argue that it would be?)

2. Did you grow up watching *Sesame Street*? What effects do you think it had on you? What role does or should education play in the matter of racism?

3. Note how at the end of paragraph 8 Fulford brings the discussion back to his central point, racism. Does that mean that what immediately precedes has been a digression?

4. Look up the letters to the editor that followed publication of this editorial in *Saturday Night* in September 1983. How valid are the responses to Fulford? Write either a counter-editorial or one that could follow Fulford's, explaining its ramifications, pushing the same subject further.

THOMAS S. SZASZ *"What Psychiatry Can and Cannot Do"*

1. Why has Szasz provided fictitious names for the patients he describes as examples? If he didn't want to use real names, why not simply refer to Mr. A., Mrs. B., and so on?

2. Why (in parts II and III) does Szasz put the words *depressed* and *depression* in quotation marks?

3. Szasz's essay is a relatively formally structured argument. Analyze its structure by writing out the opening sentence of each paragraph (sometimes an opening word or two will be enough to reveal the structure or movement).

4. Construct a formal argument about some social or other problem that you feel deeply about and about which you have some personal knowledge. Like Szasz, use some case histories to illustrate your points and support your proposition. And be sure to take into account the points your opponents would be likely to raise.

TOPICS: General and Comparative

1. Consider the ubiquitous world of advertising.

    (a) What techniques do advertisers use to try to persuade us? Examine several magazines of different kinds. What audience does each appeal to? How does the advertising in each magazine appeal to its audience?

    (b) Write a paragraph of advertising copy for some fictitious product. Then write a brief analysis of the techniques you used. What kind of reader were you aiming at? Rewrite your ad for a markedly different audience.

    (c) Translate or compose some real-estate ads according to Brink's suggestions about their real meaning. Do they use other misleading terms? Do other kinds of advertisements similarly twist language? How does one learn to decode them?

    (d) What makes a television commercial good or bad? Write an argument for or against the control of advertising on television.

2. What different kinds of persuasion do the essays in this section represent? Which persuade logically and which try to persuade emotionally? Point out instances of emotional appeal being used in addition to logic. Does that make for a stronger argument? Can it make an argument more interesting?

3. Examine some of the techniques of argument that the authors in this section use:

    (a) appeal to authority: Morgan, Brink. How does Zinsser cite authority?

    (b) analogy: Analogy is notoriously weak as an argumentative technique. How effective is the analogy at the end of Kael's third paragraph? or Gould's about a computerized war, or editing an interview? Evaluate the logic of O'Connor's comparison of literature to algebra and irregular French verbs: is the analogy sound, or could it be argued that literature is significantly different? Does Brink use analogy less as an argumentative tool than to illustrate or clarify? Compare its use in other kinds of writing, for example in Dillard's essay in section I.

    (c) wit and humor, ridicule: Kael, Gould, and Zinsser use humour and irony. Zinsser writes of "the funny story"; what connection does he see between logic and the unreasonable?

Unreasonable to whom? Is Kael ironic throughout or sometimes sarcastic? How can you distinguish? What is the effect of words and phrases like "twinkles," "operetta cheerfulness," "a spider on the valentine"? Zinsser uses *argumentum ad absurdum*—exaggerating to demonstrate the absurdity of what he opposes. How effective do you find such methods?

(d) examples: Orwell, Zinsser, Tuchman, and Szasz all use sequences of examples to support their generalizations. Are these cumulatively effective? Meigs and Brink use little narratives, illustrative anecdotes. In what other essays do you find examples, including anecdotes?

(e) questions: Both Meigs and Szasz end with rhetorical questions. How effective are these endings? Why does Szasz use so many rhetorical questions?

(f) Zinsser uses some statistics to bolster his points. How does Tuchman feel about statistics? What techniques does Morgan use? How does she debunk her opposition? By tone? logic? parody? What axioms does she accept? How does she use syllogism? Point out syllogistic structures in other essays; write them out as bare syllogisms.

4. For each of these essays, write down the *thesis*—or, for arguments, what is sometimes better thought of as the *proposition*. Which essays clearly state it? Which only imply it? Can an implied thesis or proposition sometimes be more forceful than a stated one? Where do you most often find them stated? How often do you find a thesis or proposition broken up into several parts stated at different places in an essay? Is Brink's epigrammatic final sentence part of his thesis?

5. To what degree does each of these arguments acknowledge the opposition and dispose of it? Are some fairer than others? Can you explain why? Is it sometimes a matter of audience? Are some more successful in rebuttal than others? What techniques seem to you to work best?

6. Consider also the more prominent internal strategies of development used in some of these essays. Kael, Morgan, Tuchman, Brink, and others make use of *definition*. Brink and Tuchman also use *classification*, which is often a way of defining. How does Fulford use classification? Who besides Kael uses *comparison and contrast*? Brink uses some *process analysis*. Does Morgan use process analysis in trying to explain "the descent of woman"? Not surprisingly, *cause and effect* is common in the essays in this section, for it is basic to much argument; Orwell, Kael, O'Connor, Morgan, Brink, and Fulford all use it—and is it there, perhaps less prominently, or even implicitly, in other essays? Do you find much narration and description in these essays, other than in the illustrative anecdotes?

7. Compare Morgan, Meigs, McClung (section II), Woolf (section IV), Atwood (section IV), and Cooper (section VI) on the subject of gender. Compose an imaginary conversation between two of them—or between three or four or even all six of them. Would there be much if any basic disagreement?

8. Brink stresses the importance of the individual as opposed to the masses. Note his reference to "that territory of the mind where man is utterly and adventurously alone." Why are people afraid to be alone? Do you agree that individuals are necessarily subversives? In your experience, is teaching a subversive activity? What connotation does the word *subversive* have for you? for others? for Brink? Compare Brink's quotation from Read about the need for eccentrics with what Iyer says about them (section IV). Do you believe that change, feared by so many, is not only desirable but necessary? Is Kael's mention of "the lowest common denominator of feeling" getting at the same point as Brink's reference to "ever-increasing common denominators"?

9. What is "scientific method"? Look up the term in several reference books and textbooks. Consider Szasz's essay and those by Roueché, Stephen Jay Gould, and Lewis Thomas in section IV: are they logical? Define *science*. What does science mean to you? Write an essay on the relevance or irrelevance of biology, the function of physics, the joys or dangers of chemistry, or some such topic—something you have first-hand experience of and firm opinions about.

10. What can we know? What can we prove? Compare what some of these writers have to say with Berlin's essay (section IV). Is complete objectivity possible, or should one think only of degrees of objectivity? Could you write an objective paper, or could you only try to appear objective? How would you go about trying to be totally impersonal? How important is objectivity in argument?

11. How similar are Orwell's concerns about language to those of Galbraith (section IV) and Hornyansky (section VI)? Who are the worst offenders against clarity and common sense in verbal communication? Orwell cites politicians, scientists, sociologists, psychologists, and art and literary critics. Can you cite others? Would Mitford (section IV) add morticians? Try to find examples that will enable you to distinguish among some of the kinds of *jargon*, variously referred to as *gobbledygook*, *bafflegab*, *psychobabble*, *journalese*, *bureaucratese*, *sociologese*, *educationese*, and so on. Or do they all run together? What characteristics do they *share*? In pursuing these matters, you may want to go farther afield and look at Orwell's novel *Nineteen Eighty-Four*; for example compare what Brink and Barthes, whom he quotes, say about language and what Orwell says in his appendix on "Newspeak."

12. Is Brink suggesting that people too easily take the obvious for granted, accepting what "is" as a *fait accompli*, a norm? How much control can we exercise over the way we interpret reality? Fulford says that "we are, for the most part, unable to change our instincts and feelings." Is this true, or is it rationalization? How important is the qualifying phrase "for the most part"? What are some possible exceptions that you know of? Why is the either-or dualism that Brink focusses on dangerous in contemporary society? Is it a matter of choosing between a closed and an open system? When Tuchman criticizes the use of *a* system, *a* single organizing idea, is she also attacking a simplistic either-or method? Is totalitarianism basically simplistic? Consider too that when confronted with an either-or choice—for example between two competing scientific paradigms or other logically opposed alternatives—to seek the ever-popular "happy medium" is not always the best solution: the phrase itself implies a willingness to be satisfied with mediocrity. It may represent a weak compromise, a cop-out. The best solution may for example lie much nearer one alternative than the other. Or it may lie entirely elsewhere, in some third alternative. Write a brief argument exposing the wrongheadedness of some local board or committee or governing body in settling for a "happy medium" as the solution to a seeming either-or dilemma.

13. Tuchman refers to propaganda and truth as mutually exclusive. Is this an example of either-or thinking? Fulford refers to "propagandists" shaping messages of government and media (see also the word "propagating," which he uses earlier). Are they using the word *propaganda* correctly? Is it a matter of connotation rather than denotation? Or is it not a question of being either right or wrong?

14. Fulford directly confronts the issue of the media's influence; Dryden's image (section IV) is largely a product of it; and it is strongly implicit in Arlen's essay (section VI). Compose an argument for or against the proposition that the media—the mass media—influence us too much. Draw on your own experience, but consult some other printed sources as well. (Fulford

mentions Marshall McLuhan's ideas about the media; and note that Arlen's title includes "the global village"—one of McLuhan's key phrases. Do you feel that you're living in a "global village"?) Or investigate and report on the phenomenon yourself: For a week, watch two or more television news programs and listen to the news on two radio stations. Compare them for coverage and bias. (a) What is the effect of their priorities, their decisions about what to report and when to report it? (b) What is the effect of their choice of what to omit, as well as what to include? (c) How are their presentations tailored for their respective audiences (especially the radio programs—but perhaps you'll monitor an early-morning television program as well as evening ones)? What other sources can you check these programs against?

15. Meigs discusses self-censorship. Brink refers to the banning of books in South Africa. Atwood (section IV) talks of some poetry being off-limits to students, of the banning of books in Canada, and of the dangers of self-censorship by writers. What are the implications for society of various kinds of censorship? Have women been more censored than men? Write an argumentative essay for or against some or all kinds of censorship.

16. Compare Kael's techniques as a reviewer with those of Woolf (section IV), Deacon (section V), and Cooper (section VI).

17. Examine the psychology of Meigs's essay. Examine the psychology of myth itself. What is myth? Are the different uses of the word related? Meigs is in effect decoding the myth of Pandora for her own purposes. Tuchman decodes the myths of Oedipus and Elektra in order to contradict the conventional Freudian readings of them. In what sense is Morgan, in "The Man-Made Myth," also decoding a myth, and for what purpose? Are *myth* and *truth* mutually exclusive? Or can a myth be thought of as embodying a kind of truth? Is the fable that Kingston recounts (section VI) in effect a myth that she intends us to decode?

18. Is it legitimate to use literature as a portrait of social reality? Is it logical to claim that popular plays reflect their audience's feelings and fears? Or is Fulford right when he refers to "distortion of reality, which is also called drama"? Take and defend a position on this issue. Need it be either one or the other?

19. Tuchman's essay was first delivered as a lecture, as were Brink's, Meigs's, Atwood's and Cutschall's (section IV), and Stein's (section VI). Do any stylistic features mark these as different from those intended in the first place to be read rather than heard? Or is the range from colloquial to formal equally possible in both kinds? Consider also Cooper's essay (section VI) in this respect (note the paradox in her title, "Writing Oral History").

20. Narrative uses chronological order; description often relies on spatial order. Other kinds of order include moving from specific examples to a generalization, from general to specific, from question to answer, from small to large. Arguments often use *climactic* order—moving from less important to more important, ending with the strongest point. Examine the essays in this section to see which ones use climactic order, and to what degree. How effective is it?

21. "What we call justice derives from our uneasy recognition of a social paradox: that it is impossible to be fair, and possible only to enact the law." Discuss.

22. "Boredom is the source of more social disorder than malice is, just as fear is a greater source of prejudice than hate." Discuss.

23. "Education is another name for brainwashing." Write two essays, one arguing each side of this proposition. Then analyze your own argumentative techniques. In which essay are you more convincing? Why?

24. "There is no unemployment crisis. There is only a crisis in employers' imaginations. Greater flexibility in retirement age and greater use of part-time workers would resolve many of the problems young people currently face in obtaining jobs." Write a commentary on this view.

25. Write a political speech.

IV

Writing to Explain and Inform

In his essay in a book called *The Canadian Imagination*, Northrop Frye tells the story of a southern doctor travelling with an Inuit guide in the Arctic. When a blizzard blows up and they have to bivouac, the doctor panics and shouts aimlessly, "We are lost! We are lost!" The guide looks at him thoughtfully for a moment, and then observes: "We are not lost. We are here." Frye transforms the anecdote into a commentary on identity, probing the relation between geography and the imagination and exploring the force of the perspective one brings to the definition of cultural boundaries. Using an anecdote in this fashion, making it a functional part of a commentary rather than a simple narrative ornament, constitutes a characteristic feature of much exposition. The expository writer's aim is to make a subject clear, to take a body of information and arrange the details so that they make sense, to answer the questions *how* and *why* as lucidly as possible: to explain things. A concrete anecdote often helps to get the process started or to move it along.

Aside from the anecdote, two of the chief methods by which expository writing begins are *definition* and *classification*. One writer might restrict the meanings of certain terms at the outset. Another might set up categories in order to clarify the nature of a subject—and then further divide these categories into particular subsets: classifying, for example, by size or colour, source or function, quality or reliability. Exposition is writing that attempts to explain the steps in a process, the makeup of a pattern, the causes of an event or a set of circumstances, or the applications or implications of a body of data. Among the essays that follow, Cutschall, Mitford, and Rouché trace processes. Iyer, Baker, and Cole proffer systems of classification, Atwood and Baker

223

effective analogies, Berlin an extended definition. And more than one employs an anecdote along the way.

Though exposition seems one of the most straightforward of prose forms, it is difficult to master. An intelligent simplicity is an elusive goal. Try, for example, to explain how to put on a coat—as though you were explaining to someone who couldn't differentiate between left and right—and then ask someone to try to follow your directions exactly. Or try to explain why three times four is twelve. To explain things adequately, expository writers must make use of internal definitions, helpful descriptions, comparisons, contrasts, analogies, anecdotal illustrations—in short, any techniques that will help them make their subjects clear. They try to lead their readers through snowstorms of complexity, adapting their anecdotes and analogies and other devices to the purpose at hand.

Expository essays are also to a degree attempts to persuade. But because their essential aim is to explain, a reader primarily expects information from them. And however much readers may appreciate an essayist's wit, grace, intelligence, and personality, they ultimately judge an expository essay by how much they have learned from it. As explanations, an unclear recipe and a set of inexact street directions are at the very least unhelpful. The people who try to follow them may not get lost, but they will not know exactly what they are doing or where they are. Sometimes such uncertainty turns out to be productive (can uncertainty be the mother of discovery?), but more often it simply proves confusing. And what holds for simple explanations also holds for more complex analyses and more abstract subjects. Lack of clarity dulls one's ability to absorb information and to discriminate among details; clear information, in whatever form it comes, can both stimulate and delight.

The essays in this section range, therefore, in subject, method, function, and tone. There is a piece of informative journalism and a medical whodunit; there are magazine articles, informal reflections, and a formal cultural inquiry. As the subjects vary, so do the language and the authors' attitudes. For Roueché, Gould, and Thomas, a scientific vocabulary is a natural medium of expression; Galbraith defends the use of specialized occupational words; Dryden is colloquial, Baker metaphysical and whimsical, and Mitford chillingly factual.

But is Mitford neutral and objective? Is Galbraith? Atwood? Berlin? Is, in fact, complete objectivity ever possible? Are explanations inevitably governed by bias and point of view? It is true that the reporter who strives for neutrality differs in many ways from the editorial writer who strives to persuade readers to embrace a particular social or political doctrine. The disinterested scientist and the academic investigator (neither of whom, it must be added, is likely to be *un*interested) differ in many ways from the intellectual partisan. Exposition is not polemic. But the expository language of the scientist, like the argumentative language of the partisan, can also be slanted. It is open to misuse and subject to misinterpretation. It requires care. Even a formal researcher can distort matters in the process of communicating results, just as a writer drawing only on personal experience may communicate unconsciously held biases. Given such conditions, it is a wonder that writers and readers don't feel lost more often than they do, and throw their hands up in antic despair. Sometimes they feel secure. But sometimes, after struggling to express or interpret an idea, they must be pleased even if they know with only a modest certainty where it is that they stand.

The Story of Service

Jessica Mitford

There was a time when the undertaker's tasks were clearcut and rather obvious, and when he billed his patrons accordingly. Typical late-nineteenth-century charges, in addition to the price of merchandise, are shown on bills of the period as: "Services at the house (placing corpse in the coffin) $1.25," "Preserving remains on ice, $10," "Getting Permit, $1.50." It was customary for the undertaker to add a few dollars to his bill for being "in attendance," which seems only fair and right. The cost of embalming was around $10 in 1880. An undertaker, writing in 1900, recommends these minimums for service charges: Washing and dressing, $5; embalming, $10; hearse, $8 to $10. As Habenstein and Lamers, the historians of the trade, have pointed out, "The undertaker had yet to conceive of the value of personal services offered professionally for a fee, legitimately claimed." Well, he has now so conceived with a vengeance.

When weaving in the story of service as it is rendered today, spokesmen for the funeral industry tend to become so carried away by their own enthusiasm, so positively lyrical and copious in their declarations, that the outsider may have a little trouble understanding it all. There are indeed contradictions. Preferred Funeral Directors International has prepared a mimeographed talk designed to inform people about service: "The American public receive the services of employees and proprietor alike, nine and one half days of labor for every funeral handled, they receive the use of automobiles and hearses, a building including a chapel and other rooms which require building maintenance, insurance, taxes and licenses, and depreciation, as well as heat in the winter, cooling in the summer and light and water." The writer goes on to say that while the process of embalming takes only about three hours, yet, "it would be necessary for one man to work two forty-hour weeks to complete a funeral service. This is coupled with an additional forty hours service required by members of other local allied professions, including the work of the cemeteries, newspapers, and of course, the most important of all, the service of your clergyman. These some 120 hours of labour are the basic value on which the cost of funerals rests."

Our informant has lumped a lot of things together here. To start with "the most important of all, the service of your clergyman," the average religious funeral service lasts no more than 25 minutes. Furthermore, it is not, of course, paid for by the funeral director. The "work of the cemeteries" presumably means the opening and closing of a grave. This now mechanized operation, which takes 15 to 20 minutes, is likewise not billed as part of the funeral director's costs. The work of "newspapers"? This is a puzzler. Presumably reference is made here to the publication of an obituary notice on the vital statistics page. It is, incidentally, surprising to learn that newspaper work is considered an "allied profession."

Just how insurance, taxes, licenses and depreciation are figured in as part of the 120 man-hours of service is hard to tell. The writer does mention that his operation features "65 items of service." In general, the funeral salesman is inclined to chuck in everything he does under the heading of "service." For example, in a typical list of "services" he will include items like "securing statistical data" (in other words, completing the death certificate and finding out how much insurance was left by the deceased), "the arrangements conference" (in which the sale of the funeral to the survivors is made), and the "keeping of records," by which he means his own bookkeeping work. Evidently there is some confusion here between items that properly belong in a cost-accounting system and items of *actual* service rendered in any given funeral. In all likelihood, idle time of employees is figured in and prorated as part of the "man-hours." The up-to-date funeral home operates on a 24-hour basis, and the mimeographed speech contains this heartening news:

> The funeral service profession of the United States is proud of the fact that there is not a person within the continental limits of the United States who is more than two hours away from a licensed funeral director and embalmer in case of need. That's one that even the fire fighting apparatus of our country cannot match.

While the hit-or-miss rhetoric of the foregoing is fairly typical of the prose style of the funeral trade as a whole, and while the statement that 120 man-hours are devoted to a single man- (or woman-) funeral may be open to question, there really is a fantastic amount of service accorded the dead body and its survivors.

Having decreed what sort of funeral is right, proper and nice, and having gradually appropriated to himself all the functions connected with it, the funeral director has become responsible for a multitude of tasks beyond the obvious one of "placing corpse in the coffin" recorded in our nineteenth-century funeral bill. His self-imposed duties fall into two main categories: attention to the corpse itself, and the stage-managing of the funeral.

The drama begins to unfold with the arrival of the corpse at the mortuary.

Alas, poor Yorick! How surprised he would be to see how his counter-part of today is whisked off to a funeral parlor and is in short order sprayed, sliced, pierced, pickled, trussed, trimmed, creamed, waxed, painted, rouged and neatly dressed—transformed from a common corpse into a Beautiful Memory Picture. This process is known in the trade as embalming and restorative art, and is so universally employed in the United States and Canada that the funeral director does it routinely, without consulting corpse or kin. He regards as eccentric those few who are hardy enough to suggest that it might be dispensed with. Yet no law requires embalming, no religious doctrine commends it, nor is it dictated by considerations of health, sanitation, or even of personal daintiness. In no part of the world but in Northern America is it widely used. The purpose of embalming is to make the corpse presentable for viewing in a suitably costly container; and here too the funeral director routinely, without first consulting the family, prepares the body for public display.

Is all this legal? The processes to which a dead body may be subjected are after all to some extent circumscribed by law. In most states, for instance, the signature of next of kin must be obtained before an autopsy may be performed, before the deceased may be cremated, before the body may be turned over to a medical school for research purposes; or such provision must be made in the decedent's will. In the case of embalming, no such permission is required nor is it ever sought. A textbook, *The Principles and Practices of Embalming*, comments on this: "There is some question regarding the legality of much that is done within the preparation room." The author points out that it would be most unusual for a responsible member of a bereaved family to instruct the mortician, in so many words, to "*embalm*" the body of a deceased relative. The very term "*embalming*" is so seldom used that the mortician must rely upon custom in the matter. The author concludes that unless the family specifies otherwise, the act of entrusting the body to the care of a funeral establishment carries with it an implied permission to go ahead and embalm.

Embalming is indeed a most extraordinary procedure, and one must wonder at the docility of Americans who each year pay hundreds of millions of dollars for its perpetuation, blissfully ignorant of what it is all about, what is done, how it is done. Not one in ten thousand has any idea of what actually takes place. Books on the subject are extremely hard to come by. They are not to be found in most libraries or bookshops.

In an era when huge television audiences watch surgical operations in the comfort of their living rooms, when, thanks to the animated cartoon, the geography of the digestive system has become familiar territory even to the nursery school set, in a land where the satisfaction of curiosity about almost all matters is a national pastime, the secrecy surrounding embalming can, surely, hardly be attributed to the inherent gruesomeness of the subject. Custom in this regard has within this century suffered a complete reversal. In the early days of American embalming, when it was performed in the home of the deceased, it was almost mandatory for some relative to stay by the embalmer's side and witness the procedure. Today, family members who might wish to be in attendance would certainly be dissuaded by the funeral director. All others, except apprentices, are excluded by law from the preparation room.

A close look at what does actually take place may explain in large measure the undertaker's intractable reticence concerning a procedure that has become his major *raison d'être*. Is it possible he fears that public information about embalming might lead patrons to wonder if they really want this service? If the funeral men are loath to discuss the subject outside the trade, the reader may, understandably, be equally loath to go on reading at this point. For those who have the stomach for it, let us part the formaldehyde curtain....

The body is first laid out in the undertaker's morgue—or rather, Mr. Jones is reposing in the preparation room—to be readied to bid the world farewell.

The preparation room in any of the better funeral establishments has the tiled and sterile look of a surgery, and indeed the embalmer-restorative artist who does his chores there is beginning to adopt the term "dermasurgeon" (appropriately corrupted by some mortician-writers as "demisurgeon") to describe his calling. His equipment, consisting of scalpels, scissors, augers, forceps, clamps, needles, pumps, tubes, bowls and basins, is crudely imitative of the surgeon's, as is his technique, acquired in a nine- or twelve-month post-high-school course in an embalming school. He is supplied by an advanced chemical industry with a bewildering array of fluids, sprays, pastes, oils, powders, creams, to fix or soften tissue, shrink or distend it as needed, dry it here, restore the moisture there. There are cosmetics, waxes and paints to fill and cover features, even plaster of Paris to replace entire limbs. There are ingenious aids to prop and stabilize the cadaver: a Vari-Pose Head Rest, the Edwards Arm and Hand Positioner, the Repose Block (to support the shoulders during the embalming), and the Throop Foot Positioner, which resembles an old-fashioned stocks.

Mr. John H. Eckels, president of the Eckels College of Mortuary Science, thus describes the first part of the embalming procedure: "In the hands of a skilled practitioner, this work may be done in a comparatively short time and without mutilating the body other than by slight incision—so slight that it scarcely would cause serious inconvenience if made upon a living person. It is necessary to remove the blood, and doing this not only helps in the disinfecting, but removes the principal cause of disfigurements due to discoloration."

Another textbook discusses the all-important time element: "The earlier this is done, the better, for every hour that elapses between death and embalming will add to the problems and complications encountered...." Just how soon should one get going on the embalming? The author tells us, "On the basis of such scanty information made available to this profession through its rudimentary and haphazard system of technical research, we must conclude that the best results are to be obtained if the subject is embalmed before life is completely extinct—that is, before cellular death has occurred. In the average case, this would mean within an hour after somatic death." For those who feel that there is something a little rudimentary, not to say haphazard, about this advice, a comforting thought is offered by another writer. Speaking of fears entertained in early days of premature burial, he points out, "One of the effects of embalming by chemical injection, however, has been to dispel fears of live burial." How true; once the blood is removed, chances of live burial are indeed remote.

To return to Mr. Jones, the blood is drained out through the veins and replaced by embalming fluid pumped in through the arteries. As noted in *The*

Principles and Practices of Embalming, "every operator has a favorite injection and drainage point—a fact which becomes a handicap only if he fails or refuses to forsake his favorites when conditions demand it." Typical favorites are the carotid artery, femoral artery, jugular vein, subclavian vein. There are various choices of embalming fluid. If Flextone is used, it will produce a "mild flexible rigidity. The skin retains a velvety softness, the tissues are rubbery and pliable. Ideal for women and children." It may be blended with B. and G. Products Company's Lyf-Lyk tint, which is guaranteed to reproduce "nature's own skin texture...the velvety appearance of living tissue." Suntone comes in three separate tints: Suntan; Special Cosmetic Tint, a pink shade "especially indicated for young female subjects"; and Regular Cosmetic Tint, moderately pink.

About three to six gallons of a dyed and perfumed solution of formaldehyde, glycerin, borax, phenol, alcohol and water is soon circulating through Mr. Jones, whose mouth has been sewn together with a "needle directed upward between the upper lip and gum" and brought out slightly "for a more pleasant expression." If he should be bucktoothed, his teeth are cleaned with Bon Ami and coated with colorless nail polish. His eyes, meanwhile, are closed with flesh-tinted eye caps and eye cement.

The next step is to have at Mr. Jones with a thing called a trocar. This is a long, hollow needle attached to a tube. It is jabbed into the abdomen, poked around the entrails and chest cavity, the contents of which are pumped out and replaced with "cavity fluid." This done, and the hole in the abdomen sewn up, Mr. Jones's face is heavily creamed (to protect the skin from burns which may be caused by leakage of the chemicals), and he is covered with a sheet and left unmolested for a while. But not for long—there is more, much more, in store for him. He has been embalmed, but not yet restored, and the best time to start the restorative work is eight to ten hours after embalming, when the tissues have become firm and dry.

The object of all this attention to the corpse, it must be remembered, is to make it presentable for viewing in an attitude of healthy repose. "Our customs require the presentation of our dead in the semblance of normality...unmarred by the ravages of illness, disease or mutilation," says Mr. J. Sheridan Mayer in his *Restorative Art.* This is rather a larger order since few people die in the full bloom of health, unravaged by illness and unmarked by some disfigurement. The funeral industry is equal to the challenge: "In some cases the gruesome appearance of a mutilated or disease-ridden subject may be quite discouraging. The task of restoration may seem impossible and shake the confidence of the embalmer. This is the time for intestinal fortitude and determination. Once the formative work is begun and affected tissues are cleaned or removed, all doubts of success vanish. It is surprising and gratifying to discover the results which may be obtained."

The embalmer, having allowed an appropriate interval to elapse, returns to the attack, but now he brings into play the skill and equipment of sculptor and cosmetician. Is a hand missing? Casting one in plaster of Paris is a simple matter. "For replacement purposes, only a cast of the back of the hand is necessary; this is within the ability of the average operator and is quite adequate." If a lip or two, a nose or an ear should be missing, the embalmer has at hand a variety of restorative waxes with which to model replacements. Pores and skin texture are simulated by stippling with a little brush, and over this cosmetics are laid on. Head off? Decapitation cases are rather routinely handled. Ragged edges are trimmed, and head joined to torso with a series of splints, wires and sutures. It is a good idea to have a little something at the neck—a scarf or high collar—when time for viewing comes. Swollen mouth? Cut out tissue as needed from inside the lips. If too much is removed, the surface contour can easily be restored by padding with cotton. Swollen necks and cheeks are reduced by removing tissue through vertical incisions made down each side of the neck. "When the deceased is casketed, the pillow will hide the suture incisions...as an extra precaution against leakage, the suture may be painted with liquid sealer."

The opposite condition is more likely to present itself—that of emaciation. His hypodermic syringe now loaded with massage cream, the embalmer seeks out and fills the hollowed and sunken areas by injection. In this procedure the back of the hands and fingers and the under-chin areas should not be neglected.

Positioning the lips is a problem that recurrently challenges the ingenuity of the embalmer. Closed too tightly, they tend to give a stern, even disapproving expression. Ideally, embalmers feel, the lips should give the impression of being ever so slightly parted, the upper lip protruding slightly for a more youthful appearance. This takes some engineering, however, as the lips tend to drift apart. Lip drift can sometimes be remedied by pushing one or two straight pins though the inner margin of the lower lip and then inserting them between the two front upper teeth. If Mr. Jones happens to have no teeth, the pins can just as easily be anchored in his Armstrong Face Former and Denture Replacer. Another method to maintain lip closure is to dislocate the lower jaw, which is then held in its new position by a wire run through holes which have been drilled through the upper and lower jaws at the midline. As the French are fond of saying, *il faut souffrir pour être belle.**

If Mr. Jones has died of jaundice, the embalming fluid will very likely turn him green. Does this deter the embalmer? Not if he has intestinal fortitude. Masking pastes and cosmetics are heavily laid on, burial garments and casket interiors are color-correlated with particular care, and Jones is displayed beneath rose-colored lights. Friends will say, "How *well* he looks." Death by carbon monoxide, on the other hand, can be rather a good thing from the embalmer's viewpoint: "One advantage is the fact that this type of discoloration is an exaggerated form of a natural pink coloration." This is nice because the healthy glow is already present and needs but little attention.

---

* In 1963 *Mortuary Management* reports a new development: "Natural Expression Formers," an invention of Funeral Directors Research Company. "They may be used to replace one or both artificial dentures, or over natural teeth; have 'bite-indicator' lines as a closure guide....Natural Expression Formers also offer more control of facial expression."

The patching and filling completed, Mr. Jones is now shaved, washed and dressed. Cream-based cosmetic, available in pink, flesh, suntan, brunette and blond, is applied to his hands and face, his hair is shampooed and combed (and, in the case of Mrs. Jones, set), his hands manicured. For the horny-handed son of toil special care must be taken; cream should be applied to remove ingrained grime, and the nails cleaned. "If he were not in the habit of having them manicured in life, trimming and shaping is advised for better appearance—never questioned by kin."

Jones is now ready for casketing (this is the present participle of the verb "to casket"). In this operation his right shoulder should be depressed slightly "to turn the body a bit to the right and soften the appearance of lying flat on the back." Positioning the hands is a matter of importance, and special rubber positioning blocks may be used. The hands should be cupped slightly for a more lifelike, relaxed appearance. Proper placement of the body requires a delicate sense of balance. It should lie as high as possible in the casket, yet not so high that the lid, when lowered, will hit the nose. On the other hand, we are cautioned, placing the body too low "creates the impression that the body is in a box."

Jones is next wheeled into the appointed slumber room where a few last touches may be added—his favorite pipe placed in his hand or, if he was a great reader, a book propped into position. (In the case of little Master Jones a Teddy bear may be clutched.) Here he will hold open house for a few days, visiting hours 10 A.M. to 9 P.M.

All now being in readiness, the funeral director calls a staff conference to make sure that each assistant knows his precise duties. Mr. Wilber Krieger writes: "This makes your staff feel that they are a part of the team, with a definite assignment that must be properly carried out if the whole plan is to succeed. You never heard of a football coach who failed to talk to his entire team before they go on the field. They have drilled on the plays they are to execute for hours and days, and yet the successful coach knows the importance of making even the bench-warming third-string substitute feel that he is important if the game is to be won." The winning of *this* game is predicated upon glass-smooth handling of the logistics. The funeral director has notified the pallbearers whose names were furnished by the family, has arranged for the presence of clergyman, organist, and soloist, has provided transportation for everybody, has organized and listed the flowers sent by friends. In *Psychology of Funeral Service* Mr. Edward A. Martin points out: "He may not always do as much as the family thinks he is doing, but it is his helpful guidance that they appreciate in knowing they are proceeding as they should....The important thing is how well his services can be used to make the family believe they are giving unlimited expression to their own sentiment."

The religious service may be held in a church or in the chapel of the funeral home; the funeral director vastly prefers the latter arrangement, for not only is it more convenient for him but it affords him the opportunity to show off his beautiful facilities to the gathered mourners. After the clergyman has had his say, the mourners queue up to file past the casket for a last look at the deceased. The family is *never* asked whether they want an open-casket ceremony; in the absence of their instruction to the contrary, this is taken for granted. Consequently well over 90 per cent of all American funerals feature the open casket—a custom unknown in other parts of the world. Foreigners are astonished by it. An English woman living in San Francisco described her reaction in a letter to the writer:

> I myself have attended only one funeral here—that of an elderly fellow worker of mine. After the service I could not understand why everyone was walking towards the coffin (sorry, I mean casket), but thought I had better follow the crowd. It shook me rigid to get there and find the casket open and poor old Oscar lying there in his brown tweed suit, wearing a suntan makeup and just the wrong shade of lipstick. If I had not been extremely fond of the old boy, I have a horrible feeling that I might have giggled. Then and there I decided that I could never face another American funeral—even dead.

The casket (which has been resting throughout the service on a Classic Beauty Ultra Metal Casket Bier) is now transferred by a hydraulically operated device called Porto-Lift to a balloon-tired, Glide Easy casket carriage which will wheel it to yet another conveyance, the Cadillac Funeral Coach. This may be lavender, cream, light green—anything but black. Interiors, of course, are color-correlated, "for the man who cannot stop short of perfection."

At graveside, the casket is lowered into the earth. This office, once the prerogative of friends of the deceased, is now performed by a patented mechanical lowering device. A "Lifetime Green" artificial grass mat is at the ready to conceal the sere earth, and overhead, to conceal the sky, is a portable Steril Chapel Tent ("resists the intense heat and humidity of summer and the terrific storms of winter...available in Silver Grey, Rose or Evergreen"). Now is the time for the ritual scattering of earth over the coffin, as the solemn words "earth to earth, ashes to ashes, dust to dust" are pronounced to the officiating cleric. This can today be accomplished "with a mere flick of the wrist with the Gordon Leak-Proof Earth Dispenser. No grasping of a handful of dirt, no soiled fingers. Simple, dignified, beautiful, reverent! The modern way!" The Gordon Earth Dispenser (at $5) is of nickel-plated brass construction. It is not only "attractive to the eye and long wearing"; it is also "one of the 'tools' for building better public relations" if presented as "an appropriate noncommercial gift" to the clergyman. It is shaped something like a saltshaker.

Untouched by human hand, the coffin and the earth are now united.

It is in the function of directing the participants through this maze of gadgetry that the funeral director has assigned to himself his relatively new role of "grief therapist." He has relieved the family of every detail, he has revamped the corpse to look like a living doll, he has arranged for it to nap for a few days in a slumber room, he has put on a well-oiled performance in which the concept of *death* has played no part whatsoever—unless it was inconsiderately mentioned by the clergyman who conducted the religious service. He has done everything in his power to make the funeral a real pleasure for everybody concerned. He and his team have given their all to score an upset victory over death.

Dale Carnegie has written that in the lexicon of the successful man there is no such word as "failure." So have the funeral men managed to delete the word death and all its associations from their vocabulary. They have from time to time published lists of In and Out words and phrases to be memorized and used in connection with the final return of dust to dust; then still dissatisfied with the result, have elaborated and revised the lists. Thus a 1916 glossary substitutes "prepare body" for "handle corpse." Today, though, "body" is Out and "remains" or "Mr. Jones" is In.

"The use of improper terminology by anyone affiliated with a mortuary should be strictly forbidden," declares Edward A. Martin. He suggests a rather thorough overhauling of the language; his deathless words include: "service, not funeral; Mr., Mrs., Miss Blank, not corpse or body; preparation room, not morgue; casket, not coffin; funeral director or mortician, not undertaker; reposing room or slumber room, not laying-out room; display room, not showroom; baby or infant, not stillborn; deceased, not dead; autopsy or post-mortem, not post; casket coach, not hearse; shipping case, not shipping box; flower car, not flower truck; cremains or cremated remains, not ashes; clothing, dress, suit, etc., not shroud; drawing room, not parlor."

This rather basic list was refined in 1956 by Victor Landig in his *Basic Principles of Funeral Service*. He enjoins the reader to avoid using the word "death" as much as possible, even sometimes when such avoidance may seem impossible; for example, a death certificate should be referred to as a "vital statistics form." One should speak not of the "job" but rather of the "call." We do not "haul" a dead person, we "transfer" or "remove" him—and we do this in a "service car," not a "body car." We "open and close" his grave rather than dig and fill it, and in it we "inter" rather than bury him. This is done not in a graveyard or cemetery but rather in a "memorial park." The deceased is beautified, not with makeup, but with "cosmetics." Anyway, he didn't die, he "expired." An important error to guard against, cautions Mr. Landig, is referring to "cost of the casket." The phrase, "amount of investment in the service," is a wiser usage here.

Miss Anne Hamilton Franz, writing in *Funeral Direction and Management*, adds an interesting footnote on the use of the word "ashes" to describe (in a word) ashes. She fears this usage will encourage scattering (for what is more natural than to scatter ashes?) and prefers to speak of "cremated remains" or "human remains." She does not like the word "retort" to describe the container in which cremation takes place, but prefers "cremation chamber" or "cremation vault," because this "sounds better and softens any harshness to sensitive feelings."

As for the Loved One, poor fellow, he wanders like a sad ghost through the funeral men's pronouncements. No provision seems to have been made for the burial of a Heartily Disliked One, although the necessity for such must arise in the course of human events.

Three Sick Babies

Berton Roueché

Dr. Paul M. Taylor, an assistant professor of pediatrics at the University of Pittsburgh School of Medicine, left his office on the first floor of Magee-Womens Hospital, an affiliate of the medical school, and climbed the stairs to the premature-baby nursery, on the second floor. It was twenty minutes to eleven on the morning of July 12, 1965, a Monday, and this was his regular weekday round. He was, in a way, attending physician to all the babies in the nursery. Two pediatric residents were waiting for him in the gown room. That, too, was as usual, and while Dr. Taylor scrubbed and disinfected his hands and got into a freshly laundered gown, they gave him the customary nursery news report. The weekend had been generally uneventful. All but one of the twenty-six babies in the nursery were progressing satisfactorily. The exception was one of the smallest—a twenty-five-day-old two-and-a-half-pound boy. He was in Room 227. Dr. Taylor nodded. He knew the one they meant. Well, early that morning, just after midnight, a nurse had noted that his breathing was unusually slow and his behavior somewhat apathetic. The resident on duty, seeing these signs as suggestive of septicemia, had treated the baby with penicillin and kanamycin, but he still looked and acted sick. It was probable that he would soon need artificial respiration. Meanwhile, the usual samples (blood, stool, mucus, spinal fluid) had been taken and sent along to the laboratory for culture and analysis.

Dr. Taylor heard his residents' review with no more than natural interest. Serious illness in a premature nursery is not an unusual occurrence, and a blood infection is only one of the many diseases that may afflict a premature baby during its first days of life. Trouble is inherent in the phenomenon of prematurity. For the truth of the matter is that premature birth is itself a serious affliction. A premature baby is a baby born in the seventh or eighth month of pregnancy. Its birth weight is largely determined by its relative prematurity, ranging from around two to five and a half pounds. The average term (or nine-month) baby weighs around seven pounds at birth, and it generally comes into the world alive and kicking. Premature babies begin life almost incapable of living. There is nothing more frail and fragile. Many of them are too meagerly developed to maintain normal body temperature. One in three requires immediate, and often prolonged resuscitation, and about the same number are unable to nurse, or even to swallow. Some of them are even unable to cry. All of them are exquisitely susceptible to all infection. Mental and neurological defects are also common in premature babies. One of the commonest of these is cerebral palsy. About half of all victims of the affliction are of premature birth. As recently as twenty-five years ago, most premature babies died. The technological innovations of the postwar era have greatly improved that record, but the mortality rate among newborn premature babies is still high. In even the best hospitals, some ninety percent of all two-pound babies die. So do about fifty percent of those weighing two to three pounds, around ten percent of those weighing three to four pounds, and between five and eight percent of those weighing four to five pounds. Such babies are simply too fetal to survive outside the womb. There are many causes of premature birth (including falls and blows), but most current investigators think that malnutrition is perhaps the most important cause. Prematurity would thus seem to be a socioeconomic problem, and this supposition is confirmed by statistics. The great majority of premature babies are born to women too poor to buy the nutritious food they need.

Dr. Taylor tied up the back of his gown and led the way through an inner door to the central nursing station of the nursery. Room 227 was the second room on the right. The sick baby was one of five babies being cared for there. He lay on his side in his incubator bassinet with a stomach feeding tube in his mouth, and he looked even sicker than the resident had said. There was nothing, however, that Dr. Taylor could do that hadn't already been done. He confirmed the resident's course of treatment and agreed that a respirator would probably soon be required, and then moved on to the other babies in that and the other rooms. They were all, as far as he could read the almost imperceptible manifestations of the premature, in their usual precarious but normal condition. At the end of his rounds, Dr. Taylor had lunch, and after lunch he occupied himself with his other professorial duties. Before leaving for home, he put in a call to the nursery for a report on the sick baby. The report was not comforting. The baby's condition had continued to worsen, and he had been moved to Room 229, which is reserved for babies needing constant scrupulous care. Later that evening, on his way to bed, he called the nursery again. The nurse who picked up the telephone was able to answer his question. The sick baby from Room 227 was dead.

Dr. Taylor's Tuesday-morning round was much like that of Monday. The residents' gown-room report included another sick baby. It also contained a post-mortem note on the baby from Room 227. The hospital laboratory had confirmed the general diagnosis of septicemia. A microbial culture had been grown from a sample of the baby's blood and identified as bacteria of the gram-negative type. It was one of some twenty-five species of bacteria (among them the causative organisms of typhoid fever, brucellosis, whooping cough, plague, and gonorrhea) that react negatively to the standard staining test devised in 1884 by the Danish bacteriologist Hans Christian Joachim Gram. A more specific identification was promised for the next day. Meanwhile, of course, the laboratory had been supplied with diagnostic samples from the second sick baby. This baby, also a boy, was one of the babies in Room 229. He was a term baby, three days old, but had been assigned to the premature nursery directly from the delivery room because he required artificial respiration and other intensive care. Dr. Taylor remembered the baby when he saw him. He had begun life with a severe aspiration pneumonia, stemming from an original inability to breathe, but that had been quickly controlled with penicillin, kanamycin, and dexamethasone. His trouble now was diarrhea. Diarrhea in a newborn baby is not a common complaint, and Dr. Taylor wondered if this attack might be a septic aftermath of the earlier pneumonia. But that was a question that only the laboratory could readily answer. There was no doubt about the treatment the baby was receiving. That seemed to be entirely satisfactory.

The Wednesday-morning gown-room news review contained three major items. One was that still another baby boy had become seriously ill overnight. The next item was a preliminary laboratory report on the second sick baby, which identified the cause of his diarrhea as a gram-negative bacillus. The third item was a more or less definitive laboratory report on the dead baby. After forty-eight hours of growth, the gram-negative bacteria cultured from his blood presented the colonial configuration, the fluorescent yellow-green pigmentation, and the spearmint odor generally characteristic of the type known as Pseudomonas aeruginosa.

Dr. Taylor went to Room 229 for a look at the new sick baby. He was nine days old and weighed about three pounds. His illness appeared to be a pneumonia. This illness had come on abruptly, but, like so many other premature babies, he had never been really well. He had been unable at birth to breathe spontaneously and had spent the first five or six days of his life in a respirator. It was obvious to Dr. Taylor that the baby's condition was grave. It seemed equally clear, however, that he was receiving the best of care, and a conventional course of penicillin and kanamycin had been started. Dr. Taylor left the nursery in an uneasy state of mind. His uneasiness had to do with room 229 and the sudden string of serious illnesses there. He was afraid that they might be more than merely coincidental.

Dr. Taylor was not kept in suspense for long. One of his fears was confirmed that afternoon by a call from the resident then on duty in the nursery. He called to report that the new sick baby—the three-pound nine-day-old—was dead. His illness had lasted a scant eight hours. The next morning brought another confirmation. There was a final laboratory report on the first sick baby: the cause of his death was definitely a Pseudomonas infection. There was a forty-eight-hour report on the second sick baby: the gram-negative bacteria grown from his blood had all the important charac-teristics of Pseudomonas aeruginosa. There was a twenty-four-hour report on the third sick baby: cultures grown from his blood had been identified as gram-negative bacteria. And that was too much for coincidence. It meant—it could almost certainly only mean—that a Pseudomonas epidemic had struck the premature nursery.

Pseudomonas aeruginosa is one of a group of gram-negative pathogens that have only recently come to be seriously pathogenic. Other members of this group include Escherichia coli and the several species of the Proteus and the Enterobacter-Klebsiella genera. Their rise to eminent virulence is a curious phenomenon. These microorganisms regularly reside in soil and water, and in the gastrointestinal tracts of most (if not all) human beings. Their presence in that part of the body is normally innocuous. Healthy adults are impervious to the thrust of such bacteria. The victims of Pseudomonas (and E. coli and Proteus and Enterobacter) infections are the very old, the very young, and the very debilitated (the badly burned, the postoperative, the cancerous), and in almost every case they have been receiving vigorous sulfonamide or antibiotic or adrenalsteroid therapy. Most antimicrobial drugs have little destructive effect on bacteria of the Pseudomonas group. Just the reverse, in fact. Their action, in essence, is tonic. In people rendered susceptible to the gram-negative pathogens by age or illness, the result of chemotherapy is the elimination not only of the immediately threatening pathogens but also of the natural resident bacteria that normally hold further incursions of Pseudomonas (or E. coli or Proteus or Enterobacter) in check. The virulence of Pseudomonas and its kind is thus a wry expression of perhaps the most beneficent accomplishment of twentieth-century medicine.

It is also cause for some alarm. "One of the great changes wrought by the widespread use of antibacterial agents has been the radical shift in the ecologic relations among the pathogenic bacteria that are responsible for the most serious and fatal infections," the *New England Journal of Medicine* noted editorially in July of 1967. "Whereas John Bunyan could properly refer to consumption as 'Captain of the Men of Death,' this title, according to Osler, was taken over by pneumonia in the first quarter of this century. During the last two decades, it has again shifted, at least in hospital populations, first to the staphylococcal diseases and more recently to infections caused by gram-negative bacilli. Most of the gram-negative organisms that have given rise to these serious and highly fatal infections are among the normal flora of the bowel and have sometimes been referred to as 'opportunistic pathogens.' ...Before the present antibiotic era, some of them, like Escherichia coli, although they frequently caused simple urinary-tract infections, only occasionally gave rise to serious sepsis....Strains of Proteus or Pseudomonas did so very rarely, and those of Enterobacter were not even known to produce infections in human beings before the introduction of sulfonamide drugs. Of great importance are the facts that most of these opportunistic pathogens are resistant to the antibiotics that have been most widely used, and that the infections they produce are associated with a high mortality." This mortality is anachronistically high. It is roughly that resulting from the common run of pathogenic bacteria some thirty years ago—in the days when the best defense against the many Men of Death was a strong constitution.

The most conspicuously troublesome of these ordinarily unaggressive pathogens is E. coli. It has been implicated in some ninety percent of the urinary-tract infections caused by members of this group, and it is responsible for many of the more serious cases of bacteremia, gastroenteritis, and pneumonia. It is not, however, the most opportunistic. The organism best equipped to take advantage of almost any chemotherapeutic opportunity is the Pseudomonas bacillus. Pseudomonas aeruginosa is all but invulnerable to the present pharmacopoeia. Only two antibiotics—polymyxin B and colistin—are generally effective against most Pseudomonas strains. Moreover, both must be used with great discretion to prevent severe kidney side reactions. Ps. aeruginosa is also distinctively lethal. Its mortality rate, as numerous recent outbreaks (including that in Pittsburgh in 1965) have shown, may run as high as seventy-five percent.

An investigation into the source of the Pseudomonas infections in the premature nursery at Magee-Womens Hospital was started by Dr. Taylor on Friday morning, July 16. A forty-eight-hour report from the laboratory had by then established as Ps. aeruginosa the gram-negative bacteria that had been cultured from the blood of the third sick baby, and the presence of an epidemic was now beyond dispute. The investigation began with a survey to determine the scope of the trouble. There were at that time, in addition to the surviving (or diarrheal) sick baby, twenty-eight babies in the nursery. Samples of nose, throat, and stool material were taken from each, to be dispatched to the laboratory for culture and analysis. Dr. Taylor saw this work well under way, and then walked down to his office and put in a call to a colleague named Horace M. Gezon, at the Graduate School of Public Health. Dr. Gezon (at the time professor of epidemiology and microbiology at the University of Pittsburgh Graduate School of Public Health and now chairman of the Department of Pediatrics at the Boston University School of Medicine) is an authority on hospital infections, and Dr. Taylor wanted his help. Dr. Gezon had two immediate suggestions. One was that the investigators meet at the hospital the following morning for an exchange of information and ideas. The other was that Joshua Fierer, of the Allegheny County Health Department, be invited to join the investigation. Dr. Fierer (now a postdoctoral fellow in infectious diseases at the University of Pittsburgh Department of Medicine) was an Epidemic Intelligence Service officer assigned to Allegheny County by the National Communicable Disease Center, in Atlanta.

"Dr. Taylor called me on Friday afternoon," Dr. Fierer says. "I know it was Friday, because that's when all investigations seem to begin—at the start of the weekend. I knew Dr. Taylor. I had met him with Dr. Gezon back in March—on a Friday in March. There had been an outbreak of diarrhea in the premature nursery that they thought might be a viral disease, and they called the county because we had the only virus-diagnostic laboratory in the area. That case turned out to be nothing to worry about. It got the three of us together, though, and I guess that was what brought me to mind when this new problem came up. I was delighted to be asked to participate. Pseudomonas is a very interesting organism these days. But I had to tell Dr. Taylor that I couldn't make the Saturday-morning meeting. Or, if I could, I'd be late. I had a firm commitment at the Pittsburgh Children's Zoo on Saturday morning. They had a chimpanzee out there with hepatitis.

"I got to the hospital, but I was more than late. It was after lunch, and the meeting was over and everybody had gone. I looked around the nursery, feeling kind of foolish, and said hello to the nurses, and they told me who had been at the meeting. There were six in the group, including Dr. Taylor and Dr. Gezon. The others were the two residents, a study nurse of Dr. Gezon's, and an assistant professor of epidemiology at the School of Public Health named Russell Rycheck. Dr. Rycheck was a particular friend of mine. I went over to the school and looked him up, and he gave me a good report. The meeting had naturally concentrated on the nursery. The big question, of course, was: Where had the infection come from? How had Pseudomonas been introduced into the nursery? Well, Pseudomonas is a water-dwelling organism. It can live on practically nothing in the merest drop of water. That suggested water as the probable source of the trouble, and the nursery had plenty of such sources. There were thirty incubator bassinets equipped with humidifiers drawing on water reservoirs, and there were fourteen sinks—one in each of the ten baby rooms, three in the central nursing station, and one in the gown room. And then there were the usual jugs of sterile water for washing the babies' eyes and for other medicative purposes. Dr. Gezon arranged for water samples from every possible source. That included two samples from each sink—one from the drain and one from the aerator on the faucet. The screens that diffuse the water in an aerator can provide a water bug like Pseudomonas with an excellent breeding place. For good measure, he took a swab of the respirator used in the ward. Also, Dr. Rycheck said, Dr. Gezon arranged for throat and stool samples from the two residents and from all the nurses working in the premature nursery. And he had called another meeting for Monday morning. The laboratory findings would be ready for evaluation by then.

"I made the Monday meeting. The laboratory reports were presented, and then we tried to decide what they meant. The human studies made pretty plain reading. There were two sets—the nurses and residents, and the twenty-eight seemingly well babies in the nursery. The laboratory eliminated the nurses and residents as possible carriers. Their cultured specimens were all negative for Pseudomonas. The reports on the babies confirmed what I think most of us had already suspected. This was a real epidemic. Twenty-two of the babies were negative for Pseudomonas, but six were positive. They weren't clinically sick. They didn't show any symptoms. They were, however, infected with Ps. aeruginosa. Why they weren't sick is hard to say. There were several possible explanations. The best one was that their exposure was relatively slight and their natural defenses were strong—they hadn't been weakened by antibiotics. The results of the environmental studies were very interesting. But they were also rather confusing. They showed five sink drains and three of the bassinet reservoirs to be contaminated. Everything else was negative for Pseudomonas—the water jugs, the respirator, the faucet aerators, and the other drains and bassinets. The contaminated drains were in Room 207, Room 209, Room 227, an unoccupied room, and the gown room. The contaminated bassinets were in 224, 227, and 229. All the infected babies were associated with just two rooms. They were, or had been, in either Room 227—the room where the first baby took sick—or Room 229, where he died and where the two other babies became sick. There was a contaminated sink in Room 227, but the sink in 229 was clean. There was a contaminated bassinet reservoir in each room, but only one of the bassinets was, or had been, occupied by an infected baby. There were no infected babies in two rooms—Room 209 and Room 207—that had contaminated sinks, and none in Room 224, which had a contaminated bassinet. It was all very peculiar. We had a lot of contamination and we had a lot of infected babies, but there didn't seem to be any connection between the two. The only link we could think of was the nurses. The babies had no contact with each other. The bassinets were self-contained, and none of the babies shared any equipment or medication. The nurses might have carried the infection on their hands. They could do that without becoming infected themselves. Healthy adults don't succumb to Pseudomonas. But why did they carry it only to the babies in 227 and 229?

"The meeting ended on that unsatisfactory note. Dr. Gezon was as puzzled as the rest of us. But, of course, this puzzling point was only part of the investigation. We still had an epidemic to contain. We didn't understand the mechanics of its spread, but we did know what it was, and we thought we had enough information to bring it under control. We knew who was sick and we knew that the nursery was contaminated at eight specific sites. By Monday night, the nursery was as clean as Dr. Gezon and the nursery staff knew how to make it. All the sinks were scrubbed with sodium-hypochlorite disinfectant. The bassinet reservoirs were emptied and disinfected with an iodophor, and only those in use were refilled. As a further precaution, that water was to be changed every day. Certain nurses were assigned to take exclusive care of the infected babies. Also, in the hope of dislodging their infection, all the infected babies were placed on a five-day course of colistimethate given intramuscularly, and colistin sulphate by mouth. It wasn't necessary to isolate the infected babies. They were already isolated. And it was arranged that specimens be taken every day from all the babies in the nursery, and from all the sinks and bassinets and so on. That would give us a constant focus on the course of the epidemic.

"I didn't participate in the sanitation program. They didn't need me. I would have been an extra thumb. I went back to my office and back to the regular health Department routine, but part of my mind was still out there at the nursery, and I got to thinking about something I'd read a few months before. It was a report in the *Lancet* about an outbreak of Pseudomonas in an English nursery that was traced to a catheter used to relieve throat congestion in the babies. The source of the trouble eluded detection for almost a year. What I particularly remembered about the report was a description of a new system of microbial identification. There are several different types of Ps. aeruginosa, and this report told how they could be differentiated by a laboratory procedure called pyocine typing. Pyocine typing makes use of the fact that certain strains of Pseudomonas will kill or inhibit the growth of other Pseudomonas strains, and it's a complicated procedure. Well, it occurred to me that pyocine typing might help to clarify our problem. It could at least tell us if all the sinks and all the bassinets and all the infected babies were infected with the same strain of Pseudomonas. I thought about it, and finally I called up Dr. Gezon. He saw the point at once. But, as I say, pyocine typing was then very new, and we didn't know where to turn for help. It could be that the system was being used only in England. We talked it over and decided that the best place to begin was at the Communicable Disease Center, in Atlanta. If anybody was doing pyocine typing in this country, the people there would certainly know. That was Monday evening. On Tuesday morning, I got on the phone to Atlanta and talked to one of my friends at CDC and asked him what he knew about something called pyocine typing. 'Pyocine typing?' he said, 'Why, Shulman is working on that right now. I'll switch you over to him.' Shulman was Dr. Jonas A. Shulman, and a fellow Epidemic Intelligence Service officer. He's now assistant professor of preventive medicine at Emory University. I described the case to him and asked him if he could help us out, and he was more than willing. He was eager. He wanted all the work he could get. So as soon as we finished talking I arranged for specimens of all our isolates to be air-mailed down to Atlanta. Pyocine typing takes about two days. Shulman might have something for us by Thursday.

"Before I left the hospital, I went around to the premature nursery. That *Lancet* paper was still on my mind. Not pyocine typing. What interested me now was the source of the outbreak it described—that contaminated catheter. I looked up one of the paediatric residents and asked him what went on in the delivery rooms. I was thinking about contaminated equipment that the babies might have shared. For example, did they use a regular aspirator? The resident said no. The aspirators they used were all disposable and were discarded after each use. What about the resuscitators? Did they have humidifying attachments? A humidifier would mean water, and a possible breeding place for Pseudomonas. Another no. The resuscitators used in the delivery rooms were simply bags and masks attached to an oxygen line from the wall. I asked a few more questions along those lines and got the same kind of answers, and gave up. This wasn't a case like the *Lancet* case. So I was back in the nursery again. But the more I thought about those contaminated sinks and bassinets the less convinced I was that they were the source of our trouble. I just couldn't see any plausible link between those particular sites and those nine particular babies. But if the answer wasn't a piece of contaminated equipment, what else could it be? A contaminated person? And then I got a thought—maybe a contaminated mother. It sounded only too possible. A contaminated mother could very easily transmit an infection to her baby in the course of its birth. Childbirth is not a very tidy process..

"The next question was: Which mother? I thought I could answer that. It had to be the mother of the second sick baby. Not the baby in whom the infection was first diagnosed. The significant case was the second Pseudomonas baby—the term baby who came into the nursery with pneumonia and then developed diarrhea. The first sick baby had been healthy until the day before his death. He had been healthy for over three weeks. So he was actually No. 2. It wasn't hard to reconstruct the possible course of events. The infection was introduced into the nursery by the term baby and then spread to the other babies by the nurses. Pseudomonas is a difficult organism. You can't wash it off your hands with a little soap and water, the way you can the staphylococcus bug. To get Pseudomonas off, you have to scrub and scrub and scrub. And it's also extremely resistant to most disinfectants. But what made the infected-mother theory really attractive was that it seemed to explain what the environmental theory left unexplained. It explained why the infected babies were concentrated in Room 227 and Room 229. Both of those rooms were intensive-care rooms, and there was very little traffic between them and the other rooms. However, it was just a theory. It was based on the supposition that the diarrheal baby's mother was a Pseudomonas carrier. So the next thing to do was find out. The first thing I found was that the baby had been discharged on Saturday, and that he and his mother were now at home. I got the address, and Dr. Taylor and the baby's paediatrician gave me the necessary permission. I went out to the house and introduced myself, and the mother was nice and cooperative, and I got the specimens I needed and took them back to the Health Department Lab.

"She wasn't a carrier. The preliminary laboratory report on my specimens was negative for Pseudomonas. That was the following day—Wednesday afternoon. But by then it didn't matter. We had something much more interesting to think about. The way it happened was this. I was in the nursery that afternoon, and one of the residents came over and told me they had another infected baby. New babies had been coming along every day, of course, and this one was a term baby born on Monday and sent up to the premature nursery for special care. He had had trouble breathing at birth, and had required extensive resuscitation in the delivery room. Well, a routine nasopharyngeal culture taken when he was admitted to the nursery had just been found to be positive for Pseudomonas. I looked at the resident and the resident looked at me. This was real news. That baby could not possibly have been infected in the nursery. The laboratory samples had been taken before he was even settled there. He could have been infected only in the delivery room. And there were just two possible sources of infection there. His mother was one, and the other was some piece of contaminated equipment. My guess was naturally the mother. I found out what room the new baby's mother was in, and made the necessary arrangements, and went up and took the standard nose, throat, and stool samples, and arranged for the hospital laboratory to culture them. When I got back to the nursery, Dr. Gezon was there talking to the resident, and I could tell from the look on his face that he had heard the news.

"The three of us went down to the delivery suite. We found the nurse in charge and told her what we were doing. She was terribly upset. It was most distressing to her to have us arrive in her domain on such a mission. But she was a good nurse and she cooperated perfectly. The room where the baby had been born was not in use, and she took us in and showed us around. There was a delivery table in the middle of the room, and a row of scrub sinks along the left-hand wall. On the opposite wall was a resuscitator of the type described to me the day before. It consisted of a rubber face mask and a rubber Emerson bag enclosed in a cellophane casing, and it looked very neat and clean. But something made me take it down for a closer look. There was a little dribble of water in the bottom of the Emerson bag. I showed it to Dr. Gezon, and he raised his eyebrows and passed it on to the resident. The resident took a sample of the water. There were five other rooms in the delivery suite, and luckily none of them were in use. We checked the resuscitator in every room, and every one was wet. The question was: How come? The nurse explained the delivery suite cleaning procedure. There was one central wash sink, where all delivery-room equipment was washed. Everything was washed after every use, and then sterilized by steaming in an autoclave. Including the resuscitators? No—of course not. They were made of rubber, and rubber can't stand that kind of heat. The resuscitators were washed with a detergent, rinsed with tap water, and left on the drainboard to dry. It was possible, the nurse said, that they were sometimes returned to the delivery room before they were completely dry. We asked to see the wash sink. We were all beginning to feel sort of elated. I know I was. And when we saw the sink, that just about finished us. The faucet was equipped with an aerator—a standard five-screen water-bug heaven.

"It *was* a water-bug heaven. The laboratory cultured Pseudomonas from the swab samples we took from the aerator. It also cultured Pseudomonas from five of the six resuscitator samples. You can imagine how the delivery-suite nurses felt when those reports came down. They were crushed. Dr. Gezon was able to reassure them, though. He didn't consider them guilty of ignorance. They assumed, like almost everybody else, that city drinking water is safe. It is and it isn't. It's perfectly safe to drink, but it isn't absolutely pure. This is something that has only recently been recognized. There are water bugs in even the best city water. The concentrations are much too low in ordinary circumstances to cause any trouble, but a dangerous concentration can occur in any situation—like that provided by an aerator—that enables the bugs to accumulate and breed. An aerator is a handy device, but you'd probably be better off letting the water splash. It's certainly a device that a hospital can do without.

"The laboratory gave us three reports in all. The third was on the mother of the new baby. They found her negative for Pseudomonas, and that was welcome news. A positive culture from her would have been an awkward complication. Because everything else was very satisfactory. The contaminated resuscitators seemed to explain the concentration of infected babies in Room 227 and Room 229. Seven of the ten infected babies—including the diarrheal baby and the two that died—had received at least some resuscitation in the delivery room, and it was reasonable to suppose that the three others had got their infection from the resuscitated babies by way of the nurses. There's plenty of evidence for that in the literature. I remember one report that showed that nurses' hands were contaminated simply by changing the bedding of an infected patient. It was Dr. Shulman, however, who finally pinned it down. His pyocine typing confirmed the circumstantial evidence at every point. Shulman did two groups of studies of us—one on the original material I sent him, and then another on the new infected baby and the delivery-suite material. The results of his studies were doubly instructive. They identified the delivery-room resuscitators as the source of the epidemic, and they eliminated the contaminated sinks and bassinets in the nursery. The different pyocine types of Pseudomonas aeruginosa are indicated by numbers. The Pseudomonas strain cultured from the delivery-suite aerator was identified as Pyocine Type 4-6-8. So were the isolates from the resuscitator bags. And so were those of all of the infected babies. Type 4-6-8 was also recovered from two pieces of equipment in the nursery, but I think we can safely assume that they had been contaminated indirectly from the same delivery-room source. They were a bassinet used by an infected baby and the sink in Room 227. The other contaminations in the nursery were a wild variety of types—6, 4-6, 6-8, 1-2-3-4-6-7-8, and 1-3-4-6-7-8. And where they came from wasn't much of a mystery. There was only one possible explanation. They came out of the water faucets, too."

That was the end of the formal investigation. It wasn't, however, the end of the trouble. The pockets of contamination in the sinks and elsewhere in the nursery and in the delivery suite were eliminated (and a system of ethylene-oxide sterilization set up for all resuscitation equipment), but the epidemic continued. In spite of the most sophisticated treatment (first with colis-timethate and colistin sulphate, and then with colistin in combination with polymyxin B), the infected babies remained infected. Moreover, in the course of the next few weeks twelve new infections were discovered in the nursery. In two of the new victims, the infection developed into serious clinical illness. It was not until the middle of September, when the remaining infected babies were moved to an isolated ward in another part of the hospital, that the epidemic was finally brought under control.

Hospital infections of any kind are seldom easily cured. Pseudomonas aeruginosa is only somewhat more stubborn than such other institutional pathogens as Staphylococcus aureus and the many Salmonellae. These con-fined and yet all but unextinguishable conflagrations are, in fact, the despair of modern medicine. They are also, as it happens, one of its own creations. The sullen phenomenon of hospital infection is a product equally of medical progress and of medical presumption. It has its roots in the chemotherapeutic revolution that began with the development of the sulfonamides during the middle nineteen-thirties, and in the elaboration of new life-saving and life-sustaining techniques (open-heart surgery, catheterization, intravenous feed-ing) that the new antibacterial drugs made possible, and it came into being with the failure of these drugs (largely through the development of resistance in once susceptible germs) to realize their original millennial promise. Its continuation reflects a drug-inspired persuasion that prevention is no longer superior to cure. "In the midst of the development of modern antibacterial agents, infection has flourished with a vigor that rivals the days of Semmel-weis," Dr. Sol Haberman, director of the Microbiology laboratories at Baylor University Medical Center, noted. "It would appear that the long sad history of disease transmission by attendants to the sick has been forgotten again."

Of Weirdos and Eccentrics

Pico Iyer

Charles Waterton was just another typical eccentric. In his 80s the eminent country squire was to be seen clambering around the upper branches of an oak tree with what was aptly described as the agility of an "adolescent gorilla." The beloved 27th lord of Walton Hall also devoted his distinguished old age to scratching the back part of his head with his right big toe. Such displays of animal high spirits were not, however, confined to the gentleman's later years. When young, Waterton made four separate trips to South America, where he sought the wourali poison (a cure, he was convinced, for hydrophobia), and once spent months on end with one foot dangling from his hammock in the quixotic hope of having his toe sucked by a vampire bat.

James Warren Jones, by contrast, was something of a weirdo. As a boy in the casket-making town of Lynn, Ind., he used to conduct elaborate funeral services for dead pets. Later, as a struggling preacher, he went from door to door, in bow tie and tweed jacket, selling imported monkeys. After briefly fleeing to South America (a shelter, he believed, from an imminent nuclear holocaust), the man who regarded himself as a reincarnation of Lenin settled in Northern California and opened some convalescent homes. Then, one humid day in the jungles of Guyana, he ordered his followers to drink a Kool-Aid-like punch soured with cyanide. By the time the world arrived at Jonestown, 911 people were dead.

The difference between the eccentric and the weirdo is, in its way, the difference between a man with a teddy bear in his hand and a man with a gun. We are also, of course, besieged by other kinds of deviants—crackpots, oddballs, fanatics, quacks and cranks. But the weirdo and the eccentric define between them that invisible line at which strangeness acquires an edge and oddness becomes menace.

The difference between the two starts with the words themselves: eccentric, after all, carries a distinguished Latin pedigree that refers, quite reasonably, to anything that departs from the center; weird, by comparison, has its mongrel origins in the Old English *wyrd*, meaning fate or destiny; and the larger, darker forces conjured up by the term—*Macbeth's* weird sisters and the like—are given an extra twist with the slangy, bastard suffix -o. Beneath the linguistic roots, however, we feel the difference on our pulses. The eccentric we generally regard as something of a donny, dotty, harmless type, like the British peer who threw over his Cambridge fellowship in order to live in a bath. The weirdo is an altogether more shadowy figure—Charles Manson acting out his messianic visions. The eccentric is a distinctive presence; the weirdo something of an absence, who casts no reflection in society's mirror. The eccentric raises a smile; the weirdo leaves a chill.

All too often, though, the two terms are not so easily distinguished. Many a criminal trial, after all, revolves around precisely that grey area where the two begin to blur. Was Bernhard Goetz just a volatile Everyman, ourselves pushed to the limit, and then beyond? Or was he in fact an aberration? Often, besides, eccentrics may simply be weirdos in possession of a VIP pass, people rich enough or powerful enough to live above convention, amoral as Greek gods. Elvis Presley could afford to pump bullets into silhouettes of humans and never count the cost. Lesser mortals, however, must find another kind of victim.

To some extent too, we tend to think of eccentricity as the prerogative, even the hallmark, of genius. And genius is its own vindication. Who cared that Glenn Gould sang along with the piano while playing Bach, so long as he played so beautifully? Even the Herculean debauches of Babe Ruth did not undermine so much as confirm his status as a legend.

Indeed, the unorthodox inflections of the exceptional can lead to all kinds of dangerous assumptions. If geniuses are out of the ordinary and psychopaths are out of the ordinary, then geniuses are psychopaths and vice versa, or so at least runs the reasoning of many dramatists who set their plays in loony bins. If the successful are often strange, then being strange is a way of becoming successful, or so believe all those would-be artists who work on eccentric poses. And if celebrity is its own defense, then many a demagogue or criminal assures himself that he will ultimately be redeemed by the celebrity he covets.

All these distortions, however, ignore the most fundamental distinction of all: the eccentric is strange because he cares too little about society, the weirdo because he cares too much. The eccentric generally wants nothing more than his own attic-like space in which he can live by his own peculiar lights. The weirdo, however, resents his outcast status and constantly seeks to get back into society, or at least get back at it. His is the rage not of the bachelor but the divorcé.

Thus the eccentric hardly cares if he is seen to be strange; that in a sense is what makes him strange. The weirdo, however, wants desperately to be taken as normal and struggles to keep his strangeness to himself. "He was always such a nice man," the neighbours ritually tell reporters after a sniper's rampage. "He always seemed so normal."

And because the two mark such different tangents to the norm, their incidence can, in its way, be an index of a society's health. The height of British eccentricity, for example, coincided with the height of British power, if only, perhaps, because Britain in its imperial heyday presented so strong a center from which to depart. Nowadays, with the empire gone and the center vanishing, Britain is more often associated with the maladjusted weirdo—the orange-haired misfit or the soccer hooligan.

At the other extreme, the relentless and ritualized normalcy of a society like Japan's—there are only four psychiatrists in all of Tokyo—can, to Western eyes, itself seem almost abnormal. Too few eccentrics can be as dangerous as too many weirdos. For in the end, eccentricity is a mark of confidence, accommodated best by a confident society, whereas weirdness inspires fear because it is a symptom of fear and uncertainty and rage. A society needs the eccentric as much as it needs a decorated frame for the portrait it fashions of itself; it needs the weirdo as much as it needs a hole punched through the middle of the canvas.

By the Numbers

K.C. Cole

Mathematics is all well and good, but Nature keeps dragging us around by the nose.
—Albert Einstein

One day last winter, MIT theoretical physicist Philip Morrison was talking about forces and particles, and in particular about those strange entities known as force particles. Finally Morrison said, "Look, forces and particles may not be appropriate ways to describe these things. If you read the *Physical Review*, you won't read about force particles. You'll read about Lagrangians."

A Lagrangian is not a physical thing; it is a mathematical thing—a kind of differential equation, to be exact. But physics and math are so closely connected these days that it is hard to separate the numbers from the things they describe. In fact, a month after Morrison's remark, Nobel Prize winner Burton Richter of the Stanford Linear Accelerator Center said something that eerily echoed it: "Mathematics is a language that is used to describe nature," he said. "But the theorists are beginning to think it *is* nature. To them, the Lagrangians are the reality."

Every high school student knows that nature and numbers go hand in hand. The exploration of the physical universe is open only to those who are willing to suffer total immersion in the abstract ideas of geometry and calculus. Science often deals with real things that people can see, hear, feel, and wonder about: stars, pendulums, rainbows, sounds, cells, heat, earthquakes, and elements. It hardly seems right that the only route to learning about them should be by the numbers. Yet, says Caltech's Richard Feynman, "I am sorry, but this seems to be the case. It is impossible to explain honestly the beauties of the laws of nature in a way that people can feel, without their having some deep understanding of mathematics."

The belief that truth lies in numbers goes back at least as far as the sixth century B.C., when the philosopher Pythagoras went about making such statements as "Things are numbers." And later, "There are also numbers beyond things." Pythagoras was probably the first person to formulate a physical law mathematically: the harmonic combinations of sounds that are music to our ears are based on simple, whole-number relationships. The frequency ratio 2:1 corresponds to an octave; 3:2 to a fifth. Pythagoras believed that the planets were placed in the heavens in orbits that played similar but unheard harmonies. "There is music in the spacing of the spheres," he wrote.

The Pythagoreans saw in numbers a purity and perfection impossible to achieve amid the messy complexities of everyday life. Unfortunately, they soon discovered that numbers could be messy and complicated, too—even, it turned out, "irrational." An irrational number is one that cannot be expressed as a ratio of two whole numbers, like the never-ending decimal π (3.14159...). Every soap bubble and every bit of ocean froth is built on irrational numbers. Yet the Pythagoreans were so shattered by their own discovery (was the world, at its root, irrational?) that they kept it a closely guarded secret. (It is probably just as well they did not know about "imaginary" numbers, such as the square root of minus 1, which are not only irrational but impossible.)

Several millennia later, the astronomer Johannes Kepler became so entranced by the Pythagorean ideal that he devoted his life to proving that the planets orbited in spheres enclosed in a stacking of five perfect solids. "Geometry existed before the Creation," said Kepler. "It is coeternal with the mind of God...Geometry is God himself." Even as recently as the nineteenth century, the discoverer of radio waves, Heinrich Hertz, wrote, "One cannot escape the feeling that these mathematical formulae have an independent existence and an intelligence of their own, that they are wiser than we are, wiser even than their discoverers..."

One cannot deny the astounding number of discoveries that have emerged from the mouths of equations: quarks, antimatter, even the fact that light is an electromagnetic wave. James Clerk Maxwell could not help noticing that the number 3×10^{10} kept turning up in all his equations that contained an electric field on one side and a magnetic field on the other side. The number 3×10^{10} is the velocity of light in a vacuum in centimeters per second. Even "imaginary" numbers turned out to be crucial to the theory of relativity: only through such a device could time be combined with the three dimensions of space to form a four-dimensional space-time continuum.

It should not be surprising, of course, that numbers turn up surprising relationships. Numbers *are* relationships. In fact, numbers may be one of the few ways of relating one thing to another that do not depend ultimately on sense perceptions. But if numbers reveal higher truths, they also reveal different kinds of truths from the ones we are used to. Or, as Einstein put it, "As far as the propositions of mathematics refer to reality they are not certain, and in so far as they are certain they do not refer to reality."

Strangely, however, this very quality seems to be the source of the strength in numbers. That is, mathematical descriptions do not, and cannot, exactly reflect reality. Reality is simply too complex. The glory of mathematics, on the other hand, "is that *we do not have to say what we are talking about*," says Feynman. "The glory is that the laws, the arguments, the logic are independent of what 'it' is." (Bertrand Russell gave this same idea a slightly different shading: "Mathematics may be defined as the subject in which we never know what we are talking about, nor whether what we are saying is true.")

Mathematics is different from things; it is a way of thinking about things, a method of reasoning that takes you from one step to another. The mathematical language of science is not easily translatable into other languages because it is more than a language. It is language plus logic. It is a method of connecting things that has been coded in such a way that it can be reproduced and repeated by many different people following the same path. In a sense, it *is* the path.

So many of the puzzles that confront physicists are presented in the form of numbers. There is, for example, the unexplained ratio 1/137. This is a number that keeps popping up whenever the universal constants of nature (things like the natural unit of electric charge, the velocity of light, and "Planck's constant"—a kind of universal limit of smallness) are mathematically combined. The funny thing about 1/137 is that it is dimensionless. It is not 1/137 inches or grams or seconds (or even inch-gram-seconds). It comes out 1/137 no matter what kinds of measures you put into the equation (as long as the units are consistent). Another curious correlation emerges when you compare the ratio of the electric force to the gravitational force (the number 1 divided by 4.17×10^{42}) and the ratio of the diameter of a proton to the diameter of the universe (also the number 1 divided by a number containing 42 zeros). A funny coincidence? Perhaps. But it has set at least some physicists to thinking that if the diameter of the universe is increasing as the universe expands, then perhaps the "constant" force of gravity is changing, too.

Finally, there is the matter of mass numbers. That is, why is the mass of an electron 2,000 times smaller than the mass of a proton or neutron—a relationship that fundamentally shapes the nature of the atom? Why are muons and tau particles, identical to electrons in other respects, vastly larger in their masses? "The most striking realm of ideas is where these mass numbers come from," says Feynman. "If we could find a theory to tell us where the numbers come from, then that same theory could give us many other answers."

It is unlikely that these answers will come from experiments or observations of nature. The solutions must lie in the numbers. Indeed, not so long ago, Caltech theoretical physicist David Poltizer told me that "all the recent inventions in the physics of the early universe are mathematical theorems."

Of course, searching for clues in numbers sometimes leads nowhere; Kepler's attempt to find geometrical order in the planetary orbits led to a dead end. At other times, the search is amazingly fruitful. But whether or not true knowledge of the physical world can be contained in mathematical theorems is yet another question. As Bertrand Russell suggested, "Physics is mathematical not because we know so much about the physical world, but because we know so little; it is only its mathematical properties that we can discover."

'The Feminine Note in Fiction'

Virginia Woolf

Mr Courtney is certain that there is such a thing as the feminine note in fiction; he desires, moreover, to define its nature in the book before us, though at the start he admits that the feminine and masculine points of view are so different that it is difficult for one to understand the other. At any rate, he has made a laborious attempt; it is, perhaps, partly for the reason just stated that he ends where he begins. He gives us eight very patient and careful studies in the works of living women writers, in which he outlines the plots of their most successful books in detail. But we would have spared him the trouble willingly in exchange for some definite verdict; we can all read Mrs Humphry Ward, for instance, and remember her story, but we want a critic to separate her virtues and her failings, to assign her right place in literature and to decide which of her characteristics are essentially feminine and why, and what is their significance. Mr Courtney implies by his title that he will, at any rate, accomplish this last, and it is with disappointment, though not with surprise, that we discover that he has done nothing of the kind. Is it not too soon after all to criticise the 'feminine note' in anything? And will not the adequate critic of women be a woman?

Mr Courtney, we think, feels something of this difficulty; his introduction, in which we expected to find some kind of summing-up, contains only some very tentative criticisms and conclusions. Women, we gather, are seldom artists, because they have a passion for detail which conflicts with the proper artistic proportion of their work. We would cite Sappho and Jane Austen as examples of two great women who combine exquisite detail with a supreme sense of artistic proportion. Women, again, excel in 'close analytic miniature work;' they are more happy when they reproduce than when they create; their genius is for psychological analysis — all of which we note with interest, though we reserve our judgement for the next hundred years or bequeath the duty to our successor. Yet it is worth noting, as proof of the difficulty of the task which Mr Courtney has set himself, that he finds two at least of his eight women writers 'artists'—that two others possess a strength which in this age one has to call masculine, and, in fact, that no pair of them come under any one heading, though, of course, in the same way as men, they can be divided roughly into schools. At any rate, it seems to be clear according to Mr Courtney that more and more novels are written by women for women, which is the cause, he declares, that the novel as a work of art is disappearing. The first part of his statement may well be true; it means that women having found their voices have something to say which is naturally of supreme interest and meaning to women, but the value of which we cannot yet determine. The assertion that the woman novelist is extinguishing the novel as a work of art seems to us, however, more doubtful. It is, at any rate, possible that the widening of her intelligence by means of education and study of the Greek and Latin classics may give her that sterner view of literature which will make an artist of her, so that, having blurted out her message somewhat formlessly, she will in due time fashion it into permanent artistic shape. Mr Courtney has given us material for many questions such as these, but his book has done nothing to prevent them from still remaining questions.

The Purpose of Philosophy

Isaiah Berlin

What is the subject-matter of philosophy? There is no universally accepted answer to this question. Opinions differ, from those who regard it as contemplation of all time and all existence—the queen of the sciences—the keystone of the entire arch of human knowledge—to those who wish to dismiss it as a pseudo-science exploiting verbal confusions, a symptom of intellectual immaturity, due to be consigned together with theology and other speculative disciplines to the museum of curious antiquities, as astrology and alchemy have long ago been relegated by the victorious march of the natural sciences.

Perhaps the best way of approaching this topic is to ask, what constitutes the field of other disciplines? How do we demarcate the province of, say, chemistry or history or anthropology? Here it seems clear that subjects or fields of study are determined by the kind of questions to which they have been invented to provide the answers. The questions themselves are intelligible if, and only if, we know where to look for the answers.

If you ask someone an ordinary question, say 'Where is my coat?', 'Why was Mr Kennedy elected President of the United States?','What is the Soviet system of criminal law', he would normally know how to set about finding an answer. We may not know the answers ourselves, but we know that in the case of the question about the coat, the proper procedure is to look on the chair, in the cupboard, etc. In the case of Mr Kennedy's election or the Soviet system of law we consult writings or specialists for the kind of empirical evidence which leads to the relevant conclusions and renders them, if not certain, at any rate probable.

In other words, we know where to look for the answer: we know what makes some answers plausible and others not. What makes this type of question intelligible in the first place is that we think that the answer can be discovered by empirical means, that is, by orderly observation or experiment, or methods compounded of these, namely those of common sense or the natural sciences. There is another class of questions where we are no less clear about the proper route by which the answers are to be sought, namely the formal disciplines: mathematics, for example, or logic, or grammar, or chess or heraldry, defined in terms of certain fixed axioms and certain rules of deduction etc., where the answer to problems is to be found by applying these rules in the manner prescribed as correct.

We do not know the correct proof of Fermat's Theorem, for example,—no one is known to have found it—but we know along what lines to proceed: we know what kind of methods will, and what kind of methods will not, be relevant to the answer. If anyone thinks that answers to mathematical problems can be obtained by looking at green fields or the behaviour of bees, or that answers to empirical problems can be obtained by pure calculation without any factual content at all, we would today think them mistaken to the point of insanity. Each of these major types of questions—the factual and the formal—possesses its own specialised techniques: discoveries by men of genius in these fields, once they are established, can be used by men of no genius at all in a semi-mechanical manner in order to obtain correct results.

The hallmark of these provinces of human thought is that once the question is put we know in which direction to proceed to try to obtain the answer. The history of systematic human thought is largely a sustained effort to formulate all the questions that occur to mankind in such a way that the answers to them will fall into one or other of two great baskets: the empirical, i.e. questions whose answers depend, in the end, on the data of observation; and the formal, i.e. questions whose answers depend on pure calculation, untrammelled by factual knowledge. This dichotomy is a drastically over-simple formulation: empirical and formal elements are not so easily disentangled: but it contains enough truth not to be seriously misleading. The distinction between these two great sources of human knowledge has been recognised since the first beginning of self-conscious thinking.

Yet there are certain questions that do not easily fit into this simple classification. 'What is an okapi?' is answered easily enough by an act of empirical observation. Similarly 'What is the cube root of 729?' is settled by a piece of calculation in accordance with accepted rules. But if I ask 'What is time?', 'What is a number?', 'What is the purpose of human life on earth?', 'How can I know past facts that are no longer there—no longer where?, 'Are all men truly brothers?', how do I set about looking for the answer? If I ask 'Where is my coat?' a possible answer (whether correct or not) would be 'In the cupboard', and we would all know where to look. But if a child asked me 'Where is the image in the mirror?' it would be little use to invite it to look inside the mirror, which it would find to consist of solid glass; or on the surface of the mirror, for the image is certainly not on its surface in the sense in which a postage stamp stuck on it might be; or behind the mirror (which is where the image looks as if it were), for if you look behind the mirror you will find no image there—and so on.

Many who think long enough, and intensely enough, about such questions as 'What is time?' or 'Can time stand still?', 'When I see double, what is there two of?','How do I know that other human beings (or material objects) are not mere figments of my own mind?', get into a state of hopeless frustration. 'What is the meaning of "the future tense"?' can be answered by grammarians by mechanically applying formal rules; but if I ask 'What is the meaning of "the future"?' where are we to look for the answer?

There seems to be something queer about all these questions—as wide apart as those about double vision, or number, or the brotherhood of men, or purposes of life; they differ from the questions in the other basket in that the question itself does not seem to contain a pointer to the way in which the answer to it is to be found. The other, more ordinary, questions contain precisely such pointers—built-in techniques for finding the answers to them. The questions about time, the existence of others and so on reduce the questioner to perplexity, and annoy practical people precisely because they do not seem to lead to clear answers or useful knowledge of any kind.

This shows that between the two original baskets, the empirical and the formal, there is at least one intermediate basket, in which all those questions live which cannot easily be fitted into the other two. These questions are of the most diverse nature; some appear to be questions of fact, others of value; some are questions about words and a few symbols; others are about methods pursued by those who use them: scientists, artists, critics, common men in the ordinary affairs of life; still others are about the relations between various provinces of knowledge; some deal with the presuppositions of thinking, some with the nature and ends of moral or social or political action.

The only common characteristic which all these questions appear to have is that they cannot be answered either by observation or calculation, either by inductive methods or deductive; and, as a crucial corollary of this, that those who ask them are faced with a perplexity from the very beginning—they do not know where to look for the answers; there are no dictionaries, encyclopedias, compendia of knowledge, no experts, no orthodoxies, which can be referred to with confidence as possessing unquestionable authority or knowledge in these matters. Moreover some of these questions are distinguished by being general and by dealing with matters of principle; and others, while not themselves general, very readily raise or lead to questions of principle.

Such questions tend to be called philosophical. Ordinary men regard them with contempt, or awe, or suspicion, according to their temperaments. For this reason, if for no other, there is a natural tendency to try to reformulate these questions in such a way that all or at any rate parts of them can be answered either by empirical or formal statements; that is to say efforts, sometimes very desperate ones, are made to fit them into either the empirical or the formal basket, where agreed methods, elaborated over the centuries, yield dependable results whose truth can be tested by accepted means.

The history of human knowledge is, to a large degree, a sustained attempt to shuffle all questions into one of the two 'viable' categories; for as soon as a puzzling, 'queer' question can be translated into one that can be treated by an empirical or a formal discipline, it ceases to be philosophical and becomes part of a recognised science.[1] Thus it was no mistake to regard astronomy in, say,

---

[1] The claims of metaphysics or theology to be sciences must rest on the assumption that intuition or revelation are direct sources of knowledge of facts about the world; since they claim to be forms of direct experience, their data, if their existence is allowed, belong, for our purposes, to the 'empirical' basket.

the early Middle Ages as a 'philosophical' discipline: so long as answers to questions about stars and planets were not determined by observation or experiment and calculation, but were dominated by such non-empirical notions as those, e.g., of perfect bodies determined to pursue circular paths by their goals or inner essences with which they were endowed by God or Nature, even if this was rendered improbable by empirical observation, it was not clear how astronomical questions could be settled: i.e. what part was to be played by observing actual heavenly bodies, and what part by theological or metaphysical assertions which were not capable of being tested either by empirical or by formal means.

Only when questions in astronomy were formulated in such a manner that clear answers could be discovered by using and depending on the methods of observation and experiment, and these in their turn could be connected in a systematic structure the coherence of which could be tested by purely logical or mathematical means, was the modern science of astronomy created, leaving behind it a cloud of obscure metaphysical notions unconnected with empirical tests and consequently no longer relevant to the new science, and so gradually relegated and forgotten.

So, too, in our own time, such disciplines as economics, psychology, semantics, logic itself, are gradually shaking themselves free from everything that is neither dependent on observation nor formal; if and when they have successfully completed this process they will be finally launched on independent careers of their own as natural or formal sciences, with a rich philosophical past, but an empirical and/or formal present and future. The history of thought is thus a long series of parricides, in which new disciplines seek to achieve their freedom by killing off the parent subjects and eradicating from within themselves whatever traces still linger within them of 'philosophical' problems, i.e. the kind of questions that do not carry within their own structure clear indications of the techniques of their own solution.

That, at any rate, is the ideal of such sciences; in so far as some of their problems (e.g. in modern cosmology) are not formulated in purely empirical or mathematical terms, their field necessarily overlaps with that of philosophy. Indeed, it would be rash to say of any developed high-level science that it has finally eradicated its philosophical problems. In physics, for instance, fundamental questions exist at the present time which in many ways seem philosophical—questions that concern the very framework of concepts in terms of which hypotheses are to be formed and observations interpreted. How are wave-models and particle-models related to one another? Is indeterminacy an ultimate feature of sub-atomic theory? Such questions are of a philosophical type; in particular, no deductive or observational programme leads at all directly to their solution. On the other hand, it is of course true that those who try to answer such questions need to be trained and gifted in physics, and that any answers to those questions would constitute advances in the science of physics itself. Although, with the progressive separation of the positive sciences, no philosophers' questions are physical, some physicists' questions are still philosophical.

This is one reason, but only one, why the scope and content of philosophy does not seem greatly diminished by this process of attrition. For no matter how many questions can be so transformed as to be capable of empirical or formal treatment, the number of questions that seem incapable of being so treated does not appear to grow less. This fact would have distressed the philosophers of the Enlightenment, who were convinced that all genuine questions could be solved by the methods that had achieved so magnificent a triumph in the hands of the natural scientists of the seventeenth and early eighteenth centuries.

It is true that even in that clear day men still appeared no nearer to the solution of such central, indubitably philosophical, because apparently un-answerable, questions as whether men and things had been created to fulfil a purpose by God or by nature, and if so what purpose; whether men were free to choose between alternatives, or on the contrary were rigorously determined by the causal laws that governed inanimate nature; whether ethical and aesthetic truths were universal and objective or relative and subjective; whether men were only bundles of flesh and blood and bone and nervous tissue, or the earthly habitations of immortal souls; whether human history had a discernible pattern, or was a repetitive causal sequence or a succession of casual and unintelligible accidents. These ancient questions tormented them as they had their ancestors in Greece and Rome and Palestine and the medieval west.

Physics and chemistry did not tell one why some men were obliged to obey other men and under what circumstances, and what was the nature of such obligations; what was good and what was evil; whether happiness and knowledge, justice and mercy, liberty and equality, efficiency and individual independence, were equally valid goals of human action, and if so, whether they were compatible with one another, and if not, which of them were to be chosen, and what were valid criteria for such choices, and how we could be certain about their validity, and what was meant by the notion of validity itself; and many more questions of this type.

Yet—so a good many eighteenth-century philosophers argued—a similar state of chaos and doubt had once prevailed in the realm of the natural sciences too; yet there human genius had finally prevailed and created order.

> Nature and Nature's laws lay hid in night:
> God said 'Let Newton be!' and all was light.

If Newton could, with a small number of basic laws, enable us, at least in theory, to determine the position and motion of every physical entity in the universe, and in this way abolish at one blow a vast, shapeless mass of conflicting, obscure, and only half-intelligible rules of thumb which had hitherto passed for natural knowledge, was it not reasonable to expect that by applying similar principles to human conduct and the analysis of the nature of man, we should be able to obtain similar clarification and establish the human sciences upon equally firm foundations?

Philosophy fed on the muddles and obscurities of language; if these were cleared away, it would surely be found that the only questions left would be concerned with testable human beliefs, or expressions of identifiable, everyday human needs or hopes or fears or interests. These were the proper study of psychologists, anthropologists, sociologists, economists; all that was needed was a Newton, or series of Newtons, for the sciences of man; in this way, the perplexities of metaphysics could once and for all be removed, the idle tribe of philosophical speculators eradicated, and on the ground thus cleared, a clear and firm edifice of natural science built.

This was the hope of all the best-known philosophers of the Enlightenment, from Hobbes and Hume to Helvétius, Holbach, Condorcet, Bentham, Saint-Simon, Comte, and their successors. Yet this programme was doomed to failure. The realm of philosophy was not partitioned into a series of scientific successor states. Philosophical questions continued (and continue) to fascinate and torment inquiring minds.

Why is this so? An illuminating answer to this problem was given by Kant, the first thinker to draw a clear distinction between, on the one hand, questions of fact, and, on the other, questions about the patterns in which these facts presented themselves to us—patterns that were not themselves altered however much the facts themselves, or our knowledge of them, might alter. These patterns or categories or forms of experience were themselves not the subject-matter of any possible natural science.

Kant was the first to draw the crucial distinction between facts—the data of experience as it were, the things, persons, events, qualities, relations, that we observed or inferred or thought about—and the categories in terms of which we sensed and imagined and reflected about them. These were, for him, independent of the different cosmic attitudes—the religious or metaphysical frameworks that belonged to various ages and civilisations. Thus, the majority of Greek philosophers, and most of all Aristotle, thought that all things had purposes built into them by nature—ends or goals which they could not but seek to fulfil. The medieval Christians saw the world as a hierarchy in which every object and person was called upon to fulfil a specific function by the Divine Creator; He alone understood the purpose of the entire pattern, and made the happiness and misery of His creatures depend upon the degree to which they followed the commandments that were entailed by the differing purposes for which each entity had been created—the purposes that in fulfilling themselves realised the universal harmony, the supreme pattern, the totality of which was kept from the creatures, and understood by the Creator alone.

The rationalists of the eighteenth and nineteenth centuries saw no purpose in anything but what man himself had created to serve his own needs, and regarded all else as determined by the laws of cause and effect, so that most things pursued no purposes, but were as they were, and moved and changed as they did, as a matter of 'brute' fact.

These were profoundly different outlooks. Yet those who held them saw very similar items in the universe, similar colours, tastes, shapes, forms of motion and rest, experienced similar feelings, pursued similar goals, acted in similar fashions.

Kant, in his doctrine of our knowledge of the external world, taught that the categories through which we saw it were identical for all sentient beings, permanent and unalterable; indeed this is what made our world one, and communication possible. But some of those who thought about history, morals, aesthetics, did see change and difference; what differed was not so much the empirical content of what these successive civilisations saw or heard or thought as the basic patterns in which they perceived them, the models in terms of which they conceived them, the category-spectacles through which they viewed them.

The world of a man who believes that God created him for a specific purpose, that he has an immortal soul, that there is an afterlife in which his sins will be visited upon him, is radically different from the world of a man who believes in none of these things; and the reasons for action, the moral codes, the political beliefs, the tastes, the personal relationships of the former will deeply and systematically differ from those of the latter.

Men's views of one another will differ profoundly as a very consequence of their general conception of the world: the notions of cause and purpose, good and evil, freedom and slavery, things and persons, rights, duties, laws, justice, truth, falsehood, to take some central ideas completely at random, depend directly upon the general framework within which they form, as it were, nodal points. Although the facts which are classified and arranged under these notions are not at all identical for all men at all times, yet these differences—which the sciences examine—are not the same as the profounder differences which wearing different sets of spectacles, using different categories, thinking in terms of different models, must make to men of different times and places and cultures and outlooks.

Philosophy, then, is not an empirical study: not the critical examination of what exists or has existed or will exist—this is dealt with by commonsense knowledge and belief, and the methods of the natural sciences. Nor is it a kind of formal deduction as mathematics or logic is. Its subject matter is to a large degree not the items of experience, but the ways in which they are viewed, the permanent or semi-permanent categories in terms of which experience is conceived and classified. Purpose versus mechanical causality; organism versus mere amalgams; systems versus mere togetherness; spatio-temporal order versus timeless being; duty versus appetite; value versus fact—these are categories, models, spectacles. Some of these are as old as human experience itself; others are more transient. With the more transient, the philosopher's problems take on a more dynamic and historical aspect. Different models and frameworks, with their attendant obscurities and difficulties, arise at different times. The case of contemporary problems in the explanatory framework of physics, already mentioned, is one example of this. But there are other examples, which affect the thought not just of physicists or other specialists, but of reflective men in general.

In politics, for example, men tried to conceive of their social existence by analogy with various models: Plato at one stage, perhaps following Pythagoras, tried to frame his system of human nature, its attributes and goals, following a geometrical pattern, since he thought it would explain all there was. There followed the biological pattern of Aristotle; the many Christian images with which the writings of the Fathers as well as the Old and New Testaments abound; the analogy of the family, which casts light upon human relations not provided by a mechanical model (say that of Hobbes); the notion of an army on the march with its emphasis on such virtues as loyalty, dedication, obedience, needed to overtake and crush the enemy (with which so much play has been made in the Soviet Union); the notion of the state as a traffic policeman and night watchman preventing collisions and looking after property, which is at the back of much individualist and liberal thought; the notion of the state as much more than this—as a great cooperative endeavour of individuals seeking to fulfil a common end, and therefore as entitled to enter into every nook and cranny of human experience, that animates much of the 'organic' thought of the nineteenth century; the systems borrowed from psychology, or from theories of games, that are in vogue at present—all these are models in terms of which human beings, groups and societies and cultures, have conceived of their experience.

These models often collide; some are rendered inadequate by failing to account for too many aspects of experience, and are in their turn replaced by other models which emphasise what these last have omitted but in their turn may obscure what the others have rendered clear. The task of philosophy, often a difficult and painful one, is to extricate and bring to light the hidden categories and models in terms of which human beings think (that is, their use of words, images and other symbols), to reveal what is obscure or contradictory in them, to discern the conflicts between them that prevent the construction of more adequate ways of organising and describing and explaining experience (for all description as well as explanation involves some model in terms of which the describing and explaining is done); and then, at a still 'higher' level, to examine the nature of this activity itself (epistemology, philosophical logic, linguistic analysis), and to bring to light the concealed models that operate in this second-order, philosophical, activity itself.

If it is objected that all this seems very abstract and remote from daily experience, something too little concerned with the central interests, the happiness and unhappiness and ultimate fate of ordinary men, the answer is that this charge is false. Men cannot live without seeking to describe and explain the universe to themselves. The models they use in doing this must deeply affect their lives, not least when they are unconscious; much of the misery and frustration of men is due to the mechanical or unconscious, as well as deliberate, application of models where they do not work. Who can say how much suffering has been caused by the exuberant use of the organic model in politics, or the comparison of the state to a work of art, and the representation of the dictator as the inspired moulder of human lives, by totalitarian theorists in our own times? Who shall say how much harm and how much good, in previous ages, came of the exaggerated application to social relations of metaphors and models fashioned after the patterns of paternal authority, especially to the relations of rulers of states to their subjects, or of priests to the laity?

If there is to be any hope of a rational order on earth, or of a just appreciation of the many various interests that divide diverse groups of human beings—knowledge that is indispensable to any attempt to assess their effects, and the patterns of their interplay and its consequences, in order to find viable compromises through which men may continue to live and satisfy their desires without thereby crushing the equally central desires and needs of others—it lies in the bringing to light of these models, social, moral, political, and above all the underlying metaphysical patterns in which they are rooted, with a view to examining whether they are adequate to their task.

The perennial task of philosophers is to examine whatever seems insusceptible to the methods of the sciences or everyday observation, e.g. categories, concepts, models, ways of thinking or acting, and particularly ways in which they clash with one another, with a view to constructing other, less internally contradictory, and (though this can never be fully attained) less pervertible metaphors, images, symbols and systems of categories. It is certainly a reasonable hypothesis that one of the principal causes of confusion, misery and fear is, whatever may be its psychological or social roots, blind adherence to outworn notions, pathological suspicion of any form of critical self-examination, frantic efforts to prevent any degree of rational analysis of what we live by and for.

This socially dangerous, intellectually difficult, often agonizing and thankless, but always important activity is the work of philosophers, whether they deal with the natural sciences or moral or political or purely personal issues. The goal of philosophy is always the same, to assist men to understand themselves and thus operate in the open, and not wildly, in the dark.

The Game

Ken Dryden

Once I used to wait in line like everyone else. Then one day a bank teller motioned me out of the line, and I haven't been back in one since. I feel no small guilt each time; nonetheless I continue to accept such favours. For the tellers and me, it has become normal and routine. They treat me the way they think people like me expect to be treated. And I accept.

It is the kind of special treatment professional athletes have grown accustomed to, and enjoy. It began with hockey, with teenage names and faces in local papers, with hockey jackets that only the best players on the best teams wore, with parents who competed not so quietly on the side; and it will end with hockey. In between, the longer and better we play the more all-encompassing the treatment becomes. People give, easily and naturally. And we accept. Slippers, sweaters, plant holders, mitts, baby blankets, baby clothes sent in the mail. Paintings, carvings, etchings, sculptures in clay, metal, papier-mâché. Shirts, slacks, coats, suits, ties, underwear; cars, carpets, sofas, chairs, refrigerators, beds, washers, dryers, stoves, TVs, stereos, at cost or no cost at all. After all, a special person deserves a special price. A hundred letters a week, more than 3,000 a year—"You're the best," all but a few of them say. On the street, in restaurants and theatres, we're pointed at, talked about like the weather. "There he is , the famous hockey player," your own kids announce to their friends. In other homes, your picture is on a boy's bedroom wall. Magazines, newspapers, radio, TV; hockey cards, posters, T-shirts, and curios, anywhere, everywhere, name, face, thousands of times.

And we love it. We say we don't, but we do. We hate the nuisance and inconvenience, the bother of untimely, unending autographs, handshakes, and smiles, living out an image of ourselves that isn't quite real, abused if we fail to, feeling encircled and trapped, never able to get away.

But we also feel special—head-turning, chin-dropping, forget-your-own-name special. What others buy Rolls-Royces and votes and hockey teams for, what others take off their clothes for, what others kill for, we have. All we have to do is play.

If exposure is the vehicle of celebrity, attention is what separates one celebrity from another. Guy Lafleur and Yvon Lambert are both celebrities, yet on the same ice, the same screen, Lafleur is noticed, Lambert is not. Lambert, methodical and unspectacular, has nothing readily distinctive about him. His image is passed over, his name unheard. Lafleur *is* distinctive. The way he skates, the sound of the crowd he carries with him, the goals he scores.

263

And so, too, others, for other reasons. Mario Tremblay, for his fiery, untamed spirit; Bob Gainey, for his relentless, almost palpable will: Tiger Williams, Eddie Shack, Ron Duguay, each colourful and exciting; and Dave Schultz, once king of the mountain. As sports coverage proliferates beyond games, as it becomes entertainment and moves to prime time, as we look for the story behind the story, off-ice performance becomes important. And so personas are born, and sometimes made, and cameras and microphones are there as it happens. The crazies, the clowns, the "sports intellectuals," the anti-jock rebels (Jim Bouton, Bill "Spaceman" Lee), the playboys (Joe Namath, Derek Sanderson), each a distinctive personality, each a bigger celebrity because of what he does away from the game.

TV has given us a new minimum off-ice standard. The modern player must be articulate (or engagingly inarticulate, especially southern style). It's not enough to score a goal and have it picked apart by the all-seeing eyes of replay cameras. A player must be able to put it in his own eloquent words. How did you do it? How did you feel? Live, on-camera words that cannot be edited for the morning paper.

Celebrity is a full, integrated life, earned on-ice, performed, sustained, strengthened, re-earned off-ice. As Roger Angell once put it, we want our athletes to be "good at life." Role models for children, people we want to believe earned what they have, every bit as good at things off the ice as on. If they're inarticulate, harsh and pejorative, they're suddenly just jocks. Merely lucky, less likable, less good at life, less celebrated; finally, they even seem less good *on* the ice.

At its extreme, the process creates the category of professional celebrity, people "famous for being famous," so accomplished at being celebrities that their original source of celebrity is forgotten. At the least, it encourages all celebrities to learn the *skills* of the public person. How to look good, how to sound modest and intelligent, funny and self-deprecatory, anything you want. It's a celebrity's short-cut to the real thing, but it works. Walter Cronkite *looks* trustworthy, Ronald Reagan *seems* like a nice guy. Denis Potvin *sounds* intelligent; or is he only articulate? Good enough at something to be a public person, or simply a good public person? You'll never get close enough long enough to know.

All around us are people anxious to help us look better. Not just flaks and PR types but a whole industry of journalists, commentators, biographers, award-givers. Ghost-writers who put well-paid words under our names, then disappear; charity organizers, volunteers who give time and effort so that "honorary chairmen," "honorary presidents," and "honorary directors" may look even better. Children in hospitals, old folks in old-folks' homes—we autograph their casts, shake their hands, make them props to our generosity and compassion. And never far away, photographers and cameramen record the event. It is the bandwagon momentum of celebrityhood.

In the end, for us, is an image. After thousands of confused messages, we cut through what is complex and render it simple. One image, concrete and disembodied. What agents call "Ken Dryden."

Recently, I asked an executive at an advertising agency to pretend he was trying to persuade a client to use me as a commercial spokesman for his company. We'd met two or three times, several years before, so he knew me mostly as others do. He wrote the following memo to his client: "Historically I know you have had some concerns about using an athlete...either because of potential problems developing out of their careers and public life, or due to simply their lack of availability. I think Ken is quite different from the rest. He is known as a thoughtful, articulate and concerned individual. I think it would go without saying he would not participate in any endorsation unless he was fully committed to and satisfied with the product. (His Ralph Nader exposures would assure that.) He is serious, respected and appears to be very much his own man. I don't think we could ever consider using him in humorous or light approaches (like Eddie Shack) unless it would be by juxtaposition with another...actor or player. He has good media presence....His physical presence is also commanding. He is quite tall and impressive....Other encouraging things would be his intelligence and educational background. He would be more in tune with our target audience with his credentials as a college graduate (Cornell) and a fledgling professional person (law). Also, during production, I think this intelligence and coolness would help in case of commercial production as well as helping to keep costs under control due to mental errors...."

So that's my image. Is it accurate? It doesn't matter. It's what people think, it presupposes how they'll react to me. And for the ad man and his client, how people will react is what matters.

If I don't like my image, I can do something about it. I can do things that are "good for my image." I can stop doing things that are "bad for my image." As actors remind us casually and often, I can do things to change my image. Is it too serious? If I run around the dressing room throwing water at the right moment, someone is bound to notice. A journalist with a deadline to meet and space to fill, a new angle, *news*—"Dryden misunderstood."

Want to be known as an antique collector? Collect an antique. A theatregoer? Go. Once is enough. Tell a journalist, sound enthusiastic, and, above all, play well. Then stand back and watch what happens. Clipped and filed, the news spreads like a chain letter, to other journalists who don't have time to check it out. Presto, it's part of your standard bio. And your image.

If you substitute the word "reputation" for "image," as you might have done a few years ago, you'd have something quite different. A reputation is nothing so trifling or cynical. Like an old barge, it takes time to get going. It's slow and relentless, difficult to manoeuvre, even harder to stop. An image is nothing so solemn. It is merely a commercial asset, a package of all the rights and good-will associated with "Ken Dryden"—something I can sell to whomever I want.

But it's a sticky matter. For the image I'm selling is *your* image of me. The good-will, though it relates to me, is your good-will. Whatever commercial value there is in my name, my image, it's you who puts it there. You like me or trust me, and any prospective buyer of my image, anxious to put my name alongside his product, knows that and counts on it to make you buy his product. And you might, even though it may not be in your best interest. So by selling my name, I have perhaps taken your trust and turned it against you.

I did a commercial once, six years ago. I'd decided I never would, but this one was different enough to start a web of rationalizations until I forgot the point and accepted. A fast-food chain was looking for a winter promotion; Hockey Canada, the advisory and promotional body, wanted a fundraiser and a way to deliver the message to kids and their parents that minor hockey can be approached and played differently. The idea was a mini-book done by Hockey Canada, then sold through the restaurant chain. I was to be a collaborator on the book, and its public spokesman. But after doing the TV and radio ads (for the book, but with a corporate jingle at the end), and seeing the point-of-purchase cardboard likenesses of me in the restaurants, I realized my mistake.

Since then, I have turned down endorsements for, among other things, a candy bar ("The way I see it, a full body shot of you in the net, mask up, talking, then we draw in tight on your catching glove, you open it, the bar's inside...."), a credit card company ("You may not know me without my mask, but...."), and a roll-on deodorant that would also be promoted by several other people whose names begin with the sound "dry."

It's a game—an ad game, an image game, a celebrity game—that no one really loses. Everyone needs someone to talk about— why not about us? Everyone needs heroes and villains. We earn a little money, get some exposure. The commercials are going to be done anyway. Besides, it doesn't last long. A few years and images change, celebrity cools, it's over. It all evens out.

But it doesn't. We all lose, at least a little. We lose because you think I'm better than I am. Brighter than I am, kinder, more compassionate, capable of more things, as good at life as I am at the game. I'm not. Off the ice I struggle as you do, but off the ice you never see me, even when you think you do. I appear good at other things because I'm good at being a goalie; because I'm a celebrity; because there's always someone around to say I'm good. Because in the cozy glow of success, of good news, you want me to be good. It's my angle, and so long as I play well the angle won't change. I appear bright and articulate because I'm an athlete, and many athletes are not bright and articulate. "Like a dog's walking on his hind legs," as Dr. Johnson once put it, "it is not done well; but you are surprised to find it done at all."

But you don't believe that, just as I don't believe it about celebrities I don't know. They're taller, more talented, more compassionate. They glitter into cameras and microphones, give each other awards for talent and compassion, "great human beings" every one. Wet-eyed I applaud, and believe. And all of us lose. You, because you feel less worthy than you are. Me, because once, when I was twenty-three years old and trying to learn about myself, I wanted to believe I was, or soon would be, everything others said I was. Instead, having learned much and grown older, I feel co-conspirator to a fraud.

Professional athletes do exciting, sometimes courageous, sometimes ennobling things, as heroes do, but no more than you do. Blown up on a TV screen or a page, hyped by distance and imagination, we seem more heroic, but we're not. Our achievement seems grander, but it isn't. Our cause, our commitment, is no different from yours. We are no more than examples, metaphors, because we enter every home; we're models for the young because their world is small and we do what they do.

A few years ago, Joe McGinniss, author of *The Selling of the President, 1968,* wrote a book called *Heroes.* It sketches McGinniss's own tormented trail from being *the youngest*, to *the highly acclaimed*, to *the former*—all before he was thirty. At the same time, he ostensibly searches for the vanished American hero. He talks to George McGovern and Teddy Kennedy, General William Westmoreland, John Glenn, Eugene McCarthy, author William Styron, playwright Arthur Miller—some of them heroes of his, all of them heroes to many.

But it's like chasing a rainbow. He finds that, as he gets closer, his heroes disappear. In homes and bars, on campaign trails, they're distinctly, disappointingly normal. Not wonderfully, triumphantly, down-to-earth normal, but up-close, drinking-too-much, sweating, stinking, unheroically normal. And for heroes, normal isn't enough. We are allowed one image; everything must fit.

The Greeks gave their gods human imperfections. In the modern hero, however, every flaw is a fatal flaw. It has only to be found, and it *will* be. Moving from celebrity to hero is like moving from a city to a small town. In a city, the camera's eye, though always present, is distant. In a small town, there isn't that distance. There's no place to hide.

"Whom the gods would destroy," Wilfrid Sheed wrote in *Transatlantic Blues*, "they first oversell." Superficially created, superficially destroyed—for the hero, for the celebrity, it all evens out. Except a heavy price is paid along the way. We all lose again. You, because, saddened and hurt by heroes who turn out not to be heroes at all, you become cynical and stop believing. Me, because I'm in a box. What is my responsibility? Is it, as I'm often told, to be the hero that children think I am? Or is it to live what is real, to be something else?

Recently, a friend asked me to speak to his college seminar. Near the end of two hours, we began to talk about many of these questions. A girl raised her hand. She said that a year or two earlier, on the Academy Awards, she had seen Charlton Heston receive an award for his "humanitarian" work. Heston had made the point, the girl said, that thousands of volunteers had done far more than he, that they deserved the award.

I asked the class what that story told them about Charlton Heston. That he's even modest, they decided. A few of the students laughed; then, one by one, several others joined in.

Witches

Margaret Atwood

(1980)

When I was walking through the rain in Cambridge today, lugging a heavy bag of books, having been sent to the wrong place, it was hard for me to believe that almost 20 years had passed since I first walked through Cambridge in the rain, lugging a heavy bag of books, with the deep suspicion that I had been sent to the wrong place. I had ostensibly come to Radcliffe to study Victorian literature, and that part of it was all right, since one of my fellow Canadians was teaching it here. But underneath my Victorian exterior I fancied myself a poet, a fancy that—as anyone who has ever been a graduate studentess in English will know—it was death to admit. And all the modern poetry, as well as the devices for listening thereto, were locked in Lamont Library, which was restricted to students and banned to studentesses. Getting out a book of modern poetry required somewhat the same procedures as those needed to extract a book of pornography from the X section of the Widener Library, and, being of a retiring nature, I didn't want anyone to see me doing the former under the mistaken impression that I was doing the latter. To this fact I owe my ignorance of modern American poetry, as well as my Canadian nationalism—for the Canadian poetry was not kept with the *real* poetry, but was down with Canadiana in the bowels of the Widener, underneath Ethnology and Folklore, and freely accessible to students and studentesses alike.

Walking around Cambridge today, trying to find out what I was supposed to be doing—a continuation of a lifelong endeavour—I was reminded of many happy afternoons spent in the bathtub on the third floor of 6 Appian Way (which is, alas, no more), reading Charles Dickens, scribbling dismal poems, and listening to the rain and the pitter-patter of sexual perverts as they scampered up and down the fire escape. I was also reminded of those many nights when I sat up until dawn, popping No-Nods and trying to get my term papers finished on time—for I have to confess that I actually wrote this speech this afternoon in the Greenhouse Restaurant, over a Frogurt and a cup of Sanka. It is to my habits of procrastination in things academic that I owe my success as a writer, for if I had done scholarship true justice, how would I ever have had time to write? (I did, however, learn an important distinction in graduate school: a speculation about who had syphilis when is gossip if it's about your friends, a plot element if it's about a character in a novel, and scholarship if it's about John Keats.)

It was at Radcliffe, too, that I first heard about role models. The position of dean, or was it don, was open, and there was much discussion about who should fill it. "We need a good role model," someone said. "What's that?" I asked, being from Canada. It was explained to me that, for role-modelhood, even at a university, scholarship was not the only requirement. One also had to be punctual, clean behind the ears, a good mother, well dressed, and socially presentable.

I'm afraid I'm a bad role model, but then, I long ago decided that I could be either a good role model or a writer, and for better or worse I chose writing.

Which brings me to the title of my address, a title I plucked from the air when presented with the need for one, without having the least idea of what I was going to say. I did feel, however, that it was appropriate to talk of witches here in New England, for obvious reasons, but also because this is the land of my ancestors, and one of my ancestors was a witch. Her name was Mary Webster, she lived in Connecticut, and she was hanged for "causing an old man to become extremely valetudinarious." Luckily, they had not yet invented the drop: in those days they just sort of strung you up. When they cut Mary Webster down the next day, she was, to everyone's surprise, not dead. Because of the law of double jeopardy, under which you could not be executed twice for the same offence, Mary Webster went free. I expect that if everyone thought she had occult powers before the hanging, they were even more convinced of it afterwards. She is my favourite ancestor, more dear to my heart even than the privateers and the massacred French Protestants, and if there's one thing I hope I've inherited from her, it's her neck.

One needs a neck like that if one is determined to be a writer, especially a woman writer, and especially if you are good at it. After 10 years of the Women's Movement we like to think that some of the old stereotypes are fading, but 10 years is not a very long time in the history of the world, and I can tell you from experience that the old familiar images, the old icons, have merely gone underground, and not far at that. We still think of a powerful woman as an anomaly, a potentially dangerous anomaly; there is something subversive about such women, even when they take care to be good role models. They cannot have come by their power naturally, it is felt. They must have *got it from somewhere*. Women writers are particularly subject to such projections, for writing itself is uncanny: it uses words for evocation rather than for denotation; it is spell-making. A man who is good at it is a craftsman. A woman who is good at it is a dubious proposition. A man's work is reviewed for its style and ideas, but all too often a woman's is reviewed for the supposed personality of the author as based on the jacket photograph. When a man is attacked in print, it's usually for saying what he says; when a woman is attacked in print, it's often for being who she is.

Which brings me to the next unfortunate aspect of witches. Witches were consulted in private, but their only public role was to be persecuted; or, as we say, "hunted." And here, with brief mention of the fact that in the current wave of book banning taking place in Canada, all the most prominently publicized banned writers have been women, I'd like to switch from women writers— who, after all, have it rather soft in this century, on this continent, and whose necks are strong enough to survive a little name-calling whenever they stick them out—to a larger and more alarming picture.

Witch-hunting was probably always political in nature, an attempt by the powerful to control the potentially subversive, and it still is. The difference between witch-hunting and more conventional forms of justice and punishment is that in the latter you're supposedly being punished for what you've done, but in the former it's enough to be who you are. I'm a member of Amnesty International, and I read their monthly bulletins, which I would like to give *gratis*, a year's subscription, to the next literary critic who accuses my work of being unduly pessimistic. Political witch-hunting is now a worldwide epidemic. Torture for the purposes of extracting a confession, which will in turn justify the torture, is not a thing of the past. It did not end with racks, stakes, and Grand Inquisitors, or with Cotton Mather. It's here with us now, and growing. One of the few remedies for it is free human speech, which is why writers are always among the first to be lined up against the wall by any totalitarian regime, left or right. How many poets are there in El Salvador? The answer is none. They have all been shot or exiled. The true distinction in the world today is not between the so-called left and the so-called right. It's between governments that do such things as a matter of policy, or that wink at them when they are done, and those that do not. It would be simple stupidity to suppose that North America is by nature exempt. We've had witch-hunts before, and there is every indication that we're on the verge of having them again. When times are tough, when the Black Plague strikes or the economy falters and people get restless, those in authority start looking around for someone to burn.

When you are a fiction writer, you're confronted every day with the question that confronted, among others, George Eliot and Dostoevsky: what kind of world shall you describe for your readers? The one you can see around you, or the better one you can imagine? If only the latter, you'll be unrealistic; if only the former, despairing. But it is by the better world we can imagine that we judge the world we have. If we cease to judge this world, we may find ourselves, very quickly, in one which is infinitely worse.

The Size of Thoughts

Nicholson Baker

Each thought has a size, and most are about three feet tall, with the level of complexity of a lawnmower engine, or a cigarette lighter, or those tubes of toothpaste that, by mingling several hidden pastes and gels, create a pleasantly striped product. Once in a while, a thought may come up that seems, in its woolly, ranked composure, roughly the size of one's closet. But a really *large* thought, a thought in the presence of which whole urban centers would rise to their feet, and cry out with expressions of gratefulness and kinship; a thought with grandeur, and drenching, barrel-scorning cataracts, and detonations of fist-clenched hope, and hundreds of cellos; a thought that can tear phone books in half, and rap on the iron nodes of experience until every blue girder rings; a thought that may one day pack everything noble and good into its briefcase, elbow past the curators of purposelessness, travel overnight toward Truth, and shake it by the indifferent marble shoulders until it finally whispers its cool assent—this is the size of thought worth thinking about.

I have wanted for so long to own and maintain even a few huge, interlocking thoughts that, having exhausted more legitimate methods, I have recently resorted to theoretical speculation. Would it be possible to list those features that, taken together, confer upon a thought a lofty magnificence? What *makes* them so very large? My idle corollary hope is that perhaps a systematic and rigorous codification, on the model of Hammurabi's or Napoleon's, might make large thoughts available cheap, and in bulk, to the general public, thereby salvaging the nineteenth-century dream of a liberal democracy. But mainly I am hoping that once I can coax from large thoughts the rich impulses of their power, I will be able to think them in solitude, evening after evening, walking in little circles on the carpet with my arms outspread.

In my first attempt to find an objective measure for the size of thoughts, I theorized (as most of us have, I suppose) that I had only to mount the narrow stairs to my attic, stand in the hypotenuse of sunlight that passed through the window there in midwinter, and, concentrating, punch the thought in question once quite firmly, as if it were a pillow. The total number of tiny golden dust-monads that puffed forth from the thought's shocked stuffing would indicate, I believed, its eternal, essential size.

I found this to be a crude technique, and rejected it. Next, influenced by Sir John Eccles, the famous neurophysiologist, who used the axon of the giant-squid neuron to arrive at truths about the chemistry of human nerve fibers (small truths, needless to say: all scientific truths are small), I cast about for a suitably large thought existing in a form compact enough for me to experiment on it intensively. I tried a line of Wordsworth's,

> ...steps
> Almost as silent as the turf they trod.

but it wasn't really big enough for my purposes. I tried

> O, for a beaker full of the warm South,
> Full of the true, the blushful Hippocrene...

but I wept every time I read it, and got nowhere. Finally I decided to think about Henry James's sentence "What is morality but high intelligence?" It came to seem so conveniently vast, so ideally ample, that I handled it for several days, as if it were some richly figured object carved in cool stone; and when it failed to relinquish the secret of its size after that period, I discovered that I had indirectly arrived at my first theorem regarding large thoughts, which was:

1) *All large thoughts are reluctant.* I don't think this is intentional on their part. It follows from the unhasty, liquid pace of human thinking. As an experiment, overturn half a glass of wine onto a newly starched tablecloth. Watch, wholly absorbed, as the borders of the stain search their way outward, plumping up each parched capillary of cotton, threadlet by threadlet, and then traveling on—a soundless, happy explosion, with no moving parts. Thought moves at the velocity of that stain. And since a large thought seems to wish to pierce and acknowledge and even to replenish many more shoots and plumules of one's experience, some shrunken from long neglect (for every thought, even the largest, tires, winds down, and hardens into a hibernating token of chat, a place-holder for real intellection, unless it is worried into endless, pliant movement by second thoughts, and by the sense of its own provisionality, passing and repassing through the hundreds of semi-permeable membranes that insulate learning, suffering, ambition, civility, and puzzlement from one another, and from their neighbors), its thrum of fineness will necessarily be delayed, baffled, and drawn out with numerous interstitial timidities—one pauses, looks up from the page, waits; the eyes move in meditative polygons in their orbits; and then, somehow, *more* of the thought is released into the soul, the corroborating peal of some new, distant bell—until it has filled out the entirety of its form, as a thick clay slip settles into an intricate mould, or as a ladleful of batter colonizes cell after cell of the waffle iron, or as, later, the smell of that waffle will have toured the awakening rooms of the house.

Yet I sensed that reluctance was insufficient. What else did a large thought have to have? Filled with an ambitious sort of wistfulness, I flung open the door of the island cottage where I was staying, nodded to the moon, and began to walk up the fairway of a golf course, repeating, to the pulse of my invisible feet, a large thought of Tennyson's on which I had decided to perform a few experiments:

> Witch-elms that counterchange the floor
> Of this flat lawn with dusk and bright...

The sand traps, ghostly objects shaped like white blood cells, floated slowly past. At last I reached the green, the moon-colored green, where a dark flag flapped, and looked out over the warm, white sea. I threw my arms wide, and waited. Right then my second theorem regarding large thoughts ought to have formed itself in silver characters on the far horizon, but, in fact, it reached me only some weeks later, in a public library:

2) *Large thoughts are creatures of the shade.* Not deep shade, necessarily, but the mixed and leafy shade at the floor of large forests. Small thoughts are happy to run around in their colorful swimwear under the brutallest of noons, but large thoughts really must have sizable volumes of cool, still air, to allow room for the approach and docking of their components of sadness. Nobody can frown intently at a delicate task sitting on the floor of a large forest, and large thoughts, too, evade the pointedness and single-purposiveness of a frown; instead, they assert with a general pressure, and avoid contentious-ness, and limit themselves to the suggestion that not far off, not far off, there are wholly convincing marginalia of still-undiscovered feeling, stored like heaped tapestries in unlit vaults: they exhibit, then, a lush shadiness, as do the purple fastnesses in one's lungs, or the wrought, jewelled, dark interiors of water-resistant watches. All large thoughts are also patched and played over by leaf-shadows of slight hesitation and uncertainty: this tentativeness gives the thought just enough humility for it to be true. (All that is untrue is small.) I have found that dusk—the moment of planetary shade—is the most likely time to encounter large thoughts. Because, I suppose, of some power struggle between the retina's rods and cones brought on with the coming of darkness, there is a quarter-hour or so when colors, though less distinct, seem superbly pigmented, and the important things, faces and especially the teeth of smiles, take on a soft, amiable light: it is then that large thoughts may best be observed, strolling on their sombre porches, and reciting from their codices.

As you may imagine, by the time I had successfully formulated this second theorem regarding large thoughts, I was desperately tired of them. If I felt one looming up in a page of Tolstoy, I ran off; I hid. The party seemed over: Ed Peters and the band had packed up, and the deadened balloons scudded about the floor.

I slumped in a chair. More than anything else, I wished just then for the minty breath of a slighter, gentler truth or two in my ear. A minor botanical discovery concerning a rare species of fern, perhaps; a paradox or an aperçu would do; faint harpsichord music; tricks with coins or cards; witty biographies of peripheral Victorians. What was so very contemptible about small thoughts? Where, indeed, would we be without cornish game hens such as "It is one of the chief merits of proofs that they instill a certain scepticism about the result proved," which came to rest in Bertrand Russell's lucky mind one day? Or Charles Churchill's little two-step:

> With curious art the brain, too finely wrought,
> Preys on herself, and is destroyed by thought.

Or, finally, this bit from Pater: "There is a certain shade of unconcern, the perfect manner of the eighteenth century, which may be thought to mark complete culture in the handling of abstract questions": a thought that bounds beamingly, radiantly skyward for an instant, but is then, like many fine small thoughts, snuffed out on the second bounce by a bookish delegation of counterexamples. If we exiled all that is nifty, careless, wildly exaggerated, light-footed, vulnerable, or curiously spiced from our spiritual landscape, we would be in terrible shape. I became disgusted with myself for my callousness toward the small. "Refine all epics into epigrams!" I said. "I shall measure only the flares and glimmers of the world, thimbleful by peerless thimbleful; and I shall not grudge even the jingle of a light-bulb filament the silence of an enraptured continent."

But this extreme reaction missed the point, which was, as I found out not long afterward, that:

3) *Large thoughts depend more heavily on small thoughts than you might think.* Why does velvet feel smoother than chrome? Because smoothness is a secondary inference on the part of the confused fingertip, based on its perception of many extraordinarily fleeting little roughnesses running underneath it too quickly to be individually considered. This suggestion of resistance in all truly smooth surfaces, like the sense of ornamental insurrection in all truly graceful lines, is analogous to the profusion, the anarchy, of lovely, brief insights that we often experience as we read or listen our way through a great work of the mind, a work that, once completed, will leave us filled with large, calm truths. I do not know how this happens, but it happens. The villi on the inside of our small intestine—dense groves of microscopic protuberances—constitute a total surface area dedicated to absorption of nutrients which, if flattened out, would rival the island of Manhattan in size, I am told. Large thoughts, too, disembellished and abstracted from the small thoughts that diversify their surface, become sheer and indigestible. Consider the infinitesimal hooks on the horsehairs that draw from the cello string its lavish tone; consider the grosgrain in silk; the gargoyles on a cathedral; the acanthus sprays or egg-and-dart molding along the tasteful curve of a chair; the lumps of potato that, by exception, prove the otherwise fine uniformity of a cream soup; consider the examples that enforce a moral essay; the social satire in a novel with a tragic ending; the sixteenth notes in a peaceful melody; the fanatically detailed foliage in a Dutch landscape; the incessant roadside metaphors in a work of philosophy—consider all the indefensible appliances, the snags, the friction, the plush, that seem to hinder the achievement of a larger purpose, but are, in fact, critical to it. Major truths, like benevolent madonnas, are sustained aloft by dozens of busy, cheerful angels of detail.

I have tested these three theorems—the theorem of reluctance, the theorem of shade, and the theorem of dependence—on as many of the artifacts of reason as I could while holding a steady job. My results may have a certain severe appeal. Few indeed are the hobbyists in human memory who have known the recondite craft of building a spacious, previously unthought thought of their very own: how to obtain, in arranging its long hallways and high, ornate rooms, that pull of an ever-riper deferment, by returning to it again and again, after some studied distraction—now full-face, now three-quarter view, now very near, now far off; how to gather in its huge, slow force with an encircling persistence that is three parts novelty, two parts confirming, strengthening repetition. I count Henry James, Brahms, Bellini, Burke, Bach, Pontormo. A mere eighty-six others. And now, in a mood of icy impartiality, I am going to test the size of the thought I am offering you right here, which I expect to see peter out very shortly with few surprises, wrapped up after another two or three breaths of the mind, extended perhaps by a last, gravelly spatter of instantiation, unless, O yearn! I just happen to happen upon that loose-limbed, reckless acceleration, wherein this very thought might shamble forward, plucking tart berries, purchasing newspapers, and retrieving odd bits of refuse without once breaking stride—risking a smile, shaking the outstretched hands of young constituents, loosening its tie!—no, that's all, I believe: this thought has rounded itself out, and ratified itself, despite all of its friendly intentions, as small.

Voice in the Blood: Suffering and Compassion

Colleen Cutschall

The Lakota Sioux creation myth prescribes a social and religious order and establishes a cultural identity which gives meaning to the lives of the people. Yet only in rare instances have Natives contributed their perspectives on the way mythic and cultural ideals are integrated and emulated in the sacred and secular activities of their respective societies. Ortiz's (1974) writings on the Tewa Pueblo, Fletcher and La Flesche's (1911) work on the Omaha, and Deloria's (1944) comments on the Dakota stand as cornerstones of an emic cultural anthropology. Native people are no longer isolated in a world of their own making, but are constantly subject to the information, pressures, and anxieties of a technological, fragmented, fast-paced, despiritualized world. There are Native people who live fully in both of these worlds today. There are also individuals who have been deluded and victimized by poverty both in the economic and in the spiritual sense, and by the pressures of the acculturation process. But in the last two decades we have seen Native people, more than ever before, determined to take control of their lives and regain or renew their sacred traditions for personal and collective power. We have seen the various tribes of North America unite to form positions of political strength against their common oppressor, the governments, which pre-empted their own systems of social order. In the 1970's, slogans that were popular in Indian country appealed to both the suffering and compassionate nature of Native people as well as to their inner strength, allowing them to face their trials squarely. Lakota people had not forgotten or forgiven their historical tragedies. Slogans like "We Remember Wounded Knee," "We Shall Endure," and "The Longest Walk" reflected the focus of Native people on political action.

If we accept desire, delusion, and change as universal motives for personal, social, and political suffering, then what is the Native counterpart that makes compassion efficacious? We are aware of the extremes of ritual sacrifice from North America's high cultures, such as the sacrifice of human lives among the Aztec and Natchez. We still hear of flesh being pierced or cut among the Plains tribes and of the physical and mental traumas of the vision quest among the Beaver and Ojibway. Perhaps it is time to re-examine the nature of ritualized suffering and compassion as it is experienced in and integrated into the contemporary traditions of a Native culture.

Myth prescribes a cultural pattern for ritualizing suffering and compassion through the Lakota sacred traditions of ear piercing, the vision quest, the Sundance, and spirit keeping. These are the ceremonies that build and renew the discipline required to cope with, endure and understand the nature of suffering and compassion. Wisdom, will power, resolution, and verification are the mental tools that keep suffering and compassion as opposites, holding them apart rather than allowing them to consume each other like incestuous twins. Suffering and compassion left to an undisciplined mind could easily result in mass misery keeping itself company. So ritual drama reaffirms, in a formal sense, Lakota values and the techniques for developing strength of mind. These techniques make up seven elements within the ceremonial process. The seven elements that develop strength of mind are preparation, purification, expansion or focus, resolution, illumination, verification, and reciprocation. The values are persistent among those Lakota who do not strictly adhere to or participate in the sacred traditions. For example, sharing, hospitality, and generosity are the visible values of even the poorest Lakota. The rise of these values testifies to the recognition of fundamental life as a source of suffering, one which is shared universally. The Lakota creation myth is an example of how, in mythic times, the ultimate source of creation, *Inyan*, contemplated creation within the void of darkness and the great silence. *Inyan* is considered a masculine spirit, an all-encompassing creative force. The darkness, *Hanhepi*, is a feminine spirit although not a major deity. Their opposing natures become gradually apparent as the Lakota cosmology unfolds. If myth is a model for human actions, then we need to consider what role suffering played at the dawn of time. Did the source of life, fundamental life, *Inyan*, suffer; and if so, what form did suffering assume? Following is a condensed version of what took place in the beginning.

*Inyan, the Lakota concept of the primal source, was moved by his suffering and discontent, precipitated by a desire to express his power. He desired to have control over another thing. In order to have control over the new being, **Inyan** knew that he would have to give to it a portion of his blood. The powers of **Inyan** were in his blood and his blood was blue. He was soft and formless. Out of his desire blood began to flow, taking form and materializing. **Inyan** let so much of his blood into the new creation that he began to shrink and become hard. He created our ancient mother, the great disc, **Maka**, the earth. But the powers of **Inyan** could not dwell in the waters of **Maka** and so they passed through the earth and separated, filling the silence, forming the vast blue dome. The father spirit, **Skan**, was born.*

Thus in the first few lines of the Lakota creation myth the primal method for ritualizing suffering is established. Blood is the essential element from which new or renewed life must flow. The wilful act of sacrificing one's own source of life, one's own blood, is the Lakota manner of expressing the whole self, sacrificing the physical self in order to gain a sense of one's inner self. In ceremony, which is at the core of Lakota religion, the potential exists for the individual to bind together the internal spiritual mind and the gross, physical self through formal, sacrificial observances and to gain from this experience a great strength of mind.

A child's formal initiation into the realm of Lakota spirits and spiritual beliefs occurs through the ritual piercing of its ears. From the time of birth the child is connected to this spirit realm through the wearing of the umbilical cord. Small pouches designed in the shape of turtles and lizards are still made by Lakota artisans for the purpose of keeping the cord of life. Today the cord may be kept near the child in the home and not worn continuously as it may have been in the past. As the child approaches the age of reason, five to seven years old, it has already experienced a variety of physical and mental tortures such as nightmares, accidents, and fears of abandonment. The child learns that even the most loving of parents cannot be available to deal with every possible danger. Indeed, some children learn very early to depend upon themselves to balance their own fears. Compassionate parents desiring to help their child gain this strength of mind may sponsor the ear-piercing ceremony. While an infant or toddler will respond to physical suffering by fighting off that which causes the suffering, the child approaching the age of reason is much more willing to consider the benefits and blessings that are bestowed by the ceremony.

The case of my daughter, Starlight, is illustrative. She liked the idea that there were benevolent beings in a parallel world that she could call on at any time for whatever help she might need, but only if she were willing to do something difficult. What I was emphasizing was the Lakota ideal that suffering builds great strength, that doing difficult things is a sign of sincerity that the spirits will recognize and reciprocate by being more inclined to communicate with her. Through a series of paintings I was working on at the time, she became acquainted with the names and concepts of the main Lakota gods. I also told her about the details of what she would have to endure during the ceremony, emphasizing the Lakota ideal of bravery. We discussed the *wopila*, the giving away to people who would come and see her do this difficult thing. Over the months preceding the ceremony she was able to see the enormous and intensive effort being made to assemble the items needed for the camp, the ceremony, and the *wopila*. As the sponsoring parent I bore the burden of pulling all these things together, including bringing my family into the process. There were seemingly unlimited obstacles and delays over those months and continuing right up through the ceremony. Starlight would have her ears pierced at the Sundance tree on the Sioux Valley reserve in Manitoba. It would take place on the first day, the day of the tree ceremony. She would be the first to pierce at the tree. She would do this without me by her side although my family and I would be in a procession behind her. I chose my younger sister as the woman who would be her advisor in life and instruct her in the traditions. She would take my daughter to the tree and stand by her while the piercing took place.

On the day of the ceremony the wind blew icy cold, the last breath of winter still in the air. Starlight fasted the entire day and was growing very hungry and cranky. Late in the day the tree was in place and we walked in a procession to the east gate of the sacred lodge. The people assembled and the *itancan*, or leader, addressed the people with the authority of a father, to explain what this five-year-old girl was going to do. He said this had not been done in a very long time, maybe eighty years or more. He explained that I was doing this out of great love and compassion for my daughter and he spoke of how she would benefit from doing this. The ceremony proceeded: Starlight circled the tree four times and then the *itancan* fanned her. A medicine woman, one who hears the spirits, came forward to clean Starlight's ears with buffalo wool. *Tahtanka*, the bison, is the protector of young maidens and is a symbol of prosperity to the Lakota people. For the next twenty minutes all watched as the woman struggled to get the needle through the first ear. Starlight stood tall and with a great deal of courage. There were definite signs of pain but she did not cry or whimper or fight the hand that held the needle. The woman proceeded to the second ear which was even more difficult to pierce. The needle did not want to go through and she applied more and more pressure. By this time the pain had become very upsetting and Starlight began to cry, but she did not move or fight with the woman. Once the holes had been made a new pair of earrings was to be placed in her ears. Again there was difficulty as the woman had trouble getting the earrings inserted. Finally she said they would not work and that straight wires would be needed. I was wearing a new pair of earrings and immediately removed the wires and gave them to my daughter. These were fitted and the piercing was done. Starlight cried softly as we walked in a procession before the wise, elderly women who would advise her in the role and proper behaviour of a Lakota female and in her responsibilities to the traditions. By this time even these tough older women who had been through much suffering in their life were having a hard time displaying the face of endurance for which they were known. All the people were weeping quietly. The older women praised Starlight for what she had done and thanked her with that kind of reserved respect and dignity given to those who will uphold the ideals of the people. None of the grandmothers fussed over the little girl's tears. Only when my family took her back to our lodge was this girl comforted in the way one comforts a child, but even her family expressed a new kind of respect for her and a great pride in which all could share.

The personal growth and grace demonstrated through the ritual sufferings of a small child gave to all who were there to witness a renewed sense of determination. Her courage allowed them to endure their daily sufferings with fortitude; the Sundancers could then approach their vows to suffer and pierce for the life of the people with the added strength which she had imparted to them. The act of ritual sacrifice continued through the naming ceremony and the *wopila* which followed the ear-piercing. Through her first ritual acts, Starlight had begun to fulfil her Indian name, which is the same as her English name, *the light that shines out of the darkness*. Metaphorically, *Starlight* could refer to breaking out of ignorance with the illumination of sacred knowledge. In the years to come this name may be another source of vitality that focuses, expands, and soothes the fibres of the mind. Now, at a

Sundance, when the little girls pierce their ears, Starlight is called upon to comfort them and suffer with them in their little girls' lodge. She is able to reaffirm her initial experience by showing compassion for these girls. On these occasions the older, respected women remind the girls that they will be the ones to remember these traditions and to show the people how they are carried out. They must bear the responsibility for the continuation of the tribe, for without them there could be no tribe. They are told they must uphold the home and carry on the traditions. While this may seem like an awesome task for these young girls, they are reminded that they will need the great strength which they will gain by doing these ritual acts. They are also reminded that they should be kind and take care of the people who need their help, the sick ones, the hungry ones, and anyone having a hard time. They will learn the domestic arts of feeding the people, of sewing the blankets and garments that will clothe and comfort their relatives.

It is made clear to these children that suffering is of this world and that they need the help of the Lakota spirits to minimize this suffering as well as their compassion for their fellows to help them endure these sufferings. These children were prepared mentally, emotionally, and spiritually for the ceremony. They had a desire to change from a feeble, uninformed stance to a secure state of mind capable of balancing the fears of suffering, thus providing the motivation to proceed through the ceremony. With the help of good teachers they are able to expand their understanding of what is expected of them, to externalize their internal thoughts. The parents and the teachers are formally enculturating the child. The focus and resolution come in the ceremony when the child has mastered the struggle of the duality of being and unifies the internal mind's ideal of the self with its external actions. The child wills the body to act in accordance with the mind, and in concert with the totality of the moment. The efficacy of the act is immediately apparent when the people recognize and praise the child's self-control and endurance in the face of suffering. A sacred power has been transferred to the child in whom illumination has taken place. The child has established its relationship to humanity and the world community. Verification of the new understanding is expressed through the child's and parent's reciprocation of the gift of illumination by hosting a *wopila*, the formal giving away to the people, those who supported the ceremony, the poor, the sick, and the hungry. It is, of course, expected that the ceremonial ideals will spill over into the secular life where the daily acts of kindness will be continued. The *wopila* speaks to the love that the Lakota have for fundamental life. This concept is expressed as one of the four souls, the life breath, the *niya*. The *niya* has its own great strength which is tended to in ceremony by addressing the physical needs of the people through feeding and clothing them. Outsiders observing the ceremonies are awe struck when they are expected to receive mass quantities of food and are sometimes gifted with blankets, shawls, and other items. Generosity on this scale is quite foreign to those who do not understand the traditions. They come from societies that emphasize excess consumption as a form of strength. And of course, the Lakota view is just the opposite, denying their own physical needs to gain a non-empirical ideal. This process of building mental stability and balancing desire with responsible action is expressed in myth as a concern of the gods in primordial times.

*Maka, the earth, is symbolic of materiality, desire, discontent, and the primal will of the female. In the myth she is illustrated as constantly nagging **Skan**, asking for more power. She demands to be decorated with ornaments and to own creatures over which she could exert her power. **Maka's** demands to have her own domain and all the other things she asked for were met by **Skan**. Still **Maka** was discontented because **Skan** also gave her the burden of nourishment and protection over all who were subordinate to her. **Maka** was given a companion, **Unk,** who was so disagreeable that **Maka** rejected her. **Unk** created the Circle of Evil Spirits. **Gnaski** was the smartest of **Unk's** offspring. He had no respect for anything and so he would manipulate **Maka's** desire for potency. Finally, **Skan** had enough of their games and their demands.*

> *Skan* then said to *Maka*, "Because you have listened to *Gnaski*, who advised you to do that which would provoke the Gods, and because you continually insisted on more and more demands, you shall forever care for all that exists upon the lands and protect their welfare. These animals and all created things will know you as grandmother, but they shall be for the benefit and pleasure of all the Gods and for each other." *Maka* then bowed before *Skan*, saying, "I have wrought only for my own pleasure. On all my domain are symbols, the gravel and stones beside the waters, reminders of my folly. The gods have justly humiliated me. My grievous punishment is just." *Wohpe* stood beside *Maka* and said to her, "My father has wrought to free you from vanity and from envy. The tokens placed to annoy you shall ever remind you that the greatest pleasure is in pleasing others." Seeing how meek and humble *Maka* had become, *Wohpe's* heart went out to *Maka*. Addressing her father, *Skan*, she implores him, saying, "My father, by your will I am the patron of compassion. Allow my companion *Ksa* (the spirit of wisdom) and me to abide with *Maka* while she needs us." *Skan* decrees *Wohpe* the associate of *Maka*. (Walker-Jahner, 1983, p.242; my italics)

Wohpe, who is compassion and a mediator among the gods, and *Ksa*, who is wisdom, are sent to the earth and later will dwell among the Lakota as a source of strength. It is clear that excessive desires will not be tolerated by the gods but that desires can be fulfilled. As new demands are met they will also require responsible action. The ceremonies were given to the Lakota by the gods and so they are responsible for upholding the ideals of the ceremony. *Wohpe* returns to the people in historical times and brings the gift of the pipe to the people. Since the time the Lakota received the pipe and its teachings they have been able to communicate directly to the spirits. On an individual and collective basis, the Lakota are linked to the cosmos through the pipe and through the ceremonies.

It is through the ceremonial process that one is able to activate a realization of one's sense of personal power, the *sicun*. The *sicun* is conceived as one of the four aspects of the mind or soul which gains its power through self-discipline and self-control. The *nagi*, which can be thought of as a ghost, is the individual consciousness that accumulates historicity and is the aspect of mind or soul that freely travels the inner and outer landscapes of the mind. In Lakota thought, each human being also possesses a *nagila* or little ghost. This is the presence of the mysterious life force, *taku skan skan*, that which causes all things to move. At death it reunites with the sacred totality and loses its individuality. The *nagila* is something of an alter ego, unpredictable and unconforming to rational thought. As long as the mind is strong and the other souls are well integrated, the *nagila* cannot throw one off balance or off centre. The *nagila* might be likened to *Unk* and her relatives who demand attention in a negative manner. Fundamental life has its own great strength and is the visible aspect of soul. This is the *niya*, the life breath which can be seen in steam. The *niya* is representative of the physical life without which there would be no life in an individual. One would be considered dead when this aspect of the soul departs from the body. A well-balanced individual is the result of the appropriate alignment and integration of all four souls.

Each time individuals participate in any of the major rites of the Lakota they not only acquire the security of the moment but they also retain the potency of their will and resolution in reserve. At a later time the path of determination may be recalled from memory and lead the individual into yet another illuminating experience. This process for most North Americans is less salient in adolescence, but it generally increases for the Lakota and many other traditional peoples who value the importance of dream seepage and the building of fortitude through endurance practices. They not only endure deprivations to build physical strength in the body, they are also encouraged to train their senses and their minds. In particular, they are encouraged to seek an immortal teacher and guide, to acquire supernatural assistance. The successful acquisition of supernatural assistance increases the personal potency, the *sicun*, so the Lakota becomes more attuned to the rhythms of the universe. Interacting with nature is also viewed as a source of strength. The earth mother, *Maka*, and all her creatures intercede for the Lakota and help define his relationship to all things. All living things are considered as having possession of a *nagi*. The potency of plants, animals, and supernaturals are sought by the *hanbleceya* initiate. The Lakota seeking potency through the *hanbleceya*, the vision quest, seeks to re-establish the primordial experience on a conscious physical and psychic level for the purpose of spiritual renewal. This desire for potency is the desire to be effective in this life. To the Lakota, desire is compulsory and falls within the sphere of conscious experience, while the object of the vision lies beyond it. Dreams and intuitions point to things that are unknown, hidden, mysterious, and that by their very nature are secret. The Lakota hold the dream experience in religious awe.

The naming ceremony that brought the child into the tribe, allowing the child to confront the night-fears of its carefree days, marked the emergence of the unconscious. The naming conferred a responsibility on the child and its sponsors to become versed in the complete history and philosophy of the tribe, initially responding with only a scientific and rational understanding of the night and day phenomenon. A spiritual aspirant entering into the cultural rites of passage may come to a deeper understanding and appreciation of the cosmic dualities of night and day, unconscious and conscious. Through the vision quest, the Lakota consciously reaffirm their stance in the universe through the microcosmic re-creation of the centre of the world. The umbilical cord that had, at first, attached the Lakota to the unseen world was symbolically replaced by wires in the ear-piercing. In the *hanbleceya*, the *sicun* is generated by the specific alignment of the *niya* and the mind brought into proper balance, *tawacin waste*, a good mind and a good attitude. To stand erect in a proper stance and cry for a vision is to relieve the concerns of the body and the sufferings of the unconscious mind. The Lakota offers the pipe, the gift presented to the Lakota by *Wohpe*, the beauty, the mediator and patron of compassion. The *hanbleceya*, or vision quest, is the ceremony that bestows personal potency on the individual. The knowledge gained through visions or dream seepage from the outer world can be activated in times of personal need, or sometimes used to help others in their suffering. The sacred knowledge of healing and doctoring came to the Lakota in this way, primarily through their shaman. Shamans were also knowledgable about the concept of an imbalanced mind, which the Lakota refer to as *tawacin kaptun* or the mind tipped over, out of balance. This is also a general term for neurosis and psychosis.

Sacrifice, particularly of flesh and blood, constitutes a ritual death of the concerns of the material world and a preparation for the spiritual life. A mature Lakota may choose to participate in the Sundance. The one who has experienced the ear-piercing as a child has been ritually brought into the age of reason, into the conscious world. As an adult, one may repeat that experience. Children sacrifice in the ear-piercing. A parallel process among adults involves the sacrifice of their flesh and blood. The ideal attitude is that one should dance for the people from a position of strength and knowledge. Thus young people who have already sought their visions are considered to be the best prepared to sacrifice themselves for the people in a Sundance, because a Sundancer should not expect to be supported by the strength of the others, or by the people who come to find cures and comforts for their sufferings. All the dancers should be prepared to dance by drawing on their own source of power, their *sicun*. It is interesting to note that in the contemporary Sundance one will often find the physically disabled, the diabetic, the asthmatic, and those with other health problems among the dancers. They are a constant source of consternation for the *itancan*. The responsibility of the *itancan* is to ensure that the ceremony is carried out properly and that no part of the ceremony is weakened by sick dancers. The weak tend to draw on the strength of the other dancers, causing disruptions and consequently an inappropriate focus for the offerings and prayers being made on behalf of all of the people. They become more and more concerned about their needs and sufferings and less concerned about the technique through which renewal of life and the people's desire to live will be made efficacious. One can appreciate how disastrous it would be if one were to die in the sacred lodge at the critical moment when life is being renewed. The Sundance is a collective prayer which should benefit all the people, not just one. In order that all the dancers receive this benefit, even the dancers who have health problems must by the potency of their will and resolution successfully complete their vows of sacrifice. Through coping with the sufferings of their *niya* on a daily basis, they have already gained the personal strength necessary to stay alive.

Even at the time of the death of a loved one, the Lakota express their mourning by caring for the soul of their deceased relatives, feeding and clothing a spirit post and caring for the spirit bundle that contains the essence of the deceased person, the *nagi*. After a year of mourning, the soul is released and told it can no longer remain among the living. *Tawacin waste*, a good mind and a good attitude, is not only for those who shun the turmoil of the world, but also for those who want to face it squarely. A significant life change implies that there is a loss or lack of power, impotency or death to one area of the mind or soul. Death, through the loss of a loved one, alters one's position within the community, causing one to re-evaluate one's direction in life. Myth also makes it clear that we must assume a new responsibility as well. This is the order of things that were decided when the gods battled for their potency and established a new order out of nothingness. Chaos, anxiety, confusion, impotency, and desire reigned over *Maka's* passions until she humbled herself. The distribution of goods on ceremonial occasions, such as the spirit release ritual, mirrors the feasts of the gods and the tokens given to the guests so that they might redeem their greatest desires. The give-away is recognized as the authoritative, *Skan*, response to uncontrolled desire and discontent. Thus, the suffering of the one who gives away is verified, while the guests or recipients are soothed, restored, and made potent by this ritual. The recipients lose their temporal burdens, their anxiety about such things as status and position. Their suffering is not ignored; indeed all suffering is recognized and incorporated into the living myth of ceremony. The mind is refocused on effective action. For those who bear the responsibility of keeping a soul, there is a confrontation of the final unification of the soul with all of one's relatives dwelling within the calm, spiritual waters of the universe. Death, then, is the ultimate link in the life-transformation process. When through this ceremony one confronts death, it becomes less fearful, more approachable and understandable. By releasing the soul of a beloved, one's mind expands to accept the ultimate verification of suffering, the return of the soul to its source, the final act through which life begins anew. Grace and dignity are the fruits of a lifetime of suffering. Through ceremony, the Lakota is restored and the mind behaves as *Wohpe*, the mediator and restorer of dignity and potency through compassion. For the Lakota the model of effective action comes by participating in the traditions and reciprocating with those who defend the traditions and those who are less fortunate. *Lakol wicohan*, walking the sacred red road, doing things in a culturally prescribed sacred manner, is the *sine qua non* that replaces the dried-up and disintegrated umbilical cord with which we arrived through somebody else's pain and suffering. These traditions formalize the Lakota belief system in which we are all bound and related through our suffering from birth, through life, to death and rebirth.

References: Works Consulted

Deloria, Ella C. (1944). *Speaking of Indians*. New York: Friendship Press.

Fletcher, Alice C., & La Flesche, Francis (1911). *The Omaha Tribe*. Washington: in U.S. Bureau of American Ethnology, 27th Annual Report.

Ortiz, Alfonso (1969). *The Tewa World: Space, Time, Being, and Becoming in a Pueblo Society*. Chicago & London: University of Chicago Press.

Ridington, Robin (1986). "Receiving the Mark of Honour: An Omaha Ritual of Transformation," a conference paper later revised and published in *Religion in Native North America*, ed. Christopher Vecsey. Moscow: University of Idaho Press, 1990.

Tedlock, Dennis, & Tedlock, Barbara (Eds.) (1975). *Teachings from the American Earth: Indian Religion and Philosophy*. New York: Liveright.

Walker, James R. (1983). *Lakota Myth*, ed. Elaine A. Jahner. Lincoln and London: University of Nebraska Press, in cooperation with the Colorado Historical Society.

Walker, James R. (1980). *Lakota Belief and Ritual*, ed. Raymond De Mallie & Elaine A. Jahner. Lincoln and London: University of Nebraska Press, in cooperation with the Colorado Historical Society.

Our Allotted Lifetimes

Stephen Jay Gould

J.P. Morgan, meeting with Henry Ford in E.L. Doctorow's *Ragtime*, praises the assembly line as a faithful translation of nature's wisdom:

> Has it occurred to you that your assembly line is not merely a stroke of industrial genius but a projection of organic truth? After all, the interchangeability of parts is a rule of nature....All mammals reproduce in the same way and share the same designs of self-nourishment, with digestive and circulatory systems that are recognizably the same, and they enjoy the same senses....Shared design is what allows taxonomists to classify mammals as mammals.

An imperious tycoon should not be met with equivocation; nonetheless, I can only reply "yes, and no" to Morgan's pronouncement. Morgan was wrong if he thought that large mammals are geometric replicas of smaller relatives. Elephants have relatively smaller brains and thicker legs than mice, and these differences record a general rule of mammalian design, not the idiosyncrasies of particular animals.

But Morgan was right in arguing that large animals are essentially similar to small members of their group. The similarity, however, does not reside in a constant shape. The basic laws of geometry dictate that animals must change their shape in order to work the same way at different sizes. Galileo himself established the classic example in 1638: the strength of an animal's leg is a function of its cross-sectional area (length x length); the weight that legs must support varies as the animal's volume (length x length x length). If mammals did not increase the relative thickness of their legs as they got larger, they would soon collapse (since body weight would increase so much faster than the supporting strength of limbs). To remain the same in function, animals must change their form.

The study of these changes in form is called "scaling theory." Scaling theory has uncovered a striking regularity of changing shape over the 25-millionfold range of mammalian weight from shrew to blue whale. If we plot brain weight versus body weight for all mammals on the so-called mouse-to-elephant (or shrew-to-whale) curve, very few species deviate far from a single line expressing the general rule: brain weight increases only two-thirds as fast as body weight as we move from small to large mammals. (We share with bottle-nosed dolphins the honour of greatest upward deviance from the curve.)

We can often predict these regularities from the basic physics of objects. The heart, for example, is a pump. Since all mammalian hearts work in essentially the same way, small hearts must pump considerably faster than large ones (imagine how much faster you could work a finger-sized, toy bellows than the giant model that fuels a blacksmith's forge or an old-fashioned organ). On the mouse-to-elephant curve for mammals, the length of a heartbeat increases between one-fourth and one-third as fast as body weight as we move from small to large mammals. The generality of this conclusion has recently been affirmed in an interesting study by J.E. Carrel and R.D. Heathcote on the scaling of heart rate in spiders. They used a cool laser beam to illuminate the hearts of resting spiders and drew a crab spider-to-tarantula curve for eighteen species spanning nearly a thousandfold range of body weight. Again, scaling is regular with heart rate increasing four-tenths as fast as body weight (.409 times as fast, to be exact).

We may extend this conclusion for hearts to a general statement about the pace of life in small versus large animals. Small animals tick through life far more rapidly than large animals—their hearts work more quickly, they breathe more frequently, their pulse beats much faster. Most importantly, metabolic rate, the so-called fire of life, increases only three-fourths as fast as body weight in mammals. To keep themselves going, large mammals do not need to generate as much heat per unit of body weight as small animals. Tiny shrews move frenetically, eating nearly all their waking lives to keep their metabolic fire burning at the maximal rate among mammals; blue whales glide majestically, their hearts beating the slowest rhythm among active, warm-blooded creatures.

The scaling of lifetime among mammals suggests an intriguing synthesis of these disparate data. We have all had enough experience with mammalian pets of various sizes to understand that small mammals tend to live for a shorter time than large ones. In fact, mammalian lifetime scales at about the same rate as heartbeat and breath time—between one-fourth and one-third as fast as body weight as we move from small to large animals. (*Homo sapiens* emerges from this analysis as a very peculiar animal. We live far longer than a mammal of our body size should. In [another] essay I argue that humans evolved by an evolutionary process called "neoteny"—the preservation in adults of shapes and growth rates that characterize juvenile stages of ancestral primates. I also believe that neoteny is responsible for our elevated longevity. Compared with other mammals, all stages of human life arrive "too late." We are born as helpless embryos after a long gestation; we mature late after an extended childhood; we die, if fortune be kind, at ages otherwise reached by warm-blooded animals only at the very largest sizes.)

Usually, we pity the pet mouse or gerbil that lived its full span of a year or two at most. How brief its life, while we endure for the better part of a century. As the main theme of this essay, I want to argue that such pity is misplaced (our personal grief, of course, is quite another matter; with this,

287

science does not deal). Morgan was right in *Ragtime*—small and large mammals are essentially similar. Their lifetimes are scaled to their life's pace, and all endure for approximately the same amount of biological time. Small mammals tick fast, burn rapidly, and live for a short time; large mammals live long at a stately pace. Measured by their own internal clocks, mammals of different sizes tend to live for the same amount of time.

We are prevented from grasping this important and comforting concept by a deeply ingrained habit of Western thought. We are trained from earliest memory to regard absolute Newtonian time as the single valid measuring stick in a rational and objective world. We impose our kitchen clock, ticking equably, upon all things. We marvel at the quickness of a mouse, express boredom at the torpor of a hippopotamus. Yet each is living at the appropriate pace of its own biological clock.

I do not wish to deny the importance of absolute, astronomical time to organisms. Animals must measure it to lead successful lives. Deer must know when to regrow their antlers, birds when to migrate. Animals track the day-night cycle with their circadian rhythms; jet lag is the price we pay for moving much faster than nature intended.

But absolute time is not the appropriate measuring stick for all biological phenomena. Consider the magnificent song of the humpback whale. E.O. Wilson has described the awesome effect of these vocalizations: "The notes are eerie yet beautiful to the human ear. Deep basso groans and almost inaudibly high soprano squeaks alternate with repetitive squeals that suddenly rise or fall in pitch." We do not know the function of these songs. Perhaps they enable whales to find each other and to stay together during their annual transoceanic migrations. Perhaps they are the mating songs of courting males.

Each whale has its own characteristic song; the highly complex patterns are repeated over and over again with great faithfulness. No scientific fact that I have learned in the last decade struck me with more force than Roger S. Payne's report that the length of some songs may extend for more than half an hour. I have never been able to memorize the five-minute first *Kyrie* of the B-minor Mass (and not for want of trying); how could a whale sing for thirty minutes and then repeat itself accurately? Of what possible use is a thirty-minute repeat cycle—far too long for a human to recognize; we would never grasp it as a single song (without Payne's recording machinery and much study after the fact). But then I remembered the whale's metabolic rate, the enormously slow pace of its life compared with ours. What do we know about a whale's perception of thirty minutes? A humpback may scale the world to its own metabolic rate; its half-hour song may be our minute waltz. From any point of view, the song is spectacular; it is the most elaborate single display so far discovered in any animal. I merely urge the whale's point of view as an appropriate perspective.

We can provide some numerical precision to support the claim that all mammals, on average, live for the same amount of biological time. In a method developed by W.R. Stahl, B. Günther, and E. Guerra in the late 1950s and early 1960s, we search the mouse-to-elephant equations for biological properties that scale at the same rate against body weight. For example, Günther and Guerra give the following equations for mammalian breath time and heartbeat time versus body weight.

$$\text{breath time} = .0000470 \text{ body}^{0.28}$$
$$\text{heartbeat time} = .0000119 \text{ body}^{0.28}$$

(Nonmathematical readers need not be overwhelmed by the formalism. The equations simply state that both breath time and heartbeat time increase about .28 times as fast as body weight as we move from small to large mammals.) If we divide the two equations, body weight cancels out because it is raised to the same power in both.

$$\frac{\text{breath time}}{\text{heartbeat time}} = \frac{.0000470 \, \cancel{\text{body}^{0.28}}}{.0000119 \, \cancel{\text{body}^{0.28}}} = 4.0$$

This states that the ratio of breath time to heartbeat time is 4.0 in mammals of any body size. In other words, all mammals, whatever their size, breathe once for each four heartbeats. Small mammals breathe and beat their hearts faster than large mammals, but both breath and heart slow up at the same relative rate as mammals get larger.

Lifetime also scales at the same rate as body weight (.28 times as fast as we move from small to large mammals). This means that the ratio of both breath time and heartbeat time to lifetime is also constant over the entire range of mammalian size. When we perform a calculation similar to the one above, we find that all mammals, regardless of their size, tend to breathe about 200 million times during their lives (their hearts, therefore, beat about 800 million times). Small mammals breathe fast, but live for a short time. Measured by the internal clocks of their own hearts or the rhythm of their own breathing, all mammals live the same time. (Astute readers, after counting their breaths or taking their pulses, may have calculated that they should have died long ago. But *Homo sapiens* is a markedly deviant mammal in more ways than braininess alone. We live about three times as long as mammals of our body size "should," but we breathe at the "right" rate and thus live to breathe about three times as often as an average mammal of our body size. I regard this excess of living as a happy consequence of neoteny.)

The mayfly lives but a day as an adult. It may, for all I know, experience that day as we live a lifetime. Yet all is not relative in our world, and such a short glimpse of it guarantees distortion in interpreting events ticking on longer scales. In a brilliant metaphor, the pre-Darwinian evolutionist Robert Chambers wrote in 1844 of a mayfly watching the metamorphosis of a tadpole into a frog:

Suppose that an ephemeron [a mayfly], hovering over a pool for its one April day of life, were capable of observing the fry of the frog in the waters below. In its aged afternoon, having seen no change upon them for such a long time, it would be little qualified to conceive that the external branchiae [gills] of these creatures were to decay, and be replaced by internal lungs, that feet were to be developed, the tail erased, and the animal then to become a denizen of the land.

Human consciousness arose but a minute before midnight on the geologic clock. Yet we mayflies try to bend an ancient world to our purposes, ignorant perhaps of the messages buried in its long history. Let us hope that we are still in the early morning of our April day.

Notes of a Biology-Watcher

The Hazards of Science

Lewis Thomas

The codeword for criticism of science and scientists these days is *hubris*. Once you've said that word, you've said it all; it sums up, in a word, all of today's apprehensions and misgivings in the public mind—not just about what is perceived as the insufferable attitude of the scientists themselves but, enclosed in the same word, what science and technology are perceived to be doing to make this century, this near to its ending, turn out so wrong.

Hubris is a powerful word, containing layers of powerful meaning, which is a peculiar thing when you consider its seemingly trivial history in etymology. It turned up first in popular English usage as a light piece of university slang at Oxford in the late 19th century, with the meaning of intellectual arrogance and insolence, applicable in a highly specialized sense to certain literary figures within a narrow academic community. But it was derived from a very old word, and as sometimes happens with ancient words it took on a new life of its own, growing way beyond the limits of its original meaning. Today, it is strong enough to carry the full weight of disapproval for the cast of mind that thought up atomic fusion and fission as ways of first blowing up and later heating cities, as well as the attitudes that led to strip-mining, off-shore oil wells, Kepone, food additives, SST's, and the tiny spherical particles of plastic recently discovered clogging the waters of the Sargasso Sea.

The biomedical sciences are now caught up with physical science and technology in the same kind of critical judgement, with the same pejorative word. Hubris is responsible, it is said, for the whole biologic revolution. It is hubris that has given us the prospects of behaviour control, psychosurgery, fetal research, heart transplants, the cloning of prominent politicians from bits of their own eminent tissue, iatrogenic disease, overpopulation and recombinant DNA. This last, the new technology that permits the stitching of one creature's genes into the DNA of another to make hybrids, is currently cited as the ultimate example of hubris. It is hubris for man to manufacture a hybrid, on his own.

This is interesting, for the word hybrid is a direct descendant of the ancient Greek word hubris. Hubris originally meant outrage; it was in fact a hybrid word from two Indoeuropean roots: *ud*, meaning out, and *gwer*, meaning rage. The word became *hydrida* in Latin, and was first used to describe the outrageous offspring from the mating of a wild boar with a domestic sow; these presumably unpleasant animals were, in fact, the first hybrids.

Since then the word hybrid has assumed more respectable meanings in biology, and also in literary and political usage. There have been hybrid plants and hybrid vigor, hybrid words and hybrid bills in parliament for several centuries. But always there has been a hidden meaning of danger, of presumption and arrogance, of risk. Hybrids are things fundamentally to be disapproved of.

And now we are back to the first word again, from hybrid to hubris, and the hidden meaning of two beings joined unnaturally together by man is somehow retained. Today's joining is straight out of Greek mythology: it is the combining of man's capacity with the special prerogative of the gods, and it is really in this sense of outrage that the word hubris is being used today. This is what the word has grown into, a warning, a code-word, a shorthand signal from the language itself: if man starts doing things reserved for the gods, deifying himself, the outcome will be something worse for him, symbolically, than the litters of wild boars and domestic sows were for the ancient Romans.

To be charged with hubris is therefore an extremely serious matter, and not to be dealt with by murmuring things about anti-science and anti-intellectualism, which is what many of us engaged in science tend to do these days. The doubts about our enterprise have their origin in the most profound kind of human anxiety. If we are right, and the critics are wrong, then it has to be that the word hubris is being mistakenly employed, that this is not what we are up to, that there is, for the time being anyway, a fundamental misunderstanding of science.

I suppose there is one central question to be dealt with, and I am not at all sure how to deal with it although I am certain about my own answer to it. It is this: are there some kinds of information leading to some sorts of knowledge, that human beings are really better off not having? Is there a limit to scientific inquiry not set by what is knowable but by what we ought to be knowing? Should we stop short of learning about some things, for fear of what we, or someone, will do with the knowledge? My own answer is a flat no, but I must confess that this is an intuitive response and I am neither inclined nor trained to reason my way through it.

There has been some effort, in and out of scientific quarters, to make recombinant DNA into the issue on which to settle this argument. Proponents of this line of research are accused of pure hubris, of assuming the rights of gods, of arrogance and outrage; what is more, they confess themselves to be in the business of making live hybrids, with their own hands. The mayor of Cambridge, Massachusetts, and the Attorney General of New York have both been advised to put a stop to it, forthwith.

It is not quite the same sort of argument, however, as the one about limiting knowledge, although this is surely part of it. The knowledge is already here, and the rage of the argument is about its application in technology. Should DNA for making certain useful or interesting proteins be incorporated into *Escherichia coli* plasmids, or not? Is there a risk of inserting the wrong sort of toxins, or hazardous viruses, and then having the new hybrid organisms spread beyond the laboratory? Is this a technology for creating new varieties of pathogens, and should it be stopped because of this?

If the argument is held to this level, I can see no reason why it cannot be settled, by reasonable people. We have learned a great deal about the handling of dangerous microbes in the last century, although I must say that the opponents of recombinant-DNA research tend to downgrade this huge body of information. At one time or another, agents as hazardous as those of rabies, psittacosis, plague and typhus have been dealt with by investigators in secure laboratories, with only rare cases of self-infliction of the investigators themselves, and none at all of epidemics. It takes some high imagining to postulate the creation of brand-new pathogens so wild and voracious as to spread from equally secure laboratories to endanger human life at large, as some of the arguers are now maintaining.

But this is precisely the trouble with the recombinant-DNA problem: it has become an emotional issue, with too many irretrievably lost tempers on both sides. It has lost the sound of a discussion of technologic safety, and begins now to sound like something else, almost like a religious controversy, and here it is moving toward the central issue: are there some things in science we should not be learning about?

There is an inevitably long list of hard questions to follow this one, beginning with the one that asks whether the mayor of Cambridge should be the one to decide, first off.

Maybe we'd be wiser, all of us, to back off before the recombinant-DNA issue becomes too large to cope with. If we're going to have a fight about it, let it be confined to the immediate issue of safety and security of the recombinants now under consideration, and let us by all means have regulations and guidelines to assure the public safety wherever these are indicated, or even suggested. But if possible let us stay off that question about limiting human knowledge. It is too loaded, and we'll simply not be able to cope with it.

By this time it will become clear that I have already taken sides in this matter, and my point of view is entirely prejudiced. This is true, but with a qualification. I am not so much in favor of recombinant-DNA research as I am opposed to the opposition to this line of inquiry. As a long-time student of infectious disease agents I do not take kindly the declarations that we do not know how to keep from catching things in laboratories, much less how to keep them from spreading beyond the laboratory walls. I believe we learned a lot about this sort of thing, long ago. Moreover, I regard it as a form of hubris-in-reverse to claim that man can make deadly pathogenic micro-organisms so easily. In my view, it takes a long time and a great deal of interliving before a microbe can become a successful pathogen. Pathogenicity is, in a sense, a highly skilled trade, and only a tiny minority of all the numberless tons of microbes on the earth has ever involved itself in it; most bacteria are busy with their own business, browsing and recycling the rest of life. Indeed, pathogenicity often seems to me a sort of biologic accident in which signals are misdirected by the microbe or misinterpreted by the host, as in the case of endotoxin, or in which the intimacy between host and microbe is of such long standing that a form of molecular mimicry becomes possible, as in the case of diphtheria toxin. I do not believe that by simply putting together new combinations of genes one can create creatures as highly skilled and adapted for dependence as a pathogen must be, any more than I have ever believed that microbial life from the moon or Mars could possibly make a living on this planet.

But, as I said, I'm not at all sure this is what the argument is really about. Behind it is that other discussion, which I wish we would not have to become enmeshed in. And I will tell you why.

I cannot speak for the physical sciences, which have moved an immense distance in this century by any standard, but it does seem to me that in the biologic and medical sciences we are still far too ignorant to begin making judgements about what sorts of things we should be learning or not learning. To the contrary, we ought to be grateful for whatever snatches we can get hold of, and we ought to be out there on a much larger scale than today's, looking for more.

We should be very careful with that word hubris, and make sure it is not used when not warranted. There is a great danger in applying it to the search for knowledge. The application of knowledge is another matter, and there is hubris in plenty in our technology, but I do not believe that looking for new information about nature, at whatever level, can possibly be called unnatural. Indeed, if there is any single attribute of human beings, apart from language, that distinguishes them from all other creatures on earth, it is their insatiable, uncontrollable drive to learn things and then to exchange the information with others of the species. Learning is what we do, when you think about it. I cannot think of a human impulse more difficult to govern.

But I can imagine lots of reasons for trying to govern it. New information about nature is very likely, at the outset, to be upsetting to someone or other. The recombinant-DNA line of research is already upsetting, not because of the dangers now being argued about but because it is disturbing, in a fundamental way, to face the fact that the genetic machinery in control of the planet's life can be fooled around with so easily. We do not like the idea that anything so fixed and stable as a species line can be changed. The notion that genes can be taken out of one genome and inserted in another is unnerving. Classical mythology is peopled with mixed beings—part man, part animal or plant— and most of them are associated with tragic stories. Recombinant DNA is a reminder of bad dreams.

The easiest decision for society to make in matters of this kind is to appoint an agency, or a commission, or a subcommittee within an agency, to look into the problem and provide advice. And the easiest course for a committee to take, when confronted by any process that appears to be disturbing people or making them uncomfortable, is to recommend that it be stopped, at least for the time being.

I can easily imagine such a committee, composed of unimpeachable public figures, arriving at the decision that the time is not quite ripe for further exploration of the transplantation of genes, that we should put this off for a while, maybe until next century, and get on with other affairs that make us less uncomfortable. Why not do science on something more popular?

The trouble is, it would be very hard to stop once this line was begun. There are, after all, all sorts of scientific inquiry that are not much liked by one constituency or another, and we might soon find ourselves with crowded rosters, panels, standing committees, set up in Washington for the appraisal, and then the regulation, of research. Not on grounds of the possible value and usefulness of the new knowledge, mind you, but for guarding society against scientific hubris, against the kinds of knowledge we're better off without.

It would be absolutely irresistible as a way of spending time, and people would form long queues for membership. Almost anything would be fair game, certainly anything to do with genetics, anything relating to population control, or, on the other side, research on aging. Very few fields would get by.

The research areas in the greatest trouble would be those already containing a sense of bewilderment and surprise, with discernible prospects of upheaving present dogmas. I can think of several of these, two current ones in which I've been especially interested, and one from the remote past of 40 years ago.

First, the older one. Suppose this were the mid-1930's, and there were a Commission on Scientific Hubris sitting in Washington, going over a staff report on the progress of work in the laboratory of O.T. Avery in New York. Suppose, as well, that there were people on the Commission who understood what Avery was up to and believed his work. This takes an excess of imagining, since there were vanishingly few such people around in the 1930's, and also Avery didn't publish a single word until he had the entire thing settled and wrapped up 10 years later. But anyway, suppose it. Surely, someone would have pointed out that Avery's discovery of a bacterial extract that could change pneumococci from one genetic type to another, with the transformed organisms now doomed to breed true as the changed type, was nothing less than the discovery of a gene; moreover, Avery's early conviction that the stuff was DNA might turn out to be correct, and what then? To this day, the members of such a committee might well have been felicitating each other on having nipped something so dangerous in the very bud.

But it wouldn't have worked in any case, unless they had been equally prescient about bacteriophage research and had managed to flag down phage genetics before it got going a few years later. Science can be blocked, I have no doubt of that, or at least slowed down, but it takes very fast footwork.

Here is an example from today's research on the brain, which would do very well on the agenda of a Hubris Commission. It is the work now going on in several laboratories here and abroad dealing with the endorphins, a class of small polypeptides also referred to as the endogenous opiates. It is rather a surprise that someone hasn't already objected to this research, since the implications of what has already been found are considerably more explosive, and far more unsettling, than anything in the recombinant-DNA line of work.

There are cells in the brain, chiefly in the limbic system, which possess at their surfaces specific receptors for morphine and heroin, but this is just a biologic accident; the real drugs, with the same properties as morphine, are the pentapeptide hormones produced by the brain itself. Perhaps they are switched on as analgesics at times of trauma or illness; perhaps they even serve for the organization and modulation of the physiologic process of dying when the time for dying comes. These things are not yet known, but such questions can now be asked. It is not even known whether an injection of such pentapeptides into a human being will produce a heroin-like reaction, but that kind of question will also be up for asking, and probably quite soon since the same peptides can be synthesized with relative ease. What should be done about this line of research—or rather, what should have been done about it two or three years ago when it was just being launched? Is this the sort of thing we are better off not knowing? I know some people who might think so. But if something prudent and sagacious had been done, turning off such investigations at an early stage, we would not have glimpsed the possible clue to the mechanism of catatonic schizophrenia, which was published just this month from two of the laboratories working on endorphins.

It is hard to predict how science is going to turn out, and if it is really good science it is impossible to predict. This is in the nature of the enterprise. If the things to be found are actually new, they are by definition unknown in advance, and there is no way of foretelling in advance where a really new line of inquiry will lead. You cannot make choices in this matter, selecting things you think you're going to like and shutting off the lines that make for discomfort. You either have science, or you don't, and if you have it you are obliged to accept the surprising and disturbing pieces of information, even the overwhelming and upheaving ones, along with the neat and promptly useful bits. It is like that.

And even if it were possible to call most of the shots in advance, so that we could make broad selections of the general categories of new knowledge that we like, leaving out the ones we don't have a taste for, there would always be slips, leaks, small items of shattering information somehow making their way through. I have an example of this sort of thing in mind, a small item largely overlooked in its significance, a piece of news to match in importance, for what it tells us about ourselves and our relation to the rest of nature, anything else learned in biology during the past century. This is the astonishing tale—astonishing to my ears anyway—of the true nature of mitochondria and chloroplasts.

Between them, these organelles can fairly be said to run the place. They are, from every fair point of view, in charge. The chloroplasts tap the energy of the sun, and the mitochondria make use of it. Without them we might still have a world of microbes, but we could not have eukaryotic forms of life, nor metazoans, nor any of ourselves. Now, as it turns out, both of these can be viewed as living entities, organisms rather than organelles. The mitochondria live in our cells, and the chloroplasts in the cells of plants, as symbiotic lodgers. They replicate on their own, independently of nuclear division, with their own DNA and RNA, their own ribosomes, their own membranes, and these parts are essentially similar to the corresponding parts of bacteria and blue-green algae from which they are now believed to have descended. They are, in fairness, the oldest living inhabitants of the earth, and the least changed by evolution.

Well, this is the sort of knowledge I would call overwhelming, even overturning, in its implications. It has not yet sunk in, really, but when it does it is bound to affect our view of ourselves as special entities, as selves, in charge of our own being, in command of the earth. Another way to put it is that what we might be, in real life, is a huge collection of massive colonies of the most primitive kind of bacteria, which have adapted themselves for motile life in air by constructing around themselves, like a sort of carapace, all the embellishments and adornments of the modern human form. When you settle down to think a thought, you may think it is all your own idea, but perhaps it is not so. You are sharing the notion around, with more creatures than you could count in a lifetime, and they are the ones that turned the thought on in the first place. Moreover, there is more than a family resemblance, maybe even something like identity, between the mitochondria running your cells and those in control of the working parts of any cloud of midges overhanging a summer garden, or of seagulls, or the mouse in the basement, or all the fishes in the sea. It is a startling relationship, of such strange intimacy that none of us could have counted on before the facts began coming in. Would you prefer not to know about this? It is too late for that. Or would you prefer to stop it here and learn no more, leaving matters where they stand, stuck forever with one of the great ambiguities in nature, never to know for sure how it came out?

The only solid piece of scientific truth about which I feel totally confident is that we are profoundly ignorant about nature. Indeed, I regard this as a major discovery of the past 100 years of biology. It is, in its way, an illuminating piece of news. It would have amazed the brightest minds of 18th-century enlightenment to be told by any of us how little we know, and how bewildering seems the way ahead. It is this sudden confrontation with the depth and scope of ignorance that represents the most noteworthy contribution of 20th-century science to the human intellect.

We are, at last, facing up to it. In earlier times, we either pretended to understand how things worked or ignored the problem, or simply made up stories to fill the gaps. Now that we have begun exploring in earnest, doing serious science, we are getting glimpses of how huge the questions are, and how far from being answered. Because of this, these are hard times for the human mind, and it is no wonder that we are depressed. It is not so bad being ignorant, if you are totally ignorant; the hard thing is knowing in some detail the reality of ignorance, the worst spots and here and there the not-so-bad spots, but no true light at the end of the tunnel nor even any tunnels that can yet be trusted. Hard times, indeed.

But we are making a beginning, and there ought to be some satisfaction, even exhilaration, in that. The method works. There are probably no questions we can think up that can't be answered, sooner or later, including even the matter of consciousness. To be sure, there may well be questions we can't think up, ever, and therefore limits to the reach of human intellect that we will never know about, but that is another matter. Within our limits, we should be able to work our way through to all our answers, if we keep at it long enough, and pay attention.

I am putting it this way, with all the presumption and confidence that I can summon, to raise another, last question. Is this hubris? Is there something fundamentally unnatural, or intrinsically wrong, or hazardous for the species, in the ambition that drives us all to reach a comprehensive understanding of nature, including ourselves? I cannot believe it. It would seem to me a more unnatural thing, and more of an offense against nature, for us to come on the same scene endowed as we are with curiosity, filled to overbrimming as we are with questions, and naturally talented as we are for the asking of clear questions, and then for us to do nothing about it, or worse, to try to suppress the questions. This is the greater danger for our species, to try to pretend that we are another kind of animal, that we do not need to satisfy our curiosity, that we can get along somehow without inquiry and exploration, and experimentation, and that the human mind can rise above its ignorance by simply asserting that there are things it has no need to know. This, to my way of thinking, is the real hubris, and it carries danger for us all.

The Language of Economics

John Kenneth Galbraith

I

Among the Social Sciences, and indeed among all reputable fields of learning, economics occupies a special place for the reproach that is inspired by its language. The literate layman regularly proclaims his discontent with the way in which economists express themselves. Other scholars emerge from the eccentricities of their own terminology to condemn the economist for a special commitment to obscurity. If an economist writes a book or even an article in clear English, he need say nothing. He will be praised for avoiding jargon— and also for risking the rebuke of his professional colleagues in doing so. And economists themselves, in their frequent exercises in introspection, regularly wonder whether they are making themselves intelligible to students, politicians and the general public. Committees are occasionally impaneled to consider their communication with the world at large. Invariably they urge improvement.

My purpose in this essay is to go into these charges and assess their substance. My ambition is to put a period, or at least semicolon, to this discussion. For I hope to show that the transgressions of the economists in transmitting their knowledge, though some must be conceded, are not remarkable. Some of the fault lies in the attitudes, including the insufficient diligence, of those who lead the attack. Some is in the sociology of the subject and is not wholly peculiar to economics.

The language of economics is commonly indicted on three different counts. It is of some importance that these charges, which often are mixed together, be kept separate. They are:

1. That the ideas and terminology of economics are complex and artificial and exceedingly confusing to the layman.

2. That economists are bad writers. And it is said that proficiency in obscure and difficult language may even enhance a man's professional standing.

3. That arcane concepts and obscure language are the symptoms of a deeper disorder. So far from seeking communication with the world at large, the tendency of economics is to divorce itself therefrom and construct an unreal universe of its own.

I shall take up these several charges in turn. Each calls for a progressively more detailed examination.

II

That economics has a considerable conceptual apparatus with an appropriate terminology cannot be a serious ground for complaint. Economic phenomena, ideas and instruments of analysis exist. They require names. No one can reasonably ask a serious scholar in the field to avoid reference to index numbers, the capital gains tax, the consumption function, acceleration effects, circular money flows, inflation, linear programming, the progressive income tax, the pure rate of interest or the European Common Market. Nor should he be expected to explain what these are. Education in economics is, in considerable measure, an introduction to this terminology and the ideas that it denotes. Anyone who has difficulties with the ideas should complete his education or, following an exceedingly well-beaten path, leave the subject alone. It is sometimes said that the economist has a special obligation to make himself understood because his subject is of such great and popular importance. By this rule the nuclear physicist would have to speak in monosyllables.

A physician, at least in the United States, does not tell you that a patient is dying. He says that the prognosis as of this time is without significant areas of encouragement. The dead man becomes not that to his lawyer but the decedent. Diplomats never ask. They make representations. Economists have similar vanities of expression and an accomplished practitioner can often get the words parameter, stochastic and aggregation into a single sentence.[1] But it would be hard to prove that the working terminology of the subject is more pretentious or otherwise oppressive than that of jurisprudence, gynecology or advanced poultry husbandry. One indication that it is not is the speed with which the really important words and ideas—gross national product, compensatory fiscal policy, GATT, international liquidity, product differentiation, balance of payments deficit—pass into general use.

I turn now to the quality of writing in economics.

III

Anyone who wished to contend that economists are bad writers is faced with the fact that no learned discipline unconnected with literature or the arts has had such distinguished ones. Everyone has his own test of good writing. I would urge a multiple test for economists in which particular excellence in one respect is allowed to offset lesser achievement in others.

Thus power and resourcefulness of language are important, as is purity of style. Style means that the writing is identified with personality—that it does not have the rigid homogeneity sometimes associated with scientific prose. Nor should it. Language has many dimensions. It does not convey meaning better or more accurately by being flat and colorless.

Good writing, and this is especially important in a subject such as economics, must also involve the reader in the matter at hand. It is not enough

---

[1] Arcane terminology and esoteric concepts do play a certain role in the prestige system of the subject to which I shall return.

to explain. The images that are in the mind of the writer must be made to reappear in the mind of the reader, and it is the absence of this ability that causes much economic writing to be condemned, quite properly, as abstract.

Finally, I doubt that good economic writing can be devoid of humor. This is not because it is the task of the economist to entertain or amuse. Nothing could be more abhorrent to the Calvinist gloom which characterizes all scientific attitudes. But humor is an index of man's ability to detach himself from his subject and such detachment is of considerable scientific utility. In considering economic behavior, humor is especially important for, needless to say, much of that behavior is infinitely ridiculous.

The writing of an impressive number of English-language economists qualifies by these standards. At the head of the list, I would put the work of Adam Smith. In purity and simplicity of style, and certainty in his command of language, he is inferior to John Stuart Mill. But he is more resourceful than Mill and much more amused by his subject. Smith sensed that a trip into the pin factory to see the division of labor in operation would establish the importance of the phenomenon for good. Pins, "a very trifling manufacture," were also an excellent selection; had the product been more portentous it would have competed with the process by which it was made. In competition with pins, the division of labor could not be less than triumphant. Similarly a less amused man would have stressed the penchant of businessmen for getting together to fix prices. (A halfway decent modern scholar would have isolated an instinct for antisocial behaviour.) The businessmen would then have defended themselves, not without indignation. As the men of influence and admitted respectability, their views would have prevailed; Smith would have been dismissed as anti-business. Or, more likely, he would have been ignored. Instead, in one brilliant sentence, he noted that, "People of the same trade seldom meet together, even for merriment and diversion, but the conversation ends in a conspiracy against the public, or in some contrivance to raise prices."[2] Though the tendency is wholly innocent and convivial, the impulse to wickedness is overpowering. Neither anger nor reproach is in order; only sorrow at the inability to resist an improper penny. So expressed, the indictment has never been lifted. To this day, in the United States at least, anyone observing an exchange of words between two competitors assumes it is costing the public some money. Those so engaged feel obliged to make some embarrassed comment to the same effect when they are finished. Such craftsmanship was far beyond the reach of Mill.[3]

Mill, of course, was a greatly talented writer, a standard by which others have long been judged. And to the list I would add the name of Thorstein Veblen. In one sense it is hard even to think of him in the same terms as Mill;

---

[2] Adam Smith, *Wealth of Nations* (New York, Modern Library, 1937), p.128.

[3] I have always been enchanted by another observation of Smith's: "The late resolution of the Quakers in Pennsylvania to set at liberty their negro slaves, may satisfy us that their number cannot be very great." Adam Smith, *Wealth of Nations*, Book 3 (New York: Modern Library, 1937), chapter 2.

his prose, unlike Mill's, is involuted and pretentious. One reads Veblen with the constant impression of a struggle for effect. But few men have ever so resourcefully driven home a point. What had always seemed commonplace and respectable became, after Veblen, fraudulent, ridiculous and (a favorite word of his) barbaric. This is high art. The American rich never recovered from the sardonic disdain with which Veblen analyzed their behavior. The manners of an entire society were altered as a result. After he made the phrase "conspicuous consumption" a part of the language, the real estate market in Newport was never again the same. What had been the biggest and best was henceforth the most vulgar. "Conspicuous leisure" made it difficult even for the daughters of the rich to relax. Their entertainment had thereafter to be legitimatized by charitable, artistic or even intellectual purpose or, at minimum, sexual relief. Here is Veblen's account of the effect of increasing wealth on behavior:

> ...Since the consumption of these more excellent goods is an evidence of wealth, it becomes honorific; and conversely, the failure to consume in due quantity and quality becomes a mark of inferiority and demerit.
>
> This growth of punctilious discrimination as to qualitative excellence in eating, drinking, etc. presently affects not only the manner of life, but also the training and intellectual activity of the gentleman of leisure. He is no longer simply the successful, aggressive male—the man of strength, resource, and intrepidity. In order to avoid stultification he must also cultivate his tastes, for it now becomes incumbent on him to discriminate with some nicety between the noble and the ignoble in consumable goods. He becomes a connoisseur in creditable viands of various degrees of merit, in manly beverages and trinkets, in seemly apparel and architecture, in weapons, games, dancers, and the narcotics. This cultivation of the aesthetic faculty requires time and application, and the demands made upon the gentleman in this direction therefore tend to change his life of leisure into a more or less arduous application to the business of learning how to live a life of ostensible leisure in a becoming way.[4]

The list of good if less than inspired writers—the elder Mill, Thomas Malthus, Henry George, Alfred Marshall and (subject to some reservations to be mentioned presently) John Maynard Keynes—is also an impressive one. So it would be difficult, on the general evidence, to find fault with the literary qualifications of the English-writing economists.

IV

Perhaps, however, this does not quite settle things. It will be said that when economists have gone to the technical heart of the matter, as did Ricardo in *Principles*, or as they have come up against the full complexity of modern economic problems, as did Keynes in *The General Theory*, they have become less than lucid and accessible. Some will surely think it significant that the best writer by my accounting was so nearly the first. Were Smith or Mill writing

---

[4] Thorstein Veblen, *The Theory of the Leisure Class* (New York: Macmillan, 1912), pp. 74-75.

about the economy today, they would, it will be said, be either as incomprehensible or as condescending in their prose as their contemporaries.

This confuses the problem of complex exposition or scientific perception with bad writing. Ricardo's problems were no more difficult than those which were lucidly discussed by Malthus or Mill and he did not go into them very much more deeply. Ricardo's reputation as a bad writer is greatly deserved. He was, in addition, an unscientific one. His prose was awkward, uncertain and unpredictable as to meaning conveyed, and it was his habit to state strong propositions and then qualify them to possible extinction. His natural price of labor was such as to "enable laborers, one with another, to subsist and perpetuate their race." But within a page or two the application of this heroic (and historic) law was suspended in "improving" societies, of which contemporary England was obviously one as were all others to which he had relevance. The notion of subsistence was simultaneously enlarged to include conveniences, these being any luxuries to which the worker had become or might become accustomed. And the population theory on which the proposition depended was modified to exclude Englishmen although it was deemed to have full force and effect for the Irish. This is neither good writing nor good scientific method. It is bad writing based on incomplete thought.

The writing in Keynes's *General Theory* justifies similar if somewhat less severe comment. Keynes has been widely acclaimed as a master of English prose. A good part of this applause has come from economists who are not the best of judges. Much of it approved his criticism of the Versailles Treaty, or Winston Churchill, or his pleasant memoirs on academic contemporaries. But the real test of a writer is whether he remains with a difficult subject until he has thought through not only the problem but also its exposition. This Keynes did not do. *The General Theory* is an acrostic of English prose. The fact that it was an important book should not cause anyone to say that it was well written. In a real sense it was not even finished. Though new, the ideas were not intrinsically more complex than those presented with competence by A.C. Pigou and a certain churchly eloquence by Alfred Marshall. Others writers—Mrs. Joan Robinson, Professors Hansen, Harris and Samuelson—turned Keynes's ideas into accessible English, thus showing that it could be done. A better writer—patience has a certain notoriety as a component of genius—would have done the job himself.[5] The ideas of *The General Theory* could have been stated in clear English.

The influence of this book, combined with its unintelligibility, does bring up another question. It is whether clear and unambiguous statement is the best medium for persuasion in economics. Here, I think, one may have doubts.

---

[5] Those who think this underestimates the difficulty of the ideas with which Keynes was dealing will do well to notice the carelessness of his nontechnical expression in this volume. The following is from a summary of his position in an early chapter: "The celebrated optimism of traditional economic theory, which has led to economists being looked upon as Candides who, having left this world for the cultivation of their gardens, teach that all is for the best in the best of all possible worlds provided we will let well enough alone, is also to be traced, I think, to their having neglected to take account of the drag on prosperity which can be exercised by an insufficiency of effective demand." *The General Theory of Employment Interest and Money* (New York: Harcourt, Brace, 1936), p. 33.

V

Had the Bible been in clear, straightforward language, had the ambiguities and contradictions been edited out and had the language been constantly modernized to accord with contemporary taste, it would almost certainly have been, or have become, a work of lesser influence. In the familiar or King James version it has three compelling qualities. The archaic constructions and terminology put some special strain on the reader. Accordingly, by the time he has worked his way through, say, Leviticus, he has a vested interest in what he has read. It is not something to be dismissed like a column by Alsop or even Lippmann. Too much has gone into understanding it.

The contradictions of the Old Testament also mean that with a little effort anyone can find a faith that accords with his preferences and a moral code that is agreeable to his tastes, even if fairly depraved. In consequence, dissidents are not extruded from the faith; they are retained and accommodated in a different chapter.

Finally, the ambiguities of the Scriptures allow of infinite debate over what is meant. This is most important for attracting belief, for in the course of urging his preferred variant on a particular proposition, the disputant becomes committed to the larger Writ.

Difficulty, contradiction and ambiguity have rendered precisely similar service in economics. Anyone who has worked his way through Ricardo, Marx or Keynes needs to feel that he has got something for such an effort. So he is strongly predisposed to belief. Ricardo is sufficiently replete with qualification and Marx with contradiction so that the reader can also provide himself with the interpretation he prefers.[6] All three lend themselves marvelously to argument as to what they mean. Thousands read these authors less for wisdom than because of need to participate in a suitably impressive way in arguments over what they said.

The case of Keynes is especially interesting because prior to the publication of the immensely difficult *General Theory*, he had advocated its principal conclusion—fiscal policy as an antidote for depression—in clear English in both the United States and Great Britain. He had not been greatly influential. Then in *The General Theory* he involved economists in a highly professional debate on technical concepts and their interpretation. His practical recommendations were not central to this discussion. But the participants carried his practical program to Washington and Whitehall. Would a simple, clearly argued book such as later produced by (among others) Professor Alvin Hansen have been as influential? My reluctant inclination is to doubt it.

Yet ambiguity is a tactic which not everyone should try. Economists will seize upon the ill-expressed ideas of a very great man and argue over what he had in mind. Others had better not run the risk.

---

[6] No great figure since Biblical times has lent himself to such varied interpretation as Marx. This arises partly from the manner of expression, partly from the contradiction inherent in some of the ideas and partly from the fact that so much of his work was uncompleted at his death and conflicts that might otherwise have been cleared up by revision or deletion were carried into print. It is for this reason that the interpretation and re-interpretation of Marx has been not a scholarly pursuit but a profession.

VI

So far I have been dealing with (by broad definition) classical rather than contemporary writing in economics. The time has come to consider the complex language and the difficult mathematics of the current contributions not only to *Econometrica* and *The Review of Economic Studies* but also of many of the articles in *The Economic Journal* and *The American Economic Review*. And here the question ceases to be purely one of language. These articles are obviously beyond the reach of the intelligent layman. Is it possible that they are also out of touch with reality and that it is the ambition of some scholars to construct a world of their own choosing and exclusive understanding? Doubt is not confined to noneconomists. Professor Samuelson, in his presidential address to the American Economic Association several years ago, noted that the three previous presidential addresses had been devoted to a denunciation of mathematical economics and that the most trenchant had encouraged the audience to standing applause. Once when I was in Russia on a visit to Soviet economists, I spent a long afternoon attending a discussion on the use of mathematical models in plan formation. At the conclusion an elderly scholar, who had also found it very heavy going, asked me rather wistfully if I didn't think there was still a "certain place" for the old-fashioned Marxian formulation of the labor theory of value.

What is involved here is less the language of economics than its sociology. Once this is understood, the layman can view what he does not understand with equanimity.

Professional economists, like members of city gangs, religious congregations, aboriginal tribes, British regiments, craft unions, fashionable clubs, learned disciplines, holders of diplomatic passports and, one is told, followers of the intellectually more demanding criminal pursuits, have the natural desire of all such groups to delineate and safeguard the boundary between those who belong and those who do not. This has variously been called the tribal, gang, club, guild, union or aristocratic instinct.

The differentiation of those who belong from those who do not is invariably complemented by a well-graded prestige system within the tribal group. And—a vital point—the two are closely interdependent. If the members of the tribal group are sufficiently conscious of the boundary that separates them from the rest of the world, the tribe becomes *the* world to its members. Its limits and the mental horizons of its members are coterminous. This means, in turn, that the prestige system of the tribe is the only one that has meaning to a member and it is all important. The most honorific position in the tribal group then becomes the most honorific position in the universe. If the school is all that counts, then the head boy is a person of the greatest possible grandeur. In the Barchester Close the eminence of the bishop was absolute because no one took cognizance of the world beyond. Similarly those who are privileged to the secrets of the CIA or who work in the White House. In each case, everything within depends on the exclusion of what is without.

The prestige system of economics is wholly in accord with these principles. It assigns, and for good reason, the very lowest position to the man who deals with everyday policy. For this individual, in concerning himself with the wisdom of a new tax or the need for an increased deficit, is immediately caught up in a variety of political and moral judgments. This puts him in communication with the world at large. As such, he is a threat to the sharp delineation which separates the tribal group from the rest of society and thus to the prestige system of the profession. Moreover, his achievements are rated not by his professional peers but by outsiders. This causes difficulty in fitting him into the professional hierarchy and argues strongly for leaving him at the bottom.[7, 8]

A very low position is also assigned to economists who, even though forswearing any interest in practical affairs, occupy themselves with related disciplines—urban sociology, education, the social causes of poverty or juvenile delinquency. The reason is the same. These men are also inimical to the tribal delineation for their achievements depend on the judgment of noneconomists and thus cannot be integrated into the established scale. They are assumed by their colleagues to be escaping the rigors of their own subject.

At the higher levels, economics divorces itself fully from practical questions and from the influence of other fields of scholarship with the exception of mathematics and statistics. One can think of the full prestige structure of the subject as a hollow pyramid or cone, the sides of which, though they are transparent and with numerous openings at the base, become increasingly opaque and impermeable as one proceeds to the apex. Positions near the apex are thus fully protected from external communication and influence. Work here is pure in the literal sense. Questions of practical application are excluded as also the influence of other disciplines. And this being so, tasks can be accommodated to the analytical techniques which the scholar wishes to use. These techniques may not be mathematical but the absence of extraneous practical considerations is conducive to mathematical techniques. Needless to say, communication is closely confined to those within the pyramid and

---

[7] In the United States, at least, a similar disposition is made of members who, being good teachers, are accorded the approval of their students.

[8] Thus during his life Keynes was held in rather low regard. In his *History of Economic Analysis*, which he intended to be an authoritative view of professional precedence, Professor Schumpeter affirms this judgment and bases his disapproval on Keynes's unscholarly preoccupation with useful and practical matters. He condemns Ricardo on similar grounds.

At the time of his election to the United States Senate, Professor Paul Douglas had a very high position in the prestige system of the profession and, indeed, has just completed his term as President of the American Economic Assocciation. While economists continued to take pride in his accomplishments, and especailly welcomecd his demonstration of the versatility of their craft, no grave professional importance could any longer be attached to his writing or his stand on technical issues. From being a leading economist, he became the leading economist in politics. This resolution of the matter, no doubt, is a sensible one. To fit a United States Senator into the prestige system of the profession would be very difficult. Better to compromise on purely nominal rank.

advancement to higher levels within the pyramid is exclusively by the agency of the other occupants. The standards of accomplishment which lead to recognition are thus self-perpetuating. It is no criticism of this work that it is unrelated to the real world. Such divorce is its most strongly intended feature.[9]

VII

It is not part of my present task to pass judgment on this prestige structure or to compare it with that of other learned disciplines. In a world where for pedagogic and other purposes a very large number of economists is required, an arrangement which discourages many of them from rendering public advice would seem to be well conceived. Otherwise there would be more such advice than could possibly be heard let alone used. Much of the discussion in the upper reaches of the pyramid is idle—economic models unrelated to reality are constructed, criticized, amended, on occasion commended and then, alas, completely forgotten. But, as often happens, there is no ready way of separating valueless work here from the possibly valuable and any effort to do so would be intrinsically damaging. And it is the good fortune of the affluent country that the opportunity cost of economic discussion is low and hence it can afford all kinds. Moreover, the models so constructed, though of no practical value, serve a useful academic function. The oldest problem in economic education is how to exclude the incompetent. A certain glib mastery of verbiage—the ability to speak portentously and sententiously about the relation of money supply to the price level—is easy for the unlearned and may even be aided by a mildly enfeebled intellect. The requirement that there be ability to master difficult models, including ones for which mathematical competence is required, is a highly useful screening device.[10]

What is clear from this brief excursion into the sociology of economics, and this is the matter of present importance, is how the intelligent layman or the scholar from another discipline should regard contemporary economic writing. Its relevance to the real world is not great. Much of it, and more especially that exchanged in the upper levels

---

[9] This explains why professional economists of the highest standing often come forward with proposals—for the abolition of corporations or trade unions, the outlawing of oligopoly, the enforcement of free competition, therapeutic unemployment, cathartic deflation, elimination of central banks, ending of income taxes—of the most impractical sort with no damage whatever to their reputations. No store is set by ability to assess such measures in their political and social context. On the contrary, such preoccupation is discrediting.

[10] There can be no question, however, that prolonged commitment to mathematical exercises in economics can be damaging. It leads to the atrophy of judgment and intuition which are indispensable for real solutions and, on occasion, leads also to the habit of mind which simply excludes the mathematically inconvenient factors from consideration.

of the pyramid, is not meant to be. So it may be ignored.[11] It being designed to exclude practical questions, there is no practical loss. It being designed to exclude the outside scholar, the outsider may safely take the hint. The work at the less prestigious lower edges, since it must take account of information from other disciplines and also take account of political reality, does not lend itself to highly technical and mathematical treatment. This is the part that is important to the outsider. While he may not find it easy, he is not excluded.

None of this excuses anyone from mastering the basic ideas and terminology of economics. The intelligent layman must expect also to encounter good economists who are difficult writers even though some of the best have been very good writers. He should know, moreover, that at least for a few great men ambiguity of expression has been a positive asset. But with these exceptions he may safely conclude that what is wholly mysterious in economics is not likely to be important.

---

[11] The layman may take comfort from the fact that the most esoteric of this material is not read by other economists or even by the editors who publish it. In the economics profession the editorship of a learned journal not specialized to econometrics or mathematical statistics is a position of only moderate prestige. It is accepted, moreover, that the editor must have a certain measure of practical judgment. This means that he is usually unable to read the most prestigious contributions which, nonetheless, he must publish. So it is the practice of the editor to associate with himself a mathematical curate who passes on this part of the work and whose word he takes. A certain embarrassed silence covers the arrangement.

TERMS and TOPICS

TERMS

1. **Vocabulary, Section IV:** abolition, acculturation, anarchy, arduous, attributed, attrition, beneficent, callowness, cognizance, conflagrations, convivial, cosmology, demagogue, demarcate, denizen, disparate, docility, efficacious, enraptured, entailed, entity, equably, equivocation, exquisite, extraneous, extricate, forswearing, frenetically, glib, hallmark, imperious, inference, insufferable, intercede, intractable, introspection, keystone, laity, lucid, lush, mandatory, messianic, microcosmic, motivation, pejorative, perplexity, perverts, potency, precipitated, prerogative, prescient, presuppositions, primordial, procrastinations, proliferates, proponents, qualms, quixotic, recipients, reciprocation, relegated, revamped, sagacious, sardonic, shun, speculative, sullen, torpor, transgressions, transient, trenchant, viable, vindication, virulence, wont

2. *Satire*   Ridicule of something, supposedly in order to reform it. *Satire* could also be applicable to section V, since it is often humorous. Or it could be applicable to section III, since it is a kind of criticism, or argument. Do any of the essays in this section (IV) use satire?

3. *Exposition*   One of the four traditional modes of discourse, the other three being *narration*, *description,* and *argument.* In a literary context, *exposition* refers to the providing of essential data, the who-what-where-when-why of a story. The essential meaning is the same in both instances: providing information, explaining, *exposing* the facts.

4. *Rhetoric*   The art or craft of using words effectively, whether in speaking or in writing. All of the techniques and strategies represented and discussed in this book are *rhetorical* techniques and strategies. The word *rhetoric* has also come to mean *"mere* rhetoric," empty, artificial, showy, exaggeratedly elaborate style—but that popular meaning does not apply in the context of the study of the principles of effective writing.

5. What is *language?* Consult a variety of sources for definitions (dictionaries, encyclopedias, handbooks, linguistic glossaries, and the like). You will likely find a variety of definitions. Then write a one- or two-page extended definition of the term.

6. *Jargon*   Strictly speaking, the specialized language of a particular occupation. Compare it in this respect to the terms *slang, cant,* and *argot.* The term jargon, however, is commonly broadened to mean any artificially or unnecessarily complex, fuzzy, wordy, or otherwise incomprehensible diction or style. One synonym is *gibberish.* (See quotation number 6 in the "Introduction: Audience and Purpose," and see general and comparative topic number 11 in section III.)

7. *Ambiguity*   Multiple meaning. An *ambiguous* statement is one that can be understood in more than one way. *She struck the man with the stick,* for example, or *The sparrow looked longer than the owl,* can be understood in two different ways. Poets and other writers will sometimes purposely create ambiguity, thereby forcing the reader to juggle two appropriate meanings at once. Jargon and other sloppy uses of language, however, can produce unintentional and befuddling ambiguity. Look for ambiguity in the things you read—whether in this book or elsewhere, and whether creative or unintentional. In what kinds of essay is intentional ambiguity most likely to be found? Try composing some ambiguous sentences.

TOPICS: On Individual Essays

JESSICA MITFORD   "The Story of Service"

1. Why does Mitford begin unfolding the "drama" with the words "Alas, poor Yorick!"? Who was Yorick? Why does she call it a "drama"? Where else does she play on this metaphor? What other metaphors does she use?

2. This piece constitutes Chapter 5 of Mitford's 1963 book *The American Way of Death*. What is the effect of the title of the book? of the title of this chapter? Are they in any way ironic?

3. To what extent is this an argument? How would you describe Mitford's overall purpose? What internal strategies or techniques of development does she use besides the major one of process analysis?

4. Point out some of the many instances where Mitford's style takes on a tone of barbed irony or sarcasm, and where her diction becomes decidedly loaded. (Would you call her wit, as displayed in this piece, *mordant*?) Is this the kind of moderate and objective tone that is supposedly most effective in persuasive writing? Or is it a matter of audience? Whom is she writing *for*? Whom is she writing *against*—that is, who constitutes her opposition? How does she deal with that opposition?

5. Early on, Mitford refers to the "hit-or-miss rhetoric" of a passage she quotes, and disparages "the prose style of the funeral trade as a whole" (N.B. "trade," not "profession"), but she doesn't explain. Taking your cue from the few places where she does single out specific details for criticism, write an essay analyzing the prose style of some or all of the many passages she quotes in this chapter.

6. Using Mitford's chapter as a model, write a revealing explanation of some other process, step by step and detail by detail. How is commercial ice-cream made? How is sugar refined? How is ketchup made? How is fast-food hamburger meat prepared? How are hot-dogs made? What goes on in a slaughter-house? How are chickens raised for market? What is shock therapy? How does aversion therapy work?

BERTON ROUECHÉ   "Three Sick Babies"

1. Who is John Bunyan? Who is Osler? Who is Semmelweis?

2. Note how Roueché begins with narrative (though it contains information, or "exposition"), somewhat in the manner of a police story, and then in the second paragraph shifts to almost pure exposition, background information readers need in order to understand what's going on. What is the effect of this pattern? Does it continue?

3. After Dr. Fierer comes on the scene we get continuous direct quotation until the final two paragraphs. Does Fierer in a sense, then, become the author of the essay? Considering this and the information Roueché gives about Dr. Taylor, does this essay differ significantly in kind from the interview with Gordimer (section II)? Does Roueché have greater control over what he reports?

4. Do you think Rouéché intends a kind of situational irony or irony of fate when he tells us that Dr. Fierer was delayed by "a chimpanzee...with hepatitis"? Is the effect heightened by the fact's being disclosed at the end of a paragraph?

5. The Communicable Disease Center (CDC) in Atlanta is now known as the Centers for Disease Control (CDC). What do you suppose was the reason for the change in name (and for the retention of the initials)?

6. Does having read this essay make you feel less secure or more secure about the prospect of going into hospital? Do you think Rouéché had one or the other of these results in view? If you have had experience as a patient in a hospital, try writing an essay directed at a general audience in which you explain what it was like. Make your *primary* purposes those of explaining and informing, rather than merely relating, describing, or revealing; and try to keep anything argumentative out of it altogether.

PICO IYER   "'Of Weirdos and Eccentrics'"

1. Iyer mentions Glenn Gould as an eccentric. Do you find any evidence of "eccentricity" in Gould's essay? in his playing?

2. Iyer writes of the weirdo as "outcast." How does this version of marginality differ from, say, Cooper's (section VI)?

3. Compare the comparison-and-contrast method of this essay with that of Gorman's (section V).

4. Evaluate the effectiveness of Iyer's closing analogy. Is it exact enough to work?

5. Compare Iyer's discussion of psychopathy with Szasz's discussion of mental illness (section III). Are they talking about the same sort of thing?

6. To what degree is Iyer discussing not so much individual behaviour as the pressures of contemporary urban life? Do social pressures—drugs, violence, crowding, AIDS, poverty, joblessness—increase the likelihood of "weirdness" in North America? Or is Iyer just glamourizing eccentricity by setting it off in this way? Can one overvalue individualism? Does the championing of individualism justify *any* sort of "individualistic" behaviour? Is Iyer making some points similar to those of Brink (section III)?

7. Is Iyer right about eccentricity and genius? Who are some other eccentric geniuses? Was Einstein eccentric? Wittgenstein (see Davenport's essay in section II)?

K.C. COLE   "By the Numbers"

1. Do some research into the Pythagorean theory of numbers or into Bertrand Russell's work with mathematics.

2. Is mathematics a science? Russell was a philosopher—is mathematics a philosophy, a way of looking at things? (Note that Berlin in his essay discusses Fermat's Theorem. Could Cole have brought that into his essay too? Should he have?) Is mathematics a kind of language? Is music? Is music in any way a science—especially if technology is applied to it, as Glenn Gould advocates (section III)? "Numbers *are* relationships," says Cole: irrationality, regularity, order, motion, speed—all are forms of relations or movement that numbers represent. How does language do the same thing?

3. Did *you* know that "nature and numbers go hand in hand"? Can you think of any exceptions to this general principle?

4. Explain Einstein's statement that Cole quotes halfway through the essay.

5. Write a short essay about the importance or unimportance of numbers in your life. Write an essay about "$5\frac{1}{2}$."

6. According to Galileo, "To understand the universe, you must understand the language in which it is written." Use this quotation as the beginning of an essay. It need not be about mathematics. Might it be about music? Might it be about art, as suggested in the second section of Colombo's essay (section VI)?

VIRGINIA WOOLF   "'The Feminine Note in Fiction'"

1. Is Woolf praising or attacking Courtney's book?

2. In her first sentence Woolf notes Courtney's admission that it is difficult for the masculine and feminine points of view to understand each other. In her second sentence she seems at least partly to agree with him. Is it then impossible for a man to appreciate properly or criticize fairly fiction written by women—and therefore vice versa as well?

3. When Woolf refers to "a strength which in this age one has to call masculine," what does she mean by "in this age"? Is she questioning the nature of male definitions of art? Is she attacking, from a feminist point of view, a patriarchally constructed and controlled aesthetic?

4. What is the tone of Woolf's penultimate sentence? Is there evidence for reading it as ironic, perhaps even sarcastic?

5. Is there such a thing as a "masculine note in fiction," and if so, what does it sound like?

6. Write an argument for or against the notion that women novelists write primarily for women—and contrariwise that men write primarily for other men. Do you read and enjoy fiction written by members of the opposite sex?

7. Investigate the present state of fiction. How accurate was Courtney's belief that the novel as a work of art was disappearing (whether caused by women novelists or not)?

8. The novelists Courtney discusses are as follows: Mrs. Humphry Ward (1851-1920), John Oliver Hobbes (Mrs. Pearl Craigie; 1867-1906), Lucas Malet (Mrs. St. Leger Harrison, daughter of Charles Kingsley; 1852-1931), Gertrude Atherton (U.S.; 1857-1948), Mrs. Margaret Louisa Woods (1856-1945), Mrs. Ethel Lillian Voynich (1864-1960), Elizabeth Robins (1862-1952), and Mary E. Wilkins (later Freeman; U.S.; 1852-1930). Although he calls all except Voynich artists in one degree or another, Ward and Hobbes seem to top his list; those to whom he ascribes a masculine sort of "power" are Malet and Robins, with Voynich getting some credit for "strength" as well. How good was his critical judgment? Investigate the careers and current critical reputations of these writers.

9. Write a research report on the present state of novels by women, on contemporary feminist literary theory, or on feminist critics' attitudes to Virginia Woolf.

ISAIAH BERLIN   "The Purpose of Philosophy"

1. What is Fermat's Theorem? What is the Enlightenment? Who gave it that name? What poem is Berlin quoting in paragraph 20?

2. Note the close similarity in form of the semantically diverse words *causal* and *casual*, which Berlin uses in one sentence in paragraph 18. Can you think of any other such pairs? Use each pair in a sentence.

3. To help yourself understand this essay, construct a detailed and coherent sentence outline for it.

4. Berlin's is essentially an essay in definition. What other methods or strategies does he use to define "philosophy"? The most prominent one is of course classification; in a sense his whole subject is classification (see for example paragraph 31). Explain in your own terms the two kinds of classification or categorization he points to in paragraph 30. What is he classifying, and what are the classes he decides on? Does he acknowledge that settling on the two categories is in a sense to commit the either-or fallacy that Brink criticizes (section III)? Is the setting up of a third or "intermediate basket" still perhaps an oversimplification? What are Kant's categories? Do we in the twentieth century still have our set or sets of "category-spectacles"? Do you? Should you?

5. Almost any paragraph in Berlin's essay is pregnant with possibilities for further thought. Grab one of two of his pronouncements to examine in an essay of your own. Be sure to supply concrete and specific details to clarify and support your abstractions and generalizations.

KEN DRYDEN *"The Game"*

1. What is the origin of the saying that begins "Whom the gods would destroy"?

2. If Dryden's essay is explanation, what is he explaining? Is it a work of definition?

3. Is Dryden "articulate"? Do you infer that he is also "intelligent"? Is he "modest"? Do you think he used a ghost-writer? Do you think the "image" he presents in this essay is "accurate"? If, as he says, "it doesn't matter," how can he be "his own man"—or is that his paradoxical point: he can be, because he accepts his image for what it is? When he says of a self-deprecating remark, "But you don't believe that," do you believe him? Is he genuinely "self-deprecatory"? After reading this piece, do you consider Dryden in any way a victim of his own "image"? How is his "reputation" different from his "image"—or is it, since he refused to play the "game" after doing only one commercial? Look and listen for other instances of "the game" and "playing the game" used metaphorically in contemporary rhetoric—for example "the game of life," with its "winners and losers."

4. If you're among those who attend to the "image" of sports heroes, do you feel that you've had a "fraud" perpetrated on you?

5. Do you discern any irony, of whatever kind, in this essay? What is the effect of the closing anecdote?

6. Many a hero in the great literature of the past supposedly possessed a "tragic flaw" which brought about his downfall—for example Oedipus and Othello. Do modern heroes, including sports heroes, have tragic or fatal flaws? In an essay, explore the nature of modern heroism, perhaps by comparing a modern hero or heroine with some from the past.

7. Write an essay in which you explain how some other public figures can be thought of as "metaphors."

MARGARET ATWOOD   "Witches"

1. Why do you suppose modern poetry in the library should have been off-limits to female students? And why should Canadian poetry have been exempt from this restriction?

2. How important is irony in this piece? Point out instances of Atwood's verbal and other witticisms. What is their function? Do they merely help to establish a tone, a *persona*? Do they make a point, or several points? Is Atwood weaving a spell?

3. To what degree is this piece feminist? From the whole talk, how much can you infer about the sort of audience she was speaking to?

4. Write an essay about "role models" in your life. Are you a role model for anyone?

5. Write a short essay that begins with a personal anecdote about revisiting a place after several years and then moves on to discuss some topic growing out of that experience.

NICHOLSON BAKER   "The Size of Thoughts"

1. Did you find Baker's vocabulary intimidating? How many of these words did you have to look up: *nodes, corollary, codification, relinquish, replenish, intellection, thrum, interstitial, contentiousness, fastnesses, codices, aperçu, peripheral, insurrection, profusion, recondite*? What do such words contribute to the tone and texture of this essay? Which of them do you want in your working vocabulary? What is the effect of terms like *nifty* and *peter out* occurring among the others?

2. Who was Hammurabi? What is the point of the reference to "the nineteenth-century dream of a liberal democracy"? What poet does Baker quote after Wordsworth?

3. Baker divides thoughts into three classes, by size; then he focusses on one of the categories, large thoughts, and defines them in terms of three criteria. What other internal strategies does he use?

4. But of course thoughts do not, literally, have size, physical bulk. Baker is using *synaesthesia*, metaphorically mixing the senses, as when one speaks of the taste of defeat or the smell of victory. Try classifying and defining the colours of anger, the dimensions of pain, the taste of numbers, the smells of sorrow, the textures of prose, the colour or touch of sounds, the sounds of colours. Write an essay categorizing thoughts according to their colours.

5. What are Brahms, Bellini, Bach, and Pontormo doing among the builders of large thoughts? Who might some of the "mere eighty-six others" be? Is Baker serious here? Is it likely that your or anyone else's list would coincide or even overlap much with his? Or are his three criteria personal, subjective? Is objectivity possible with this subject? How do the lines from Tennyson qualify as a "large thought" according to Baker's criteria? As evidenced here, are some of Baker's own thoughts large? Or is he content with thinking small ones?

6. What does Baker mean by saying "(all scientific thoughts are small)" and "(All that is untrue is small)"? Why does he put these statements in parentheses?

7. This essay is so complexly rich with figurative language that it both invites and defies comment. Try taking one section—a sentence or two, for example the image of the spreading wine-stain—and analyzing as thoroughly as you can how its metaphors work. Then write a brief speculative or metaphysical piece of your own in which you try to use language as imaginatively as he does.

COLLEEN CUTSCHALL   *"Voice in the Blood: Suffering and Compassion"*

1. In the first paragraph Cutschall uses the term *emic*, implying that her own approach will be of that sort—that is, an internal study of a particular culture and the interrelations of its elements, as opposed to an *etic* approach, which is external and generalized, attempting to fit the elements of a particular culture into some already established general classification. What are some of the possible strengths and weaknesses of each approach?

2. What is the social or psychological function of ritual and ceremony? Compare the Lakota rituals described here with parallel or divergent rituals and ceremonies among other cultural groups.

3. In what way does a current secular ritual such as Hallowe'en represent the survival of ancient customs in modern life? (You may want to read Shirley Jackson's well-known short story "The Lottery" in connection with this question.)

4. How does Cutschall's analysis of funerary customs differ from Mitford's? Examine purpose and tone as well as details of cultural difference.

5. Cutschall retells, in a kind of cyclic way, several stages of the Lakota creation myth. What is the effect of using narrative to interrupt her explanations of religious practice—or are her explanations in a way better understood as interruptions of the narrative? What connections is she establishing between individual and communal experience? between childhood and adulthood? between daily life and myth and history?

6. What role or roles do children have in Lakota society as Cutschall describes it? Compare the assumptions here about the place of children with those for example of Mukherjee or White (section I), Gordimer (section II), O'Connor (section III), or Swift (section VII).

7. Write an essay analyzing the nature and purpose of some ritual or ceremony that you participated in as a child or that you still participate in.

STEPHEN JAY GOULD   *"Our Allotted Lifetimes"*

1. What are the principal internal strategies Gould uses? Does he classify? define? compare and contrast? provide examples and illustrations? Does he rely only on scientific evidence, or does he explain his point in other ways as well? Does the analogy between heart and bellows (paragraph 5) help you understand the point he is making?

2. Does the essay flow smoothly? Examine each paragraph to see if its beginning provides a transitional hook to the preceding paragraph or refers to the overall topic, or both. Do any paragraph openings lack one or both of these devices? If so, what then maintains coherence and unity?

3. Does the fact that Gould concludes with the mayfly, which is not a mammal, damage either the consistency or the structural integrity of his essay? Or does it usefully broaden the perspective—as well as provide him with an effective metaphor to end on?

4. Compare the ways in which scientist Gould and nonscientist Dillard (section 1) approach nature.

5. Build the beginning of your next essay around a longish quotation—dialogue or not—from some published work.

LEWIS THOMAS "Notes of a Biology-Watcher: The Hazards of Science"

1. Thomas begins almost as if his main interest were in the history of the words *hubris* and *hybrid*. Browse in an etymological dictionary until you find two or three interesting words that are similarly related etymologically but whose current meanings do not at first glance appear related (for example *savour, savant; safe, salute; grammar, glamour*). Then write a short essay tracing the history of their meanings.

2. If Thomas thinks that "the question about limiting human knowledge" is "too loaded" (paragraph 14), why does he later turn to a direct discussion of it and give an extended answer to it? Is this an example of artful artlessness? Analyze the structure and strategy of Thomas's whole extended beginning.

3. Read Milton's *Paradise Lost*, Book VII, lines 5-38, 66ff., 167-68, and Book XII, lines 553-87, and write an essay discussing the statements of Raphael, Michael, and Adam alongside those of Thomas.

4. Imagine yourself a non-scientist member of a "Hubris Commission." Four cases are put before you:

   (1) A team of scientists seems to be on the verge of discovering a way to convert lead into gold. How would you react?

   (2) A scientist is experimenting with ants—enormously strong creatures for their size—in an attempt to breed larger ones to serve as "workhorses" and thus conserve energy. Should he be allowed to continue?

   (3) A parapsychologist claims to have proof that a human being, properly trained, can appreciably raise the temperature of objects hundreds of miles away. Should he be locked up?

   (4) A medical institute conducting research on aging wants a huge grant, claiming to be hot on the track of a way to double or even triple human life-expectancy. Should they get the money, or should they be turned off?

   Write a brief brief on one of these cases for presentation to the committee.

JOHN KENNETH GALBRAITH "The Language of Economics"

1. If Galbraith's vocabulary sent you to the dictionary unusually often, is that a good thing or a bad thing? Here are a few of his larger words: *portentous, involuted, punctilious, stultification, equanimity, coterminous, honorific, inimical, sententiously, esoteric*. Do you want any of these in your working vocabulary? Which of them are now in your recognition vocabulary?

2. Is part II, in its brevity, sufficient to accomplish its purpose? Try putting the words *parameter, stochastic* and *aggregation* into a single sentence (not, of course, the way Galbraith does, or we do here).

3. Explain in your own words what Galbraith finds so good about the two statements he quotes from Adam Smith in part III (one in footnote 3).

4. Need Galbraith have used so many and such long discursive footnotes? Are they in themselves an element of his style in this essay? Using Galbraith's announced principles, analyze his own prose style.

5. In part V, is Galbraith's analogy between the Bible and the writings of economists clear and valid? What does it suggest about modern economic theory?

6. In parts VI and VII, is Galbraith being intentionally ironic in spots? If so, where did the irony begin? What is the final, overall tone of this essay?

7. Veblen may have dealt what he called"conspicuous consumption" a heavy blow, but it did not disappear. Write an essay on one or more kinds of conspicuous consumption in today's society. Or write a confessional essay about conspicuous consumption's part in your own behaviour (you may wish to be ironically self-mocking—remember Forster's essay in section I). Or write an argumentative essay in which you try to justify at least some forms of conspicuous consumption.

8. Write an essay anatomizing a passage of prose from some professional journal. Evaluate the necessity and effectiveness of the language and style of the passage.

TOPICS: General and Comparative

1. What is the thesis of each essay in this section? What is each writer trying to explain? What for example is Baker's purpose? Are any theses implied rather than stated? Note also where theses are stated. Does Roueché's thesis appear only at the end? Are some stated—in different form—both near the beginning and near the end? Note how Gould calls attention to his "main theme"—but not until almost halfway through the essay; is that actually his thesis? Note that Thomas, like Forster in section I, puts his thesis in the form of a question which he then proceeds to answer. In your own essays, think carefully about the form and the placement of your thesis.

2. Consider the tone of the essays in this section. Atwood is informal and partly ironic; Roueché is objective and intense; Berlin is formal; Baker is openly subjective and playful—but is he also quite serious? Is Galbraith formal and academic as well as wry? How would you characterize Cole's tone? Try ordering these essays on a scale running from formal to informal or colloquial, on another running from objective to subjective, and on yet another running from sober to sardonic. What is the effect of each tonal choice?

3. These essays are expository—written to explain and inform. But expository writing is often also argumentative, at least implicitly if not explicitly. Mitford is openly, even blatantly argumentative. Gould says he wants to "argue" his main theme; but is his essay primarily argumentative? Galbraith makes clear at the beginning that his essay is argument as well as exposition; analyze its argumentative structure. Clearly Thomas's essay is not only informative but also argumentative: compare his rhetorical techniques with those of one or more of the other essays in this section that are written to persuade; then compare them with the techniques of the essays in section III. Is there anything argumentative about Iyer's essay? Cole's? Berlin's? Woolf's?

4. Because they deal with something that takes place during a period of time, process essays often use narrative; they also often use cause and effect. Examine the process essays in this section to see how much and in what ways and for what reasons they use narrative and cause-and-effect techniques.

5. Could Dryden's essay just as well be in the "Writing to Reveal" section as here? What, if anything, gets revealed, as opposed to explained? Is Atwood's intention partly to reveal something about herself? How about Baker, Thomas, and Galbraith? What is Mitford striving to reveal? How does she accomplish the revelation?

6. How important are titles? What should a title do? Evaluate the titles of the essays in this section—and in the other sections too. How effective are they? How are they effective? Try classifying them according to their kinds and the way they work. Does Cole's title constitute an allusion, or is it just a conveniently familiar phrase? Do you believe that Atwood "plucked" her title "from the air" before she'd even planned her talk? How effective does her title turn out to be? In how many ways does she apply it? Try the tactic yourself: find a title at random (perhaps by sticking your finger into a dictionary or other book with your eyes closed, or arranging a pile of letter-tiles from a word game) and see if from it, by processes of association and the like, you can generate material for a short essay.

7. Do Thomas and Gould write the way you would expect scientists to write? How *should* scientists write? Does it depend on their audience on a given occasion? Do you feel legitimately included in their audiences here? Faced with the complexities of subjects like medicine, biology, mathematics, and economics, how do writers strive to be clear? Does their use of a technical vocabulary help, or does it hinder? Does the medical terminology Rouché uses annoy you or does it add authenticity? Does Berlin help you understand the function of philosophy? How does his purpose differ from that of Davenport in section II? Are Cole and Galbraith intent on getting you to understand mathematics and economics, respectively, or are they content with more modest aims? Galbraith tries to distinguish between the clarity of a necessary technical language and the ambiguity that much jargon creates. How effective is he? Is the distinction valid? Write a short informative essay on a technical subject. Don't shy away from technical terminology, however; use it so that it will help rather than hinder non-specialist readers.

8. Eiseley (section I) mentions "the passion of modern men for the precision of machines" and their dislike of "vagueness of any sort." Cole refers to numbers as different from "the messy complexities of everyday life." Is mathematics always true, certain, dependable? Do "irrational" numbers fit into logical science? Do non-linear equations? (You might wish to write an essay explaining the "logic" of "chaos theory.") How can mathematicians talk, rationally, about "imaginary" or "impossible" numbers? Would it have bothered Wittgenstein (see Davenport in section II)? How might a mathematician answer Berlin's question, "What is a number?" Try answering it yourself. Is it a "philosophical" question, according to Berlin's definition? Do some of the questions Berlin uses as examples sound similar to those of Wittgenstein? How central is *language* to the problems of philosophy that Berlin discusses (see for example paragraph 22)?

9. Note what Berlin says about "the history of thought" being "a long series of parricides." He outlines history as a succession of patterns, models, categories. How would such a view sit with Tuchman (section III)? Would she find it too neat and tidy? Or is Berlin's view really neat and tidy at all? Note that she cites him in support of her position. Does his essay reveal the same attitudes or assumptions as appear in what she quotes from another of his works?

10. Explain the difference between a base-3 number system and a base-10 number system. Are there advantages to each? Or explain the differences between a diatonic scale, a 12-tone scale, a pentatonic scale, and a chromatic scale.

11. Classify the books in your own or a friend's personal collection. What does the classification reveal? Or write an essay classifying your closest friends and acquaintances. Decide on what criteria you will use—gender, age, size, intelligence, interests, national or ethnic background, and so on. Which scheme of classification yields the most interesting or useful results?

12. Write an essay defining happiness, courage, romance, friendship, or some other abstract idea. If necessary divide your topic into parts and focus selectively. Provide plenty of examples and illustrations.

13. Write an essay explaining the causes of a particular election result, of the outcome of a particular battle, of a notable athletic victory or defeat, or of some similar event. Choose an event small enough to be manageable. Do whatever research is necessary. You will probably need to use some narration.

14. Write an essay interpreting a body of statistics. Consider such topics as the differences in the cost of food from place to place, ethnic distribution in your area over a twenty-year span, the unemployment figures for your province during the last decade, or the spread and control of an epidemic disease.

15. If you know how to tie flies, write a brief instructional process essay on how to tie a particular kind—perhaps a Harger's Orange? Or explain how to make spaghetti sauce; how to fix the gears on a ten-speed bike; how to play soccer; how to get from Winnipeg to Thunder Bay; how to drink soup through a straw; how to tie shoes; how to fly a kite; how to peel a tomato; how to play dominoes; how to throw a boomerang; how to write a good paragraph; how to eat grapefruit; how to darn stockings; how to beat inflation; how to tune a guitar; how to use dental floss; how to prune a fruit tree; how to make an omelette; how to analyze a poem; how to polish brass; how to polish apples; how to win friends and influence people; how to use a dictionary; how to re-pot a root-bound plant; how to eat an artichoke; how to make croutons; how to change a spark-plug; how to trim a moustache; how to give up smoking; how to sew on a button; how to.... Consider beginning your essay with "It's not so difficult to...," or words to that effect.

V

Writing to Amuse

In an essay called "Humour as I See It," published in 1916 in *Further Foolishness,* Stephen Leacock reflects characteristically on his own craft:

> Until two weeks ago I might have taken my pen in hand to write about humour with the confident air of an acknowledged professional. But that time is past. Such claim as I had has been taken from me. In fact I stand unmasked. An English reviewer writing in a literary journal, the very name of which is enough to put contradiction to sleep, has said of my writing, "What is there, after all, in Professor Leacock's humour but a rather ingenious mixture of hyperbole and meiosis?"
>
> The man was right. How he stumbled upon this trade secret I do not know. But I am willing to admit, since the truth is out, that it has long been my custom in preparing an article of a humorous nature to go down to the cellar and mix up half a gallon of meiosis with a pint of hyperbole. If I want to give the article a decidedly literary character, I find it well to put in about half a pint of paresis. The whole thing is amazingly simple.

Writing humorously, he underlines the difficulties of writing about humour: the almost overwhelming impulse to become solemn, the easy reliance on categories of humorous techniques, the temptation to cap the humorist's jokes with other jokes that usually fall flat. There are good reasons why one should not write about humorous writing at all, but instead just sit back and enjoy it.

Yet humour often has serious implications, and writers of humour do use various techniques, and there is an art to good storytelling: all of these subjects are worthy of comment. Involved in good storytelling are such matters as a writer's control over intonation, careful pacing, and use of dramatic pauses. Because intonation is particularly important in a work striving to amuse, it is necessary for a writer to orchestrate a written work so that readers can adequately gauge the tone. The techniques of hyperbole (exaggeration) and meiosis (understatement) will both work to this end. But not always. A writer, or even a speaker, must place some trust in a reader's or an audience's ability to adjust to changes in tone, and such trust is often betrayed. Humourless persons often fail to perceive a speaker's ironic tone or ironic intent. Responding literally is the surest way to kill the humour of a situation, and literal (often outraged) responses are usually out of all proportion to the original comment. "Letters to the Editor" columns frequently fill up with such misspent energy. And readers who fail to find a written work funny—if indeed it is funny—have often, like those mistaken listeners, simply failed to *hear the voice*—to catch the cadence and intonations—of the speaker who transcribed his ironic observations onto the page.

People use several different terms when talking about events or things that amuse, and the terms are often confused. Here are some of them:

humorous (How neutral a term is this?)

funny (Why does this word imply both simple amusement and strangeness?)

ironic (Are there any limits to this term?)

comic (Has this term become codified by modern criticism?)

laughable (Does this imply any humour at all?)

risible (Is this term more formal than others—or funny in itself?)

witty (Does this imply intellectual enjoyment only?)

amusing (Does this imply distant superiority?)

wry (In what way does this suggest emotional release?)

sardonic (Does this differ from *wry*?)

smart (Is this a culturally biased word?)

whimsical (Is this word socially biased?)

facetious (Has this word become a slur?)

capricious (How does this relate to humour or enjoyment?)

farcical (Why is this word associated with drama?)

droll (Does this word now sound oddly archaic?)

sarcastic (What does this imply that *ironic* does not?)

satiric (Is humour a necessary element here?)

There are other terms as well, all of which imply different variations of response. And we have to be careful to distinguish among these differences. People often confuse *sarcastic* (which means "flesh-tearing") with *ironic*, even though irony need not be aggressive. *Comic*, similarly, is synonymous with neither *ironic* nor *satiric*, nor even with *witty*. Whereas *wit* usually involves verbal cleverness (not necessarily with intent to amuse), *comic*—like some of the other terms on the list—can refer to visual incongruity rather than verbal, or in a much more general way to a genial acceptance of the complexities and possibilities of life.

When one tries to distinguish *comedy* from *irony* and *satire*—either in substance and intent or in form—other problems arise, and still more literary categories spring into being. Irony and sarcasm can be formal techniques in the context of satiric writing, which many critics think of as essentially reformative. So can innuendo. So can burlesque, parody, and travesty. But irony can also refer to a whole attitude of human expectations, a shrugging resignation in the face of the difference between human desires and the way things are.

To contemplate theories of humour is to encounter further disagreement. A number of theorists see *wit*, for example, as a kind of indirect savagery, and they define both satiric humour and humour of the farcical, slipping-on-a-banana-peel kind as psychological sublimation of violence. These writers stress the implicit viciousness of humorous writing. By contrast, someone like Leacock, who in "A, B, and C" expresses a sympathy (not unalloyed) for human fallibility, stresses how humour emerges from our awareness of the close relation between sorrow and joy. Some people call humour elitist or escapist; others claim that it is necessary for sanity, for survival, for openness, for flexibility, and for the ability to deal sensibly with reality. All of these are large claims, and perhaps no single theory adequately explains why people find things funny or why they laugh.

Whatever the impulse behind it, humorous writing—whether reformative or reflective in nature, whether sympathetic or angry—will work only when the writer carefully controls what he or she has to say. Letting things get out of hand—letting more anger than amusement show, pushing the ridiculous too hard or for too long—will get in the reader's way. Uncontrolled invective will simply appear frivolous—laughable rather than mirthful—or else vicious or simply embarrassing. Sometimes the reformative impulse of humour has to declare itself, of course. Thomas Chandler Haliburton, in his 1836 work *The Clockmaker*, notes that "When reason fails to convince, there is nothin' left but ridicule." Ritter's wry amusement at contemporary urban pretensions, Murdoch's stylized annoyance with cliché, Leacock's humanizing of dull textbooks: these represent various shades of attack. But how closely, how *literally*, can one accept what these essays say? Possibly not at all. Humour works at tangents, works with two levels of reality in mind. The humour derives from our sense of an author's control over such disparity and from our sense of an author's engaging eye for incongruities in language, form, and human behaviour. Because language is often the medium for such incongruities, it is also a frequent topic of humour as well. Trillin's reflections on the pain of living literally, Thurber's attack on our linguistic cruelty to animals, and Le Guin's echoing of scientific reporting all take language comically—in order, one might say, to take language (and life) seriously. Through humour they find a way of dealing with life's absurdities and ironies, and enduring. Through burlesque and exaggeration, through puns and ironic asides, they probe cultural values, social attitudes, and the idiosyncrasies of character. They also amuse.

Bicycles

Erika Ritter

It wasn't always like this. There was a time in the life of the world when adults were adults, having firmly put away childish things and thrown away the key.

Not any more. The change must have come about innocently enough, I imagine. Modern Man learning to play nicely in the sandbox with the other grown-ups. Very low-tension stuff.

Now, in every direction you look, your gaze is met by the risible spectacle of adults postponing adolescence well into senility by means of adult toys: running shoes, baseball bats, roller skates, and—bicycles!

But the attitude is no longer the fun-loving approach of a bunch of superannuated kids, and I'm sure you can envision how the evolution occurred. Jogging progressed from a casual encounter with the fresh air to an intensive relationship, attended by sixty-dollar jogging shoes and a designer sweatband. Playing baseball stopped being fun unless you had a Lacoste (as opposed to low-cost) tee-shirt in which to impress your teammates. And where was the thrill in running around a squash court unless it was with a potentially important client?

As for bicycles—well, let's not even talk about bicycles. On the other hand, maybe we *should* talk about them, because there's something particularly poignant about how it all went wrong for the bicycle, by what declension this once proud and carefree vehicle sank into the role of beast of burden, to bear the weight of sobersided grown-ups at their supposed sport.

First, there was the earliest domestication of the North American bicycle (*cyclus pedalis americanus*) in the late Hippie Scene Era of the 1960s. This was the age of the no-nuke whole-grain cyclist, who saw in the bicycle the possibility of Making a Statement while he rode. A statement about pollution, about materialism, about imperialism, about militarism, about—enough already. You get the picture: two wheels good, four wheels bad.

Thus it was that the basic bicycle gradually evolved into a chunky three-speed number from China, bowed down under a plastic kiddie carrier, army surplus knapsacks, and a faded fender-sticker advising Make Tofu, Not War. And a rider clad in a red plaid lumber-jacket, Birkenstock sandals, and an expression of urgent concern for all living things.

Once the very act of bicycle riding had become an act of high moral purpose, it was an easy step to the next phase of the bicycle's journey along the path of post-Meanderthal seriousness.

I'm speaking of the era of the high-strung thoroughbred bicycle, whose rider had also made advances, from pedalling peacenik to a hunched and humorless habitué of the velodrome, clad in leather-seated shorts, white crash helmet, and fingerless gloves, whizzing soundlessly, and with no hint of joy, down city streets and along the shoulders of super-highways, aboard a vehicle sculpted in wisps of silver chrome. A vehicle so overbred, in its final evolutionary stages, that it began to resemble the mere exoskeleton of a conventional cycle, its flesh picked away by birds of carrion.

Having been stripped of any connection with its innocent and leisurely origins, the bicycle now no longer bore the slightest resemblance to the happy creature it once had been. And in the mid-Plastic Scene Era, another crippling blow was struck by the upscale name-brand cyclist, who came along to finish what the fanatical velodromist had refined. Namely, the complete transformation of an ambling and unhurried mode of transit into a fast, nerve-wracking, expensive, and utterly competitive display of high speed, high technology, and high status.

The Upscale Cyclist was looking for a twelve-speed Bottecchia that matched his eyes, something that he'd look trendy upon the seat of, when riding to the office (the office!), and he was ready to pay in four figures for it.

Not only that, he was also prepared to shell out some heavy bread for those status accessories to complete the picture: the backpack designed by the engineers at NASA, the insulated water-bottle to keep his Perrier chilled just right, the sixteen-track Walkman that would virtually assure him the envy of all his friends.

So much for the cyclist. What of his poor debased mount?

Not surprisingly, amongst the breed of bicycle, morale is currently low, and personal pride all but a thing of the past. And yet...and yet, there are those who say that *cyclus pedalis americanus* is an indomitable creature, and that it is the bicycle, not its rider, who will make the last evolution of the wheel.

In fact, some theorize that the present high incidence of bicycle thievery, far from being evidence of crime, is actually an indication that the modern bicycle has had enough of oppressive exploitation and man's joyless ways, and is in the process of reverting to the wild in greater and greater numbers.

There have always remained a few aboriginal undomesticated bicycles—or so the theory goes—and now it is these free-spirited mavericks, down from the hills at night, who visit urban bike-racks, garages, and back porches to lure tame bicycles away with them.

Costly Kryptonite locks are wrenched asunder, expensive accoutrements are shrugged off, intricate gear systems are torn away, and lo—look what is revealed! Unadorned, undefiled *cyclus* in all his pristine glory, unfettered and unencumbered once more, and free to roam.

A wistful fantasy, you might say? The maundering illusions of someone who's been riding her bicycle too long without a crash helmet? I wonder.

Just the other day, there was that piece in the paper about a bicycle that went berserk in a shopping centre, smashing two display windows before it was subdued. And did you hear about the recent sighting of a whole herd of riderless bicycles, all rolling soundlessly across a park in the night?

It all kind of gets you to thinking. I mean, do *you* know where your ten-speed is tonight?

Literally

Calvin Trillin

September 12, 1981

My problem with country living began innocently enough when our well ran dry and a neighbor said some pump priming would be necessary.

"I didn't come up here to discuss economics," I said. Actually, I don't discuss economics in the city either. As it happens, I don't understand economics. There's no use revealing that, though, to every Tom, Dick and Harry who interrupts his dinner to try to get your water running, so I said, "I come up here to get away from that sort of thing." My neighbor gave me a puzzled look.

"He's talking about the water pump," Alice told me. "It needs priming."

I thought that experience might have been just a fluke—until, on a fishing trip with the same neighbor, I proudly pulled in a fish with what I thought was a major display of deep-sea angling skill, only to hear a voice behind me say, "It's just a fluke."

"This is dangerous," I said to Alice, while helping her weed the vegetable garden the next day. I had thought our problem was limited to the pump-priming ichthyologist down the road, but that morning at the post office I had overheard a farmer say that since we seemed to be in for a few days of good weather he intended to make his hay while the sun was shining. "These people are robbing me of aphorisms," I said, taking advantage of the discussion to rest for a while on my hoe. "How can I encourage the children to take advantage of opportunities by telling them to make hay while the sun shines if they think that means making hay while the sun shines?"

"Could you please keep weeding those peas while you talk," she said. "You've got a long row to hoe."

I began to look at Alice with new eyes. By that, of course, I don't mean that I actually went to a discount eye outlet, acquired two new eyes (20/20 this time), replaced my old eyes with the new ones and looked at Alice. Having to make that explanation is just the sort of thing I found troubling. What I mean is that I was worried about the possibility of Alice's falling into the habit of rural literalism herself. My concern was deepened a few days later by a conversation that took place while I was in one of our apple trees, looking for an apple that was not used as a *dacha* by the local worms. "I just talked to the Murrays, and they say that the secret is picking up windfalls," Alice said.

"Windfalls?" I said. "Could it be that Jim Murray has taken over Exxon since last time I saw him? Or do the Murrays have a natural-gas operation in the back forty I didn't know about?"

"Not those kinds of windfalls," Alice said. "The apples that fall from the tree because of the wind. They're a breeding place for worms."

"There's nothing wrong with our apples," I said, reaching for a particularly plump one.

"Be careful," she said. "You may be getting yourself too far out on a limb."

"You may be getting yourself out on a limb yourself," I said to Alice at breakfast the next morning.

She looked around the room. "I'm sitting at the kitchen table," she said.

"I meant it symbolically," I said. "The way it was meant to be meant. This has got to stop. I won't have you coming in from the garden with small potatoes in your basket and saying that what you found was just small potatoes. 'Small potatoes' doesn't mean small potatoes."

"Small potatoes doesn't mean small potatoes?"

"I refuse to discuss it," I said. "The tide's in, so I'm going fishing, and I don't want to hear any encouraging talk about that fluke not being the only fish in the ocean."

"I was just going to ask why you have to leave before you finish your breakfast," she said.

"Because time and tide wait for no man," I said. "And I mean it."

Had she trapped me into saying that? Or was it possible that I was falling into the habit myself? Was I, as I waited for a bite, thinking that there were plenty of other fish in the sea? Then I had a bite—then another. I forgot about the problem until after I had returned to the dock and done my most skilful job of filleting.

"Look!" I said, holding up the carcass of one fish proudly, as Alice approached the dock. "It's nothing but skin and bones."

The shock of realizing what I had said caused me to stumble against my fish-cleaning table and knock the fillets off the dock. "Now we won't have anything for dinner," I said.

"Don't worry about it," Alice said. "I have other fish to fry."

"That's not right!" I shouted. "That's not what that means. It means you have something better to do."

"It can also mean that I have other fish to fry," she said. "And I do. I'll just get that other fish you caught out of the freezer. Even though it was just a fluke."

I tried to calm myself. I apologized to Alice for shouting and offered to help her pick vegetables from the garden for dinner.

"I'll try to watch my language," she said, as we stood among the peas.

"It's all right, really," I said.

"I was just going to say that tonight it seems rather slim pickings," she said. "Just about everything has gone to seed."

"Perfectly all right," I said, wandering over toward the garden shed, where some mud seemed to be caked in the eaves. I pushed at the mud with a rake, and a swarm of wasps burst out at me. I ran for the house, swatting at wasps with my hat. Inside, I suddenly had the feeling that some of them had managed to crawl up the legs of my jeans, and I tore the jeans off. Alice found me there in the kitchen, standing quietly in what the English call their smalls.

"That does it," I said, "We're going back to the city."

"Just because of a few stings?"

"Can't you see what happened?" I said. "They scared the pants off me."

A, B, and C

**The Human Element
in Mathematics**

Stephen Leacock

The student of arithmetic who has mastered the first four rules of his art, and successfully striven with money sums and fractions, finds himself confronted by an unbroken expanse of questions known as problems. These are short stories of adventure and industry with the end omitted, and though betraying a strong family resemblance, are not without a certain element of romance.

The characters in the plot of a problem are three people called A, B, and C. The form of the question is generally of this sort:

"A, B, and C do a certain piece of work. A can do as much work in one hour as B in two, or C in four. Find how long they work at it."

Or thus:

"A, B, and C are employed to dig a ditch. A can dig as much in one hour as B can dig in two, and B can dig twice as fast as C. Find how long, etc., etc."

Or after this wise:

"A lays a wager that he can walk faster than B or C. A can walk half as fast again as B, and C is only an indifferent walker. Find how far, and so forth."

The occupations of A, B, and C are many and varied. In the older arithmetics they contented themselves with doing "a certain piece of work." This statement of the case, however, was found too sly and mysterious, or possibly lacking in romantic charm. It became the fashion to define the job more clearly and to set them at walking-matches, ditch-digging, regattas, and piling cord wood. At times they became commercial and entered into partnership, having with their old mystery a "certain" capital. Above all they revel in motion. When they tire of walking-matches—A rides on horseback, or borrows a bicycle and competes with his weaker-minded associates on foot. Now they race on locomotives; now they row; or again they become historical and engage stagecoaches; or at times they are aquatic and swim. If their occupation is actual work they prefer to pump water into cisterns, two of which leak through holes in the bottom and one of which is water-tight. A, of course, has the good one; he also takes the bicycle, and the best locomotive, and the right of swimming with the current. Whatever they do they put money on it, being all three sports. A always wins.

In the early chapters of the arithmetic, their identity is concealed under the names John, William, and Henry, and they wrangle over the division of marbles. In algebra they are often called X, Y, and Z. But these are only their Christian names, and they are really the same people.

Now to one who has followed the history of these men through countless pages of problems, watched them in their leisure hours dallying with cord wood, and seen their panting sides heave in the full frenzy of filling a cistern with a leak in it, they become something more than mere symbols. They appear as creatures of flesh and blood, living men with their own passions, ambitions, and aspirations like the rest of us. Let us view them in turn. A is a full-blooded blustering fellow, of energetic temperament, hotheaded and strong-willed. It is he who proposes everything, challenges B to work, makes the bets, and bends the others to his will. He is a man of great physical strength and phenomenal endurance. He has been known to walk forty-eight hours at a stretch, and to pump ninety-six. His life is arduous and full of peril. A mistake in the working of a sum may keep him digging a fortnight without sleep. A repeating decimal in the answer might kill him.

B is a quiet, easy-going fellow, afraid of A and bullied by him, but very gentle and brotherly to little C, the weakling. He is quite in A's power, having lost all his money in bets.

Poor C is an undersized, frail man, with a plaintive face. Constant walking, digging, and pumping has broken his health and ruined his nervous system. His joyless life has driven him to drink and smoke more than is good for him, and his hand often shakes as he digs ditches. He has not the strength to work as the others can; in fact, as Hamlin Smith has said, "A can do more work in one hour than C in four."

The first time that ever I saw these men was one evening after a regatta. They had all been rowing in it, and it had transpired that A could row as much in one hour as B in two, or C in four. B and C had come in dead fagged and C was coughing badly. "Never mind, old fellow," I heard B say, "I'll fix you up on the sofa and get you some hot tea." Just then A came blustering in and shouted, "I say, you fellows, Hamlin Smith has shown me three cisterns in his garden and he says we can pump them until tomorrow night. I bet I can beat you both. Come on. You can pump in your rowing things, you know. Your cistern leaks a little, I think, C." I heard B growl that it was a dirty shame and that C was used up now, but they went, and presently I could tell from the sound of the water that A was pumping four times as fast as C.

For years after that I used to see them constantly about town and always busy. I never heard of any of them eating or sleeping. Then owing to a long absence from home, I lost sight of them. On my return I was surprised to no longer find A, B, and C at their accustomed tasks; on inquiry I heard that work in this line was now done by N, M, and O, and that some people were employing for algebraical jobs four foreigners called Alpha, Beta, Gamma, and Delta.

Now it chanced one day that I stumbled upon old D, in the little garden in front of his cottage, hoeing in the sun. D is an aged labouring man who used occasionally to be called in to help A, B, and C. "Did I know 'em, sir?" he answered. "Why, I knowed 'em ever since they was little fellows in brackets.

Master A, he were a fine lad, sir, though I always said, give me Master B for kindheartedness-like. Many's the job as we've been on together, sir, though I never did no racing nor aught of that, but just the plain labour, as you might say. I'm getting a bit too old and stiff for it nowadays, sir—just scratch about in the garden here and grow a bit of a logarithm, or raise a common denominator or two. But Mr. Euclid he use me still for them propositions, he do."

From the garrulous old man I learned the melancholy end of my former acquaintances. Soon after I left town, he told me, C had been taken ill. It seems that A and B had been rowing on the river for a wager, and C had been running on the bank and then sat in a draught. Of course the bank had refused the draught and C was taken ill. A and B came home and found C lying helpless in bed. A shook him roughly and said, "Get up, C, we're going to pile wood." C looked so worn and pitiful that B said, "Look here, A, I won't stand this, he isn't fit to pile wood to-night." C smiled feebly and said, "Perhaps I might pile a little if I sat up in bed." Then B, thoroughly alarmed, said, "See here, A, I'm going to fetch a doctor; he's dying." A flared up and answered, "You've no money to fetch a doctor." "I'll reduce him to his lowest terms," B said firmly, "that'll fetch him." C's life might even then have been saved but they made a mistake about the medicine. It stood at the head of the bed on a bracket, and the nurse accidentally removed it from the bracket without changing the sign. After the fatal blunder C seems to have sunk rapidly. On the evening of the next day, as the shadows deepened in the little room, it was clear to all that the end was near. I think that even A was affected at the last as he stood with bowed head, aimlessly offering to bet with the doctor on C's laboured breathing. "A," whispered C, "I think I'm going fast." "How fast do you think you'll go, old man?" murmured A. "I don't know," said C , "but I'm going at any rate."—The end came soon after that. C rallied for a moment and asked for a certain piece of work that he had left downstairs. A put it in his arms and he expired. As his soul sped heavenward A watched its flight with melancholy admiration. B burst into a passionate flood of tears and sobbed, "Put away his little cistern and the rowing clothes he used to wear. I feel as if I could hardly ever dig again."—The funeral was plain and unostentatious. It differed in nothing from the ordinary, except that out of deference to sporting men and mathematicians, A engaged two hearses. Both vehicles started at the same time, B driving the one which bore the sable parallelopiped containing the last remains of his ill-fated friend. A on the box of the empty hearse generously consented to a handicap of a hundred yards, but arrived first at the cemetery by driving four times as fast as B. (Find the distance to the cemetery.) As the sarcophagus was lowered, the grave was surrounded by the broken figures of the first book of Euclid.—It was noticed that after the death of C, A became a changed man. He lost interest in racing with B, and dug but languidly. He finally gave up his work and settled down to live on the interest of his bets.—B never recovered from the shock of C's death; his grief preyed upon his intellect and it became deranged. He grew moody and spoke only in monosyllables. His disease became rapidly aggravated, and he presently spoke only in words

333

whose spelling was regular and which presented no difficulty to the beginner. Realising his precarious condition he voluntarily submitted to be incarcerated in an asylum, where he abjured mathematics and devoted himself to writing the History of the Swiss Family Robinson in words of one syllable.

Some Approaches to the Problem of the Shortage of Time

Ursula K. Le Guin

The Little Tiny Hole Theory

The hypothesis put forward by James Osbold of the Lick Observatory, though magnificently comprehensive, presents certain difficulties to agencies seeking practical solutions to the problem. Divested of its mathematical formulation, Dr. Osbold's theory may be described in very approximate terms as positing the existence of an anomaly in the space-time continuum. The cause of the anomaly is a failure of reality to meet the specifications of the General Theory of Relativity, although only in one minor detail. Its effect on the actual constitution of the universe is a local imperfection or flaw, that is, a hole in the continuum.

The hole, according to Osbold's calculations, is a distinctly spacelike hole. In this spatiality lies its danger, since the imbalance thus constituted in the continuum causes a compensatory influx from the timelike aspect of the cosmos. In other words, time is running out of the hole. This has probably been going on ever since the origin of the universe 12 to 15 billion years ago, but only lately has the leak grown to noticeable proportions.

The propounder of the theory is not pessimistic, remarking that it might be even worse if the anomaly were in the timelike aspect of the continuum, in which case space would be escaping, possibly one dimension at a time, which would cause untold discomfort and confusion; although, Osbold adds, "In that event we might have time enough to do something about it."

Since the theory posits the hole's location somewhere or other, Lick and two Australian observatories have arranged a coordinated search for local variations in the red shift which might aid in pinpointing the point/instant. "It may still be a very small hole," Osbold says. "Quite tiny. It would not need to be very large to do a good deal of damage. But since the effect is so noticeable here on Earth, I feel we have a good chance of finding the thing perhaps no farther away than the Andromeda Galaxy, and then all we'll need is what you might call a Dutch boy."

The Nonbiodegradable Moment

A totally different explanation of the time shortage is offered by a research team of the Interco Development Corporation. Their approach to the problem, as presented by N. T. Chaudhuri, an internationally recognised authority on the ecology and ethology of the internal combustion engine, is chemical rather than cosmological. Chaudhuri has proved that the fumes of incompletely burned petroleum fuel, under certain conditions—diffused anxiety is the major predisposing factor—will form a chemical bond with time, "tying down" instants in the same manner as a nucleating agent "ties down" free atoms into molecules. The process is called chronocrystallisation or (in the case of acute anxiety) chronoprecipitation. The resulting compact arrangement of instants is far more orderly than the pre-existent random "nowness," but unfortunately this decrease in entropy is paid for by a very marked increase in bioinsupportability. In fact the petroleum/time compound appears to be absolutely incompatible with life in any form, even anaerobic bacteria, of which so much was hoped.

The present danger, then, as described by team member F. Gonzales Park, is that so much of our free time, or radical time properly speaking, will be locked into this noxious compound (which she refers to as petropsychotoxin or PPST) that we will be forced to bring up the vast deposits of PPST which the U.S. Government has dumped or stored in various caves, swamps, holes, oceans, and back yards, and deliberately break down the compound, thus releasing free temporal radicals. Senator Helms and several Sunbelt Democrats have already protested. Certainly the process of reclaiming time from PPST is risky, requiring so much oxygen that we might end up, as O. Heiko, a third member of the team, puts it, with plenty of free time but no air.

Feeling that time is running out even faster than the oil wells, Heiko himself favors an "austerity" approach to the problem, beginning with a ban on aircraft flying in excess of the speed of sound, and working steadily on down through prop planes, racing cars, standard cars, ships, motorboats, etc., until, if necessary, all petroleum-powered vehicles have been eliminated. Speed serves as the standard of priority, since the higher the velocity of the petroleum-fuelled vehicle, and hence the more concentrated the conscious or subliminal anxiety of the driver/passengers, the more complete is the petrolisation of time, and the more poisonous the resultant PPST. Heiko, believing there is no "safe level" of contamination, thinks that probably not even mopeds would eventually escape the ban. As he points out, a single gas-powered lawnmower moving at less than 3 mph can petrolise three solid hours of a Sunday afternoon in an area of one city block.

A ban on gas guzzlers may, however, solve only half the problem. An attempt by the Islamic League to raise the price of crude time by $8.50/hr was recently foiled by prompt action by the Organisation of Time Consuming States; but West Germany is already paying $18.75/hr—twice what the American consumer expects to pay for his time.

Bleeding Hearts? The Temporal Conservation Movement

Willing to listen to the cosmological and chemical hypotheses but uncommitted to either is a growing consortium of scientists and laypersons, many of whom have grouped themselves into organisations such as Le Temps Perdu (Brussels), Protestants Concerned at the Waste of Time (Indianapolis), and the driving, widespread Latin-American action group Mañana. A Mañanista spokesperson, Dolores Guzman McIntosh of Buenos Aires, states the group's view: "We have—all of us—almost entirely wasted our time. If we do not save it, we are lost. There is not much time left." The Mañanistas have so far carefully avoided political affiliation, stating bluntly that the time shortfall is the fault of Communist and Capitalist governments equally. A growing number of priests from Mexico to Chile have joined the movement, but the Vatican recently issued an official denunciation of those "who, while they talk of saving time, lose their own souls." In Italy a Communist temporal-conservation group, Eppur Si Muove, was recently splintered by the defection of its president, who after a visit to Moscow stated in print: "Having watched the bureaucracy of the Soviet Union in action I have lost faith in the arousal of class consciousness as the principal means towards our goal."

A group of social scientists in Cambridge, England, continues meanwhile to investigate the as yet unproven link of the time shortage with shortage of temper. "If we could show the connection," says psychologist Derrick Groat, "the temporal conservation groups might be able to act more effectively. As it is they mostly quarrel. Everybody wants to save time before it's gone forever, but nobody really knows how, and so we all get cross. If only there were a substitute, you know, like solar and geothermal for petroleum, it would ease the strain. But evidently we have to make do with what we've got." Groat mentioned the "time stretcher" marketed by General Substances under the trademark Sudokron, withdrawn last year after tests indicated that moderate doses caused laboratory mice to turn into Kleenex. Informed that the Rand Corporation was devoting massive funding to research into a substitute for time, he said, "I wish them luck. But they may have to work longer hours at it!" The British scientist was referring to the fact that the United States has shortened the hour by ten minutes while retaining twenty-four per day, while the EEC countries, foreseeing increasing shortages, have chosen to keep sixty minutes to the hour but allow only twenty hours to the "devalued" European day.

Meantime, the average citizen in Moscow or Chicago, while often complaining about the shortage of time or the deteriorating quality of what remains, seems inclined to scoff at the doomsday prophets, and to put off such extreme measures as rationing as long as possible. Perhaps he feels, along with Ecclesiastes and the President, that when you've seen one day, you've seen 'em all.

The Trouble with Man Is Man

James Thurber

Man has gone long enough, or even too long, without being man enough to face the simple truth that the trouble with Man is Man. For nearly three thousand years, or since the time of Aesop, he has blamed his frailties and defects on the birds, the beasts, and the insects. It is an immemorial convention of the writer of fables to invest the lower animals with the darker traits of human beings, so that, by age-old habit, Man has come to blame his faults and flaws on the other creatures in this least possible of all worlds.

The human being says that the beast in him has been aroused, when what he actually means is that the human being in him has been aroused. A person is not pigeon-toed, either, but person-toed, and what the lady has are not crow's-feet but woman-wrinkles. It is our species, and not any other, that goes out on wildcat strikes, plays the badger game, weeps crocodile tears, sets up kangaroo courts. It is the man, and not the shark, that becomes the loan shark; the cat burglar, when caught, turns out not to be a cat but a man; the cock-and-bull story was not invented by the cock and the bull; and the male of our species, at the height of his arrogant certainties, is mansure and not cocksure, just as, at his most put-upon, he is woman-nagged and not hen-pecked.

It is interesting to find in one dictionary that "cowed" does not come from "cow" but means, literally, "with the tail between the legs." I had naturally assumed, too, that Man blamed his quailing, or shrinking with fear, on the quail, but the dictionary claims that the origin of the verb "to quail" is uncertain. It is nice to know that "duck," meaning to avoid an unpleasant task, does not derive from our web-footed friend but from the German verb "tauchen," meaning "to dive." We blame our cowardice, though, on poultry, when we say of a cringing man that he "chickened out."

Lest I be suspected by friends and colleagues, as well as by the F.B.I. and the American Legion, of wearing fur or feathers under my clothing, and acting as a spy in the midst of a species that is as nervous as a man and not as a cat, I shall set down here some of the comparatively few laudatory phrases about the other animals that have passed into general usage. We say, then, that a man has dogged determination, bulldog tenacity, and is the watchdog of this or that public office, usually the Treasury. We call him lionhearted, or as brave as a lion, as proud as a peacock, as lively as a cricket, as graceful as a swan, as busy as a bee, as gentle as a lamb, and we sometimes observe that he has the memory of an elephant and works like a beaver. (Why this should make him dog-tired instead of beaver-tired I don't know.)

As I sit here, I suddenly, in my fevered fancy, get a man's-eye view, not a bird's-eye view, of a police detective snooping about a brownstone house, back in the prohibition days. He has been tipped off that the place is a blind tiger that sells white mule, or tiger sweat, and he will not believe the denials of the proprietor, one Joe, whose story sounds fishy. The detective smells a rat and begins pussyfooting around. He is sure that this is a joint in which a man can drink like a fish and get as drunk as a monkey. The proprietor may be as wise as an owl and as slippery as an eel, but the detective is confident that he can outfox him.

"Don't hound me. You're on a wild-goose chase," insists Joe, who has butterflies in his stomach, and gooseflesh. (The goose has been terribly maligned by the human being, who has even gone so far as to pretend that the German jack-boot strut is the goose step. Surely only the dog, the cat, and the bug are more derogated than the goose.) "You're as crazy as a loon," Joe quavers.

"Don't bug me," says the cop, and the bloodhound continues his search. Suddenly he flings open a door, and there stands the proprietor's current mouse, a soiled dove, as naked as a jay bird. But the detective has now ferreted out a secret panel and a cache of currency. "There must be ten thousand clams here," he says. "If you made all this fish legitimately, why do you hide it? And don't try to weasel out."

"In this rat race it's dog eat dog," the proprietor says, as he either is led off to jail or pays off the cop.

The English and American vocabularies have been vastly enlarged and, I suppose, enriched by the multitudinous figures of speech that slander and libel the lower animals, but the result has been the further inflation of the already inflated human ego by easy denigration of the other species. We have a thousand disparaging nouns applicable only to human beings, such as scoundrel, rascal, villain, scalawag, varlet, curmudgeon, and the like, but an angry person is much more apt to use, instead of one of these, such words as jackal, jackass, ape, baboon, gorilla, skunk, black sheep, louse, worm, lobster, crab, or shrimp. Incidentally, the word "curmudgeon" seems to derive from the French "*coeur méchant*," so that an old curmudgeon is nothing worse than an old naughty heart.

The female of our species comes out of slight, slur, insult, and contumely wearing more unfavorable tags and labels than the male. The fishwife, for example, has no fishhusband. The word "shrew" derives from the name of a small furred mammal with a malignant reputation, based on an old, mistaken notion that it is venomous. Shrews are, to be sure, made up of both males and females, but the word is applied only to the female human being. Similarly, "vixen," meaning an ill-tempered person, was originally applied to both sexes (of human beings, not of foxes), but it is now aimed only at the woman. When a man, especially a general or other leader, is called a fox, the word is usually employed in a favorable sense.

Both "shrew" and "vixen" are rarely used any more in domestic altercations. For one thing, neither implies mental imbalance, and our species is fond of epithets and invective implying insanity. The list of such slings and arrows in Roget's Thesaurus contains, of course, such expressions as "off one's rocker" and "off one's trolley," but once again the lower forms of life are accused of being "disturbed," as in "mad as a March hare," "bats," "batty," "bats in the belfry," "crazier than a bedbug," and so on. (My favorite phrase in this Roget category gets away from bugs and bats, and rockers and trolleys; it is "balmy in the crumpet.")

Every younger generation, in its time and turn, adds to our animalistic vocabulary of disparagement. A lone male at a dance is no longer a stag turned wolf when he dogs the steps of a girl; he's a bird dog. And if the young lady turns on him, she no longer snaps, "Get lost!" or "Drop dead!" but, I am told, "Clean out your cage!" Since I heard about this two years ago, however, it may well be old hat by now, having given way to something like "Put your foot back in the trap!" or "Go hide under your rock!" or "Crawl back into the woodwork!"

I am afraid that nothing I can say will prevent mankind from being unkind to catkind, dogkind, and bugkind. I find no record of any cat that was killed by care. There are no dogs where a man goes when he goes to the dogs. The bugs that a man gets out of his mechanisms, if he does get them out, are not bugs but defects caused by the ineptitude, haste, or oversight of men.

Let us all go back to counting sheep. I think that the reason for the prevalent sleeplessness of Americans must be that we are no longer counting sheep but men.

On Pioneering

Walter Murdoch

Hail, ye faithful, much-enduring readers!...But perhaps I had better explain. I spent a vacation recently in reading nearly three hundred Odes to Western Australia; and I wonder whether anybody ever spent a vacation in this way before, since the world began. I am now convalescent, thank you; except that I find a certain difficulty in not beginning sentences with "Hail!" the symptoms of odeshock have practically disappeared.

They mostly began with "hail" or "all hail" and many of them threw in an extra "hail" whenever their feelings got the better of them or the metre seemed to call for an extra syllable. They hailed everything and everybody; they hailed the country, they hailed the centenary, they hailed our wool, our wheat, our gold, our pearling industry, our wildflowers, the men of a century ago and the generations yet unborn. One of them exhorted his readers, at intervals, to "shout a loud hooray," and the variation was so pleasing that I felt inclined to take him at his word. Another invited us all to "shout and sing, and make the welkin blithely ring," but most of them were content with something less noisy than this. They were satisfied with hailing.

Of the earnest patriotism of these poets there can be no question; they have boundless faith in their land. We are a young people—"the debutante of nations," one of our singers calls us; and another, whose grammar is his servant, not his master, says, "the youngest of all thy fair sisters art thee"— and, being young, we are apt to be shy and to have too much respect for our elders. Our poets teach us a truer faith,

> Hail, beauteous land! hail, bonzer West Australia;
> Compared with you, all others are a failure.

That is the kind of thing, and it undoubtedly warms the cockles of the heart, though some may object to the rhyme—but then Western Australia is a puzzling name to fit into rhyme; one minstrel ingeniously solves the problem by turning it round:

> Hail, Groperland! Australia West!
> Of earth's fair places thou art best.

There is no doubt about the fervour of this; and most of these poems are fervid. We are the salt of the earth; other people are its scum. We inhabit the loveliest of lands; other countries are more or less blots on the landscape. Even the size of our State comes in for its meed of praise:

> Hail to Westralia!
>> Hail to its bigness!
> Hail to its motto
>> "Cygnis insignis."

We have done wonderful things—especially Lord Forrest, who comes into scores of odes; this, for instance is the country

> Where the purest water flows up-hill
> In accordance with Lord Forrest's will.

Wonderful man! wonderful country! wonderful poets! Hail, every one of you! All hail, in fact.

But what most of these bards praise most loudly and continuously is the character and achievements of the men of a century ago—the pioneers. So far as I am concerned, the net result is that I never want to hear another word about pioneers as long as I live. That being so, you may object, why write an essay about them?—but I hope this essay will turn out before it is done, not to be about the pioneers at all, but about a quite different subject. Anyhow, I am tired of them,

> Those souls of priceless rarity,
> Pioneers of our State,

who seem to have been physically almost as remarkable as they were in soul:

> Lean they were, with eyes aflame,
> These strong and sturdy men from hame.

"From hame" does not mean that they came from Scotland; it only means that the bard was bothered for a rhyme. (But what was the matter with "they came"?) When I try to discover from the odes what, exactly, these persons with flaming eyes and priceless souls did when they arrived, I get no very adequate account of their achievements. One poet does, indeed, endeavour to describe their doings with some exactness.

> They stopped at Mount Eliza,
> They camped beneath a tree,
> They said to one another,
> "This is good enough for me."

But I rather doubt the accuracy of this; the idiom has a too modern sound. It is wiser, perhaps, to keep to general statements, such as—

> They founded here a mighty State,
> On January 26th, 1828.

I suppose this is substantially true, though the poet seems to have antedated the event; and I suppose it is also true that they came to an inhospitable land, where—

> The native with his waddy, his boomerang and spear
> Held sway o'er its vast spaces by ignorance and fear.

And they got the better of him. At all events, whatever they did and whatever they were, it is in their honour that most of the odes beat the big drum.

> Then give to them the honour,
>   For that they well deserve,
> And do your best endeavour
>   To hand on the preserve.

By all means. Give them the honour they deserve; and give others the honour they, in their turn, deserve. The centenary celebrations are not to be arranged, I take it, for the glorification of the passengers on the *Parmelia* or of Thomas Peel's syndicate, but rather for public rejoicing that Western Australia has reached a certain stage in her journey—that she has survived the teething troubles (or weathered the storms, if that seems a more dignified way of putting it) of her first century; and for public thankfulness to whatsoever powers, human or divine, have guided her steps so far. Why anybody should pick out for special gratitude the men and women who happened to be the first on the spot it is a little difficult to see. We might as well go farther back and sing paeans of praise to the Angles and Saxons and Jutes, calling them souls of priceless rarity. Or why not sing hymns in honour of Adam, with eyes aflame, and also Eve, his beauteous dame?

The men and women who first came to settle in Australia were of British stock, and of an honourably adventurous strain. They came here to better their fortunes, lured by fantastic accounts of the country (Fraser's report dwelt on the "superiority of the soil"—and also on its "permanent humidity," a feature not conspicuous in my garden). Captain Stirling described it as "the land, out of all that I have seen in various quarters of the world, that possesses the greatest natural attractions." Vast tracts of this land were to be granted to each settler for next to nothing, and they were to cultivate cotton, tobacco, sugar and flax, to rear horses for the East Indian trade, and to establish large herds of cattle and swine for the supply of salt junk to His Majesty's shipping. They were to make fortunes easily and quickly. The land did not come up to their expectations, and they had but a thin time of it for many years after their arrival.

I do not wish to say a word against them; only, I do not see why special praise is due to them. They showed a spirit of adventure, which is the common

343

birthright of our race—and of other races. They showed great courage in coming out to a remote and unknown world; courage, thank Heaven, is not an uncommon virtue. Are we not all born of women who have sailed gallantly into the perilous sea of marriage and faced death to bring us into the world? Everywhere in our country to-day, not only in remote and lonely places in the backblocks, but in the heart of our cities, too, men and women are confronting their fate with a high courage worthy of all honour. Those pioneers endured many hardships without whimpering; all praise to them for that; but why not praise also the innumerable persons who in our midst today are enduring hardships without whimpering, and who, because they do not whimper, are unhonoured and unsung? To single out the pioneers for special glorification is to libel humanity; it is to imply that virtue has been lost. The world is as full today as ever it was of the shining virtues of courage in danger and fortitude in adversity. Did the war show that our nation—or any nation—had lost its ancient hardihood? It is impossible to read the newspapers intelligently without being proud to belong to the indomitable human race; but the best examples do not get into the newspapers. They are to be found in all sorts of odd places; in the lonely bush and in the crowded slum; the heroic is everywhere at home.

Of course if, misled by the glamour of the past, you like to talk nonsense about the pioneers, and represent them as souls of priceless rarity stalking about with eyes aflame, I suppose no great harm is done. They were probably decent people, of average intelligence, fairly industrious and not without grit and resourcefulness; very like the normal Australian of to-day. The mistake made by the writers of some of these odes was to suppose that, to write poetry, you must talk nonsense. It is not so. Poetry and nonsense are incompatible. And this nonsense about pioneers gets, after a time, on one's nerves; hence this protest. The world is young; and we are all pioneers.

What a Canadian Has Done for Canada

William Arthur Deacon

Canada is a convenient, far-off place of which the English novelist sometimes avails himself, possibly to the satisfaction of his English patrons, but frequently to the amusement of his Canadian readers. This Dominion affords refuge for criminals fleeing from justice; a place where sudden death may overtake the villain of the story at a fit distance from the scene of the hero's triumph and happiness; a remote spot to which a jilted suitor may be packed off, and whence he can return presently with a fortune. Up till recently the vagueness of the allusions to such incidents protected the English novelist: we smiled at the transparency of the conventional device of "a legendary place," but were unable to object pointedly because almost anything may happen almost anywhere provided "corroborative detail intended to give artistic verisimilitude" be carefully avoided.

Lately the list toward realism has upset the balance somewhat, and English novelists are starting to describe scenes and events which betray their ignorance of localities and conditions and to supply Canadian reviewers with material for many a jest. About four years ago, for instance, an English writer of standing put his hero on a horse at Montreal in the morning, and had him riding into Edmonton the same night. It was stated that the horse was very tired—a conservative enough estimate of its condition considering that it had covered a distance which a fast train travels in about four days. Last year May Wynne, in *The Ambitions of Gill*, wound up her book with a chapter entitled "In Far Muskoka," where the hero was represented as living the life of a prospector completely isolated from other human beings. Actually, Muskoka is the most popular of Canadian summer resorts and yields no minerals except the minted coins that tourists spend with commendable freedom. The heroine, seeking her beloved, walks miles to his cabin through the wilderness, which in the description resembles an English park more than the reality. In that country covered with evergreens, whose largest branches grow close to the ground, it would be impossible to see "at some distance a herd of deer feeding quietly beneath the trees." And the final touch is added when she comes upon "some wild boars looking for truffles," as there are neither wild boars nor truffles anywhere in North America.

As an aid to checking this tendency by showing how the Canadian scene should not be used, we may consider *Empty Hands* by Arthur Stringer, a native author and until recently a resident in Canada, but now a naturalized citizen of the United States. His book caps the climax for absurdities about Canadian woods life. On one score, however, I am very pleased with him. The literary world has long been in dire need of a second Munchausen; and though Stringer owes something to *Robinson Crusoe, Swiss Family Robinson*, and *The Admirable Crichton*, his narrative partakes far more of the bold, sweeping mendacities of the great Baron. Certainly Oscar Wilde would never have written his lament on "The Decay of Lying" if he had foreseen the mighty renaissance of that ancient and delightful art that was to come in 1924. Because a fairy story loses half its charm when it is accepted as fact; and because Stringer, being a Canadian by birth, may be mistaken for a realist by readers in other countries, I hasten to correct any such erroneous impression, and to proclaim him for the rightful monarch he is—The Prince of the "Canada Fakers" he once denounced in an article under that title in the New York *Herald*.

Like all fairy stories, the scene is laid in a place hard to locate on any mundane map, no one point in Canada fulfilling all the conditions. From seven scattered paragraphs I gather that the author means northern Manitoba. "North of the Pas," "the Land of Little Sticks" and "on the fringe of the Barren Grounds" seem to indicate this; yet on page 53 Hudson's Bay is spoken of as "hundreds of miles away...to the north," which is true of Toronto but not of the barrens far north of the Pas. Yet the mistiness of the location serves as useful cover enabling the author to bring together the strangest collection of northern and southern fauna and flora ever seen outside a zoo or a museum.

In the timber-lands at the fringe of the Barrens, then, is a mining camp; and it is the purpose of the author to turn naked into the wilds a young Canadian engineer of 30 and a wealthy and useless, though somewhat or-namental, New York society girl of 19, as hero and heroine who shall create civilization with its many inventions out of the raw material afforded by Nature. The launching is accomplished by the girl getting caught in the rapids leading out of Barrier Lake while she is fishing in her canoe before breakfast. Grimshaw, the camp-boss, still in his pyjamas, sees her go and rushes to her aid by rowing a York-boat. Now a small York-boat is 30 feet long, carries four tons of freight and a crew of eight to twelve men. Why he did not take one of the other canoes is one of the myriad entrancing mysteries in the book. But single-handed he propels the York-boat down the lake at break-neck speed, and the two of them shoot the seven miles of rapids. The hero is evidently an acrobat too, for his boat springing a leak, he, standing, tossed by the furious waves, removes both parts of his pyjamas to mend the leak. He also "steers" the drifting boat by means of a sweep, though this is physically impossible. The girl's bathing suit rips and comes off, though such garments usually stand contact with water. Both craft are lost, so the people reach shore at the lower end of the rapids naked and without baggage.

Though they started shortly after dawn, and were hurled down at light-ning speed, they reach the bottom of the rapids late in the afternoon. I, having shot a seven-mile rapid in about half an hour, deplore this dilatoriness; but am forced to admire the efficiency and speed of the hero once he is on land. Between, say, 4:30 P.M. and dark he manages to cut and weave clothes for them both out of willow branches; erects a substantial log house and puts a roof on; makes beds out of "armful after armful of cat-tails"; makes a barricade for the door; catches two fish with his hands—one a five pound maskalonge, not native to that section of the country; makes a bone knife, bark platter and drinking cup; cleans the fish; goes out and inspects timber, climbing uplands to do so; notes bear and moose indications; digs cedar roots, though no cedars grow that far north; collects punk and bird feathers.

The author is careful to tell us that the seven miles of land separating the twain from the camp (where Mr. Endicott, Claire's father and Grimshaw's employer, is at the moment) is impassable on account of rock faces and muskeg. As a matter of fact, a long, precipitous rapid could not flow through a muskeg. The walls of the river were high and rocky, and any rock can be scaled or walked around. But the story must go on; hence this mythical screen cutting the castaways off from their kind. And in the book it is three months before an aeroplane can reach them.

Miracles now happen thick and fast. The accomplishment of the first evening is a mere nothing to this superwoodsman, who makes errors in woodlore discreditable to a boy scout. After supper on the first full day in camp, Grimshaw attacks a bull moose of 1,000 pounds weight and actually succeeds in drawing blood by striking it on the neck with his deer-rib knife. The bull is infuriated, as it has every right to be, strikes the man with its "fore-paws," knocks him down and jumps on him. An ordinary moose with hard, sharp hoofs would certainly have killed him; but this one, doubtless because equipped by the author with "paws," only succeeds in giving him "a bruise or two" which cause him no trouble. Claire, witnessing the first part of this unequal combat, leaps on the animal's back and "paralyzes" it by thrusting her wooden, stone-tipped spear through its spine, a moose's spine being about as soft as reinforced concrete sewer-pipe. The beast was possibly paralyzed with astonishment, went into hysteria and suffered a nervous breakdown. Anyway, Grimshaw kills it—with the deer-rib. There were two bull moose when Grimshaw came up, but the author makes a concession to realism by telling us that "the other one got away." Hardly less wonderful is the episode of a later day when Grimshaw kills a caribou by sticking a spear into her rump.

Of all the necessities, conveniences and sheer luxuries manufactured by the marvellous Grimshaw, it must be remembered that most of them were the products of the first six days' toil. He worked very hard. On the second full day in camp, for instance, he got breakfast of berries and bannocks made of parched bulrush bulbs pounded between stones into flour, and broiled moose meat; rewashed the heavy-haired skin, and laid it out for scraping; split the moosehead and saved the brains; washed and stretched the intestines for fish lines; dug out the precious white sinew along the spine; found the prow of his boat with some iron on it; made wooden, stone-tipped tongs to handle hot metal; made a stone hammer; made a kiln; made charcoal in the kiln; made a forge of stone, chinked with clay; made a bellows for the forge out of moose-hide; made a leg-bone into a draft conductor; got two slabs of tamarack; charred the slabs; resmoked the moose-hide over the fire, dressing it with a mixture of fish-fat and brains; drilled holes through the slabs; fixed leg-bone to slat; fitted and sewed discs of moose-hide; finished bellows and forge; made another kiln of charcoal; from the iron he made a chisel, a knife, an axehead, two sewing-awls and a spearhead. Then he called it a day, and laid off!

About two weeks after landing they had plenty of time to build a fine, large log-house, whitewashed and decorated, divided into rooms, having windows, a planed floor, furniture, a brick chimney and bake-oven, and a fireplace of glazed tiles. They possessed two iron table knives, forks and spoons of bone, a razor made from a single "medium-sized" nail (presumably a wire nail), cups, saucers and plates of glazed earthenware ornamented with colored designs, storage crocks, pails and tubs, wash basins, candles, curtains and rugs, willow chairs, tooth brushes, scented toilet soap, scissors, and the following articles all of solid gold: a comb, hair pins, buttons, a ring and a frying pan—the last of which is made out to be a *useful* cooking implement. In the third month preparations for winter were so complete that time hung heavily upon their hands, and one wonders why they did not make a Mah Jongg set, or construct a radio and get the news from home, or even send a message to Dad, seven miles away, telling him where they were.

"In all this world I don't suppose a man and a woman have ever been thrown together as we've been thrown together in this wilderness," remarks Claire, and I cannot help agreeing with her that the author did throw his characters together somewhat heedlessly. He calls their life "a splendid crudity," and spoke more truly than he knew. For within nine days the girl, who had probably never even dressed herself, had become an expert cook, dressmaker, archer, hunter and woodsman. Her first attempt at sewing resulted in the satisfactory cutting-out and making of garments. She eats birch-buds in the fall, though they grow only in spring. She put a fish in a jack-pine to protect it from mink, marten and wolverine, whereas all of them can climb and the marten *lives* in trees. But she was a greenhorn and can be excused for her author's faults.

With Grimshaw the case is different. "By instinct and training a woodsman...he preferred to remember only his woodcraft." The trouble is that he remembers it wrongly so much of the time! Thus, Stringer gravely assures us that he found and used swamp-elm, box-elder, Canada-balsam, wild plums, wild rice, elk, maskalonge, ironwood and cedar, none of which are to be found in that part of Canada—the last three being beyond the margin of possibility by several hundred miles. For the author has fixed his latitude by the introduction of a vast herd of 10,000 to 15,000 caribou, and these are only to be found in these numbers on the Barrens and in the forest at their southern extremity. If Stringer had limited his caribou herd to ten or twelve animals we might suppose they were woodland caribou, which go farther south, but even then most of these items would be beyond the geographical limits. Further-more, he speaks of "partridge *and* Canada grouse," evidently ignorant of the fact that the two names are synonymous. His famous woodsman loses his companion in a swamp, notes her steps going in, and goes home thinking she is dead—*without circling the swamp to pick up any out trail*, which any second-rate woodsman would have done. Of course she did emerge on the other side of the swamp. Ignorant of woodlore as he was, Grimshaw might have been sure that Stringer could not afford to spoil the story by letting her die.

After that revelation I am almost ashamed to mention other lapses, such as Claire's coming on a "slashing" in the primeval forest, where no man had been to cut it. A slain bear is disembowelled first, though the custom is to skin the animal first so that the hide will be kept clean. He does not seem to know that spruce grows in swamps. He refers to a "tanned" jacket as "rawhide." He calls the same beast an elk and a caribou alternately, and knotted tamarack poles turn into hemlock by the same carelessness of pen. And the author's reiterated contention that salt and green vegetables are essential to life is groundless.

"Stretching it" used to be a synonym for the kind of fiction this author has fabricated, and a literal case of it occurs in what the castaways made out of the original moose-hide. It is an elastic substance, but could hardly be "stretched" to cover more than half of the articles made, which include a "knee-length," two-piece suite for Claire, a two-piece suit for Grimshaw "with trousers that reached almost to his moccasin tops," moccasins for both with double-ply soles, thongs for rabbit snares, withes and binding-strings for tying clothing, strings for forge tongs, the whole bellows-cover, strings for two bows and sundry fish lines. The same tendency to stretch is found in Grimshaw's hair which, a month after landing, has grown "half-way to his shoulders." This feat will enable him to earn his living henceforth with the Seven Sutherland Sisters, for since the appearance of Stringer's book he will have to give up his old profession. In spite of his miracles, no one would hire him as assistant guide after reading of his ignorance of elementary woodlore. His gormandizing in itself is disgusting, for we learn that four days after getting "several hundred pounds" of meat from the moose, he and Claire are eating the last of it.

Yet I have a tender spot for him. I see him on that third day clad only in willow sticks—the leaves must all have withered and blown away by that time—standing before his hot forge while the summer sun blistered his skin. The black-flies and mosquitoes would be all over his body having a regular Christmas dinner. The author does not tell us so, but I know the North. The sparks were flying out from the forge and burning him dreadfully. Oh! Why did not the author "stretch" the moose-skin far enough to make a blacksmith's apron for him? I see him dancing around bare-footed on the hot rocks, burned and blistered all over; and the girl blowing the bellows, and forcing more heat at him. And I am very sorry for poor, ignorant, wonder-working Grimshaw.

But, while they cannot have any respect for the hero, Canadians owe a boundless debt to Mr. Stringer. They have writhed for years under the misrepresentations of English and American authors, who have written absurd tales purporting to depict life in the Canadian woods. There was only one way to stop it: to tell such a "whopper" as to elevate the myth to a place among the great imaginative classics of the world. Stringer has done that. He has "stretched" credence till it burst asunder and his imagination soared to the heights of the divinely unbelievable. It is a matter for national pride that one of our native authors has made two people "disappear" down a rapid as Lewis Carroll took Alice down the rabbit-hole, has made his hero slay a moose with the rib of a deer as an earlier fighter slew a thousand Philistines with the jaw-bone of an ass—has, in short, achieved a *tour de force* in that superlative kind of untruth we love under the name of fairy-story, and, at the same time, has erected a monument of unconscious humor. I hereby tender the country's thanks to Arthur Stringingus.

Man, Bytes, Dog

James Gorman

Many people have asked me about the Cairn Terrier. How about memory, they want to know. Is it I.B.M.-compatible? Why didn't I get the I.B.M. itself, or a Kaypro, Compaq, or Macintosh? I think the best way to answer these questions is to look at the Macintosh and the Cairn head on. I almost did buy the Macintosh. It has terrific graphics, good word-processing capabilities, and the mouse. But in the end I decided on the Cairn, and I think I made the right decision.

Let's start out with the basics:

MACINTOSH:
Weight (without printer): 20 lbs.
Memory (RAM): 128K
Price (with printer): $3,090

CAIRN TERRIER:
Weight (without printer): 14 lbs.
Memory (RAM): Some
Price (without printer): $250

Just on the basis of price and weight, the choice is obvious. Another plus is that the Cairn Terrier comes in one unit. No printer is necessary, or useful. And—this was a big attraction to me—there is no user's manual.

Here are some of the other qualities I found put the Cairn out ahead of the Macintosh:

PORTABILITY: To give you a better idea of size, Toto in "The Wizard of Oz" was a Cairn Terrier. So you can see that if the young Judy Garland was able to carry Toto around in that little picnic basket, you will have no trouble at all moving your Cairn from place to place. For short trips it will move under its own power. The Macintosh will not.

RELIABILITY: In five to ten years, I am sure, the Macintosh will be superseded by a new model, like the Delicious or the Granny Smith. The Cairn Terrier, on the other hand, has held its share of the market with only minor modifications for hundreds of years. In the short term, Cairns seldom need servicing, apart from shots and the odd worming, and most function without interruption during electrical storms.

COMPATIBILITY: Cairn Terriers get along with everyone. And for communications with any other dog, of any breed, within a radius of three miles, no additional hardware is necessary. All dogs share a common operating system.

SOFTWARE: The Cairn will run three standard programs, SIT, COME, and NO, and whatever else you create. It is true that, being microcanine, the Cairn is limited here, but it does load the programs instantaneously. No disk drives. No tapes.

Admittedly, these are peripheral advantages. The real comparison has to be on the basis of capabilities. What can the Macintosh and Cairn do? Let's start on the Macintosh's turf—income-tax preparation, recipe storage, graphics, and astrophysics problems:

	Taxes	Recipes	Graphics	Astrophysics
Macintosh	yes	yes	yes	yes
Cairn	no	no	no	no

At first glance it looks bad for the Cairn. But it's important to look beneath the surface with this kind of chart. If you yourself are leaning toward the Macintosh, ask yourself these questions: Do you want to do your own income taxes? Do you want to type all your recipes into a computer? In your graph, what would you put on the x axis? The y axis? Do you have any astrophysics problems you want solved?

Then consider the Cairn's specialties: playing fetch and tug-of-war, licking your face, and chasing foxes out of rock cairns (eponymously). Note that no software is necessary. All these functions are part of the operating system:

	Fetch	Tug-of-War	Face	Foxes
Cairn	yes	yes	yes	yes
Macintosh	no	no	no	no

Another point to keep in mind is that computers, even the Macintosh, only do what you tell them to do. Cairns perform their functions all on their own. Here are some of the additional capabilities that I discovered once I got the Cairn home and housebroken:

WORD PROCESSING: Remarkably, the Cairn seems to understand every word I say. He has a nice way of pricking up his ears at words like "out" or "ball." He also has highly tuned voice-recognition.

EDUCATION: The Cairn provides children with hands-on experience at an early age, contributing to social interaction, crawling ability, and language skills. At age one, my daughter could say "Sit," "Come," and "No."

CLEANING: This function was a pleasant surprise. But of course cleaning up around the cave is one of the reasons dogs were developed in the first place. Users with young (below age two) children will still find this function useful. The Cairn Terrier cleans the floor, spoons, bib, and baby, and has an unerring ability to distinguish strained peas from ears, nose, and fingers.

PSYCHOTHERAPY: Here the Cairn really shines. And remember, therapy is something that computers have tried. There is a program that makes the computer ask you questions when you tell it your problems. You say, "I'm afraid of foxes." The computer says, "You're afraid of foxes?"

The Cairn won't give you that kind of echo. Like Freudian analysts, Cairns are mercifully silent; unlike Freudians, they are infinitely sympathetic. I've found that the Cairn will share, in a nonjudgmental fashion, disappointments, joys, and frustrations. And you don't have to know BASIC.

This last capability is related to the Cairn's strongest point, which was the final deciding factor in my decision against the Macintosh—user friendliness. On this criterion, there is simply no comparison. The Cairn Terrier is the essence of user-friendliness. It has fur, it doesn't flicker when you look at it, and it wags its tail.

TERMS and TOPICS

TERMS

1. **Vocabulary, Section V:** abjured, accoutrements, affiliation, altercations, amiable, anomaly, archetype, austerity, blustering, boisterous, cater, consortium, contumely, dallying, decorum, denigration, deranged, derogated, dilatoriness, disparaging, diversion, divested, entropy, eponymously, err, garrulous, gormandizing, immemorial, incarcerated, indomitable, ineptitude, lamentable, lapse, maundering, mavericks, mundane, noxious, parsimony, pettifoggery, plaintive, posits, precarious, predisposing, pristine, propounder, purporting, reiterated, revel, reverting, risible, scoff, sundry, superseded, sybil, tour de force, tyranny, unencumbered, unfettered, unostentatious, unpalatable, verisimilitude, veritable, wrangle

2. *Meiosis* (see the introduction to this section) and *litotes* (see "A Note to the Reader"), two forms of understatement, are also kinds of *irony* (see Terms, section II). Is *hyperbole* (overstatement, exaggeration) also a kind of irony? What is *paresis*?

3. Differentiate among the terms in each of the following groups: (a) witty, comic, humorous; (b) caricature, burlesque, parody, travesty, satire, lampoon; (c) adage, aphorism, axiom epigram, maxim, motto, proverb, saw, saying.

4. Find out the meanings of *spoonerism* and *malapropism* and record several examples of each. Why are spoonerisms and malapropisms funny, whereas ordinary solecisms usually are not?

5. *Invective* Direct verbal abuse; vituperation. Explain the difference between invective and sarcasm. Can invective be called a kind of *satire*?

6. *Pun* Wordplay that depends on a word's having two different meanings or on two words having similar sounds but different meanings. For example, one could say of inflation that "it never reigns but it poors." Consult a good dictionary or glossary of literary terms to find out about the various kinds of puns. Puns are usually considered a product of wit; but wit is not always humorous. Are puns always humorous? A pun is a figure of speech. Can a pun also be a kind of *allusion* (see "A Note to the Reader")?

7. What do the terms *pacing* and *cadence* mean when applied to prose? Are they just other words for *rhythm* (see "A Note to the Reader"), or do they rather refer to certain *features* of rhythm?

TOPICS: On Individual Essays

ERIKA RITTER "Bicycles"

1. Is this piece meant merely to amuse? Or is Ritter using humour to score a point or few? If it is satiric, is it narrowly aimed, or more like scatter-shot? Does its world of allusions—to designer sweatbands, tofu, Perrier, and so on—make it a comedy of middle-class fads? What are some of her other allusions? What is Kryptonite? What does *upscale* mean? What is the point of the terms "Hippie Scene Era," "post-Meanderthal," and "mid-Plastic Scene Era"?

2. Is this essay a "wistful fantasy"? If so, or partly so, what prompts the wistfulness? What is the point of the three short opening paragraphs? Is their implication borne out by the rest of the piece? Does Ritter mean that bicycles are "childish things"? Is she focusing on a contrast between past and present, or between adults and children? Compare what she is saying in this regard with other essays in this book, for example Fisher and White (section I).

3. Write a short essay in which you personify or animate some familiar object, as Ritter does with bicycles. Does such a technique automatically lead to humour?

4. Write an essay on the proposition "Inflation is good only for the bicycle industry."

CALVIN TRILLIN   *"Literally"*

1. Does Trillin's sketch have any serious purpose, or is it purely a *jeu d'esprit*? Do you believe that something even a little like this actually happened, or do you think Trillin is making up the whole thing? Do some of the instances of verbal confusion he describes seem more likely than others?

2. The word *literally* is often used when *figuratively* would be correct. For example someone says, "He literally blew his top!" Unless the *he* in question is Mt. St. Helens or its like, this should be something like "Figuratively speaking, he blew his top." Is Trillin perhaps satirizing this colloquial tendency? That is, one could say of a diligent farmer, "He literally makes hay while the sun shines," and mean it—literally. Would it also be true figuratively?

3. Metaphors are much more common in our language than most people might think. Analyze your own everyday speech or something informal you've recently written (a letter?) for metaphors you've used without consciously realizing you were being metaphorical. If you refer to the *leg* of a table or an *arm* of the sea, are you being metaphorical? Is a dead metaphor nevertheless still a metaphor? Bring some dead or moribund metaphors back to life by using them in fresh ways.

4. From various reference books, draw up a list of metaphorical aphorisms, proverbs, saws, even appropriate clichés and slang expressions. Then create a narrative context in which several of them can be intended or interpreted literally instead of (or as well as) figuratively. Are you necessarily limited to rural or nature-oriented expressions? Why does Trillin choose that kind?

STEPHEN LEACOCK   *"A, B, and C: The Human Element in Mathematics"*

1. In the third paragraph from the end Leacock splits an infinitive ("to no longer find"). Is this necessary?

2. Point out some instances of wordplay in Leacock's essay.

3. By means of a humorous excess of imagination, Leacock makes fun of the apparent lack of imagination of those who set mathematical problems. Write a brief essay satirizing some similar unimaginativeness that you find in one of your textbooks. Or write a sketch in which, like Leacock, you personify some abstract concepts or labels—perhaps some other mathematical concepts, or the symbols of some elements or chemicals, or a few acronyms, or even punctuation marks. Use your imagination.

4. Retell some familiar fable or fairy tale in words of one syllable. Or write a narrative or descriptive paragraph of 100-200 words using only monosyllables. Try to keep it from sounding artificial.

5. Write an essay on one of the following topics: "The Human Element in Concrete Design," "The Human Element in F# Minor," "The Human Element in Cobalt Blue," "The Human Element in Garbage."

URSULA K. LE GUIN   *"Some Approaches to the Problem of the Shortage of Time"*

1. Is Le Guin's real subject a sort of psychological ecology, the common human feeling that there aren't enough hours in the day to accomplish what one wants to do? Or is time merely the agency by which to parody something else?

2. Is Le Guin parodying the "modelling" done by scientists—especially social scientists—in their attempts to analyze or account for a set of phenomena?

3. Is she satirizing anything or anyone, or just having fun? Is she mocking science? or economists who set up competing theories? or the human tendency to seek or accept answers even if they don't make sense, or to climb aboard social or scientific bandwagons? or the lack of logic in human thought?

4. How does Le Guin establish the illusion of seriousness? Does she ever break that illusion?

5. The book this work comes from is subtitled *Short Stories by Ursula K. Le Guin.* How can it be thought of as a "story"? Should we have put it in section VI, "Choosing a Form"? Would you have read it any differently if we had? Or if we'd put it in section II, or III, or IV?

JAMES THURBER   *"The Trouble with Man Is Man"*

1. Identify the allusion at the end of Thurber's first paragraph.

2. What is the serious observation underlying all the verbal play in Thurber's essay?

3. Can you think of any other terms that Thurber could have cited? (Would *slothful* be a fair addition?) Has contemporary slang added, as Thurber predicts it will, to the "animalistic vocabulary of disparagement"? You may want to write a brief essay expanding on what Thurber has to say.

4. Is Thurber being fair? What are the origins of some of the terms he criticizes? He cites ten of the "comparatively laudatory phrases about other animals"—can you think of any more? Could you write an opposing argument, or is he right about the large imbalance?

5. Thurber once said, during an interview, that "The wit makes fun of other persons; the satirist makes fun of the world; the humorist makes fun of himself." Do you agree?

6. Write a brief essay or report on some other common family of metaphors or other associative terms that run through English slang and cliché and proverbs. Perhaps try other elements of nature, or food, or nautical terminology. You may want to consult not only standard dictionaries, but also dictionaries of proverbs, and of similes, and especially one or more of the dictionaries of slang compiled by Eric Partridge.

WALTER MURDOCH   "On Pioneering"

1. Is Murdoch's title at first partly misleading? How long was it before you realized how broadly it applies?

2. Have you recently suffered an affliction similar to Murdoch's "odeshock"? *Adshock*, perhaps, from perusing glossy magazines or spending an evening watching television? Or *edshock*, from reading too many Letters to the Editor or from overexposure to Educationists' jargon? Or *idshock*, from listening to some fanatically Freudian friends? Using Murdoch's essay as a model, write a short essay satirizing something of this sort. You may wish, like Murdoch, to delay your full thesis until near the end.

3. Murdoch ends by turning his satire into a serious statement about everyday human beings. Write a short essay praising some similarly "unhonoured and unsung" people from everyday life—perhaps streetcar conductors? (See MacLennan, section I.) Perhaps you would also like to try your hand at composing an ode to them.

WILLIAM ARTHUR DEACON   "What a Canadian Has Done for Canada"

1. Why is Deacon's essay funny?

2. Compare Deacon's essay to Mark Twain's essay on "Fenimore Cooper's Literary Offenses." Do you think Deacon is indebted to Twain? Is his tone different from Twain's?

3. Compare Deacon's reviewing method with that of one or more of Kael, Cooper, and Woolf. Is his piece, strictly speaking, a "review" at all?

4. Should real settings be represented realistically in fiction? Investigate a novel or story set in or near the place where you live: does it represent scenes accurately? What does *accurately* mean in this context? To what degree should such authenticity be expected or insisted on? Compare film: many films are shot, say, in Vancouver or Toronto, but purport to be taking place in Seattle, St. Louis, New York, and so on: does this matter aesthetically? or in some other way? (You might want to consult Pierre Berton's 1975 book *Hollywood's Canada*.)

5. To what degree is Deacon attacking not so much a book as the colonized mind? How do stereotypes ("the wilderness," etc.) serve a political purpose?

6. Write an amusingly critical essay on a book or film in order to expose stereotypes in it.

JAMES GORMAN   "Man, Bytes, Dog"

1. Is the allusiveness of the title in any way functional, or is it just witty, amusing?

2. This piece is a model of one kind of comparison-and-contrast essay, or report, in which the overall purpose is to demonstrate the superiority of one thing over one or more other similar things. The seemingly absurd disparity between the two things Gorman is comparing, however, suggests that his main purpose is to entertain. But see if you can construct a serious thesis statement that would fit this piece. Is Gorman indulging in satire? If so, does he possibly have more than one target?

3. Write a humorous comparative evaluation of two widely different kinds of things—much more different than the proverbial apples and oranges or bananas, each of which is a fruit,

after all. Compare peanut butter with a lawnmower, a grandmother with a guitar, a Shakespeare sonnet with a sports car, a...but you can think up your own unlikely pairing. Does the comparison lead you to any serious implications about one or both of your items? Devise an inventive title for your essay.

TOPICS: General and Comparative

1. How do writers of humour establish and control a desired tone? Point out examples in the essays in this section. How would you characterize the tone of each? How soon does the tone of each essay become clear?

2. How do other writers in this book use humorous techniques or establish an ironic frame of reference? Consider for example the ironic understatement of MacLennan's essay (section I), the puns in the essays by Haig-Brown (section I) and Colombo (section VI), the exaggerated punctuation at the beginning of Lewis Thomas's essay in section VI, Frayn's use of parodic form (section VI), the tone of the essays by Dylan Thomas, White, and Forster (section I), Lane (section II), Glenn Gould and Morgan (section III), and Hornyansky (section VI), the irony and sarcasm in the essays by Zinsser (section III), Mitford, and Atwood (section IV). In what way might Davenport's essay (section II) be considered humorous?

3. A common theory of humour claims that it depends on *incongruity* of some kind. Test this idea against each of the essays in this section. Consider for example Ritter's exaggeration, Leacock's absurdly reductive literal-mindedness, Le Guin's poker-faced tone, Gorman's understatement. In what way are puns and irony examples of incongruity? Can you suggest any other constant or frequent ingredients of humour?

4. To what extent is humour culturally, economically, or otherwise biased? Consider for example the essays by Deacon and Ritter. Does some humour depend on intellectual or social differences?

5. Note that much humour depends to some degree on language as subject matter. Does Trillin's essay—whether it has any overtly serious purpose or not—make you think about some of the oddities of our language, or of the way we use it? Thurber's essay focusses on a peculiarity of the way we use English. Compare Trillin's and Murdoch's attitudes toward language with those of Galbraith (section IV), Hornyansky, Cooper, and Stein (section VI).

6. How do people respond to humour? Can one take any of the essays in this section *literally*? How do you recognize irony? Why is much humour not simply dismissed as "lying"?

7. Consider humour as a weapon. In his book *Writing Well*, Zinsser says that "Humor is the secret weapon of the nonfiction writer. It is secret because so few writers realize that it is often their best tool—sometimes their only tool—for making an important point" (p. 158). Why is humour (satire, jokes, cartoons) a way of dealing—even from inside—with a society that, like the one Brink describes in section III, "is built upon the lie"? Is Zinsser in his own essay (section III) using satire and irony in that way? What other writers in this book use humour to make serious and important points?

8. Compare Leacock's use of caricature with that of Dylan Thomas (section I) or Lane (section II). Compare it with the creation or rendition of *character* in the pieces by Fisher and Mukherjee (section I).

VI

Choosing a Form

The nine examples in this last section constitute a varied group. By turns expository and argumentative, humorous and narrative, they reveal the virtues (some would say vices) of a number of stylistic idiosyncrasies, and they therefore draw attention to the personality of literary form. Writing is not a mechanical act but a practised art, and the skilled writer to a degree invents a way into a new subject, breaking standard rules of order and syntax, developing other standards, honing fresh combinations of words and fresh ways to communicate. This observation does not mean that standards are pointless, that mechanics do not matter, or that every pretense at style should be tolerated. Indeed, Hornyansky's essay reads as a powerful tribute to the meanings that people should remember to respect in the words they use. Yet it is by no means stylistically staid. In method and in intent, it champions clarity and vigour together.

Other approaches to language and usage, possibly less conventional but not intrinsically more vital, emerge in the essays by Colombo, Stein, Frayn, Cooper and Arlen. Colombo cleverly defines form; Hornyansky discusses it. Frayn plays with it, both musically and visually, in the process of writing what starts out to be a film review (what does it end up as?). Cooper demonstrates how political it can be. Kingston and MacEwen probe the further reaches of the essay form by putting what they have to say in the shape of fable and story. Thomas wittily demonstrates the virtues of punctuation; and the concrete poems that Colombo examines emphasize the power that language can have when people actually see words—as visual objects—as well as when they decode, by the ordinary process we call "reading," what words more conventionally have to say. (A novelist once asked one of us if the word *castle* would be as interesting if it had no *t* in it; for him, it wouldn't, for lodged visually in the *t* were the crenellated walls and turrets of the castles of his imagination.)

And in Stein's lecture and Arlen's reflections on, or of, the medium of television there sounds another inflection of the art of communication: they rely heavily for their meaning on cadence and oral association. The reader of these essays has to think aurally. Voice matters. And the page, in a curious way, intervenes.

Everyone knows that words, whether lodged on the page or freed from it in some sort of utterance, have the capacity to convey meaning. But good writers also know that words are not the sole agency for conveying meaning, that good writing often borrows from other modes of expression for some of its finest effects. Music is one such mode, and there are also the visual arts, including film; and there is even mathematics. How the borrowing takes place is another question. It has become a commonplace for critics to praise "musical" and "cinematic" and "visual" literary styles—though it is not always easy to know what they mean. Or to recognize the criteria that elicit their praise. For example, critics laud rhythmic prose—and in this might be praising "musicality"—but they condemn overly apparent metrical patterns and disconcertingly obvious rhymes. Not all sound patterns prove laudable. Clearly it is the intrusiveness that bothers the critics, not the rhythm per se. They are uneasy whenever any single pattern of sound or structure takes over; they will be equally bothered by clusters of words ending in *-tion*, by strings of prepositional phrases, by monotonously similar sentence lengths, and by excessive alliteration. A good writer, however, might still be able to take any one of these flaws and turn it, in a special context, into a stylistic strength.

Music has long been an obvious analogy for writers and critics to use. It has led them to think of rhythm as a product of movement and sound, providing ways to talk about the aural effects of language and ways to produce these effects on the page. More recently, film has provided a related analogy, one that adds the element of visual perspective to those of sound and movement, that transforms rhythm into a visual notion, and that makes *leitmotif*, for example, a visual as well as a musical technique. (Think of the sound patterns in Prokofiev's *Peter and the Wolf*; think of the light patterns in the film *Doctor Zhivago*.) And though there has not yet appeared a "scientific" ("mathematical"? Certainly not "formulaic"!) school of prose style, the division between the sciences and the art of writing is not necessarily greater than that between writing and the other arts. Science, indeed, may be among the most potent contributors to current stylistic change. Explications of entropy and quantum physics have already had some effect on literary style—most evident so far, perhaps, in interrupted, nonlinear fictional forms—and the influence might go further and deeper than many humanities-trained critics now realize.

But there remains a difficulty of interpretation and assessment. How can one validly distinguish between faddishness and creative experiment? For conservative critics there is no problem here: they see no distinction. But not many writers can accept that judgment. Casual reflection might suggest that *topic* determines *style*, and that to talk about a chaotic universe would require a kind of linguistic chaos. Yet even the essays collected here would say otherwise. Hornyansky, conservative by persuasion, is at least relaxed and idiomatic if not actually radical in style. And Stein, the most idiosyncratic stylist, is discussing what many would consider a commonplace. Possibly by refashioning the commonplace, her style freshens it as well. Possibly, too, by opting for a relatively conservative style before he innovates with form, Colombo gives an illusion of familiarity to the subject of experimental literary form.

The point is that writing depends on sound and sight and texture and movement as well as on grammar and syntax and vocabulary; the overall form an idea takes in speech and writing is as great a part of its meaning as the sum of the definitions a reader or listener attaches to a series of separate words. Good writers, knowing enough about the ordinary rules of coherent discourse to know when to break them to gain an effect, choose their form. It is not accidental. It is personal. And it is clear enough in execution to be shared.

Matters of time, taste, and fashion affect the distinctions we make among personal styles. Every writer, moreover, has to guard against defending quixotic notions and idiosyncratic styles simply on the grounds of "personality." Solipsism is not a literary virtue, if it is a virtue of any sort at all. And time often modifies the enthusiasms of fashion and taste. But over time, and transcending the individuality of style, the virtues of vitality and clarity persist. If writers begin with a subject to talk about and the intelligence to deal with it, then the two problems they face are these: how to present their subject so that it is fresh and alive, and how to make it clear. Vitality. Clarity. The trouble with an experimental style is that it often sacrifices clarity, and the trouble with a conventional style is that it often sacrifices vitality. Writers who claim, in the name of the other virtue, that they must make such sacrifices— that they can be vital only by being obscure, or be clear only by being conventional—are rationalizing, not excusing or explaining their act. Vitality and clarity are not mutually exclusive. Balance is all.

We know that poets, of all writers, squeeze the maximum of meaning from the words they bring together, which might suggest that the kind of balance they achieve could prove instructive for essayists as well. We do not ask essay-writers to be poets. Yet many of the techniques poets use, once (and by some critics still) considered out of bounds for the essayist, have become widely acceptable in prose, even praiseworthy. Puns, echoes, creative ambiguities, and the resuscitation of obscure or archaic meanings in the context of the contemporary and everyday: these are not the standard equipment of explication. Yet a stylist with a particular subject might find them appropriate. What is praiseworthy is a writer's ability to use any technical means available to make a subject clearer than it was before, to help a reader understand it better. Fiction included. Experiments, of course, are not intrinsically more valuable than standard forms. Indeed, writing obscurely on the grounds that a subject is dense and therefore requires it is as wrongheaded as assuming a difficult idea can be made simple by ignoring its complexities.

Good writers do not make such mistakes. Instead, they address the problem they are trying to solve. They neither underestimate its difficulty nor inflate it; they neither impose rigid and simplistic solutions upon it nor allow it to dissipate in clouds of generalization. They keep in mind, rather, that they must direct their words in an appropriate manner to the audience they want to reach. At the same time, they bring to their subject the range of their personal understanding and the force of their personal style. Good writers invest themselves in their words, and shape ideas the way they choose. They often make "unsafe" choices—choices that force readers to adjust their stylistic expectations. But "safe" writers often commit far more grievous assaults on the language: they uncritically adopt the evasive passive voice, as bureaucratese does; they equate length of word with height of style, and sound like a thesaurus in search of meaning; they parrot jargon in an attempt to feather themselves in the colour and prestige of the sciences; they confuse effusive writing with emotional commitment, pedantic writing with accuracy, mechanical and predictable writing with openness. Writers who follow such practices shirk their obligation to convey meaning. By contrast, good writers say what they mean and mean what they say. In the process of communicating, they call attention to the rewards to be gained, by writer and reader alike, from actually learning the craft.

Communicating through Form

John Robert Colombo

What We Mean by Form

> Form follows function.
> Content has its own shape.
> "Good form" versus "bad form".
> Form versus content.
> Manner or matter.
> Substance or style.
> Formal, informal; material, immaterial.
> Chaos, cosmos; chance, control.
> Form as a vessel; content as a liquid.
> Freedom regardless of form; the freedom to conform.
> A matter, question, problem, possibility of form.
> The necessity of form; the irrelevancy of form.
> A formula; a formlessness.
> Transcendental form; immanent form.
> "The earth was without form."

These are only a few of the phrases we regularly use when we talk about form. There are many more, but most of these concepts cancel each other (if not themselves) out. The alleged dichotomy between form and content, which is one of the hoariest of metaphysical problems, has puzzled philosophers down through the ages, and there is no reason to believe that it will ever be solved. In fact, there is no reason to believe that it is even a "problem." Perhaps it is only an issue—a platform on which you take a stand and defend it whether you actually believe in it or not. It has been argued, quite convincingly, that the words "form" and "content" have no meaning whatsoever.

One difficulty facing anyone making an inquiry into the meaning of form is that we think with words (or, at the very least, we formulate and communicate our thoughts using words to help us along). But like children with an unlimited supply of lettered blocks, we raise up immense and often shaky structures which spell out imponderables and then topple of their own weight. Some of these constructions have no obvious relation to reality and are of various orders of complexity.

At random: We can have pure forms that are antilogies, like the phrase "a formless form." We can have nonexistent things (about which we know a great deal), like "unicorns." We can have impossible things, like "phlogiston" and "sky hooks." We can have no-longer-existing things, like Napoleon I and the dodo. And we can have things like "god" and "angel" and "sin" and "grace," which may or may not have any objective meaning. Is our concept of form one of these? And if it is, which one?

No definition of "form" will be found in this essay. Everyone has his own rule-of-thumb meaning, and we all know we can recognize a single shape or a recurring pattern or an ordering principle when we see one. More general inquiries into form in reading matter are helped along not by narrowing down the concept but by expanding it as much as possible. Instead, what will be found in this essay are instances of infracted forms. Forms are not as much seen as over-seen. A form is exposed when another is imposed upon it, with a *moiré* screen. The patterned lines of such a screen, when placed over another pattern of lines, "generate" a third pattern. This is purely an optical illusion. The pattern does not exist, except perceptually, and what exists objectively are the two parents of that illusion, the two original patterns. The "third thing" is an interesting distortion, a child with a subjective existence only. This applies to many of the instances discussed in this essay.

Much modern art has the perception of pattern or the hunt for meaning as its organizing principle. As Paul Valery wrote, "I write half the poem, the reader writes the other half." There are numerous essays and books that discuss the serious arts, and the reader has only to turn to authors like Harold Rosenberg (*The Anxious Object* and *The Tradition of the New*) to fit many of these ideas into their proper perspective. But there are nooks and crannies that have not been swept clean and which, to my knowledge, have not been examined from the point of view of form and the new directions contemporary art is taking. The instances of violated forms I will be discussing are all literary and, in the main, poetic. But the inquiry could quite easily be extended to the other arts as well, music and painting and cinema in particular, and even into modern social concerns.

Art and the Environment

My starting point is that, strictly speaking, there is no content in art that is separate from the world. All art is entirely formal. By this I mean that art is an attitude to life and that the object of this attitude is life itself. To some extent, to be a human being one must be something of an artist. And to be an artist, one must work in the public, accessible world of people and their perceptions. At various times art has been other and different things. In fact, there is no single "art" but many "arts." At one point in history, art was craftsmanship and little more. The English word "art" derives from this sense of the artist as artisan or artificer. Art was something well done. At various other points in history, art (even the artist) was equated with expression, communication, madness, divine inspiration, problem-solving, information-accumulation, or what-have-you. Usually it was a number of these combined. Today it is perfectly possible for the artist to create works of art that are co-extensive with the world itself. It is, in a parallel fashion, perfectly possible for the art-fancier to react to the world as if it were a work of art itself. Was it Claes Oldenburg, the pop artist, who signed the southern-most tip of Manhattan Island, as he would a canvas, to "aesthetically claim" both this object and this way of seeing things?

With art so fully an attitude to life, everything that exists can be declared to be a work of art. Not all works are good ones, of course, but with this environmental approach as a background, it is possible to criticize one part of the ecology along aesthetic lines and retain some standard of objectivity. The Vancouver painter, Iain Baxter, photographs cityscapes and landscapes and then labels them. Bad views are marked "ART"—Aesthetically Rejected Things. Good views are stamped "ACT"—Aesthetically Claimed Things. Behind this seemingly facile gesture lies a deep and overwhelming idea: that the world itself is a single work of art. This is, at core, a religious notion. The world is not "the work of God" so much as "the artwork of God." In a small way this has been recognized with landscapes. A brilliant sunset is called "a lovely Turner", a gentle countryside "a fine Constable." Nature imitates art, as Oscar Wilde observed, but in even more fundamental a sense than he imagined.

The "deep focus" of art may thus include all reaction, since nothing is exclusive to the aesthetic experience. The American composer, John Cage, has a composition called "4′ 33″ " which is four minutes and 33 seconds of silence. He "performs" this composition at the keyboard. At the premiere, his audience was first surprised, then moved to irritation, and finally taken to a state of self-knowledge. The realization slowly dawned on those present that the random noises which accompany a musical concert in a hall—the shuffling of feet, coughing, etc.—are an accepted part of the auditory experience and can, as such, for a short while anyway, be contemplated singly.

This view, that art is co-extensive with the environment, that the artist is in a sense the "stage-manager of reality," is sometimes called Expanded Art. It is close to the positions taken by Susan Sontag, with her stress on surface value and "against interpretation"; Andy Warhol, whose Campbell's soup labels are not representational so much as presentational; and Marshall Mc-Luhan, who sees art as an anti-environment which exposes the invisible "wrap-around" of the environment. Expanded Art gives a rationale for such contemporary art movements as underground films, camp, happenings, environmental sculptures, endless paintings, interminable poems, sidewalk theatre, dance as movement, etc. Various phrases are commonly used to identify these contemporary artistic tendencies: Ecological Art, Environmental Art, Conceptual Art, Earth Art, and so on.

One of the pleasures of this new approach to art is that one can respond to a work (or a nonwork) on the simplest of levels. In fact, one's response is often joyous, and incredibly naive. It is like the nursery rhyme about the man and woman who live in Fife.

> In a cottage in Fife
> Lived a man and his wife,

365

> Who, believe me, were comical folk;
>> For, to people's surprise,
>> They both saw with their eyes,
> And their tongues moved whenever they spoke!
>> When quite fast asleep,
>> I've been told that to keep
> Their eyes open they could not contrive;
>> They walked on their feet,
>> And 'twas thought what they eat
> Helped, with drinking to keep them alive!

Reading Forwards, Backwards, Up or Down

One way in which we too are "comical folk" is that we accept all our conventions, and work within them. We seldom make fun of them, or if we do, we consider this "bad form." One convention of literacy in the Western world is that, without blinking or appearing to notice it, you are reading this page from the left-hand margin to the right-hand margin, moving from line to line in a downward direction. Why not read from right to left, as the Hebrews do? Or down rather than across, as the Chinese do? What difference does it make? Little, really, except that Westerners are inclined to "scan" the world in a similar fashion, and look at reality from left to right, from top to bottom, "placing" things in this total form. For the eye, focussed on the printed page, at least half of the movement is wasted effort. Our eyes "scan" across the page, taking in information, and then sweep back, disregarding the information that is available on the return leg of the round trip. The ancients, who read less than we do, were more concerned about this than we are, and some ancient inscriptions are carved into rock both forwards and backwards in alternate lines, just as a field is ploughed. The Greek word for "the turning of an ox" is *boustrophedon*, and boustrophedonic writing is prose which appears in this backwards-and-forwards, continuous fashion. Strictly speaking, alternate "return" lines should appear in a second set of characters in which the actual letter-forms are reversed. (Many of these matters are discussed in Herbert Spencer's *The Visible Word* [London: Lund Humphries, 1968].) But making do with the standard set of characters, here are the first four lines of Lincoln's "Gettysburg Address" in a boustrophedonic treatment.

> Fourscore and seven years ago our fathers brought forth
> dna ytrebil ni deviecnoc noitan wen a tnenitnoc siht no
> dedicated to the proposition that all men are created
> gnitset raw livic taerg a ni degagne era ew woN .lauqe

Why resurrect a form of writing as weird as boustrophedon? No one practises it today. Since it was once a form of writing, at variance with our own practice, why not reuse it if it can be made to serve a useful purpose? What follows is a found poem (a free-verse arrangement of a passage of someone else's prose) that has been given a semi-boustrophedonic treat-ment—"semi" because, given the difficulty the eye encounters when forced to read a line backwards, the line has been arranged to be read in the standard way but with the words in the backwards order. Thus only the word order is boustrophedonic. One hold-over of this principle today is the Hungarian custom of referring to an individual by his last name first. (In English, this is customary only with alphabetical listings.) Thus, in Hungarian, the former Prime Minister of Canada is "Diefenbaker John." The found poem "Budapest" grew out of this convention.

BUDAPEST
day present the to time that from
from that time to the present day
capital hungarian the of record the
the record of the hungarian capital
advance uninterrupted of one been has
has been one of uninterrupted advance
as such externals in merely not
not merely in externals such as
town the of reconstruction the slums of removal the
the removal of slums the reconstruction of the town
trade and industry communications of development the
the development of communications industry and trade
buildings public important of erection the and
and the erection of important public buildings
elevation physical and moral mental the in also but
but also in the mental moral and physical elevation
inhabitants the of
of the inhabitants
gain important another besides
besides another important gain
statesman hungarian the of view of point the from
from the point of view of the hungarian statesman
improvement and increase progressive the namely
namely the progressive increase and improvement
population the of element magyar the of status of
of status of the magyar element of the population

The text of "Budapest" was given in—or taken from—the Eleventh Edi-tion of the *Encyclopaedia Britannica*. The same 1911 edition supplies texts for the four found poems that follow. (They form part of a group, called *The Great Cities of Antiquity*, which treats each of 76 ancient cities mentioned in the *E.B.* in a characteristic style.) What is more appropriate for the capital of Japan than a (found) haiku?

KIOTO

Clear water
ripples everywhere
throughout the city.

For such a picturesque place as the capital of Thailand, only a delicate and romantic form like the (found) triolet would do.

BANGKOK

The climate has without a doubt
In occupation of Siam
Becoming king it was chosen
The climate has without a doubt
It was seized by the warrior
Become hotter and less humid
The climate has without a doubt
In occupation of Siam

Since the ancient capital of Persia, now Iran, is a closed book, archaeologically and historically, only a short poem is necessary. The entry in the *E.B.* begins and ends with the two words which open and close this brief poem. Luckily they happen to be evocative words.

PERSEPOLIS

Persepolis
ruins.

Two words are used to recreate the rise and fall of Persepolis, and only two words, united in a single graphic design, are needed to dramatize the fate of Pompeii in 79 A.D. This poem is both "found" and "concrete," and shows how Expanded Art can combine two modes of poetry and two types of art—graphics and poetry—to make a singleness of effect. (For those unused to "reading" this kind of poetry, the "X" might be seen as lava.)

POMPEII
X
VES
UVIUS
POMPEII
XXXXXXXXX

Oddities of Shape

One difference between prose and poetry is that prose runs to the edge of the page and poetry does not. Purely typographical considerations play a large role in our appreciation of a passage of writing, and poets have occasionally given their poems typographical "shapes" consistent with the subjects or themes of their poems. The original inspiration might be derived from inscriptions in books and on monuments. "Emblematic poems" were popular in the late-sixteenth century, and the practice has persisted as a minor genre until our time. "Shaped whimseys" were very popular in the late-nineteenth century, and Carolyn Wells has collected a number of these in *A Whimsey Anthology* (New York: Charles Scribner's Sons, 1906). The ones reproduced here are oddities, perhaps, but Stéphane Mallarmé and Apollinaire both took the conceit and raised it from a curiosity to a cultural product. George Herbert, John Donne, Dylan Thomas, Edward Lear, John Hollander—all have tried their hand at "Shaped poems." "The Wine Glass" is based on Proverbs xxiii: 29-30.

                    THE WINE GLASS
          Who hath woe? Who hath sorrow? Who
            hath contentions? Who hath wounds
              without cause?   Who hath redness
                of eyes? They that tarry long
                  at   the   wine!   They   that
                    go   to   seek   mixed   wine!
                  Look   not   thou   upon   the
                    wine   when   it   is   red,
                      when it giveth
                        its colour
                          in the
                           cup,
                          when it
                        moveth itself
                          aright.
                            At
                         the last it
                    biteth like a serpent
              and stingeth like an adder!

"The Wine Glass" is a kind of collaboration between the author of Proverbs (said to be Solomon himself) and the anonymous nineteenth-century poet or designer or scribe who first gave the passage its picturesque shape. A characteristic of "Shaped poetry" is that it is impossible to read such poems without experiencing both a perception and an apperception. The reader experiences both the poem and his consciousness of experiencing the poem. Such experiments encourage self-awareness, self-consciousness. This response is close to the Distancing Effect discussed by the German playwright, Bertolt Brecht.

The following poem is an original, rhymed composition set in the shape of a sinister creature. A Stegomyia is a genus of mosquito, one variety of which carries Yellow Fever. Certainly the point of "The Stegomyia" is a moralistic one: Wash up, kiddies, or you will suffer!

THE STEGOMYIA

I
t
s

b
i
l
l

is
long
and wick-
ed, and
is
filled
with deadly

juice   and   you
needn't try   to dodge   it   for   it
won't   be   any use;

it
will
chase
you up
and catch
you and
with woe will
fill your cup;
oh, the steg-
omyia'll get
you if you
don't clean
up
!

Even if "Avoirdupois" is not strictly a poem, it is a fine example of the way in which an argument can be typographically visualized and given a concrete form. The poem could, as well, be presented orally. A stand-up comedian would give each line a different vocal emphasis—the lightness of the ashes, the monstrous size of the bill. The form seems to mirror the content. Or is it *vice versa*?

AVOIRDUPOIS

The length of this line indicates the ton of coal as dug by the miner.
This one indicates the ton shipped to the dealer.
The small dealer gets a ton like this.
This is the one you pay for.
This is what you get.
The residue is:
Cinders and
Ashes.
And this line will give you some conception of the size of the BILL.

Tricks and Teasers

Moving into the area of the poem-as-puzzle, we have "Greetings, in Season." The poem is more than the letters of the alphabet arranged in an aesthetically pleasing pattern. Examine the anonymous composition closely and you will find that a letter is missing. Which one? The point of the poem turns on a pun that identifies the missing letter. A clue: It's a Christmas greeting. (The answer is given at the end of this essay.)

GREETINGS, IN SEASON

A B C D E
F G H I J
K M N O P
Q R S T U
V W X Y Z

During the Victorian Era, versifiers by the hundreds tried their hands at typographical extravagances like "O I C." The title, and indeed the whole poem, must be sounded phonetically. These verses have to be "worked out." As constructions, they differ from rebuses only in that a rebus actually introduces a tiny picture of what the substituted word means, whereas a typographical poem uses symbols instead of signs.

O I C

I'm in a 10der mood today
    & feel poetic, 2;
4 fun I'll just—off a line
    & send it off 2 u.

I'm sorry you've been 6 O long:
    Don't B disconsol8;
But bear your ills with 42de,
    & they won't seem so gr8.

Perhaps the most unusual novel ever written is a book called *Gadsby*, published in 1939. The author was Ernest Vincent Wright, who subtitled his work "A Story of Over 50,000 Words Without Using the Letter E." The ingenious and industrious author decided to write a work which avoided the most common letter in the English alphabet—e. He tied down the e-key on his typewriter, and avoided "the" and "ed" endings and hundreds of other everyday words and phrases. He wrote what must be the longest lipogram ever created. (A lipogram is a work so constructed that a single letter has been consistently avoided.) Imagine the problems that Wright faced. Why, even this sentence alone contains six! David Kahn, in *The Code-Breakers: The Story of Secret Writing* (London: Weidenfeld and Nicholson, 1967), goes into further details about the significance of Wright's experiment, and he reproduces the opening paragraph:

> Upon this basis I am going to show you how a bunch of bright young folks did find a champion; a man with boys and girls of his own; a man of so dominating and happy individuality that Youth is drawn to him as is a fly to a sugar bowl. It is a story about a small town. It is not a gossipy yarn; nor is it a dry, monotonous account, full of such customary "fill-ins" as "romantic moonlight casting murky shadows down a long, winding country road." Nor will it say anything about twinklings lulling distant folds; robins carolling at twilight, nor any "warm glow of lamplight" from a cabin window. No. It is an account of up-and-doing activity; a vivid portrayal of Youth as it is today; and a practical discarding of that worn-out notion that "a child don't know anything."

Works which can be read every-which-way to yield differing meanings have been dubbed "Jesuitical verses." The work that follows is the "all-around platform," and was popular in the 1860s in the United States when the Secessionists and the Abolitionists were arguing it out. For the Secessionist view, read the first column down. For the Abolitionist view, read the second column down. For the Democratic platform, read everything all together.

THE PLATFORM

(Read down or across)

Hurrah for	The old Union
Secession	Is a curse
We fight for	The Constitution
The Confederacy	Is a league with hell
We love	Free speech
The rebellion	Is treason
We glory in	A free press
Separation	Will not be tolerated
We fight not for	The negro's freedom
Reconstruction	Must be obtained
We must succeed	At every hazard
The Union	We love

We love not	The negro
We never said	Let the Union slide
We want	The Union as it was
Foreign intervention	Is played out
We cherish	The old flag
The stars and bars	Is a flaunting lie
We venerate	The habeas corpus
Southern chivalry	Is hateful
Death to	Jeff Davis
Abe Lincoln	Isn't the Government
Down with	Mob law
Law and order	Shall triumph.

From works so formed that three points of view are simultaneously meaningful, it is not much of a leap to a work with a point of view that is logically impossible. "Resolutions Passed by the Board of Councilmen, Canton, Mississippi" pops up time and time again in different places. The former premier of Ontario, Mitch Hepburn, used to tell the same tale but in terms of a jail rather than a school. Here the form of the work is a series of mutually dependent propositions. The form of the syllogism is preserved, but the spirit is violated in intent.

1. Resolved, by this Council, that we build a new Jail.
2. Resolved, that the new Jail be built out of the materials of the old Jail.
3. Resolved, that the old Jail be used until the new Jail is finished.

Juggling the Letters

Out of the twenty-six letters of the English alphabet, a million books could be constructed. Out of a half-a-dozen letters, what can be made? A word, a short phrase perhaps. With some juggling, the letters could be arranged and rearranged to make different words and phrases, different meanings. This accounts for the perpetual fascination of the anagram. An anagram is a word or phrase that has been transformed into another by the simple transposition of letters. For instance, "Evangelists" can be perversely rearranged without loss or substitution or addition of letters into "Evil's Agents."

Here are some others. "The Mona Lisa" may be altered into the following comment: "No hat, a smile."

To the anagramist, "Nova Scotia and Prince Edward Island" presents intriguing possibilities, including "The Canadian Provinces: Lands I Dread!"

Even the word "Anagrams" itself can be so treated. It becomes "Ars Magna," Latin for "Great Art."

Creating anagrams is a test of patience and wit. C. C. Bombaugh, in *Oddities and Curiosities of Words and Literature* (New York: Dover Publications, 1961), edited by Martin Gardner, takes anagrams a step further, into the area of magic squares, and writes:

This word, Time, is the only word in the English language which can be thus arranged, and the different transpositions thereof are all at the same time Latin words. These words, in English as well as in Latin, may be read either upward or downward. Their signification as Latin words is as follows: Time—fear thou; Item—likewise; Meti—to be measured; Emit—he buys.

```
T I M E
I T E M
M E T I
E M I T
```

A cousin of the anagram is the palindrome. In the anagram, the letters are reordered to create a different sense. In the palindrome, the letters are merely read backwards to repeat the same sense. This often results in such awkward English that the reader might confuse it initially with doubletalk. Take these two examples:

Trash? Even interpret Nineveh's art.
Red root put up to order.

Both sound preposterous, and as imponderable as the predictions of Nostradamus. Not all palindromes are laughable, for a few have a poetic quality that lends them memorability and has ensured their survival through the years. There is no basis for the following palindromes in the Bible, but there is a popular tradition that maintains the following conversation took place in Eden. Adam's first words to Eve were:

Madam, I'm Adam.

And Eve's reply? This too is palindromial and has been preserved:

Name no one man.

In the same fashion, Napoleon's last words—spoken in English!—are reputed to be:

Able was I ere I saw Elba.

Thousands of palindromes have been written. There is something uncanny about them, almost magical.

Concrete Poetry

"The only unfortunate thing about concrete poetry," Emmet Williams once said, "is the phrase concrete poetry. The word 'concrete' is misleading. The stress should be on the word 'poetry'." Williams is the editor of *An Anthology* of *Concrete Poetry* (New York: Something Else Press, 1967) and a world authority on the subject. Even he would balk at defining this fairly recent development in contemporary art. "The medium is the message" might well have been coined to answer the question, "What is concrete poetry?"

In any discussion of form in art, the work of the Brazilian poet Pedro Xisto is of particular interest. The two examples of his work that follow come from Xisto's *Logogrammes*, or word-forms, published in 1966.

At first glance, "Epithalamium II" looks like a corporate symbol. In fact, it is a simple poem of great subtlety. It is also quite memorable and mnemonic; once seen, it is unlikely to be soon forgotten. As well, Xisto's poem has the virtues of brevity and wit. The theme of the poem is one's interpretation of it. The "h" can represent "he" or "homo," man. The "e" can represent "Eve" or "elle." The "s" surely represents the uniting of the two figures in a forceful yet graceful way. It is also a serpent, perhaps, and is the poem "set" in the Garden of Eden? Together, the man and the woman are united in a sexual union. Do they become a she? Is there a female child of the union? Or is this another incarnation of the Eternal Feminine? Whatever the poet intended, all these (and many more) are valid readings of this simple-seeming concrete poem.

The second poem is a "logogram", and a splendid, classical one at that. The image is one of solid repose. It could be looked upon as many things, including an Art Deco design, a geometric construction, or rafters against a wall. In actual fact, the title of the poem is a dead giveaway. It is called "Zen," and this word can be traced continuously throughout the composition. Less is more.

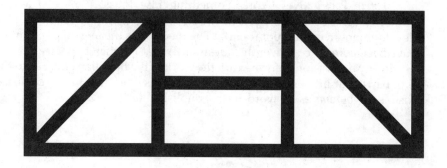

```
                    l                    e

                    o              e

              l   love

              o    e   evol    l

        love    e        o

              e   evol    l

        e   e        o

  e              l
```

* Concrete poem "Blues" by bpNichol. Used by permission of the author. (From *New Direction in Canadian Poetry*, Holt, Rinehart and Winston of Canada, Limited, 1971.)

David Kahn writes in *The Code-Breakers:*

Three-quarters of English text is "unnecessary." English could theoretically express the same things with one-quarter its present letters if it were
wholly non-redundant. A literary curiosity demonstrates graphically how
a few letters carry most of the information of a text while the others are
redundant.

DEATH AND LIFE

cur	f	w	d	dis	and	p
A sed	iend	rought	eath	ease		ain.
bles	fr	b	br	and		ag

A New Category for Artists

Today, in the West, the artist is regarded as now a craftsman, now a creator,
but seldom as a realizer. Some of the newer art forms, like film, suggest that
this new category of "realizer" should be created for the artist. In what way
is a film director a creative artist? All the elements he works with—the script,
the dialogue, the setting, the story, the actors, even the camera work—are the
contributions of other individuals, often interpretative artists of the highest
calibre. But with the *auteur,* or "author," theory, the director is the one who
gives the film its final stamp. He imposes his personality on all its parts and
makes them work together as a single whole—the artist is the "entrepreneur
of reality," whose task it is to reveal aesthetic possibilities within situations or
with objects not always of his own making.

The anthropologist Edmund Carpenter has described how the Eskimo
sculptor does not carve his stone into the shape of a seal but, by cutting away,
"releases" the seal from the stone. Chinese artists have made "natural stone
paintings" which involve finding suitable rocks and then cutting them to
reveal previously existing patterns. Perhaps the best-known Western expression of this search for a naturally satisfying form is the taste for driftwood.
This is "low art," perhaps, and appropriate for living room tables and mantles.
Found "high art" is the *objet trouvé,* the discovery of Dada that any object, taken
from its original context and placed in another, acquires new and interesting
aesthetic possibilities.

Word-plays like the ones that follow must be low on any artistic totem-
pole. But if nothing else, these one-liners are interesting examples of juggled
forms, "realized" possibilities. Placing one word within another is like inject-
ing one form into another:

PREJEWDICE

Disguising a given formal order by giving it the trappings of another period
is another way of having fun with forms. (This example comes from the first
edition of the *Encyclopaedia Britannica,* 1768.)

Miffiffippi

Making a word reflexive—that is, making it comment upon itself—can be the
operative device behind any number of word-plays:

CXNSXRSHXP

They can get quite short:
  Ha!t

They can imitate natural objects:
  mountAin

They can look pretty:
  sn[＊]w

Occasionally an innocent typo can subtly shift letters to bring home a different message:

  UNITED STATES OF AMERCIA

This is not a misspelling of "AMERICA" but a way of drawing attention to the fact that the "CIA" is a part of American life and "deforms" the very symbol of the country. Finally, finding one complete word within another is a kind of punning that is especially appropriate in an essay on Expanded Art:

  E(ART)H

So the search for form is an on-going process, and one that will never end—as long as there is a human being with an interest in art alive in the world. Man may think he imposes his "sense of form" on the world, but the chances are fifty-fifty that the world imposes its "sense of form" on him too.

[Note. The poem "Greetings, In Season" is missing the letter L.   There is no L.   Noel.]

Is Your English Destroying Your Image?

Michael Hornyansky

When I let it slip among ordinary company that I'm a professor of English, you can guess what the reaction is: "Oh-oh," they say with nervous smiles, "I'd better watch my language." No use explaining that I don't teach composition. If English professors hit the front page, or confront public awareness at all, it's not when they have had profound or brilliant ideas about literature, but when they are testily muttering that their latest crop of freshmen can neither read nor write. And the truth is, of course, that we are—we must be—concerned with language. It is the medium both of the works we study, and of our attempts to teach it. If language should decay far enough, the study of literature becomes difficult or impossible. I won't play for headlines by pretending this is the condition we have reached; but such a condition is at least imaginable, as things are going. So I worry a good deal about language, myself. And I think the most useful way to put my worries before you is to pursue that automatic reaction: "Oh-oh, I'd better watch my language."

It's a touchy area. People are as anxious about the impression their words make as they are about their clothes or their faces or their waistlines. If you catch someone in an error, he is mortified. If you suggest he doesn't speak well, you wound his vanity as sharply as if you claim he has no sense of humour. Sniping at other people's mistakes is a favourite sport of those who write letters to the *Globe and Mail*; and there are always other correspondents to jeer at the snipers. And even when there are no English teachers (official or amateur) within earshot, private citizens go on fretting over what words to use, and whether they're using them properly. I know of a group which spent hours wrangling over whether a certain person should be described as *responsible* for the task assigned to him, or whether that didn't seem to wag the finger at him needlessly. They finally settled on *accountable* instead—a word in fashion these days, but one which to my mind conveys a good deal less personal dignity and freedom than *responsible* does. That's how it often goes: the questions we're least certain about are the ones that arouse our stronger feelings. And when it comes to language, most of us are uncertain. The frequency of little check-up phrases in our normal speech—"you know? eh? like? see what I mean?"—is a symptom not so much of sloppiness, but of concern about whether we're getting through.

This is why I thought of offering some helpful hints. I don't aim to give you a lesson in grammar. Think of this chapter as an essay in linguistic psychology, not in rules. Remember my title: "Is your English destroying your image?" I put it that way not to be cute or disarming, but because that's the form our anxiety takes. I shall be asking not just what errors we make, but why we make them, and how they affect our view of each other; and after that, how to set about improving matters. To tell you that this is Right and that is Wrong (even if I had the confidence to do so) wouldn't be much help, anyway. Far better in the long run to try to understand why some things work and others don't—so we can judge for ourselves instead of carrying around a list of lapses. I say "we" because I talk for a living, and I am reminded daily of how my words can undermine rapport, or on good days virtually magic people into understanding me. I dare to advise you not because I'm a professor, but because I've been there, and I have some practical knowledge of what can go wrong and how to cure it.

If I am to write about mistakes in our use of language, I had best begin by establishing what makes a mistake—what standards to measure by. There are two possible misconceptions here. At one extreme is the idea of Correctness. Some people still hold to the notion that there is such a thing as Correct English: the King's English, possibly the Queen's, existing as a heavenly paradigm to which only educated people and professors have access. (Francophones are even more prone to think of Correct French, because they have an official Academy to act as its guardian and legislator; but as they are beginning to discover, their hopes are misplaced.) There are several reasons why this mystical notion won't do. One is that educated people—even teachers; even, heaven knows, Her Majesty—do not always speak well. How can we be certain when to follow them? Worse still, the belief that a correct pattern exists can become, in a curious way, a cause of errors: for the people who most firmly believe in the King's English are usually hazy about *what precisely it is*, and in their anxiety to be proper they lean over backwards, into slips that would not befall a more natural stance. No, the idea of Correct English has at best a social validity. By speaking like the Queen you may prove your loyalty and your place in society, but you do not exempt yourself from error. In fact there is no enduring pattern of correctness. As most people have come to realize, language changes, constantly and irresistibly—and correctness, if it's a workable idea at all, must change too. The purists are remembered as quaint defenders of the last ditch: like Jonathan Swift, rejecting the uncouth expression "mob," because all right-speaking people knew it should be *mobile vulgus*. (Swift also won a few, however. See Dwight Macdonald, *Against the American Grain*, Vintage, 1962, p. 323.) Or like the person who answers the telephone with "Hello: it is I, Clifton Webb."

At the other extreme is the notion that since language constantly changes, then anything goes—there are no rules at all, Usage is king. It will not be so easy to persuade you that this too is a misconception. The barometer of our times is set at Change. A recent letter to the *Globe* condemns the declared policy of Ontario's Minister of Education to return to the 3 R's: "[he] invites our children to take firm, confident steps backward into the future. Pity." (Ray MacLain, *Globe*, 25 Feb. 1975.) The CBC's news-readers, once modestly reliable (meaning they could be counted on to apologize for errors), have lost their supervisor of broadcast language, and now commit cheerfully such bar-barisms as "It sounds like he's going to reform." This is the age of Humpty Dumpty, who claimed that words meant what he wanted them to mean; it was simply a question of who was to be master. You will recall what happened to Humpty Dumpty. But his fragmented soul is still with us: it lives on in the third edition of Webster's *New International Dictionary* (1961), which makes no attempt to distinguish acceptable usage from colloquial, slang, or illiterate. "If it is used, it is usage": that is Webster's principle in a nutshell—and a nutshell is where it belongs. To see the enterprise mercilessly analysed, read Dwight Macdonald's patient and savage review called "The String Untuned." (Reprinted in *Against the American Grain*, p. 289.)

Those who appeal to usage as the final arbiter seem to march under the banners of Life and Progress. In fact they are making a mystique of change, supposing that since it is normal it must also be good. Happily, the letter columns of the newspaper do feature other correspondents, who realize that change may be not growth but decay, and that mere growth is not always welcome, in language as in life.

> It is fatuous (publicists please note: this word does not yet mean stout or plump) to argue that the language is undergoing positive and dynamic change in the hands of our public figures. Only fools would unreservedly maintain so.
>
> (C.C.J. Bond, *Globe*, 17 Feb. 1975)

(I expect a later correspondent observed that it wasn't their *hands* but their mouths that did the damage.) Not all change is progress. Some of it has to be resisted, and when possible reversed. If the last ditch needs defending, I'll take my place alongside Sam Johnson:

> If the changes we fear be thus irresistible, what remains but to acquiesce with silence, as in the other insurmountable distresses of humanity? It remains that we retard what we cannot repel, that we palliate what we can-not cure.
>
> (Preface to the *Dictionary*)

That final sentence, by the way, is a grand example of how to project the image of Doctor Johnson.

But I don't think the situation's quite so desperate. One can take account of a flood without drowning in it or becoming flotsam. Call me Noah. I think that even for a language in flux, certain firm criteria can be proposed. They are based on this assumption: *that language is a means of giving a precise pattern to thought and feeling, and a means of conveying that pattern to other people.* I do not claim this is the only assumption possible. Language is commonly used for several other purposes. It is used to make up for, or disguise, the absence of thought, and to mask one's feelings; and it may communicate nothing more than a soothing assurance of togetherness. But for this purpose, as politicians (and some married couples) know, almost any noise will do: there is no question of Good Usage, or Correctness. Language can also be used deliberately to deceive. Here the question is skill, not usage. An assumption more likely to mislead us is one I've already alluded to: that language is above all a badge of social position. Here usage does matter. But which usage is socially acceptable (and that is the criterion, even though it may be called "proper"; for instance, there was a time not long ago when saying *ain't* and droppin' your final g's were the signals of aristocratic talk)—that is a question that varies rapidly with time and place, so that no general criteria can be proposed. One has to play it by ear, or find a member of the desired club who knows the passwords and is willing to tell, like Nancy Mitford or Henry Higgins.

My concern, however, is language that communicates thought and feeling—the kind I am trying to use now. This is where it makes some sense to apply standards of proper, or good, usage. And the standards I propose are these three: *Clarity*, *Impact*, and *Idiom*. (Not *correctness*, as you see, but bases upon which we can decide what *is* correct, or at least what is preferable.) *Is it clear? Does it hit home? Is it English?* These are the only reasonable standards I can find; and since they apply, so far as I can see, to a language at any time, they need not be surrendered under the pressure of change.

Clarity is of course what we aim at when we want to express thoughts with cool precision: easy to talk about, hard to achieve. It will govern our choice of words, the design of our sentences and arguments. It is the standard that causes Humpty Dumpty to fall, or at least to remain babbling to himself in a private lingo: for we all should know from experience that if we use words arbitrarily, instead of in their agreed senses, we will not make contact. Clarity also governs the gradual smoothing out of inflections (that is, variations in the form of a word according to its grammatical function, like *who/whose/ whom*). Presumably it was in the interest of clarity that primitive tongues established remarkably complex systems of inflection (and of syntax generally); but as the history of our language shows, the complicated patterns that make French or German (or Latin) hard for us to learn have not proved necessary for speakers of English. Indeed, if clarity were our sole guide, we might wind up saying *he loves she*, or *you did hurt I*—in fact we're well on the way to that. But I proposed three standards, not one.

The second of them, *Impact*, is our aim when we want to persuade or impress rather than to inform; when instead of taking our cue from logicians or astronauts, we speak like witch doctors, advertising men, or poets. We know that by choosing certain words over others (not because they're more exact, but because they're fresh, arresting, expressive of likeness not essence) and by combining them in unexpected ways, we can charge our speech, and make it strike home as clarity alone would never do. We say, "John's a tiger." In point of literal fact, John is a featherless biped rather short on hair; but one simple and over-used metaphor conveys more about how he *strikes* us than would paragraphs of careful analysis. Again, however, impact by itself is not a sufficient guide. Without clarity squeezing the brakes, impact may run riot and collapse into nonsense or mumbo-jumbo—as poetry has been known to do, or advertising slogans, or slang. And there is no dull thud to compare with yesterday's impact: I mean, *lamp the frail with the solo cheater, will ya? Bro-ther, she just don't connect.* And neither do you, I imagine—though thirty years ago you would have followed me without trouble.

The mention of slang brings us at once to my third criterion, the tricky one: *Idiom*. I might have defined idiom as "the sense of linguistic fitness possessed by one who has grown up speaking a language"—I might have defined it so, if I hadn't learned better from experience. For I teach third and fourth-generation Canadians who have spoken English (sort of, you know?) since the crib, yet who have no more sense of English idiom than a recent arrival from the Old Country.

You might suspect that under the mask of idiom I am actually dragging correctness in through the back door. Not so. By asking "Is it English?" I do not mean to ask, is it *proper* English—but whether it is English rather than Transylvanian or Tagalog. Thus, we accept as idiomatic "That's all right by me," but do not (yet) accept "By me you are lovely" (which is fine in German). This also demonstrates that idiom is not equivalent to usage: for there are some usages which although clear, and even fashionable for a while, are ultimately rejected as unidiomatic. By idiom in general, then, we mean the ground rules or *customs* of a particular language, developed over the centuries—no matter whether all its speakers know them or not. These rules (like those that distinguish Canadian football from the American and the British games) set limits to the ways in which a given language works, the kinds of "play" that are legitimate—limits that may have little connection with clarity or force; indeed, they almost set up an independent standard for clarity and force. I would suppose that idiom arises from the same motive as slang: a sense of clubbiness, of "the way we do things" (as against the way outsiders—aliens and foreigners—handle them). The difference is that in slang the club is narrower, the motive keener and more restless, so that fashions in slang change very swiftly—as I shall be noting later on. Idioms do change, but not too far and not too fast, for the club they signify is the main coherent body of speakers of a language; and the changes are not mindless accidents (as the proponents of Usage seem at times to suggest) but organic and adaptive. We may be able to explain why particular idioms arise; but they are unlikely to be logical or even grammatical, even in French. In short, idiom is the human side of language, balancing between the poles of emotion and reason (as we ourselves do). The idiomatic speaker recognizes that his language has a living identity. He will be so intimately acquainted with its every nerve and fibre that he knows instinctively how it prefers to behave, and will not force it into unnatural postures.

You see that these three standards of good usage are flexible, not absolute. I trust you will find them reasonable, not arbitrary. And you will realize that they work together in odd and unpredictable ways, so that we cannot apply them unimaginatively or with stickling accuracy. It should also be even clearer why I have chosen to discuss not "the mistakes we make in grammar," but (using the adman's idiom) the linguistic images we project: there are territories where grammar has little relevance. I shall assume that for the most part we *hope* to project the image of educated people—an image of clear thought, charged only with the emotion we consciously intend, and conveying by the way a perfect familiarity with the structure and temperament of our language. In short, the picture of people in control of themselves. But the fact is that we very easily go wrong, in the sense of transmitting unexpected and damaging pictures of ourselves, because our language is not wholly under our control. My main concern, therefore, will be the images we actually do project without intending them.

I'll start with a group of images that convey—well, I was going to say Ignorance, which has a nice honest ring to it; but it's not quite adequate, because in a way all the faulty images involve some ignorance. Let's try a few, and see what they have in common. First, the image of the Illiterate (the uneducated, the rube, the rough diamond). It is the most obvious, and should be the simplest to avoid; yet even in the guarded speech of Academe you may catch such expressions as *irregardless, equally as good as, a little ways further on, with regards to, anyways, most everyone*. I do not include in this category expressions which are linguistically O.K. but socially taboo, like *ain't*. I am pointing only at those which violate one or more of my three criteria, principally the test of clarity. For instance, *with regards to* is unclear because it's ambiguous; it belongs at the end of a letter—with regards to Auntie May, Uncle Harry, and Roger the dog—whereas *with regard to* is rather pompous but clear enough. A complaint about how *bad prisoners are treated* (on CBC Viewpoint, 17 March 1975) leaves us confused between bad prisoners and bad treatment. Or take the formula beloved of the newspaper reader: "Hey, I see where René Lévesque's been elected." *Where*? Well, in his constituency; where else?

These are the obvious errors, the ones that schoolteachers have hammered away at for years. Then why are they as common as ever? Partly carelessness, no doubt, and partly, yes, ignorance, for education of any kind is the perpetual caulking of a leaky boat. But I think there is another reason, much stronger than these: inverted snobbery, the wish not to seem better than anyone else. Illiteracy is an image often assumed for this purpose. When a mechanic reports that "she's runnin' real good," it takes a pretty stuffy professor to reply that "it is indeed running rather well." Instead, with tact and democratic sympathy, he agrees that she sure is running purty smooth, by the sound of her. For he knows that grammar varies inversely as virility; and that if you *continue on* down to the stadium, you'll find that nobody there plays well. He-men play *good*. In that quaint dream of pioneer society to which we North Americans so desperately cling, careful speech is the mark of the sissy or the dude or the schoolmarm (who isn't even a Real Woman until she takes off her glasses and drops her g's). Fluency is suspect, suggesting a flim-flam man at work: which is one reason why our politicians burble, haw, and drone.

As I shall bear witness, I have every sympathy with changing your tune to fit your environment. Boswell's memory of Dr. Johnson, addressing a baffled stable-boy as if he were a meeting of the Royal Society, should be a warning to us all. By all means let us keep up the fiction that we're all simple country folk—if it makes us talk simply, it can't be all bad. But there are times in the real world when talking like Gary Cooper does not meet the necessities of the situation. Another risk: if we don't watch what we're doing, our assumed illiteracies may become chronic, and we'll find ourselves (at a Home and School meeting, say) unable to shift gears. For instance, in the past ten years it has become chic among fairly well-educated British journalists and authors to imitate the laxer kind of Americanism—at first in a campy way, half-sneering, but then trendily, and at last unconsciously. So that now you find columnists in the London *Observer* "spending money like it was going out of style" (as it is, of course; but the locution doesn't harmonize with the rest of their column), and authors, *veddy* conservative and precise by nature, striving for the Chandler image and descending to vilely un-British depths:

> This man had hooked her *helplessly*. Who now talked *like* he did and some-
> times more wildly. (My italics)

That's from a thriller by William Haggard (*The Bitter Harvest*, Cassell, 1971, p. 142), whose normal style is literate and careful. By odd contrast, I find two American authors of fast, tough thrillers being surprisingly choosy. Ross Macdonald has his hero (Lew Archer, in *The Moving Target*) announce that he's the "new-type detective," and soften the illiteracy by carefully putting in the hyphen. John D. MacDonald (in the Travis McGee books) is liberal with illiteracies, but uses *horrid* either in the British slang sense or, it may be, in the original Latin sense.

All right: I've oversimplified the North American scene. Pioneer simplicity is not our only dream, or even the dominant one. We have a strong contrary tendency, to inflate and load down our language with impressive sonorities: to talk like judges and senators rather than cowboys. And for this too there is a trap. It's a subspecies of illiteracy: call it the image of a *narrow education*—specifically, an education short on etymology in Latin, Greek, or even English. I am not saying educated people all ought to know Latin or Greek (though I opine wistfully that if they knew one or the other, preferably a bit of Latin, they would use English in a less wooden way). I am saying that when English words are imported from those tongues, it is useful to know what they've brought with them. The expression *continue on*, for example, occurs even in ivied towers; but it doesn't take a classical education to know that *continue* means to *go on*, not just go. The word *major* is generally believed to be a powerful synonym for *big* or *important* or *significant*, so that one hears visiting pundits speak continually of Very Major Problems. At the risk of offending them, let me spell it out: *major* began life as a Latin comparative, and the comparative flavour is still there—it means either *bigger* or *rather big*. And neither a "very bigger problem" nor a "very rather big" one makes much sense. Or take four common words which afford a handy test of a man's breadth of education: *phenomenon, criterion, stratum,* and *medium*. Two are

Greek, two are Latin; and they behave accordingly when they become plural. Yet I have heard a respected literary scholar in a national broadcast refer to "an interesting phenomena"; to appreciate the full effect of this, imagine hearing it in the voice W.C. Fields. *Criteria* and *strata* are likewise frequently used as if they were singular. They were not; they are not. And everyone these days knows (without pausing to think about it) that *a media* is something you communicate to the masses with. In fact there is only one Media: it's where the Medes came from.

Now I grant you there is a line past which this sort of objection becomes precious. But I think we ought to draw that line with care. For instance, the spelling (and pronunciation) *chaise lounge* is a peculiarly insensitive gaffe to allow ourselves in a country with Francophone leanings. And on our own monoglot ground, "between the three of us" should sound wrong (to the idiomatic ear) not because grammarians say so, but because *between* was once *bi tweyen*, or *by two*. "By two the three of us" becomes a study in vulgar fractions. Keep *between* for intimate moments *à deux*; it was made for you and me.

Pretentiousness in our speech is bedevilled by other dangers. Consider the image of Fogginess, shrouding the speaker who would like to make clear distinctions but has forgotten how. He says, "To me this is a semantic problem in that the confusion centres around a verbal misunderstanding." Sounds impressive at first; but there are three dead give-aways. *Semantic* is a favourite word with people who can't convey their meaning and want to shift the blame. *In that*, as my students seem to know by instinct, is a dandy way of implying a subtle connection when you are actually going to repeat the identical idea in different words. And *centres around*, as the critics have pointed out long ago, betrays a confusion in basic geometry. Nothing centres *around* anything. Things may *revolve around*, if they must, but if they centre at all, they centre *on*.

A frequent cause of fog is choosing the wrong word in a pair: *continual* for *continuous*, *differential* for *different*, *lie* for *lay*, and so on. (For a charmingly outdated list, see Fowler's *Dictionary of Modern English Usage* under "Pairs and Snares.") The normal result is haziness of outline, but at times it may be something more risky: "Oh, I was just laying around." One of Richard Needham's correspondents cripples his indignation with this kind of error:

> When the Government takes over Bell Canada—as *regretfully* they will one day—does anyone seriously think that either service or costs will improve?
> (Needham, *Globe*, 25 Feb. 1975; My italics)

Regretfully imputes an emotion to the government which does it too much honour. And come to think of it, what does a cost do when it improves? *Nutritional*, much in people's mouths lately, is either ambiguous or an unnecessary variant of *nutritious*. And *disinterested* has virtually lost its useful idiomatic meaning of "impartial." I have had people tell me no thanks, they were disinterested in football—the perfect qualification for a referee, but I was looking for someone to use the other ticket. The most common confusion is that of *infer* with *imply*. I am quite aware that even a good dictionary gives *imply* as one meaning of *infer*. That simply proves you cannot always trust dictionaries. The words are so obviously meant for each other as opposites (the speaker *folding in* an extra meaning, the listener *taking it in*) that I mistrust the judgment of a person who mixes them up. Perhaps the most noticeable symptom of the foggy speaker, or woofer, is an addiction to *facts* and *factors*. He speaks of a *fact* when he means an opinion, a risk, or a possibility; and he says *factor* when he senses that something is important but doesn't know how or why. Allow me to offer you a brief cautionary tale about factors. Originally, you recall, factors were the men in charge of trading posts for the Hudson's Bay Company; but they proved to be such willing workers that when the Company retrenched, the factors went forth and multiplied—and became factotums.

Remember that I am speaking of inadvertent fogginess. Conscious or deliberate blurring of outlines belongs to propaganda. No doubt we condition ourselves to be its victims if we use, or even listen to without comment, such expressions as "the military *internationalization* of Arab oil" (proposed in a bloodless way by a U.S. commentator not long ago). Others have pointed out that the use of woolly abstractions (*defoliation* being one of the mildest) to disguise ugly particulars is one of the sorry consequences of the war in Vietnam. A senior American journalist (Edwin Newman, in *Strictly Speaking*, Bobbs-Merrill, 1974) has been so appalled by it as to cry out against the murder of the language; once *that* murder is accomplished, it makes others easier to excuse or condone. I think it is fair to describe this as the Nazification of English. It is the process that caused George Steiner virtually to give up on language altogether (see *Language and Silence*, Atheneum, 1967). I shall content myself with this brief reminder that the seemingly trivial effects which I am discussing do border on sombre realities; and that if I choose to play it light, that's because lightness makes for more clarity than does indignation.

Close kin to fogginess is the image of what appears to be the absent mind—which cannot remember how it started, three words ago. It goes to pieces over what the grammarian calls Agreement, because it forgets both the person and the number of what it was talking about. Try this: "Bell Canada refunds your money without question if you tell *them* you reached a wrong number." How many Bells are ringing here, and for whom? Or this advice from a TV golfer: "*a person* of short stature should take care in grasping *their* club. *He* (or *she*) should grasp *their* club firmly..." Who grasps whose club, exactly? Does the owner know? But I'm being unfair. The difficulty in both cases has to do with pronouns which won't do precisely the job we intend. For one thing, speakers of English feel the lack of a genuinely impersonal pronoun like *on* in French: the nearest we can come to *on dit* is "they say," or "it is said." Actually *on* derives from *homo*, the Latin word for *man*—just as the impersonal *man* in German is connected with the masculine *Mann*—but in French the derivation is so masked by time that I doubt if most French speakers recognize it. Our convention in English is that *he* does duty for both *he* and *she*, and can be used impersonally. Evidently this was felt to be awkward or misleading even before the voice of women was heard, and so it has been replaced by something even more awkward, the explicit *he or she*, or in some places *s/he*. English does have the alternative *one*: "one should grasp one's club..." But one hesitates to do much of this, largely because the British are prone to use *one* as a coy or playful self-effacement for *I* and *me*. Perhaps you recall the courtship of Princess Anne, when in interviews with the press Captain Phillips proved far too well-bred to draw attention to himself, and therefore became *oneself*: one belonged, one gathered, to the nation.... When the princess replied in kind, the two dear things practically faded from sight.

In such a cleft stick, what is the average speaker to do? I'd advise him to rely on *they*, and to avoid awkwardness by carrying the plural through: for instance "When you tell *them*, Bell Canada *refund* your money." Besides, it's good psychology to treat corporate entities like Bell or the government as plurals rather than monoliths; it helps remind us they're made of people, and can be reached. Another device is to stop being so impersonal, and use *you* instead: "If you're short, grasp your club." And try to stay out of ambiguous situations like "Everybody thinks they're in charge."

There are clearer test cases for this image (the absent or sieve-like mind). One is the formula so many people find irresistible, especially politicians talking to us on television: *as far as [X] is concerned...* By beginning the formula, one stands pledged to follow through, eventually, with the rest of it. But usually the windbag who starts out with a really big X, "*as far as* low-rental housing developments and their location within the metropolitan area within the foreseeable future, by which I mean until the next election, ah..."—well, such a man is lost. He's forgotten his launch platform, and we could wait for weeks without hearing a whisper of *concern*. Strip it down, and he's left with a silly dangle—"as far as housing." (If this is your problem, let me recommend some safe and easy alternatives, like *as for, as to, concerning,* or even *with regard to.* You might play it Edward G. Robinson style: "You wanna know about housing? Okay, I'll tell ya.") The other telltale habit is the mixed metaphor, as in "We promise to *harness* those *bottlenecks,*" or (to quote an Ontario cabinet minister) "One bad apple can give the whole thing a black eye." Perhaps it is too kind to blame these unconscious jokes on forgetfulness. A truer explanation may be that such speakers are totally deaf to metaphor, and largely deaf to wit as well. A *bad apple* no longer carries for them any memory of fruit, it's just a phrase filed under Crook or Rascal (in the same fashion, I suspect, as jokes are filed under subject headings and "injected" into their speeches at apt moments).

More seductive (and for the discriminating judge, more damaging) is the image of would-be elegance, which produces Genteelisms, like *between you and I.* A little grammar is a dangerous thing. The cause of trouble is something I've already mentioned: a misplaced faith in the King's English, a striving to be correct at any cost. The effect is the same as lifting one's pinkie at a formal teacup—exaggerated propriety, more ludicrous than honest ignorance. (The British used to have a word for such behaviour: *refained.* The Refained Speaker is so anxious not to sound like a Cockney—"the rine in Spine styes minely in the pline"—that he converts *all* his i's to a's; so he cannot even say *refined*.) The psychology of such errors is plain enough. Because one got scolded as a child for saying "Us kids are going to the store" or "Me and Jimmy got whipped," one assumes that *us* and *me* are always wrong. The result is Refained Grammar, like *between you and I*. Educated people, I suppose because they are conscious of having to set an example, are specially prone to this trick. I have heard my own colleagues say, "This report was prepared by Professor Perkins and I." If they reversed the order and said "by I, and Professor Perkins" they might notice the error—but they wouldn't do that, it would be impolite to put themselves first. Or take "you must be tolerant with *we* ordinary mortals": that came from an instructor in English. (No, an English department does not have faultless speakers; what makes it unusual is that the mistakes are more likely to be noticed.) A brilliant philosopher of my acquaintance will construct noble sentences rotten at the core: "Distinctions of this order are of major importance to he who cares about logic." *Him who cares about his image, I bid take note.* And then there is the *whom* problem, which the *New Yorker* used to love so well. "The lady in question, whom our informants advise us is known as Lou..." Whom is? Well, in my view *whom* is a booby trap. My advice is to drop it. It's on the way out, and the tactful speaker may avoid it even when it's technically correct. A question like "Whom do you mean?" really deserves the answer it gets from Pogo: "*Youm*, that's whom."

Now for a cluster of images which offend chiefly against Idiom. In doing so they also becloud clarity and muffle impact, for my three criteria intertwine so subtly that to hurt one is to hurt all. This fact strikes me as good presumptive evidence of having hit upon the right criteria.

The image which I confess most quickly riles me is that of the Pseudo-Immigrant—the speaker who blurs or disfigures the native idiom. The irony here, as I've already suggested, is that this speaker has known no other idiom since birth. *Genuine* foreigners who learn our language from the ground up can, of course, put him to shame—as Conrad and Nabokov have demonstrated for the written word. It is not always easy to decide what is idiomatically wrong, and what is merely illiterate or malaprop. What to do with this sentence, spoken by an old friend of mine: "We are enough individuals that we could never expect unanimity"? *Hein*? Does he mean, "There are so many of us that somebody is bound to vote No," or does he mean, "We're so different we'll never agree completely"? I suspect, but I can't be sure. What I do feel sure of is that he's not at home in the language. And that's what he has in common with the speaker who gets his meaning across but sounds all wrong: "If you would have broken that tackle, you may have gone all the way." A clear case of the conditional so *imperfect* as to be totally loused up; and a very common blooper among sports announcers and "colour commentators."

The most treacherous ground of all may be the use of prepositions, for it is here that English idiom hits a peak of unreason. Small wonder that they drive foreigners to despair; but a daily wonder that they also baffle a great many native high-school graduates, who speak of having *a preference to blondes* (or sometimes *an attraction for blondes*, lucky them), *an interest for snowmobiles* (let the finance company handle that one), or *an insight of the problem* (part of the problem being that they will spell "insight" with a C). And the chances are strong that they will compound the crime by leaning significantly on the faulty preposition: "an insight OF the problem." That's a habit they learn from their elders, who may choose the right prepositions but then try to project an image of profound deliberation by weighing them down: "I don't have detailed data ON that, Chief, but my office can get the figures FOR you." A clear and simple case of lead-swinging.

The pseudo-foreign flavour comes back strong with the unidiomatic choice of tenses, as in "Did you have dinner yet?" Did I have dinner yet: let a man ask me that but once, and his image by me is irreparably flawed. A host who understood English idiom (and human feelings) would ask, "Have you had dinner?"—by which he would delicately but unmistakably convey that there was (yet) more in the kitchen. By replying, "No, I haven't," I would likewise convey implicitly that although I had not dined up to that moment, I lived in hopes. That is what is so perfectly splendid about the Present Perfect. But our Alien wouldn't understand; in his world, I eat or I ate. And if I reply in the only language he knows, "No I didn't," it's all over and done with—dinner has fled, there is nothing but bleakness and starvation. I've *had it.*

This did-you-have-dinner-yet is the thin end of a great clumsy wedge. Pretty soon we'll be saying things like "Are you in this country since long?" and "Yes, my god, I was here since I am a child." It's full of rich ethnic flavour, no doubt, the stuff of which warm situation comedies are made, but it sticks in my craw. Why should I have these uncouth alien notions of time and sequence thrust upon me, when English idiom allows me to specify time within time, before time, and after time with infinite subtlety and satisfaction? Take for example this snatch of song from *Camelot:*

> If ever you would leave me,
> It wouldn't be in springtime.

I object to Mr. Lerner's lyrics because they warp idiom, and therefore wreak confusion. What he means, in his schmaltzy Transylvanian heart, is, "If ever you *should* leave me"—that is, it hasn't happened so far, and with luck it may not happen at all. But he says instead, "If ever you *would*," which conveys something precise but quite different. To the idiomatic ear, it suggests a pitiable stretch of Time Past (*not* time to come), during which You were accustomed in a habitual and rather heartless way to leave Me—though not (one infers) for very long at a time, and never (one knows) between March and June. Given that opening clause, the verse ought really to unfold like this:

> If ever you would leave me
> I knew you had a reason—
> Like wishing to deceive me,
> Or wild duck's being in season.

Another form of idiom-smashing that attracts educated people is what I call Literalism. This is the habit of using a word for what it looks as if it should mean, rather than what idiom has brought it to mean. The most familiar example is *presently*. A man who asks me for a job, and says he is *presently completing* his thesis, already has one strike against him. Sure, to a foreign eye it appears to mean "at present." But as speakers of English we inherit the English genius for delay (as Samuel Johnson observes, "languages are the pedigree of nations"), and when we say "any moment now" we mean tomorrow. Once upon a time there was a good old four-letter word, *anon*, which meant *in one, at once*; but it soon became clear that you couldn't trust a tapster who said "anon, anon, sir," so somebody introduced the precise Latin word *presently* to mean *now*, and all was plain for a while. But the barman dragged his heels again, and *presently* became *some other time*. Now, if you want prompt action, you must specify *immediately*, or *on the double*. And if you mean *at present*, why not say it? It takes not one millisecond longer.

A slightly different case is presented by *momentarily* and *hopefully*. The idiomatic meaning—the only meaning given in a reliable Scottish dictionary, *Chambers's*—of *momentarily* is "for a moment, briefly," as in the poignant phrase, "momentarily she was mine; then, alas, she slipped through my fingers and was gone." (Feminist readers will substitute *he*.) So the fellow who says, with eyes aglow, "She will be mine momentarily," may be in for a big disappointment—and anyone who talks that way deserves it. He means *in a moment*. Other people abuse the word to mean *at the moment*. Thornton Wilder has even used it to mean *by the moment*, or *moment by moment*—and he does it in a stage direction, so there's no way out:

> The children lean forward and all watch the funeral in silence growing *momentarily* more *solemnized*.
> (*The Long Christmas Dinner*, Harper and Row, 1963, p. 95)

He wrote that in 1931. *Solemnized* is a bonus boner, which happily hasn't caught on. It will do fine as a reminder that if we wish to keep our language undefiled, we cannot always trust reputable authors.

As for *hopefully*, it appears to be a more recent immigrant from Germany by way of New York. But in German it was *hoffentlich*, and meant "hopingly": a detached, impersonal adverb that English hasn't invented yet—because English has other ways of being impersonal. If we want to say "hopingly" we can use *I hope, one hopes*, or even *it is to be hoped*, which ought to be impersonal enough for anybody. When we say *hopefully*, we mean in our idiomatic way that whoever is speaking or acting is *full of hope*. A famous example: "it is better to travel hopefully than to arrive." The man who tells us "She will be mine, hopefully, within the week *(ja)*" may thus be a decent modest fellow by German standards; but in English he's taking an awful lot for granted, for he implies that it's *she* who is so keen. And when the Hon. John Turner advertises in a British newspaper that his four children "require a kind and loving nannie

391

[sic], *hopefully* with previous experience," any nanny worth her salt will perceive that it isn't only the children who need her help.

Momentarily, then, is misused through literalness and unawareness of idiom, as is *presently* (examples of what *Chambers's Dictionary* calls folk-etymology, or "popular unscientific attempts at etymology"). But the case of *hopefully* suggests an additional dimension, at least to my sensibilities. I connect it first with other personal adverbs misapplied in a general, impersonal way—*regretfully* instead of *regrettably*, maybe *pitifully* a while ago. What's happening here is the transfer of a private emotion to "the public sector," so that its source can no longer be traced. No wonder these usages prevail among businessmen and politicians. *Who* is full of hope, or regret, or pity? Not me, not you, not anyone: it has been shifted into a quality of the objective environment, as if there were a something, a process out there which had taken on sentience. Is it fanciful to connect this with other hints of personal abdication, such as is implied by a *decision-making process*? If a process can feel hope or regret, it can surely make decisions. And when decisions are made by a process, no single person can be held responsible; it *happens*, objectively and inexorably, like the march of history. No doubt, the original motive for the phrase was to imply (without promising) the breaking down of tyranny, the sharing of decisions by a number of persons (as in *participatory democracy*). In practice, however, both phrases are cop-outs, and in neither case does anything get decided or done. These are the phrases of people who have no policies, no self-reliance, no confidence — and who deserve none. The only way to bring about decisions and actions is to find some *person* who can *decide*, and *act*.

What disturbs me more than the standard lies and distortions of such propaganda language is this curious appearance of an inexorable process *out there*, because in common parlance we do not merely take part in a *decision-making process*, we are *plugged into it*. Immediately I am reminded of other locutions with the same metallic flavour: "This really turns me on, you know?" and, "Man, she turns me off" (which isn't an action by "her," exactly, nor yet a response by "me"). Who, or what, is speaking? *Where is the switch*? The image I detect here is Mechanism—half surrender to, half propitiation of the great, half-glimpsed machine which we half adore, half fear. By using the language of machines to describe our hopes, actions, reactions, by transferring to a humming external process what was once our private domain of striving, do we placate the Computer Politic, the World Machine, or do we program ourselves for sacrifice? Machines, as I understand them, have languages but no idioms. What I am expressing is not the modern fear that the robots are coming, but the fear that we are *robotizing, dehumanizing, depersonalizing* ourselves through words as ugly as the process they describe.

Another troublesome question under the general head of idiom has to do with the set of sub-idioms we call Slang. There are two opposite causes of concern: whether it is proper to use slang at all, or more commonly the question of *which* slang is fashionable or "in." The motive in both cases is *togetherness* (a piece of manufactured slang which never quite made it), the wish to confirm one's belonging to a group: in the first case the large group, the great club of all those who Speak Properly (and whose slang is called idiom); in the second case the small exclusive group, the tribe of the elite who share a secret attitude (and whose exclusiveness must be assured by continual changes in the password), like adolescents or pop musicians or anglers or astronomers. To those who ask the first question I reply cheerfully, "Yes, by all means use slang—if you know the risks." Those who worry about the second are not likely to ask me, because I am obviously no swinger; all the same, one or two of my random reflections may prove edifying.

Those who ask whether slang is permissible in polite society are really preoccupied with correctness, on which I've already offered my view. Applying my kind of standards, I would repeat that in our democratic, colloquial society you are more likely to be censured for using no slang at all. But of course there are risks in using it too. Some sober groups may find your flip ways unacceptable; argot that suits one milieu may draw sneers in another. My own preference for the simple and colloquial as salt to my discourse leads many of my colleagues to dismiss me as frivolous, unscholarly, simple-minded—a reflection to which I shall return. And slang of all kinds is in constant danger of not being clear, because impact, not clarity, presides at its birth. A current fad leans heavily but ambiguously on the simple word *to*. "To me, he's a wonderful person." (Great, but how does he behave to others?) "To the majority of immigrants, their perception of education is quite different from our own" (a spokesman for the Toronto Board of Education, quoted by Canadian Press, 17 Feb. 1975). Here *to* implies a perception *of a perception*. He means "most immigrants look on education in a way native Canadians don't," but he says, "most immigrants don't look at their perceptions as we would look at *their perceptions*"—which is true, perhaps, but not useful. A short way off is the modish use of *into*: "Yeah, I'm into the hard stuff," "I'm into medieval studies," "I'm into people." The obvious risk is that the literal meaning may overturn the slang one, as with the earnest boy who confides that he's really getting into girls now. Or take the curious American insistence on *human beings* as if they were a species of achievement. "Bruce is a superb human being," they affirm glowingly. (The hell you say; and here I was, expecting a stoat.)

This approaches the image of the Hopeless Square, who keeps treading on verbal land-mines because he is unaware of slang meanings. Scientific colleagues have complained to me of inexplicable merriment in their classes when they speak of a *crude model*; and we all recall the visiting Britisher who apologizes for *knocking up* his hostess at 2 a.m. Words like *cool* and *hot* have a perpetual but fluctuating slang sense: so that Marshall McLuhan's attempt to give them specific content with regard to the media runs into difficulties. The other way to look hopelessly square is to use argot that is out of date (or *old hat*, if you get me). For instance, a few years back *no way* was the all-purpose surfboard of the young, until like so many other passwords it sank from sight. But it did not quite disappear, for adults (in those days when youth could do no wrong) snatched at it eagerly, and have never let go—with the result that instead of being in the swim as they hoped, they are now quaintly stranded on an antique beach.

On the other hand, I observe with an agreeable sense of irony how the whirligig of time brings back the exile. *Groovy*, which I helped to bury 30 years ago, is suddenly alive and well. *Chap*, which in those early days was laughably British and probably a bit effeminate, is now a perfectly normal fella, even in New York. And although *gay* is at the moment unfit for any but its slang use, a fact I deplore, it seems possible that at last *queer* can be reinstated—and perhaps *fruit* as well.

One particular area which I would hesitate to call trendy in itself has undeniably provoked trendy convulsions in language: I mean of course the movement to liberate women. It took me a long time to realize that *consciousness raising* was not a phase of transcendental meditation but a specific manoeuvre in the feminist campaign. And I doubt that *chauvinism* will be fit for its original duty in my lifetime. But the silly edge of this argot shows when the new consciousness starts in on the unsexing of *métiers*. The *Globe* for Valentine's Day carried advertisements for "a Bodyman-woman, a Foreperson and, the most intriguing of all, a Parts man-woman." (Quoted in Letters, 18 Feb. 1975.) Richard Needham notes other transformations: cowboy into cattleperson, bus boy into dining-room attendant, governess into child mentor. Everyone keeps his own list. And because this kind of neurotic fiddling quickly invites a backlash, as we say, everyone keeps a list of put-downs. I have already demonstrated my impartiality, I hope, in various ways. So let me register my objection to the plague of *persons* where hateful sexist English reads *-man*. In *spokesman*, *chairman*, *barman*, and so on we don't even pronounce it "man," but "mun." I am reminded of a special British expression in which *person* is not neutral but insulting: "She's more of a *person*, really..." I am also reminded of the ultimate achievement in desexing language, the invention of a columnist that would replace *human* with the triumphant neuter *huperson*. (And *Mädchen* is neuter, I recall. Do liberated Ger-persons object?)

Trendiness annoys me above all not merely because it is seductive and always has been, but because it seduces us back into the screwloose religion of change. The man who deplores a return to the 3 R's as a step back toward the cave is suffering from delirium *trendens*. He belongs to the McLuhanite fringe who scream that print is dead, the book is buried, and citizens of the global village must be expert in the new mysteries of film and tape and incantation. I never know how much to blame on the ancient sage himself, because I'm never sure what he means or how serious he is. But risking naiveté, let me suggest, to his disciples at least, that if the universe around the corner is electronic all the way, then we've got to find someone else who can write the *script*, and someone who can read it, and someone else who can use the camera properly (the emptiness of handheld scriptless impromptu inaudible film happenings having at last registered on the most glazed watcher).

Are we lapsing into barbarism? Will we soon be unable to communicate except by coos and grunts and formulas? I don't really think so—though there are portents, dammit: such as my wife's hitchhiker, a braw school-leaver of nineteen, personable and polite. When she asked him to find out what was causing the noisy rattle he checked, diagnosed, and reported, "The uh thing...is, like...Uhhh..." Aghast, she conferred: did he mean the back door on the wagon was not properly shut? He heaved a great smiling sigh of relief. "Yuh," he said, having got through. No, what I fear is that well before that, we shall have lost touch with the past. That is the other purpose and glory of language, which the usage-mongers and the progress-peddlers and the flux-worshippers forget. The gift of my tongue does not merely enable me to "interrelate" with my contemporaries; it makes me a citizen of the entire human commonwealth, of an empire across time. I will not exchange that for a wilderness of global villages.

I remember that when I sang "We Three Kings" as a child I repeated the line, "Star with royal beauty *dight*," as generations of children had done before me. Later I learned with pleasure the ancient words to "This Endris Night." But I am hard put to excavate them now. Within one generation *dight* has vanished, replaced by "royal beauty *bright*." And in "Jingle Bells"—now sanctified as a *carol*, together with "Silver Bells"—who sings now of a one-horse open *shay*? (But it's still listed, glory be, in the *Dictionary of Canadian English* as a by-form of *chaise*.) How much longer before the only readers capable of grasping ancient documents (like *Sunshine Sketches of a Little Town* or *The Great Gatsby*) are eccentric antiquarians? You zealots of the flood, explain to me how it is that words can be preserved intact through the centuries, down the ringing grooves of change, and crumble only within our own half-life? I can guess. It is because, through the efforts of traditionalists and tories and purists who refused, God bless them, to believe that all our yesterdays were irrelevant, the barbarous babble current at any one time in the past was not allowed to prevail or prescribe. *Barbarous*: a good honest word. In Greek it meant "stammering," and they used it of foreigners' talk. We should know better. We know that stammering begins at home; and that barbarism begins inside the citadel.

To return, more calmly, from sermon to images. Let me round off my survey by asking what we should project, instead of all these inadvertent and regrettable images. I wonder how many readers will agree with my suggestion that there is no single answer, no proper image for all seasons. There is a whole range of good, desirable, effective impressions we can make with our words. It is our business to choose among them, and the one we choose should depend on the job we want to do and the audience we address. You can see the truth of this when it comes to accent. Only a very narrow-minded speaker would claim that the proper way to pronounce your English is the way they do it in Aburrdeen, or Suhhbiton, or Long Guyland, or Arnpryre. I propose quite seriously that the same is true for grammar, within limits, and above all for style. The style, or *register*, which you use to a bridge partner is not appropriate when you address a tax consultant or a bus driver—though each style may be free of errors. I remember a lady who taught grade nine, and told me of a boy who told her: "Look, I talk the way my father talks. What does my father *do*? He drinks. If I talked the way *you* talk, I'd get beat to a pulp." That boy was *right*. I suspect he was also clever enough to be leading a double or triple life by now, with a perfectly idiomatic language for each (as butlers used to do in England).

But let's take an example closer to hand. I wouldn't mind a small bet that some of you think there is such a thing as a Professorial Style—correct, dignified, formal, impressive, like a god talking. There is, of course; I've put in some examples of it myself, just to prove I can. But what I'd bet on is that you have a sneaky feeling that it's *the* proper style—that we should all aim to talk or write that way, and that when I depart from it (as I do) my image suffers. This is where people go wrong—professors most of all. That formal, god-like style is only too easy to reach; and if reached too often it becomes no style at all, but a disease. This is where Humpty Dumpty's remark does make sense. The question is who is to be master—you, or the style. A man at the mercy of his own style is as comic, and as much to be pitied, as a man at the mercy of drink. Your style ought to express *what you are*, and you are not the same person on all occasions, in every company. If you seem to be, you are a bore.

I see where I am heading. The image which I have really been deploring all along, an image which embraces all the unhappy ones I've described, is the image not of the Poor Boob, but of the Zombie. What I mourn over is not the mistakes, but the *numbness*, to every aspect of language, which they imply. I regret the sort of mind that measures sense by the syllable, and accepts as oratory flannel a yard wide. To such a mind, ideas expressed in a simple, playful way are (necessarily) simple and obvious ideas, not worth having. I regret likewise the mind that must cloak metaphors in prose, apparently believing that naked metaphor is indecent—the progeny of Knowlton Nash, those newsmouths that say "climb off his *legislative* high horse," or "this promises to become a *political* hot potato." I regret above all the mind insensitive to humour and wordplay of all kinds—not just the reflex groan at a bad pun, but the total inability to grasp a good one. I regret the mind which wears a superior smile when you play with a deliberate error (for instance, a friend of mine habitually says, "Oh, it was a congenital evening," and people exchange secret smiles because they think *he's* slipped). I regret, in sum, the mind to which all languages are dead languages, including its own.

Notes on Punctuation

Lewis Thomas

There are no precise rules about punctuation (Fowler lays out some general advice (as best he can under the complex circumstances of English prose (he points out, for example, that we possess only four stops (the comma, the semicolon, the colon and the period (the question mark and exclamation point are not, strictly speaking, stops; they are indicators of tone (oddly enough, the Greeks employed the semicolon for their question mark (it produces a strange sensation to read a Greek sentence which is a straightforward question: Why weepest thou; (instead of Why weepest thou? (and, of course, there are parentheses (which are surely a kind of punctuation making this whole matter much more complicated by having to count up the left-handed parentheses in order to be sure of closing with the right number (but if the parentheses were left out, with nothing to work with but the stops, we would have considerably more flexibility in the deploying of layers of meaning than if we tried to separate all the clauses by physical barriers (and in the latter case, while we might have more precision and exactitude for our meaning, we would lose the essential flavor of language, which is its wonderful ambiguity)))))))))))).

The commas are the most useful and usable of all the stops. It is highly important to put them in place as you go along. If you try to come back after doing a paragraph and stick them in the various spots that tempt you you will discover that they tend to swarm like minnows into all sorts of crevices whose existence you hadn't realized and before you know it the whole long sentence becomes immobilized and lashed up squirming in commas. Better to use them sparingly, and with affection, precisely when the need for each one arises, nicely, by itself.

I have grown fond of semicolons in recent years. The semicolon tells you that there is still some question about the preceding full sentence; something needs to be added; it reminds you sometimes of the Greek usage. It is almost always a greater pleasure to come across a semicolon than a period. The period tells you that that is that; if you didn't get all the meaning you wanted or expected, anyway you got all the writer intended to parcel out and now you have to move along. But with a semicolon there you get a pleasant little feeling of expectancy; there is more to come; read on; it will get clearer.

Colons are a lot less attractive, for several reasons: firstly, they give you the feeling of being rather ordered around, or at least having your nose pointed in a direction you might not be inclined to take if left to yourself, and, secondly, you suspect you're in for one of those sentences that will be labeling the points to be made: firstly, secondly and so forth, with the implication that you haven't sense enough to keep track of a sequence of notions without having them numbered. Also, many writers use this system loosely and incompletely, starting out with number one and number two as though counting off on their fingers but then going on and on without the succession of labels you've been led to expect, leaving you floundering about searching for the ninethly or seventeenthly that ought to be there but isn't.

Exclamation points are the most irritating of all. Look! they say, look at what I just said! How amazing is my thought! It is like being forced to watch someone else's small child jumping up and down crazily in the center of the living room shouting to attract attention. If a sentence really has something of importance to say, something quite remarkable, it doesn't need a mark to point it out. And if it is really, after all, a banal sentence needing more zing, the exclamation point simply emphasizes its banality!

Quotation marks should be used honestly and sparingly, when there is a genuine quotation at hand, and it is necessary to be very rigorous about the words enclosed by the marks. If something is to be quoted, the *exact* words must be used. If part of it must be left out because of space limitations, it is good manners to insert three dots to indicate the omission, but it is unethical to do this if it means connecting two thoughts which the original author did not intend to have tied together. Above all, quotation marks should not be used for ideas that you'd like to disown, things in the air so to speak. Nor should they be put in place around clichés; if you want to use a cliché you must take full responsibility for it yourself and not try to job it off on anon., or on society. The most objectionable misuse of quotation marks, but one which illustrates the dangers of misuse in ordinary prose, is seen in advertising, especially in advertisements for small restaurants, for example "just around the corner," or "a good place to eat." No single, identifiable, citable person ever really said, for the record, "just around the corner," much less "a good place to eat," least likely of all for restaurants of the type that use this type of prose.

The dash is a handy device, informal and essentially playful, telling you that you're about to take off on a different tack but still in some way connected with the present course—only you have to remember that the dash is there, and either put a second dash at the end of the notion to let the reader know that he's back on course, or else end the sentence, as here, with a period.

The greatest danger in punctuation is for poetry. Here it is necessary to be as economical and parsimonious with commas and periods as with the words themselves, and any marks that seem to carry their own subtle meanings, like dashes and little rows of periods, even semicolons and question marks, should be left out altogether rather than inserted to clog up the thing with ambiguity. A single exclamation point in a poem, no matter what else the poem has to say, is enough to destroy the whole work.

The things I like best in T.S. Eliot's poetry, especially in the *Four Quartets*, are the semicolons. You cannot hear them, but they are there, laying out the connections between the images and ideas. Sometimes you get a glimpse of a semicolon coming, a few lines farther on, and it is like climbing a steep path through woods and seeing a wooden bench just at a bend in the road ahead, a place where you can expect to sit for a moment, catching your breath.

Commas can't do this sort of thing; they can only tell you how the different parts of a complicated thought are to be fitted together, but you can't sit, not even take a breath, just because of a comma,

Lives and Likenesses

Michael Frayn

Mr. Ken Russell seems to have hit upon a simple but important new biographical principle in his films for "Monitor" on B.B.C. Television. According to sympathetic critics, he makes each film in the style of the artist it is about.

Thus, according to Peter Black, "his Elgar was straightforward and sentimentalised, his Debussy misty and complex." His Douanier Rousseau, similarly, was naïve and primitive. In fact it was considerably *more* naïve and primitive than Rousseau. It takes a real hardened professional to get as naïve and primitive as that. These amateur innocents like Rousseau never knew the tricks of the trade.

Writers have obviously been missing an opportunity. In fact, it's rather presumptuous, when you come to think about it, for old Strachey to have written "Queen Victoria" in his own style and not Queen Victoria's. And why didn't Mr. Alan Bullock couch his study of Hitler rather more in the familiar Nuremberg vein? A touch of egomania here?

Now Mr. Russell has shown the way, no doubt the idea will be taken up. Here are trailers for one or two biographies I hope to be seeing in the book-shops soon.

Firstly I should like to say this—and I make no apology for mentioning it: Harold Wilson was born—and I choose that word advisedly—on the eleventh of March 1916. Not on the tenth, or the twelfth, as some people would like you to believe—and here I intend no disrespect to the many men and women up and down the country who I know *were* born on the tenth or the twelfth, and who have given loyal and unstinting service to the community, and whose special needs—I say this to them now—have not been forgotten.

But—and it's a big but—if this book is to make any real headway, if we're really going to bring it up to date, we simply cannot afford—and this cannot be said too often—we simply cannot afford to sit back and rest content with our progress so far. Because make no mistake—and there's none of us who doesn't make mistakes at times—if we're forced to go on breaking off like this for modifications, concessions, and reassuring asides, we shan't reach Mr. Wilson's first birthday until about Chapter 23.

A (indef. art.) man who might with some justice be called the
AARDVARK (noun) of English letters, whose
AARONIC (adj.) pronouncements upon anything from the

AASVOGEL (noun) to the

ABACA (noun) often took his companions

ABACK (adv.), and frequently caused them to

ABANDON (verb) themselves to mirth, Dr. Johnson was never known to let anyone

ABASE (verb) or

ABASH (verb) him, and would wallow agreeably

ABASK (adv.) in what others might have found to be a veritable conversational

ABATTOIR (noun).

Mozart:
Chapter No. 21 in D Minor

In 1779 Mozart returned to Salzburg. In the year 1779 Mozart returned to Salzburg. Back to his native city in the year after 1778 Wolfgang Amadeus Mozart came.

And was made court organist, was appointed organist at the court, the organ-player at the court he was created. Having come back to Salzburg in 1779 he became court organist, the court organist is what he became after his return to Salzburg in 1779.

He was oppressed with debts. He owed money. Goods and services had been credited to him for which he had not yet paid. He was oppressed with debts, debts weighed him down. Money was outstanding. He owed. Money was what he owed.

In 1779 Mozart returned to Salzburg. Back to his home town came he. And was appointed court organist.

To Salzburg, the well-known town in Austria. That was where, in 1779, Mozart returned.

A Life of T.S. Eliot:
Acknowledgments

How can I begin to thank
Professor Pomattox, or Doctor Frack,
The Misses Fischbein, or Monsignor Blum?
Words lose their meaning, and grow slack.

Some typed upon Remingtons in obscure rooms.
Some made suggestions.
Some read the proofs. Some wept. One smiled:
"The world is full of questions."

Mrs. Crupper came and went
With tiny jars of liniment.

The finished pages flutter to the floor.
La lune éternue et s'endort.
All this, and so much more,
And so much more.

Composition as Explanation

Gertrude Stein

There is singularly nothing that makes a difference a difference in beginning and in the middle and in ending except that each generation has something different at which they are all looking. By this I mean so simply that anybody knows it that composition is the difference which makes each and all of them then different from other generations and this is what makes everything different otherwise they are all alike and everybody knows it because everybody says it.

It is very likely that nearly every one has been very nearly certain that something that is interesting is interesting them. Can they and do they. It is very interesting that nothing inside in them, that is when you consider the very long history of how every one ever acted or has felt, it is very interesting that nothing inside in them in all of them makes it connectedly different. By this I mean this. The only thing that is different from one time to another is what is seen and what is seen depends upon how everybody is doing everything. This makes the thing we are looking at very different and this makes what those who describe it make of it, it makes a composition, it confuses, it shows, it is, it looks, it likes it as it is, and this makes what is seen as it is seen. Nothing changes from generation to generation except the thing seen and that makes a composition. Lord Grey remarked that when the generals before the war talked about the war they talked about it as a nineteenth century war although to be fought with twentieth century weapons. That is because war is a thing that decides how it is to be when it is to be done. It is prepared and to that degree it is like all academies it is not a thing made by being made it is a thing prepared. Writing and painting and all that, is like that, for those who occupy themselves with it and don't make it as it is made. Now the few who make it as it is made, and it is to be remarked that the most decided of them usually are prepared just as the world around them is preparing, do it in this way and so I if you do not mind I will tell you how it happens. Naturally one does not know how it happened until it is well over beginning happening.

To come back to the part that the only thing that is different is what is seen when it seems to be being seen, in other words, composition and time-sense.

No one is ahead of his time, it is only that the particular variety of creating his time is the one that his contemporaries who also are creating their own time refuse to accept. And they refuse to accept it for a very simple reason and that is that they do not have to accept it for any reason. They themselves that is everybody in their entering the modern composition and they do enter it, if they do not enter it they are not so to speak in it they are out of it and so they do enter it; but in as you may say the non-competitive efforts where if you are not in it nothing is lost except nothing at all except what is not had, there are naturally all the refusals, and the things refused are only important if unexpectedly somebody happens to need them. In the case of the arts it is very definite. Those who are creating the modern composition authentically are naturally only of importance when they are dead because by that time the modern composition having become past is classified and the description of it is classical. That is the reason why the creator of the new composition in the arts is an outlaw until he is a classic, there is hardly a moment in between and it is really too bad very much too bad naturally for the creator but also very much too bad for the enjoyer, they all really would enjoy the created so much better just after it has been made than when it is already a classic, but it is perfectly simple that there is no reason why the contemporaries should see, because it would not make any difference as they lead their lives in the new composition anyway, and as every one is naturally indolent why naturally they don't see. For this reason as in quoting Lord Grey it is quite certain that nations not actively threatened are at least several generations behind themselves militarily so aesthetically they are more than several generations behind themselves and it is very much too bad, it is so very much more exciting and satisfactory for everybody if one can have contemporaries, if all one's contemporaries could be one's contemporaries.

There is almost not an interest.

For a very long time everybody refuses and then almost without a pause almost everybody accepts. In the history of the refused in the arts and literature the rapidity of the change is always startling. Now the only difficulty with the *volte-face* concerning the arts is this. When the acceptance comes, by that acceptance the thing created becomes a classic. It is a natural phenomena a rather extraordinary natural phenomena that a thing accepted becomes a classic. And what is the characteristic quality of a classic. The characteristic quality of a classic is that it is beautiful. Now of course it is perfectly true that a more or less first rate work of art is beautiful but the trouble is that when that first rate work of art becomes a classic because it is accepted the only thing that is important from then on to the majority of the acceptors the enormous majority, the most intelligent majority of the acceptors is that it is so wonderfully beautiful. Of course it is wonderfully beautiful, only when it is still a thing irritating annoying stimulating then all quality of beauty is denied to it.

Of course it is beautiful but first all beauty in it is denied and then all the beauty of it is accepted. If every one were not so indolent they would realise that beauty is beauty even when it is irritating and stimulating not only when it is accepted and classic. Of course it is extremely difficult nothing more so than to remember back to its not being beautiful once it has become beautiful. This makes it so much more difficult to realise its beauty when the work is being refused and prevents every one from realising that they were convinced that beauty was denied, once the work is accepted. Automatically with the acceptance of the time-sense comes the recognition of the beauty and once the beauty is accepted the beauty never fails any one.

Beginning again and again is a natural thing even when there is a series.

Beginning again and again and again explaining composition and time is a natural thing.

It is understood by this time that everything is the same except composition and time, composition and the time of the composition and the time in the composition.

Everything is the same except composition and as the composition is different and always going to be different everything is not the same. Everything is not the same as the time when of the composition and the time in the composition is different. The composition is different, that is certain.

The composition is the thing seen by every one living in the living they are doing, they are the composing of the composition that at the time they are living is the composition of the time in which they are living. It is that that makes living a thing they are doing. Nothing else is different, of that almost any one can be certain. The time when and the time of and the time in that composition is the natural phenomena of that composition and of that perhaps every one can be certain.

No one thinks these things when they are making when they are creating what is the composition, naturally no one thinks that is no one formulates until what is to be formulated has been made.

Composition is not there, it is going to be there and we are here. This is some time ago for us naturally.

The only thing that is different from one time to another is what is seen and what is seen depends upon how everybody is doing everything. This makes the thing we are looking at very different and this makes what those who describe it make of it, it makes a composition, it confuses, it shows, it is, it looks, it likes it as it is, and this makes what is seen as it is seen. Nothing changes from generation to generation except the thing seen and that makes a composition.

Now the few who make writing as it is made and it is to be remarked that the most decided of them are those that are prepared by preparing, are prepared just as the world around them is prepared and is preparing to do it in this way and so if you do not mind I will again tell you how it happens. Naturally one does not know how it happened until it is well over beginning happening.

Each period of living differs from any other period of living not in the way life is but in the way life is conducted and that authentically speaking is composition. After life has been conducted in a certain way everybody knows it but nobody knows it, little by little, nobody knows it as long as nobody knows it. Any one creating the composition in the arts does not know it either, they are conducting life and that makes their composition what it is, it makes their work compose as it does.

Their influence and their influences are the same as that of all of their contemporaries only it must always be remembered that the analogy is not obvious until as I say the composition of a time has become so pronounced that it is past and the artistic composition of it is a classic.

And now to begin as if to begin. Composition is not there, it is going to be there and we are here. This is some time ago for us naturally. There is something to be added afterwards.

Just how much my work is known to you I do not know. I feel that perhaps it would be just as well to tell the whole of it.

In beginning writing I wrote a book called *Three Lives* this was written in 1905. I wrote a negro story called *Melanctha*. In that there was a constant recurring and beginning there was a marked direction in the direction of being in the present although naturally I had been accustomed to past present and future, and why, because the composition forming around me was a prolonged present. A composition of a prolonged present is a natural composition in the world as it has been these thirty years it was more and more a prolonged present. I created then a prolonged present naturally I knew nothing of a continuous present but it came naturally to me to make one, it was simple it was clear to me and nobody knew why it was done like that, I did not myself although naturally to me it was natural.

After that I did a book called *The Making of Americans* it is a long book about a thousand pages.

Here again it was all so natural to me and more and more complicatedly a continuous present. A continuous present is a continuous present. I made almost a thousand pages of a continuous present.

Continuous present is one thing and beginning again and again is another thing. These are both things. And then there is using everything.

This brings us again to composition this the using everything. The using everything brings us to composition and to this composition. A continuous present and using everything and beginning again. In these two books there was elaboration of the complexities of using everything and of a continuous present and of beginning again and again and again.

In the first book there was a groping for a continuous present and for using everything by beginning again and again.

There was a groping for using everything and there was a groping for a continuous present and there was an inevitable beginning of beginning again and again and again.

Having naturally done this I naturally was a little troubled with it when I read it. I became then like the others who read it. One does, you know, excepting that when I reread it myself I lost myself in it again. Then I said to myself this time it will be different and I began. I did not begin again I just began.

In this beginning naturally since I at once went on and on very soon there were pages and pages and pages more and more elaborated creating a more and more continuous present including more and more using of everything and continuing more and more beginning and beginning and beginning.

I went on and on to a thousand pages of it.

In the meantime to naturally begin I commenced making portraits of anybody and anything. In making these portraits I naturally made a continuous present an including everything and a beginning again and again within a very small thing. That started me into composing anything into one thing. So then naturally it was natural that one thing an enormously long thing was not everything an enormously short thing was also not everything nor was it all of it a continuous present thing nor was it always and always beginning again. Naturally I would then begin again. I would begin again I would naturally begin. I did naturally begin. This brings me to a great deal that has been begun.

And after that what changes what changes after that, after that what changes and what changes after that and after that and what changes and after that and what changes after that.

The problem from this time on became more definite.

It was all so nearly alike it must be different and it is different, it is natural that if everything is used and there is a continuous present and a beginning again and again if it is all so alike it must be simply different and everything simply different was the natural way of creating it then.

In this natural way of creating it then that it was simply different everything being alike it was simply different, this kept on leading one to lists. Lists naturally for a while and by lists I mean a series. More and more in going back over what was done at this time I find that I naturally kept simply different as an intention. Whether there was or whether there was not a continuous present did not then any longer trouble me there was or there was, and using everything no longer troubled me if everything is alike using everything could no longer trouble me and beginning again and again could no longer trouble me because if lists were inevitable if series were inevitable and the whole of it was inevitable beginning again and again could not trouble me so then with nothing to trouble me I very completely began naturally since everything is alike making it as simply different naturally as simply different as possible. I began doing natural phenomena what I call natural phenomena and natural phenomena naturally everything being alike natural phenomena are making things be naturally simply different. This found its culmination later, in the beginning it began in a center confused with lists with series with geography with returning portraits and with particularly often four and three and often with five and four. It is easy to see that in the beginning such a conception as everything being naturally different would be very inarticulate and very slowly it began to emerge and take the form of anything, and then naturally if anything that is simply different is simply different what follows will follow.

So far then the progress of my conceptions was the natural progress entirely in accordance with my epoch as I am sure is to be quite easily realised if you think over the scene that was before us all from year to year.

As I said in the beginning, there is the long history of how every one ever acted or has felt and that nothing inside in them in all of them makes it connectedly different. By this I mean all this.

The only thing that is different from one time to another is what is seen and what is seen depends upon how everybody is doing everything.

It is understood by this time that everything is the same except composition and time, composition and the time of the composition and the time in the composition.

Everything is the same except composition and as the composition is different and always going to be different everything is not the same. So then I as a contemporary creating the composition in the beginning was groping toward a continuous present, a using everything a beginning again and again and then everything being alike then everything very simply everything was naturally simply different and so I as a contemporary was creating everything being alike was creating everything naturally being naturally simply different, everything being alike. This then was the period that brings me to the period of the beginning of 1914. Everything being alike everything naturally would be simply different and war came and everything being alike and everything being simply different brings everything being simply different brings it to romanticism.

Romanticism is then when everything being alike everything is naturally simply different, and romanticism.

Then for four years this was more and more different even though this was, was everything alike. Everything alike naturally everything was simply different and this is and was romanticism and this is and was war. Everything being alike everything naturally everything is different simply different naturally simply different.

And so there was the natural phenomena that was war, which had been, before war came, several generations behind the contemporary composition, because it became war and so completely needed to be contemporary became completely contemporary and so created the completed recognition of the contemporary composition. Every one but one may say every one became consciously became aware of the existence of the authenticity of the modern composition. This then the contemporary recognition, because of the academic thing known as war having been forced to become contemporary made every one not only contemporary in act not only contemporary in thought but contemporary in self-consciousness made every one contemporary with the modern composition. And so the art creation of the contemporary composition which would have been outlawed normally outlawed several generations more behind even than war, war having been brought so to speak up to date art so to speak was allowed not completely to be up to date, but nearly up to date, in other words we who created the expression of the modern composition were to be recognized before we were dead some of us even quite a long time before we were dead. And so war may be said to have advanced a general recognition of the expression of the contemporary composition by almost thirty years.

And now after that there is no more of that in other words there is peace and something comes then and it follows coming then.

And so now one finds oneself interesting oneself in an equilibration, that of course means words as well as things and distribution as well as between themselves between the words and themselves and the things and themselves, a distribution as distribution. This makes what follows what follows and now there is every reason why there should be an arrangement made. Distribution is interesting and equilibration is interesting when a continuous present and a beginning again and again and using everything and everything alike and everything naturally simply different has been done.

After all this, there is that, there has been that that there is a composition and that nothing changes except composition the composition and the time of and the time in the composition.

The time of the composition is a natural thing and the time in the composition is a natural thing it is a natural thing and it is a contemporary thing.

The time of the composition is the time of the composition. It has been at times a present thing it has been at times a past thing it has been at times a future thing it has been at times an endeavour at parts or all of these things. In my beginning it was a continuous present a beginning again and again and again and again, it was a series it was a list it was a similarity and everything different it was a distribution and an equilibration. That is all of the time some of the time of the composition.

Now there is still something else the time-sense in the composition. This is what is always a fear a doubt and a judgement and a conviction. The quality in the creation of expression the quality in a composition that makes it go dead just after it has been made is very troublesome.

The time in the composition is a thing that is very troublesome. If the time in the composition is very troublesome it is because there must even if there is no time at all in the composition there must be time in the composition which is in its quality of distribution and equilibration. In the beginning there was the time in the composition that naturally was in the composition but time in the composition comes now and this is what is now troubling every one the time in the composition is now a part of distribution and equilibration. In the beginning there was confusion there was a continuous present and later there was romanticism which was not a confusion but an extrication and now there is either succeeding or failing there must be distribution and equilibration there must be time that is distributed and equilibrated. This is the thing that is at present the most troubling and if there is the time that is at present the most troublesome the time-sense that is at present the most troubling is the thing that makes the present the most troubling. There is at present there is distribution, by this I mean expression and time, and in this way at present composition is time that is the reason that at present the time-sense is troubling that is the reason why at present the time-sense in the composition is the composition that is making what there is in composition.

And afterwards.

Now that is all.

Writing Oral History
SISTREN Theatre Collective's *Lionheart Gal*

Carolyn Cooper

Lionheart Gal: Life Stories of Jamaican Women is an experiment in narrative form that exemplifies the dialogic nature of oral/scribal and Creole/English discourse in Jamaican literature. For *Lionheart Gal* is dialogic in the old-fashioned, literal sense of that word: the text, with three notable exceptions, is the product of a dialogue in Creole and English between each woman of Sistren and Honor Ford Smith, the sister confessor, who herself confesses all in solitary script, immaculate in English.

In the fashionably modern, Bakhtinian sense of the word dialogic, *Lionheart Gal* is impeccably subversive. For it engenders an oral, Creole subversion of the authority of the English literary canon. Further, its autobiographical form—the lucid verbal flash—articulates a feminist subversion of the authority of the literary text as fiction—as transformative rewriting of the self in the *persona* of distanced, divine omniscience. *Lionheart Gal*, like much contemporary feminist discourse, does not pretend to be authoritative. Indeed, the preferred narrative mode of many feminist writers is the guise of intimate, understated domestic writing by women: letters, diaries or what Sistren, in an oral/Creole context, simply calls testimony. The simultaneously secular and religious resonances of 'testimony' intimate the potential for ideological development from the purely personal to the political that is the usual consequence of this process of communal disclosure.

It is important to distinguish between actual letters and diaries written by women, and the literary use of this sub-genre as fictional frame. For the artifice of these feminist narrative forms is that they are artless, the author having receded in Joycean detachment to pare, and perhaps paint her fingernails, leaving the tape-recorder or word-processor on automatic. For example, Alice Walker in *The Color Purple* describes herself as 'A.W., author and medium', and courteously 'thank[s] everybody in this book for coming'.[1] She presumably ghost writes the text.

With *Lionheart Gal* this feminist illusion of narrative artlessness is complicated by the mediating consciousness of Honor Ford Smith, the editorial *persona* who performs a dual function in the making of the text. As testifier, Honor records her own story in 'Grandma's Estate'. As amanuensis, she transcribes the testimonies of the other Sistren (except for 'Ava's Diary' and 'Red Ibo'), shaping the women's responses to her three leading questions:

'How did you first become aware of the fact that you were oppressed as a woman? How did that experience affect your life? How have you tried to change it?'[2]

The full weight of that unprepossessing 'with' on the title page—'SISTREN with Honor Ford Smith, editor'—is revealed in the polemical 'Introduction', particularly in the section 'How This Book Was Made'. The editorial explanation of the collaborative process is an illuminating sub-text, as interesting as the stories themselves. For the 'Introduction' offers an ideological frame for the stories that defines the boundaries of their meaning: the stories assume a sociological authority that the improvisational authorial process cannot readily support. The sociologist, Herman McKenzie, in his review of the text, issues an instructive caveat:

> There are methodological doubts, however, which make me feel that perhaps it is wiser to view these stories as illustrative of generalizations previously arrived at by other means, rather than as providing an independent basis for such generalizations about women in Jamaica.[3]

Editorial intervention in the making of the text is clearly an important issue in *Lionheart Gal*. Evelyn O'Callaghan argues that 'the life stories related in *Lionheart Gal* stand somewhere *between* fiction and research data. These stories have been so shaped by selection, editing, rewriting and publication that they have become to a large extent..."fictionalized".'[4] As editor, Honor seems to doctor the text—less in the pejorative sense of that word and more in the sense of obstetrician. This metaphor signifies both the active creativity of the labouring woman telling her story, and the somewhat more passive efficiency of the enabling mid-wife dilating the passage of the text. This distinction between text and story, between ideological necessity and narrative autonomy, is central to the problem of authorship and authority in *Lionheart Gal*.

In her 'Introduction' Honor acknowledges a methodological uncertainty in the making of *Lionheart Gal:* a tension between illustration and testimony—what I call text and story:

> This book started life as a documentation of the work of the theatre collective. The first section was to put the work in the context of Jamaican society and focus on the conditions of life of Jamaican women. It was to include testimonies from Sistren as illustrations of predetermined themes and then discuss how we work on our plays. Soon it was clear that the testimonies would not sit neatly into an introductory section. They refused to become supporting evidence of predetermined factors. They threatened to take over the entire project and they would not behave.

> So, in the end we gave up trying to trim them and silence them and we decided to change the nature of the entire project. (pp. xxvi-xxvii)

Lionheart Gal does not entirely transcend its ambiguous origins in social history; but perhaps it oughtn't to. For as Herman McKenzie concedes in his lively critique, the hybrid nature of the text is a major source of its appeal:

> The collection, therefore, while its mode of presentation (and appeal) places it firmly within the arts, suggests conclusions that challenge social scientists to consider both the problems as well as potential contributions, not to say advantages, of this approach.[5]

Indeed, the ideological frame does not totally circumscribe the range of meanings of the stories. For *Lionheart Gal* is literary less by intent than intuition. Somewhat like *Jane and Louisa Will Soon Come Home* (whose author Erna Brodber once artlessly described herself as 'innocent of literature'),[6] *Lionheart Gal* subverts the conventional generic boundaries between literature and social document, between autobiography and fiction, between the oral and the scribal traditions.

As story, *Lionheart Gal* is for the most part clearly oral. The language of narration is Creole, employing proverb, earthy metaphors and folk tale structures, particularly repetition and apparent digression. In addition, the rural setting of many of the stories reinforces the sense of a 'folk' perspective. The life stories illustrate what Derek Walcott calls the 'symmetry' of the folk tale: 'The true folk tale concealed a structure as universal as the skeleton, the one armature from Br'er Anancy to King Lear. It kept the same digital rhythm of three movements, three acts, three moral revelations'.[7] In the case of *Lionheart Gal*, narrative structure is shaped by Honor's three informing questions which compress female experience into riddle. Decoding the riddle is the key to identity and the moral of the fable.

As text, *Lionheart Gal* somewhat ironically affirms the authority of the written word. Documenting the ideological development of the women of the Sistren Theatre Collective cannot, apparently, be fully accomplished in the medium of theatre. The plays do not adequately speak for themselves: thus the scribal intention of the original project. Further, the search for what Honor calls a 'throughline for each story' (p.xxviii) superimposes on these misbehaving oral accounts a decidedly scribal narrative necessity. The circular line of oral narration becomes diametrically opposed to the ideological, scribal throughline.

This oral/scribal contradiction is quintessentially Creole/English. For, as Honor observes somewhat evangelically in her 'Introduction':

> Those who speak standard English easily are usually middle class. They usually write in English, but a few also write in Patwah (usually poetry or drama only). Those who are working-class and speak Patwah, write English too—or at least very few write Patwah (usually poetry or drama). This means that Patwah is written for performance, which is excellent, but what is not excellent is that it is not written for silent reflection or for purposes other than entertainment. Yet we all know that Jamaican people reflect all the time in their heads or in conversations in Patwah, and we also

know that reflection is part of the process of gaining control over one's own life. So, why are certain kinds of written language still dominated totally by English? (pp. xxviii-ix)

This is the seminal/ovular question. But Honor's own written performance, both in 'Grandma's Estate'[8] and the elaborate 'Introduction' serves to confirm not the appropriateness of the Creole mother tongue, but the imperial authority of the English father tongue—more often phallic pen—as the instrument of serious, written reflection. But perhaps it is indelicate to notice: the subversive subverted.

In an unpublished 1986 conference paper, entitled 'Creole and the Jamaican Novelist: Redcam, DeLisser and V.S. Reid', Victor Chang, more sceptical than Honor, poses a series of challenging questions to our writers, which *Lionheart Gal* as story, if not as text, eloquently answers:

> We have been increasingly told that the resources for expression in Creole are no more limited than in Standard English. If this is so, why then is it not used for internal musing and reflection? Could it be that there is still a persistent belief that Creole just will not serve in certain situations, that certain registers require Standard English, or that our writers still have yet to learn to manipulate the Creole with total freedom? Perhaps it could be argued that the very spoken nature of the Creole, its very physicality, militates against its use for inner reflection and introspection.[9]

Recognising the dialogic nature of oral/scribal and Creole/English discourse in the story/text *Lionheart Gal* and seeking to narrow the social distance between the language of the stories and the language of textual analysis, I wish to engage in an experimental Creole subversion of the authority of English as our exclusive voice of scholarship. My analysis of the testimonies of the women of Sistren—their verbal acts of introspective self-disclosure—will now proceed in Creole.

'We come together and talk our life story and put it in a lickle scene'. (p. 72) A so Ava seh Sistren start off: a tell one anodder story. So yu tell, me tell, so tell di whole a we find out seh a di one story we a tell. Oman story. Di same ting over an over. But it no easy fi get up tell people yu business ma! It tek plenty heart. So Foxy seh eena fi her story. She seh:

> Plenty women used to talk bout di children dat we have and di baby-faada problem. At first me was shy to talk about myself. Di impression women always give me is dat dem is a set of people who always lap dem tail, tek yuh name spread table cloth. Me did feel sort a funny at di time, having children fi two different man, especially since me never like Archie. Me never discuss it wid nobody. When me come meet Didi and hear she talk bout her baby faada and how she hate him after she get pregnant, me say, 'Well if yuh can say your own me can say mine, for we actually deh pon di same ting.' Me and she start talk bout it. (p. 253)

An a di same Foxy she come find out seh dat di tings dem dat happen to we jus because we a oman, dem deh tings supposin fi call 'politics', jus like any a di odder big tings deh, weh a gwan eena 'politricks' as di one Tosh him

413

seh. Den wat a way dem kill him off ee! Me no know if a big Politics dat, or a lickle politics, but someting mus eena someting. But dat is anodder story. An di ile dat fry sprat cyaan fry jack, so small fry all like me no suppose fi business eena dem deh tings.

So hear how Foxy seh she start fi find out bout dis oman politics:

> Tings develop so-till we start meet more people and talk bout woman and work and woman and politics. We discuss what is politics and how it affect woman. After we done talk ah get to feel dat di little day-to-day tings dat happen to we as women, is politics too. For instance, if yuh tek yuh pick-ney to hospital and it die in yuh hand—dat is politics. If yuh do someting to yuh own child dat damage him or her fi di future, dat is politics. If yuh man box yuh down, dat is politics. But plenty politicians don't tink dose tings have anything to do wid politics. (p. 253)

A true. For yu cyaan understan 'di little day-to-day tings dat happen to we as women' if yu no understan seh dat di whole ting set up gainst plenty oman from di day dem born. Tek for instance how so much a di oman dem weh a tell dem story eena *Lionheart Gal* jus find out seh dem pregnant. Yes! It come een like a big surprise. Grab bag. A no nuttin dem plan for. A no like how yu hear dem people pon radio and t.v. a tell yu seh 'Two is better than too many'—like seh pickney is sums: add an multiply an divide an subtract! Wear yu down to nuttin. Nought. Dat a weh pregnant do plenty oman. Not even oman good. Young gal. Force ripe an blighted.

But even though life hard, di oman dem still a try. Hear how Barbara put it:

> Di pregnancy a never someting me plan or choose. It just happen. Nadine born '71. After she born, me did just love her. Me always feel a tenderness inside me dat me no waan do notten fi hurt her. At di same time me no pet her till she spoil. (p. 138)

But oman an pickney cyaan live pon so-so love. An a when di oman dem start fi try fi find lickle work dat story come to bump. For a den di politics beat dem down. Ongle certain kind a people fi do certain kind a work. An dawg nyam yu supper if *yu* no one a dem. All yu fi do a fi look after odder people business. Yu no have no business fi look after. Dat a weh happen to Doreen. Never even get a chance fi go a day school. Pure evening school, an nah learn nuttin:

> Me did waan learn, for me did waan be nurse, or a teacher, but me couldn't grasp notten. Me know definitely seh if me no pass di exam, me nah go get di job me did want. As di months pass by and me see seh me couldn't manage di work in di evening school, me know dere and den seh me nah go noweh in life. After school, ah used to walk past di residential areas and wish it was in deh me live. Sometime me used to pretend seh me live deh and dat me get fi go a school like dem pickney. (p. 92)

So now when pickney problem jine aan pon no-get-fi-go-a-no-good-school, cyaan get no work, haffi a siddown wait pon man fi set yu up, dat a when de politics get hot. Dat a Didi story. Hear her:

Sometime when yuh no have notten and yuh have di pickney dem and dem a look to yuh fi food and fi shelter, yuh haffi do sometings weh yuh no really waan fi do, just fi survive. Sometimes a better yuh cyaan do, mek yuh tek certain man. Sometime yuh really in need. A man might use dat fi ketch yuh. Yuh might know a so it go, but yuh in need. Yuh want it, so yuh haffi tek it. (p. 201)

But a no all di time yu cyan tek it. For might-as-well turn eena livin hell. For now man all waan beat yu if yu no mek up yu mind fi do weh *him* seh. An if yu married to him, dat no mek no difference. It could a all worse, for now him directly feel dat him own yu. Dat a di prekkeh Yvonne get herself een. She seh:

Ah say ah have me three pickney now and ah married. Dem time deh when yuh married, dem say yuh married fi life. Ah never expect fi me and him separate. Me depress and unhappy. Everyting just get confuse inna me brain. Me feel seh me life mash up tru me never understand bout sex and man. Me never know what me could a do bout di problem. Me say is everyday problem. It cyaan change. Me grow in it. A so life hard. Me no chat to nobody more dan so. Me no know no odder woman fi talk to. Me never have no consideration. Me, like me unconscious. (p. 151)

Dem deh blow good fi kill yu. Lick yu down flat. Di ongle ting fi bring yu back from grave-side a fi find out seh a no yu one. Odder oman eena di ring wid yu a go help yu pen up di bull. So yu talk, act out yu lickle scene, an nex ting—yu eena book.

So how dem mek di book? Accorden to di ring-leader, Honor, di whole ting start off wid she a ask di Sistren dem question bout how dem grow up, an di different different tings dat happen to dem fi mek dem find out seh life hard. An dem go roun and roun, an talk an talk, like dem a play 'Show me yu Motion'. All dis time dem a tape everyting dem seh. Den Honor she listen back to di tape an fix-up fix-up wat she tink di Sistren dem a seh, an dem gwan talk an talk so tell dem en up wid las version. An den dem write it down.

Plenty a di story dem soun like a so di oman dem talk. But some a dem mek me wonder. Dem no soun so caseer. Tek for instance 'Ava's Diary'. It kind a mix-up mix-up. It come een like seh how she talk a her yard eena war wid how dem did want her fi talk an write a school; an di school nah win! See't ya now:

Since me and the children are alone, if a man come to me other than him, I would have to leave them and go out with him. Therefore I have decided not to have any relationship with another man for the time being.

Bertie know seh me no have no man friend, so him come if him want to come, till me and him start to talk good and him start come intensively. (p. 271)

Den now, 'Grandma's Estate' and 'Red Ibo'. Me never like how di two a dem jus prims up demself eena so-so English. An dem no inna no talkin business me dear; a pure write dem a write. School definitely win out yasso.

An it look like seh Honor did know seh people a go ask her bout it, for she try fi clear up herself. She seh:

> With the two middle-strata members of the group, the oral interviews did not work well. Accustomed to standard English and the conventions of academic expression, their stories sounded stilted when spoken, full of jargon, and hollow. Both 'Red Ibo' and 'Grandma's Estate' were written responses to the interview questions. (p. xxviii)

An yu know, me think me understan: Parson christen dem pickney first. But me still seh, supposin dem did gi we di chance fi hear wat dem did *seh*? Maybe notten never did wrong wid it. Den nex ting: It no soun like seh dem a seh seh dem cyaan *talk* good, dem cyan ongle *write* good? Me no know; me just a wonder.

Den again, yu no see seh fi dem story no personally deal wid no man an oman business to dat; no lickle rudeness. But me nah seh dem faint-a-heart because dem nah tell people di whole a fi dem personal an private business—like di odder lionheart gal dem! Is jus dat fi dem story come een like seh yu a try fi explain yu self, yu know seh people a listen, so yu haffi fix it up. 'Red Ibo' story all soun like seh she a preach. But no testimony meeting! Everybody a testify inna dem owna way. But me dear mek me lef it. For puss an dawg no have di same luck, an me no waan nobody seh a bad mind me bad mind mek me a ask dem ya lickle question.

An still for all, yu haffi gi it to dem. A true seh Ella an Red Ibo story soun like book. But wat is fi-yu cyaan be un-fi-yu. An more time dem still ketch a nice lickle roots vibe inna di English. Hear how Red Ibo she start off fi her story cultural: 'When I think of childhood, I think of a village squatting on hillslopes with a river running through it and a bridge and a fording midway along the road which ran by the river'. (p.221) An a Ella granny nearly spoil up di poor lickle pickney. No want her fi ask no question bout her people dem. She fi go read book. Not even play di lickle pickney cyaan play. Poort ting. She seh:

> I packed leaves of croton and pimento into a basket I found in the kitchen. I twisted a piece of cloth into a cotta and put it on my head. I placed the basket on top of it and practised walking while balancing it on my head. Then I stepped off down the pathway arriving with my produce under Grandma's window. 'Lady, Lady, yuh want anyting to buy, maam?' I readjusted the basket, which proved difficult to control.
>
> At first there was no answer, so I repeated 'Lady, Lady, yuh want anyting to buy, maam?'
>
> My grandmother pushed her head through the window.
>
> 'Ella! Come inside at once and put down that basket!'
>
> I obeyed.
>
> 'What do you think you are doing, Miss?'
>
> 'Playing market woman, Grandma,' I said, not sure what I had done wrong.

'Never let me see you doing that again.'

'Why grandma?' I asked. 'What is wrong with market ladies?'

'Ladies? They are not ladies. They are women. Go and take a seat in your room.'

(pp. 180-81)

A so it go. *Lionheart Gal* is a serious book. An oonu better read it. It might a lickle hard fi ketch di spellin fi di first, but after yu gwan gwan, it not so bad. Den one ting sweet me: Yu know how some a fi we people simple; from dem see sinting set down eena book dem tink it important. So now plenty a dem who never go a none a Sistren play, dem same one a go read Sistren book, because book high. Dem a go get ketch. For a six a one, half a dozen a di odder: oman problem, man problem, pickney problem. Plenty politics. An whole heap a joke! For yu know how we know how fi tek bad tings mek joke. Stop yu from mad go off yu head. Doreen know how it go. Hear her nuh:

All my life, me did haffi act in order to survive. Di fantasies and ginnalship were ways of coping wid di frustration. Now me can put dat pain on stage and mek fun a di people who cause it.

Go deh, Sistren! Last lick sweet.

NOTES

1. Alice Walker, *The Color Purple* (1982; New York: Washington Square Press, 1983), p. 253.

2. SISTREN with Honor Ford Smith, editor, *Lionheart Gal: Life Stories of Jamaican Women* (London: The Women's Press, 1986), p. xxvii. Subsequent references cited parenthetically in text.

3. Herman McKenzie, Review of *Lionheart Gal, Jamaica Journal*, 20, 4 (Nov. 1987-Jan.1988), p. 64.

4. Evelyn O'Callaghan, Review of *Lionheart Gal, Journal of West Indian Literature*, 2,1 (Dec. 1987), p. 93.

5. McKenzie, op.cit., p. 63.

6. In an unpublished talk to students in the West Indian Literature class, Department of English, U.W.I., Mona, 1984.

7. Derek Walcott, 'What the Twilight Says: An Overture' in *Dream on Monkey Mountain and Other Plays* (New York: Farrar, Straus and Giroux, 1970), p. 24.

8. Ella *does* use Creole when she role plays as the market lady '"Lady, Lady, yuh want anything to buy, maam?" I readjusted the basket, which proved difficult to control.' (p.180). A Freudian slip?

9. Victor Chang, 'Creole and the Jamaican Novelist: Redcam, Delisser and V.S. Reid', Sixth, Annual Conference on West Indian Literature, U.W.I., St. Augustine, 1986, p. 5.

Life and Death in the Global Village

Michael J. Arlen

He was shot in secrecy, away from cameras. No strange slow-motion scenes, as when the young Japanese student, sword in hand, rushed across the stage to lunge at a Socialist politician, or when Verwoerd, the South African, was shot at and for whole crazy moments (it seems so long ago; so many people shot at since then) the cameras swirled and danced around the tumbling, stampeding bodies of the crowd—and then John Kennedy was killed, his life made to disappear right there before us, frame by frame, the projector slowing down, s-l-o-w-i-n-g d-o-w-n, s—l—o—w—i—n—g d—o—w—n, as we watched (three consecutive days we watched), gathered in little tight-gutted bands around the television set, meals being cooked somehow, children put to bed, sent out to play, our thoughts of abandonment and despair and God knows what else focusing on the images of the television set, television itself taking on (we were told later) the aspect of a national icon, a shrine, an exorciser of grief; we were never so close (we were told later) as in those days just after Dallas. It could not have been quite close enough, it seems, or lasted long enough. The man who was shot in Memphis on Thursday of last week was standing on a second-floor balcony of a motel, the Lorraine, leaning over the railing of the balcony in front of his room, which was No. 306. (We have been told it was No. 306.) He was shot once and killed by a man who fired his rifle (a Remington 30.06), apparently, from inside a bathroom window of a rooming house some two hundred feet away. The address of the rooming house is 420 South Main Street. There was no film record of the act, no attendant Zapruder to witness for us the body falling and other memorabilia, but most of us found out about it by television, and it is by television that most of us have been connected with whatever it is that really happened, or is happening now. Television connects—the global village. We sit at home—We had been out, actually, a party full of lawyers, and had come back early and turned on the eleven-o'clock news. "I have a dream..." young Dr. King was chanting, "that one day on the red hills of Georgia..." CBS's Joseph Benti said that Dr. King had been shot and killed, was dead. The President was speaking. "I ask every citizen to reject the blind violence that has struck Dr. King, who lived by non-violence," he said. They showed us pictures of Dr. King in Montgomery. They showed us pictures of the outside of the Lorraine Motel.

The telephone rang. A friend of my wife's. "Have you heard?" she said. I said we'd heard. "It so horrible," she said. And then, "I can't believe it." And then, "I feel we're all mad." I held the phone against my ear, mumbling the usual things, feeling, in part, her grief, her guilt, her sense of lunacy—whatever it was—and, in part, that adrenalin desire we strangers have who have been separate in our cabins all the long sea voyage to somehow touch each other at the moment that the ship goes down. She talked some more. "I'm keeping you from watching," she said at last. I mumbled protests, and we said good-by and disconnected. We will all meet for dinner three weekends hence and discuss summer rentals on the Vineyard.

All over the country now the members of the global village sit before their sets, and the voices and faces out of the sets speak softly, earnestly, reasonably, sincerely to us, in order once again (have four and a half years really gone by since Dallas?) to bind us together, to heal, to mend, to take us forward. The President appears. His face looks firmer, squarer, straighter now than it has looked in months. "We can achieve nothing by lawlessness and divisiveness among the American people," he says. "It's only by joining together and only by working together we can continue to move toward equality and fulfillment for all of our people." The Vice-President speaks. "The cause for which he marched and worked, I am sure, will find a new strength. The plight of discrimination, poverty, and neglect must be erased from America," he says. Former Vice-President Richard Nixon is expected to release a statement soon. There are brief pictures of a coffin being slid onto a plane. The Field Foundation, one hears, has just undertaken to donate a million dollars to the civil-rights movement. Dr. Ralph Bunche asks for "an effort of unparalleled determination, massiveness, and urgency to convert the American ideal of equality into reality."

The television sets hum in our midst. Gray smoke, black smoke begins to rise from blocks of buildings in Washington and Chicago. Sirens whine outside our windows in the night. The voices out of Memphis seem to be fainter now; the pictures of that little nondescript motel, the railing, the bathroom window are already being shown to us less frequently today. Down below us on the sidewalk, six blue-helmeted policemen are gathered in a group. Three police cars are parked farther down the street. The television beams out at us a Joel McCrea movie. Detroit and Newark have been remembered. Responsible decisions have been made in responsible places. The President is working now "to avoid catastrophe." The cartoons are on this morning. The air is very bright outside. The day is sunny. All day long the sirens sound. The television hums through its schedule. There is a circus on Channel 4. Back from the dime store, my daughter asks one of the helmeted policemen if anything has happened. He seems surprised. No, nothing, he says. A squad car drives slowly, slowly by. A bowling exhibition is taking place on Channel 7. Another movie—and then the news. Great waves of smoke, clouds, billowing waves are suddenly pouring out of buildings. The sounds of bells and sirens. Mayor Daley speaks. Mayor Daley declares a curfew. Six Negro boys are running down a street, carrying armfuls of clothes.

419

Police cars streak by. More smoke. The news is over. We are re-enveloped in a movie. We sit there on the floor and absorb the hum of television. Last summer it inflamed our passions, did it not? This time the scenes of black men running past the smoking buildings of Chicago are handled briefly, almost dreamily—a light caress by cameras and announcers. The coffin—one wonders where the coffin is at present, who is with it. Boston University announces that ten new scholarships for "underprivileged students" have just been created. The Indian Parliament pays tribute. The voices of reason and reordering rise out of the civic temples of the land and float through the air and the airwaves into our homes. Twenty-one House Republicans have issued an "urgent appeal" for passage of the new civil-rights bill. "With whom will we stand? The man who fired the gun? Or the man who fell before it?" Senator Edward Brooke, of Massachusetts, asks. The City Council of Chicago meets and passes a resolution to build a "permanent memorial." Senator Robert Kennedy deplores the rise in violence.

There was a moment the other evening when (just for a few seconds) everybody stopped talking, when (just for a few seconds) the television stopped its humming and soothing and filling of silences and its preachments of lessons-we-have-just-learned and how-we-must-all-march-together—and (just for a few seconds) Mrs. King appeared; she was speaking about her husband, her dead husband. She spoke; she seemed so alive with him—it's marvelous how that sometimes happens between people; he really had been alive, and one knew it then—and for a few scant moments, just at that time, and afterward, sitting there looking at the set, that very imperfect icon, that very imperfect connector of people (will somebody really have the nerve to say this week that we are a nation "united in grief"?), one could almost hear the weeping out there, of real people in real villages, and the anger, this time, of abandonment.

And then the sounds came back—the sounds of one's own life. The weather man came on. A Negro minister on Channel 13 was talking about the need to implement the recommendations of the President's new Commission on Civil Disorders. He *had* been alive...hadn't he? Later that night, one could hear the sirens—very cool and clear—and, somewhere nearby (around the corner? blocks away?), the sounds of footsteps running.

On Mortality

Maxine Hong Kingston

As you know, any plain person you chance to meet can prove to be a powerful immortal in disguise come to test you.

Li Fu-yen told a story about Tu Tzu-chun, who lived from A.D. 558 to 618, during the Northern Chou and Sui dynasties. Tu's examiner was a Taoist monk, who made him rich twice, and twice Tu squandered his fortune though it took him two lifetimes to do so. The third time the Taoist gave him money, he bought a thousand li of good land, plowed it himself, seeded it, built houses, roads, and bridges, then welcomed widows and orphans to live on it. With the leftover money, he found a husband for each spinster and a wife for every bachelor in his family, and also paid for the weddings. When he met the Taoist again, he said, "I've used up all your money on the unfortunates I've come across."

"You'll have to repay me by working for me," said the Taoist monk. "I need your help on an important difficult task." He gave Tu three white pills. "Swallow these," he said, pouring him a cup of wine. "All that you'll see and feel will be illusions. No matter what happens, don't speak; don't scream. Remember the saying 'Hide your broken arms in your sleeves'."

"How easy," said Tu as he swallowed the pills in three gulps of wine. "Why should I scream if I know they're illusions?"

Level by level he descended into the nine hells. At first he saw oxheads, horsefaces, and the heads of generals decapitated in war. Illusions. Only illusions, harmless. He laughed at the heads. He had seen heads before. Soon fewer heads whizzed through the dark until he saw no more of them.

Suddenly his wife was being tortured. Demons were cutting her up into pieces, starting with her toes. He heard her scream; he heard her bones crack. He reminded himself that she was an illusion. *Illusion*, he thought. She was ground into bloodmeal.

Then the tortures on his own body began. Demons poured bronze down his throat and beat him with iron clubs and chains. They mortar-and-pestled and packed him into a pill.

He had to walk over mountains of knives and through fields of knives and forests of swords. He was killed, his head chopped off, rolling into other people's nightmares.

He heard gods and goddesses talking about him, "This man is too wicked to be reborn a man. Let him be born a woman." He saw the entrance of a black tunnel and felt tired. He would have to squeeze his head and shoulders down into the enclosure and travel a long distance. He pushed head first through the entrance, only the beginning. A god kicked him in the butt to give him a move on. (This kick is the reason many Chinese babies have a blue-gray spot on their butts or lower backs, the "Mongolian spot.") Sometimes stuck in the tunnel, sometimes shooting helplessly through it, he emerged again into light with many urgent things to do, many messages to deliver, but his hands were useless baby's hands, his legs wobbly baby's legs, his voice a wordless baby's cries. Years had to pass before he could regain adult powers; he howled as he began to forget the cosmos, his attention taken up with mastering how to crawl, how to stand, how to walk, how to control his bowel movements.

He discovered that he had been reborn a deaf-mute female named Tu. When she became a woman, her parents married her to a man named Lu, who at first did not mind. "Why does she need to talk," said Lu, "to be a good wife? Let her set an example for women." They had a child. But years later, Lu tired of Tu's dumbness. "You're just being stubborn," he said, and lifted their child by the feet. "Talk, or I'll dash its head against the rocks." The poor mother held her hand to her mouth. Lu swung the child, broke its head against the wall.

Tu shouted out, "Oh! Oh!"—and he was back with the Taoist, who sadly told him that at the moment when she had said, "Oh! Oh!" the Taoist was about to complete the last step in making the elixir for immortality. Now that Tu had broken his silence, the formula was spoiled, no immortality for the human race. "You overcame joy and sorrow, anger, fear, and evil desire, but not love," said the Taoist, and went on his way.

The Holyland Buffet

Gwendolyn MacEwen

'The most amazing thing I saw in all my travels,' Kali was saying, 'was that streetcar in Cairo.'

'I thought you never travelled,' said Ibrahim the Syrian, who was sitting across the table from her in a new vegetarian restaurant called Mythological Foods. 'When you get mad, you always swear that you're going to pack up and go to India. But you never go, so I assumed you never travel.'

'Ah but I have, you know. I have been to two holy lands—Israel and Egypt. I have also been to Greece, which is not really a holy land. But to get back to that streetcar—'

'Tell me about Israel,' Ibrahim said. 'I want to comprehend the enemy.'

'On my first day there I took a walk alone along the beach at Jaffa, which means *The Beautiful*. Some boy about eleven or twelve came up and asked me the time—everybody there asks you the time, don't ask me why—and when I told him he attacked me and threw me to the ground and starting punching me all over. We punched and kicked for a while until he finally got bored and walked away. I never knew what it was all about, except that because I was wearing shorts I probably offended him.'

'Bloody aggressive Israelis,' Ibrahim said. 'That's all they know, how to punch and kick their way through the world.'

'The boy was a Palestinian Arab,' Kali said. 'He thought *I* was an Israeli.'

'Then the story is entirely different,' said Ibrahim. 'It needs re-examining.'

The mythological food arrived at their table and they dug in. Ibrahim showed her how to eat a dish of dark brown powder with an indescribable smell.

'This is *zaatar*,' he said. 'We've been eating it for centuries in the East. You dip the bread first in the olive oil to moisten it, then into the *zaatar*—so.' He popped a piece into her mouth. 'Jesus Christ ate this all the time,' he said. 'Him and his disciples. This is the bitter herbs they wrote about. Anyway, tell me more about Israel.'

'It's really the streetcar I want to talk about,' Kali said.

'Never mind the streetcar.'

'Well I was walking through this village called Lifta, outside Jerusalem, and I was wearing shorts again, so I looked like a *sabra* again, and a whole tribe of little Arab boys came screaming up the mountain path toward me and started pelting me with stones. Stoned outside of Jerusalem, can you imagine, in the twentieth century, and me a Kanadian. In the clinic they put something called a spider clamp into my head where the worst wound was, and covered it with bandages that looked like a turban. They said now I looked like an Arab, and told me not to do anything exciting for a few days. I tried not to do anything exciting, but the Israelis are hooked on speed—I mean anything that goes fast, the faster the better. So I had this wild motorcycle ride with a guy who thought he was doing me a favour by giving me a ride up to Tiberias, and every moment I thought I was going to die, which was of course the whole point, the thrill. Then I walked around Tiberias with the spider clamp rusting in my skull, holding my thoughts together as it were, keeping my head from flying apart in a hundred directions; then I brooded and felt biblical in a small hotel, and the next day another guy offered me a ride in his motor-boat in Lake Tiberias. I should have known better. He rode at top speed to the middle of the lake and informed me that now, two minutes either way, meant the difference between Israel and Jordan, life or death. Then he laughed and laughed like a madman and started going around in crazy wild circles. Can you imagine—this maniac in the middle of the Sea of Galilee and us going round and round and the laughter so loud they could probably hear it on both shores....'

'Bloody insane Israelis,' said Ibrahim, and passed her a plate of ripe green figs.

'Well all the guys are on the make over there,' Kali said, 'and I was a female tourist travelling alone, so what could I expect? Come on, it would be the same in your country.'

Ibrahim addressed his full attention to the figs.

'Oh wait,' Kali remembered, 'I knew I forgot something, I forgot to tell you about the Holyland Buffet...'

'*What?*'

'The Holyland Buffet. It was this crazy little place at the foot of the Mount of Loaves and Fishes. Nothing more than a little shack, really, with a counter in the front and a few shelves behind full of orange drinks and cigarettes and halvah bars. I must have been the first person the owner had seen for days, because—'

'Wait!' Ibrahim cried. 'Wait wait wait! I have a cousin in Jordan who has a place called the Holyland Buffet, just outside of Bethlehem!'

'Well this one was in Israel.'

'It's impossible that there are two!' Ibrahim cried, his face getting very red. 'It's just impossible!'

'Well, I didn't know if the guy who ran this one was Arab or Israeli. Anyway, as I was saying, I must have been the first person or maybe just the first woman he'd seen for days because he leaned over the counter after he served me my drink and clutched my wrists and pleaded *Come with me to Haifa! The lights, the cabarets, the people!* I said that I couldn't, and I didn't even know him. He said that didn't matter, we'd have a wonderful time anyway. *To Haifa, to Haifa together!* I wonder where he is today; what a beautiful man....'

'There can't be two Holyland Buffets,' Ibrahim said, and proceeded not to listen to her as she went on.

424

'And then there was old Ephraim, the painter who lived in the old village of Safed in the mountains. He wanted to seduce me too, although he went on for hours about Eisenstein and Isadora Duncan and Stanislavsky and all the others he had known who were black-listed in the States. Now in Israel the tourist bureau warned tourists against having their portraits done by the infamous communist Ephraim, so he ended up with more business than anyone....'

'Let's change the subject,' said Ibrahim, dejectedly sipping a Turkish coffee. 'What about Egypt?'

'At last we're getting to what I wanted to tell you in the first place. The streetcar—'

'Who cares about a streetcar? What happened in Egypt?'

'Well of course, it's even worse there for a woman to walk around alone. When I went every day to the museum in Cairo because there was so much to see, the guards thought I must have been playing some really sexy game with them; it was inconceivable that I would go alone to a museum every day—why? What was my *real* reason? I could not possibly have travelled half-way around the world to stare at statues and mummies of the dead lords of Egypt, the gold of Tutankhamon, the most exquisite sculpture imaginable. No, I was indeed a tart, a slut, a whore. So they kept plying me with sugary tea and cigarettes, and they smiled and joked among themselves, and when I didn't want more sugary tea they offered me *Misra-Cola* and more cigarettes and endless offers of escorted tours around Cairo. Within a few days I had acquired a reputation of being one of the loosest women in the city, a tramp, an easy lay; and of course each one of them boasted to the others of his conquest of this piece of garbage, this foreigner. I don't know how I got to actually see what I wanted to see in the museum, but somehow I did.'

'Would you like some *halvah*?' Ibrahim asked. 'It's the lovely kind with chocolate marbled all through it. Here, have some.' And he popped a piece into her mouth. 'Now, what else?'

'The pyramids,' Kali said. 'Not the pyramids themselves—what can one say? But the washrooms, the horrible little washrooms that had no doors on the cubicles and no doors closed to the outside, and you had to pay the guard—a man—to go and pee, and you sat there in the shameless light of day staring at the Great Pyramid of Giza from the vantage point of a toilet seat, for Christ's sake. I remember it well; I have tried to forget.'

The waiter at Mythological Foods produced the bill for the meal, and Ibrahim frowned darkly as he checked it over.

'It's amazing and disgusting what they think they can charge for food that has been eaten since before Jesus Christ walked the earth, before Ulysses set sail from Ithaca, before there even was a Holy Land,' he said.

He paid, and they left. Outside the sky was a frail blue, the colour of Roman glass.

'But you come back from these travels, and it's wonderful,' Kali mused. 'You come back to Kanada, and the jet going from East to West interferes with the world's turning. You realize there are other times, arrested sunsets, moments that go on forever, cities whose walls trap time....'

'That bill was too high,' Ibrahim muttered. 'We'd have gotten a better meal at the Holyland Buffet. The one my cousin owns. In Jordan.'

They waited for a streetcar; they were both going in the same direction.

'*Now* will you listen to my story, the one I was going to tell you in the first place?' Kali asked.

'All right, but make it fast.'

'Well there I was, standing in the middle of Cairo one afternoon, hot, mad, and completely disoriented, with people screaming all around me and donkeys braying and a chaos that exists nowhere else in the world—when what should I see?'

'I don't know. What did you see?'

'What should I see, coming toward me with the slowness and grace of a dream, its colours an unmistakable dark-red and yellow, the sign on its metal forehead a magic name recalling a distant, mythic land....'

'What did you *see*?' Ibrahim's mood was black.

'*A King Street streetcar.*'

'A what?'

'A King Street streetcar. From Toronto, Kanada. The city gives old ones away to Egypt and I guess other places, when they're too worn out to use here. There it was, coming toward me, this great, fabulous beast. Try to imagine it, Ibrahim, try to imagine what I felt.'

But Ibrahim was too angry about the meal, about the bill, about the second Holyland Buffet which was in the country of the enemy, and about the coldness of the day in this country of his exile, to pay much attention to what she said.

TERMS and TOPICS

TERMS

1. **Vocabulary, Section VI:** abdication, amanuensis, arbiter, arbitrary, articulates, artifice, artless, chic, communal, condone, criterion, deploying, dilating, disarming, edifying, evangelically, extrication, fatuous, flim-flam, gaffe, generic, hoariest, immanent, impeccably, imponderables, imputes, indolent, inexorable, inflection, mediating, memorabilia, metaphysical, milieu, militates, monoliths, mortified, mystical, mystique, nondescript, omniscience, ovular, palliate, propitiation, pundits, rapport, rube, sanctified, schmaltzy, seminal, sombre, subversive, tack, testily, transcend, uncouth, unethical, unstinting, wallow, zealots.

2. What is a concrete poem? What is meant by *concrete language*? (See "A Note to the Reader.") Does a concrete poem have to use concrete language?

3. Distinguish between the words *simplistic* and *solipsistic*. How does *simplistic* differ from *simple*? How does *solipsistic* differ from *personal, private,* or *subjective*?

4. What is the difference between a *motif* and a *leitmotif*? What are some other terms that, like *leitmotif,* literary criticism has adopted from the visual and plastic arts and from music?

5. *Metre, alliteration, assonance, consonance* and *rhyme* are defined in "A Note to the Reader." They are all common devices in poetry. How much can a writer of prose use such devices? Are there some kinds of essays in which a writer should avoid them all, others where they can be used in a limited way, and others where they can be used with abandon? Carefully examine several essays of different kinds in this book to determine to what extent these devices are present in them. What are the differences between poetry and prose? See if you can find one or more pieces of writing (not in this book) that it would be difficult if not impossible to classify as either poetry or prose. Write a paragraph of prose—perhaps describing a scene or an action—in which you make deliberate use of metre, alliteration, assonance, consonance, and rhyme. Are you tempted to think of the result as poetry? or at least poetic prose?

6. What does the term *reading* mean? What is the relation between reading and writing? Should readers try to reproduce in themselves the experience the writer had while writing? How important is it that readers "hear" an essay that is written down? Should writers always read aloud what they have written? Do you make it a practice to read your essays aloud—whether anyone else is around or not—before you consider them finished? How can readers learn to be conscious of *voice* in what they read? What exactly is *voice*? How much attention should readers pay to the *appearance* of an essay on the page? How can a reader "read" a concrete poem?

Topics: On Individual Essays

JOHN ROBERT COLOMBO   *"Communicating through Form"*

1. What is Dada? What is Art Deco? Prepare a research report on one of these or some other movement in twentieth-century art.

2. Explain in your own words, with concrete examples, the difference between *perception* and *apperception*. What is the difference between a *symbol* and a *sign*?

3. Advertising often picks up innovations in the arts. Find several ads that make use of the kinds of "infracted forms" Colombo discusses. Write an essay exploring "violated forms" of other than a literary kind, for example in music, painting, photography, or film. How could they exist also in "modern social concerns," as Colombo says they do?

4. Colombo says that "today it is perfectly possible...to react to the world as if it were a work of art itself." Possible, yes—but, considering what the word *art* means, is it legitimate to do so, to adopt "this way of seeing things"? Compose an argument answering this question.

5. Try making an anagram of your own name.

6. Write a lipogram of at least one hundred words avoiding one of the vowels. Then write one avoiding *r*, *s*, or *t*. Write a paragraph in which each word contains an *a*, then one with each word having an *e*; an *i*; a *t*; an *o*; an *n*. Write five univocalic sentences—each using only one of the five vowels; for example: Jack has a swayback nag that balks at a caravan march.

7. Compose a concrete poem.

MICHAEL HORNYANSKY   *"Is Your English Destroying Your Image?"*

1. Identify the literary allusions in "Call me Noah" and "A little grammar is a dangerous thing." Are these allusions amusing? Point out and explain some of Hornyansky's many other allusions.

2. In the fourth paragraph Hornyansky clarifies the meaning of "mistake" as he wants it understood. What other terms does he find it necessary to define? Show how he uses classification in this essay.

3. This is a long essay. Examine Hornyansky's topic sentences to see how well each also works transitionally, helping to maintain coherence between paragraphs.

4. Do you agree that "lightness makes for more clarity than does indignation"? Why should this be so? Which would make for more *impact*? Is Hornyansky correct when he says that his three criteria are always subtly intertwined?

5. Hornyansky says he likes to use "the simple and colloquial as salt to my discourse." Point out several examples of his doing that, and evaluate the overall effectiveness of the technique. Examine also his use of metaphors.

6. In the third paragraph Hornyansky uses *magic* as a verb—which ordinarily it isn't—thereby adding vigour and freshness to the sentence. Compose half-a-dozen sentences using nouns as verbs, then another half-dozen using adjectives as verbs. You may then want to try building paragraphs around one or more of the sentences.

7. From your everyday reading and listening, gather more words and phrases that create images of Fogginess and Mechanism. Find some examples—perhaps in your textbooks—of the "Professorial" or "God-like" style that Hornyansky calls a "disease." Can you think of any other "images" to add to those he lists?

8. Keep score for a week, recording the number of times you see or hear *hopefully* misused. Compare several dictionaries to see what, if anything, they say about the usage of such terms as *ain't, like* as a conjunction, *disinterested, due to, irregardless, good* as an adverb, *media, infer, hopefully, presently, momentarily.* Write a brief report on your findings. You may want to classify the various dictionaries according to how they treat such matters.

9. Hornyansky doesn't refer to passive voice. Show how passive voice is often weak in the same way that such phrases as "a decision-making process" are weak. Does Hornyansky use much passive voice?

10. Do you agree that *whom* is best avoided? If not, construct a brief argument for its retention. Or try an ironic argument, if you agree with Hornyansky.

11. Write a persuasive essay either agreeing or disagreeing with Hornyansky's stand on "sexist English."

LEWIS THOMAS   *"Notes on Punctuation"*

1. Is there a significant difference between *precision* and *exactitude* as Thomas uses them at the end of his first paragraph?

2. How can one use a comma "with affection"? Do you agree with Thomas's preference for the semicolon over the colon? Why or why not?

3. Thomas is a scientist (see his essay in section IV); why should he be writing about punctuation? And discussing poetry?

4. Is this essay argumentative? Is Thomas trying to convince his readers that punctuation is important, that it shouldn't be considered as something accidental or added on but rather as part of *what* is being said because it tells readers *how to read* what is being said? If so, does he succeed? Does he also communicate the *pleasures* of punctuation?

5. Apply Thomas's advice to your own writing. For practice, compose sentences—preferably many of them—that experiment with each of the marks in the various ways suggested by Thomas's remarks and examples. Could a single sentence contain all the marks?

MICHAEL FRAYN   *"Lives and Likenesses"*

1. What signs indicate the original occasion for this essay? What differentiates it as a review from that of Kael in section III? Is Frayn's piece also argumentative?

2. Are the examples Frayn offers examples of different things, or is it all one essay? If it is all of a piece, what holds it together? Show how the *forms*—the patterns and the organization—of the sentences in each example are related to what that example is saying.

3. When do you first know that this is going to be a humorous essay? The subtitle of the collection from which it comes is "Satirical Essays by Michael Frayn." What or whom is this essay satirizing?

4. Frayn's use of *form* as part of *content*—the *how* as part of the *what*—is obvious. For fun, try devising an appropriate form to tell part of the life of a famous media personality, sports star, politician, or artist—someone identified with a particular form (Bogart? K.D. Lang? Harry Belafonte? Nixon? Margaret Thatcher? Picasso? Tom Thomson? Wayne Gretzky? Schoenberg?). Or write a book review (would it have to be a negative one?) that parodies the style or some of the book's mannerisms, or a gossip column in the form of a dialogue over the back fence or by the office water-cooler, or a piece on a famous cook or on dieting in the form of a recipe, or.... But you can probably find a better subject yourself.

GERTRUDE STEIN   "Composition as Explanation"

1. Analyze the reflexive quality of this essay, the way it turns in upon itself, uses itself as part of its own subject. Discuss the effect of the "constant recurring and beginning" Stein refers to and makes much use of. What is the function of all the repetition? Is there any pattern to it? What does it have to do with what she says about time? Try your own hand at writing a paragraph that conveys the feeling of a "continuous present." Perhaps make it a portrait, a description of someone you know well.

2. Try to explain how *romanticism* and *war* function in this discussion of composition. What does Stein mean by "the authenticity of the modern composition"? What exactly does she mean by "composition"?

3. Does Stein adequately define *distribution* and *equilibration*? Define them yourself in order to help explain what she means.

4. Stein uses the word *phenomena* as both a singular noun and a plural noun. Is this deliberate, or a careless or carefree handling of the language?

5. Some of Stein's sentences at first sound like nonsense, but if you read them over and over again they begin to make a kind of sense that would be impossible with more conventional sentences. Analyze two or three sentences to show how this happens. How does her style force a reader to look closely at individual words and at the specific functions of parts of speech?

CAROLYN COOPER   "Writing Oral History: SISTREN Theatre Collective's Lionheart Gal"

1. Find a copy of *Lionheart Gal* and read it. Compare it with an "oral history" that comes from your area—for instance one of the books of Canadian oral history compiled by Barry Broadfoot.

2. Cooper calls *Lionheart Gal* "impeccably subversive"—subversive in what sense? Is her own essay also subversive?

3. Compare the diction of the first half of the essay to that of the second half. What features mark the word choice, syntax, and so on? Many of the phrases—for example *last lick sweet* and *di ile dat fry sprat cyaan fry jack*—are proverbs. Why does a critic so adept at the vocabulary of critical theory move into proverbs when she shifts to Creole? What is the function of proverbial utterance in "Patwah" (patois)?

4. The last half of Cooper's essay asks to be *heard*. Find a recording of Jamaican speech sounds—for example the folk poetry of Louise Bennett—to get some sense of the cadences of this essay. Of what significance is *sound* to the effect of an essay?

5. Cooper writes about the political marginalization that derives from race, class, gender, and linguistic distinctness. Compare her strategy for combatting such marginalization with that of some other writer, such as Cutschall, Brink, or Gordimer.

6. Compare Cooper's representation of women's experience with those of Meigs, Atwood, and Morgan.

7. Finally, here is a glossary of at least some of the Creole terms that might cause difficulties for readers unfamiliar with the tongue. (Note that we did not put it with the essay, since that would have invited immediate translation by the reader. How would such translation have affected your reading of the essay? What elements of its effectiveness would likely have been lost?) You may also wish to consult F.G. Cassidy and R.B. Le Page, *Dictionary of Jamaican English* (Cambridge Univ. Press, 1967).

a = is, be, am, are, it is, there are, to, at, in, of
aan = on
a her yard = in her home
caseer = right, "kosher"
cotta = pad, for the head, on which to place a load
cyaan = can't
dat = that
deh = there
dem = they, them, those
den = then
di = the
ee = eh
eena = in, into
faada = father
fi = for, to
get ketch = get caught
gi = give
ginnalship = trickery
gwan = go on
gwan gwan = get going
haffi = have to
ile = oil
jack = food fish
jine = join
ketch = catch
lap = fold

lickle = little
mash up true = really messed up
mek me lef it = let me leave it
nah = not
notten = nothing
noweh = nowhere
nyam = eat
odder = other
oman = woman, women
ongle = only
oonu = you (pl.)
pickney = child
pon = upon
prekkeh = trouble
red ibo = light-skinned person with African hair, features
roots vibe = echo sense of the folk or "root" culture
seh = say, that
sinting = something
sprat = bait fish
sweet me = pleases me
tell dem en up = until they end up
tek = take
waan = want
weh = what
yasso = here, this time

MICHAEL J. ARLEN   *"Life and Death in the Global Village"*

1. The book in which this and other of Arlen's columns from the late 1960s are collected is called *Living-Room War*. In his introduction to the book, many of whose pieces are about the war in Vietnam and its daily exposure on television, Arlen says he doesn't fully agree that the war is "necessarily made 'real'" to viewers by being brought into their living rooms, claiming that it is "also made less 'real'—diminished," because it is seen on a small screen with its "picture of men three inches tall shooting at other men three inches tall, and trivialized, or at least tamed, by the enveloping cozy alarums of the household." How does this idea help you appreciate the way he treats the assassination of Martin Luther King as he saw it reported on television?

2. At the end of the fourth paragraph Arlen reports that "Robert Kennedy deplores the rise in violence." Consider the adventitious irony and poignancy accruing to this remark from the fact that only two months later Kennedy himself was assassinated in Los Angeles.

3. What is the effect of the ending, his reference to "the sounds of footsteps running"?

4. Consider the *form* or style Arlen chooses to write in: it is marked by (among other things) the play with "slowing down," the many ellipses and parentheses, the short and sometimes fragmentary sentences and quotations (as well as a few unusually long ones, such as the first). How does such a style help convey not only the nature of the event itself but also the way the event was perceived by him and millions of others? What effect do cadence and movement have on meaning?

5. Make your medium your message. Compose an essay about commercial television's news coverage of some major event—not necessarily a violent one. Use judicious amounts of direct quotation from reporters and commentators as well as interviewees. And find some way to incorporate (perhaps parenthetically?) words, phrases, and sentences from the commercials that occur before and after parts of the news stories, especially if (as often happens) the juxtaposition makes the commercial appear in some way ironic or otherwise relevant to the news, or just outrageously inappropriate. That is, create your own juxtapositions for the effects you want. And try mixing present tense in, as Arlen does, for a sense of immediacy.

MAXINE HONG KINGSTON   *"On Mortality"*

1. A *fable* is a brief story told to make a moral point or to illustrate something about human nature; the point is usually stated explicitly at the end. What other characteristics do fables sometimes have? How does a *parable* differ from a fable? How do these forms work? Compare Kingston's fable with others you know, such as Aesop's or Thurber's, and perhaps with Christ's parables in the Bible. Would it be accurate to call all of these *allegorical*? How is a fable or a parable different from a *myth* or *legend* or *folktale* or *fairy tale*?

2. What does Kingston's piece suggest about the nature of *illusion*? What does it suggest about the need for *perspective*, for seeing something from another's point of view—namely that of the opposite sex?

3. The original form of the story was obviously not the same as that in which Kingston relates it. For one thing, it wasn't in English. Do you think she has done much more than simply translate it? What else might she have changed, or added—and why? Do you believe that Tu actually lived from A.D. 558 to 618? What is the effect of Kingston's use of such a matter-of-fact

tone for the recounting of such extravagant and horrific events? Do you find yourself virtually compelled to seek significance beyond the literal level?

GWENDOLYN MacEWEN "The Holyland Buffet"

1. This piece appears in a book descriptively subtitled *An Anthology of Travel Writing*, which also includes straightforward accounts, extracts from journals, poetry, impressionistic prose-poems, and photographs. A note tells us that "The Holyland Buffet" is "from a new book of short stories" by MacEwen, but adds that "all of the events" in it "are true and happened to her." Is it then fiction, or fact? Is it an imaginative autobiographical narrative cast in the *form* of a third-person short story? Or is it a "story"? Does it differ essentially in kind from, say, White's "Once More to the Lake" (section I)? Does it have a plot? Does it have a thesis? Compare it as travel writing with some of the other pieces in this book. Is White's essay (story?) in any sense travel writing? Mukherjee's (section I)? How about Huxley's essay (section II)?

2. Analyze this work as a story—that is, in terms of plot, character, setting, style, and structure. Is the narrative point of view (a) omniscient, (b) limited to one of the characters, or (c) objective, "dramatic"? Who is the protagonist? Does it contain any elements of what you might call fantasy? Does it use conversation to *reveal*, in the manner of some of the essays in section II?

3. Why "Mythological Foods"? Why "Kanada" and "Kanadian" with a K? Why the name "Kali"? *Is* there a "Mount of Loaves and Fishes"? If not, what might MacEwen be suggesting by the name? *Are* there two Holyland Buffets? How many "Holylands" are there? Why might Greece be, to some, "really a holy land"?

4. As has often been said, "It all depends on your point of view." Explain how this piece dramatizes that truism. One of Rooney's bits of advice (section II) reads: "You aren't the only one who doesn't understand the situation in the Middle East." Is MacEwen's intention partly to illustrate such a point?

5. Write a "story," a fictionalized account, in the third person, based on your own personal experience—perhaps about something that happened to you while you were travelling. What do you find yourself doing differently than you would if you were writing a straightforward first-person report?

TOPICS: General and Comparative

1. Colombo says he will provide no definition of the word *form*. What is your own "rule-of-thumb meaning" for it? How does your dictionary define it? How could it possibly be argued that *form* and *content* "have no meaning whatsoever," as Colombo in his first paragraph says it has been? Are *form* and *content* in the arts inseparable in the same way Brink at the end of his fourth paragraph says *thought* and *action* are (section III)? Test his analogy. Consider the question of form with respect to other essays in this book—and not just those in section VI. To what degree is *method* part of *meaning*? The meaning of Arlen's narrative comes largely through the way he delivers it, and Frayn in his biographical sketches clearly uses form—*style*—to echo the content of what he says. Do Davenport and Lane (section II) manipulate meaning through the style they use? Does Ludwig (section II)? How does Cooper combine

style and substance? How do White's diction and syntax (section I) reflect his shifting point of view?

2. Consider punctuation: it is part of form. It is most often simply a visual sign of an author's intended aural pacing, but it can be crucial. Some of the oddity of Stein's prose is due simply to the absence of conventional punctuation. Since it was originally given as a lecture, try reading a paragraph or two aloud, several times: does oral delivery make it clearer? Try supplying the punctuation necessary to make it more like conventional writing. Does that make it clearer? If so, however, given her idiosyncratic style and what she is using it to say, is anything lost by adding punctuation? (For fun, listen to a record of Victor Borge's comic skit on "oral punctuation.") At the other extreme, Lewis Thomas offers good advice about the different punctuation marks, and in each instance he uses the particular mark in the process of saying something about it. That is, he adopts—or constructs—a *form* of expression that enables him to illustrate the point he is making while he is making it. Form joins function. When he seems to overdo it, for example with parentheses, is it for humour or emphasis rather than because he is insensitive to the nuances of punctuation? Examine the punctuation of other writers to see if they punctuate as Thomas recommends. Try to evaluate and explain any notable departures from the principles he outlines.

3. Hornyansky sometimes demonstrates the very fault he is discussing. Write a short paragraph discussing some weakness or error of style in which you add to the point by purposely committing the error or weakness yourself. Then write another paragraph in which you use the same technique to demonstrate a stylistic or rhetorical strength. That is, give some advice about writing in such a way that you demonstrate what you're writing about while you're writing about it. Some possible subjects: sentence length or variety, passive voice, placement of topic sentences, vigorous verbs, clichés, slang, wordiness, rhetorical questions, metaphors—perhaps even punctuation.

4. Narration is often used for exposition. Arlen's essay, for example, is overall a narrative. How, within that mode, does he engage your interest in and attention to other matters than the mere sequence of events? That is, how does he make it *expository*? Kingston's fable is itself expository, and appears inside an essay form; MacEwen's story is expository, as are the narratives of personal experience by White and others in section I. Roueché's essay (section IV) is largely narrative; Brink's essay (section III) includes a fable, and Atwood (section IV), Hornyansky, and others use anecdotes to help make their expository points. Examine the way these writers use narrative (and descriptive) elements in their essays. How do they introduce them? How do they comment on them?

5. Note how some writers use graphic devices to help control the structure of their essays. Colombo, for example, uses boldface headings, or subtitles, for the sections of his essay. Galbraith (section IV) uses Roman numerals, as do Szasz (section III) and Eiseley (section I). Baker (section IV) numbers his three criteria. Which writers in this book use simply a little extra white space to mark a break or division? Is that method equally effective but less obtrusive? Are numerals somehow more formal? Does it depend on the length or complexity of the essay?

6. Write an essay about violence and the media. Many different approaches are possible. Explore the dual subject until you find a focus that appeals to you. Take into account not only Arlen's essay but also those by Zinsser, Fulford, and Brink in section III, and possibly other sources as well. Plan carefully: decide on your overall purpose and your major internal strategies, and draw up an outline. If your essay is to be at all long or complex, consider dividing it into sections, whether numbered or not.

7. Hornyansky refers to the word *togetherness,* saying he's glad it didn't succeed in becoming established. Kael uses the word scornfully in her review (section III). Is Hornyansky also concerned with the concept, or only with the word? How do you feel about the word—and the concept? Are the two separable? Write a short expressive essay on the subject.

8. In the next essay you write, make a conscious effort to introduce rhythm and sound patterns. How far dare you go? What considerations seem to determine how far you can go?

9. Cooper's review and Cutschall's paper (section IV) are also in part research essays. Note the various ways the authors refer to and otherwise handle material that comes from other sources. Is it smoothly integrated? Note too their different methods of documenting sources. Cooper uses the once-traditional "note" method, with superscript numbers referring to footnotes or, here, endnotes. Cutschall uses a version of the now more common "parenthetical" method, with name and date (and sometimes page) given in the text, and a list of references provided at the end.

10. Choose a subject that interests you, such as athletics, home movies, blackberrying, Cézanne, dog shows, English kings, forensic medicine, snowmobiles, *Genesis,* whole numbers, sound waves, or seismography. First define your subject closely, narrowing it to a topic that can be handled in a short essay. Then cast yourself in a range of writer's roles, and write a series of short essays, say two or three pages each, all on the same subject, but varying in emphasis and approach as you alter your purpose and your audience in the following ways:

   (a) *Relate and describe.* Write a personal narrative which illustrates your involvement with the subject, but keep your emphasis on the subject rather than on yourself. Build descriptive elements into your story in such a way that they add to, but do not overpower, the narrative itself. Use some metaphorical language.

   (b) *Reveal.* Interview several people about your subject, taking notes. Then use some or all of your notes in an essay which explores the subject but also reveals aspects of personality—either your own or that of the person or persons who supplied the most striking perspective.

   (c) *Persuade.* Treat your subject argumentatively. Perhaps try to convince a reader of its virtues or shortcomings, or try to defend it against some attack which you can imagine being mounted against it. In any event, be sure to take into account what an opposing argument might say. If your subject is suitable, you might try writing an extended advertisement for it. Don't be afraid to use satire or irony if they are appropriate to your intentions.

   (d) *Explain and inform.* Explain some particular feature of your subject. Use descriptive and narrative elements if they help you to be clear about the point you are trying to elucidate, but keep them minimal. Do not let yourself be drawn into an argumentative stance; be as objective as possible.

   (e) *Amuse.* Treat your subject humorously. (Your central point can be serious, but the tone should be light.) Decide in advance which devices of humour will be appropriate to your purpose, but don't therefore automatically discard other promising ideas that inspiration gives you as you write.

   When you have finished these essays, look back over them and consider the differences among them. To what audience does each essay appeal? Which essays are the most (and least) successful? Why? How and why have you varied their form? Have you been technically experimental? Where? Why? Now write one more essay, one in which you analyze your own writing style (as these five short essays reveal it) and explore how and why your style varies.

VII

Reading for Style

The word *style* refers to the overall choice and arrangement of sounds, words, phrases, sentences, and paragraphs in any piece of writing. Style consists of everything having to do with the way a writer writes something—that is, with *manner* as opposed to *matter*. But style and subject (manner and matter, form and content, method and meaning, medium and message) do not so easily separate from each other. The way something is said or written inevitably influences the effect of what it says; method is a part of meaning.

Though one can refer to styles as ornate or simple, convoluted or straightforward, styles do not fall into absolute categories; they are as individual as good writers, and as subject to time and imagination. Fashion and taste influence style; so do regional and cultural variations, changing standards of usage, the development of new words and new meanings in the language and the loss of old ones. A good style is an appropriate style; the best style on a given occasion is the one that most aptly chooses and arranges words to convey a particular intended shade of meaning.

Reading for style means listening for the sound patterns, looking closely at the choice of words and the shape of sentences, pausing to reflect on the intricate relations between form and substance.

How long is a sentence? Like any piece of string, a given sentence is long enough to get from one end to the other. Most sentences are of moderate size, doing what they have to do efficiently but without rushing. Some sentences are short, blunt. Or even deliberate fragments. Some sentences start straightforwardly but linger into length, stopping to savour a forceful modifier, pausing in a participial aside, branching into a subordinate clause that might lead along a different path or supply a cogent, pointed, adjectival detail that adds subtlety or complexity to the principal idea. Other sentences, pausing almost before they begin, keeping the main idea in abeyance while they stake out the ground in which that idea stands, hold back, until the very end, the completing word or phrase. And not all sentences are of the same or even similar shape; some even reverse standard order to achieve effects, or begin with a conjunction. In the juxtapositions they permit, the specific words they use, and the (often parallel) arrangements they construct, lie the individual meanings which each sentence conveys.

To read for style is to read with an eye for the way the actual form of a sentence designs its meaning. Not uncommonly, for example, negative structures design an oblique shade of meaning, and not the simple opposite of a positive. Who would argue that the opposite of "not understood" is necessarily a straightforward "understood," or that "not unknown" means precisely the same as "known"? (Parenthetically, one might observe that the interrogative form of a rhetorical question is itself a stylistic device. Note, too, that imperative structures use a deliberate artifice. Even simple declaration is often not so simple, as writers who effectively use modal forms of the verb must realize, and as those who use irony, with whatever degree of skill, at least ought to know.) Gone are the days when inversions were commonplace, but the practice still exists for special occasions—perhaps for those moments when into one's mind there springs an insistent cliché. "Who's to say," a questioner might ask, "that even dialogue might not enter an unsuspecting paragraph?" To which "Indeed!" is probably as good an answer as any. *Style* embraces all these strategies, its arms open to metaphor—and to parataxis—and to metaphor—and to rhythm—and to metaphor—and to repetition—and to →T*y*P*o*gR*a p*H*i*CA*l*← manipulation—

> and to white space

—and to numerous other devices, techniques, artifices, designs—and to anticlimax, probably.

Not all paragraphs are long, or end lamely. Some rely heavily on adverbs. Some seek coherence unsuccessfully.

Some are only one sentence long—though not frequently.

Style embraces all such matters. *Style* notices repetitions: *style* delights in anaphora sometimes, and in chiasmus and other balanced structures. *Style* delights in patterns of sound and the sound of patterns—sighing in soft sibilants, or languishing in loving murmurs, monotones of moonlight; or rattling rickety-tick in a regular metre and resonant rhyme; or ripping apart in rough bits, each bite a curt blast, clatter mattering more to meaning than one might at first think.

Such words, all words, have shape, length, and histories as well. They can be as short as a cough or as big as hate, as sesquipedalian as polysyllabic construction permits or as small as one or two dots of sound. They can be *good*, *wicked*, Germanic; they can be *contentious*, *acquiescent*, Latinate. Or they can flow like *alcohol* or leap like *kangaroos* from other sources, adventitiously enriching the stock of similes available to users of the language and widening still further the reach of style.

Reading for style is (to commandeer an analogy) like learning to recognize the kinds of nails, wood, and mortar used to construct something: a bungalow, a cabin, a cubist castle. The rudiments for every builder are the same, but the choices, and the sequence of choices, produce edifices of infinite variety. Just so does every writer start on a level plain. But stylistic choices of all kinds work wonders on that stark terrain, and the results can be extraordinary. For only some readers, however, will the process of recognizing the literary wood and nails be an end in itself. For most, reading for style will help them design better buildings—help them reach for those effects that, as writers of prose, they want to achieve.

Here then are a few essays and prose extracts for you to practise on and discuss. Arranged in two chronological groups, they also illustrate some of the changes that have taken place in English style over the centuries. Not all of them make useful models for twentieth-century writers, but all of them are intrinsically interesting. Read them for style.

Note: For ease of reading, we have modernized the mechanics (spelling, punctuation, capitalization) of most of the selections from earlier than about 1750.

Ecclesiastes 3:1-8

from The Bible, Authorized (King James) Version (1611)

To every thing there is a season, and a time to every purpose under the heaven:

A time to be born, and a time to die; a time to plant, and a time to pluck up that which is planted;

A time to kill, and a time to heal; a time to break down, and a time to build up;

A time to weep, and a time to laugh; a time to mourn, and a time to dance;

A time to cast away stones, and a time to gather stones together; a time to embrace, and a time to refrain from embracing;

A time to get, and a time to lose; a time to keep, and a time to cast away;

A time to rend, and a time to sew; a time to keep silence, and a time to speak;

A time to love, and a time to hate; a time of war, and a time of peace.

St. Luke 15

from The Bible: The Prodigal Son

Then drew near unto him all the publicans and sinners for to hear him.

And the Pharisees and scribes murmured, saying, This man receiveth sinners, and eateth with them.

And he spake this parable unto them, saying,

What man of you, having an hundred sheep, if he lose one of them, doth not leave the ninety and nine in the wilderness, and go after that which is lost, until he find it?

And when he hath found it, he layeth it on his shoulders, rejoicing.

And when he cometh home, he calleth together his friends and neighbours, saying unto them, Rejoice with me; for I have found my sheep which was lost.

I say unto you, that likewise joy shall be in heaven over one sinner that repenteth, more than over ninety and nine just persons, which need no repentance.

Either what woman having ten pieces of silver, if she lose one piece, doth not light a candle, and sweep the house, and seek diligently till she find it?

And when she hath found it, she calleth her friends and her neighbours together, saying, Rejoice with me; for I have found the piece which I had lost.

Likewise, I say unto you, there is joy in the presence of the angels of God over one sinner that repenteth.

And he said, A certain man had two sons:

And the younger of them said to his father, Father, give me the portion of goods that falleth to me. And he divided unto them his living.

And not many days after the younger son gathered all together, and took his journey into a far country, and there wasted his substance with riotous living.

And when he had spent all, there arose a mighty famine in that land; and he began to be in want.

And he went and joined himself to a citizen of that country; and he sent him into his fields to feed swine.

And he would fain have filled his belly with the husks that the swine did eat: and no man gave unto him.

And when he came to himself, he said, How many hired servants of my father's have bread enough and to spare, and I perish with hunger!

I will arise and go to my father, and will say unto him, Father, I have sinned against heaven, and before thee,

And am no more worthy to be called thy son: make me as one of thy hired servants.

And he arose, and came to his father. But when he was yet a great way off, his father saw him, and had compassion, and ran, and fell on his neck and kissed him.

And the son said unto him, Father, I have sinned against heaven, and in thy sight, and am no more worthy to be called thy son.

But the father said to his servants, Bring forth the best robe, and put it on him; and put a ring on his hand, and shoes on his feet:

And bring hither the fatted calf, and kill it; and let us eat, and be merry:

For this my son was dead, and is alive again; he was lost, and is found. And they began to be merry.

Now his elder son was in the field: and as he came and drew nigh to the house, he heard music and dancing.

And he called one of the servants, and asked what these things meant.

And he said unto him, Thy brother is come; and thy father hath killed the fatted calf, because he hath received him safe and sound.

And he was angry, and would not go in: therefore came his father out, and intreated him.

And he answering said to his father, Lo, these many years do I serve thee, neither transgressed I at any time they commandment: and yet thou never gavest me a kid, that I might make merry with my friends:

But as soon as this thy son was come, which hath devoured thy living with harlots, thou hast killed for him the fatted calf.

And he said unto him, Son, thou art ever with me, and all that I have is thine.

It was meet that we should make merry, and be glad: for this thy brother was dead, and is alive again; and was lost, and is found.

Nicholas Breton

from *The Good and the Bad* (1616)

A Worthy Gentleman

A worthy gentleman is a branch of the tree of honour, whose fruits are the actions of virtue, as pleasing to the eye of judgment as tasteful to the spirit of understanding. Whatsoever he doeth it is not forced, except it be evil, which either through ignorance unwillingly, or through compulsion unwillingly, he falls upon. He is in nature kind, in demeanour courteous, in allegiance loyal, and in religion zealous; in service faithful, and in reward bountiful. He is made of no baggage stuff, nor for the wearing of base people; but it is woven by the spirit of wisdom to adorn the court of honour. His apparel is more comely than costly, and his diet more wholesome than excessive; his exercise more healthful than painful, and his study more for knowledge than pride; his love not wanton nor common, his gifts not niggardly nor prodigal, and his carriage neither apish nor sullen. In sum, he is an approver of his pedigree by the nobleness of his passage, and in the course of his life an example to his posterity.

An Unworthy Gentleman

An unworthy gentleman is the scoff of wit and the scorn of honour, where more wealth than wit is worshipped of simplicity; who spends more in idleness than would maintain thrift, or hides more in misery than might purchase honour; whose delights are vanities and whose pleasures fopperies, whose studies fables and whose exercise worse than follies. His conversation is base, and his conference ridiculous; his affections ungracious, and his actions ignominious; his apparel out of fashion, and his diet out of order; his carriage out of square, and his company out of request. In sum, he is like a mongrel dog with a velvet collar, a cart-horse with a golden saddle, a buzzard kite with a falcon's bells, or a baboon with a pied jerkin.

John Donne

Meditation XVII (1624)

Nunc lento sonitu dicunt.　　　　Now this Bell tolling softly for another,
Morieris.　　　　　　　　　　　says to me, Thou must die.

Perchance he for whom this bell tolls may be so ill as that he knows not it tolls for him; and perchance I may think myself so much better than I am as that they who are about me, and see my state, may have caused it to toll for me, and I know not that. The church is catholic, universal; so are all her actions;

all that she does belongs to all. When she baptizes a child, that action concerns me, for that child is thereby connected to that head which is my head too, and engrafted into that body whereof I am a member. And when she buries a man, that action concerns me: All mankind is of one author, and is one volume; when one man dies, one chapter is not torn out of the book, but translated into a better language; and every chapter must be so translated. God employs several translators; some pieces are translated by age, some by sickness, some by war, some by justice; but God's hand is in every translation, and his hand shall bind up all our scattered leaves again, for that library where every book shall lie open to one another. As therefore the bell that rings to a sermon calls not upon the preacher only, but upon the congregation to come, so this bell calls us all—but how much more me, who am brought so near the door by this sickness. There was a contention as far as a suit (in which both piety and dignity, religion and estimation, were mingled) which of the religious orders should ring to prayers first in the morning; and it was determined that they should ring first that rose earliest. If we understand aright the dignity of this bell that tolls for our evening prayer, we would be glad to make it ours by rising early, in that application, that it might be ours as well as his whose indeed it is. The bell doth toll for him that thinks it doth; and though it intermit again, yet from that minute that that occasion wrought upon him, he is united to God. Who casts not up his eye to the sun when it rises? but who takes off his eye from a comet when that breaks out? Who bends not his ear to any bell which upon any occasion rings? but who can remove it from that bell which is passing a piece of himself out of this world? No man is an island, entire of itself; every man is a piece of the continent, a part of the main. If a clod be washed away by the sea, Europe is the less, as well as if a promontory were, as well as if a manor of thy friends or of thine own were. Any man's death diminishes me, because I am involved in mankind. And therefore never send to know for whom the bell tolls; it tolls for thee. Neither can we call this a begging of misery or a borrowing of misery, as though we were not miserable enough of ourselves but must fetch in more from the next house, in taking upon us the misery of our neighbours. Truly it were an excusable covetousness if we did, for affliction is a treasure, and scarce any man hath enough of it. No man hath affliction enough that is not matured and ripened by it, and made fit for God by that affliction. If a man carry treasure in bullion, or in a wedge of gold, and have none coined into current monies, his treasure will not defray him as he travels. Tribulation is treasure in the nature of it, but it is not current money in the use of it except we get nearer and nearer our home, heaven, by it. Another may be sick too, and sick to death, and this affliction may lie in his bowels, as gold in a mine, and be of no use to him; but this bell, that tells me of his affliction, digs out and applies that gold to me, if by this consideration of another's danger I take mine own into contemplation, and so secure myself by making my recourse to my God, who is our only security.

443

Sir Francis Bacon

Of Marriage and Single Life (1625)

He that hath wife and children hath given hostages to fortune, for they are impediments to great enterprises, either of virtue or mischief. Certainly the best works, and of greatest merit for the public, have proceeded from the unmarried or childless men, which both in affection and means have married and endowed the public. Yet it were great reason that those that have children should have greatest care of future times, unto which they know they must transmit their dearest pledges. Some there are, who though they lead a single life, yet their thoughts do end with themselves, and account future times impertinences. Nay, there are some other that account wife and children but as bills of charges. Nay more, there are some foolish rich covetous men that take a pride in having no children, because they may be thought so much the richer. For perhaps they have heard some talk, "Such an one is a great rich man," and another except to it, "Yea, but he hath a great charge of children," as if it were an abatement to his riches. But the most ordinary cause of a single life is liberty, especially in certain self-pleasing and humorous minds, which are so sensible of every restraint as they will go near to think their girdles and garters to be bonds and shackles. Unmarried men are best friends, best masters, best servants, but not always best subjects, for they are light to run away; and almost all fugitives are of that condition. A single life doth well with churchmen, for charity will hardly water the ground where it must first fill a pool. It is indifferent for judges and magistrates, for if they be facile and corrupt, you shall have a servant five times worse than a wife. For soldiers, I find the generals commonly in their hortatives put men in mind of their wives and children, and I think the despising of marriage amongst the Turks maketh the vulgar soldier more base. Certainly wife and children are a kind of discipline of humanity; and single men, though they be many times more charitable, because their means are less exhaust, yet on the other side they are more cruel and hard-hearted (good to make severe inquisitors), because their tenderness is not so oft called upon. Grave natures, led by custom, and therefore constant, are commonly loving husbands; as was said of Ulysses, *Vetulam suam praetulit immortalitati*[1] Chaste women are often proud and froward, as presuming upon the merit of their chastity. It is one of the best bonds both of chastity and obedience in the wife, if she think her husband wise, which she will never do if she finds him jealous. Wives are young men's mistresses, companions for middle age, and old men's nurses. So as a man may have a quarrel to marry when he will. But yet he was reputed one of the wise men that made answer to the question, when a man should marry? "A young man not yet, an elder man not at all." It is often seen that bad husbands have very good wives, whether it be that it raiseth the price of their husband's kindness when it comes, or that the wives take a pride in their patience. But this never fails if the bad husbands were of their own choosing, against their friends' consent, for then they will be sure to make good their own folly.

---

[1] Vetulam...: He preferred his old wife to immortality (i.e., he went home to Penelope instead of staying with Calypso).

John Milton

from *Areopagitica* (1644)

Good and evil we know in the field of this world grow up together almost inseparably; and the knowledge of good is so involved and interwoven with the knowledge of evil, and in so many cunning resemblances hardly to be discerned, that those confused seeds which were imposed upon Psyche as an incessant labour to cull out and sort asunder, were not more intermixed. It was from out the rind of one apple tasted that the knowledge of good and evil, as two twins cleaving together, leaped forth into the world. And perhaps this is that doom which Adam fell into of knowing good and evil — that is to say, of knowing good by evil.

As therefore the state of man now is, what wisdom can there be to choose, what continence to forbear, without the knowledge of evil? He that can apprehend and consider vice with all her baits and seeming pleasures, and yet abstain, and yet distinguish, and yet prefer that which is truly better, he is the true warfaring Christian. I cannot praise a fugitive and cloistered virtue, unexercised and unbreathed, that never sallies out and seeks her adversary, but slinks out of the race where that immortal garland is to be run for, not without dust and heat. Assuredly we bring not innocence into the world, we bring impurity much rather; that which purifies us is trial, and trial is by what is contrary. That virtue therefore which is but a youngling in the contemplation of evil, and knows not the utmost that vice promises to her followers, and rejects it, is but a blank virtue, not a pure; her whiteness is but an excremental whiteness—which was the reason why our sage and serious poet Spenser (whom I dare be known to think a better teacher than Scotus or Aquinas), describing true temperance under the person of Guion, brings him in with his palmer through the cave of Mammon and the bower of earthly bliss, that he might see and know, and yet abstain.

Sir Thomas Browne

from *Hydriotaphia. Urn Burial: or, a Discourse of the Sepulchral Urns Lately Found in Norfolk* (1658)

What song the Sirens sang, or what name Achilles assumed when he hid himself among women, though puzzling questions, are not beyond all conjecture.[1] What time the persons of these ossuaries entered the famous nations of the dead, and slept with princes and counsellors, might admit a wide solution. But who were the proprietaries of these bones, or what bodies these ashes made up, were a question above antiquarism; not to be resolved by man, nor easily perhaps by spirits, except we consult the provincial guardians, or tutelary observators. Had they made as good provision for their names as they have done for their relics, they had not so grossly erred in the art of perpetuation. But to subsist in bones, and be but pyramidally extant, is a fallacy in duration. Vain ashes which in the oblivion of names, persons, times, and sexes, have found unto themselves a fruitless continuation, and only arise unto late posterity, as emblems of mortal vanities, antidotes against pride, vainglory, and madding vices. Pagan vainglories which thought the world might last forever, had encouragement for ambition; and, finding no Atropos unto the immortality of their names, were never damped with the necessity of oblivion. Even old ambitions had the advantage of ours, in the attempts of their vainglories, who acting early, and before the probable meridian of time, have by this time found great accomplishment of their designs, whereby the ancient heroes have already outlasted their monuments and mechanical preservations. But in this latter scene of time, we cannot expect such mummies unto our memories, when ambition may fear the prophecy of Elias, and Charles the Fifth can never hope to live within two Methuselahs of Hector.

[1] According to Suetonius, Tiberius asked such puzzling questions of grammarians.

Joseph Addison

The Spectator, No. 105: Saturday, June 30, 1711

My friend Will Honeycomb values himself very much upon what he calls the Knowledge of Mankind, which has cost him many disasters in his youth, for Will reckons every misfortune that he has met with among the women, and every rencounter among the men, as parts of his education, and fancies he should never have been the man he is had not he broke windows, knocked down constables, disturbed honest people with his midnight serenades, and beat up a lewd woman's quarters when he was a young fellow. The engaging in adventures of this nature Will calls the studying of mankind, and terms this Knowledge of the Town the Knowledge of the World. Will ingenuously confesses that for half his life his head ached every morning with reading of men overnight, and at present comforts himself under certain pains which he endures from time to time, that without them he could not have been acquainted with the gallantries of the age. This Will looks upon as the learning of a gentleman, and regards all other kinds of science as the accomplishments of one whom he calls a scholar, a bookish man, or a philosopher.

For these reasons Will shines in mixt company, where he has the discretion not to go out of his depth, and has often a certain way of making his real ignorance appear a seeming one. Our club however has frequently caught him tripping, at which times they never spare him. For as Will often insults us with the Knowledge of the Town, we sometimes take our revenge upon him by our Knowledge of Books.

He was last week producing two or three letters which he writ in his youth to a coquet lady. The raillery of them was natural, and well enough for a mere Man of the Town; but, very unluckily, several of the words were wrong spelt. Will laughed this off at first as well as he could; but finding himself pushed on all sides, and especially by the Templar, he told us, with a little passion, that he never liked pedantry in spelling, and that he spelt like a gentleman and not like a scholar. Upon this Will had recourse to his old topic of showing the narrow-spiritedness, the pride, and ignorance of pedants, which he carried so far that upon my retiring to my lodgings, I could not forbear throwing together such reflections as occurred to me upon that subject.

A man who has been brought up among books, and is able to talk of nothing else, is a very indifferent companion, and what we call a pedant. But, methinks, we should enlarge the title, and give it everyone that does not know how to think out of his profession and particular way of life.

What is a greater pedant than a mere Man of the Town? Bar him the playhouses, a catalogue of the reigning beauties, and an account of a few fashionable distempers that have befallen him, and you strike him dumb. How many a pretty gentleman's knowledge lies all within the verge of the court? He will tell you the names of the principal favourites, repeat the shrewd sayings of a man of quality, whisper an intrigue that is not yet blown upon by common fame; or, if the sphere of his observations is a little larger than ordinary, will perhaps enter into all the incidents, turns, and revolutions in a game of ombre. When he has gone thus far he has shown you the whole circle of his accomplishments, his parts are drained, and he is disabled from any further conversation. What are these but rank pedants? And yet these are the men who value themselves most on their exemption from the pedantry of colleges.

I might here mention the military pedant who always talks in a camp, and is storming towns, making lodgments, and fighting battles from one end of the year to the other. Everything he speaks smells of gunpowder; if you take away his artillery from him, he has not a word to say for himself. I might likewise mention the law pedant that is perpetually putting cases, repeating the transactions of Westminster Hall, wrangling with you upon the most indifferent circumstances of life, and not to be convinced of the distance of a place or of the most trivial point in conversation but by dint of argument. The state pedant is wrapt up in news and lost in politics. If you mention either of the kings of Spain or Poland, he talks very notably; but if you go out of the *Gazette*, you drop him. In short, a mere courtier, a mere soldier, a mere scholar, a mere anything, is an insipid pedantic character, and equally ridiculous.

Of all the species of pedants which I have mentioned, the book pedant is much the most supportable; he has at least an exercised understanding and a head which is full though confused, so that a man who converses with him may often receive from him hints of things that are worth knowing, and what he may possibly turn to his own advantage, though they are of little use to the owner. The worst kind of pedants among learned men are such as are naturally endued with a very small share of common sense and have read a great number of books without taste or distinction.

The truth of it is, learning, like travelling, and all other methods of improvement, as it finishes good sense, so it makes a silly man ten thousand times more insufferable by supplying variety of matter to his impertinence and giving him an opportunity of abounding in absurdities.

Shallow pedants cry up one another much more than men of solid and useful learning. To read the titles they give an editor or collator of a manuscript, you would take him for the glory of the commonwealth of letters, and the wonder of his age, when perhaps upon examination you find that he has only rectified a Greek particle or laid out a whole sentence in proper commas.

They are obliged indeed to be thus lavish of their praises, that they may keep one another in countenance; and it is no wonder if a great deal of knowledge which is not capable of making a man wise has a natural tendency to make him vain and arrogant.

Lady Mary Wortley Montagu

Letter to the Countess of Mar

Pera of Constantinople, March 10, O.S. 1718

I have not written to you, dear Sister, these many months—a great piece of self-denial. But I know not where to direct, or what part of the world you are in. I have received no letter from you since that short note of April last, in which you tell me that you are on the point of leaving England, and promise me a direction for the place you stay in; but I have in vain expected it till now, and now I only learn from the gazette that you are returned, which induces me to venture this letter to your house at London. I had rather ten of my letters should be lost than you imagine I don't write, and I think 'tis hard fortune if one in ten don't reach you. However, I am resolved to keep the copies as testimonies of my inclination to give you, to the utmost of my power, all the diverting part of my travels, while you are exempt from all the fatigues and inconveniences.

In the first place, I wish you joy of your niece, for I was brought to bed of a daughter five weeks ago. I don't mention this as one of my diverting adventures, though I must own that it is not half so mortifying here as in England, there being as much difference as there is between a little cold in the head, which sometimes happens here, and the consumptive coughs so common in London. Nobody keeps their house a month for lying-in, and I am not so fond of any of our customs to retain them when they are not necessary. I returned my visits at three weeks' end, and about four days ago crossed the sea which divides this place from Constantinople to make a new one, where I had the good fortune to pick up many curiosities.

I went to see the Sultana Hafiten, favourite of the late Emperor Mustapha, who you know (or perhaps you don't know) was deposed by his brother, the reigning Sultan, and died a few weeks after, being poisoned, as it was generally believed. This lady was immediately after his death saluted with an absolute order to leave the seraglio and choose herself a husband among the great men at the Porte. I suppose you may imagine her overjoyed at this proposal. Quite contrary: these women, who are called and esteem themselves queens, look upon this liberty as the greatest disgrace and affront that can happen to them. She threw herself at the Sultan's feet and begged him to poniard her rather than use his brother's widow with that contempt. She represented to him in agonies of sorrow that she was privileged from this misfortune by having brought five princes into the Ottoman family; but all the boys being dead and only one girl surviving, this excuse was not received, and she was compelled to make her choice. She chose Bekir Effendi, then secretary of state, and above fourscore years old, to convince the world that she firmly intended to keep the vow she had made of never suffering a second husband to approach her bed; and since she must honour some subject so far as to be called his wife, she would choose him as a mark of her gratitude, since it was he that had presented her at the age of ten years old to her last lord. But she never permitted him to pay her one visit, though it is now fifteen years she has been in his house, where she passes her time in uninterrupted mourning with a constancy very little known in Christendom, especially in a widow of twenty-one, for she is now but thirty-six. She has no black eunuchs for her guard, her husband being obliged to respect her as a queen and not enquire at all into what is done in her apartment, where I was led into a large room, with a sofa the whole length of it, adorned with white marble pillars like a *ruelle*, covered with pale blue figured velvet on a silver ground, with cushions of the same, where I was desired to repose till the Sultana appeared, who had contrived this manner of reception to avoid rising up at my entrance, though she made me an inclination of her head when I rose up to her. I was very glad to observe a lady that had been distinguished by the favour of an Emperor to whom beauties were every day presented from all parts of the world. But she did not seem to me to have ever been half so beautiful as the fair Fatima I saw at Adrianople, though she had the remains of a fine face, more decayed by sorrow than time.

But her dress was something so surprisingly rich I cannot forbear describing it to you. She wore a vest called *donalma*, and which differs from a *caftan* by longer sleeves and folding over at the bottom. It was of purple cloth strait to her shape and thick set on each side down to her feet and round the sleeves, with pearls of the best water, of the same size as their buttons commonly are. You must not suppose that I mean as large as those of my Lord ——, but about the bigness of a pea; and to these buttons large loops of diamonds in the form of those gold loops so common on birthday coats. This habit was tied at the waist with two large tassels of smaller pearls, and round the arms embroidered with large diamonds; her shift fastened at the bottom with a great diamond shaped like a lozenge; her girdle as broad as the broadest

English ribbon, entirely covered with diamonds. Round her neck she wore three chains which reached to her knees: one of large pearl at the bottom of which hung a fine coloured emerald as big as a turkey-egg, another consisting of two hundred emeralds closely joined together, of the most lively green, perfectly matched, every one as large as a half-crown piece and as thick as three crown pieces, and another of small emeralds, perfectly round. But her earrings eclipsed all the rest: they were two diamonds, shaped exactly like pears, as large as a big hazel-nut. Round her *talpoche* she had four strings of pearl, the whitest and most perfect in the world, at least enough to make four necklaces every one as large as the Duchess of Marlborough's, and of the same size, fastened with two roses consisting of a large ruby for the middle stone, and round them twenty drops of clean diamonds to each. Besides this, her head-dress was covered with bodkins of emeralds and diamonds. She wore large diamond bracelets and had five rings on her fingers, all single diamonds, (except Mr. Pitt's) the largest I ever saw in my life. 'Tis for jewellers to compute the value of these things, but according to the common estimation of jewels in our part of the world, her whole dress must be worth above a hundred thousand pounds sterling. This I am very sure of, that no European queen has half the quantity, and the Empress's jewels, though very fine, would look very mean near hers.

She gave me a dinner of fifty dishes of meat, which (after their fashion) were placed on the table but one at a time, and was extremely tedious, but the magnificence of her table answered very well to that of her dress. The knives were of gold, the hafts set with diamonds. But the piece of luxury that grieved my eyes was the table-cloth and napkins, which were all tiffany embroidered with silks and gold in the finest manner in natural flowers. It was with the utmost regret that I made use of these costly napkins, as finely wrought as the finest handkerchiefs that ever came out of this country. You may be sure that they were entirely spoiled before dinner was over. The sherbet (which is the liquor they drink at meals) was served in china bowls, but the covers and salvers massy gold. After dinner water was brought in gold basins, and towels of the same kind with the napkins, which I very unwillingly wiped my hands upon, and coffee was served in china with gold *soucoupes*.

The Sultana seemed in very good humour, and talked to me with the utmost civility. I did not omit this opportunity of learning all that I possibly could of the seraglio, which is so entirely unknown amongst us. She assured me that the story of the Sultan's throwing a handkerchief is altogether fabulous, and the manner on that occasion no other but he sends the *kyslar aga* to signify to the lady the honour he intends her. She is immediately complimented upon it by the others, and led to the bath, where she is perfumed and dressed in the most magnificent and becoming manner. The Emperor precedes his visit by a royal present, and then comes into her apartment. Neither is there any such thing as her creeping in at the bed's foot. She said that the first he made choice of was always after the first in rank, and not the mother of the eldest son, as other writers would make us believe. Sometimes the Sultan diverts himself in the company of all his ladies, who stand in a circle round him, and she confessed that they were ready to die with envy and jealousy of the happy she that he distinguished by any appearance of preference. But this seemed to me neither better nor worse than the circles in most courts, where the glance of the monarch is watched and every smile is waited for with impatience and envied by those who cannot obtain it.

She never mentioned the Sultan without tears in her eyes, yet she seemed very fond of the discourse. "My past happiness," said she, "appears a dream to me, yet I cannot forget that I was beloved by the greatest and most lovely of mankind. I was chosen from all the rest to make all his campaigns with him. I would not survive him if I was not passionately fond of the princess, my daughter, yet all my tenderness for her was hardly enough to make me preserve my life. When I lost him, I passed a whole twelvemonth without seeing the light. Time hath softened my despair, yet I now pass some days every week in tears devoted to the memory of my Sultan." There was no affectation in these words. It was easy to see she was in a deep melancholy, though her good humour made her willing to divert me.

She asked me to walk in her garden, and one of her slaves immediately brought her a *pellice* of rich brocade lined with sables. I waited on her into the garden, which had nothing in it remarkable but the fountains, and from thence she showed me all her apartments. In her bed-chamber her toilet was displayed, consisting of two looking-glasses, the frames covered with pearls, and her night *talpoche* set with bodkins of jewels, and near it three vests of fine sables, every one of which is at least worth a thousand dollars (two hundred pounds English money). I don't doubt these rich habits were purposely placed in sight, but they seemed negligently thrown on the sofa. When I took my leave of her, I was complimented with perfumes, as at the Grand-Vizier's, and presented with a very fine embroidered handkerchief. Her slaves were to the number of thirty, besides ten little ones, the eldest not above seven years old. These were the most beautiful girls I ever saw, all richly dressed; and I observed that the Sultana took a great deal of pleasure in these lovely children, which is a vast expense, for there is not a handsome girl of that age to be bought under a hundred pounds sterling. They wore little garlands of flowers, and their own hair braided, which was all their head-dress; but their habits all of gold stuffs. These served her coffee kneeling, brought water when she washed, etc. 'Tis a great part of the work of the older slaves to take care of these girls, to learn them to embroider and serve them as carefully as if they were children of the family.

Now do I fancy that you imagine I have entertained you all this while with a relation that has, at least, received many embellishments from my hand? This is but too like (say you) the Arabian Tales: these embroidered napkins! and a jewel as large as a turkey's egg! You forget, dear sister, those very tales were written by an author of this country and (excepting the enchantments) are a real representation of the manners here. We travellers are in very hard circumstances. If we say nothing but what has been said before us, we are dull and we have observed nothing. If we tell any thing new, we are laughed at as fabulous and romantic, not allowing for the difference of ranks, which afford difference of company, more curiosity, or the changes of customs that happen every twenty years in every country. But people judge of travellers exactly with the same candour, good nature, and impartiality they judge of their neighbours upon all occasions. For my part, if I live to return amongst you, I am so well acquainted with the morals of all my dear friends and acquaintance that I am resolved to tell them nothing at all, to avoid the imputation (which their charity would certainly incline them to) of my telling too much. But I depend upon your knowing me enough to believe whatever I seriously assert for truth, though I give you leave to be surprised at an account so new to you.

But what would you say if I told you that I have been in a harem where the winter apartment was wainscoted with inlaid work of mother-of-pearl, ivory of different colours, and olive wood, exactly like the little boxes you have seen brought out of this country; and those rooms designed for summer, the walls all crusted with japan china, the roofs gilt, and the floors spread with the finest Persian carpets! Yet there is nothing more true; such is the palace of my lovely friend, the fair Fatima, whom I was acquainted with at Adrianople. I went to visit her yesterday, and if possible she appeared to me handsomer than before. She met me at the door of her chamber, and, giving me her hand with the best grace in the world, "You Christian ladies," said she with a smile that made her as beautiful as an angel, "have the reputation of inconstancy, and I did not expect, whatever goodness you expressed for me at Adrianople, that I should ever see you again; but I am now convinced that I have really the happiness of pleasing you, and if you knew how I speak of you amongst our ladies, you would be assured that you do me justice if you think me your friend." She placed me in the corner of the sofa, and I spent the afternoon in her conversation with the greatest pleasure in the world.

The Sultana Hafiten is what one would naturally expect to find a Turkish lady, willing to oblige, but not knowing how to go about it; and 'tis easy to see in her manner that she has lived excluded from the world. But Fatima has all the politeness and good breeding of a court, with an air that inspires at once respect and tenderness; and now I understand her language, I find her wit as agreeable as her beauty. She is very curious after the manners of other countries, and has not the partiality for her own so common to little minds. A Greek that I carried with me, who had never seen her before (nor could have been admitted now if she had not been in my train), showed that surprise at her beauty and manner which is unavoidable at the first sight, and said to me in Italian, "This is no Turkish lady; she is certainly some Christian." Fatima guessed she spoke of her, and asked what she said. I would not have told, thinking she would have been no better pleased with the compliment than one of our court beauties to be told she had the air of a Turk; but the Greek lady told it her, and she smiled, saying, "It is not the first time I have heard so. My mother was a Poloneze taken at the siege of Caminiec, and my father used to rally me, saying he believed his Christian wife had found some Christian gallant, for I had not the air of a Turkish girl." I assured her that if all the Turkish ladies were like her, it was absolutely necessary to confine them from public view for the repose of mankind, and proceeded to tell her what a noise such a face as hers would make in London or Paris. "I can't believe you," replied she agreeably; "if beauty was so much valued in your country as you say, they would never have suffered you to leave it." Perhaps, dear Sister, you laugh at my vanity in repeating this compliment, but I only do it as I think it very well turned, and give it to you as an instance of the spirit of her conversation.

Her house was magnificently furnished and very well fancied, her winter rooms being furnished with figured velvet on gold grounds, and those for summer with fine Indian quilting embroidered with gold. The houses of the great Turkish ladies are kept clean with as much nicety as those in Holland. This was situated in a high part of the town, and from the windows of her summer apartment we had the prospect of the sea, the islands, and the Asian mountains.

My letter is insensibly grown so long, I am ashamed of it. This is a very bad symptom. 'Tis well if I don't degenerate into a downright story-teller. It may be our proverb, that knowledge is no burden, may be true as to one's self, but knowing too much is very apt to make us troublesome to other people.

Jonathan Swift

A Modest Proposal

For preventing the children of poor people in Ireland from being a burden to their parents or country, and for making them beneficial to the public. (1729)

It is a melancholy object to those who walk through this great town, or travel in the country, when they see the streets, the roads, and cabin-doors crowded with beggars of the female sex, followed by three, four, or six children, *all in rags*, and importuning every passenger for an alms. These mothers instead of being able to work for their honest livelihood, are forced to employ all their time in strolling, to beg sustenance for their helpless infants, who, as they grow up, either turn thieves for want of work, or leave their dear Native Country to fight for the Pretender in Spain, or sell themselves to the Barbadoes.

I think it is agreed by all parties, that this prodigious number of children, in the arms, or on the backs, or at the heels of their mothers, and frequently of their fathers, is in the present deplorable state of the kingdom a very great additional grievance; and therefore whoever could find out a fair, cheap, and easy method of making these children sound useful members of the common-wealth would deserve so well of the public, as to have his statue set up for a preserver of the nation.

But my intention is very far from being confined to provide only for the children of professed beggars; it is of a much greater extent, and shall take in the whole number of infants at a certain age, who are born of parents in effect as little able to support them, as those who demand our charity in the streets.

As to my own, part, having turned my thoughts, for many years, upon this important subject, and maturely weighed the several schemes of other projectors, I have always found them grossly mistaken in their computation. It is true a child, just dropped from its dam, may be supported by her milk for a solar year with little other nourishment, at most not above the value of two shillings, which the mother may certainly get, or the value in scraps, by her lawful occupation of begging, and it is exactly at one year old that I propose to provide for them, in such a manner, as, instead of being a charge upon their parents, or the parish, or wanting food and raiment for the rest of their lives, they shall, on the contrary, contribute to the feeding and partly to the clothing of many thousands.

There is likewise another great advantage in my scheme, that it will prevent those voluntary abortions, and that horrid practice of women murdering their bastard children, alas, too frequent among us, sacrificing the poor innocent babes, I doubt, more to avoid the expense, than the shame, which would move tears and pity in the most savage and inhuman breast.

The number of souls in this kingdom being usually reckoned one million and a half, of these I calculate there may be about two hundred thousand couple whose wives are breeders, from which number I subtract thirty thousand couples, who are able to maintain their own children, although I apprehend there cannot be so many under the present distresses of the kingdom, but this being granted, there will remain an hundred and seventy thousand breeders. I again subtract fifty thousand for those women who miscarry, or whose children die by accident, or disease, within the year. There only remain an hundred and twenty thousand children of poor parents annually born: the question therefore is, how this number shall be reared, and provided for, which, as I have already said, under the present situation of affairs, is utterly impossible by all the methods hitherto proposed, for we can neither employ them in handicraft, or agriculture; we neither build houses (I mean in the country) nor cultivate land; they can very seldom pick up a livelihood by stealing till they arrive at six years old, except where they are of towardly parts, although, I confess, they learn the rudiments much earlier, during which time they can however be properly looked upon only as *probationers*, as I have been informed by a principal gentleman in the County of Cavan, who protested to me, that he never knew above one or two instances under the age of six, even in a part of the kingdom so renowned for the quickest proficiency in that art.

I am assured by our merchants, that a boy or a girl, before twelve years old, is no saleable commodity, and even when they come to this age, they will not yield above three pounds, or three pounds and half-a-crown at most on the Exchange, which cannot turn to account either to the parents or kingdom, the charge of nutriment and rags having been at least four times that value.

I shall now therefore humbly propose my own thoughts, which I hope will not be liable to the least objection.

I have been assured by a very knowing American of my acquaintance in London, that a young healthy child well nursed is at a year old a most delicious, nourishing, and wholesome food, whether stewed, roasted, baked, or boiled, and I make no doubt that it will equally serve in a fricassee, or ragout.

I do therefore humbly offer it to public consideration, that of the hundred and twenty thousand children, already computed, twenty thousand may be reserved for breed, whereof only one fourth part to be males, which is more than we allow to sheep, black-cattle, or swine, and my reason is that these children are seldom the fruits of marriage, a circumstance not much regarded by our savages, therefore one male will be sufficient to serve four females. That the remaining hundred thousand may at a year old be offered in sale to the persons of quality, and fortune, through the kingdom, always advising the mother to let them suck plentifully in the last month, so as to render them plump, and fat for a good table. A child will make two dishes at an entertainment for friends, and when the family dines alone, the fore or hind quarter will make a reasonable dish, and seasoned with a little pepper or salt will be very good boiled on the fourth day, especially in winter.

I have reckoned upon a medium, that a child just born will weigh 12 pounds, and in a solar year if tolerably nursed increaseth to 28 pounds.

I grant this food will be somewhat dear, and therefore very proper for landlords, who, as they have already devoured most of the parents, seem to have the best title to the children.

Infants' flesh will be in season throughout the year, but more plentiful in March, and a little before and after, for we are told by a grave author, an eminent French Physician, that fish being a prolific diet, there are more children born in Roman Catholic countries about nine months after Lent, than at any other season; therefore reckoning a year after Lent, the markets will be more glutted than usual, because the number of Popish infants is at least three to one in this kingdom, and therefore it will have one other collateral advantage by lessening the number of Papists among us.

I have already computed the charge of nursing a beggar's child (in which list I reckon all cottagers, labourers, and four-fifths of the farmers) to be about two shillings *per annum*, rags included, and I believe no gentleman would repine to give ten shillings for the carcass of a good fat child, which, as I have said, will make four dishes of excellent nutritive meat, when he hath only some particular friend, or his own family to dine with him. Thus the Squire will learn to be a good landlord, and grow popular among his tenants; the mother will have eight shillings net profit, and be fit for work till she produces another child.

Those who are more thrifty (as I must confess the times require) may flay the carcass; the skin of which, artificially dressed, will make admirable gloves for ladies, and summer boots for fine gentlemen.

As to our City of Dublin, shambles may be appointed for this purpose, in the most convenient parts of it, and butchers we may be assured will not be wanting, although I rather recommend buying the children alive, and dressing them hot from the knife, as we do roasting pigs.

A very worthy person, a true lover of his country, and whose virtues I highly esteem, was lately pleased, in discoursing on this matter, to offer a refinement upon my scheme. He said, that many gentlemen of this kingdom, having of late destroyed their deer, he conceived that the want of venison might be well supplied by the bodies of young lads and maidens, not exceeding fourteen years of age, nor under twelve, so great a number of both sexes in every country being now ready to starve, for want of work and service: and these to be disposed of by their parents if alive, or otherwise by their nearest relations. But with due deference to so excellent a friend, and so deserving a patriot, I cannot be altogether in his sentiments; for as to the males, my American acquaintance assured me from frequent experience, that their flesh was generally tough and lean, like that of our schoolboys, by continual exercise, and their taste disagreeable, and to fatten them would not answer the charge. Then as to the females, it would, I think with humble submission, be a loss to the public, because they soon would become breeders themselves: and besides, it is not improbable that some scrupulous people might be apt to censure such a practice (although indeed very unjustly) as a little bordering upon cruelty, which, I confess, hath always been with me the strongest objection against any project, however so well intended.

But in order to justify my friend, he confessed that this expedient was put into his head by the famous Psalmanazar, a native of the island Formosa, who came from thence to London, above twenty years ago, and in conversation told my friend, that in his country when any young person happened to be put to death, the executioner sold the carcass to persons of quality, as a prime dainty, and that, in his time, the body of a plump girl of fifteen, who was crucified for an attempt to poison the emperor, was sold to his Imperial Majesty's Prime Minister of State, and other great Mandarins of the Court, in joints from the gibbet, at four hundred crowns. Neither indeed can I deny, that if the same use were made of several plump young girls in this town, who, without one single groat to their fortunes, cannot stir abroad without a chair, and appear at the playhouse and assemblies in foreign fineries, which they never will pay for, the kingdom would not be the worse.

Some persons of a desponding spirit are in great concern about that vast number of people, who are aged, diseased, or maimed, and I have been desired to employ my thoughts what course may be taken, to ease the nation of so grievous an encumbrance. But I am not in the least pain upon that matter, because it is very well known, that they are every day dying, and rotting, by cold, and famine, and filth, and vermin, as fast as can be reasonably expected. And as to the younger labourers they are now in almost as hopeful a condition. They cannot get work, and consequently pine away for want of nourishment, to a degree, that if at any time they are accidentally hired to common labour, they have not strength to perform it; and thus the country and themselves are in a fair way of being soon delivered from the evils to come.

I have too long digressed, and therefore shall return to my subject. I think the advantages by the proposal which I have made are obvious and many, as well as of the highest importance.

For first, as I have already observed, it would greatly lessen the number of Papists, with whom we are yearly over-run, being the principal breeders of the nation, as well as our most dangerous enemies, and who stay at home on purpose with a design to deliver the kingdom to the Pretender, hoping to take their advantage by the absence of so many good Protestants, who have chosen rather to leave their country, than stay at home, and pay tithes against their conscience, to an Episcopal curate.

Secondly, The poorer tenants will have something valuable of their own, which by law may be made liable to distress, and help to pay their landlord's rent, their corn and cattle being already seized, and *money a thing unknown*.

Thirdly, Whereas the maintenance of an hundred thousand children, from two years old, and upwards, cannot be computed at less than ten shillings a piece *per annum*, the nation's stock will be thereby increased fifty thousand pounds *per annum*, besides the profit of a new dish, introduced to the tables of all gentlemen of fortune in the kingdom, who have any refinement in taste, and the money will circulate among ourselves, the goods being entirely of our own growth and manufacture.

Fourthly, The constant breeders, besides the gain of eight shillings sterling *per annum*, by the sale of their children, will be rid of the charge of maintaining them after the first year.

Fifthly, This food would likewise bring great custom to taverns, where the vintners will certainly be so prudent as to procure the best receipts for dressing it to perfection, and consequently have their houses frequented by all the fine gentlemen, who justly value themselves upon their knowledge in good eating; and a skilful cook, who understands how to oblige his guests, will contrive to make it as expensive as they please.

Sixthly, This would be a great inducement to marriage, which all wise nations have either encouraged by rewards, or enforced by laws and penalties. It would increase the care and tenderness of mothers toward their children, when they were sure of a settlement for life, to the poor babes, provided in some sort by the public to their annual profit instead of expense. We should see an honest emulation among the married women, which of them could bring the fattest child to the market; men would become as fond of their wives, during the time of their pregnancy, as they are now of their mares in foal, their cows in calf, or sows when they are ready to farrow, nor offer to beat or kick them (as it is too frequent a practice) for fear of a miscarriage.

Many other advantages might be enumerated: For instance, the addition of some thousand carcasses in our exportation of barrelled beef; the propagation of swine's flesh, and improvement in the art of making good bacon, so much wanted among us by the great destruction of pigs, too frequent at our tables, which are no way comparable in taste or magnificence to a well-grown, fat yearling child, which roasted whole will make a considerable figure at a Lord Mayor's feast, or any other public entertainment. But this and many others I omit, being studious of brevity.

Supposing that one thousand families in this city, would be constant customers for infants' flesh, besides others who might have it at merry-meetings, particularly weddings and christenings, I compute that Dublin would take off annually about twenty thousand carcasses, and the rest of the kingdom (where probably they will be sold somewhat cheaper) the remaining eighty thousand.

I can think of no one objection, that will possibly be raised against this proposal, unless it should be urged that the number of people will be thereby much lessened in the kingdom. This I freely own, and was indeed one principal design in offering it to the world. I desire the reader will observe, that I calculate my remedy *for this one individual Kingdom of Ireland, and for no other that ever was, is, or, I think, ever can be upon earth.* Therefore let no man talk to me of other expedients: *Of taxing our absentees at five shillings a pound: Of using neither clothes, nor household furniture, except what is of our own growth and manufacture: Of utterly rejecting the materials and instruments that promote foreign luxury: Of curing the expensiveness of pride, vanity, idleness, and gaming in our women: Of introducing a vein of parsimony, prudence and temperance: Of learning to love our Country, wherein we differ even from* LAPLANDERS, *and the inhabitants of* TOPINAMBOO: *Of quitting our animosities and factions, nor act any longer like the Jews, who were murdering one another at the very moment their city was taken: Of being a little cautious not to sell our country and consciences for nothing: Of teaching landlords to have at least one degree of mercy toward their tenants. Lastly, of putting a spirit of honesty, industry, and skill into our shopkeepers, who, if a resolution could now be taken to buy our native goods, would immediately unite to cheat and exact upon us in the price, the measure, and the goodness, nor could ever yet be brought to make one fair proposal of just dealing, though often and earnestly invited to it.*

Therefore I repeat, let no man talk to me of these and the like expedients, till he hath at least some glimpse of hope that there will ever be some hearty and sincere attempt to put them in practice.

But as to myself, having been wearied out for many years with offering vain, idle, visionary thoughts, and at length utterly despairing of success, I fortunately fell upon this proposal, which as it is wholly new, so it hath something solid and real, of no expense and little trouble, full in our own power, and whereby we can incur no danger in *disobliging* ENGLAND. For this kind of commodity will not bear exportation, the flesh being of too tender a consistence to admit a long continuance in salt, *although perhaps I could name a country, which would be glad to eat up our whole nation without it.*

After all I am not so violently bent upon my own opinion, as to reject any offer, proposed by wise men, which shall be found equally innocent, cheap, easy, and effectual. But before something of that kind shall be advanced in contradiction to my scheme, and offering a better, I desire the author or authors will be pleased maturely to consider two points. First, as things now stand, how they will be able to find food and raiment for an hundred thousand useless mouths and backs. And secondly, there being a round million of creatures in human figure, throughout this kingdom, whose whole subsistence put into a common stock would leave them in debt two millions of pounds sterling; adding those who are beggars by profession to the bulk of farmers, cottagers, and labourers with their wives and children, who are beggars in effect; I desire those politicians who dislike my overture, and may perhaps be so bold to attempt an answer, that they will first ask the parents of these mortals, whether they would not at this day think it a great happiness to have been sold for food at a year old, in the manner I prescribe, and thereby have avoided such a perpetual scene of misfortunes, as they have since gone through, by the oppression of landlords, the impossibility of paying rent without money or trade, the want of common sustenance, with neither house nor clothes to cover them from the inclemencies of the weather, and the most inevitable prospect of entailing the like, or greater miseries upon their breed for ever.

I profess in the sincerity of my heart that I have not the least personal interest in endeavouring to promote this necessary work, having no other motive than the *public good of my country, by advancing our trade, providing for infants, relieving the poor, and giving some pleasure to the rich.* I have no children by which I can propose to get a single penny; the youngest being nine years old, and my wife past child-bearing.

Samuel Johnson

The Rambler, No. 58: Saturday, October 6th, 1750

> *Improbae*
> *Crescunt divitiae, tamen*
> *Curae nescio quid semper abest rei.*   Horace.

> But, while in heaps his wicked wealth ascends,
> He is not of his wish possessed;
> There's something wanting still to make him blessed.   Francis.

As the love of money has been in all ages one of the passions that has given great disturbance to the tranquillity of the world, there is no topic more copiously treated by the ancient moralists than the folly of devoting the heart to the accumulation of riches. They who are acquainted with these authors need not be told how riches incite pity, contempt, or reproach whenever they are mentioned; with what numbers of examples the danger of large possessions is illustrated; and how all the powers of reason and eloquence have been exhausted in endeavours to eradicate a desire which seems to have entrenched itself too strongly in the mind to be driven out, and which, perhaps, had not lost its power even over those who declaimed against it, but would have broken out in the poet or the sage if it had been excited by opportunity and invigorated by the approximation of its proper object.

Their arguments have been, indeed, so unsuccessful, that I know not whether it can be shown that, by all the wit and reason which this favourite cause has called forth, a single convert was ever made; that even one man has refused to be rich, when to be rich was in his power, from the conviction of the greater happiness of a narrow fortune; or disburthened himself of wealth, when he had tried its inquietudes, merely to enjoy the peace and leisure and security of a mean and unenvied state.

It is true, indeed, that many have neglected opportunities of raising themselves to honours and to wealth, and rejected the kindest offers of fortune. But, however their moderation may be boasted by themselves or admired by such as only view them at a distance, it will be, perhaps, seldom found that they value riches less, but that they dread labour or danger more than others. They are unable to rouse themselves to action, to strain in the race of competition, or to stand the shock of contest; but though they therefore decline the toil of climbing, they nevertheless wish themselves aloft and would willingly enjoy what they dare not seize.

Others have retired from high stations, and voluntarily condemned themselves to privacy and obscurity. But even these will not afford many occasions of triumph to the philosopher; for they have commonly either quitted that only which they thought themselves unable to hold, and prevented disgrace by resignation, or they have been induced to try new measures by general inconstancy which always dreams of happiness in novelty, or by a gloomy disposition which is disgusted in the same degree with every state, and wishes every scene of life to change as soon as it is beheld. Such men found high and low stations equally unable to satisfy the wishes of a distempered mind, and were unable to shelter themselves in the closest retreat from disappointment, solicitude, and misery.

Yet though these admonitions have been thus neglected by those who either enjoyed riches or were able to procure them, it is not rashly to be determined that they are altogether without use. For since far the greatest part of mankind must be confined to conditions comparatively mean, and placed in situations from which they naturally look up with envy to the eminences before them, those writers cannot be thought ill employed that have administered remedies to discontent almost universal by showing that what we cannot reach may very well be forborne, that the inequality of distribution at which we murmur is for the most part less than it seems, and that the greatness which we admire at a distance has much fewer advantages and much less splendour when we are suffered to approach it.

It is the business of moralists to detect the frauds of fortune, and to show that she imposes upon the careless eye by a quick succession of shadows which will shrink to nothing in the grip; that she disguises life in extrinsic ornaments which serve only for show and are laid aside in the hours of solitude and of pleasure; and that when greatness aspires either to felicity or to wisdom it shakes off those distinctions which dazzle the gazer and awe the supplicant.

It may be remarked that they whose condition has not afforded them the light of moral or religious instruction, and who collect all their ideas by their own eyes and digest them by their own understandings, seem to consider those who are placed in ranks of remote superiority as almost another and higher species of beings. As themselves have known little other misery than the consequences of want, they are with difficulty persuaded that where there is wealth there can be sorrow, or that those who glitter in dignity and glide along in affluence can be acquainted with pains and cares like those which lie heavy upon the rest of mankind.

This prejudice is, indeed, confined to the lowest meanness and the darkest ignorance; but it is so confined only because others have been shown its folly and its falsehood, because it has been opposed in its progress by history and philosophy and hindered from spreading its infection by powerful preservatives.

The doctrine of the contempt of wealth, though it has not been able to extinguish avarice or ambition or suppress that reluctance with which a man passes his days in a state of inferiority, must at least have made the lower conditions less grating and wearisome, and has consequently contributed to the general security of life by hindering that fraud and violence, rapine and circumvention, which must have been produced by an unbounded eagerness of wealth arising from an unshaken conviction that to be rich is to be happy.

Whoever finds himself incited by some violent impulse of passion to pursue riches as the chief end of being must surely be so much alarmed by the successive admonitions of those whose experience and sagacity have recommended them as the guides of mankind, as to stop and consider whether he is about to engage in an undertaking that will reward his toil, and to examine, before he rushes to wealth through right and wrong, what it will confer when he has acquired it; and this examination will seldom fail to repress his ardour and retard his violence.

Wealth is nothing in itself. It is not useful but when it departs from us; its value is found only in that which it can purchase, which, if we suppose it put to its best use by those that possess it, seems not much to deserve the desire or envy of a wise man. It is certain that, with regard to corporal enjoyment, money can neither open new avenues to pleasure nor block up the passages of anguish. Disease and infirmity still continue to torture and enfeeble, perhaps exasperated by luxury or promoted by softness. With respect to the mind, it has rarely been observed that wealth contributes much to quicken the discernment, enlarge the capacity, or elevate the imagination, but may, by hiring flattery or laying diligence asleep, confirm error and harden stupidity.

Wealth cannot confer greatness, for nothing can make that great which the decree of nature has ordained to be little. The bramble may be placed in a hot-bed, but can never become an oak. Even royalty itself is not able to give that dignity which it happens not to find, but oppresses feeble minds though it may elevate the strong. The world has been governed in the name of kings, whose existence has scarcely been perceived by any real effects beyond their own palaces.

When, therefore, the desire of wealth is taking hold of the heart, let us look round and see how it operates upon those whose industry or fortune has obtained it. When we find them oppressed with their own abundance, luxurious without pleasure, idle without ease, impatient and querulous in themselves, and despised or hated by the rest of mankind, we shall soon be convinced that if the real wants of our condition are satisfied there remains little to be sought with solicitude or desired with eagerness.

Hester Lynch Thrale Piozzi

from *British Synonymy* (1794)

BLISS, HAPPINESS, FELICITY

Are three the strongest words mankind have been able to invent for a sensation they know so very little about; and we may observe that the first of these has been long ago nearly discarded from common talk, as too sublime and perfect, being now used only in a solemn sense, and with allusion to eternity—But if FELICITY could be ever found on earth, it might most justly be expected from a marriage of two persons eminently qualified to make each other's HAPPI-NESS, in a union first formed by love, continued by friendship, and so cemented by virtue as may give the partners a well-founded hope of everlasting BLISS in the world to come.

Thomas Carlyle

from *Sartor Resartus* (1833-1834)

"Men are properly said to be clothed with Authority,[1] clothed with Beauty, with Curses, and the like. Nay, if you consider it, what is Man himself, and his whole terrestrial Life, but an Emblem; a Clothing or visible Garment[2] for that divine ME of his, cast hither, like a light-particle, down from Heaven? Thus is he said also to be clothed with a Body.

"Language is called the Garment of Thought: however, it should rather be, Language is the Flesh-Garment, the Body,[3] of Thought. I said that imagination wove this Flesh-Garment; and does not she? Metaphors are her stuff: examine Language; what, if you except some few primitive elements (of natural sound), what is it all but Metaphors, recognised as such, or no longer recognised; still fluid and florid, or now solid-grown and colourless? If those same primitive elements are the osseous fixtures in the Flesh-Garment, Language,—then are Metaphors its muscles and tissues and living integuments. An unmetaphorical style you shall in vain seek for: is not your very *Attention* a *Stretching-to?*[4] The difference lies here: some styles are lean, adust, wiry, the muscle itself seems osseous; some are even quite pallid, hunger-bitten and dead-looking; while others again glow in the flush of health and vigorous self-growth, sometimes (as in my own case) not without an apoplectic tendency. Moreover, there are sham Metaphors, which overhanging that same Thought's-Body (best naked), and deceptively bedizening, or bolstering it out, may be called its false stuffings, superfluous show-cloaks (*Putz-Mäntel*), and tawdry woollen rags: whereof he that runs and reads may gather whole hampers,—and burn them."

Than which paragraph on Metaphors did the reader ever chance to see a more surprisingly metaphorical? However, that is not our chief grievance; the Professor continues:

"Why multiply instances? It is written, the Heavens and the Earth shall fade away like a Vesture;[5] which indeed they are: the Time-vesture of the Eternal. Whatsoever sensibly exists, whatsoever represents Spirit to Spirit, is properly a Clothing, a suit of Raiment, put on for a season, and to be laid off. Thus in this one pregnant subject of CLOTHES, rightly understood, is included all that men have thought, dreamed, done, and been: the whole Eternal Universe and what it holds is but Clothing, and the essence of all Science lies in the PHILOSOPHY OF CLOTHES."

[1] See Shakespeare's *Measure for Measure*, II.ii.118.

[2] Here and elsewhere Professor Teufelsdröckh echoes Section II of Jonathan Swift's *A Tale of a Tub*.

[3] See Job 10:11.

[4] The word *attention, attend,* is from the Latin *ad-*(toward) + *tendere* (to stretch).

[5] See Psalms 102:26.

Thomas Chandler Haliburton

from "Yankee eating and horse feeding" (1835)

Did you ever heer tell of Abernethy, a British doctor? said the Clockmaker. Frequently, said I, he was an eminent man, and had a most extensive practice. Well, I reckon he was a vulgar critter that, he replied, he treated the honble. Alder Gobble, secretary to our Legation at London, dreadful bad; and I guess if it had been me he had used that way, I'd a fixed his flint for him, so that he'd think twice afore he'd fire such another shot as that are agin—I'd a made him make tracks, I guess, as quick as a dog does a hog from a potato field—he'd a found his way out of the hole in the fence a plagy sight quicker than he came in, I reckon. His manner, said I, was certainly rather unceremonious at times, but he was so honest, and so straightforward, that no person was, I believe, ever seriously offended at him. *It was his way.* Then his way was so plagy rough, continued the Clockmaker, that he'd been the better, if it had been hammered and mauled down smoother; I'd a levelled him as flat as a flounder. Pray what was his offence? said I—Bad enough you may depend. The honble. Alder Gobble was dyspeptic, and he suffered great oneasiness arter eatin, so he goes to Abernethy for advice. What's the matter with you? said he. Why, says Alder, I presume I have the Dyspepsy—Ah! said he, I see, a yankee swallowed more dollars and cents than he can digest. I am an American citizen, says Alder, with great dignity, I am Secretary to our Legation at the Court of St. James. The devil you are, said Abernethy, then you'll soon get cured of your Dyspepsy. I dont see that are inference, said Alder, it don't follow from what you predicate at all—it ant a natural consequence I guess, that a man should cease to be ill, because he is called by the voice of a free and enlightened people to fill an important office. (The truth is, you could no more trap Alder than you could an Indian, he could see other folks' trail, and made none himself; he was a real diplomatist, and I believe our diplomatists are allowed to be the best in the world.) But I tell you it does follow, said the Dr. for in the company you'll have to keep, you'll have to eat like a christian. It was an everlasting pity Alder contradicted him, for he broke out like mad. I'll be d——d, said he, if ever I saw a yankee that didnt bolt his food whole like a Boa Constrictor. How the devil can you expect to digest food, that you neither take the trouble to dissect, nor time to masticate? Its no wonder you lose your teeth, for you never use them; nor your digestion, for you overload it; nor your saliva, for you expend it on the carpets, instead of your food. Its disgusting, its beastly. You Yankees load your stomachs as a Devonshire man does his cart, as full as it can hold, and as fast as he can pitch it with a dung fork, and drive off—and then you complain that such a load of comfort is too heavy for you. Dispepsy, eh, infernal guzzeling you mean. I'll tell you what, Mr. Secretary of Legation, take half the time to eat, that you do to drawl out your words, chew your food half as much as you do your filthy tobacco, and you'll be well in a month.

Elizabeth Rigby (later Lady Eastlake)

from *Letters from the Shores of the Baltic* (1841)

Of all the pleasures and luxuries which the blessings of modern peace have brought in their train, none are more universally desired, pursued, attained, and abused than those of travelling. Of all the varying motives which impel the actions of mankind, at this or any time, none are so multifarious, so relative, so contradictory, and so specious as those of travelling. The young and ardent, borne on the wings of hope—the listless and vapid, pushed forward on the mere dancing wire of fashion—the restless and disappointed, urged onward by the perpetual spur of excitement, all bring a different worship to the same idol. If there be good angels watching our movements from above, gazing, as the deaf, on the busy dance of life, and insensible to the jarring tones which impel it, how utterly incomprehensible must those inducements appear to them which drive tens of thousands annually from their native shores, to seek enjoyments which at home they would not have extended a hand to grasp, to encounter discomforts which at home would have been shunned as positive misfortunes, to withhold their substance where it ill can be spared, to spend it where it were better away—which lead individuals voluntarily to forsake all they can best love and trust, to follow a phantom, to double the chances of misfortune, or at best but to create to themselves a new home to leave it again, in sorrow and heaviness of heart, like the old one! But such is human nature;—seldom enjoying a good but in anticipation, seldom prizing happiness till it is gone; and such the reflections, inconsistent if true, of one who, self-condemned, is following in the motley herd of these emigrants, and who has now outwardly quitted all of England, save a narrow blue strip on the horizon which a finger may cover.

Thomas Babington Macaulay

from *The History of England from the Accession of James the Second* (1849-1861)

It is curious that the two most remarkable battles that perhaps were ever gained by irregular over regular troops should have been fought in the same week; the battle of Killiecrankie, and the battle of Newton Butler. In both battles the success of the irregular troops was singularly rapid and complete. In both battles the panic of the regular troops, in spite of the conspicuous example of courage set by their generals, was singularly disgraceful. It ought also to be noted that, of these extraordinary victories, one was gained by Celts over Saxons, and the other by Saxons over Celts. The victory of Killiecrankie indeed, though neither more splendid nor more important than the victory of Newton Butler, is far more widely renowned; and the reason is evident. The Anglosaxon and the Celt have been reconciled in Scotland, and have never been reconciled in Ireland. In Scotland all the great actions of both races are thrown into a common stock, and are considered as making up the glory which belongs to the whole country. So completely has the old antipathy been extinguished that nothing is more usual than to hear a Lowlander talk with complacency and even with pride of the most humiliating defeat that his ancestors ever underwent. It would be difficult to name any eminent man in whom national feeling and clannish feeling were stronger than in Sir Walter Scott. Yet when Sir Walter Scott mentioned Killiecrankie he seemed utterly to forget that he was a Saxon, that he was of the same blood and of the same speech with Ramsay's foot and Annandale's horse. His heart swelled with triumph when he related how his own kindred had fled like hares before a smaller number of warriors of a different breed and of a different tongue.

John Ruskin

from *The Stones of Venice* (1851-1853)

And now I wish that the reader, before I bring him into St. Mark's Place, would imagine himself for a little time in a quiet English cathedral town, and walk with me to the west front of its cathedral. Let us go together up the more retired street, at the end of which we can see the pinnacles of one of the towers, and then through the low grey gateway, with its battlemented top and small latticed window in the centre, into the inner private-looking road or close, where nothing goes in but the carts of the tradesmen who supply the bishop and the chapter, and where there are little shaven grassplots, fenced in by neat rails, before old-fashioned groups of somewhat diminutive and excessively trim houses, with little oriel and bay windows jutting out here and there, and deep wooden cornices and eaves painted cream colour and white, and small porches to their doors in the shape of cockleshells, or little, crooked, thick, indescribable wooden gables warped a little on one side; and so forward till we come to larger houses, also old-fashioned, but of red brick, and with gardens behind them, and fruit walls, which show here and there, among the nectarines, the vestiges of scattering, and now settling suddenly into invisible places among the bosses and flowers, the crowd of restless birds that fill the whole square with that strange clangour of theirs, so harsh and yet so soothing, like the cries of birds on a solitary coast between the cliffs and the sea.

John Henry Newman

from *The Idea of a University* (1852)

Knowledge is one thing, virtue is another; good sense is not conscience, refinement is not humility, nor is largeness and justness of view faith. Philosophy, however enlightened, however profound, gives no command over the passions, no influential notives, no vivifying principles. Liberal Education makes not the Christian, not the Catholic, but the gentleman. It is well to be a gentleman, it is well to have a cultivated intellect, a delicate taste, a candid, equitable, dispassionate mind, a noble and courteous bearing in the conduct of life—these are the connatural qualities of a large knowledge; they are the objects of a University; I am advocating, I shall illustrate and insist upon them; but still, I repeat, they are no guarantee for sanctity or even for conscientiousness, they may attach to the man of the world, to the profligate, to the heartless, pleasant, alas, and attractive as he shows when decked out in them. Taken by themselves, they do but seem to be what they are not; they look like virtue at a distance, but they are detected by close observers, and on the long run; and hence it is that they are popularly accused of pretense and

Reading for Style

hypocrisy, not, I repeat, from their own fault, but because their professors and their admirers persist in taking them for what they are not, and are officious in arrogating for them a praise to which they have no claim. Quarry the granite rock with razors, or moor the vessel with a thread of silk; then may you hope with such keen and delicate instruments as human knowledge and human reason to contend against those giants, the passion and the pride of man.

Henry David Thoreau

from *Walden* (1854)

Time is but the stream I go a-fishing in. I drink at it; but while I drink I see the sandy bottom and detect how shallow it is. Its thin current slides away, but eternity remains. I would drink deeper; fish in the sky, whose bottom is pebbly with stars. I cannot count one. I know not the first letter of the alphabet. I have always been regretting that I was not as wise as the day I was born. The intellect is a cleaver; it discerns and rifts its way into the secret of things. I do not wish to be any more busy with my hands than is necessary. My head is hands and feet. I feel all my best faculties concentrated in it. My instinct tells me that my head is an organ for burrowing, as some creatures use their snout and fore-paws, and with it I would mine and burrow my way through these hills. I think that the richest vein is somewhere hereabouts; so by the divining rod and thin rising vapors I judge; and here I will begin to mine.

Catharine Parr Traill

from *The Canadian Settler's Guide* (1855)

MASQUINONGE

Scale and clean your fish, if possible before the skin becomes dry and hard; but should it not come to your hands for some time after being taken out of the water, lay it on some clean stones, in a cool place, and throw over it a bowl or two of cold salt and water: this will render the scales less difficult to remove. With a sharp knife remove the gills and the inside. Few people cook the head of the masquinonge unless the fish is to be boiled, or baked whole, when the head and tail are tied and skewered so as to form a circle. Be careful, in cleaning this fish, not to wound your flesh with his sharp teeth or fins, as the cut is difficult to heal. Take out the roe, and throw it into salt and water. It should be floured, peppered, and salted, and fried as a garnish to the dish, but requires to be thoroughly done through: if it be soft and jelly-like, it is not sufficiently cooked. If you design to fry the fish, it must be cut in pieces, quite through the thickness of the fish, about three inches in width; dry on a board;

467

flour the pieces, and sprinkle with salt and pepper; or, beat up an egg, dip the pieces in the egg, and strew crumbs of bread, and lay them in the boiling lard: this is the best way. But sometimes the Canadian housewife may be obliged to resort to a more homely method, that of frying some slices of fat pork, to obtain the dripping in which to cook her fish; and if well attended to, even thus, her fish will be no despicable dish for a hungry family.

FIRE

Among the casualties that bring danger and alarm into a Canadian settler's homestead, there is none more frequent than fire—none more terrible; but, one, where a little presence of mind, and knowing what best to do on the spur of the moment, may save both life and property. As a timely care will often do more by preventing the danger, than much exertion after it has occurred, I will warn those whose houses are heated by stoves, to have the pipes taken down, especially where there are elbows or turns in them, twice during the long winter months; have a sheet of tin or iron nailed down on the floor below the stove:—this is less troublesome than a box, as in old times was the custom, filled with sand. The kitchen stoves are, from their construction, less liable to take fire than any other: the dampers being pushed in will stop the draught from ascending into the pipe. If it is a chimney that is on fire, after throwing water on the logs, hang up a cloth, rug, blanket, or anything you can get hold of, made wet, in front of the chimney, and keep the doors shut; a wisp of wet straw, or old woollen rags tied on a long staff, and put up the chimney, may extinguish the fire. All houses should have a ladder at hand; there are usually ledges left on the roof, near the chimney, to facilitate cleaning them; a bunch of pine-boughs, or a bundle of straw fastened to a rope, and drawn up and down by two persons, is the common chimney-sweep of a Canadian house. A quantity of salt thrown on the fire will damp flame. A mass of fire may be put out or kept down by covering it and pressing it down; and many a child has been saved by being wrapped tightly up, so as to exclude the access of air. Even a cotton garment, if pressed closely and the air excluded, has been safely used to smother fire; but linen or woollen is best of anything for this purpose. A table-cover, carpet, rug, any large thing should be caught up, unhesitatingly, to extinguish fire.

One of the great causes of destruction of houses by fire, in Canada, may be traced to the want of care in removing ashes, among which some live embers will often be hidden. No wooden vessel, pail, or box should be used to take ashes away in, and no ash-barrel should stand on the verandah, or near a wall. A proper ash-shed, away from the house, should be made, and an earthen or stone floor should be below the ash-barrels.

Sometimes people are exposed to considerable peril in new clearings, from the running of fire in the woods, or new fallows. In such case, where there is any danger of the fire getting to the homestead or standing crops, and there is no near supply of water, much can be effected by beating out the advancing flames, and still more by opening the earth with hoes, spades, or better still, by men yoking up the cattle and ploughing a few furrows, so as to interpose the new earth between the advancing fire and the combustible matter. Women, yes, weak women and children have battled against a wall of advancing fire, and with hoes and other instruments have kept it back till help could be obtained. This subject may seem out of place to dwell upon, but I have seen many instances where, if women had not roused themselves to exertion, *all* would have been lost.

Frances Anne (Fanny) Kemble

from "A Letter to the Editor of the London *Times*" (1853, 1863)

I do not believe the planters have any disposition to put an end to slavery, nor is it perhaps much to be wondered at that they have not. To do so is, in the opinion of the majority of them, to run the risk of losing their property, perhaps their lives, for a benefit which they profess to think doubtful to the slaves themselves. How far they are right in anticipating ruin from the manumission of their slaves I think questionable, but that they do so is certain, and self-impoverishment for the sake of abstract principle is not a thing to be reasonably expected from any large class of men. But, besides the natural fact that the slaveholders wish to retain their property, emancipation is, in their view of it, not only a risk of enormous pecuniary loss, and of their entire social status, but involves elements of personal danger, and, above all, disgust to inveterate prejudices, which they will assuredly never encounter. The question is not alone one of foregoing great wealth or the mere means of subsistence (in either case almost equally hard); it is not alone the unbinding the hands of those who have many a bloody debt of hatred and revenge to settle; it is not alone the consenting suddenly to see by their side, upon a footing of free social equality, creatures toward whom their predominant feeling is one of mingled terror and abhorrence, and who, during the whole of their national existence, have been, as the earth, trampled beneath their feet, yet ever threatening to gape and swallow them alive. It is not all this alone which makes it unlikely that the Southern planter should desire to free his slaves: freedom in America is not merely a personal right; it involves a political privilege. Freemen there are legislators. The rulers of the land are the majority of the people, and in many parts of the Southern states the black free citizens would become, if not at once, yet in process of time, inevitably voters, landholders, delegates to state Legislatures, members of Assembly—who knows?—senators, judges, aspirants to the presidency of the United States. You must be an American, or have lived long among them, to conceive the shout of derisive execration with which such an idea would be hailed from one end of the land to the other.

That the emancipation of the negroes need not necessarily put them in possession of the franchise is of course obvious; but, as a general consequence, the one would follow from the other; and at present certainly the slaveholders are no more ready to grant the political privilege than the natural right of freedom. Under these circumstances, though the utmost commiseration is naturally excited by the slaves, I agree with you that some forbearance is due to the masters. It is difficult to conceive a more awful position than theirs: fettered by laws which impede every movement toward right and justice, and utterly without the desire to repeal them—dogged by the apprehension of nameless retributions—bound beneath a burden of responsibility for which, whether they acknowledge it or not, they are held accountable by God and men—goaded by the keen consciousness of the growing reprobation of all civilized Christian communities, their existence presents the miserable moral counterpart of the physical condition of their slaves; and it is one compared with which that of the wretchedest slave is, in my judgement, worthy of envy.

Robert Louis Stevenson

from "An Apology for Idlers" (1877)

There is no duty we so much underrate as the duty of being happy. By being happy, we sow anonymous benefits upon the world, which remain unknown even to ourselves, or, when they are disclosed, surprise nobody so much as the benefactor. The other day, a ragged, barefoot boy ran down the street after a marble, with so jolly an air that he set every one he passed into a good humour; one of these persons, who had been delivered from more than usually black thoughts, stopped the little fellow and gave him some money with this remark: 'You see what sometimes comes of looking pleased.' If he had looked pleased before, he had now to look both pleased and mystified. For my part, I justify this encouragement of smiling rather than tearful children; I do not wish to pay for tears anywhere but upon the stage; but I am prepared to deal largely in the opposite commodity. A happy man or woman is a better thing to find than a five-pound note. He or she is a radiating focus of goodwill; and their entrance into a room is as though another candle had been lighted. We need not care whether they could prove the forty-seventh proposition; they do a better thing than that, they practically demonstrate the great Theorem of the Liveableness of Life. Consequently, if a person cannot be happy without remaining idle, idle he should remain. It is a revolutionary precept; but thanks to hunger and the workhouse, one not easily to be abused; and, within practical limits, it is one of the most incontestable truths in the whole Body of Morality. Look at one of your industrious fellows for a moment, I beseech you. He sows hurry and reaps indigestion; he puts a vast deal of activity out to interest, and receives a large measure of nervous derangement in return. Either he absents himself entirely from all fellowship, and lives a recluse in a garret, with carpet slippers and a leaden inkpot; or he comes among people swiftly and bitterly, in a contraction of his whole nervous system, to discharge some temper before he returns to work. I do not care how much or how well he works, this fellow is an evil feature in other people's lives. They would be happier if he were dead. They could easier do without his services in the Circumlocution Office, than they can tolerate his fractious spirits. He poisons life at the well-head. It is better to be beggared out of hand by a scapegrace nephew, than daily hag-ridden by a peevish uncle.

And what, in God's name, is all this pother about? For what cause do they embitter their own and other people's lives? That a man should publish three or thirty articles a year, that he should finish or not finish his great allegorical picture, are questions of little interest to the world. The ranks of life are full; and although a thousand fall, there are always some to go into the breach. When they told Joan of Arc she should be at home minding women's work, she answered there were plenty to spin and wash. And so, even with your own rare gifts! When nature is 'so careless of the single life,' why should we coddle ourselves into the fancy that our own is of exceptional importance? Suppose Shakespeare had been knocked on the head some dark night in Sir Thomas Lucy's preserves, the world would have wagged on better or worse, the pitcher gone to the well, the scythe to the corn, and the student to his book; and no one been any the wiser of the loss. There are not many works extant, if you look the alternative all over, which are worth the price of a pound of tobacco to a man of limited means. This is a sobering reflection for the proudest of our earthly vanities. Even a tobacconist may, upon consideration, find no great cause for personal vainglory in the phrase; for although tobacco is an admirable sedative, the qualities necessary for retailing it are neither rare nor precious in themselves. Alas and alas! you may take it how you will, but the services of no single individual are indispensable. Atlas was just a gentleman with a protracted nightmare! And yet you see merchants who go and labour themselves into a great fortune and thence into the bankruptcy court; scribblers who keep scribbling at little articles until their temper is a cross to all who come about them, as though Pharaoh should set the Israelites to make a pin instead of a pyramid; and fine young men who work themselves into a decline, and are driven off in a hearse with white plumes upon it. Would you not suppose these persons had been whispered, by the Master of the Ceremonies, the promise of some momentous destiny? and that this lukewarm bullet on which they play their farces was the bull's-eye and centrepoint of all the universe? And yet it is not so. The ends for which they give away their priceless youth, for all they know, may be chimerical or hurtful; the glory and riches they expect may never come, or may find them indifferent; and they and the world they inhabit are so inconsiderable that the mind freezes at the thought.

Catherine Helen Spence

"The Dangerous Classes" (1878)

It is not an uncommon thing for educated people to give the title of the dangerous class to the discontented poor—to the proletariat who has no stake in the country, who has nothing to lose, and may reasonably imagine that he has everything to gain by a social or political revolution. So far from education acting as a universal safeguard against the possibility of physical force and against the danger of large numbers clutching at the wealth and attacking the privileges of the minority it sometimes brings a profounder discontent than ignorance, and it enables masses to combine for more effective action than was possible in the time when life was harder and its prizes much less attainable by those who seemed born to do the rough work of life. But it is a mere conventionalism to restrict the term dangerous classes to the poor and the numerous. Every class is dangerous which has unchecked power, which exacts all its legal rights and forgets its national and social duties. The self-indulgent rich are the dangerous class until they have been brought under the will of the indignant and envious poor, and it is quite possible for the very hope and strength of our English nation and colonies—the intelligent middle class—to be dangerous to the safety of the state if it holds in its hands the supreme power and uses it for selfish or for class interests.

Looking back on the history of France, who were the dangerous classes during the century that preceded the Revolution? The despotic sovereign, the idle and luxurious nobles, who parted with their political power as a check on the monarch on condition of retaining all their social privileges and their insolent authority over all beneath them, and the church, which banded itself with the strong, and never as a political or social power helped the weak and oppressed—these were responsible for the long-gathered vengeance which they provoked. Had these dangerous classes either from within or from without awakened to a sense of public duty toward those whom they believed Providence had set under them would not the French Revolution have been a progressive movement instead of a frightful catastrophe? After the turning-point which led to the subversion of the monarchy, of the aristocracy, and the church the dangerous classes were the unchecked ignorant but not more selfish—probably much less selfish—Democrats. They were violent, they were cruel, their hands were stained with much innocent blood, but there was a wonderful cleanness with regard to money, and, with all their excuses, a love of the republic strong and inspiring. But this one class was a dangerous class, because it had no restraining power within the commonwealth. Its sole danger was from foreign foes, only to be withstood by enormous armies hastily levied and poorly equipped, but fired by real national enthusiasm and recruited from the new peasant proprietors of the soil, who felt they had so much to fight for that life could be thrown away gloriously for the sake of France.

The army and the general of the army next took the position of the dangerous classes, and a military despotism dependent for its continuance on foreign conquest, drained France of blood and money and at last left her at the mercy of a European coalition which made her take back her Bourbons and stay the march of freedom for herself and for Europe. After this the dangerous classes were the despotic and superstitious abettors of the retrograde movement and all the middle class who for the sake of peace or place or emolument strengthened the hands of the unwise government. The dangerous classes under Louis Philippe were the bourgeois and the bureaucrats, who derived all the advantages of peace and security, and were careless about the miseries of the poor or the freedom of the press. And again we see that in the time of Louis Napoleon the dangerous classes were not so much the discontented poor as the self-indulgent rich, and still more the apathetic peasant and bourgeois, who could carry any measure, but who thought of their own private interests and not of their public duties. In the discussion which has been lately carried on in the *Nineteenth Century* as to whether the popular judgment on political matters is more correct than that of the higher orders the weight of argument was in favour of the popular judgment being more quickly responsive to generous sympathy and to broad principles of justice, but too easily led by mistakes in public policy from one-sided ideas of the right and the wrong of a national quarrel. If the blood of England is up, England will go to war for an idea, though it is a wrong one.

It has been because England has had so long the right of public meeting, the right of petition, and a free anonymous press, that what in other countries would produce revolution in her leads to reform, sometimes slow, sometimes rapid. A measure apparently lost this session is merely delayed to the next; all means of agitation and of discussion are still open, and the greatest victories of freedom have been won by patience. Even without universal suffrage the power of the non-voter is felt in the country, and the curiously anomalous nature of the constitution, which cannot be imitated by foreign nations or even by English colonies tempers the actual absolute supremacy of the House of Commons, while the unrecognized powers—the press and the non-voters, comprising a very large proportion of the adult population—exert through public opinion a constant influence which cannot be defied. The recognized checks on the Commons—the Queen and the Lords—only maintain power by never straining it. The unrecognized powers have a reserve force, which it is to the interest of the Queen, Lords, and Commons to respect, and not to permit them to strain. In our attempts to make a brand new House of Lords or an Upper House respectable enough to delay or to modify democratic legislation, all the English colonies find it extremely difficult to adjust the balance of power so as to make the check beneficial and not hurtful. The rough-and-ready criterion of wealth is often the only one taken into consideration in choosing a representative for the Council, and it is fancied that a man who has managed his own affairs well will be the best man to manage the affairs of the colony. But our rich men often have been so engrossed with the adding of pound to pound and flock to flock and acre to acre that broad political principles, either of honour or of large expediency, are lost in the hand-to-mouth kind of legislation which suits personal interests and personal convenience. A selfish plutocracy in a rising colony is as dangerous a class as a selfish democracy; indeed we think that the transparently fallacious arguments of a rich man against property taxation have less excuse than equally one-sided arguments from the working man's point of view. Whilst condemning utterly Mr Berry's extreme measures one cannot help seeing that the proceedings of the Upper House in Victoria made them a dangerous class, and if the war goes on *à l'outrance* and the persistence of the Council leads to their being shorn of their legitimate powers then the unchecked democracy, now a source of infinite peril to the state, will be emphatically *the* dangerous class until some other constitutional mode of representing the opinions which contain the complementary or the modifying portions of political truth can be devised and carried out.

With regard to the attitude of the press towards both bodies of the legislature the public takes the opinions of journalists for what they are worth, and anonymity neither strengthens nor weakens their effect. And the correspondence columns of every respectable journal are open to bona fide opponents; those who consider themselves aggrieved can either anonymously or with the full privilege of their name and character combat the arguments of the leading article by counter-arguments. The compulsory signature of articles in France and other countries was not devised for the protection of the people from being overawed by the imposing "we," but for the convenience of the despotic government in order that an obnoxious writer—obnoxious probably in proportion to his truthfulness—might be silenced, fined, or imprisoned. In spite of the sensitive view of some non-members to press criticism from impecunious anonymous writers, they are only prevented from becoming the dangerous classes by the freedom of criticism—by its being possible to blame, to ridicule, or to denounce them. If the German press could freely condemn or laugh at Prince Bismarck he and his supporters would not be the dangerous class there, with the probability that suppressed public opinion may ere long turn the tables and give birth to a strong and very dangerous class in the Fatherland of the future. Free criticism, free public meetings, and a free press are the only safeguards for any nation from the mischievous sway of any one preponderating power.

Oscar Wilde

from *The Decay of Lying* (1889)

Cyril. The theory is certainly a very curious one, but to make it complete you must show that Nature, no less than Life, is an imitation of Art. Are you prepared to prove that?

Vivian. My dear fellow, I am prepared to prove anything.

Cyril. Nature follows the landscape painter, then, and takes her effects from him?

Vivian. Certainly. Where, if not from the Impressionists, do we get those wonderful brown fogs that come creeping down our streets, blurring the gas-lamps and changing the houses into monstrous shadows? To whom, if not to them and their master, do we owe the lovely silver mists that brood over our river, and turn to faint forms of fading grace, curved bridge and swaying barge? The extraordinary change that has taken place in the climate of London during the last ten years is entirely due to this particular school of Art. You smile. Consider the matter from a scientific or a metaphysical point of view, and you will find that I am right. For what is Nature? Nature is no great mother who has borne us. She is our creation. It is in our brain that she quickens to life. Things are because we see them, and what we see, and how we see it, depends on the Arts that have influenced us. To look at a thing is very different from seeing a thing. One does not see anything until one sees its beauty. Then, and then only, does it come into existence. At present, people see fogs, not because there are fogs, but because poets and painters have taught them the mysterious loveliness of such effects. There may have been fogs for centuries in London. I dare say there were. But no one saw them, and so we do not know anything about them. They did not exist till Art had invented them. Now, it must be admitted, fogs are carried to excess. They have become the mere mannerism of a clique, and the exaggerated realism of their method gives dull people bronchitis. Where the cultured catch an effect, the uncultured catch cold. And so, let us be humane, and invite Art to turn her wonderful eyes elsewhere. She has done so already, indeed. That white quivering sunlight that one sees now in France, with its strange blotches of mauve, and its restless violet shadows, is her latest fancy, and, on the whole, Nature reproduces it quite admirably. Where she used to give us Corots and Daubignys, she gives us now exquisite Monets and entrancing Pissarros. Indeed, there are moments, rare, it is true, but still to be observed from time to time, when Nature becomes absolutely modern. Of course she is not always to be relied upon. The fact is that she is in this unfortunate position: Art creates an incomparable and unique effect, and, having done so, passes on to other things. Nature, upon the other hand, forgetting that imitation can be made the sincerest form of insult, keeps on repeating this effect until we all become absolutely wearied of it. Nobody of any real culture, for instance, ever talks nowadays about the beauty of a sunset. Sunsets are quite old-fashioned. They belong to the time when Turner was the last note in art. To admire them is a distinct sign of provincialism of temperament. Upon the other hand they go on. Yesterday evening Mrs. Arundel insisted on my going to the window, and looking at the glorious sky, as she called it. Of course I had to look at it. She is one of those absurdly pretty Philistines, to whom one can deny nothing. And what was it? It was simply a very second-rate Turner, a Turner of a bad period, with all the painter's worst faults exaggerated and over-emphasized. Of

475

course, I am quite ready to admit that Life very often commits the same error. She produces her false Renés and her sham Vautrins, just as Nature gives us, on one day a doubtful Cuyp, and on another a more than questionable Rousseau. Still, Nature irritates one more when she does things of that kind. It seems so stupid, so obvious, so unnecessary. A false Vautrin might be delightful. A doubtful Cuyp is unbearable. However, I don't want to be too hard on Nature. I wish the Channel, especially at Hastings, did not look quite so often like a Henry Moore, grey pearl with yellow lights, but then, when Art is more varied, Nature will, no doubt, be more varied also. That she imitates Art, I don't think even her worst enemy would deny now. It is the one thing that keeps her in touch with civilised man. But have I proved my theory to your satisfaction?

Cyril. You have proved it to my dissatisfaction, which is better. But even admitting this strange imitative instinct in Life and Nature, surely you would acknowledge that Art expresses the temper of its age, the spirit of its time, the moral and social conditions that surround it, and under whose influence it is produced.

Vivian. Certainly not! Art never expresses anything but itself. This is the principle of my new æsthetics; and it is this, more than that vital connection between form and substance, on which Mr. Pater dwells, that makes music the type of all the arts.

Mary Kingsley
from Travels in West Africa (1897)

INTRODUCTION

Relateth the various causes which impelled the author to embark upon the voyage.

It was in 1893 that , for the first time in my life, I found myself in possession of five or six months which were not heavily forestalled, and feeling like a boy with a new half-crown, I lay about in my mind, as Mr. Bunyan would say, as to what to do with them. "Go and learn your tropics," said Science. Where on earth am I to go, I wondered, for tropics are tropics wherever found, so I got down an atlas and saw that either South America or West Africa must be my destination, for the Malayan region was too far off and too expensive. Then I got Wallace's *Geographical Distribution* and after reading that master's article on the Ethiopian region I hardened my heart and closed with West Africa. I did this the more readily because while I knew nothing of the practical condition of it, I knew a good deal both by tradition and report of South East America, and remembered that Yellow Jack was endemic, and that a certain naturalist, my superior physically and mentally, had come very near getting starved to death in the depressing society of an expedition slowly perishing of want and miscellaneous fevers up the Parana.

My ignorance regarding West Africa was soon removed. And although the vast cavity in my mind that it occupied is not even yet half filled up, there is a great deal of very curious information in its place. I use the word curious advisedly, for I think many seemed to translate my request for practical hints and advice into an advertisement that "Rubbish may be shot here." This same information is in a state of great confusion still, although I have made heroic efforts to codify it. I find, however, that it can almost all be got in under the following different headings, namely and to wit:—

The dangers of West Africa.
The disagreeables of West Africa.
The diseases of West Africa.
The things you must take to West Africa.
The things you find most handy in West Africa.
The worst possible things you can do in West Africa.

I inquired of all my friends as a beginning what they knew of West Africa. The majority knew nothing. A percentage said, "Oh, you can't possibly go there; that's where Sierra Leone is, the white man's grave, you know." If these were pressed further, one occasionally found that they had had relations who had gone out there after having been "sad trials," but, on consideration of their having left not only West Africa, but this world, were now forgiven and forgotten. One lady however kindly remembered a case of a gentleman who had resided some few years at Fernando Po, but when he returned an aged wreck of forty he shook so violently with ague as to dislodge a chandelier, thereby destroying a valuable tea-service and flattening the silver teapot in its midst.

No; there was no doubt about it, the place was not healthy, and although I had not been "a sad trial," yet neither had the chandelier-dislodging Fernando Po gentleman. So I next turned my attention to cross-examining the doctors. "Deadliest spot on earth," they said cheerfully, and showed me maps of the geographical distribution of disease. Now I do not say that a country looks inviting when it is coloured in Scheele's green or a bilious yellow, but these colours may arise from lack of artistic gift in the cartographer. There is no mistaking what he means by black, however, and black you'll find they colour West Africa from above Sierra Leone to below the Congo. "I wouldn't go there if I were you," said my medical friends, "you'll catch something; but if you must go, and you're as obstinate as a mule, just bring me—" and then followed a list of commissions from here to New York, any one of which—but I only found that out afterwards.

All my informants referred me to the missionaries. "There were," they said, in an airy way, "lots of them down there, and had been for years." So to missionary literature I addressed myself with great ardour; alas! only to find that these good people wrote their reports not to tell you how the country they resided in was, but how it was getting on towards being what it ought to be, and how necessary it was that their readers should subscribe more freely, and not get any foolishness into their heads about obtaining an inadequate supply of souls for their money. I also found fearful confirmation of my medical friends' statements about its unhealthiness, and various details of the distribution of cotton shirts over which I did not linger.

From the missionaries it was, however, that I got my first idea about the social condition of West Africa. I gathered that there existed there, firstly the native human beings—the raw material, as it were—and that these were led either to good or bad respectively by the missionary and the trader. There were also the Government representatives, whose chief business it was to strengthen and consolidate the missionary's work, a function they carried on but indifferently well. But as for those traders! well, I put them down under the dangers of West Africa at once. Subsequently I came across the good old coast yarn of how, when a trader from that region went thence, it goes without saying where, the Fallen Angel without a moment's hesitation vacated the infernal throne (Milton) in his favour. This, I beg to note, is the marine form of the legend. When it occurs terrestrially the trader becomes a Liverpool mate. But of course no one need believe it either way—it is not a missionary's story.

Naturally, while my higher intelligence was taken up with attending to these statements, my mind got set on going, and I had to go. Fortunately I could number among my acquaintances one individual who had lived on the Coast for seven years. Not, it is true, on that part of it which I was bound for. Still his advice was pre-eminently worth attention, because, in spite of his long residence in the deadliest spot of the region, he was still in fair going order. I told him I intended going to West Africa, and he said, "When you have made up your mind to go to West Africa the very best thing you can do is to get it unmade again and go to Scotland instead; but if your intelligence is not strong enough to do so, abstain from exposing yourself to the direct rays of the sun, take 4 grains of quinine every day for a fortnight before you reach the Rivers, and get some introductions to the Wesleyans; they are the only people on the Coast who have got a hearse with feathers."

My attention was next turned to getting ready things to take with me. Having opened upon myself the sluice gates of advice, I rapidly became distracted. My friends and their friends alike seemed to labour under the delusion that I intended to charter a steamer and was a person of wealth beyond the dreams of avarice. The only thing to do in this state of affairs was to gratefully listen and let things drift. They showered on me various preparations of quinine and other so-called medical comforts, mustard leaves, a patent filter, a hot-water bottle, and last but not least a large square bottle purporting to be malt and cod-liver oil, which, rebelling against an African temperature, arose in its wrath, ejected its cork, and proclaimed itself an efficient but not too savoury glue.

Not only do the things you have got to take, but the things you have got to take them in, present a fine series of problems to the young traveller. Crowds of witnesses testified to the forms of baggage holders they had found invaluable, and these, it is unnecessary to say, were all different in form and material.

With all this *embarras de choix* I was too distracted to buy anything new in the way of baggage except a long waterproof sack neatly closed at the top with a bar and handle. Into this I put blankets, boots, books, in fact anything that would not go into my portmanteau or black bag. From the first I was haunted by a conviction that its bottom would come out, but it never did, and in spite of the fact that it had ideas of its own about the arrangement of its contents, it served me well throughout my voyage.

. . . .

John Millington Synge

from *The Aran Islands* (1907)

I am in Aranmor, sitting over a turf fire, listening to a murmur of Gaelic that is rising from a little public-house under my room.

The steamer which comes to Aran sails according to the tide, and it was six o'clock this morning when we left the quay of Galway in a dense shroud of mist.

A low line of shore was visible at first on the right between the movement of the waves and fog, but when we came further it was lost sight of, and nothing could be seen but the mist curling in the rigging, and a small circle of foam.

There were few passengers; a couple of men going out with young pigs tied loosely in sacking, three or four young girls who sat in the cabin with their heads completely twisted in their shawls, and a builder, on his way to repair the pier at Kilronan, who walked up and down and talked with me.

In about three hours Aran came in sight. A dreary rock appeared at first sloping up from the sea into the fog; then, as we drew nearer, a coast-guard station and the village.

A little later I was wandering out along the one good roadway of the island, looking over low walls on either side into small flat fields of naked rock. I have seen nothing so desolate. Grey floods of water were sweeping everywhere upon the limestone, making at times a wild torrent of the road, which twined continually over low hills and cavities in the rock or passed between a few small fields of potatoes or grass hidden away in corners that had shelter. Whenever the cloud lifted I could see the edge of the sea below me on the right, and the naked ridge of the island above me on the other side. Occasionally I passed a lonely chapel or schoolhouse, or a line of stone pillars with crosses above them and inscriptions asking a prayer for the soul of the person they commemorated.

I met few people; but here and there a band of tall girls passed me on their way to Kilronan, and called out to me with humorous wonder, speaking English with a slight foreign intonation that differed a good deal from the brogue of Galway. The rain and cold seemed to have no influence on their vitality, and as they hurried past me with eager laughter and great talking in Gaelic, they left the wet masses of rock more desolate than before.

A little after midday when I was coming back one old half-blind man spoke to me in Gaelic, but, in general, I was surprised at the abundance and fluency of the foreign tongue.

. . . .

As we talked he sat huddled together over the fire, shaking and blind, yet his face was indescribably pliant, lighting up with an ecstasy of humour when he told me anything that had a point of wit or malice, and growing sombre and desolate again when he spoke of religion or the fairies.

. . . .

Afterwards he told me how one of his children had been taken by the fairies.

One day a neighbour was passing, and she said, when she saw it on the road, 'That's a fine child'.

Its mother tried to say 'God bless it', but something choked the words in her throat.

A while later they found a wound on its neck, and for three nights the house was filled with noises.

'I never wear a shirt at night,' he said, 'but I got up out of my bed, all naked as I was, when I heard the noises in the house, and lighted a light, but there was nothing in it.'

Then a dummy came and made signs of hammering nails in a coffin.

The next day the seed potatoes were full of blood and the child told his mother that he was going to America.

That night it died, and 'Believe me,' said the old man, 'the fairies were in it.'

When he went away, a little bare-footed girl was sent up with turf and the bellows to make a fire that would last for the evening.

She was shy, yet eager to talk, and told me that she had good spoken Irish, and was learning to read it in the school, and that she had been twice to Galway, though there are many grown women in the place who have never set a foot upon the mainland.

. . . .

In spite of the charm of my teacher, the old blind man I met the day of my arrival, I have decided to move on to Inishmaan, where Gaelic is more generally used, and the life is perhaps the most primitive that is left in Europe.

I spent all this last day with my blind guide, looking at the antiquities that abound in the west or north-west of the island.

. . . .

Then he sat down in the middle of the floor and began to recite old Irish poetry, with an exquisite purity of intonation that brought tears to my eyes though I understood but little of the meaning.

480

On our way home he gave me the Catholic theory of the fairies.

When Lucifer saw himself in the glass he thought himself equal with God. Then the Lord threw him out of heaven, and all the angels that belonged to him. While He was 'chucking them out,' an archangel asked Him to spare some of them, and those that were falling are in the air still, and have the power to wreck ships, and to work evil in the world.

From this he wandered off into tedious matters of theology, and repeated many long prayers and sermons in Irish that he had heard from the priests.

. . . .

I am settled at last on Inishmaan in a small cottage with a continual drone of Gaelic coming from the kitchen that opens into my room.

Early this morning the man of the house came over for me with a four-oared curagh—that is, a curagh with four rowers and four oars on either side, as each man uses two—and we set off a little before noon.

It gave me a moment of exquisite satisfaction to find myself moving away from civilisation in this rude canvas canoe of a model that has served primitive races since men first went to sea.

. . . .

My room is at one end of the cottage, with a boarded floor and ceiling, and two windows opposite each other. Then there is the kitchen with earth floor and open rafters, and two doors opposite each other opening into the open air, but no windows. Beyond it there are two small rooms of half the width of the kitchen with one window apiece.

The kitchen itself, where I will spend most of my time, is full of beauty and distinction. The red dresses of the women who cluster round the fire on their stools give a glow of almost Eastern richness, and the walls have been toned by the turf-smoke to a soft brown that blends with the grey earth-colour of the floor. Many sorts of fishing-tackle, and the nets and oil-skins of the men, are hung upon the walls or among the open rafters; and right overhead, under the thatch, there is a whole cowskin from which they make pampooties.[1]

Every article on these islands has an almost personal character, which gives this simple life, where all art is unknown, something of the artistic beauty of mediæval life. The curaghs and spinning-wheels, the tiny wooden barrels that are still much used in the place of earthenware, the home-made cradles, churns, and baskets, are all full of individuality, and being made from materials that are common here, yet to some extent peculiar to the island, they seem to exist as a natural link between the people and the world that is about them.

---

[1] A kind of cowhide slipper or sandal worn particularly by Aran Islanders.

Ambrose Bierce

from *The Devil's Dictionary* (1911)

ABSURDITY, *n*. A statement or belief manifestly inconsistent with one's own opinion.

ALONE, *adj*. In bad company.

CONSULT, *v.t.* To seek another's approval of a course already decided upon.

DEBAUCHEE, *n*. One who has so earnestly pursued pleasure that he has had the misfortune to overtake it.

FRIENDLESS, *adj*. Having no favors to bestow. Destitute of fortune. Addicted to utterance of truth and common sense.

LOQUACITY, *n*. A disorder which renders the sufferer unable to curb his tongue when you wish to talk.

PLATITUDE, *n*. The fundamental element and special glory of popular literature. A thought that snores in words that smoke. The wisdom of a million fools in the diction of a dullard. A fossil sentiment in artificial rock. A moral without the fable. All that is mortal of a departed truth. A demi-tasse of milk-and-morality. The Pope's-nose of a featherless peacock. A jelly-fish withering on the shore of the sea of thought. The cackle surviving the egg. A desiccated epigram.

RESPONSIBILITY, *n*. A detachable burden easily shifted to the shoulders of God, Fate, Fortune, Luck or one's neighbor. In the days of astrology it was customary to unload it upon a star.

Margaret Laurence

from *The Prophet's Camel Bell* (1963)

May they not just possibly be true, the tales of creatures as splendidly strange as minotaurs or mermaids? Will there be elephants old as forests, white peacocks with crests of azure, jewel-eyed birds as gaudy as the painted birds in the tombs of pharaohs, apes like jesters, great cats dark and secretive as Bast,[1] men who change into leopards at the flick of a claw?

Nothing can equal in hope and apprehension the first voyage east of Suez, yourself eager for all manner of oddities, pretending to disbelieve in marvels lest you appear naïve but anticipating them just the same, prepared for anything, prepared for nothing, burdened with baggage—most of it useless, unburdened by knowledge, assuming all will go well because it is you and not someone else going to the far place (harm comes only to others), bland as eggplant and as innocent of the hard earth as a fledgling sparrow.

There you go, rejoicing, as so you should, for anything might happen and you are carrying with you your notebook and camera so you may catch vast and elusive life in a word and a snapshot. There you go, anxious, as you may well be, for anything might happen and so you furtively reassure yourself with pages from the first-aid book in which it says the best thing to do for snakebite is to keep the patient quiet until the doctor arrives—luckily, you do not notice that it does not tell you what to do if there is no doctor within a hundred miles.

And in your excitement at the trip, the last thing in the world that would occur to you is that the strangest glimpses you may have of any creature in the distant lands will be those you catch of yourself.

[1] Ancient Egyptian cat-goddess.

Barry Lopez

from "A Reflection on White Geese" (1982)

At rest on the water the geese drank and slept and bathed and preened. They reminded me in their ablutions of the field notes of a Hudson's Bay trader, George Barnston. He wrote of watching flocks of snow geese gathering on James Bay in 1862, in preparation for their annual two-thousand-mile, non-stop thirty-two-hour flight to the Louisiana coast. They finally left off feeding, he wrote, to smooth and dress their feathers with oil, like athletes, biding their time for a north wind. When it came they were gone, hundreds of thousands of them, leaving a coast once "widely resonant with their petulant and incessant calls" suddenly as "silent as the grave—a deserted, barren, and frozen shore."

Barnston was struck by the way snow geese did things together. No other waterfowl are as gregarious; certainly no other large bird flies as skillfully in such tight aggregations. This quality—the individual act beautifully integrated within the larger movement of the flock—is provocative. One afternoon I studied individual birds for hours as they landed and took off. I never once saw a bird on the water move over to accommodate a bird that was landing; nor a bird ever disturbed by another taking off, no matter how tightly they were bunched. In no flight overhead did I see two birds so much as brush wing tips. Certainly they must; but for the most part they are flawlessly adroit. A flock settles gently on the water like wiffling leaves; birds explode vertically with compact and furious wingbeats and then stretch out full length, airborne, rank on rank, as if the whole flock had been cleanly wedged from the surface of the water. Several thousand bank smoothly against a head wind, as precisely as though they were feathers in the wing of a single bird.

from "Landscape and Narrative" (1984)

I think of two landscapes—one outside the self, the other within. The external landscape is the one we see—not only the line and color of the land and its shading at different times of the day, but also its plants and animals in season, its weather, its geology, the record of its climate and evolution. If you walk up, say, a dry arroyo in the Sonoran Desert you will feel a mounding and rolling of sand and silt beneath your foot that is distinctive. You will anticipate the crumbling of the sedimentary earth in the arroyo bank as your hand reaches out, and in that tangible evidence you will sense a history of water in the region. Perhaps a black-throated sparrow lands in a paloverde bush—the resiliency of the twig under the bird, that precise shade of yellowish-green against the milk-blue sky, the fluttering whir of the arriving sparrow, are what I mean by "the landscape." Draw on the smell of creosote bush, or clack stones together in the dry air. Feel how light is the desiccated dropping of the kangaroo rat. Study an animal track obscured by the wind. These are all elements of the land, and what makes the landscape comprehensible are the relationships between them. One learns a landscape finally not by knowing the name or identity of everything in it, but by perceiving the relationships in it—like that between the sparrow and the twig. The difference between the relationships and the elements is the same as that between written history and a catalog of events.

The second landscape I think of is an interior one, a kind of projection within a person of a part of the exterior landscape. Relationships in the exterior landscape include those that are named and discernible, such as the nitrogen cycle, or a vertical sequence of Ordovician limestone, and others that are uncodified or ineffable, such as winter light falling on a particular kind of granite, or the effect of humidity on the frequency of a blackpoll warbler's burst of song. That these relationships have purpose and order, however inscrutable they may seem to us, is a tenet of evolution. Similarly, the speculations, intuitions, and formal ideas we refer to as "mind" are a set of relationships in the interior landscape with purpose and order; some of these are obvious, many impenetrably subtle. The shape and character of these relationships in a person's thinking, I believe, are deeply influenced by where on this earth one goes, what one touches, the patterns one observes in nature—the intricate history of one's life in the land, even a life in the city, where wind, the chirp of birds, the line of a falling leaf, are known. These thoughts are arranged, further, according to the thread of one's moral, intellectual, and spiritual development. The interior landscape responds to the character and subtlety of an exterior landscape; the shape of the individual mind is affected by land as it is by genes.

One can also analyze style in works of fiction. For further practice in reading for style, here are the openings of several novels:

John Lyly

from *Euphues: The Anatomy of Wit* (1578)

There dwelt in Athens a young gentleman of great patrimony and of so comely a personage that it was doubted whether he were more bound to Nature for the lineaments of his person, or to Fortune for the increase of his possessions. But Nature, impatient of comparisons, and as it were disdaining a companion or copartner in her working, added to this comeliness of his body such a sharp capacity of mind that not only she proved Fortune counterfeit, but was half of that opinion that she herself was only current. This young gallant, of more wit than wealth, and yet of more wealth than wisdom, seeing himself inferior to none in pleasant conceits, thought himself superior to all in honest conditions, insomuch that he thought himself so apt to all things that he gave himself almost to nothing but practising of those things commonly which are incident to these sharp wits: fine phrases, smooth quips, merry taunts, using jesting without mean, and abusing mirth without measure. As therefore the sweetest rose hath his prickle, the finest velvet his brack,[1] the fairest flower his bran, so the sharpest wit hath his wanton will, and the holiest head his wicked way. And true it is that some men write and most men believe that, in all perfect shapes, a blemish bringeth rather a liking every way to the eyes than a loathing any way to the mind. Venus had her mole in her cheek, which made her more amiable; Helen her scar on her chin, which Paris called *cos amoris*, the whetstone of love; Aristippus his wart; Lycurgus his wen. So likewise in the disposition of the mind, either virtue is overshadowed with some vice, or vice overcast with some virtue. Alexander valiant in war, yet given to wine. Tully eloquent in his glosses, yet vainglorious. Solomon wise, yet too, too wanton. David holy, but yet an homicide. None more witty than Euphues, yet at the first none more wicked. The freshest colours soonest fade, the teenest[2] razor soonest turneth his edge, the finest cloth is soonest eaten with moths, and the cambric sooner stained than the coarse canvas: which appeared well in this Euphues, whose wit being like wax, apt to receive any impression, and bearing the head[3] in his own hand, either to use the rein or the spur, disdaining counsel, leaving his country, loathing his old acquaintance, thought either by wit to obtain some conquest, or by shame to abide some conflict; who, preferring fancy before friends, and his present humour before honour to come, laid reason in water, being too salt for his taste, and followed unbridled affection, most pleasant for his tooth. When parents have more care how to leave their children wealthy than wise, and are more desirous to have them maintain the name than the nature of a gentleman;

when they put gold into the hands of youth, where they should put a rod under their girdle; when instead of awe they make them past grace, and leave them rich executors of goods and poor executors of godliness; then is it no marvel that the son, being left rich by his father's will, become reckless by his own will.

[1] Flaw, break.   [2] Keenest.   [3] Headstall, bridle.

Daniel Defoe

from *Moll Flanders* (1722)

My true name is so well known in the records or registers at Newgate, and in the Old Bailey, and there are some things of such consequence still depending there, relating to my particular conduct, that it is not to be expected I should set my name or the account of my family to this work; perhaps, after my death, it may be better known; at present it would not be proper, no, not though a general pardon should be issued, even without Exceptions and reserve of persons or crimes.

Henry Fielding

from *Joseph Andrews* (1742)

It is a trite but true observation, that examples work more forcibly on the mind than precepts: and if this be just in what is odious and blameable, it is more strongly so in what is amiable and praiseworthy. Here emulation most effectually operates upon us, and inspires our imitation in an irresistible manner. A good man therefore is a standing lesson to all his acquaintance, and of far greater use in that narrow circle than a good book.

Jane Austen

from *Pride and Prejudice* (1813)

It is a truth universally acknowledged, that a single man in possession of a good fortune, must be in want of a wife.

Edward Bulwer-Lytton, Lord Lytton

from *Paul Clifford* (1840)

It was a dark and stormy night; the rain fell in torrents—except at occasional intervals, when it was checked by a violent gust of wind which swept up the streets (for it is in London that our scene lies), rattling along the housetops, and fiercely agitating the scanty flame of the lamps that struggled against the darkness.

Herman Melville

from *Moby-Dick; or, The Whale* (1851)

Call me Ishmael. Some years ago—never mind how long precisely—having little or no money in my purse, and nothing particular to interest me on shore, I thought I would sail about a little and see the watery part of the world. It is a way I have of driving off the spleen, and regulating the circulation. Whenever I find myself growing grim about the mouth; whenever it is a damp, drizzly November in my soul; whenever I find myself involuntarily pausing before coffin warehouses, and bringing up the rear of every funeral I meet; and especially whenever my hypos get such an upper hand of me, that it requires a strong moral principle to prevent me from deliberately stepping into the street, and methodically knocking people's hats off—then, I account it high time to get to sea as soon as I can. This is my substitute for pistol and ball. With a philosophical flourish Cato throws himself upon his sword; I quietly take to the ship. There is nothing surprising in this. If they but knew it, almost all men in their degree, some time or other, cherish very nearly the same feelings towards the ocean with me.

Mrs. (Elizabeth) Gaskell

from *Cranford* (1853)

In the first place, Cranford is in possession of the Amazons; all the holders of houses, above a certain rent, are women. If a married couple come to settle in the town, somehow the gentleman disappears; he is either fairly frightened to death by being the only man in the Cranford evening parties, or he is accounted for by being with his regiment, his ship, or closely engaged in business all the week in the great neighbouring commercial town of Drumble, distant only twenty miles on a railroad. In short, whatever does become of the gentlemen, they are not at Cranford. What could they do if they were there? The surgeon has his round of thirty miles, and sleeps at Cranford; but every man cannot be a surgeon. For keeping the trim gardens full of choice flowers without a weed to speck them; for frightening away little boys who look wistfully at the said flowers through the railings; for rushing out at the geese that occasionally venture into the gardens if the gates are left open; for deciding all questions of literature and politics without troubling themselves with unnecessary reasons or arguments; for obtaining clear and correct knowledge of everybody's affairs in the parish; for keeping their neat maid-servants in admirable order; for kindliness (somewhat dictatorial) to the poor, and real tender good offices to each other whenever they are in distress, the ladies of Cranford are quite sufficient. "A man," as one of them observed to me once, "is so in the way in the house!" Although the ladies of Cranford know all each other's proceedings, they are exceedingly indifferent to each other's opinions. Indeed, as each has her own individuality, not to say eccentricity, pretty strongly developed, nothing is so easy as verbal retaliation; but some-how good-will reigns among them to a considerable degree.

Charles Dickens

from *Hard Times* (1854)

"Now, what I want is, Facts. Teach these boys and girls nothing but Facts. Facts alone are wanted in life. Plant nothing else, and root out everything else. You can only form the minds of reasoning animals upon Facts; nothing else will ever be of any service to them. This is the principle on which I bring up these children. Stick to Facts, Sir!"

from *A Tale of Two Cities* (1859)

It was the best of times, it was the worst of times, it was the age of wisdom, it was the age of foolishness, it was the epoch of belief, it was the epoch of incredulity, it was the season of Light, it was the season of Darkness, it was the spring of hope, it was the winter of despair, we had everything before us, we had nothing before us, we were all going direct to Heaven, we were all going direct the other way—in short, the period was so far like the present period, that some of its noisiest authorities insisted on its being received, for good or for evil, in the superlative degree of comparison only.

George Eliot

from *Adam Bede* (1859)

With a single drop of ink for a mirror, the Egyptian sorcerer undertakes to reveal to any chance comer far-reaching visions of the past. This is what I undertake to do for you, reader. With this drop of ink at the end of my pen, I will show you the roomy workshop of Mr. Jonathan Burge, carpenter and builder, in the village of Hayslope, as it appeared on the eighteenth of June, in the year of our Lord 1799.

Lewis Carroll

from *Alice's Adventures in Wonderland* (1865)

Alice was beginning to get very tired of sitting by her sister on the bank and of having nothing to do: once or twice she had peeped into the book her sister was reading, but it had no pictures or conversations in it, "and what is the use of a book," thought Alice, "without pictures or conversations?"

Mark Twain

from *Adventures of Huckleberry Finn* (1884)

You don't know about me, without you have read a book by the name of "The Adventures of Tom Sawyer," but that ain't no matter. That book was made by Mr. Mark Twain, and he told the truth, mainly. There was things which he stretched, but mainly he told the truth. That is nothing. I never seen anybody but lied, one time or another, without it was Aunt Polly, or the widow, or maybe Mary. Aunt Polly—Tom's Aunt Polly, she is—and Mary, and the Widow Douglas, is all told about in that book—which is mostly a true book; with some stretchers, as I said before.

Stephen Crane

from *The Red Badge of Courage* (1895)

The cold passed reluctantly from the earth, and the retiring fogs revealed an army stretched out on the hills, resting. As the landscape changed from brown to green, the army awakened, and began to tremble with eagerness at the noise of rumors. It cast its eyes upon the roads, which were growing from long troughs of liquid mud to proper thoroughfares. A river, amber-tinted in the shadow of its banks, purled at the army's feet; and at night, when the stream had become of a sorrowful blackness, one could see across it the red, eyelike gleam of hostile camp-fires set in the low brows of distant hills.

Joseph Conrad

from *Lord Jim* (1900)

He was an inch, perhaps two, under six feet, powerfully built, and he advanced straight at you with a slight stoop of the shoulders, head forward, and a fixed from-under stare which made you think of a charging bull. His voice was deep, loud, and his manner displayed a kind of dogged self-assertion which had nothing aggressive in it. It seemed a necessity, and it was directed apparently as much at himself as at anybody else. He was spotlessly neat, apparelled in immaculate white from shoes to hat, and in the various Eastern ports where he got his living as ship-chandler's water-clerk he was very popular.

Henry James

from *The Beast in the Jungle* (1903)

What determined the speech that startled him in the course of their encounter scarcely matters, being probably but some words spoken by himself quite without intention—spoken as they lingered and slowly moved together after their renewal of acquaintance. He had been conveyed by friends, an hour or two before, to the house at which she was staying; the party of visitors at the other house, of whom he was one, and thanks to whom it was his theory, as always, that he was lost in the crowd, had been invited over to luncheon. There had been after luncheon much dispersal, all in the interest of the original motive, a view of Weatherend itself and the fine things, intrinsic features, pictures, heirlooms, treasures of all the arts, that made the place almost famous; and the great rooms were so numerous that guests could wander at their will, hang back from the principal group, and, in cases where they took such matters with the last seriousness, give themselves up to mysterious appreciations and measurements. There were persons to be observed, singly or in couples, bending toward objects in out-of-the-way corners with their hands on their knees and their heads nodding quite as with the emphasis of an excited sense of smell. When they were two they either mingled their sounds of ecstasy or melted into silences of even deeper import, so that there were aspects of the occasion that gave it for Marcher much the air of the "look round," previous to a sale highly advertised, that excites or quenches, as may be, the dream of acquisition. The dream of acquisition at Weatherend would have had to be wild indeed, and John Marcher found himself, among such suggestions, disconcerted almost equally by the presence of those who knew too much and by that of those who knew nothing. The great rooms caused so much poetry and history to press upon him that he needed to wander apart to feel in a proper relation with them, though his doing so was not, as happened, like the gloating of some of his companions, to be compared to the movements of a dog sniffing a cupboard. It had an issue promptly enough in a direction that was not to have been calculated.

James Joyce

from *A Portrait of the Artist as a Young Man* (1916)

Once upon a time and a very good time it was there was a moocow coming down along the road and this moocow that was coming down along the road met a nicens little boy named baby tuckoo. . . .

Virginia Woolf

from *The Waves* (1931)

The sun had not yet risen. The sea was indistinguishable from the sky, except that the sea was slightly creased as if a cloth had wrinkles in it. Gradually as the sky whitened a dark line lay on the horizon dividing the sea from the sky and the grey cloth became barred with thick strokes moving, one after another, beneath the surface, following each other, pursuing each other, perpetually.

Aldous Huxley

from *Brave New World* (1932)

A squat grey building of only thirty-four storeys. Over the main entrance the words, CENTRAL LONDON HATCHERY AND CONDITIONING CENTRE, and, in a shield, the World State's motto, COMMUNITY, IDENTITY, STABILITY.

Joyce Cary

from *The Horse's Mouth* (1944)

I was walking by the Thames. Half-past morning on an autumn day. Sun in a mist. Like an orange in a fried fish shop. All bright below. Low tide, dusty water and a crooked bar of straw, chicken-boxes, dirt and oil from mud to mud. Like a viper swimming in skim milk. The old serpent, symbol of nature and love.

Rose Macaulay

from *The Towers of Trebizond* (1956)

"Take my camel, dear," said my aunt Dot, as she climbed down from this animal on her return from High Mass.

Patrick White

from *Riders in the Chariot* (1961)

"Who was that woman?" asked Mrs. Colquhoun, a rich lady who had come recently to live at Sarsaparilla.

"Ah," Mrs. Sugden said, and laughed, "that was Miss Hare."

"She appears an unusual sort of person." Mrs. Colquhoun ventured to hope.

"Well," replied Mrs. Sugden, "I cannot deny that Miss Hare is *different*."

But the postmistress would not add to that. She started poking at a dry sponge. Even at her most communicative, talking with authority of the weather, which was her subject, she favoured the objective approach.

Mrs. Colquhoun was able to see for herself that Miss Hare was a small, freckled thing, whose stockings, at that moment, could have been coming down. To tell the truth, Mrs. Colquhoun was somewhat put out by the postmistress's discretion, but could not remain so indefinitely, for the war was over, and the peace had not yet set hard.

Miss Hare continued to walk away from the post office, through a smell of moist nettles, under the pale disc of the sun. An early pearliness of light, a lamb's-wool of morning promised the millennium, yet, between the road and the shed in which the Godbolds lived, the burnt-out blackberry bushes, lolling and waiting in rusty coils, suggested that the enemy might not have withdrawn. As Miss Hare passed, several barbs of several strands attached themselves to the folds of her skirt, pulling on it, tight, tight, tighter, until she was all spread out behind, part woman, part umbrella.

Patricia Grace

from *Mutuwhenua: The Moon Sleeps* (1978)

The days before my wedding were full and busy ones but more so for my mother than for any of us. It was summer, with the sun skidding day after day across a flawless ice-blue sky, taking with it all moisture from creeks and pastures, draining the hills and gullies to a sleek ivory. It was the nearest we would get to a white Christmas in these parts.

Earlier, the ti kouka far at the back of the house had given warning of this dryness, spilling out streamer after streamer of cream flowers from among its many bundles of speared leaves.

The ti kouka had been brought down from the bush when my father was a small boy; in front of it stands a ngaio tree that was planted at the time I was born.

From without it has a peaceful appearance, the ngaio tree, with its tidy rounded shape and its even green. Not until you get in close to it do you discover the pained twisting of its limbs and the scarring on the patterned skin, but even so it is a quiet tree. I was named after it. A new name in our family, but I was given one of the old names as well.

Margaret Atwood

from *The Handmaid's Tale* (1985)

We slept in what had once been the gymnasium. The floor was of varnished wood, with stripes and circles painted on it, for the games that were formerly played there; the hoops for the basketball nets were still in place, though the nets were gone. A balcony ran around the room, for the spectators, and I thought I could smell, faintly like an afterimage, the pungent scent of sweat, shot through with the sweet taint of chewing gum and perfume from the watching girls, felt-skirted as I knew from pictures, later in mini-skirts, then pants, then in one earring, spiky green-streaked hair. Dances would have been held there; the music lingered, a palimpsest of unheard sound, style upon style, an undercurrent of drums, a forlorn wail, garlands made of tissue-paper flowers, cardboard devils, a revolving ball of mirrors, powdering the dancers with a snow of light.

Terms and Topics

TERMS

1. **Vocabulary, Section VII**: abatement, abettors, ablutions, acquisition, aggregations, antipathy, apathetic, apt, arrogating, bedizening, blemish, bourgeois, brogue, chimerical, clannish, cleaving, comeliness, commiseration, complementary, conjecture, consequence, continence, debauchee, demeanour, derisive, desiccated, despotic, dictatorial, discretion, disdaining, dispersal, distempers, dogged, emolument, emulation, endemic, execration, executors, expedients, extant, fopperies, forbearance, forestalled, fractious, furtively, gregarious, hypocrisy, incredulity, ineffable, inquietude, inscrutable, insipid, integuments, intrinsic, inveterate, lineaments, lolling, loquacity, manifestly, manumission, meanness, metaphysical, millennium, minotaurs, motley, niggardly, odious, officious, osseous, patrimony, peevish, Philistines, platitude, plutocracy, portmanteau, precepts, pretense, prodigal, proficiency, proletariat, protracted, provocative, pungent, quenches, quickens, rapine, reparation, retributions, retrograde, rudiments, sanctity, scapegrace, shambles, specious, subsistence, superlative, taint, taunts, temperance, tenet, trite, unbridled, unceremonious, vainglory, vapid, vivifying, wanton, zealous

2. The term *diction* refers to a writer's choice of words and the various ways we can describe them: big, small, long, short, learned, simple, Latinate, Anglo-Saxon, strong, weak, etc. See "A Note to the Reader" and (for "levels") Terms, section I.

3. Diction can also be classified as *abstract* or *concrete*, *general* or *specific* (see "A Note to the Reader" for definitions and examples).

4. *Hypotaxis* (hypotactic style) refers to the subordination of phrases and clauses. *Parataxis* (paratactic style) refers to the coordination of elements, especially if without connectives. Omitting connectives, as in "I came, I saw, I conquered," is called *asyndeton*; using connectives between all elements, rather than just the last two items of a series, is called *polysyndeton*.

5. *Parallelism* (see Terms, section I) is a highly effective stylistic device. You will find it in many of the selections in this section, sometimes in conjunction with a *series* of three or more words, phrases, or clauses, or occasionally in conjunction with *balance*, a symmetry or near-symmetry of two words, phrases, or clauses (see for example the reference to *chiasmus* in "A Note to the Reader").

6. Kinds of sentences: the traditional four are *simple* (one subject, one verb—a single independent clause), *compound* (two independent clauses), *complex* (one independent clause and at least one dependent or subordinate clause), and *compound-complex* (at least two independent clauses and at least one subordinate clause). But this classification can be misleading unless you remember that a *simple* sentence may be quite long and seemingly complicated, and that a *compound* or *complex* or even *compound-complex* sentence can be relatively short and seemingly uncomplicated.

7. A *loose* sentence (not, here, a pejorative term) makes its main point early and then adds on subordinate elements, often at some length. A *periodic* sentence holds its main point in

abeyance until the end. An intermediate sort of sentence can be thought of as having a certain *degree* of *periodicity*. These are sometimes referred to, respectively, as ***right-branching, left-branching***, and ***mid-branching*** sentences.

8. Sentences are also classified according to their purpose: ***declarative*** (making statements), ***interrogative*** (asking questions), ***imperative*** (giving commands), and ***exclamatory*** (expressing strong feeling or emphasis).

9. ***Anaphora*** refers to the repetition of the opening word or words of successive phrases or clauses—for example the repeated "it is not alone" in the excerpt by Fanny Kemble.

10. *Etymology* (see "A Note to the Reader" and Topic I on Lewis Thomas's "Notes of a Biology Watcher"). Look up the origins and histories of the following words. The first group are all from Ecclesiastes, the second from Samuel Johnson, the third from several authors, as indicated:
   (a) season, purpose, die, plant, pluck, heal, weep, laugh, mourn, dance, keep, sew, speak, love, hate, war, peace
   (b) copiously, incite, solicitude, extrinsic, felicity, affluence, avarice, admonitions, corporal, exasperated, diligence
   (c) adroit (Lopez), arroyo (Lopez), candid (Newman), gaudy (Laurence), oblivion (Browne), tawdry (Carlyle)

TOPICS: On Individual Selections

NICHOLAS BRETON   *"A Worthy Gentleman," "An Unworthy Gentleman"*

1. Point out the ways in which the two separate paragraphs parallel each other.
2. Compare the ways in which other writers use techniques of character-drawing similar to those of Breton: for example Lane, Davenport, Addison, Montagu.

JOHN DONNE   *Meditation XVII*

1. How does Donne contrive to create the effect of a church bell tolling throughout this meditation? What is the effect?
2. Point out some of the images by which Donne repeatedly emphasizes the relation between part and whole.
3. What does he mean by "translation"? What relevance does the metaphor of *writing* have to the condition he is trying to explain?
4. "The bell doth toll for him that thinks it doth." Discuss.
5. Compare Donne's comments on "treasure" here to Johnson's on "money," "riches," "wealth," and Bacon's on "charges."

SIR FRANCIS BACON   *"Of Marriage and Single Life"*

1. On what features does the effectiveness of the opening sentence depend?
2. What is Bacon's attitude to women? Compare it to those of others, for example Montagu.

3. Can you think of any examples from earlier or later history that either support or counter Bacon's claim in his second sentence?

4. What does the term "liberty" mean as Bacon uses it?

JOSEPH ADDISON   Spectator No. 105

1. In effect, Addison's first three paragraphs serve as an introduction to his "reflections" on pedantry. Is that disproportionately long? Does the character sketch stand on its own—and if so, does "Spectator No. 105" amount to two separate essays stuck together?

2. Would you characterize Addison's style here as "straightforward"? Compare and contrast its clarity and directness with those of some of the other selections—perhaps that by Johnson.

LADY MARY WORTLEY MONTAGU   Letter to the Countess of Mar

1. What are the signs of personal relation in this letter?

2. To what degree do the descriptions depend on concrete detail? Try rewriting a descriptive passage in general terms.

3. Show how a narrative passage, as opposed to a descriptive one, can serve as a moral exemplum.

4. Examine the author's use of active and passive voice. Note for example how in the third paragraph she mixes active and passive voice to help define the position of women in Turkish society as being acted upon and having limited power of choice, especially in matters of love and marriage. Is there an implicit contrast with the power of English women?

5. To what degree is motherhood a focal point in this letter, a subject around which almost everything else develops?

JONATHAN SWIFT   "A Modest Proposal"

1. Swift's essay is a masterpiece of sustained irony. Some inattentive readers have thought Swift was serious, failing to note that he had adopted a *persona* (Latin for actor's mask; see also Terms, section II) for the occasion. But point out the places where Swift deliberately lets the mask slip.

2. What specific political issues is Swift addressing?

3. Define the word *projectors* as Swift uses it. What is the force of the word *other* modifying it?

4. How do the verbs in the passive voice—for example in the first few paragraphs—serve an ironic purpose?

5. Consider Swift's deliberate use of stereotypes. What is the force of his references to nationalities and faiths—American, French, Irish, Roman Catholic (Papists), Formosa (Mandarins)?

6. What is the effect of enumerating, using statistics, when applied to the lives of human beings? What is the difference (first sentence of paragraph 6) between *couple* and *couples*?

7. Contrast the speaker's attitude toward marriage with that of Bacon and Montagu.

8. Explain the ending—what is its effect?

9. Write a contemporary modest proposal on some local subject, perhaps a social or political program or proposal that you think is wrongheaded. Like Swift, adopt a persona; wear a mask. Propose just the opposite of what you really think should be done—but, like Swift, try to find some way of making your serious point clear as well.

SAMUEL JOHNSON   *Rambler No. 58*

1. Examine the effect of the recurrence of words referring to comparative sizes and stations, such as *great, greater, greatest, greatness, little, lower, lowest, more, less, fewer.*

2. Find instances of passive voice in Johnson's essay. What is their effect in their immediate context? Do they affect the overall tone?

3. To what degree does Johnson rely on abstraction as opposed to concreteness?

HESTER LYNCH THRALE PIOZZI   *"Bliss, Happiness, Felicity"*

1. Does it strike you as odd that the title serves as the subject of the opening clause?

2. Is the author's primary purpose—definition, clarifying the distinctions between the meanings of similar words—served or undermined by her inclusion of moral and philosophical ideas?

CATHARINE PARR TRAILL   *"Masquinonge," "Fire"*

1. Are the instructions for cleaning and frying the fish clear? What parts go beyond straightforward step-by-step directions? Why?

2. Is the piece on "Fire" also a set of instructions? How does it differ in kind from the other one?

3. Is the conclusion of "Fire" effective? Is it a digression, as Traill seems to suggest?

CATHERINE HELEN SPENCE "   *The Dangerous Classes"*

1. What are Spence's primary and secondary purposes in this essay? Is she arguing? explaining? correcting mistaken views?

2. Do you think that writing from the point of view of an Australian enables Spence to view England and France with greater objectivity?

3. In her review in section IV Virginia Woolf refers to women writers with "a strength which in this age one has to call masculine." Do you think Spence is such a writer? If so, try to account for her strength. Is it a matter of diction (though she depends heavily on the verb *be*)? sentence structure (note how often she begins sentences with *And* and *But*)? economy? or what? How does she achieve emphasis?

TOPICS: On the Openings of Novels

Examine the openings of these and other works of fiction to establish how each uses various elements of style to begin setting up issues, perspectives, ideas, attitudes. Here are some specific questions on the excerpts included in this section:

1. Judging from the extract from Lyly's *Euphues*, how would you characterize the style known as *euphuism*? What are its principal features? Do any of the later selections share some of these features? If so, how do they differ?

2. In the opening of Defoe's *Moll Flanders*, do the assertions of truth, the hints at possibilities, and the recurrent use of negative words raise questions about the reliability of his narrator?

3. How does Fielding make use of cliché? And how does Bulwer-Lytton seemingly fall into clichés? (You may want to look into the anthologies for the annual Bulwer-Lytton bad-writing contest.)

4. In Austen's famous opening sentence, notice how the tension between the absolutes (*truth, universally*) and the modal (*must*) creates irony.

5. Note the abrupt three-word sentence with which Melville begins *Moby-Dick*. What is the effect, then, of the leisurely, rambling, self-indulgent sentences which follow it? Comment on Ishmael's imagery. Do his remarks about his *spleen* (melancholy) and *hypos* (hypochondrias) paint him as a gloomy and weak sort, or is he being humorous? What seem to you the principal purposes of this opening paragraph?

6. How does the style of Gaskell's opening lead up to and underscore the implications of that final word *degree*? Of what consequence are the repetitions of the word *Cranford*, the cumulative series of *for* phrases, the several alternatives signalled by *or*, the balance achieved by forms of qualification (*although, pretty strongly, somehow*, etc.)?

7. Does Dickens, in the opening of *A Tale of Two Cities*, echo Ecclesiastes? How and for what reason does the style emphasize *comparison*? And how does the speaker of the opening paragraph of *Hard Times*, by contrast, insist upon the force and consequence of *absolutes*?

8. Does George Eliot wish to set herself up as something of a "sorcerer," or is she simply using a convenient analogy as a way of getting started? Would this analogy be impossible for a writer today, in an age of typewriters and word-processors? Do you like being addressed as "reader"?

9. Does Carroll's opening of *Alice* necessarily establish the work as a children's book?

10. What are the various effects of Twain's use of Huck Finn's vernacular point of view? Is it incongruous to use as a narrator of a work of literature someone who doesn't appear to be literate? Compare Twain's use of vernacular with Haliburton's.

11. Analyze Crane's opening paragraph to see what makes it work. Why does the landscape change from brown to green? Is the army metaphorically personified (see Terms, section I)? Does Crane succeed in revivifying the dead metaphor of "brows . . . of hills"?

12. Consider the kinds and forms of the first four sentences of Conrad's *Lord Jim*, and the details of physical description and the inferences of character drawn from them. What do the words *perhaps, seemed*, and *apparently* convey? What is suggested about Jim by his being just "under

six feet"—and why didn't Conrad just write "five-feet ten or eleven" and have done with it? What is the tone of the final words, "very popular"?

13. Compare the level of formality produced by James's diction, sentence structure, and sentence length with that of some of the other openings. What is the effect of James's style—for example is it an attempt to represent an unusually subtle and probing intellectuality?

14. What verbal perspective is created by the language (spoken by the hero's father) that Joyce uses to begin his *Portrait*?

15. In Woolf's opening paragraph, what does the rhythm—especially of the last sentence—suggest? What can you say about the speed or tempo of the prose? What is represented in the progress from absence, to crease, to line, to bars? What is the effect of casting the whole in italics?

16. What is the force of the block capitals in Huxley's opening? (Perhaps note also Carlyle's use of them.) Of the abstract nouns? Of the connections drawn between adjectives (*squat grey, only thirty-four*)?

17. Do the fragments in Cary's opening paragraph have something to do with the narrator's being an artist? What about the things he sees—and the way he sees them?

18. What is the effect of the incongruity in Rose Macaulay's opening sentence?

19. Comment on the lengths of White's sentences. Note how the character Miss Hare (why "hare"?) is constructed by sensory effects rather than by speech. How does the contrast with Mrs. Colquhoun, who uses conventional forms of speech, emphasize Miss Hare's unconventionality?

20. In Grace's opening paragraph, what does the conjunction of *summer* and *Christmas* tell you? Are the Maori terms *ti kouka* and *ngaio* therefore less puzzling than they might otherwise have been? What do the qualities of style suggest about the first-person narrator?

21. Analyze the effect of Atwood's use of tense in the opening paragraph of *The Handmaid's Tale*. What is the force of the phrase "a palimpsest of unheard sound"—is it an instance of synaesthesia? How do the images of pleasure in game and dance intensify the sense of loss?

TOPICS: General and Comparative

1. When reading for style, watch for recurrent features; repetition (of vocabulary, of structure, of sound, etc.) will often signal or stress a writer's points and priorities. Note for example how the following *repetitions* or *recurrent patterns* contribute to the effect of certain selections:

   (a) anaphora (see Terms): Kemble

   (b) parallel structures: Johnson

   (c) balanced structures: Macaulay

   (d) inversions, reversals: Breton

   (e) pattern of contrasts: Ecclesiastes

   (f) sound patterns, alliteration: Laurence (first sentence)

   (g) "for" clauses: Bacon

   (h) rhetorical questions: Addison (fifth paragraph)

(i)   adverbs: Lopez (a)

(j)   adjectives: Ruskin

(k) concrete nouns: Traill

(l)   first-person pronoun: Thoreau

(m) negative structures: Newman

(n) key terms: Spence (the title phrase throughout, and at the end the word *free*)

Now look for more examples of such repetitions and recurrent patterns in these and other selections in this book. When you find them, analyze them; try to account for their use and their effects. For example, contrast the different effects to be achieved by extensive *parallelism*—in the passage from Ecclesiastes, in Breton, in Bacon, in Johnson, in Rigby, in Macaulay, in . . . .

2. Investigate the ways in which diction—word choice—influences the way a passage achieves its effect.

(a) Contrast the predominantly Germanic vocabulary of the King James translation of St. Luke with the predominantly Latinate vocabulary of Sir Thomas Browne or Samuel Johnson. What is the effect of Addison's or Stevenson's combining of Germanic and Latinate vocabularies?

(b) Track down the origins of the following words in the *Oxford English Dictionary*:

Bacon: *girdle, garter, shackle, froward*

Addison: *lewd, disaster, raillery, pedant, dint*

Montagu: *mortifying, lozenge, bodkin, hazel-nut*

Traill: *scale, gill, cook, roe, garnish, jelly, crumb, pipe, box, sand, rug, staff, hoe*

(c) Consider the effect of words from other sources; for example *masquinonge* (Traill), *caftan, sherbet, soucoupes* (Montagu), embarras de choix (Kingsley), tobacco (Stevenson), pampooties (Synge).

(d) Examine the way particular authors use verbs, for example Milton, Addison, and Lopez.

(e) In the first excerpt by Lopez, what does *wiffling* mean, or suggest associatively?

(f) For Sam Slick, Haliburton deliberately contrives a vernacular full of solecisms, proverbial utterances, epigrams, mundane similes. What features of personality is Haliburton thereby emphasizing: native wit? salt-of-the-earth morality? rural wisdom? uneducated brashness? unmannerly ignorance?

3. How does imagery, both literal and figurative, contribute to style? For example consider the following:

(a) the way Breton uses a series of similes to intensify his second portrait

(b) the way Donne uses the image of continent and island

(c) the way Milton uses an extended metaphor

(d) the seeming scarcity of figurative language in Swift's "A Modest Proposal" (point out the obvious instances of it, and describe their effect): does literal imagery make up for the lack? (or is Carlyle's Teufelsdröckh correct in saying "An unmetaphorical style you shall in vain seek for"?)

(e) the way Johnson in his penultimate paragraph uses the image of the oak and the bramble as an illustrative example, similar to a parable

(f) the way Carlyle has Teufelsdröckh push metaphors

(g) the way Newman in his final sentence uses impossible images to make a moral point

(h) the degree to which Thoreau's paragraph depends on metaphor

(i) the degree to which Lopez uses literal as opposed to figurative images; point out all his metaphors

4. What is the effect of sentence length? For example:

(a) Why does Ruskin spin out his second sentence to such a length?

(b) What is the effect of the successive short sentences in Thoreau and Wilde?

(c) Donne's sentences are predominantly long; but note the two shorter ones a little past the middle. What is the effect of this sudden shift?

(d) Why does Swift use such a long sentence (ignore the capitalized *Of*'s in the fifth paragraph from the end)?

(e) The capitalized *But* after the dash in the middle of Piozzi's paragraph makes it somewhat ambiguous, but in effect it is one long sentence. Would it be better broken up, with each of the three independent clauses standing as a sentence?

(f) Browne's sentences don't vary much in length. What is the effect of this near uniformity of length? Is the same true of Macaulay's paragraph?

(g) Addison's sentences, in contrast, vary almost rhythmically. Again, what is the effect? Is the same true of Newman's excerpt? of Stevenson's?

5. What effects does the length of paragraphs have? Are long paragraphs harder to read? Do short paragraphs seem choppy? Or is each appropriate to certain kinds of material or occasion? Are modern paragraphs generally shorter than earlier ones? Try for example to account for the following:

(a) Donne's meditation is all one paragraph, as is Bacon's essay.

(b) Addison uses a variety of paragraph lengths, as do Swift and Johnson.

(c) The first paragraph of Kemble's excerpt is quite long, as are all of Spence's.

(d) Synge uses predominantly short paragraphs, many consisting of only one fairly short sentence.

(e) The two paragraphs of Lopez's second selection are virtually identical in length.

6. Contrast the uses and effects of different kinds of sentences. First the classification according to purpose: By far, most sentences in English are declarative. The other forms—interrogative, imperative, and exclamatory—gain some of their effect by departing from the declarative norm. But not all uses of any one of them are alike. Consider for example the following:

(a) All of Bacon's sentences are declarative (even the one that ends with a question mark); but try contrasting them with, say, those of Breton, or Browne, or Newman, or Thoreau, or Kemble, or Synge (when the old man says "Believe me, the fairies were in it," is he being imperative?). Ruskin's first sentence is declarative in form, but is it imperative in spirit? And his second is imperative in form, but is it declarative in spirit? Most of Bierce's definitions aren't even complete sentences, but could they be classified as anything other than declarative?

(b) Newman concludes with an imperative sentence; and Traill's first extract is mainly imperative (as befits instructions), but why isn't the second one as well?

(c) Laurence opens with interrogatives; and note the interrogative sentences in Stevenson, Spence, and Wilde.

(d) Note the exclamatory sentences in Rigby and Stevenson.

7. Next, loose sentences and periodic sentences: Most sentences are loose; it is the natural, comfortable way to make sentences. Periodic sentences are usually the result of a conscious intent to be different; they stand out as, in a way, unnatural—and therefore usually aren't used often. Consider the following, for example:

(a) Ruskin's second sentence is decidedly loose, and unusually long as well. What is its effect?

(b) Milton uses several periodic or partly periodic sentences. Do they seem strained, or are they rhetorically effective?

8. Finally, the classification by grammatical type. Consider the following, for example:

(a) the predominance of compound-complex sentences in Donne, and the fairly high ratio also in Bacon (are there any simple sentences in either of these?)

(b) the predominance of complex sentences in Browne (and note the long fragment in mid-paragraph: Why does he allow it? Is it effective?)

(c) the predominance of complex sentences in the first part of Addison's essay, but the consistent mixture of types thereafter (and note his frequent use of compound predicates)

(d) the fact that all Newman's sentences are simple, compound, or compound-complex (compound sentences often being in effect simple sentences joined)

(e) the thorough mixture of types in Thoreau's paragraph (try listing their successive types in order to get a sort of picture of the rhythm of the paragraph in this respect; does it match that from sentence length?)

What grammatical types are Rigby's five sentences? What kind are most of Johnson's? Are there as many simple sentences sprinkled through Wilde's excerpt as you might have expected? in Synge's?

9. What are the techniques by which *contrast* works? Consider for example the force of each of the following:

(a) *yet* and *but* in Bacon and Montagu, *but* in Spence, *than* in Breton

(b) negation in Milton and Newman

(c) the irony in Stevenson, and especially in Swift, and the litotes at the beginning of Spence's essay

(d) the competing ranges of vocabulary in Montagu, Stevenson, and Spence

(e) Haliburton's contrast between the measured English speech of The Squire ("I" in this passage) and the Yankee twang of Sam Slick ("the Clockmaker") and between the bumptiousness of Alder Gobble and the pompousness of Abernathy

(f) the wit in Wilde, with the implicit contrast between the cultured and the uncultured

(g) the contrast between fancy and reality in Laurence

10. What determines *tone*? How would you characterize the tone of each selection, and why? Consider for example the following:

(a) Ecclesiastes: Would you call this sombre? pessimistic? optimistic? or perhaps just realistic? What are the effects of the almost incantatory and poetic repetition and rhythm?

(b) Could Donne's meditation be called elegiac? Is it Donne's faith alone that enables him to be glowingly optimistic about such a subject? Does the style itself contribute to optimism, or is it in ironic contrast with the optimism?

(c) What creates the matter-of-factness of Bacon's essay?

(d) Milton is arguing against the policy of prior censorship of books. Does he sound argumentative? Is his tone here one of confidence—and if so, what does he do stylistically to create that feeling?

(e) Would you call Addison's tone friendly, folksy? Where would you put this on a scale of one (frivolous) to ten (deadly serious)?

(f) How should a careful reader be able to spot the fact that Swift is being ironic? Do you find "A Modest Proposal" morbid, in spite of the devastating irony? Is it at any point downright laugh-provoking?

(g) Carlyle's tone is difficult to pin down, partly because he pretends to be editing and commenting on philosophical fragments written by professor Diogenes Teufelsdröckh. Carlyle's own purpose is to attack the mechanistic and utilitarian spirit of the age, urging instead a sort of Calvinistic German transcendentalism.

(h) How does Haliburton establish Sam Slick as a garrulous storyteller? Consider the rhythms and the speed of the passage.

(i) Does the way Rigby ends her introductory paragraph by admitting that she is "self-condemned" add weight to or detract from her criticism of the motives of travellers?

(j) How does Traill succeed—if she does—in making her instructive paragraphs other than simply dry and matter-of-fact?

(k) Is Kemble serious when, at the end of her excerpt, she professes to have more pity for the slaveholders than for the slaves?

(l) What is Stevenson's tone? (This excerpt is approximately the concluding quarter of his essay.) Does Stevenson make you feel good by praising idleness, or bad by belittling individual achievement?

(m) How serious is Wilde? Are Vivian's aesthetic pronouncements patently absurd, or is there a degree of truth in them? What does the dialogue form contribute to the effect?

(n) How does Kinglsey's humour and irony affect her expression of her views on such subjects as Africa, missions, medicine, the role of women, travelling?

(o) What mood or atmosphere or feeling does Synge create in this (slightly abridged) opening of his book? How does he create it? Does the cadence of his prose contribute?

(p) Do you find Bierce's cynicism pleasant, or unpleasant?

(q) What is the tonal effect of Laurence's repeated use of *you, your,* and *yourself* in this opening passage of her book?

11. What effects does allusion achieve? Consider the following, for example:

    (a) The Bible is a common source of allusion; note for example in St. Luke 15: "the prodigal son" (quoted not from the text but from a heading at the top of the page); "killed the fatted calf." Shakespeare is also a common source. (The excerpt from Carlyle contains allusions to both the Bible and Shakespeare—and to Swift as well.) Yet another common source is history.

    (b) Why is Donne's Meditation XVII alluded to so often ("no man is an island"; Hemingway's *For Whom the Bell Tolls*)?

    (c) Why does Bacon allude to Ulysses?

    (d) What does Milton gain by alluding to Spenser?

    (e) Identify the several allusions in Browne's paragraph.

    (f) Stevenson alludes to Dickens's *Little Dorrit* (in which the Circumlocution Office appears), to Joan of Arc, to Shakespeare, to Atlas, and to the Bible (Pharaoh and the Israelites). What is the result, for the reader, of such wide-ranging references?

    (g) Is Kingsley's opening allusion to Bunyan functional, or just fun?

12. Show how style affects the way a particular subject is treated. Consult the Thematic Table of Contents for two or more authors handling the same or similar subjects and compare and contrast the ways in which they do it.

13. Consider punctuation. Find examples of authors (especially the more recent ones) using punctuation in what you think particularly effective ways—or in ways different from the way you use it. Note for example Newman's dash and semicolons, Kemble's dashes. Comment on Traill's punctuation—and perhaps contrast it with Spence's. Is Stevenson's punctuation an aid to rhythm? to clarity? How about Kingsley's? Does Lopez use too many dashes—or does each pay its way?

14. Consider the politics of style: What are the assumptions behind such features as balances, parallels, closures (rhythms of conclusions)? In "A Note to the Reader" we define tone as "an author's attitude toward his or her subject and audience"; is tone then dependent on a writer's *purpose* on a given occasion? Is the notion of "style" subject to fashion? Is it only a way of preserving the status quo? What is meant by "received style," or "received standard" style (or pronunciation)? Is style itself ever rebellious? Consider for example how style itself can constitute part of the way an author reacts to present paradigms of power and constructs or suggests alternatives. Such a stylistic role is perhaps most noticeable in the selection by Haliburton, but how is it present also in such others as those by Montagu, Swift, Spence, Wilde, and Synge? You may wish to refer also to the essay by Cooper in section VI.

Notes on Authors and Sources

ADDISON, JOSEPH (1672-1719). English poet, dramatist (*Cato*), critic, and statesman, known principally for his periodical essays in Richard Steele's *The Tatler* (1709-1711) and especially in *The Spectator* (1711-1712,1714), a joint production with Steele.

ARLEN, MICHAEL J. (b. 1930). English-born writer and television critic; author of *The Camera Age: Essays on Television* (1981) and *Passage to Ararat* (1975), which won a National Book Award. "Life and Death in the Global Village" first appeared in *The New Yorker* and was collected in *Living-Room War* in 1969.

ATWOOD, MARGARET (b. 1939). Canadian poet and writer of novels, stories, and criticism; *The Circle Game* (1966) won a Governor General's Award. Among her novels are *Surfacing* (1972), *Bodily Harm* (1981), and *Cat's Eye* (1988). "Witches" was collected in *Second Words: Selected Critical Prose* (1982).

AUSTEN, JANE (1775-1817). English novelist, known for her incisive use of irony. Besides *Pride and Prejudice* (1813), her best-known works are *Sense and Sensibility* (1811), *Mansfield Park* (1814), and *Emma* (1816).

BACON, SIR FRANCIS (1561-1626). English philosophical writer and statesman (he became Lord Chancellor in 1618). In addition to *The Essays, or Counsels, Civil and Moral*, best known in their third edition (1625), he wrote *The Advancement of Learning* (1605), *Novum Organum* (1620), and *The New Atlantis* (1627).

BAKER, NICHOLSON (b. 1957). American writer, contributor to *The Little Magazine, Story Quarterly, The New Yorker*, and *The Atlantic*, where "The Size of Thoughts" appeared in March 1983. His story "K.590" was included in *The Best American Short Stories (1982); The Mezzanine*, his first novel, appeared in 1988.

BERLIN, SIR ISAIAH (b. 1909). Latvian-born British teacher, philosopher, and writer—often about political theory and the history of ideas. Among his better known works are *The Hedgehog and the Fox: An Essay on Tolstoy's View of History* (1957) and *Four Essays on Liberty* (1969). "The Purpose of Philosophy" first appeared in *Insight* in 1962 and was collected in *Concepts and Categories: Philosophical Essays* (1978).

BIERCE, AMBROSE (1842-c.1914). Sardonic American journalist and author, best known for such Civil War tales as "An Occurrence at Owl Creek Bridge" and *The Devil's Dictionary* (whose definitions began accumulating in 1881 and were first collected under the title *The Cynic's Word Book* in 1906). Late in 1913 he disappeared into Mexico during that country's Civil War.

BRETON, NICHOLAS (c.1555-1626). English author of a large number and variety of works, including *The Soul's Heavenly Exercise* (1601), *The Passionate Shepherd* (1604), and *The Fantasticks* (1626). His "character" writings appeared in *The Good and the Bad, Or Descriptions of the Worthies and Unworthies of this Age* (1616).

BRINK, ANDRÉ (b. 1935). South African novelist, playwright, and essayist, author of *Looking on Darkness* (1974), *A Dry White Season* (1979), and *A Chain of Voices* (1982). "The Intellectual and His World," the 1980 Graduation address, University of the Witwatersrand, was collected in *Mapmakers: Writing in a State of Siege* (1983).

BROWNE, SIR THOMAS (1605-1682). English medical doctor and author of *Urn Burial* (1658), *Religio Medici* (1642), and *Pseudodoxia Epidemica*, commonly known as *Vulgar Errors* (1646).

BULWER-LYTTON, EDWARD GEORGE EARLE LYTTON, FIRST BARON LYTTON (1803-1873). Prolific English novelist, dramatist, and poet, no longer much read. The best-known of his novels are probably *Pelham* (1828), *Eugene Aram* (1832), and *The Last Days of Pompeii* (1834).

CARLYLE, THOMAS (1795-1881). Scots-born scholar and translator of German literature, author of the exuberant *Sartor Resartus: The Life and Opinions of Herr Teufelsdröckh* ("Professor of Things in General" at the University of Weissnichtwo; "Sartor Resartus" means "the tailor retailored"); it first appeared in *Fraser's Magazine*, 1833-1834. He also wrote *The French Revolution: A History* (1837), *On Heroes, Hero-Worship and the Heroic in History* (1841), and *Past and Present* (1843).

CARROLL, LEWIS (CHARLES LUTWIDGE DODGSON) (1832-1898). A mathematician at Oxford (*Euclid and His Modern Rivals*, 1879), much better known as author of *Alice's Adventures in Wonderland* (1865), *Through the Looking-Glass and What Alice Found There* (including the poem "Jabberwocky"; 1871), and *The Hunting of the Snark: An Agony in Eight Fits* (1876).

CARY, JOYCE (1888-1957). Irish-born English novelist, best known for his early novels set in Africa (e.g. *Mister Johnson*, 1939) and two trilogies, the first comprising *Herself Surprised* (1941), *To Be a Pilgrim* (1942), and *The Horse's Mouth* (1944).

COLE, K. C. (b. 1946). American free-lance writer and magazine editor. Among his books are *Vision: In the Eye of the Beholder* (1978), *Between the Lines* (1982), and *Sympathetic Vibrations: Reflections on Physics As a Way of Life* (1984). "By the Numbers" first appeared in *Discover* magazine in January 1984.

COLOMBO, JOHN ROBERT (b. 1936). Canadian poet, translator, and anthologist, compiler of *Colombo's Canadian Quotations* (1974) and devotee of "found poetry." "Communicating Through Form" appeared in *A Media Mosaic*, ed. Walt McDayter, in 1971.

CONRAD, JOSEPH (1857-1924). Polish-born writer of novels, short stories, and essays. After twenty years as a seaman, he settled in England in 1894 to become a professional writer of such works as *The Nigger of the "Narcissus"* (1897), *Lord Jim* (1900), "Youth" and *Heart of Darkness* (1902), *Nostromo* (1904), *The Secret Agent* (1907), and *Under Western Eyes* (1911).

COOPER, CAROLYN (b. 1950). Jamaican professor and critic, specializing in Black American and Caribbean literature and in feminist literary theory. "Writing Oral History: SISTREN Theatre Collective's *Lionheart Gal*" is included in *After Europe: Critical Theory and Post-Colonial Writing*, ed. Stephen Slemon and Helen Tiffin, 1989.

CRANE, STEPHEN (1871-1900). American journalist, war correspondent, and writer of fiction—and some poetry; best known for his realistic Civil War novel *The Red Badge of Courage* (1895) and such stories as "The Open Boat" (1897) and "The Bride Comes to Yellow Sky" (1898).

CUTSCHALL, COLLEEN. Lakota-Sioux Professor of Native Studies and Artist in Residence at the University of Brandon. The paper "Voice in the Blood: Suffering and Compassion" was delivered as a lecture at the November 1987 meeting of the American Anthropology Association, in Chicago, at a session entitled "Suffering and Compassion."

DAVENPORT, GUY (b. 1927). American teacher, scholar, poet, critic, and artist. Among his works are *Da Vinci's Bicycle: Ten Stories by Guy Davenport* (1979) and *The Jules Verne Steam Balloon* (1987). "Wittgenstein" was collected in *The Geography of the Imagination* (1981).

DEACON, WILLIAM ARTHUR (1890-1977). Canadian critic, influential in setting up the Governor General's Awards in 1937; literary editor of *Saturday Night* (1922-1928) and the *Globe and Mail* (1936-1960), and author of *The Four*

Jameses (1927). "What a Canadian Has Done for Canada" first appeared in *Saturday Night* and was collected in *Poteen: A Pot-Pourri of Canadian Essays* in 1926.

DEFOE, DANIEL (1659-1731). Prolific English author of novels, histories, satires, and miscellaneous journalism. Known principally for *The Life and Strange and Surprising Adventures of Robinson Crusoe* (1719) and *The Fortunes and Misfortunes of the Famous Moll Flanders* (1722), he also wrote, among other works, *The Shortest Way with the Dissenters* (1702), *A Journal of the Plague Year* (1722), and *Roxana, or The Fortunate Mistress* (1724).

DICKENS, CHARLES (1812-1870). One of the pre-eminent English novelists of the Victorian period. Dickens's huge output includes such favourites as *The Pickwick Papers* (1836-1837), *Oliver Twist* (1837-1839), *Nicholas Nickleby* (1838-1839), *The Old Curiosity Shop* (1840-1841), *A Christmas Carol* (1843), *David Copperfield* (1849-1850), *Bleak House* (1852-1853), and *Great Expectations* (1860-1861). He also ran the weekly periodicals *Household Words* (1850-1859) and *All the Year Round* (1859-1870).

DILLARD, ANNIE (b. 1945). American essayist who often writes about herself and nature; author of *Living by Fiction* (1978), *Pilgrim at Tinker Creek* (which won a Pulitzer Prize in 1975), *An American Childhood* (1987), and *Teaching a Stone to Talk*, in which "Living Like Weasels" was collected in 1982.

DONNE, JOHN (1572-1631). English poet and churchman, born a Catholic but later Dean of St. Paul's. His early worldly poetry contrasts with his later religious works such as *Devotions upon Emergent Occasions* (1624), which he wrote in a fever on what was nearly his death-bed, and from which Meditation XVII comes. Among his better-known poems are "The Canonization," "A Valediction: Forbidding Mourning," and the Holy Sonnets.

DRYDEN, KEN (b. 1947). Canadian hockey star, now retired; played 1030 NHL games. "The Game," adapted from his 1984 book *The Game*, appeared in *Saturday Night* magazine.

EISELEY, LOREN (1907-1977). American anthropologist; author of *Darwin's Century* (1958), *The Firmament of Time* (1960), *The Invisible Pyramid* (1970), and other books on nature and modern life. "The Creature from the Marsh" is taken from *Night Country* (1971).

ELIOT, GEORGE (MARY ANN EVANS) (1819-1880). Prominent Victorian English novelist, poet, and essayist. Among her novels are *The Mill on the Floss* (1860), *Silas Marner* (1861), *Middlemarch* (1871-1872), and *Daniel Deronda* (1874-1876). She also wrote a volume of essays called *The Impressions of Theophrastus Such* (1879).

FIELDING, HENRY (1707-1754). English novelist who began as a writer of topical comic plays (e.g., *Tom Thumb*, 1730). When his political satire brought censorship in the form of the theatre Licensing Act of 1737, he turned to other forms. Best known for *Joseph Andrews* (1742) and *Tom Jones* (1749), he also wrote many periodical essays. In addition he was a lawyer and magistrate who instituted what amounted to the beginnings of an effective English police force.

FISHER, M. F. K. (b. 1908). American writer, principally about gastronomy and travel; author of *How to Cook a Wolf* (1942), *The Gastronomical Me* (which includes "A Thing Shared"; 1943), and *An Alphabet for Gourmets* (1949), which were collected with two other works in 1954 as *The Art of Eating*, and *Sister Age*, a collection of stories (1983).

FORSTER, E. M. (1879-1970). English novelist and critic, best known for *A Room with a View* (1908), *A Passage to India* (1924), the stories in *The Celestial Omnibus* (1911), and *Aspects of Fiction* (1927). "My Wood" appeared in *Abinger Harvest*, a collection of his essays, in 1936.

FRAYN, MICHAEL (b. 1933). English columnist, novelist, and dramatist; among his works are *The Russian Interpreter* (1966), *Sweet Dreams* (1973), and the plays *Noises Off* (1982) and *Benefactors* (1984). "Lives and Likenesses" first appeared in *The Observer* and was collected in 1983 in *The Original Michael Frayn*.

FULFORD, ROBERT (b. 1932). Canadian journalist and (under the pseudonym Marshall Delaney) film critic; author of *Crisis at the Victory Burlesk* (1968) and other books, including his autobiography, *Best Seat in the House* (1988). From 1968 to 1988 he was editor of *Saturday Night*, where "White Lies" appeared in September 1983.

GALBRAITH, JOHN KENNETH (b. 1908). Canadian-born U.S. diplomat and economist; author of *The Affluent Society* (1958) and *The Scotch* (1964). "The Language of Economics" appeared in *Fortune* magazine (December 1962) and was republished in *Economics, Peace & Laughter*, ed. Andrea D. Williams, in 1971.

GASKELL, MRS. ELIZABETH (1810-1865). English novelist, known principally for *Mary Barton* (1848), *Cranford* (1853), and *North and South* (1855)—and for her biography of a friend, *The Life of Charlotte Brontë* (1857).

GORDIMER, NADINE (b. 1923). South African writer of social criticism, television documentaries, and fiction, including *A World of Strangers* (1958), *The Conservationist* (1974), *July's People* (1981), and *A Sport of Nature* (1987), and several collections of short stories, including a volume of selected stories, *No Place Like* (1978). The interview by Jannika Hurwitt (here somewhat abridged) first appeared in *The Paris Review* in 1980 and has been collected in *Women Writers at Work: The* Paris Review *Interviews* (1989).

GORMAN, JAMES (b. 1949). American writer of humorous pieces and of pieces about science—sometimes of humorous pieces about science. Author of *First Aid For Hypochondriacs* (1982) and *The Total Penguin* (1990). "Man, Bytes, Dog" appeared in *The New Yorker* July 2, 1984.

GOULD, GLENN (1932-1982). Canadian pianist and music commentator, famous for his interpretive performances, especially of Bach. *Conversations with Glenn Gould*, ed. Jonathan Cott, and *The Glenn Gould Reader*, ed. Tim Pope, both appeared in 1984—the latter including "Music and Technology," which first appeared in *Piano Quarterly* (Winter 1974-75).

GOULD, STEPHEN JAY (b. 1941). American teacher and frequent writer about geology, paleontology, and evolution; author of *Ever Since Darwin* (1977) and *Hen's Teeth and Horse's Toes* (1983). He has won awards for *The Mismeasure of Man* (1981) and for *The Panda's Thumb* (1980), in which "Our Allotted Lifetimes" was collected after having first appeared, like much of his work, in his column in *Natural History* magazine.

GRACE, PATRICIA (b. 1937). Born in Wellington, New Zealand, of Ngati Raukawa, Ngati Toa, and Te Ati Awa descent; author of several essays, stories, and novels, including *Waiariki* (1975), *The Dream Sleepers and Other Stories* (1980), and *Potiki* (1986).

HAIG-BROWN, RODERICK (1908-1976). English-born Canadian essayist, novelist, and magistrate; author of several books for children, including *Saltwater Summer* (1948), and a number of books on the art of fishing, including *Fisherman's Fall* (1964), from which "Behind the Salmon" is taken.

HALIBURTON, THOMAS CHANDLER (1796-1865). Nova Scotia-born satirist, historian, and judge, often called the "father of American humour." He moved to England in 1856 and became an MP. Author of many essays, pamphlets, and stories (e.g., *The Old Judge*, 1849), he is best known for his several epigrammatic and anecdotal sketches of "Sam Slick," including *The Clockmaker* (first series 1836, in which "Yankee eating and horse feeding" appeared) and *The Attaché* (1843-1844).

HORNYANSKY, MICHAEL (b. 1927). Canadian folklorist, children's writer (*The Golden Phoenix*, 1958), and professor of English. His essay on usage appeared in *In the Name of Language!*, ed. Joseph Gold, in 1975.

HURWITT, JANNIKA. American freelance writer, a contributor to *The Paris Review*, *The Village Voice*, and other magazines.

HUXLEY, ALDOUS (1894-1963). English satirist, essayist, and novelist, long a United States resident; best known for his moral fable *Brave New World* (1932) and novels like *Point Counter Point* (1928) and *Island* (1962). "Usually Destroyed" was collected in *Adonis and the Alphabet* (1956), called *Tomorrow and Tomorrow and Tomorrow* in the American edition.

IYER, PICO (b. 1957). English-born American journalist, author of *Video Nights in Kathmandu* (1989) and frequent contributor to such magazines as *Time*, *Partisan Review*, and *The Village Voice*. "Of Weirdos and Eccentrics" appeared in the January 18, 1988, issue of *Time*.

JAMES, HENRY (1843-1916). Prolific American writer whose novels and stories often focus on Americans in Europe, as in *The American* (1877), *The Portrait of a Lady* (1881), and *The Ambassadors* (1903), and occasionally on Europeans in America, as in *The Europeans* (1878). Other works include "The Turn of the Screw" (1898) and *The Golden Bowl* (1904). He lived most of his life in England, and became a British subject in 1915.

JOHNSON, SAMUEL (1709-1784). The pre-eminent literary figure in England in the mid-eighteenth century, author of a tragedy, *Irene* (1736), the long poems *London* (1738) and *The Vanity of Human Wishes* (1749), periodical essays in *The Rambler* (1750-1752) and *The Idler* (1758-1760), the philosophical fiction *Rasselas, Prince of Abyssinia* (1759), critical biography in *The Lives of the English Poets* (1779-1781), and *A Dictionary of the English Language* (1755). He is also famous as the subject of James Boswell's *The Life of Samuel Johnson* (1791).

JOYCE, JAMES (1882-1941). Irish novelist and short story writer who left Ireland for the Continent in 1904. Probably the most influential "modern" writer, Joyce published some poetry and a play, but his reputation rests on his collection of stories, *Dubliners* (1914), the autobiographical novel *A Portrait of the Artist as a Young Man* (1916), and the experimental novels *Ulysses* (1922) and *Finnegans Wake* (1939).

KAEL, PAULINE (b. 1929). Widely printed American film critic; author of *Kiss Kiss Bang Bang* (1968), in which her comments on *The Sound of Music* were collected, and other works, including *Going Steady* (1970) and *Reeling* (1976).

KEMBLE, FRANCES ANNE (1809-1893). Born into the prominent English acting family (daughter of Charles Kemble, niece of Sarah Siddons), Fanny Kemble is known principally as a great actress. But she also wrote some poetry (published in 1844) and interesting autobiographical works, including *Journal of a Residence on a Georgian Plantation in 1838-1839* (1863), in which her letter to the *Times* was included as an appendix.

KINGSLEY, MARY (1862-1900). Niece of English writers Charles and Henry Kingsley, Mary Kingsley largely educated herself while staying home to care

511

for her ailing parents. In 1892, after their death, she took a short trip to the Canary Islands and, briefly, Africa, to which she returned for longer periods in 1893 and 1895, experiences she wrote about engagingly in *Travels in West Africa* (1897) and polemically in *West African Studies* (1899). She died of typhoid fever caught while nursing Boer prisoners of war in South Africa.

KINGSTON, MAXINE HONG (b. 1940). American writer and English teacher, of Chinese ancestry; author of the award-winning books *The Woman Warrior: Memoirs of a Girlhood Among Ghosts* (1976) and *China Men* (1980), from which "On Mortality" comes, and *Tripmaster Monkey: His Fake Book* (1989).

LANE, MARGARET (b. 1907). English reporter, novelist, and biographer of Beatrix Potter, Edgar Wallace, Charlotte Brontë, and other literary figures. "The Ghost of Beatrix Potter" appeared in her *Purely for Pleasure* (1966).

LAURENCE, MARGARET (1926-1987). Canadian author of fiction, memoirs, and essays. Her travel book, *The Prophet's Camel Bell* (1963) records her residence in East Africa. Her later fictions (among them: *The Stone Angel*, 1964; *A Bird in the House*, 1970; *The Diviners*, 1974) focus more on the social values of her native Manitoba.

LEACOCK, STEPHEN (1869-1944). Canadian humorist and professor of economics and political science; widely known as a humorous lecturer and as the author of *Sunshine Sketches of a Little Town* (1912) and other works. *Literary Lapses*, in which "A, B, and C" appeared, was first published in 1910.

LE GUIN, URSULA K. (b. 1929). American writer of speculative fiction, essays, and poems, noted for such works as her Earthsea trilogy (*A Wizard of Earthsea*, 1968; *The Tombs of Atuan*, 1971; *The Farthest Shore*, 1972), *The Lathe of Heaven* (1971), and *The Dispossessed* (1974). "Some Approaches to the Problem of Time" first appeared in *Omni* in 1979 and is collected in *The Compass Rose* (1982).

LOPEZ, BARRY (b. 1945). American essayist and nature writer, a contributing editor of *Harper's*; noted for *Of Wolves and Men* (1979) and *Arctic Dreams* (1986). "A Reflection on White Geese" and "Landscape and Narrative" are collected in *Crossing Open Ground* (1988).

LUDWIG, JACK (b. 1922). Canadian novelist, professor, and sports observer, now resident in New York; his works include a novel, *Above Ground* (1968), and a book of essays, *Games of Fear and Winning* (1976), which includes his comments on the Calgary Stampede.

LYLY, JOHN (1554-1606). English poet, dramatist, and novelist, best known for England's first prose novel, *Euphues: The Anatomy of Wit*, and its sequel, *Euphues and His England* (1580), and the style thereafter called *euphuism*. He also wrote such plays as *Alexander and Campaspe* (1584), *Endimion, the Man in the Moon* (1591), and *The Woman in the Moon* (1597).

MACAULAY, DAME ROSE (1881-1958). English poet, novelist, essayist, and travel writer. Her works include *Potterism* (1920), *Told by an Idiot* (1923), *They Were Defeated* (1932), and *The Pleasure of Ruins* (1953).

MACAULAY, THOMAS BABINGTON (1800-1859). Indefatigable and highly popular English essayist, historian, and politician. In addition to his *History of England* (1849-1861), he is known for *Essays Critical and Historical* (1834) and the poems *Lays of Ancient Rome* (1842). As a Whig MP he helped pass the important first Reform Bill, in 1834.

MacEWEN, GWENDOLYN (1941-1987). Canadian poet, dramatist, and fiction writer; among her books are *The Shadow-Maker*, winner of a Governor General's Award in 1969, *Magic Animals: Selected Poems Old and New* (1974), and *The Fire-Eaters* (1976). "The Holyland Buffet" first appeared in *Views From the North: An Anthology of Travel Writing*, ed. Karen Mulhallen, in 1984.

MacLENNAN, HUGH (b. 1907). Canadian novelist and essayist. His novels include *Barometer Rising* (1941), *The Watch that Ends the Night* (1959), and *Voices in Time* (1980). "The Street-Car Conductor" appeared in his *Thirty and Three* (1955).

McCLUNG, NELLIE (1873-1951). Canadian novelist and polemicist, often advocating temperance and women's rights. Among her books are *Sowing Seeds in Danny* (1908) and the autobiographical *Clearing in the West: My Own Story* (1935). "A Gentlemen of the Old School" is Chapter XIII of *The Stream Runs Fast: My Own Story* (1945).

MEIGS, MARY (b. 1917). American-born writer now resident in Canada; author of *The Medusa Head* (1983) and *Lily Briscoe, A Self-Portrait* (1981). "Pandora Was a Feminist" appeared in *Women and Words: The Anthology Les Femmes et les Mots: Une Anthologie* in 1984.

MELVILLE, HERMAN (1819-1891). One of the foremost nineteenth-century American writers. Besides *Moby-Dick; or, The Whale*, he wrote, among other books, *Typee: A Peep at Polynesian Life* (1846), *Omoo: A Narrative of Adventures in the South Seas* (1847), *The Piazza Tales* (including "Benito Cereno" and "Bartleby the Scrivener"; 1856), *Battle-Pieces, and Aspects of the War* (Civil War poems, 1866), and *Billy Budd, Foretopman* (published 1924).

MILTON, JOHN (1608-1674). English poet and pamphleteer, known chiefly for the great epic poem *Paradise Lost* (1667). Other poetic works include "On the Morning of Christ's Nativity" (1629), *Comus* (1634; 1637), *Lycidas* (1637), *Paradise Regained* (1671), and *Samson Agonistes* (1671), as well as several notable sonnets. As a staunch fighter for liberty and an anti-Royalist (and as Oliver Cromwell's Latin secretary during the Commonwealth), he wrote many religious, political, and other prose works, including *The Doctrine and Discipline of Divorce* (1643), *Of Education* (1644), *Areopagitica: A Speech for the Liberty of Unlicensed Printing* (1644), and *The Tenure of Kings and Magistrates* (1649).

MITFORD, JESSICA (b. 1917). Member of a well-known English family, long resident in the United States; author of many books and articles, including *Kind and Unusual Punishment: The Prison Business* (1973) and *Poison Penmanship: The Gentle Art of Muckraking* (1979). Her first major success was *The American Way of Death* (1963), in which "The Story of Service" is the fifth chapter.

MONTAGU, LADY MARY WORTLEY (1689-1762). Aristocratic English writer and traveller, best known for her *Letters* (mostly adaptations of actual letters, a common form of travel writing), especially those written while her husband was ambassador to Turkey. On her return to England in 1718 she introduced and fought for the acceptance of inoculation against smallpox.

MORGAN, ELAINE (b. 1920). Welsh playwright, feminist sociological writer, and author of *Falling Apart* (1977). "The Man-Made Myth" is the opening chapter of *The Descent of Woman* (1972).

MUKHERJEE, BHARATI (b. 1940). Bengali-born Canadian novelist, now resident in the United States; author of *Wife* (1975) and *Jasmine* (1989). "Intimations" is a chapter in her part of *Days and Nights in Calcutta* (1977, rev. 1986), an autobiographical account of a year in India which she wrote in collaboration with her husband, Clark Blaise.

MURDOCH, WALTER (1874-1970). Australian newspaper essayist. "On Pioneering" appeared in *Speaking Personally* in 1930, and again in his *Collected Essays* in 1941.

NEWMAN, JOHN HENRY (1801-1890). English churchman who became part of the Oxford Movement (*Tracts for the Times*, 1833-1841) and turned Roman Catholic in 1845; made a Cardinal in 1879. He wrote *Apologia pro Vita Sua* (1864) to defend himself against an attack by Charles Kingsley, and the long poem *The Dream of Gerontius* (1865). His lectures and essays as rector of Dublin's Catholic University became in 1873 *The Idea of a University Defined and Illustrated*.

O'CONNOR, FLANNERY (1925-1964). American novelist and short story writer; author of *Wise Blood* (1952) and *Everything that Rises Must Converge* (1965). Her essay on education appeared in *Mystery and Manners*, ed. Sally and Robert Fitzgerald, in 1969.

ORWELL, GEORGE (ERIC ARTHUR BLAIR) (1903-1950). English novelist, essayist, and social critic; born in Bengal. Author of many books, including *Down and Out in Paris and London* (1933), the autobiographical novel *Burmese Days* (1934), the satirical fable *Animal Farm* (1945), the dystopia *Nineteen Eighty-Four* (1949), and many essays. "Politics and the English Language," written in 1946, was collected in *Shooting an Elephant and Other Essays* in 1950.

PIOZZI, HESTER LYNCH (THRALE) (1741-1821). As Mrs. Thrale, she was a close friend of Samuel Johnson, leading to her *Anecdotes of the Late Samuel Johnson* (1786). Her *British Synonymy*, subtitled *An Attempt at Regulating the Choice of Words in Familiar Conversation*, was intended particularly as an aid to foreigners living in England.

RIGBY, ELIZABETH (LADY EASTLAKE) (1809-1893). English writer, a frequent contributor to the *Quarterly Review* on subjects as various as literature, religion, lady travellers, art and architecture, music, and the Franco-Prussian War. She became Lady Eastlake in 1849 when she married the painter Sir Charles Eastlake (1793-1865). She translated works on art and in 1883 published essays on *Five Great Painters*.

RITTER, ERIKA (b. 1948). Canadian dramatist and humorist, author of *Automatic Pilot* (a play that won the 1980 Chalmers award) and *The Passing Scene* (1982). "Bicycles" was collected in *Urban Scrawl* in 1984.

ROONEY, ANDREW A. (b. 1919). American columnist and television writer, producer, and performer. His television essays have been collected in *A Few Minutes with Andy Rooney* (1981), his newspaper columns in several other books, including *And More by Andy Rooney* (1982) and *Pieces of My Mind* (1984), which includes "A Penny Saved Is a Waste of Time."

ROUECHÉ, BERTON (b. 1911). American medical journalist; author of *Eleven Blue Men* (1953), *The Incurable Wound* (1957), and other "narratives of medical detection." "Three Sick Babies" appeared in his *The Orange Man* in 1971.

RUSKIN, JOHN (1819-1900). English historian and critic of art and architecture. In addition to many essays, he published *Modern Painters* (5 volumes, 1843-1860), *The Seven Lamps of Architecture* (1849), and *The Stones of Venice* (1851-1853). In 1841 he wrote the popular story *The King of the Golden River* (1851). As a critic of modern social and scientific trends he wrote such works as *Unto this Last* (1860), *Sesame and Lilies* (1865), and *Fors Clavigera* (1871-1878).

SHEEHAN, LAURENCE (b. 1940). American writer on sports and other subjects; his "The Christmas Tree Lot Murders" was among the *Best Detective Stories of the Year* in 1977. His essays, often humorous, appear in *Harper's*, *Golf Digest*, *Tennis*, and other magazines. "How to Play Second Base" first appeared in *The Atlantic Monthly* in September 1974.

SPENCE, CATHERINE HELEN (1825-1910). Scots-born Australian feminist novelist and journalist; her fiction includes *Clara Morison* (1854) and a novel considered too radical for its time, *Handfasted* (published posthumously, 1984); several of her social critiques, including "The Dangerous Classes," were collected by Helen Thomson in *Catherine Helen Spence* (1987).

STEIN, GERTRUDE (1874-1946). American writer, trained in psychology and medicine, who became a literary leader among the exiles who settled in Paris in the 1920s, whom she called "the lost generation"; author of *The Autobiography of Alice B. Toklas* (1933) and many other works. "Composition as Explanation," one of a series of lectures delivered in England, was first published in 1926 in a volume of the same title.

STEVENSON, ROBERT LOUIS (1850-1894). Scots writer and traveller known popularly for *Treasure Island* (1883), *A Child's Garden of Verses* (1885), *The Strange Case of Dr. Jekyll and Mr. Hyde* (1886), and *Kidnapped* (1886); among his many other works are *Travels with a Donkey in the Cevennes* (1879), *The Silverado Squatters* (1883), and *The Merry Men and Other Tales and Fables* (1887). "An Apology for Idlers" was collected in *Virginibus Puerisque and Other Papers* in 1881.

SWIFT, JONATHAN (1667-1745). Dublin-born satirist and churchman, became Dean of St. Patrick's Cathedral in 1713. Famous for his ironic masterpiece *A Modest Proposal* (1729) and *Gulliver's Travels* (1726), he wrote many other works, including *The Battle of the Books* and *The Tale of a Tub* (1704), *Verses on the Death of Dr. Swift* (1731), and *A Complete Collection of Polite and Ingenious Conversation* (1738).

SYNGE, JOHN MILLINGTON (1871-1909). Irish playwright, poet, and travel writer. On the advice of poet William Butler Yeats, he travelled to the Aran Islands, off the west coast of Ireland, to absorb the spirit of traditional Irish society. *The Aran Islands* appeared in 1907, but Synge is perhaps better known for such plays as *Riders to the Sea* (1904), and *The Playboy of the Western World* (1907).

SZASZ, THOMAS (b. 1920). American psychiatrist and author of *The Myth of Mental Illness* (1974), *Ceremonial Chemistry* (1974), and other books on psychiatry and public attitude. "What Psychiatry Can and Cannot Do" appeared in *Harper's Magazine* in 1964, and in his *Ideology and Insanity* (1970).

THOMAS, DYLAN (1914-1953). Welsh poet (*Deaths and Entrances*, 1946), scriptwriter (*Under Milk Wood*, 1954), and story writer (*Portrait of the Artist as a Young Dog*, 1955). "Memories of Christmas" was first broadcast by the BBC Welsh Home Service in 1945 and printed in *The Listener*, and collected in *Quite Early One Morning* in 1954.

THOMAS, LEWIS (b. 1913). American medical doctor, president (1973-1980) and then chancellor of Memorial Sloan-Kettering Cancer Center in New York; author of *The Lives of a Cell*, which won a 1974 National Book Award, *The Medusa and the Snail* (1979), from which "Notes on Punctuation" comes, and *Late Night Thoughts on Listening to Mahler's Ninth Symphony* (1983). His "Notes of a Biology-Watcher: The Hazards of Science" first appeared in the *New England Journal of Medicine*, 10 February 1977, and in an altered form in *The Medusa and the Snail*.

THOREAU, HENRY DAVID (1817-1862). American transcendentalist, naturalist, and author who made his living primarily as a pencil manufacturer, teacher, and surveyor. Known mainly for *Walden, or Life in the Woods* (1854), he also published *A Week on the Concord and Merrimack Rivers* (1849). Jailed for a day in 1845 for refusing to pay a tax to a government engaged in the Mexican War, he explained his principles in "Civil Disobedience" (1849), which later would help influence Gandhi and others to adopt strategies of passive resistance. Works published posthumously include "Life Without Principle" (1863) and *A Yankee in Canada* (1866).

THURBER, JAMES (1894-1961). American cartoonist, humorist, journalist, and playwright, long a staff member of *The New Yorker*; among his many works are *The Seal in the Bedroom* (1932), *Fables for Our Time* (1943), and *The Wonderful O* (1957). "The Trouble with Man Is Man" first appeared in *The New Yorker* and was collected in *Lanterns & Lances* (1961).

TRAILL, CATHARINE PARR (1802-1899). One of seven children born into a literary family in England (her sisters include the writers Agnes Strickland and Susanna Moodie). She is known primarily for her children's books—*The Young Emigrants* (1826), *The Canadian Crusoes* (1852)—and for the pioneer guidebooks she wrote after emigrating to Canada in 1832: *The Backwoods of Canada* (1836) and *The Female Emigrant's Guide* (1854).

TRILLIN, CALVIN (b. 1935). American reporter and columnist; author of *An Education in Georgia* (1964), *U.S. Journal* (1970), *American Fried: Adventures of a Happy Eater* (1974), and *Killings* (1984). "Literally" is from *Uncivil Liberties*, a 1982 collection of his columns from *The Nation*, where it appeared on 12 September 1981.

TUCHMAN, BARBARA (1912-1989). American historian; winner of Pulitzer Prizes for *Stilwell and the American Experience in China* (1970) and *The Guns of August* (1971); author also of *The Proud Tower* (1966) and *A Distant Mirror: The Calamitous 14th Century* (1978). "Is History a Guide to the Future?" was collected in *Practicing History* (1981).

TWAIN, MARK (SAMUEL LANGHORNE CLEMENS) (1835-1910). Prolific American writer and humorist, best known for *The Adventures of Tom Sawyer*

(1876) and *Adventures of Huckleberry Finn* (1885). Other works include "The Notorious Jumping Frog of Calaveras County" (1865), *Life on the Mississippi* (1883), and *A Connecticut Yankee in King Arthur's Court* (1889). In his later years he wrote such darker works as "The Man that Corrupted Hadleyburg" (1900), *What Is Man?* (1906), and *The Mysterious Stranger* (published 1916).

UPDIKE, JOHN (b. 1932). American writer of novels, short stories, poems, and essays; among his many works are *Rabbit, Run* (1960), *Pigeon Feathers and Other Stories* (1962), *The Centaur* (1963, winner of a National Book Award), and *The Coup* (1978). In 1982 his novel *Rabbit Is Rich* won a Pulitzer Prize and two other awards. "Central Park," which originally appeard in *The New Yorker*, was collected in *Assorted Prose* in 1965.

WHITE, E.B. (1899-1985). American poet, essayist, letter writer; author of *Charlotte's Web* (1952) and other books for children, and collections of essays and sketches such as *Quo Vadimus? or The Case for the Bicycle* (1938) and *The Points of My Compass* (1962). "Once More to the Lake," written in 1941, appeared in *One Man's Meat* (1944) and later in *Essays of E. B. White* (1977).

WHITE, PATRICK (1912-1990). English-born Australian author, winner of the 1973 Nobel Prize for fiction. His several books include *The Aunt's Story* (1948), *Voss* (1957), *A Fringe of Leaves* (1976), and *The Burnt Ones* (1964), a collection of short stories.

WILDE, OSCAR FINGAL O'FLAHERTIE WILLS (1854-1900). Flamboyant wit and man of letters of the *fin de siècle* English literary scene, born in Dublin. Proponent of the Aesthetic Movement ("Art for Art's Sake"), he wrote numerous successful works, including *The Happy Prince and Other Tales* (1888), *The Picture of Dorian Gray* (1890), *The Importance of Being Earnest* (1895), and *The Ballad of Reading Gaol* (1898).

WOOLF, VIRGINIA (1882-1941). English novelist and essayist, best known for *Mrs Dalloway* (1925), *To the Lighthouse* (1927), *A Room of One's Own* (1929), and the essays in the two volumes of *The Common Reader* (1925, 1932). Her review of W. L. Courtney's *The Feminine Note in Fiction* appeared in the *Guardian*, January 25, 1905, and has been collected in Volume One of *The Essays of Virginia Woolf* (1986), ed. Andrew McNeillie.

ZINSSER, WILLIAM (b. 1922). American feature writer, editor, and teacher; author of *On Writing Well* (3rd ed. 1985), *Pop Goes America* (1966), and *Writing with a Word Processor* (1983). "Nobody Here but Us Dead Sheep" first appeared in *Life* magazine 22 August 1969.

Index of Terms

(See also the alternative tables of contents.)

Index of Authors